The Historical Books

THE COMPLETE PORTRAIT
OF THE MESSIAH

Volume 3

Other volumes in The Complete Portrait of the Messiah series

Also available from Time to Revive and Laura Kim Martin

reviveDAILY: A Devotional Journey from Genesis to Revelation, Year 1
reviveDAILY: A Devotional Journey from Genesis to Revelation, Year 2

The Historical Books

THE COMPLETE PORTRAIT
OF THE MESSIAH

Volume 3

Kyle Lance Martin

Time to Revive and reviveSCHOOL

Richardson, Texas

The Historical Books

Published in conjunction with
Iron Stream Media
100 Missionary Ridge
Birmingham, AL 35242
IronStreamMedia.com

Library of Congress Control Number: 2023905973

978-1-63204-100-5 (hardback)
978-1-63204-101-2 (eBook)

1 2 3 4 5—27 26 25 24 23

DEDICATION

Greetings friends and colaborers of the Lord Jesus Christ!

I am writing to you with an excitement that is beyond words. For I would like to dedicate this book to individuals like yourselves whose desire to grow closer to Jesus and go deeper in the Word of God brings such JOY to my heart. And my prayer for each one of you is that the Holy Spirit will reveal more of Himself to you in this in-depth time of studying the Word of God daily. Jesus said, "Blessed are those who hunger and thirst for righteousness, for they will be satisfied" (Matthew 5:6 NASB). So as you embark on this journey of studying each book of the Bible, may you experience a freshness and a fulfillment that can only come from the Spirit of God. You will have days that you won't want to wake up early and read. There will be moments when life throws you a situation that delays your personal devotional time with Him. But please press in and allow the Holy Spirit to strengthen your every step. This will allow you to exercise your faith muscles and walk out what you are learning in this. From my experience, obedience will bring education to life!

It will be quite a strenuous commitment, yet it's a part of an intentional strategy to equip the saints for His return. And your participation with revive-SCHOOL is a unique part of this preparation.

May the Lord receive all the glory, honor, and fame in this pursuit of righteousness.

Praying,
Dr. Kyle Lance Martin

Contents

WEEK 37

WEEK 38

WEEK 39

WEEK 40

WEEK 44

WEEK 45

WEEK 46

WEEK 47

WEEK 48

reviveSCHOOL History and Introduction

In January of 2015, our ministry, Time to Revive, was invited from our home base in Richardson, Texas, to Goshen, Indiana, to help equip the local church to learn how to go out and share the gospel in their community. We called it reviveINDIANA. During this frigid first trip in January, our intention was to help facilitate a week of prayer and outreach as a form of training, which we hoped would lead to an intentional week of outreach later that year. Little did we know that God had other plans.

The week of prayer and outreach started with about 450 people from various churches in the community and, to our surprise, quickly swelled to over 3,000. And by the end of that first week, the Holy Spirit confirmed to a group of us, including local pastors, that the Time to Revive team should stay for 52 straight days! Imagine the phone calls we had to make to our spouses telling them we were going to stay a "little" longer.

Over the course of these seven weeks, the local church witnessed God move in mighty ways, and each person involved could tell you miraculous testimonies of how they witnessed, firsthand, how God was moving. The 52 days culminated on March 4 of that year where an estimated 10,000 people showed up to brave the cold temperatures and go out and share the love of Jesus Christ.

All the while, word of this was spreading throughout the state, and it led to the Time to Revive team being invited to seven different cities in Indiana over the course of the next seven months. We continued to witness the local body of believers in these various communities encouraged and equipped to continue to take out their faith and share with others. The gospel wasn't intended to stay only in the church building. Jesus commissioned each one of us to go and make disciples in our own Jerusalem, Judea, and Samaria and to the ends of the earth. Back in Goshen, the local body continued to go out regularly after those initial 52 days while keeping track of the days since that first amazing week. A couple of years later in 2017, the local believers invited our team to celebrate their 1,000th day of outreach in their community. It was during that time when a local man shared with us a dream he had, which led us to start a two-year Bible study in the community. Similar to the Apostle Paul as he taught 12 disciples in Ephesus to study the Word of God on a daily basis, Time to Revive's desire was to also provide in-depth teaching that would focus on where the Messiah is found in every book of the Bible from Genesis to Revelation. We knew this would deepen their commitment to sharing the gospel as well as deepen their relationship with the Lord and with those whom they were discipling.

> But when some became hardened and would not believe, slandering the Way in front of the crowd, he withdrew from them and met separately with the disciples, conducting discussions every day in the lecture hall of Tyrannus. —Acts 19:9

This local Bible study started with 12 men who signed up and committed to study the Word of God in a barn on a county road in Goshen, Indiana. And on January 1, 2018, we launched reviveSCHOOL with 54 men in this initial group. They studied the Scriptures daily, using the online resources, then gathered in the barn to discuss them in person. Each student studied the Bible daily using these resources:

- a Scripture reading plan to stay on track,
- a 29-minute teaching video (by Kyle Lance Martin, Indiana pastors, and TTR teachers),
- a devotion (written by Laura Kim Martin),
- reading guide questions to help facilitate discussion and critical thinking,
- lesson plans to summarize the daily teaching, and
- a painting of each book of the Bible by Mindi Oaten.

Upon the completion of the two-year study in the Word, Time to Revive celebrated over 200 students who had joined reviveSCHOOL with a graduation ceremony in January 2020. Plans were made for these individuals to take the Word and launch reviveSCHOOL groups not only in the United States but also throughout various nations. However, with worldwide travel restrictions due to the COVID-19 pandemic, this travel didn't happen. Thankfully, God had another plan, His plan was "above and beyond" all that Time to Revive could ask or think of (Ephesians 3:20–21).

With all the reviveSCHOOL materials already available online, the Holy Spirit spread the word to pastors and leaders of nations all throughout the world. Believers were hungry for biblically sound teaching and resources to grow closer to the Lord. As exemplified in Acts 19 with Paul and the disciples, and all the people of Asia, the Word of God through reviveSCHOOL truly spread—from a barn in Indiana to the nations.

> And this went on for two years, so that all the inhabitants of Asia, both Jews and Greeks, heard the message about the Lord. —Acts 19:10

By God's grace, reviveSCHOOL has become an outlet for individuals to gain fresh insight into the Messiah all throughout the Scriptures, as well as to develop an understanding of the role of Israel from a biblical perspective.

I am humbled and honored that you would select reviveSCHOOL for your learning. When we started with 12 guys in a Bible study, we had no idea that reviveSCHOOL would be as far reaching as it has become. Our team would delight in knowing that you are studying the Word of God and using the resources with reviveSCHOOL. We pray that through these resources you will grow closer to the Lord and that you are inspired to walk out the plans that God has for your life by exposing others to the love of Christ.

To God be the glory!
Dr. Kyle Lance Martin

For further information about how to sign up for this two-year study in the Word of God or if you would like to launch a reviveSCHOOL group in your community, state/province, or country, please go online to www.reviveSCHOOL.org.

How to Use this Bible Study Series

The Complete Portrait of the Messiah Bible study series contains multiple components for each lesson. These components work together to provide an in-depth study of how Jesus is revealed throughout the whole of Scripture. Below is a description of each component and how you can use each one to maximize your study experience.

Teaching Notes & Video Lessons
The teaching notes summarize the main points of each video lesson and include a QR code to access the video teaching. If you have access to the internet via your phone or tablet, you can scan the QR code to watch the video lesson.*

The Daily Word Devotional
Dig deeper into personal application for each lesson through "The Daily Word" devotion. This day-by-day devotion encourages you with thoughts for application and further Scripture readings.

Reading Guide Questions
These questions will guide you into a more detailed exploration of each lesson's content. Examine the concepts of the daily Scripture readings in more detail.

The Bible Art Collection
This Bible study series is augmented by a one-of-a-kind, especially inspired series of original artwork created by artist Mindi Oaten. These 66 acrylic paintings creatively depict the revelation of Christ in each book of the Bible. Viewing each of these original art pieces will inspire and further enrich your understanding of Jesus throughout all of the Scriptures. These can be found at https://www.mindioaten.com/pages/mindi-oaten-art-bible-art-collection or https://www.reviveschool.org/

About the Cover

1 Samuel
"The Anointed One"

Artist Notes: Mindi Oaten

The books of Samuel begin the transition of Israel from a theocracy (ruled by God through priests) to a monarchy (ruled by a king, good or bad). The paintings symbolically reflect three key figures: Samuel the prophet, Saul the failed king, and David the great king.

Intro to a Diptych

A diptych is a piece of art created in two parts. Typically, the two panels are closely related, though it may also be the same piece that is continued on a separate panel. Traditionally, diptychs were hinged like books that could be folded. In modern art, it is common for artists to create two separate panels designed to hang next to each other. The Samuel paintings hung together represent a diptych.

Red Velvet Chair

The people refused to listen to Samuel. "No!" they said. "We must have a king over us. Then we'll be like all the other nations: our king will judge us, go out before us, and fight our battles." —1 Samuel 8:19–20

When planning my composition, I needed a background to place the crown. I wanted to display a kingly feel, so I chose to paint royal cloth draped over a chair, a royal seat. As I painted, the Lord reminded me of our heavenly position, seated in Christ, coheirs with Him as a royal priesthood. This symbolizes the transition from theocracy to monarchy as demanded by the Israelites so that they looked "like the other nations." They wanted a human king instead of the unseen divine *King*.

Horn of Oil

The horn of oil represents the prophet Samuel. He anointed both Saul and David as kings. Samuel is a major figure in this book.

Crown

*Samuel took the flask of oil, poured it out on Saul's head, kissed him, and said, "Hasn't the L*ORD *anointed you ruler over His inheritance?"*
—1 Samuel 10:1

The crown is a symbol of the first kingship of Israel. Samuel anointed Saul as king because the people wanted a human king, rejecting the Lord as divine *King*.

The Lyre/Harp

The lyre (better known as a harp) represents David, the worshipper. David was often called to play the lyre whenever evil spirits troubled Saul (1 Samuel 16:16). David is also the author of many of the psalms.

Sling and Five Stones

These were the tools David chose to defeat the giant Goliath. It only took one stone, but he came prepared with five.

Sky/Rain and Sheep in the Pasture

*"Now, therefore, present yourselves and see this great thing that the L*ORD *will do before your eyes. Isn't the wheat harvest today? I will call on the L*ORD *and He will send thunder and rain, so that you will know and see what a great evil you committed in the L*ORD*'s sight by requesting a king for yourselves." Samuel called on the L*ORD*, and on that day the L*ORD *sent thunder and rain. As a result, all the people greatly feared the L*ORD *and Samuel. They pleaded with Samuel, "Pray to the L*ORD *your God for your servants, so we won't die! For we have added to all our sins the evil of requesting a king for ourselves."* —1 Samuel 12:16–19

God manifested judgment through thunder and rain to show the people that he indeed was God. We must obey Him and not turn to an earthly king to be saved. Heed this lesson of obedience in 1 Samuel about following the Lord's commandments and not the way of man.

Flower—The Olive Branch: Anointing

I chose the olive branch as my "flower piece" of the garden, a representation of oil to anoint kings.

*In reviveSCHOOL, the theme name for Jesus in 1 Samuel is *Anointed One*.

Lesson 1: Joshua 1—2

Commander: Transferring Leadership

Teaching Notes

Intro

After studying the five books of the Pentateuch and the four Gospels, we're now starting a new section in the books of history. We have completed 200 lessons so far. We're now going to study 12 historical books, beginning with the book of Joshua. We will study Joshua to Nehemiah (1405 BC to 424 BC), a period of almost 1,000 years. The Israelites were coming into possession of the Promised Land after 430 years in Egypt as slaves (Exodus 12:40–41) and 40 years wandering in the wilderness.[1]

The historical books can be divided into three groups:

Pre-Exile *(before captivity)*	Exile *(during captivity)*	Post-Exile *(after captivity)*
Joshua, Judges, Ruth	Esther	Ezra
1, 2 Samuel		Nehemiah
1, 2 Kings		
1, 2 Chronicles		

The historical books can also be divided as:

Pre-Kingship	Kingship	Post-Kingship
Joshua	1, 2 Samuel	Ezra
Judges	1, 2 Kings	Nehemiah
Ruth	1, 2 Chronicles	Esther

Joshua (meaning "Jehovah saves" or "the Lord is salvation") was the understudy of Moses (Numbers 27:18–23), and a foreshadow of the coming of Christ. The one word for the book of Joshua is *Commander*. The author of the book was

---

[1] John MacArthur, *The MacArthur Bible Commentary* (Nashville: Thomas Nelson, 2005), 255.

Joshua, although some think it was the high priest Eleazar or his son Phinehas.[2] Joshua became the leader of the Israelites at the age of 90. He died at the age of 110 (Joshua 24:29). Through the book of Joshua we see the faithfulness of God and the fulfillment of God's promises about Israel possessing the Promised Land.

Teaching

Joshua 1:1: We see a clear transition from Moses' leadership to Joshua's. Charles Wesley explained, "God buries His workmen but carries on His work."[3] J. Oswald Sanders said, "A work originated by God and conducted on spiritual principles will surmount the shock of a change of leadership and indeed will probably thrive better as a result."[4]

MacArthur explains that God prepared Joshua to assume leadership through his training under Moses:[5]

1. Through service (Exodus 17:10; 33:11)
2. Through soldiering (Exodus 17:9–13)
3. Through scouting (Numbers 13–14)
4. Through supplication and commission by Moses (Numbers 27:15–17)
5. Through the sovereignty of God (Numbers 27:18)
6. Through the Spirit's presence (Numbers 27:18; Deuteronomy 34:9)
7. Through separation from Moses (Numbers 27:18–23; Deuteronomy 31:7–8; 13:15)
8. Through selflessness in following the Lord (Numbers 32:12)

Joshua 1:2–3: God repeated His promise that the Israelites would enter the land He had given them under Joshua's leadership (Genesis 12:7; 13:14–15; 15:18–21). Everywhere they stepped would be God's land. They had to walk into the land and claim it . . . step by step.

Romans 10:15 seems to support this instruction and fulfill it: "And how can they preach unless they are sent? As it is written: How beautiful are the feet of those who announce the gospel of good things." Can you imagine if everyone

---

[2] Thomas L. Constable, *Expository Notes of Dr. Thomas Constable: Joshua*, 2, http://planobiblechapel.org/tcon/notes/pdf/joshua.pdf.

[3] This phrase appears on the monument to the Wesleys in Westminster Abbey. See "John, Charles & Samuel Wesley," Westminster Abbey, https://www.westminster-abbey.org/abbey-commemorations/commemorations/john-charles-samuel-wesley.

[4] J. Oswald Sanders, *Spiritual Leadership* (Chicago: Moody, 1967), 132.

[5] MacArthur, 257.

who shares the gospel could picture this moment and understand that *everywhere* they go, God has already prepared the way?

Joshua 1:4–5: Verse 4 outlines all the boundaries of the land that God gave the Israelites. If you use an Old Testament map and compare these boundaries to the present-day borders of Israel, it's obvious they don't match up. The lands of Lebanon, Syria, Gaza, and Jordan, were all included in the land that God promised the Israelites. This is why it's so important this land not be divided today, because it still belongs to God and His people. Sadly, we think that we can achieve peace in the Middle East by dividing the land and giving some of it away, but that goes against everything God promised. That's not a racial comment, but a reading of God's Word.

In verse 5, God promised Joshua that He would be with him as long as he lived. God made this promise to others as well, including: Jacob (Genesis 28:15), Gideon (Judges 6:16), and the Jewish exiles returning from Babylon (Isaiah 41:10; 43:5). God promises to always be with us through His Son—Emmanuel (Matthew 1:23). He is always with us (Matthew 28:20), and He will never leave us (Hebrews 13:5). The language in the historical books is the same as in the New Testament. God is always the same . . . yesterday, today, and tomorrow.

Joshua 1:6–9: Verse 6 is the first of several instances in chapter 1 where God told Joshua to "be strong and courageous." God had given different sections of the land to the various tribes, but the Israelites would first have to conquer the land. God told Joshua again to "be strong and very courageous" while observing (or possibly meditating on the Word inside them) all the instructions given to Moses.

One of the issues the church faces today is that it doesn't always have the Spirit of God within it, so it strays to the left or the right. Success is found when we are in the Word of God and we allow Him to dictates our steps and where we are to go.

Joshua 1:10–18: Joshua sent the officers among the people to tell them to get ready to cross into the Promised Land in three days. He told the Reubenites, the Gadites, and the half tribe of Manasseh that they could stay in the land they were in on the east side of the Jordan River (vv. 12–15), but that they still had to fight for the Promised Land. Joshua was announcing that the Israelites' journey had come to an end and the time of whining was over, because God had prepared the way for them into the Promised Land. Everyone agreed to follow Joshua's leadership (v. 16). They were committed until the end.

Closing

We are going to walk through some incredible stories of God moving among His people in the days to come. Welcome to the study of Joshua.

The Daily Word

After Moses' death, Joshua became the leader of the Israelites. The Lord commanded Joshua to lead the people over the Jordan River and into the Promised Land. Before crossing into the new land, the Lord gave Joshua promises of His faithfulness: "I have given you every place where the sole of your foot treads. No one will be able to stand against you. I will be with you. I will not leave you. You will succeed in whatever you do. I am with you wherever you go."

As you walk with the Lord in faith, God's promises stand true for your life as well. His Word is the same yesterday, today, and tomorrow. When the Lord calls you to do something or go somewhere, whether it's to pray with someone at the park or to quit your job and begin another one, God is with you wherever you go. However, God instructed Joshua to "not depart from the book of instruction." When God leads you in faith, remember to stay grounded in the Word of God. He doesn't want you to walk in faith and then go on your own. Rather, the Lord longs for you to read and follow His Word as you walk in faith, remembering His faithful promises. It's in the truth of God's Word that you will remain strong and courageous. Today, walk in faith, knowing the Lord your God is with you wherever you go.

No one will be able to stand against you as long as you live. I will be with you, just as I was with Moses. I will not leave you or forsake you. . . . Above all, be strong and very courageous to carefully observe the whole instruction My servant Moses commanded you. —Joshua 1:5, 7

Further Scripture: Genesis 28:15; Matthew 28:20; Hebrews 13:5

Questions

1. In verse 8, God says, "This book of instruction must not depart from your mouth." What do you think that means? What does it mean to meditate on it day and night?

2. Why do you think the spies went to Rahab for lodging?

3. The Israelite spies were afraid of going into the Promised Land (Numbers 13:28–29). Why then do you think the Canaanites feared the Israelites entering their land (Joshua 2:9–11)?

4. Can you think of another time in Scripture when God's people were told to mark their house to escape death (Exodus 12:23)?

5. What did the Holy Spirit highlight to you in Joshua 1—2 through the reading or the teaching?

Lesson 2: Joshua 3—4

Commander: Breaking Camp

Teaching Notes

Intro

In Joshua 2, Joshua sent two spies into the city of Jericho. Remember Joshua 1:11 where he commands the people to prepare to move in three days? This was going to be a big week for the Israelites, because they were going into the Promised Land. The spies encountered Rahab, who helped hide them. Because of her help, she and her family were to be spared when the Israelites took the city. This is the backdrop for what happened in chapter 3.

Teaching

Joshua 3:1–2: Joshua started early in the morning. It seems that men of God in the Bible rose early in the morning (Exodus 24:4; 2 Chronicles 29:20; Psalm 57:8; Mark 1:35). Joshua left the Acacia Grove with all the Israelites. They went to the Jordan River and camped out. After three days, the officers went throughout the camp instructing the people. When they saw the ark of the covenant, they were to break camp and follow.

Joshua 3:3: I love this verse because when I wanted to see God move, He led me to these verses. We must break camp in order to do Gods work. I think a lot of people have a desire to break camp but they are afraid to do it.

Joshua 3:4: The Israelites were to keep a distance of 1,000 yards (or half a mile away) from the ark. When you break camp, you should fully expect it to not look the way you want it to look. You have to have faith to break camp and go into the unknown. In some regards, there had to have been some excitement in the camp. The Israelites were finally at the starting line! They were to expect it to be like nothing they had ever seen.

Joshua 3:5: Joshua told the people to consecrate themselves because the Lord would be among them the next day. They were to make sure they were not connected to anything unclean. This is a pattern of sanctification that God established for His people. Warren Wiersbe wrote that this meant that "everybody bathed and changed their clothes and that the married couples devoted themselves wholly to the Lord."[1] They were to keep themselves pure.

It is almost like saying that this was a new beginning. Sin is pictured as defilement and is to be washed away (2 Samuel 12:20; Psalm 51:2). Spiritually speaking, God needed the Israelites to get ready. It is similar to the picture of baptism we see in Romans 6.

Joshua 3:6–7: The priests were to take the ark and go ahead of the people. Once you break camp, you need get your feet wet! In other words, you need to move forward. God exalted Joshua (just as He did with Moses) in the sight of Israel so they would know that he was their leader. Actually, God used Joshua *and* the priest to show that He was with the Israelites.

Joshua 3:8–9: Joshua was to command the priest. When they reached the edge of the Jordan, they were to stand in the water. If you want to see God move in your life, you need to be obedient to His will! Does this sound like the Red Sea all over again? To me this is a radical story. The reality is you need to walk by faith (2 Corinthians 5:7). Nobody had a clue what would happen. In faith alone, the priest had to get into the water. In order to get your feet wet, you have to walk by faith (Hebrews 11:6), even when it doesn't make sense to walk by faith (James 1:22).

Joshua 3:10: Joshua said, "Look at what God is going to do." God was going to dispose of seven people groups in the land. As the Israelites crossed over, God said He was going to rid the land of their enemies. I think we don't share the gospel because we are afraid of the enemy, afraid that God won't take care of things.

Joshua 3:11–13: Joshua chose 12 men, one from every tribe of Israel. These men come into play in chapter 4. Joshua told the Israelites that when the priests stood in the river, the waters would be cut off and would "stand up in a mass" (v. 13) (like a wall).

Joshua 3:14–17: The people broke down their camps to cross the Jordan. As soon as the priest stood in the river, the water stopped and rose up in a mass that extended 18 miles. Remember two million people needed to cross the river. The priest stood in the middle of the Jordan as the people began to cross on dry

---

[1] Warren W. Wiersbe, *Be Strong: Putting God's Power to Work in Your Life* (Colorado Springs: David C. Cook, 1993), 61.

ground until all Israel reached the opposite shore. When you are willing to break camp and get your feet wet, you can expect a miraculous sign.

Joshua 4: Joshua summoned the 12 men and instructed them to each take one of the large stones from the middle of the Jordan River (v. 8). These men were to stack these stones at the edge of their camp to serve as a reminder to the Israelites of what God had done.

Joshua told the Israelites that all people of the earth who saw the stones would know that God was mighty and to always fear Him (v. 24). Joshua also picked up 12 stones and placed them in the middle of the Jordan River where the ark of the covenant had been (v. 9). After everyone reached the opposite bank, the priests finished crossing. As soon as the priest stood on dry ground, the river resumed its flow (v. 18).

Closing

All people should know that the Lord is mighty. The reality is that the Israelites were crossing into a whole new season. They were claiming their inheritance. And Joshua served as a type of Christ: "But as it is written: What eye did not see and ear did not hear, and what never entered the human mind—God prepared this for those who love Him. Now God has revealed these things to us by the Spirit, for the Spirit searches everything, even the depths of God" (1 Corinthians 2:9–10).

God is preparing these deep things through our relationship with him. God has an inheritance waiting for us. The only way to receive this inheritance is to walk in faith (Psalm 47:4).

The Daily Word

The Israelites looked ahead at the Promised Land and saw the Jordan River in their path. Joshua received orders from the Lord on how they would cross over. First the Israelites had to break camp, leaving a place of comfort. Then the priests had to stand in the water with both feet. When they followed these instructions, they witnessed God's miraculous hand—the Jordan River dried up, allowing thousands of Israelites to walk across the riverbed.

Breaking camp and standing in the water . . . that's what the Israelites were instructed to do as they walked in faith. What does that mean for you today? Where in your life do you need to break up what is comfortable? Has the Lord asked you to move away from the job you've held for decades? Maybe you need to say something to someone that's been on your heart for months. It's time to break camp. And then go all in. Don't just sort-of do it. Be confident to the Lord's calling. *Stand in the water with both feet.* Move to another state. Invite a friend who hasn't spoken to you out for dinner. Just go for it. If the Lord is leading you to do it, then He will be with you. As you move in obedience and in faith to His leading, you will witness God's mighty hand, His mighty power, and His mighty provision in your life. Walk it out in bold obedience! God is with you.

When the people broke camp to cross the Jordan, the priests carried the ark of the covenant ahead of the people. Now the Jordan overflows its banks throughout the harvest season. But as soon as the priests carrying the ark reached the Jordan, their feet touched the water at its edge and the water flowing downstream stood still, rising up in a mass that extended as far as Adam, a city next to Zarethan. —Joshua 3:14–16

Further Scripture: 1 Chronicles 16:8; Proverbs 3:5–6; Isaiah 42:16

Questions

1. What is the significance of the Israelites following the ark (Exodus 13:21–22; John 16:7, 13)?
2. Why do you think that God exalted Joshua in the sight of all Israel?
3. Why did the Lord command the stones to be taken out from under where the priests were standing firm (Matthew 7:24)?
4. Why do you think the priests had to step into the river before God parted the water?
5. What did the Holy Spirit highlight to you in Joshua 3—4 through the reading or the teaching?

Lesson 3: Joshua 5—6

Commander: The Wall Fell

Teaching Notes

Intro

I feel like we have covered a lot of ground already! There is still a lot of meat! Remember the Israelites were actually in the Promised Land. Today we are going to talk about the Israeli army. Let's set the background: Joshua was getting ready to attack Jericho. Jericho is on the west bank of the Jordan River.

Teaching

Joshua 5:13–14: An angel of the Lord (a man with a sword) appeared in front of Joshua. Joshua's first question was, are you for us or against us? I think this is a natural question, but it's not one I would ask! The angel replied, "Neither . . . I have now come as the commander of the Lord's army" (v. 14). Joshua immediately bowed down on his knees.

The real question is, who is the *Commander* of the Lord's army? I want to paint a picture of who the *Commander* of the Lord's army is. Similar to Jesus coming to Joshua as the *Commander*, the Lord also shows up to others in the Old Testament. To Abraham, the Lord dined with him (Genesis 18:1–8), and to the three Hebrew men, Jesus stood with them in the fire (Daniel 3:25–26). Most would call this a pre-incarnate appearance of Christ. Christ was tangibly showing up throughout the Old Testament (Numbers 22:23; 1 Kings 22:19; 1 Chronicles 21:15; Job 32:5–6; Psalm 148:2).

Joshua 5:15: Joshua was instructed to remove his sandals, for he was on holy ground. This reminds us of Moses and his encounter with the burning bush in Exodus 3:5. Joshua was getting ready to go fight, so Jesus showed up as the *Commander*. God always shows up with how we need to hear from the Lord!

Joshua 6:1–2: Jericho was strongly fortified because of the Israelites. No one was entering or leaving. The Lord had already given Joshua victory. There was nothing to worry about! The Lord is going to fight our battles. It's already a done deal

(Exodus 15:3; Psalm 46:7–11)! How does this apply to us? I think it is important to remember that the victory has already been won. The world, flesh, and Satan have already been defeated on the cross.

Joshua 6:3–5: Joshua was given the game plan. The Israeli army was to march once around the city for six days. On the seventh day, they marched around the city seven times. The priests then blew their trumpets, and Joshua gave the order for the army of men to shout.

This is how funny this is to me: they say Jericho was less than half a mile all the way around. It probably didn't take too long to walk around. Can you imagine watching people hike around your city not saying anything? What I love about God's plan is that in our eyes, it is completely foolish. I love this plan because only God can do it (2 Chronicles 16:9)!

These trumpets being used were not the normal silver trumpets that signified important times. These were shofars, which were normally blown at a celebration, a jubilee when something new was coming (Hebrews 11:30). People are required to walk by faith; by faith the walls of Jericho fell down.

Joshua 6:6–9: Joshua summoned the priests and told them the plan. The priests with trumpets were behind the army and the rear guard went behind the ark (Isaiah 52:12). This was God's game plan. Wiersbe wrote, "I quoted J. Hudson Taylor's words about three different ways to serve the Lord: (1) to make the best plans we can and hope they succeed; (2) to make our own plans and ask God to bless them; or (3) to ask God for His plans and then do what He tells us to do."[1]

My challenge to you is to consider, where are you at in the planning of your life? Do you make plans or do you seek God's guidance?

Joshua 6:10: Joshua commanded the men to not let their voice be heard. They were to hike around the city wall completely silent. It seems foolish! We need to be able to control our tongue and our body (James 3:1–2). It seems like this would have been hard. There is a time to be silent (Ecclesiastes 3:7; Luke 23:9). Jesus modeled the practice of silence over and over again.

Joshua 6:11–18: The Israelites set out to complete God's game plan. They walked around the city for six days in silence. Early on the seventh day, they marched around the city seven times. The priests blew the trumpets and the men shouted. Everything was to be destroyed, except Rahab and her family, who were spared for helping the spies that previously went into Jericho. The men in the army were

---

[1] Warren W. Wiersbe, *Be Strong: Putting God's Power to Work in Your Life* (Colorado Springs: David C. Cook, 1993), 89.

not to keep anything. In fact, if one person were to keep anything destruction would be brought on everyone.

Joshua 6:19–21: All the metals were to be dedicated to the Lord and put into His treasury. Once the men shouted, the walls crumbled. After the walls fell the army went forth and captured the city.

Joshua 6:22–26: Joshua wanted to honor what the Israelite spies' promised Rahab, so Rahab was spared. The army brought Rahab and her family out of the city. They were placed outside the camp. Then the army burnt the city to the ground. After the city was demolished, Joshua imposed a curse. Joshua prophesied that if anyone attempted to rebuild Jericho that man's two sons would die (1 Kings 16:34).

Closing

Joshua's fame spread throughout the land. There are a lot of images here we can go through. When we depend upon the Lord to get us through the battle, it works! Christ gives us the spiritual weapons to win our battles:

> 2 Corinthians 10:2–6: "I beg you that when I am present I will not need to be bold with the confidence by which I plan to challenge certain people who think we are behaving in an unspiritual way. For though we live in the body, we do not wage war in an unspiritual way, since the weapons of our warfare are not worldly, but are powerful through God for all demolition of strongholds. We demolish arguments and every high-minded thing that is raised up against the knowledge of God, taking every thought captive to obey Christ. And we are ready to punish any disobedience, once your obedience had been confirmed."

> Ephesians 6:10–12: "Finally, be strengthened by the Lord and His vast strength. Put on the full armor of God so that you can stand against the tactics of the devil. For our battle is not against flesh and blood, but against the rulers, against the authorities, against the world powers of this darkness, against the spiritual forces of evil in the heavens."

We are to daily put on the armor of God so we are ready to face any battle that comes our way.

The Daily Word

The Lord gave Joshua the plans for taking over Jericho, bringing victory out of destruction. Joshua listened to the Lord and, as commander, gave the plan to the Israelites. They followed the instructions from the Lord, even though they appeared to be strange, and not your average orders for taking over a city. Joshua trusted the Lord and responded with obedience.

The Lord knows the battles you face each day. While you are not likely marching around a city, it may feel as though you are facing the same kind of battle in a relationship you have had for years. You may feel as though you have dealt with the same struggle with the temptation to sin over and over. The Lord says you will face battles. Today, are you ready to stomp out anger and jealousy? Are you ready to defeat the power of drugs or alcohol in your life? Are you ready to let go of control and give it to the Lord? It is time to seek the Lord for the game plan. Ask Him how to overcome the battle you face. He promises He will fight for you. He promises victory in His name. Today, stop and seek His face, trust the plan He gives you, and respond with obedience.

The Lord said to Joshua, "Look, I have handed Jericho, its king, and its fighting men over to you. March around the city with all the men of war, circling the city one time. Do this for six days. . . . on the seventh day, march around the city seven times, while the priests blow the trumpets." —Joshua 6:2–4

Further Scripture: Exodus 15:2; Psalm 46:10; Hebrews 11:30

Questions

1. What was the response of the people living in the land when they heard what the Lord had done for the Israelites? How long had they been afraid (Joshua 2:9–11)?

2. Why did the Israelite men need to be circumcised a second time? Why could this have been a dangerous thing to do (Genesis 34:25: Joshua 5:8)? Do you believe that God was testing their faith? Why?

3. When did the manna cease for the Israelites? What were they eating now?

4. Who was the *Commander* of the army of the Lord in verse 14? (Note: He did not instruct Joshua not to bow down to Him.)

5. What were the details of how to defeat Jericho in Joshua 6? What was the purpose of God giving these particular directions (Deuteronomy 7:24; Joshua 6:2)?

6. In Joshua 6:2 the Lord said that Jericho had already been defeated. How, as Christians, has the victory already been won for us (2 Chronicles 20:15; John 12:31, 16:33; 1 Corinthians 15:57; Colossians 2:13–15)?

7. What did the Holy Spirit highlight to you in Joshua 5—6 through the reading or the teaching?

Lesson 4: Joshua 7—8

Commander: Blatant Sin Against God

Teaching Notes

Intro

How do you pick a movie to watch? Action? Drama? The book of Joshua has all that. Yesterday, we looked at Joshua 6 and the Israelites taking over Jericho because it was the Lord's plan. There was plenty of action involved in the story. Today's passage brings drama. The Israelites knew they were in God's hands as they went into the Promised Land. Unfortunately, they didn't always remain faithful to that knowledge.

Teaching

Joshua 7:1: Verse 1 points out that unfaithfulness. God had commanded the Israelites to destroy *everything* in Jericho except for Rahab and her family and the things that were to be dedicated to God (Joshua 6:17–19). However, one of the Israelites did not follow those instructions and instead chose to keep some of the silver, gold, bronze, and iron objects from God's treasury. Achan, the guilty man, was from the tribe of Judah, so he shared his lineage with Christ. God's "anger burned," not just at Achan but against all the Israelites. Why did God's anger burn against them all? Wiersbe explains that "Israel was *one people in the Lord* and not just an assorted collection of tribes, clans, families, and individuals."[1] Achan's name means "trouble," and, according to verse 25, he was known as the man who troubled Israel. *Nelson's Commentary* explains that the phrase "committed a trespass" (NKJV) can be understood as "committed a treacherous violation."[2]

---

[1] Warren W. Wiersbe, *Be Strong: Putting God's Power to Work in Your Life* (Colorado Springs: David C. Cook, 1993), 102.

[2] Earl D. Radmacher, Ronald B. Allen, and H. Wayne House, eds., *Nelson's New Illustrated Bible Commentary* (Nashville: Thomas Nelson, 1999), 284.

Joshua 7:2–5: After the victory at Jericho, Joshua sent out men to Ai as scouts. The name "Ai" means "ruin,"[3] and was a small city (12,000 people; Joshua 8:25). The word for "spies" in the Hebrew contains the idea of feet in its meaning,[4] bringing us again to the idea of feet moving forward. The spies reported there were so few people that Joshua didn't need to send a large number of troops, only 2,000 or 3,000. Remember that 40,000 soldiers went into Jericho to take that city (see Joshua 4:13). However, the smaller army of 3,000 fled from Ai. This is evidence of man's plan rather than God's plan (Proverbs 16:18). Thirty-six Israelite soldiers were killed as they fled, and the entire Israelite people's "hearts melted and became like water" (v. 5). Note how the people of Jericho lost heart over the power of the Israelite's God (Joshua 2:11). Now, the same thing happened to the Israelites as they faced their first defeat in the second battle they ever fought.

Joshua 7:6–9: Joshua and the elders tore their clothes, put dust on their heads, and fell face down on the ground in mourning (Genesis 37:34; Judges 20:26; Psalm 6:6; Isaiah 32:12; Lamentations 2:10; Ezra 9:5). Joshua didn't understand why they had lost the battle (v. 7). The Israelites had questioned what they were doing while they were in the wilderness (Exodus 16:3; Numbers 20:3–5). Now, Joshua complained as well, even questioning what this would do to God's reputation (vv. 8–9). Daniel had this same concern when he was in prayer and fasting and called out to the Lord to listen and take action without delay (Daniel 9:16–19).

Joshua 7:10–12: In response, God asked why Joshua was on the ground (v. 10). God explained, "Israel has sinned" and "violated" His covenant. They had stolen from God the things that had been set apart for Him (v. 11). Each sin God reported, He blamed on "they"—all the Israelites. *Nelson's Commentary* explains, "God had consistent standards for both Israel and the Canaanites. . . . He could not allow Israel to accommodate corruption, even that of one man, especially when the instructions concerning the infraction were so clear."[5] God explained that this was the reason the Israelites could not stand against Ai (v. 12). God would not be with them unless they took care of the guilty."

Joshua 7:13–15: God told Joshua to consecrate the people and get them ready to come before Him in order to take care of the sin that had separated Israel from Him (v. 13). They were to present themselves before the Lord, tribe by

---

[3] Radmacher et al., 284.

[4] Radmacher et al., 284.

[5] Radmacher et al., 285.

tribe, family by family, and then, based on the one God called out, man by man (v. 14). The guilty would have to be burned in retribution (v. 15). *Nelson's Commentary* says the guilty person had "a blatant and senseless disregard for God's will."[6] When we put this into New Testament context, it means when we choose to sin, we are saying the cross isn't good enough for us to live for. Achan was being deceitful and got caught!

Joshua 7:16–19: The tribes came forward, and the tribe of Judah was selected (possibly determined through the priest's ephod (1 Samuel 23:6, 9; 30:7–8)). The clans of Judah came forward and the Zerahite clan was selected (v. 17), and then Zabdi was selected. Then, Zabdi's family was brought forward, man by man. Achan was selected (v. 18). Achan confessed what he had done (vv. 19–21). Joshua sent men to Achan's tent to get the things he had stolen, and put them before the Lord. Then they took Achan and his family to the Valley of Achor, stoned them to death, and burned their bodies (vv. 22–26). Achan said that he saw it, he coveted it, he stole it, and he hid it. We always try to hide sin.

Closing

God always knows our sin. We cannot hide it from Him:

- Psalm 139:7: "Where can I go to escape Your Spirit? Where can I flee from Your presence?"
- Jeremiah 16:17: "For My gaze takes in all their ways. They are not concealed from Me, and their guilt is not hidden from My sight."

But we have good news. Because of the New Testament, we are guaranteed God's forgiveness for our sins.

The Daily Word

After the Israelites were struck down during the first battle with the city of Ai, Joshua discovered that "Achan son of Carmi, son of Zabdi, son of Zerah, of the tribe of Judah" had been unfaithful to the plan the Lord had given the Israelites during the destruction of Jericho. Achan had disobeyed orders and taken some of what had been set apart. Therefore, when the Israelites went to battle against Ai, they were not protected by the Lord, and men died. The Israelites became discouraged. Despite all this, the Lord instructed Joshua, "Do not be afraid or discouraged." God had a new plan for defeating Ai.

---

[6] Radmacher et al., 285.

Unfortunately, sin and disobedience exist in the world. You make choices, and those around you make choices that affect the outcome of everyday life. Sometimes you just want to throw in the towel because things are just so discouraging. But God's grace is strong in your weakness. God's power is at work within you. God has a plan for good, not for calamity. When you come before Him and trust Him, He promises to work all things together for good. *So do not be afraid or discouraged.* Seek the Lord, and He will guide your next steps. Keep your head up, friend, and do not give up! God loves you and will never leave you or forsake you!

The Lord said to Joshua, "Do not be afraid or discouraged. Take the whole military force with you and go attack Ai. Look, I have handed over to you the king of Ai, his people, city, and land." —Joshua 8:1

Further Scripture: Psalm 37:24; Isaiah 41:10; Jeremiah 29:11

Questions

1. After having just defeated Jericho, why was Israel defeated at Ai? Do you see a connection to the firstfruits belonging to God (Deuteronomy 26:1–10)?

2. What was Achan's sin? Do you think God was just in punishing Achan's whole family for his sin? What had to be done to be restored back to fellowship with God?

3. The Israelite army had gone from victory, to defeat, to victory. How did they defeat Ai the second time they fought them?

4. What do you notice about what God told them to do after defeating Ai (Joshua 8:1b–2)? Achan could have had all the wealth he wanted if he had just waited. Are there times when you get impatient for something? How can you learn to wait for God's timing (Psalm 27:11–14; Isaiah 64:4)?

5. How was building an altar at Mount Ebal a fulfillment of Deuteronomy 27? How do you see the many acts of obedience after the victory at Ai?

6. What did the Holy Spirit highlight to you in Joshua 7—8 through the reading or the teaching?

Lesson 5: Joshua 9—10

Commander: Believing in God and
Believing God

Teaching Notes

Intro

While we're in the book of Joshua, we'll have two chapters to consider each day. That creates a small inner turmoil for me, because it means each day I have to decide which chapter to teach on. The historical books feel like constant ongoing action. Chapter 9 opens with six people groups who formed an alliance against Joshua and the Israelites. However, the Gibeonites tried to deceive the Israelites by looking like meek and poor foreigners. Israel bought into this deception and made peace (vv. 1–15). Three days later, the Israelites found out the Gibeonites were their neighbors, not foreigners, and realized the Gibeonites had deceived them. The Israelites felt they couldn't kill the Gibeonites as their enemies because of the peace between them, so they allowed them to live. The Gibeonites became the woodcutters and water carriers for the Israelite community (vv. 16–27).

Teaching

Joshua 10:1–5: This is the first reference to Jerusalem in Scripture (v. 1). Dale Davis explains that according to information recorded in the Amarna letters between 1406 and 1340 BC, "Jerusalem was the center of political activity in the fourteenth century BC and was always conscious of its own security."[1] The name "Jerusalem" meant "The Founding (or Possession) of Peace."[2] In this case, the king of Jerusalem was trying to figure out how to keep the city safe, and he became angry that the city of Gibeon had sought safety from the Israelites, basically pulling out of the alliance that had been formed against the Israelites (v. 2). King Adoni-zedek, who was not a good guy, sent for the other kings in the alliance for support in fighting the Gibeonites (vv. 3–4). *Nelson's Commentary* states that these five kings made "political and military calculations" to

---

[1] Dale Ralph Davis, *No Falling Words* (Grand Rapids: Baker Book House, 1988), 95.

[2] Thomas L. Constable, *Expository Notes of Dr. Thomas Constable: Joshua*, 85, http://planobiblechapel.org/tcon/notes/pdf/joshua.pdf.

determine how they could take the large city of Gibeon with its large numbers of warriors.[3] This coalition of kings from Canaanite (or Amorites) besieged the city of Gibeon (v. 5).

If you keep up with what's going on in the Middle East today, you'll see this same pattern continues as each country tries to gain the support of another nation so they will have more power and influence. It's the common theme of what happens there. And when the Antichrist comes into play, Israel will be totally deceived. But that also means that the Messiah is coming! There's this crazy foreshadow here of what we see today.

Joshua 10:6–8: The Gibeonites called out to Joshua for help (v. 6). Joshua and the Israelites' entire fighting force came from Gilgal (v. 7). Wiersbe notes there are three "calls" for help in this passage: (1) Adoni-zedek called the other kings for help against the Gibeonites; (2) the Gibeonites called out to Joshua for help against this coalition; and (3) Joshua called out to the Lord.[4] God promised, no one would be able to stand against them (v. 8) and Joshua believed God (Romans 14:23; 10:17). The more we listen to the Holy Spirit, the more we are able to walk out our faith.

Wiersbe points out that because "they believed God's promise and knew that the victory was assured," they marched at night for a surprise attack on the coalition.[5] The Israelites' journey was twenty miles long and up steep terrain,[6] but they moved quickly because of their trust in God's promises (v. 9). One of Israel's prime ministers said, "We don't believe in miracles; we depend upon them." Joshua caught the coalition by surprise, and God threw their enemy into confusion, defeating them, chasing them, and raining down hail upon them. More died from God's hailstones than from the sword (vv. 10–11). I always wonder why none of the Israelites were struck by the hailstones.

Joshua 10:12–15: Joshua prayed before the people of Israel of God's might in the battle, asking that the sun stand still and the moon stop (vv. 12–13a). His prayer was confirmed in the Book of Jasher (v. 13b), which has not survived, and is mentioned in 2 Samuel 1:18.[7] How did these miracles happen? *Nelson's Commentary* proposes three possibilities: (1) Since the sun doesn't actually move, some suggest God stopped the rotation of the earth; (2) some suggest "God

---

[3] Earl D. Radmacher, Ronald B. Allen, and H. Wayne House, eds., *Nelson's New Illustrated Bible Commentary* (Nashville: Thomas Nelson, 1999), 289.

[4] Warren W. Wiersbe, *Be Strong: Putting God's Power to Work in Your Life* (Colorado Springs: David C. Cook, 1993), 135–36.

[5] Wiersbe, 136.

[6] Radmacher et al., 290.

[7] Radmacher et al., 290.

caused an unusual refraction of light in the earth's atmosphere that caused the sun to remain visible" for a longer period of time than normal; and (3) some suggest Joshua's prayer was actually for the sun to stop rather than stand still to keep the sun off his exhausted soldiers.[8] Regardless of how you view this, God responded to a man's prayer by using His power over His creation to change nature's action at the precise moment it was needed.[9] Verse 14 says, "The LORD listened to the voice of a man, because the LORD fought for Israel." Joshua and his men returned to Gilgal with the Lord (v. 15).

Joshua 10:16–21: The defeated kings fled and hid in a cave. When Joshua found out where they were, he told his men to roll large stones in front of the cave and place guards outside it. The rest of his men were told to keep fighting, pursuing and attacking the enemy until they were destroyed. However, a few survivors escaped and hid in some of the fortified cities. This is important because they didn't complete what they were supposed to do, and this will impact things to come later in the book of Joshua.

Joshua 10:22–28: Then Joshua had the kings brought out of the cave, and Joshua had his military commanders put their feet on the necks of the kings (Psalm 8:6; 110:1; 1 Corinthians 10:15). Joshua encouraged his commanders because this had been the Lord's work. Then the kings were executed and hung on five trees. In the evening, their bodies were taken down and sealed again inside the cave. On the same day, Joshua also captured the city of Makkedah and executed its king as well.

We keep talking about the stones because they provide reminders of what has happened along the journey.

Closing

Joshua didn't just believe in God, but he believed God and acted on that belief.

The Daily Word

After the Israelites conquered and destroyed both Jericho and Ai, the people of Gibeon feared for their lives. In an effort to save their lives, they carried out a crafty plan and tricked Joshua and the Israelites. The plan worked, and the Israelites, without seeking the Lord's wisdom, swore an oath to allow the Gibeonites to live in their land. Eventually, Joshua and the Israelites learned the truth, and the Gibeonites never found the freedom they desired. Instead, as a result of their

---

[8] Radmacher et al., 290.

[9] Radmacher et al., 290.

deceitful ways, they served as woodcutters and water carriers for the rest of their lives.

In the moment, lying and deception can seem like the easier choice to make. Like the Gibeonites, fear of what lies ahead may overtake you to the point your flesh thinks lying is the best and only choice. Your flesh may say, "It's only a small lie. It's easier this way, and besides, no one will ever know." Eventually someone will uncover the truth, and then you will face the consequences. But if you walk in the power of the Spirit, you will not give in to the deeds of the flesh, like lying and deceiving. *When you live honestly, you live securely.* Remember, as you make choices, the Lord delights in those who are honest.

We greatly feared for our lives because of you, and that is why we did this. Now we are in your hands. Do to us whatever you think is right.
—Joshua 9:24–25

Further Scripture: Proverbs 10:9; Proverbs 12:22; Galatians 5:16

Questions

1. Why did the people of Gibeon resort to deception? How did they deceive the Israelites?

2. Why didn't Joshua and the Israelites destroy the Gibeonites? What should they have done first (Joshua 9:14)? Can you think of a time when you didn't consult the Lord and had a negative outcome?

3. In Joshua 10:13, the Lord made the sun stand still. Why? What was the result?

4. Why did Joshua have his commanders step on the necks of the captured kings? What did he tell them (Joshua 10:25; Psalm 110:1; Romans 16:20)?

5. What did the Holy Spirit highlight to you in Joshua 9—10 through the reading or the teaching?

Lesson 6: Joshua 11—12

Commander: Completing God's Plan

Teaching Notes

Intro

As we move further into the book of Joshua, we're watching Joshua, the commander, lead the people into the Promised Land. Most of the time, God was doing the work while the Israelites were following His plan. In Joshua 11, we move from the south to the conquest in the north.

Teaching

Joshua 11:1–5: Jabin was king of Hazor, a city of 30,000 to 40,000 people.[1] When word that the Israelites' had moved north was shared with him, he sent word to the other northern kings, and they gathered together to attack the Israelites (vv. 1–3). In the list of groups that came together were the Jebusites, who *should not* have been there. Remember they were already wiped out by the Israelites, except for the few survivors who escaped (Joshua 10:20). Verse 4 describes the size of their armies: "They went out with all their armies—a multitude as numerous as the sand on the seashore—along with a vast number of horses and chariots." The historian Josephus estimated "the combined armies of the Canaanite tribes totaled 300,000 armed footmen, 10,000 horsemen, and 20,000 chariots."[2] *Nelson's Commentary* points out that "only in the battles of Jericho and Ai did the Israelites initiate the action."[3] In the beginning, God showed His power by limiting the size of the Israelites' force.[4] The northern coalition camped at the waters of Merom before they attacked (v. 5).

---

[1] Richard S. Hess, *Joshua: An Introduction and Commentary* (Tyndale Old Testament Commentaries series) (Leicester, England, and Downer's Grove, IL: InterVarsity, 1996), 208.

[2] Flavius Josephus, *The Works of Flavius Josephus*, trans. William Whiston (London: T. Nelson and Sons, 1866; repr. Peabody, MA: Hendrickson, 1988), 5:1:18.

[3] Earl D. Radmacher, Ronald B. Allen, and H. Wayne House, eds., *Nelson's New Illustrated Bible Commentary* (Nashville: Thomas Nelson, 1999), 292.

[4] Radmacher et al., 292.

Joshua 11:6–11: God reminded Joshua that he had nothing to fear in the northern coalition. Joshua was told to cut the hamstring muscles of the horses and burn the chariots of this army (v. 6). The Israelites surprised the coalition armies and God gave them the battle. The Israelites followed the surviving armies in all directions, leaving no survivors (vv. 7–9). Joshua also captured the city of Hazor, executed the king, struck down all the people, and burned the city (vv. 10–11). Interestingly, there is archaeological evidence of the destruction of Hazor in the fifteenth century BC.[5]

Joshua 11:12–15: In Israel today, there are many "tells," or mounts, in which cities are built upon former cities. Note that the Israelites only destroyed the city of Hazor, so these other cities are probably at the bottom of many of these tells (vv. 12–13). From all these cities, the Israelites took the things of value and the cattle for themselves. They left no one alive, just as God has commanded Moses, who commanded Joshua (vv. 14–15).

The annihilation of whole groups of people make us uncomfortable, especially people who are concerned about human rights. Was it necessary? Or did Joshua become bloodthirsty in the process? *Nelson's Commentary* explains that God told Moses the destruction of Canaan was because "the Canaanites were being judged by God for their wickedness"[6] (Deuteronomy 20:16– 20). God is an extreme God when He wants to set His people apart. Look at what He did to His Son so we could be with Him.

Joshua 11:16–23: These verses provide a summary of Joshua's conquests—the hill country, the Negev, Goshen, and the foothills (vv. 16–17). Joshua took it all, even land like the Negev that is mostly desert. Joshua had been a man of action for a long time (v. 18). Wiersbe explains that this long time lasted seven years, based on the fact that Caleb was 40 years old at Kadesh-barnea (Deuteronomy 2:14) and it was 38 years later when they crossed the Jordan River (Joshua 14:7). Caleb was 85 (Joshua 14:10), when the Israelites' conquest of the Promised Land was completed (so 40+38=78 was Caleb's age at the beginning of the conquest and 85 at the end; 85–78=7 years).[7]

No cities made peace with the Israelites except the Gibeonites, and all the others were annihilated as God commanded (vv. 19–21). In verse 22, no Anakim (the giants the Israelite spies were afraid of), were left except in Gaza, Gath, and

---

[5] Douglas Petrovich, "The Dating of Hazor's Destruction in Joshua 11 by Way of Biblical, Archaeological, and Epigraphical Evidence," *Journal of the Evangelical Theological Society* 51:3 (September 2008):489–512.

[6] Radmacher et al., 292.

[7] Warren W. Wiersbe, *The Bible Exposition Commentary: Joshua–Esther* (Colorado Springs: David C. Cook, 2003), 67.

Ashod (v. 22). Gaza is home to the Palestinians. In Joshua's command, the size of the armies and the enemies didn't matter. All that mattered was the size of his God. Joshua took all the land because that's what God told him to do (v. 23). He believed in his God. And, "the land had rest from war" (v. 23b).

Closing

The fulfillment of prophecy was happening through the leadership of Joshua. James Montgomery Boice identified the following qualities of Joshua's leadership[8]:

1. Joshua did not let short-term gains deter him from long-range objects. He found the five kings, defeated the armies, and then killed the kings.
2. Joshua understood the need others have for visible encouragement. He had his commanders put their feet on the kings' necks to encourage them.
3. Joshua took no shortcuts but pursued the campaign in a step-by-step progression that took seven years.
4. Joshua didn't allow his early errors to unsettle or defeat him, such as the defeat at Ai and the sin in the camp (Philippians 3:13–14).
5. Joshua believed God implicitly—he was strong and courageous.
6. Joshua obeyed completely (Joshua 11:15).

These are good qualities for anyone in leadership for God.

The Daily Word

News of the Israelites' victories in battle spread throughout the northern cities of the Promised Land. As a result, Jabor, the king of Hazor, gathered all the neighboring kings and their armies to attack Israel together. The combined army was as numerous as the grains of sand on the seashore. Joshua heard of this coming attack, and the Lord reminded Joshua not to fear. Then He gave Joshua the strategy for victory. God's battle plan included both God and man. God would hand the armies over to the Israelites, but He still gave the Israelites a battle plan.

The Lord says you will face battles. You may lie in bed at night wondering how you will face tomorrow. The Lord sees you and knows the battles you face. He says do not worry about tomorrow—do not fear. He has a plan for you, and He goes before you. Trust in His plan. Even if the plan seems unusual, follow Him. The Lord told Joshua to hamstring the horses and burn the chariots, and

---

[8] James Montgomery Boice, *Expositional Commentary: Joshua* (Grand Rapids: Baker Book House, 2006), n.p.

the Israelites found victory. Follow the Lord's ways, and you will find victory in the battle.

The Lord said to Joshua, "Do not be afraid of them, for at this time tomorrow I will cause all of them to be killed before Israel. You are to hamstring their horses and burn up their chariots." . . . The Lord handed them over to Israel, and they struck them down. —Joshua 11:6, 8

Further Scripture: Deuteronomy 20:4; Proverbs 21:31; 1 Corinthians 15:57–58

Questions

1. At the beginning of Joshua 11, many kings and their armies were gathering to fight against Israel. Have you ever felt like those around you were gathering to fight against you?

2. Read Joshua 11:4–5 and Revelation 19:19. What similarities do you see?

3. What does Joshua 11:9, 12, and 15 remind you of from the Pentateuch (Exodus 39:42; 40:16, 19, 21, 23)? What was God's reason for instructing the Israelites to kill everyone in these cities (Deuteronomy 20:16–18; Joshua 11:11)?

4. The Lord hardened the hearts of the Canaanites (Joshua 11:20). Where else have we read about God hardening hearts (Exodus 9:12; 10:1; 14:8; Deuteronomy 2:30; John 12:40)?

5. In chapter 12, Joshua retold the defeat of Sihon and Og, the Amorite kings on the east side of the Jordan, and listed the 31 kings and their cities the Israelites conquered. Why do you think he did this (Deuteronomy 8:2; Psalm 77:11; 105:5)?

6. What did the Holy Spirit highlight to you in Joshua 11—12 through the reading or the teaching?

Lesson 7: Joshua 13—14

Commander: Caleb's Unaltering Confidence

Teaching Notes

Intro

As we continue to move through the book of Joshua, we've seen a lot of killing and a lot of obedience. The Israelites were living out God's instructions to Joshua to "be strong and courageous." Moses prepared Joshua to take the land, and the people supported Joshua's leadership. In all of these things, God continued to intervene so the Israelites would have the victory. Joshua 13 states that Joshua had become old and there were still lands that had not been claimed (vv. 1–7). In the rest of the chapter, the lands that had been conquered were handed out to the tribes of Reuben, Gad, and half the tribe of Manasseh as their inheritance. In chapter 14, the giving out of the land to the other tribes of Israel continues. Joshua is an image of the coming provision of salvation through Jesus.

Teaching

Joshua 14:1–5: Eleazar the high priest, Joshua, and the heads of the families within each of the tribes handed out the land by lots as God had told Moses to do (vv. 1–2). This group provided the inheritances to nine-and-a-half tribes since Moses had already given inheritances to two-and-a-half tribes before they entered the Promised Land (v. 3). The Levites (the priestly tribe) received no land inheritance but were given cities and pasture lands for their cattle and livestock. The inheritance was received through the obedience of Joshua and the Israelites.

Joshua 14:6–9: In verse 6, the story seems to make a right turn. The descendants of Judah approached Joshua, and Caleb spoke to him. Remember that Joshua and Caleb were the only two of the original spies who were allowed to enter the Promised Land. Caleb is described as the son of Jephunneh the Kenizzite, a non-Israelite group descended from Esau through Kenaz (Genesis 15:19; 36:11, 15).[1] Some scholars suggest there was a group that associated themselves with

---

[1] Donald K Campbell, "Joshua," in *The Bible Knowledge Commentary: Old Testament*, ed. John F. Walvoord and Roy B. Zuck (Colorado Springs: David C. Cook, 1985), 357.

Judah at an early stage (Numbers 13:6), making Caleb a generation removed from a non-Israelite family.[2]

Caleb reminded Joshua of all they had been through as they scouted the Promised Land (vv. 6–9). Caleb pointed out he had brought back "an honest report," unlike the other spies (v. 7). He also stated the other spies had come back with reports that caused the people to fear, but he had remained loyal to his God (v. 8) (Numbers 13:30). He reminded Joshua that because of his honest report, he and his tribe had been promised a special inheritance (v. 9). Numbers 14:24 says "But since my servant Caleb has a different spirit and has followed Me completely, I will bring him into the land where he has gone, and his descendants will inherit it."

Joshua 14:10–12: Caleb was 40 years old when the Lord spoke this word to Moses, and now, 45 years later, Caleb was still waiting on this promise from God to be fulfilled (v. 10). At 85, Caleb was ready to receive that fulfillment. His strength for battle and for the work was as strong as it was at 40 (v. 11). Therefore, Caleb asked for the hill country God had promised him 45 years earlier (v. 12). The land Caleb asked for was the land of the Anakim—the giants. Caleb wanted to go in with God's help. F. B. Meyer said,

> Amid the marchings and the counter marchings, the innumerable deaths, the murmurings and rebellions of the people, [Caleb] retained a steadfast purpose to do only God's will to please Him, to know no other leader and to heed no other voice. . . . He would be no party to Miriam's jealous spite. He would not be allured by the wiles of the girls of Moab. Always strong and true and pure and noble; like a rock in a changeful sea, like a snow-capped peak in a change of cloud and storm and sun. A man in whose strong nature weaker men could hide, and who must have been a tower of strength to that new and young generation which grew up to fill the vacant places in the van of Israel. The Nestor of the Hebrew camp, in him the words of the Psalmist were anticipated, that he bore fruit in old age, and to the last was fat and flourishing.[3]

---

[2] Earl D. Radmacher, Ronald B. Allen, and H. Wayne House, eds., *Nelson's New Illustrated Bible Commentary* (Nashville: Thomas Nelson, 1999), 280.

[3] Frederick B. Meyer, *Joshua and the Land of Promise* (New York: Fleming H. Revell, n.d.; reprint ed., Fort Washington, PA: Christian Literature Crusade, 1977), 2; available online at http://www.baptistbiblebelievers.com/LinkClick.aspx?fileticket=l7VECJdnV9U%3d&tabid=306&mid=1008.

This is such an amazing image. Amidst life, Caleb held on. Amidst life, Caleb and Joshua didn't waver in what they felt called to do. Caleb was ready to take the next step to fulfill God's promise to him. Jacobson questioned why Caleb didn't look for a "softer" or easy place to settle. His explanation states: "It would have been natural for Caleb to ask for a 'soft spot'—a portion of land already conquered where he could settle down and spend the rest of his life raising a few vegetables or flowers. Instead, at 85, he asked for the very section that had struck terror into the hearts of the ten spies."[4] I wonder if Caleb had these moments while waiting for the blessing that he would receive—actually hanging on to the Word of God!

Joshua 14:13–15: Joshua's response to Caleb's request begins in verse 13. Joshua blessed Caleb and gave him Hebron as his inheritance. Hebron is one of the very few Jewish sites that is sacred today (Numbers 13:21–22). Jacob and Caleb had gone into this land as spies. This was the only piece of land Abraham had owned, and he and his wife Sarah were buried there, as well as Isaac, Rebecca, and Jacob. Eventually, even Joseph asked for his bones to be buried there. This is the closest thing to a Jewish sacred site at the time, and it was going to be given to Caleb because "he remained loyal to the Lord" (v. 14).

James Montgomery Boice explains that the Nephilim were giants (Genesis 6:4), and the Anakim were descendants of Nephilim. Three of Anak's (Anakim) descendants lived in Hebron: Ahiman, Sheshai, and Talmai (Numbers 13:22), so there were still giants in the land. Even though the Israelites had conquered it, there was still work to do.[5] Yet there was also the promise of peace—"rest from war"[6] (v. 15).

Alan Redpath summarizes this transfer of land: "The majority measured the giants against their own strength; Caleb and Joshua measured the giants against God. The majority trembled; the two triumphed. The majority had great giants but a little God. Caleb had a great God and little giants."[7] Caleb believed just as much as Joshua did. Because of Caleb's radical faith, Caleb was not complicated.[8] He understood he had a role to fulfill and kept his eyes on God, not the giants.

---

[4] Henry Jacobsen, *Claiming God's Promises*, new ed. Bible Knowledge series (Wheaton: Scripture Press, 1963), 100.

[5] James Montgomery Boice, *Joshua: Expositional Commentary* (Grand Rapids: Baker Book House, 2006), n.p.

[6] Alan Redpath, *Victorious Christian Living* (Grand Rapids: Baker Book House, 2003), 197–98.

[7] Redpath, 173.

[8] John Cawood, "The Godly Features of Caleb," *Confident Living*, 44:10 (November 1986): 53–55.

Closing

John Cawood identified four leadership qualities in Caleb:

1. "Uncompromising convictions"—For 45 years, Caleb held to the promise God had given him.
2. "Unreserved commitment"—He was totally sold out to God.
3. "Unalterable courage"—He found courage through his complete dependence upon God.
4. "Unwavering confidence"—He never lost his confidence in God.

What if Caleb had never received the promise? Crazy as it is, most people in Scripture never saw the fulfillment of the promise (Hebrews 11:32–40), but their faith never wavered.

The Daily Word

Forty-five years after spying out the land in Canaan, Caleb reminded Joshua about the inheritance the Lord promised him. Even after years of wandering in the wilderness without seeing the fulfillment of God's promise, Caleb remained loyal to the Lord his God. Joshua recognized Caleb's loyalty to the Lord and blessed him, giving Hebron as an inheritance.

Even at the age of eighty-five, Caleb remained strong in the Lord. You may be young or you may be growing older in years, but like Caleb, you are called to keep your eyes on the Lord. Remain steadfast and immovable. You may have hard days. You may feel as though you have giants to face. You may even be wandering in a wilderness. Continue to remain faithful to the Lord. Today, *believe God is at work*. He has not forgotten you, and His promises still stand. Great is His faithfulness.

Here I am today, 85 years old. I am still as strong today as I was the day Moses sent me out. My strength for battle and for daily tasks is now as it was then. Now give me this hill country the Lord promised me on that day, because you heard then that the Anakim are there, as well as large fortified cities. Perhaps the Lord will be with me and I will drive them out as the Lord promised. —Joshua 14:10–12

Further Scripture: Psalm 33:11; Isaiah 46:4; 1 Corinthians 15:58

Questions

1. According to Joshua 13:6, who would drive out the inhabitants of the land that had not yet been possessed by the Israelites? Do you trust God to drive out your enemies who possess "territory" that belongs to you?

2. A notation in Joshua 13:22 reminds us that the Israelites killed Balaam, son of Beor, while on the east side of the Jordan. Why do you think this is mentioned (Numbers 31:16; 2 Peter 2:15; Revelation 2:14)?

3. What do we know about the Anakim (Genesis 6:4; Numbers 13:33; Deuteronomy 9:2)?

4. Caleb asked Joshua for his inheritance as promised by Moses, and Hebron was given to him. What events happened there in the past (Genesis 23:2; 35:27)?

5. The last verse of chapter 14 explains how Hebron's name was formerly Kiriath-arba. Why was it called that? Who was Arba (Joshua 15:13)?

6. What did the Holy Spirit highlight to you in Joshua 13—14 through the reading or the teaching?

Lesson 8: Joshua 15—16

Commander: Asking for Inheritance

Teaching Notes

Intro

We're going to talk about land allotment today. Yesterday, we looked at Caleb's request for his promised land of Hebron. Joshua 13—19 focus on the land allotments given to each of the tribes of Israel. Judah's land allotment, in chapter 15, was the most extensive. Since Reuben, the oldest son, messed up and slept with his father's concubine, he lost his firstborn rights. The next two sons, Simeon and Levi, also messed up when they massacred the Shechemites. Genesis 34 records these actions as a "stench on the land." The fourth son, Judah, was given the right to rule as the next in line (Genesis 49:8–12). Judah's kingship rule will go on forever until the Messiah comes.

Teaching

Joshua 15:1–12: Borders were important because it was an issue of stewardship—taking care of the land they had been given and protecting that land from outside invaders. Judah's southern border was at the northern tip of the Dead Sea and ran to the border with Egypt to the south, the southernmost tribe of Israel. The eastern border was along the Dead Sea. The northern border began at the mouth of the Jordan River and ended at the Mediterranean Sea.

Joshua 15:13–19: Caleb asked for the land promised to him, land that still had giants in it (Joshua 14). Caleb drove out the giants and then marched against Debir. Caleb promised to give his daughter in marriage to the person who captured Kiriath-sepher (the father of Anak). Othniel, either Caleb's nephew or youngest brother, took the challenge and captured Kiriath-sepher and then married Caleb's daughter Achsah. Othniel later became one of Israel's judges.[1] In some sense, Caleb's son-in-law became the leader and deliverer after Joshua (Judges 3:9). Caleb's daughter Achsah persuaded her husband to ask Caleb for a blessing of springs of water.

---

[1] Warren W. Wiersbe, *The Bible Exposition Commentary: Joshua–Esther* (Colorado Springs: David C. Cook, 2003), 70.

Hess notes that Achsah's request for springs is reminiscent of Rebekah's meeting with Isaac. Consider these similarities[2]:

1. Both approached riding on an animal.
2. Both dismounted.
3. Both asked for something.
4. Both received what they asked for.

What's cool about this is that it proves we will not be denied our inheritance in Christ when we ask for it. Our inheritance is more than land, more than springs of water—it is complete in Jesus. We have always been given an inheritance, but we don't always ask for the full inheritance.

Joshua 15:20–32: In verses 20–32, the 29 outermost cities of the tribe of Judah are given.

Joshua 15:33–47: In these verses, the 39 cities and their villages in the Judean foothills are listed.

Joshua 15:48–60: In these verses, the 38 cities and their villages in the hill country are given.

Joshua 15:61–62: The six cities and their villages of the wilderness are given.

Joshua 15:63: But the descendants of Judah could not drive out the Jebusites who lived in Jerusalem. This was right on the border between Judah and Benjamin. A few survivors ran away to the walled cities, and they showed back up in Jerusalem (Joshua 10:20). The verse continues, "So the Jebusites live in Jerusalem among the descendants of Judah to this day." That seems to be part of the reason for the problem in Jerusalem now. Because the Israelites didn't clean house then, there is still no peace in Israel today.

    Nelson's Commentary explains the Jebusites lived in Jerusalem before the Israelites arrived and were able to hold on to the city, "because the tribe of Judah did not follow through on its obligation to destroy them completely. God did not want Israel to make peace with the inhabitants of the land, but instead to drive them out and utterly destroy them."[3] At first, Jerusalem did not belong to either the tribe of Benjamin or the tribe of Judah.

---

[2] Richard S. Hess, *Joshua: An Introduction and Commentary*, Tyndale Old Testament Commentaries series (Leicester, England, and Downer's Grove, IL: InterVarsity, 1996), 245.

[3] Earl D. Radmacher, Ronald B. Allen, and H. Wayne House, eds., *Nelson's New Illustrated Bible Commentary* (Nashville: Thomas Nelson, 1999), 295.

Judges 1:8: "The men of Judah fought against Jerusalem and captured it. They put the city to the sword and set it on fire."

Judges 1:28: "When Israel became stronger, they made the Canaanites serve as forced labor but never drove them out completely."

The city of Jerusalem belonged to the Jebusites until the time of David—all because Judah and Benjamin did not drive out the Jebusites as they were instructed.

Closing

In one of these cities, one of Caleb's daughters asked for more. It is a reminder to us all that we can, and should, ask God for more . . . more of His Spirit, more of His presence, more of His grace.

The Daily Word

Caleb marched against the inhabitants of Debir. He promised his daughter Achsah as a wife to whoever captured Kiriath-sepher. Othniel captured and struck down Kiriath-sepher, and he received Achsah as his wife. Achsah persuaded her new husband to ask her father for a field. Achsah knew her father had more to give the newly married couple, so she asked for even more. She asked for a blessing and for springs of water. Without hesitating, her father gave her both the upper and lower springs.

In a similar way, your Heavenly Father has even more gifts for you. As you walk with Him in integrity, He will not withhold good things. He has more power, grace, wisdom, and joy to give, even beyond what you can imagine. Jesus is your daily source of living water. As you believe in Him, it lives within you. The Lord says to abide in Him, asking whatever you wish, and it will be done for you. Today, confidently ask the Lord for even more. May His living water spring up within you today!

She replied, "Give me a blessing. Since you have given me land in the Negev, give me the springs of water also." So he gave her the upper and lower springs. —Joshua 15:19

Further Scripture: Psalm 84:11; John 15:7; Revelation 21:6

Questions

1. How did Caleb's faith rub off on his family and in-laws (Joshua 15:13–19; Judges 3:7–11)? What did Caleb's daughter have the faith to ask him?

2. How do you think the older generation should minister to the younger generation in the church?

3. In Joshua15:20–62, the tribe of Judah was receiving their inheritance. What can we as believers claim because we have received our inheritance in Christ? What is the future inheritance we have to look forward to (Ephesians 1:3; 1 Peter 1:3–6)?

4. What did the Holy Spirit highlight to you in Joshua 15—16 through the reading or the teaching?

Lesson 9: Joshua 17—18

Commander: Division of Land

Teaching Notes

Intro

All we do is talk about land! God, from the very beginning with Abraham, kept promising land and lots of it. The Israelites finally got to the Promised Land under the leadership of Joshua. They were having to fight people for land.

Teaching

Joshua 17:1–13: Joshua divided up the land for the tribe of Manasseh. There was a West Manasseh group and an East Manasseh group. Why was there an east and west? The river divided the land, and half the tribe decided to settle on the eastern side of the Jordan rather than enter the Promised Land.

Joshua 17:14–18: These verses lay out additional inheritances for the tribes of Manasseh and Ephraim.

Joshua 18:1: This verse begins with more of the real estate business. The entire community gathered at Shiloh. Shiloh was in the middle of the whole terrain, and it was where the Israelites had set up the tent of meeting. Remember, the tent of meeting was a portable tent and was also referred to as the tabernacle. The Israelites wanted the entire community to be able to experience the presence of God. In time, the tabernacle lead to the temple, and the temple lead to Jesus (1 Samuel 4; Psalm 78:60; Jeremiah 7:14).

I want to walk through the history here. Two men built the tent of meeting in Shiloh (Exodus 31:2–3, 6). These two guys were the general contractors. After the tent was completed, it was taken on a progression throughout the Promised Land:

- Gilgal (Joshua 5:10)
- Gilgal (Joshua 10:15, 43)
- Shiloh (Joshua 18:1)
- Bethel (Judges 20: 27–28)

- Shiloh (1 Samuel 1:3)
- Mizpah (1 Samuel 7:9–10)
- Gilgal (1 Samuel 10:8)
- Gibeon (1 Chronicles 16:39–40)

This tent eventually ended up in Jerusalem where Solomon later built the temple. The tent was moving; it was a lot of work for people to set up and take down. To experience the presence of God, sometimes we have to go out of our way for Him.

Joshua 18:2: Five tribes had already received their inheritances. There were seven more who had not received their inheritance. It was almost as if they were choosing not to.

Joshua 18:3: Joshua asked them, "How long are you going to wait?" *Nelson's Commentary* says, "It was not enough to defeat the inhabitants of the land; they also had to take possession of it."[1] *Nelson's Commentary* goes on to point out that "this laziness disobeyed God's instructions in Joshua 13:1 and showed a lack of faith in His promises."[2] Seven more tribes had not gone after the land! Let's call out the ones who have not inhabited the land:

1. Benjamin (Joshua 18:11–28)
2. Simeon (Joshua 19:1–9)
3. Zebulun (Joshua 19: 10–16)
4. Issachar (Joshua 19:17–23)
5. Asher (Joshua 19:24–31)
6. Naphtali (Joshua 19:32–39)
7. Dan (Joshua 19:40–48)

You can see the progression that was coming, but I think it was because Joshua called them out.

In 2 Kings 5:8–11, Naaman was told go into the water seven times and his leprosy would be healed. He left the prophet disappointed and angry. He wanted an instant miracle from the prophet himself. The Israelites wanted their inheritance just handed to them. We have a part to play in our relationship with God. That is why it is called a relationship. In order to get to know God, we have got to pour into Him as well.

---

[1] Earl D. Radmacher, Ronald B. Allen, and H. Wayne House, eds., *Nelson's New Illustrated Bible Commentary* (Nashville: Thomas Nelson, 1999), 297.

[2] Radmacher et al., 297.

Look at Jonah 1:1–3. Sometimes we think that something can only look a certain way, but God continues to show us it has to be His way. In Luke 6:46–48, Jesus asked, "Why do you call Me 'Lord, Lord,' and don't do the things I say?" When we do not do what the Lord says in His timing, we have to face the ramifications of our disobedience.

Joshua 18:4: Joshua instructed these seven tribes of the Israelites to appoint three men from each tribe, a total of 21 men. These men were to be sent out to survey the land, write down their observations, and report back their findings. Joshua was a good leader because these tribes were procrastinators, and they needed his direction.

Joshua 18:5: The land was to be divided into seven portions. Judah was to remain in the south and Joseph's family was to reside in the north.

Joshua 18:6–7: Joshua instructed the 21 men that they were to report back on what they found, and then Joshua would cast lots for each tribe in the presence of God. These lots would determine what portion of land each tribe would inherit. Keep in mind the Levites would receive no land because they received the priesthood as their inheritance.

Joshua 18:8–10: As the men prepared to go, Joshua repeated his directions to them. Essentially, they were to go, stay focused, and come back. The 21 men left and wrote down their observations of the towns they were assigned. When they came back together, they put together a document divided into seven sections. Joshua cast lots for the seven Israelite tribes at Shiloh, and then divided the land accordingly.

Closing

By the end of chapter 18, the Promised Land was being divided among the Israelites. At the heart of this, Joshua wanted to make sure the Israelites experience the fulfillment of prophecy that went through Abraham, Isaac, and Jacob. Joshua was a good leader; he was clear in what he instructed the people to do.

The Daily Word

The entire Israelite community came together at Shiloh. Seven tribes of Israel had not yet divided up their inheritance. Joshua wondered how long the people would delay going out and receiving what the Lord had given them. Therefore he instructed the tribes to go and survey the land, write descriptions of it, and then return to him. Joshua waited for them to return at the Tent of Meeting. Then, in the presence of the Lord, they cast lots.

As believers of Jesus, you have the opportunity to have a relationship with Him and to daily abide in Him as your source of strength, peace, joy, and guidance. But like the Israelites, you have to *go* after it. The Lord longs for you to pursue His presence daily. In order to know Jesus more, you must spend time in His presence, read His Word, observe it, and write it down. What is keeping you from this today? Why do you delay? Maybe you are busy and keep getting sidetracked. *Go!* Start today! Do not delay seeking the Lord and all He has for you in His presence!

So Joshua said to the Israelites, "How long will you delay going out to take possession of the land that the Lord, the God of your fathers, gave you? Appoint for yourselves three men from each tribe, and I will send them out. They are to go and survey the land, write a description of it for the purpose of their inheritance, and return to me." —Joshua 18:3–4

Further Scripture: Psalm 27:7–8; Romans 13:11; James 4:8

Questions

1. What were Ephraim and Manasseh upset about? How did Joshua respond?
2. What was the difference between how Ephraim and Manasseh responded in taking their inheritance and how Caleb responded (Joshua 14:11–12)?
3. Why do you think there were still seven tribes that did not yet have possession of their inheritance (Joshua 2–3; Proverbs 12:27; Hebrews 11:6)?
4. What is the difference between having an inheritance and having possession of that inheritance (Joshua 2:6; 18:3; Matthew 25:34)?
5. What did the Holy Spirit highlight to you in Joshua 17—18 through the reading or the teaching?

Lesson 10: Joshua 19—20

Commander: The Tribe of Asher

Teaching Notes

Intro

I feel like all we've been talking about is real estate. Up until this point, the Israelites had not been given their land. They were finally given the Promised Land. Caleb and Joshua finally got to experience the Promised Land! There were seven tribes that had not taken possession of their lands. Today, we are going to talk about more of the Israelites' inheritance, which was more than just the land. There were more components within the land. We are going to talk about the tribe of Asher today. Prophetically, this is an incredibly rich tribe.

Teaching

Joshua 19:1–9: The first lot came out for the tribe of Benjamin and the second lot came out for the tribe of Simeon. When you start to understand the land inheritances, everything in the Old Testament makes more sense.

Joshua 19:10–16: The third lot came out for the tribe of Zebulun. Remember those 21 men who were told to go, survey, record, and come back? These men were experiencing the results of their work.

Joshua 19:17–23: The fourth lot came out for the tribe of Issachar. Their inheritance was located to the south of the Sea of Galilee.

Joshua 19:24–31: The fifth lot came out for the tribe of Asher (Ezekiel 47:21–23). The land of Asher was a long narrow strip along the Mediterranean Sea. Unlike most of the other tribes' territories, Asher's borders were not drawn from one border city to another. The New American Bible Commentary describes Asher's territory as "'a kaleidoscope totality,' this 'indiscriminate mingling of two sorts of materials' shows that 'from the standpoint of the national claim on territory, both boundary cities and interior cities serve same basic function."[1] Therefore the borders were hard to define (Judges 1:29–31). The borders seemed to be constantly moving. In Joshua 21:30–31, the Levitical cities are listed (1 Kings 9:11–13). This gives a picture of how difficult it is to define Asher's borders:

- Asher was Jacob's eighth son by Leah's maidservant Zilpa. He was the second child Zilpa bore to Jacob. The name Asher meant "happiness."
- According to Deuteronomy 27:13–16, the representatives of Asher, along with five other tribes' representatives, declared curses over the Israelites under Moses' command. There were 12 curses these tribes released over the Israelites.
- In Deuteronomy 33:24, Jacob proclaimed that Asher would be most blessed and favored (Genesis 49:20). One of the blessings Jacob bestowed to Asher was that he would dip his foot in olive oil to signify prosperity and blessing from the Lord.
- The tribe of Asher couldn't drive out the Canaanites (Judges 1:31–32). They didn't do what God told them to do. Were they going to receive the blessings or the tension from their disobedience (Judges 5:17)?

Joshua 19:32–39: The sixth lot came out for Naphtali.

Joshua 19:40–48: The seventh lot came out for Dan.

Closing

I feel like many times, the people of Asher missed out on blessings because they did not do what God wanted them to do. As we walk with the Lord, He pours out His blessings. Are you doing what God wants you to?

The Daily Word

The tribes of Israel continued to mark their inheritance of land. Each tribe had land with boundaries. Each allotment was different, and each tribe was responsible to care for their assigned land. The territory of the Danites slipped out of control. They had to fight for their plot of land and take possession of it.

When the Lord gives you land, a home, or even relationships or children, you are responsible to care for them. Sometimes, like the Danites, the things God entrusts you to steward can get out of control. *Is there anything in your life*

---

[1] David M. Howard, *The New American Bible Commentary* (Nashville: Broadman & Holman, 1998), 372.

that you own or are responsible for that feels out of control? Maybe you have a hard relationship or struggle raising children. Perhaps your home is falling apart, and you don't have the resources to keep up. You may not know what to do next. Remember, the Lord cares for you, and He has entrusted you to care for the things He has given you. Seek Him in the middle of the chaos, and trust Him to give you the wisdom to steward them well and with excellence. Don't give up! The Danites had to fight for their plot of land. You may have to press in, pray hard, and fight the battle before you. Remember, the Lord will be with you. In Him you have victory!

When the territory of the Danites slipped out of their control, they went up and fought against Leshem, captured it, and struck it down with the sword. So they took possession of it, lived there, and renamed Leshem after their ancestor Dan. —Joshua 19:47

Further Scripture: Galatians 6:9; James 1:5; 1 Peter 4:10

Questions

1. What do you think the phrase "according to their families" means in dividing up the land?
2. In Joshua 19:9, why was the share of the land of the sons of Judah too large for them if it was given according to their families?
3. Who were the leaders of the designated cities of refuge (Numbers 35:6)?
4. Why was Dan allowed to take Leshem if it was not in his territory (Joshua 19:47)?
5. What did the Holy Spirit highlight to you in Joshua 19—20 through the reading or the teaching?

Lesson 11: Joshua 21—22

Commander: Building an Altar as a Reminder

Teaching Notes

Intro

The takeaway for me, from our study of Joshua, is that we have the *Commander* of the Lord's army going to war for us. Everywhere we go, Jesus says, "I'm with you, and I'll be with you." That had to be the confidence Joshua had as he went through the Promised Land. Joshua was a great commander and warrior as he led the Israelites in and out of battle, but he also cared about his people. In Joshua 22, we'll see this caring side of Joshua.

Teaching

Joshua 22:1–8: Joshua called the tribes of Reuben, Gad, and the half tribe of Manasseh before him (v. 1). He congratulated them for how they listened to God's commands and provided support for the other tribes (vv. 2–3). In other words, they had finished well. They had done everything they had been asked to do (Colossians 3:23–24). In verse 4, Joshua basically gave them an honorable discharge and sent them back to their homes (Romans 5:1). As Christians, we are no longer at war with the world, we can rest in Christ.

Verse 5 is the key and heart of this chapter. Joshua encouraged these tribes to continue to obey God's command and instruction as they received their inheritances—to love God completely, walk in His ways, keep His commands, remain faithful to Him, and serve Him with their whole heart and soul. He encouraged them to remain faithful because they were going back across the Jordan River and would be surrounded by unconquered peoples. The river created a geographical division between the tribes. Joshua blessed them and sent them home (v. 6). Normally, the high priest would have given the blessing (Numbers 6:22–27), but in this case, Joshua did. Then, Joshua sent them on their way, with their share of the spoils from the battles. They were incredibly blessed as they returned home because they had done their job (vv. 7–8).

Joshua 22:9–12: As the two and a half tribes traveled home, they stopped and built a large stone altar (v. 10). When the Israelites on the western side of the

Jordan heard about the altar, they questioned why the eastern tribes had done this (v. 11). Wiersbe describes the impact of this new altar as creating "honest concern" for the eastern Israelites.[2] Based on this information, the Israelites gathered at Shiloh (where the presence of the Lord was) to go to war against the eastern tribes (v. 12).

Joshua 22:13–20: The Israelites sent the priest and ten family leaders to the eastern tribes (vv. 13–15). In verses 16–18, they asked the eastern tribes what they were doing, because they were sinning against God. Verse 17 refers to the sin of aligning with the god Peor (Numbers 25:3), which suggests the Israelites still carried the remorse of that sin with them. The Israelites were asking if these two and a half tribes were now rebelling, turning against God. In verse 20, the emissaries reminded the eastern tribes about the sin of Achan (Joshua 7).

Joshua 22:21–25: The eastern tribes' response was unexpected. Wiersbe describes their response as "a humble submission."[3] Isn't it amazing that when you've done nothing wrong, you have nothing to hide? The eastern tribes had nothing to hide, so they responded honestly and humbly. They said that if they had rebelled against God, or even created an altar for offerings, they should be punished (vv. 22–23). They explained that they had built the altar so future generations on both sides of the river would remember their shared faith (v. 24). Further, they realized that since the Jordan River created a division between them, each side could question the faith of the other (v. 25).

Joshua 22:26–29: The eastern tribes (Reuben, Gad, and half of Manasseh) continued, saying they had built the altar "to be a witness between us and you, and between the generations after us, so that we may carry out the worship of the Lord in His presence with our burnt offerings, sacrifices, and fellowship offerings" (v. 27).

Joshua 22:30–34: Wiersbe describes this as a "happy agreement."[4] The altar was named, "It is a witness between us that the Lord is God." The Israelites on the western side of the Jordan River were pleased and did not go to war against the other tribes on the eastern side. Constable points out that, "probably the Israelites should not have allowed this altar to stand" because "God had not

---

[2] Warren W. Wiersbe, *The Bible Exposition Commentary: Joshua–Esther* (Colorado Springs: David C. Cook, 2003), 76.

[3] Wiersbe, 77.

[4] Wiersbe, 79.

ordained it."[5] In fact, "other people would misunderstand its existence—as some had already done . . . the practice of building altars resulted in the weakening of tribal ties and allegiance to Yahweh, rather than strengthening them."[6] Sometimes people will go along with anything to have peace. Peace must come from purity (James 3:17). Peace cannot be faked or based on land. As Matthew Henry said, "Peace is such a precious jewel that I would give anything but truth."

As we pray for peace in Jerusalem (Psalm 122), it cannot be faked. It can only come from the Messiah.

Closing

When you go after peace, make sure that it comes from the Lord and that it is pure.

The Daily Word

After the tribes spread out to their inherited cities and pasture lands, word came that the Reubenites, Gadites, and half the tribe of Manasseh had built an altar on the frontier of the land of Canaan. Because of past sins and experiences, the Israelites assumed they built the altar as an act against God. However, before attacking and going to war against them, they sent Phinehas and ten leaders to seek more understanding of the altar. It turned out they built the altar with pure motives so future descendants would know about their relationship with the Lord God of Israel. When Phinehas and community leaders reported the truth about the altar to the Israelites, they were pleased and praised God. No one spoke about going to war with the decedents of Reuben, Gad, and Manasseh again.

As you have relationships with people, you will face conflict. That's part of life. As you face conflict, before responding in action, seek understanding. Listen to the person you are in conflict with. Then make your decision after you understand the entire situation. Don't just assume and take action. If the Israelites had done that, they would have found themselves at war for no reason. *Is there a situation in your life today in which you need to seek further understanding?* You may be amazed at how the Lord works it out when you take the time to understand.

When Phinehas the priest and the community leaders, the heads of Israel's clans who were with him, heard what the descendants of Reuben, Gad, and

---

[5] Thomas L. Constable, *Expository Notes of Dr. Thomas Constable: Joshua*, 131, http://planobiblechapel.org/constable-notes/.

[6] Constable, 131.

Manasseh had to say, they were pleased. . . . The Israelites were pleased with the report, and they praised God. —Joshua 22:30, 33

Further Scripture: Proverbs 15:1; Matthew 5:9; Matthew 18:15–16

Questions

1. Why did the Levites not get any territory? What did they get instead as their inheritance (Numbers 18:20)?

2. In Joshua 22:8, who were the brethren they were referring to (Joshua 1:14)?

3. In Joshua 22:10, why did the tribe of Reuben, Gad, and the half tribe of Manasseh build an altar (Joshua 22:26–28)? Why did the children of Israel gather for war against them?

4. Why did they call the altar "Witness"?

5. What did the Holy Spirit highlight to you in Joshua 21—22 through the reading or the teaching?

Lesson 12: Joshua 23—24

Commander: God Sent the Hornet

Teaching Notes

Intro

It is amazing that this is our last lesson in Joshua. We have flown through the book of Joshua in 12 lessons. This has felt like an action movie, and it will continue into our study on Judges as well. The word we've focused on for the book of Joshua is *Commander.* Mindi's painting brings into focus for us the breaking of the camp under the new leadership of Joshua and then moving into the Promised Land. Every battle they went into, they had the *Commander,* the Lord, with them. At the end of the book, Joshua encouraged them to build a memorial of stones as a constant reminder of all that God had done for them. In Joshua 23 and 24 there are two speeches. First, Joshua's farewell address was given in which Joshua reminded the people of all that God had done (Joshua 23). This actually shows the fulfillment of God's promise to Abraham in Genesis. He encouraged the people to be strong and obedient to God because everything God had promised had been fulfilled (Joshua 23:14). The second speech is found in Joshua 24.

Teaching

Joshua 24:1–5: Joshua brought together the 12 tribes, the leaders, and the judges, at Shechem (Genesis 12:6–7), where the tabernacle and God's presence was located at that time (v. 1). Joshua explained God had used pagans (Terah and Nahor) in His plan (v. 2). God can use ANY of us. The first five verses provided a review of their history, covering Genesis through Exodus 15. George Santayana said, "Those who cannot remember the past are condemned to repeat it." And author Norman Cousins describes history as a "vast early warning system." Sadly, the book of Judges is a cycle of sin and disobedience because the people didn't heed the first five verses of Joshua 24.

Joshua began to outline God's involvement with the Israelites through Terah, Nahor, and Abraham, through the journey from the land beyond the Euphrates River into Canaan, and through Abraham's descendants (vv. 2–3a). Joshua outlined the progression of his heritage through Isaac, Jacob, and Esau (vv. 3b–4).

Verses 4–5 include the timing of the Israelites' move to Egypt. Joshua was telling the people what they already knew. They knew their history, but knowing about it did not mean they would remember all they had experienced, and all God had done for them. For some reason, the "memory stones" could not be lodged in their hearts. Joshua's last message was, "Don't forget all this!" It is almost as though Joshua knew what was to come.

Being at Shechem for his farewell address was significant. Clarence Macartney explained the significance of Shechem this way: "If you were to put Plymouth Rock and Yorktown and Lexington and Independence Hall together, you would not have what Shechem is to Israel."[1] Shechem was part of God's prophetic word to Israel, and this event showed that they were now walking that prophecy out. We've all had those moments when God has spoken to us, and the place where we were, at that time, becomes our "Shechem." The giving of Joshua's words at Shechem is also a reminder to us to remember and treasure those places in our own lives.

Joshua 24:6–13: This provides another historical record, which covers Exodus 12 to Joshua 22 (with a little bit of historical backtracking). Joshua reminded his listeners (most had not been there when it happened) about God saving the Israelites from the Egyptian army by parting the Red Sea (vv. 6–7). In these verses, Joshua switched to third person, including his audience in what they had experienced. In verse 8, Joshua reminded them of going into the Promised Land and annihilating the people there. Joshua included the Amorites, Balak king of Moab, and Jericho, along with the other groups (vv. 9–11).

Verse 12 states God sent the "hornet" ahead. (Exodus 23:28.) God going ahead of the Israelites is a constant theme in Joshua. Here are a couple of options of what the hornet referred to: "(1) symbolic of the pharaoh of Egypt, whose symbols were a bee or a hornet; (2) symbolic of God's terror or panic among the Canaanites; (3) actual hornets."[2] (Joshua 2:9–11, 24; 5:1; 6:27). Whichever option is correct, clearly God was making a way for Israel. Possibly the answer is found in Exodus 23:

> "I will send the hornet in front of you, and it will drive the Hivites, Canaanites, and Hittites away from you" (v. 28).
>
> "I am going to send an angel before you to protect you on the way and bring you to the place I have prepared. Be attentive to him and

---

[1] Clarence Macartney, *The Greatest Texts of the Bible* (Nashville: Abingdon, 1947), 74–75.

[2] Earl D. Radmacher, Ronald B. Allen, and H. Wayne House, eds., *Nelson's New Illustrated Bible Commentary* (Nashville: Thomas Nelson, 1999), 301.

> listen to his voice. Do not defy him, because he will not forgive your acts of rebellion, for My name is in him. But if you will carefully obey him and do everything I say, then I will be an enemy to your enemies and a foe to your foes. For My angel will go before you and bring you to the land of the Amorites, Hittites, Perizzites, Canaanites, Hivites, and Jebusites, and I will wipe them out" (vv. 20–23).

The Hebrew term for "hornet" could be a reference to the preincarnate Christ. Joshua 5:13–15 records Joshua encountering a man who had come as "commander of the Lord's army." Moses talked about God sending the hornet (Deuteronomy 7:17–22). The progression shows God sent an angel, later called a hornet, and possibly the preincarnate Christ.

This message was so important because Joshua wanted the people of Israel to understand that even though Joshua would not be with them, God would! The *Commander* of the Lord's Army—the HORNET—would be with them.

This is a reminder to us in reviveSCHOOL to slow down in our reading of Scripture and go deeper. When we go deeper, we are more prepared. In this case, Joshua was stripping away all the different messages to make one point—God was with them.

Joshua 24:15: This is the verse we see on walls and quilts and is the takeaway verse from Joshua: "As for me and my family, we will worship Yahweh." That section of the verse comes after Joshua told the people they would have to decide who they were going to follow—Yahweh or the pagan gods of their forefathers. Then Joshua answered the question himself . . . he and his family chose Yahweh.

Joshua 24:26–33: Joshua set up a memorial stone to commemorate what God had done (vv. 26–27). Then he sent the Israelites away and died at the age of 110 (vv. 28–29). Joseph's bones were brought up from Egypt (v. 32) and Eleazar, son of Aaron, died (v. 33). All of the leaders are now dead, and no one is left to take the baton.

Closing

If we are not careful, the church adds all this other stuff to the message that is not important. At the end of Joshua's life, he wanted them to do one thing . . . to worship the Lord their God. Nothing else was as important to Joshua as that, and this was the message of his last words to the Israelites.

The Daily Word

Joshua spoke to the Israelites before his death, reminding them of God's powerful faithfulness over the years. Once again, he encouraged them how to live—fear the Lord, worship Him in sincerity and truth, get rid of other gods. Simply put, obey Yahweh. Then Joshua placed a memorial stone under an oak tree as witness to not deny the Lord their God, the Rock of their salvation. It's as though Joshua were saying, "Please just keep your eyes on the Rock."

Have you ever walked into a home and seen a plaque with, "As for me and my family, we will worship the Lord"? Or maybe you have these words in your own home and pass by them daily. *What does it mean for you to worship the Lord as a family?* Today, ask the Lord: "Have I gotten away from worshipping the Lord in Spirit and truth? Do I have other gods besides the one and only Jesus Christ, the Rock of my salvation? Am I obeying You?" If the Spirit brings anything to mind, turn from it and fix your eyes on Jesus. Refocus on the Lord Jesus and seek Him with all your heart, soul, mind, and strength. He loves you, and He's all you need!

Therefore, fear the Lord and worship Him in sincerity and truth. Get rid of the gods your fathers worshiped beyond the Euphrates River and in Egypt, and worship Yahweh. . . . As for me and my family, we will worship Yahweh. —Joshua 24:14, 15

Further Scripture: Proverbs 4:25–27; Luke 10:27; 1 Peter 1:22

Questions

1. Why had Israel received rest from all their enemies as mentioned in Joshua 23:1 (Joshua 1:13; 21:44; 22:4)?

2. What was Joshua reminding the Israelites about when he said that they had seen what God had done for them? How does this encourage you in your circumstances?

3. What was the secret of Joshua's success (Joshua 23:6, 14)?

4. What was the importance of Joshua giving his "farewell address" at Shechem (Genesis 12:6–7; 33:18–20)?

5. How many times in Joshua 24 did the Israelites affirm their desire to serve the Lord (Joshua 24:16–18, 21, 24)? What did Joshua do as result of this affirmation from the people? What does it mean to serve God?

6. What did the Holy Spirit highlight to you in Joshua 23—24 through the reading or the teaching?

Lesson 13: Judges 1—2

Judge: The Cycle of Disobedience

Teaching Notes

Intro

We just wrapped up Joshua, the first of the historical books, and now we're moving into Judges. The first verse of Judges explains Joshua had died, so Judges presents a new season for the Israelites. The book of Judges feels a little chaotic. Mindy's new painting is a little dark with a snake and a skull, but that's what we're talking about in the book of Judges. Judges is about multiple leaders, or judges.

The author of the book is believed to be Samuel (1 Samuel 10:25). *Nelson's Commentary* said Israel's judges "did not normally hold court, listen to complaints, or make legal decisions (except for Deborah). Rather, they were political leaders who delivered Israel from foreign threat or oppression."[1] The book was probably written after Saul had been anointed king but before the reign of David.[2] Interestingly, Judges can refer to both the book of the Bible, or to the period of about 300 years in which the judges were in place when chaos reigned in Israel. The book of Judges was a sequel to the book of Joshua. Within this book, 15 judges are named.

Chuck Swindoll suggests these reasons for the period of Judges in which there was great apostasy in Israel[3]:

1. There was tremendous political and religious turmoil because the tribes of Israel were continuously trying to obtain the rest of the Promised Land

---

[1] Earl D. Radmacher, Ronald B. Allen, and H. Wayne House, eds., *Nelson's New Illustrated Bible Commentary* (Nashville: Thomas Nelson, 1999), 309.

[2] Thomas L. Constable, *Expository Notes of Dr. Thomas Constable: Judges*, 3, http://planobiblechapel.org/tcon/notes/pdf/judges.pdf.

[3] Chuck Swindoll, *Judges: Why Was Judges So Important?*, available online at https://www.insight.org/resources/bible/the-historical-books/judges.

they hadn't completely conquered. There was a halfway obedience to God's commands.

2. The tribes of Israel began fighting against each other. In fact, the tribes of Manasseh (Judges 12) and Benjamin (Judges 20–21) were almost wiped out.

3. A cycle of sin, punishment, repentance, and forgiveness took place. God's people rebelled through idolatry and disbelief, so God brought judgment through foreign oppression. Then God would raise up a deliverer or judge who brought the people back to God in repentance. However, within a couple of chapters, the people fell back into sin and the cycle started over again.

The image is of one who came to save the people, not hammer them into obedience. This is a picture of the coming Savior. In her painting, Mindi used the bitten apple to represent the Israelites' cycle of sin that we all have from the fall in Genesis; the snake to represent how sin is always coming after us; and the skull represents death. Each supports the theme of the book—God will not allow sin to go unpunished.

The book of Exodus explains how Israel became God's people and followed Him in the wilderness. In the book of Joshua, He led them to conquer the Promised Land, and the book ended with Joshua's speech warning against forgetting what God had done (Joshua 24). And in Judges, God had to discipline His people for following other gods, for disobeying His law, and for immorality.

Teaching

Judges 1:1–18: Leadership was turned over to Judah and Simeon (vv. 1–3). In verses 4–5, the Israelites were still trying to conquer the rest of the Promised Land (Joshua 3:10). They pursued Adoni-bezek, captured him, and cut off his thumbs and big toes so he could no longer hold a sword or run in battle. *Nelson's Commentary* explains that "the practice of mutilating vanquished enemies is recorded in ancient sources . . . and was practiced by Adoni-bezek himself."[4] Adoni-bezek died from the wounds (vv. 6–7). They seized Jerusalem, but not everyone died (v. 8) (Joshua 15:63). Judges gives a picture of Jerusalem that is incomplete without the information in Joshua. Then, Judah struck down the three giants in Hebron—Sheshai, Ahiman, and Talmai (v. 10). Remember that Caleb used marriage to his daughter as the prize to whomever delivered the land, which was Othniel (vv. 11–14). She asked for and received the double portion of springs of water (upper and lower) on the Negev Desert (vv. 15–16). Othniel became the first judge. In verses 17–18, several towns were captured.

---

[4] Radmacher et al., 306.

Judges 1:19–34: They took possession of the hill country but could not drive out the people in the valley who had "iron chariots" (v. 19). They failed due to a complete lack of faith on the Israelites' part. Joshua 1:3 says the Lord would drive the people out. In Joshua 1:3–7, God said that everywhere they stepped, He would be with them and would give them the land. Failure didn't just happen to Judah. Several tribes failed: Benjamin (v. 21); Manasseh (v. 27); Ephraim (v. 29); Zebulon (v. 30); Asher (v. 31); Naphtali (v. 33); and Dan (v. 34). These tribes failed because they didn't trust God. They were told to completely destroy the inhabitants of the land so their faith would not be pulled away from God, but they failed (Deuteronomy 20:16–18). When they didn't obey wholeheartedly, Deuteronomy 20:18 came true (Joshua 6:17; 11:14; Judges 2:11–12).

Closing

In Judges 2:1–4, the Angel of the Lord (Christ Jesus) came and told the people not to make a covenant with the inhabitants of the land. Even that was not enough to save the Israelites from the cycle of disobedience and rebellion (Judges 2:16). That leads us to our word for this study—*Judge*. These God-appointed judges in the book of Judges lead to the *Judge*.

The function of our *Judge* is found in Colossians 1:13–14: "He has rescued us from the domain of darkness and transferred us into the kingdom of the Son He loves. We have redemption, the forgiveness of sins, in Him."

If you want to get off the cycle of sin, just look to the *Judge*—Jesus Christ.

The Daily Word

Despite Joshua's warnings to have no other gods and worship the Lord only, the Israelites did not listen. They did what was evil in the Lord's sight and worshipped Ba'al and other gods, abandoning the Lord, the God of their fathers. They lived in disobedience to the Lord and did not keep their eyes on Him. And as a result, they failed in battle and found themselves in chaos. However, despite their sin, the Lord raised up judges to help save the people from their enemies. The Lord rescued them from darkness. In the same way, God the Father saw the chaos and sin of the world and sent His Son Jesus to come rescue you. Jesus came to save you from darkness and the power of sin. He came to bring life and hope, even in the midst of your chaos. *Will you turn to Jesus and allow Him to rescue you?* Or will you press on in your own strength, your own wisdom, and try it in your own power? Friend, allow Jesus to help you. Today, believe and receive His love, grace, and power. He is there for you because He loves you.

Whenever the Lord raised up a judge for the Israelites, the Lord was with him and saved the people form the power of their enemies while the judge was still alive. —Judges 2:18

Further Scripture: 1 Corinthians 10:13; Colossians 1:13–14; 1 Thessalonians 1:10

Questions

1. After Joshua died, why do you think God told Israel that Judah should go up first to fight the Canaanites (Genesis 49:8–9; Revelation 5:5)?

2. From who did Caleb's daughter, Achsah, request to ask Caleb about giving them land? Who wound up asking him? How did Caleb respond?

3. In Judges 2, why did the people of Israel weep after hearing from the Angel of the Lord? What did they do after hearing this word?

4. What were some sins of the new generation after Joshua?

5. Even during the Israelites' rebellion, how did God show His compassion for them? What was His purpose for leaving the nations in the land that had not been driven out?

6. What did the Holy Spirit highlight to you in Judges 1—2 through the reading or the teaching?

Lesson 14: Judges 3—4

Judge: Facing God's Tests

Teaching Notes

Intro

Today, we're looking at Judges 3—4 and will be looking at how the Israelites passed the test. How did they do once they were no longer following Joshua's leadership?

Teaching

Judges 3:1–4: Verse 1 seems to bring something new to us. Joshua had been told to conquer all the land, but Judges 3:1 states that God let some nations test Israel. We'll see how Israel did on this test. Note that God grades on a different scale than we understand. This would teach the younger generations of Israel to fight in battles (v. 2). These younger generations had not experienced war before, so this provided a reality check. They were soft and God needed to toughen them up.

Think about whether we too need a reality check. Have we forgotten what it cost to stand where we do today?

Fragmented groups of Philistines, Canaanites, Sidonians, and Hivites were left behind as part of this test (vv. 3–4). Does God still test us today?

1. Exodus 13:17–18 states God did not lead the Israelites on the shortest route past the Philistines in case they changed their minds and wanted to return to Egypt.

2. Deuteronomy 8:1–2 describes the wilderness journey as a test to see if they trusted God.

3. 2 Corinthians 13:5: "Test yourselves to see if you are in the faith. Examine yourselves. Or do you yourselves not recognize that Jesus Christ is in you? —unless you fail the test."

Judges 3:5–8: Instead of removing these nations (v. 4), the Israelites chose to live among them. They married pagan daughters, married their own daughters to pagan sons, and they worshipped pagan gods (vv. 5–6). They specifically inter-married with the Canaanites and other pagan groups. They mixed their families and took on the worship of other gods. They compromised the integrity of their marriages by marrying outside of their own beliefs. They moved from relation-ship to compromise, to idolatry, to captivity. They did something that seemed small, but was "evil in the sight of the Lord." They began to worship the Baals and Asherahs and ended up in idolatry (v. 7). As a result of their sin, God was angry and sold them to the king of Mesopotamia, into slavery (v. 8).

Why did God seek justice? Some people look at this and wonder how a loving God could punish those He loves. This was a corporate (national) sin over time. It wasn't one sin that happened once or twice. We understand a judge is one who brings justice; and justice brings liberation. God loves us too much to allow us to continue in sin. God can be angry and discipline us to bring us back to where we should be, and never lose an ounce of love! God will never shy away from justice. Sin will tip us out of balance, but the Holy Spirit brings that balance back. Why? Because He loves us—even through sometimes tough love is required.

Judges 3:9–11: The people of Israel cried out to God, and the Lord raised up a deliverer—Othniel, Caleb's younger brother (v. 9). Othniel, as a man, was not the deliverer; God was the deliverer. The Spirit of the Lord came upon Othniel, and *then* he became the judge of Israel, and he went out to war against Meso-potamia (v.10). God's Spirit empowered Othniel to do what he did. They were in captivity for eight years (v.8), and then they walked in peace for the next 40 years (v. 11).

Judges 3:12–31: Again, the Israelites sinned (v. 12), and God handed them over to Moab for 18 years (vv. 13–14). And once again the people cried out to God so He raised up Ehud as the next judge. Ehud actually killed the king of Moab, and the people of Israel were released. Israel then had 80 years of peace (v. 30). Then Shamgar became judge and delivered Israel by striking down the Philis-tines (v. 31).

When we think of the deliverer (our word for Exodus), we usually think of Jesus. These judges provide a picture of Christ coming as our *Deliverer*.

Judges 4:1–10: The cycle continues. Israel sinned and God gave them to the king of Canaan (vv. 1–2). Again, Israel cried out for deliverance against Sisera, the commander of the kings army, who had 900 chariots and had oppressed them for 20 years (v. 3). God raised up Deborah, a prophetess who could discern the will of God and speak it to others, as His next judge (v. 4). The Israelites would come to her for judgment (v. 5). She commanded Barak to take 10,000

Israelite troops to Mount Tabor (v. 6). God promised He would deliver Sisera, the Canaanite commander, to him (v. 7). Barak knew that Deborah was hearing from God, and he agreed to go if she went with him (v. 8). Deborah agreed to go, but told Barak he would not get the honor because God would use a woman to kill Sisera (v. 9). Barak and Deborah took 10,000 men from the tribes of Zebulun and Naphtali to prepare to face Sisera's army (v. 10).

Judges 4:11–24: They went into battle against Sisera, and God sent rains during the dry season to stop Sisera's iron chariots due to the mud (Judges 5:4b). Sisera's entire army was cut down by the sword. There were no survivors, except Sisera who fled from the battle. Sisera hid in the tent of Heber. While Sisera slept, Heber's wife Jael drove a tent peg into his temple on the side of his head. When Sisera died, Israel was set free through the actions of three people—Barak, Deborah, and Jael. None of them took action because they wanted glory. Barak didn't mind serving under female leadership or not receiving glory. He only wanted to see God set the people free. Are we willing to do what God tells us to do without receiving any glory or recognition?

Closing

How did Israel pass the test God gave them? God used people to do His will. Jesus has set us free. I believe God is calling us to be the deliverers in our communities and across the nation.

The Daily Word

Without Joshua as commander, a theme emerged among the nation of Israel. First the Israelites did what was evil in the Lord's sight, serving other gods and forgetting the Lord their God. Then an enemy would rise up and oppress the Israelites. In response, they would cry out to the Lord. The Lord would hear their cries and grant mercy by raising up a judge to deliver them in battle. This happened over and over and over. The judges did not focus on their own reputations or glory. Rather, they answered the call the Lord put on their lives so the people of Israel could walk in freedom.

The Lord loves you deeply. Even when you continue to walk in sin or seek the things of this world instead of the Lord's ways, Jesus is still there. When you cry out to Him, He will answer. Jesus will deliver you. Today, *if you feel stuck in a place of defeat, cry out to the Lord like the Israelites did*. Allow Jesus to deliver you. Then, as you walk in deliverance and freedom, the Spirit of God will use you to help others just as He used the judges in the past. The Lord is calling out followers of Christ to help deliver and bring others to victory in Jesus' name. Be ready and available!

The Israelites cried out to the Lord. So, the Lord raised up Othniel son of Kenaz, Caleb's youngest brother, as a deliverer to save the Israelites. —Judges 3:9

Further Scripture: Psalm 32:7; Psalm 34:17; 1 Corinthians 15:57

Questions

1. The Lord left nations among the Israelites for what purpose (Joshua 23:12–13; Judges 2:21–22; 3:1, 4)? Do you think there is any comparison to this "test" and the parable in Matthew 25:14–30? Have you ever felt tested by the Lord?

2. In Judges 3:5–6, the Israelites lived among the nations they were to utterly destroy (Joshua 11:14–15). What were the consequences? What consequences have you seen when you didn't obey God's instructions? What is the purpose for these consequences?

3. According to Judges 3:9, how did their circumstances change? What empowered this deliverer (Judges 3:10)? Who actually gave Israel the victory?

4. What pattern or cycle are you already seeing in the Book of Judges? How do you think the test is going so far (Judges 3:1)?

5. What judges were written about in chapters three and four? How were they similar to each other? How were they different? Is God looking for certain qualities in those He calls to serve His purpose? If so, what are those qualities?

6. What did the Holy Spirit highlight to you in Judges 3—4 through the reading or the teaching?

Lesson 15: Judges 5—6

Judge: All About the Name

Teaching Notes

Intro

What's in a name? God is very intentional in the names He gives people. In this lesson, we'll talk about some interesting situations with some even more interesting characters as we look at the fourth and fifth judges of Israel. We'll continue to look at Deborah and then meet Gideon. Through Gideon, we'll look at the mystery of his name . . . "mighty warrior" and "the Lord saves." Chapter 5 contains the Song of Deborah. I remember a time when God gave me a vision that showed the Lord putting His hand on my mother's womb and saying that this one was His mighty warrior. The vision wrecked me so much that I began to cry and weep. When I told my dad about my vision, he shared with me about a time in Turkey when a man came and put his hands on my mother's belly and said that she was carrying a mighty warrior. Growing up, they always referred to me as a mighty warrior. We're going to talk about people who were born in crazy times of adversity, but God had marked them for such a time as that. Every one of you who are listening to this have been marked by God and called to do something significant in the kingdom.

Teaching

Judges 5:1: Deborah and Barak celebrated their victory with a song (v. 1). In Exodus we see Miriam and Moses picking up their instruments to sing songs, and King David celebrates when Israel captures back the Ark of the Covenant. Deborah's name literally means "bee." God used Deborah as a judge to bring a sting to the enemies of God. Deborah was a poet and prophetess. Barak's name means "lightning." *Barak* is also a Hebrew word for praise. Psalm 34:1 says, "I will *barak* the Lord at all times; His *barak* will always be on my lips." The connotation of the word means to worship and bow down. Psalm 95:6 says, "Come, let us *barak*; let us kneel before the Lord our Maker."

Judges 5:2–6: In verse 2, *barak* is used again: "When the leaders lead in Israel, when the people volunteer, praise (*barak*) the Lord." What Deborah and Barak were doing was confirming their names—it was a prophetic act showing that they were living out their names. God used Deborah to lead the troops to sting like a bee and Barak to lead the troops to strike light lightning! They were now praising (barak) the Lord. Barak literally means to bless, to kneel, to bless abundantly, to salute, to thank, to boast in, and to pronounce blessing. In verse 3, a different Hebrew word is used for praise—*zamar*, which means to make music, to praise in song. Sometimes in church, we say we'll praise the Lord, and we use that word for all kinds of praise. In Hebrew, there are multiple words for praise. The third judge, Shamgar, is named (v.6).

Judges 5:7–9: Deborah arose as "a mother in Israel" (v. 7). God is raising up godly fathers and mothers to speak into our lives (I Corinthians 4:15–17). Verse 8 records what had happened in Israel—they had done evil in the sight of God, and been put under the rule of Jabin, king of the Canaanites (Judges 4:1–3). Verse 9 is a model of godly leadership. Their hearts were with the people in leadership. It was humble leadership that submitted to one another (Ephesians 5:19–21). Deborah and Barak used this as a teachable moment to the people of what the nation's response should be to God.

Judges 5:10–11, 21, 31: Another Hebrew word for praise—*sinch*, which means to consider, muse, sign, speak of, or talk (v.10). Verse 11 uses still another Hebrew word for the concept of praise—*dabar*, which means to speak, assert, declare, preach, talk, or utter. Deborah's and Barak's names were prophetic. The word *dabar* is from the Hebrew root word debir, meaning to speak, and is getting ridiculously close to sounding like the name Deborah. Deborah is living out her prophetic destiny as a speaker and mother to Israel. Deborah (*dabar, debir*) is living out the call to "sing a new song." This is one of the coolest verses—"March on, my soul, in strength!" (v. 21). The land had peace for 40 years. Deborah and Barak were peace-makers (Matthew 5:9).

Judges 6:1–10: Again, Israel did evil in God's sight. As the result, God handed them over to Midian for seven years (v. 1). Remember that Moses' father-in-law was a priest to the Midianites. They were descendants of Abraham's concubine Keturah. The name Midian means judgment, and God used the Midianites to bring judgment on the Israelites. It got so bad that the Israelites had to hide from Midian attacks in the mountain and caves (vv. 2–5). God allowed the Midianites to bring havoc onto the disobedient Israelites. Because of the attacks, Israel became so poverty-stricken that they cried out to God (vv. 6–7). God sent them an unnamed prophet who reminded them that God had delivered them from

Egypt and given them their land (vv. 8–9). There were about 130 years between the death of Joshua and Gideon's rise, and about 220 years since Israel's deliverance from Egypt. You can see the progression in these 200+ years as people drifted in and out of the things of God. The prophet reminded them that God had told them not to fear the gods of the Amorites but they had disobeyed Him (v. 10).

Judges 6:11–21: The times were so desperate that the Angel of the Lord found Gideon hiding in the wine vat while he threshed wheat (v. 11). The Angel called him a "mighty warrior" (v. 12). Romans 4:17 says, "God calls forth those things which are not, as though they were." Gideon responded pitifully in verse 13, accusing God of handing them over to Midian. God completely disregarded Gideon's concerns and complaints, and just said, "Go!" (v. 14). In the church, God doesn't really concern Himself with our comfort zone. He wants us to move in the power of the Holy Spirit to bring justice and balance into the world. But Gideon questioned God's instructions (v. 15). God answered, "I will be with you!" (v. 16). The name Gideon is from the Hebrew word *gada*, which means to hew down, break off, chop down, or cut into pieces. These words are prophetic of what Gideon would be called to do. Gideon asked for a sign to prove he was hearing from God (vv. 17–18). Doesn't this seem comical that the Angel of the Lord was kept waiting while Gideon fixed food for him? Yet, in this time of forced famine, this food offering cost Gideon a lot (v. 19). The Angel told Gideon what to do with the prepared food, then touched the tip of his staff to the meat and bread which were consumed by a fire coming up from the rock (vv. 20–21).

Judges 6:22–28: This is an amazing encounter between Gideon and the Lord. In the next couple of verses, God told Gideon to destroy the altar to Baal and the pole of Asherah, and to take a young bull along with a seven-year-old bull from his father (v. 25). The Lord was taking Gideon to a prophetic place in which the sacrifice of the first bull would cut off the curse on his family through his father's idol worship, and the sacrifice of the second bull would remove the iniquity of the seven years of Midianite torture. Gideon's father was an avid Baal worshiper, so Gideon "cut down" (just as his name said he would) the Asherah pole, tore up the altar to Baal, and sacrificed the bulls on a new altar he made to the Lord (vv. 27–28).

Closing

Your name has so much meaning, and you were born for such a time as this. It's no mistake—you were born for a purpose. I'm excited about the Baal altars and Asherah poles that you'll be called to cut down. We need righteous men and women to rise up and balance the death of the sin in the world.

The Daily Word

The Lord called out Gideon as Israel's fifth judge to deliver the people after their season of disobedience. Gideon didn't see how the Lord could use him; he was from the weakest family in the weakest tribe of Manasseh and was the youngest in his father's home. But the Lord saw Gideon as a mighty warrior. The Lord reminded Gideon that He would be with him. Along the way, Gideon asked for signs and confirmations from the Lord for this calling, and God answered his request with signs and wonders.

If you have ever felt inadequate for the Lord's call on your life, then you are in good company with Gideon. Remember, *the Lord has plans for you in His kingdom*. It's not because of your educational degrees or business success, and it's not even because of your family heritage. Rather, because He created you perfectly and wonderfully, He has plans for you. As He calls you, do not be afraid. He wants to use you daily in the kingdom of God, and He will send you as you listen to the Holy Spirit within you. He is always with you. But like Gideon, you may have times in your life when you ask the Lord for confirmation and throw out a fleece before Him. Watch the Lord confirm your steps as you seek His face. Walk it out in faith as God's mighty warrior.

He said to Him, "Please, Lord, how can I deliver Israel? Look, my family is the weakest in Manasseh, and I am the youngest in my father's house." "But I will be with you," the Lord said to him. "You will strike Midian down as if it were one man." —Judges 6:15–16

Further Scripture: 1 Samuel 17:37; Jeremiah 32:27; Hebrews 13:20, 21

Questions

1. When reading the Song of Deborah and Barak, they sang about Jael and her defeat of Sisera. Does Judges 5:26–27 bring to mind Genesis 3:15? Why?

2. Judges 6:1 records that the sons of Israel again did what was evil in the sight of the Lord, and the Lord gave them into the hands of Midian (Deuteronomy 31:16–18). When they cry out to the Lord this time, how does the Lord respond (Judges 6:7–10)? Why do you think God sent the prophet before He began to deliver them?

3. The Midianites and Amalekites would let Israel plant their crops, but they would come and take or destroy the harvest (Judges 6:3–4). How does this compare with when they took possession of this land in Joshua 24:13?

4. When the angel of the Lord appeared to Gideon, Gideon had trouble with the phrase, "The Lord is with you." Why was that? Do you think Gideon had heard the Song of Moses in Deuteronomy 32? Had Gideon been brought up in a household where the Lord was worshipped faithfully (Judges 6:25)?

5. How do you think Gideon knew what to offer to the Lord (Judges 6:19)? What does the fire coming out of the rock and consuming the offering indicate? Why do you think Gideon named the altar he built, "The Lord is Peace" (Leviticus 26:6; Judges 6:24)?

6. What did the Holy Spirit highlight to you in Judges 5—6 through the reading or the teaching?

Lesson 16: Judges 7—8

Judge: Faith Even in Weakness

Teaching Notes

Intro

Mindi's picture does an incredible job of portraying not just the book of Judges, but the period of the judges as well. It was 300 years of chaos in Israel, seen in cycles of disobedience and rebellion against God, receiving God's judgment, until they cried out for Him to save them. God, listening, raised up of a judge to be the nation's deliverer, which saw them restored back to Himself. And then, the chaotic cycle began again. The judges God raised up were a foreshadow of Christ. Gideon was the fifth judge after Othniel, Ehud, Shamgar, and Deborah. In chapter 6, Gideon carefully considered what God had called him to do because he felt he was not capable. Twice, Gideon set out a fleece to make sure of God's intentions for his life. It brings up the question of whether we need a fleece in our lives as well to affirm what God wants us to do when we feel we're not capable. In Judges 6, Gideon had an encounter with the pre-incarnate Christ, and since he was always committed to the Lord, God was getting him ready for more. Despite all of Gideon's complaints, questions, and doubts, he ended up walking through what God had called him to do. And, God was still able to use Gideon, despite everything.

Teaching

Judges 7:1–4: Wiersbe uses a simple, three-point outline for this chapter: "God tests our faith"; "God encourages our faith"; and, "God honors our faith."[1] Gideon's army camped beside the spring of Harod, and God told Gideon if his army was too large the Israelites might claim the victory as their own (vv. 1–2). God wants us to have utter dependence upon Him (2 Corinthians 12:9). God told Gideon to send home all who were afraid, and 22,000 left (v. 3). Two-thirds of Gideon's army bailed out. Wiersbe refers to this as "the first sifting."[2] Wouldn't

---

[1] Warren W. Wiersbe, *Be Available: Accepting the Challenge to Confront the Enemy* (Colorado Springs: David C. Cook, 1994), 74–78.

[2] Wiersbe, 75.

that have been depressing to see 22,000 soldiers leave. The army they would face had 135,000 soldiers (Judges 8:10). Inrig says, "God doesn't want to just give us victory. He is concerned with teaching us trust. In fact, if our victories make us self-reliant, they are ultimately more disastrous than defeat."[3] God's question was, "Do you trust Me when things get tougher?" People are facing that every day.

Remember in the Pentateuch study, we discovered there were various reasons soldiers could leave a battle and not fight besides cowardice: if they had just built a new house; if they were engaged to be married; or, if they had planted a vineyard.

Judges 7:4–8: God sifted the troops a second time, reducing the 10,000 soldiers to 300, based on the way they drank water from the spring, either lapping with their tongues or using their hands to bring water to their mouths. This was a true test of faith. It's like what Winston Churchill said after World War II, "Never in the field of human conflict was so much owed to so many by so few." This is a good example of that quote. God wanted these 300 men under the leadership of Gideon, the deliverer, to have victory over the Midianites.

Judges 7:9–14: In the process of testing our faith, God will encourage our faith. Many people give up during the testing and never make it to verse 9. We tend to live in the posture that we're the weakest, the youngest, the least capable. God promised Gideon that He had already given him victory (v. 9). This was the third time God made that promise, but He also gave Gideon three signs— Judges 6:20–21, 36–38, 39–40. Then, God told Gideon to take his servant Purah to walk beside him in the battle since he was still afraid (v. 10). Davis and Whitcomb described Gideon's position this way: "Gideon is no fearless all-pro linebacker, no General Patton and John Wayne rolled into one huge ball of true grit."[4] He was going up against 135,000 enemy soldiers.

Verse 12 describes the enemy soldiers as "a swarm of locusts" and their camels as "innumerable as the sand on the seashore." Gideon heard a Midianite man telling his friend about a dream in which a loaf of barley bread fell from above and turned the tent upside down (v. 13). A dream means that it had taken place while asleep; a vision means that it had taken place while awake. The friend responded that God had given Gideon victory over the Midianites (v. 14). Some people deny theologically that dreams from God still happen today (1 Kings 3:5; Joel 2:28; Matthew 2:13; Acts 2:17). Have the last days come? If not, then dreams are still relevant today. God can speak to us in dreams. If what we hear doesn't contradict God's Word, then God could be speaking to us. And God can speak through dreams of non-believers.

---

[3] Gary Inrig, *Hearts of Iron, Feet of Clay* (Grand Rapids: Discovery House, 1979), 125.

[4] John J. Davis and John C. Whitcomb, *A History of Israel*, reprint ed. (Grand Rapids: Baker Book House, 1980), 106–7.

Judges 7:15–25: God will honor our faith. When Gideon heard the Midianite's dream, then he called his troops to battle. He gave each man a trumpet in one hand and a pitcher with a torch inside it in the other, and then he told them to watch him to know what to do. Gideon was acting like an army general. When they saw him outside the camp, they blew their trumpets and busted the pitcher to expose their lights. They yelled out and chased the Midianite soldiers who turned on each other, killing each other with Midianite swords. The Israelites called on more of their own tribes and they pursued the Midianites so that none escaped.

Closing

Hebrews 11:6 says, "Now without faith it is impossible to please God, for the one who draws near to Him must believe that He exists and rewards those who seek Him." We are all Gideons. God honored Gideon for his leap of faith and he succeeded.

The Daily Word

As Gideon answered the call from the Lord, he formed a mighty army and prepared to fight the Midianites. Amidst the preparations, the Lord told Gideon that his army was too large. God cut the army from 32,000 down to a mere 300 men. The Lord promised Gideon that He would deliver the Midianites into the hand of Gideon using just 300 men. Gideon walked God's promise out in faith, trusting the calling on his life. The Lord continued to confirm and equip Gideon to overcome each doubt and fear along the way. And through it all, because of Gideon's weakness, the Lord received the glory.

God's strength is made evident in your weakness. He promises that in your weakness, He is strong. Therefore you can boast in His strength and not in your own. Remember as you walk out your calling for the day, no mountain is ever too large for the Lord. There is no marriage too broken, no job is too difficult, and no sickness too far gone for the Lord. Like Gideon, the Lord wants you to trust Him. In your weakness, have faith in the impossible, and follow His ways. Draw near to Him, and He will deliver you from your situation. Trust. Trust. Trust.

The Lord said to Gideon, "You have too many people for Me to hand the Midianites over to you, or else Israel might brag: 'I did it myself.'"
—Judges 7:2

Further Scripture: Judges 7:7–8; 2 Corinthians 12:9; Hebrews 11:6

Questions

1. Why did God reduce Gideon's army from 32,000 men to 300 (Judges 7:2–8)?

2. What happened that gave Gideon courage to attack the Midianites (Judges 7:13–15)? Have you had a dream from the Lord that gave you courage for your task? How does being in community and hearing what others are hearing from the Lord encourage you?

3. Why do you think that officials in Succoth told Gideon to first catch Zebah and Zalmunna before they would feed his army? What punishment did they receive?

4. Why did Gideon request one gold earring from each man's plunder? What did he do with them? Did this end up being a positive thing? Why or why not?

5. What did the Holy Spirit highlight to you in Judges 7—8 through the reading or the teaching?

Lesson 17: Judges 9—10

Judge: Taking a Stand Against Evil

Teaching Notes

Intro

What I love about the book of Judges is to see how these guys messed up bad and yet God chooses to still use them. I pray as you're walking through Judges that you'll find hope from these examples of how God will be able to use you as well. Today, we'll be looking at Abimelech, the son of Jerubbaal (also known as Gideon). Abimelech was not a judge at all but was an enemy of God.

Gideon was hiding from the enemy when God called him, and he followed God's instructions exactly as he led a small army of Israelites against a much larger enemy. In Judges 8:22, Gideon and his grandson were asked to rule over the Israelites. But Gideon answered that only the Lord would rule over them (Judges 8:23). God brought deliverance through Gideon. Notice how the people were inclined to follow this man. They were ready to make him their king. Often when someone is used mightily by God, their pride can rear up and take over. Gideon stayed humble and obedient to God. But then, he asked for an earring from each of the soldiers from their plunder. The earrings had been used in pagan worship, but Gideon used them to create an ephod, the garment of a priest, for his son. The ephod became a point of worship. Judges 8:27 records the results: "Then all Israel prostituted themselves with it there, and it became a snare to Gideon and his household." Toward the end of Gideon's life, the people began to slip farther and farther away from God.

Teaching

Judges 9:1–6: Abimelech was the son of Gideon, whose other name Jerubbaal meant "let Baal contend." Abimelech's mother was one of Gideon's concubines who was a Canaanite. As the son of a concubine, Abimelech wasn't one of Gideon's 70 sons and had no inheritance from Gideon. The 70 sons were living well; Abimelech was not. Abimelech struggled with jealousy and a desire for power (James 3:13–16). Out of his desire for power, Abimelech stepped way over the bounds of God's laws. He went to Shechem to talk to his mother's Canaanite clan, and asked if they wanted to be ruled by Gideon's 70 sons, or by one of their own—him (vv. 1–2). The Canaanite clan convinced the rest of the lords in Shechem that Abimelech was the right person to rule since he was part of their family (v. 3). Abimelech was given 70 pieces of silver from Baal's temple offering, which he used to hire assassins to murder his 70 brothers on one stone (vv.4–5a). Can you imagine what it would have looked like to see 70 bodies sacrificed on a stone altar? The men of Shechem then made Abimelech their king (v. 6). They anointed him their king, but he was NOT God's king. Jotham, the youngest of Gideon's sons, hid and survived the massacre (v. 5b). His escape shows the sovereignty of God.

Joshua 9:7–21: When Jotham found out that Abimelech had become king, he shouted the parable about trees from the top of Mount Gerizim (v.7). Within the parable:

> *The Trees* represented the men of Shechem, productive human beings who were looking for someone to lead.
> *The Olive Tree* produced oil and refused to stop doing what it was created to do to become king.
> *The Fig Tree* produced sweet fruit and refused to stop doing what it was created to do to become king.
> *The Grapevine* produced grapes and refused to stop doing what it was created to do to become king.

Notice that everyone was doing what was right in their own lives (Judges 17:6). Isn't this true in America? We're so busy and so focused on what we're doing that brambles are popping up all around us to reign over us.

> *The Bramble* produced nothing but was willing to become the king, and threatened the trees' safety if it was not made king.

In verse 16, Jotham provided an ultimatum. If the people of Shechem had acted out of their faith in making Abimelech the king, if they had done right by Jerubbaal and his family, they would be able to rejoice in what they had done (vv. 17–19). But, if they had not acted out of their faith and had not done right by Jerubbaal and his family, they would be consumed by fire from one another (v. 20). Simply put, if they had not acted for God, if they continued to walk this out, they would destroy each other. The fire of God was going to come to these men through their dissent.

Judges 9:22–55: After Abimelech had been king for three years, God sent an evil spirit between the king and the lords of Shechem. The people of Shechem rebelled against Abimelech by placing robbers to ambush trade caravans as they passed through the mountains (vv. 22–25). Abimelech lost tax monies and tariffs as well as his reputation through the attacks. A man named Gaal (whose name meant "loathsome") saw an opportunity to take power from Abimelech. He went with the lords of Shechem to harvest grapes and celebrate in the house of their god (vv. 26–27). Gaal began to conspire to murder Abimelech (vv. 28–29). Zebul, the ruler of the city, found out about Gaal's plan and let Abimelech know, and helped arrange an ambush against Gaal and his followers (vv. 35–36). War began between them. Abimelech killed Gaal in battle and many of the men of Shechem who followed Gaal were also killed (vv. 37–45).

After the battle, the lords and the people of Shechem entered the tower of the temple to El-berith. When Abimelech heard that they had gathered there, he used an axe to cut a branch from a tree and told all the people with him to do the same thing. They took the branches inside the tower and set them afire. About 1,000 men and women died in the tower (vv. 46–49). The curse of Jotham from Mt. Gerizim was fulfilled through this fire.

The other part of the curse was that Abimelech would be consumed by fire too. Abimelech went to Thebez and the people there took shelter in another tower. Abimelech approached the tower to burn it as well, but a woman dropped a millstone from an upper window that landed on Abimelech's head, fracturing his skull. Abimelech called for his armor-bearer to kill him with the sword so no one would say he had been killed by a woman. The armor-bearer did as he was told, and when Abimelech was dead, the people returned home (vv. 50–55).

Judges 9:56–57: God's plan and purpose cannot be thwarted by people. We will always see the hand of God bringing the scales of justice.

Judges 10:1–6: God raised Tola, son of Puah, as judge who "began to deliver Israel." He judged for 23 years (vv. 1–2). After Tola, God raised Jair the Gileadean who judged for 22 years (vv. 3–5).

That's a period of 45 years in which the Israelites were under judges, doing what they were supposed to do. But then, the Israelites again did evil in God's sight (v. 6). Notice that each time the Israelites turned from God, the depth of their sin went deeper and the list of pagan gods they worshiped became longer. Their sin progressively got worse.

Closing

What does this look like for us today? There will always be Abimelechs, jealous and hungry for power, in the world. There will always be people who are hungry for power and jealous of what others have. But are we moved by that? Do we stand up like Jotham and speak God's message against this? God is looking for us to take a stand against the chaos of our world.

My challenge is that, as we move through Judges, we don't miss the fact that God is just. And in His justice there is mercy and love as we walk this out.

The Daily Word

Gideon's son Abimelech did not receive the power he thought he deserved over the people. As a result, he reacted out of bitterness and jealousy toward his family. He murdered seventy of Gideon's sons (and Abimelech's own brothers) minus Jotham, who escaped. Even though Abimelech continued to do evil and turned away from God, God is sovereign, and His hand was and is upon Israel. In the midst of battle, Abimelech was fatally struck by a millstone. The Lord was present in the battle and delivered the Israelites to victory.

This is a story about a man losing his mind and acting completely apart from the Lord's plan. But even so, the Lord remained in control. The crazy, selfish plans of man cannot overcome God's sovereignty. He is always there, showing His grace and mercy. You may need to hear this today. *God will not give up on you*, just as He never gave up on the Israelites. He is there even in the unseen, hard moments of battle. And He is victorious. Even when crazy surrounds you, you are surrounded by the Lord God Almighty. Praise His name!

In this way, God turned back on Abimelech the evil that he had done against his father, by killing his 70 brothers. And God also returned all the evil of the men of Shechem on their heads. So the curse of Jotham son of Jerubbaal came on them. —Judges 9:56–57

Further Scripture: Psalm 135:6; Proverbs 16:4; Colossians 1:17

Questions

1. Why did Abimelech kill 70 of his half-brothers? Why would the citizens of Shechem be alright with that? (Judges 9:1–6)
2. Read the parable spoken by Jotham. How do you interpret it? Can you remember a time when you may have settled for less?

3. How did God punish Abimelech and the people of Shechem? Do you think that was justified? Why?

4. Why did the Lord turn Israel over to the Philistines and Ammonites? (Judges 10:6–8)

5. Who does the Lord say He rescued the Israelites from in the past (Judges 10:11–12)? Why did He say He would not help them now? (Judges 10:13)

6. What did the Holy Spirit highlight to you in Judges 9—10 through the reading or the teaching?

Lesson 18: Judges 11—12

Judge: Lawlessness or Righteousness

Teaching Notes

Intro

Jesus the Messiah is the *Judge* of the Old Testament and the New Testament, of the days past and the days to come. In Mindi's painting, she shows peace through the poppy, and that the enemy wants to steal, kill, and destroy through the idolatry of the Israelites. When the Holy Spirit came on each of the judges, it tipped the scale to favor Israel. Again and again, we see the crazy era that the book of Judges took place in—an era of pendulum swings from "lawless living" to "righteous reform" and back to "lawless living." Idolatry was rampant with gods and idols from seven different nations (Judges 10:11). Seven is a number that symbolizes completion and which shows that the Israelites had been exposed to the full wickedness of all the nations that were left in their land.

Teaching

Judges 11:1–11: Jephthah was a great warrior, but he was the son of a prostitute (v. 1). He had a lot of baggage, because of the things of the past that he couldn't shake off. Even his brothers turned on him (v. 2). The Israelites condemned prostitution. Prostitutes were not allowed in the house of worship, and the children of prostitutes were shunned and could not enter the house of worship. The actions of the parents followed children into their lives. Jephthah was a mighty warrior, but he carried shame from his mother's actions. The thrust for today's lesson, however, is that our past does not define us. The Bible states that there is no condemnation for those who are in Christ Jesus (Romans 8:1).

Jephthah fled to the land of Tob (the name means goodness) and lawless men joined him (v. 3). In other translations, these men were called scoundrels and adventurers. Jay Vernon McGee preached on Jephthah and described the process Jephthah went through in this chapter: he was exiled, exalted, and excited.[1] We've already seen Jephthah being exiled.

---

[1] Jay Vernon McGee, "07 Judges 11–15—J Vernon McGee—Thru the Bible," YouTube, https://www.youtube.com/watch?v=5wIWIkgCZSs.

I don't believe that Jephthah understood the goodness of God, and probably had preconceived notions of who Yahweh was. But when the Ammonites made war against Israel, the elders of Gilead went to Tob to get Jephthah and bring him back as their army commander (vv. 4–6). Jephthah responded in the spirit of rejection (v. 7). The elders explained they had no other options (v. 8). Jephthah agreed to go with the condition that if God gave him victory, he would be made the leader of Gilead (v. 9). They agreed, swearing God as their witness (v. 10). Jephthah went with them and repeated his terms in the presence of God before all the people (v. 11). Jephthah was finally exalted, and he was ready to be the leader God called him to be.

The name Jephthah means to open, to release. God was raising Jephthah up to open the doors of victory once again, and to bring freedom and release to the people.

Judges 11:12–22: Jephthah sent a message to the king of the Ammonites asking why they had come to fight in his land (v. 12). The Ammonites responded that Israel had taken their land (v. 13). This was a half-truth. Charles Ellicott explains,

> This was a very plausible plea, but was not in accordance with facts. The Israelites had been distinctly forbidden to war against the Moabites and Ammonites; but when Sihon, king of the Amorites, had refused them permission to pass peaceably through his land, and had even come out to battle against them, they had defeated him and seized his territory. It was quite true that a large district in this territory had *originally* belonged to Moab and Ammon, and had been wrested from them by Sihon; but that was a question with which the Israelites had nothing to do, and it was absurd to expect that they would shed their blood to win settlements for the sole purpose of restoring them to nations which regarded them with the deadliest enmity.[2] (Numbers 21:21–26; Deuteronomy 2:19)

Jephthah responded that the Israelites were not supposed to fight the Ammonites and he reminded them of historical events (vv. 14–22).

Judges 11:23–40: Chemosh was the national deity of the Ammonites and Moabites. His name meant the destroyer, subduer, and fish god. King Solomon would introduce the worship of Chemosh to Israel, and King Josiah years later

---

[2] Charles J. Ellicott, *Ellicott's Bible Commentary for English Readers: Judges 11:13*, StudyLight. org, www.studylight.org/commentaries/ebc/judges-11.html.

would eradicate the practice from Israel. Jephthah questioned why the Ammonites wanted land that their god, Chemosh, had not given them and why they had waited over 300 years to try to get it back (vv. 24, 26). But the Spirit of the Lord came upon Jephthah, who traveled throughout the area into the land of the Ammonites (v. 29). Jephthah grew excited and made the vow to the Lord that if God gave him victory over the Ammonites, he would offer whoever came out of his house first as a burnt offering to the Lord (vv. 30–31). Notice that God didn't ask for this; Jephthah made this rash decision. God did not and does not require human sacrifice. Our God does not do that because it's not in His nature. Jephthah was mixing religions by vowing to the God Yahweh, with the demands of the other gods in the area. After victory against the Ammonites (vv. 32–33), his daughter came out to greet him on his return (v. 34). Jephthah tore his clothes in grief as he realized his vow would take the life of his daughter, a vow he thought he could not take back (v. 35). Once again, notice Jephthah's lack of understanding of who God is as a loving, caring, forgiving God.

Sadly, the daughter's understanding of the Lord was no better than her father Jephthah's, so she asked only that her father would allow her two months to wander in the mountains while she grieved her virginity before he carried out his vow (v. 37). He agreed, and at the end of two months, she returned, and Jephthah kept his vow (vv. 38–39). The young women of Israel commemorated Jephthah's daughter for four days every year (v. 40).

What a reminder this is for us who are parents to teach our children who God really is—to paint the picture of our loving, merciful God correctly.

Judges 12:1–6: The men of the tribe of Ephraim came to Jephthah because he had not asked them to fight the Ammonites with him and threatened to burn his house down with him in it (v. 1). Ephraim wanted part of the spoils from the battle. Jephthah explained that they had been asked but had refused to go, so he had to fight without them (vv. 2–3). Sadly, Gilead and Ephraim went to war against each other, and Gilead defeated Ephraim. Forty-two thousand soldiers from Ephraim were killed in battle.

Closing

It is hard to know how to tie this lesson up. All the craziness, the misunderstandings of God, the cross fighting between the tribes of Israel—it's all hard to get a handle on. One thing we can take away from this is that we need to become people who walk in freedom and release ourselves from old ways of thinking, old teachings, and old ideas of who we think God is. God is not waiting to strike people down. He is the God of love. My prayer is that we begin to see God as the *Judge* who focuses on the big picture, who determines what is fair, and who reigns in righteousness and justice.

The Daily Word

Jephthah became a great warrior and leader for the Israelites. The Book of Hebrews even mentions his faith. He boldly and uniquely led the Israelites to defeat the Ammonites. Even though Jephthah was the son of a prostitute, he did not let his past define him. He honored his vow to the Lord during difficult and unlikely circumstances and led the Israelites through battle as he walked by faith.

Your past does not define you. You may have experienced abuse or come from a broken family. But praise God! Your family history does not define you. As you trust Jesus and walk with Him, remember, *you are a child of God*. You are a new creation—the old things have passed away and new things have come. He formed you in your mother's womb, and He has plans for you. He will work all things together for good for those who trust in Him. Today, walk in who you are in Christ!

Jephthah the Gileadite was a great warrior, but he was the son of a prostitute, and Gilead was his father. —Judges 11:1

Further Scripture: Romans 8:28; 2 Corinthians 5:17; Hebrews 11:32–34

Questions

1. Jephthah was chased away by his half-brothers, but when the war began, the elders called him back to help and then to rule over them. In your opinion, why did they ask Jephthah and not his brothers to help and to rule?
2. Why do you think the tribe of Ephraim refused to come and help Jephthah? Why did they become angry and threaten to kill him (Judges 12:1–6)?
3. How did the people of Ephraim try to escape? What were the results? How many lost their lives?
4. In Judges 11:27, how was the Lord referenced?
5. What did the Holy Spirit highlight to you in Judges 11–12 through the reading or the teaching?

Lesson 19: Judges 13—14

Judge: The Appearance of the Pre-Incarnate Christ

Teaching Notes

Intro

As we start today, I want to make a disclaimer. This is the Word of God—I didn't make it up. There are stories in the rest of Judges that are really crazy. It's what makes it so exciting to study God's Word. Our prayer is that this study is refreshing and that we keep our eyes on God in the midst of the craziness in the book of Judges.

Teaching

Judges 13:1–5: Once again, the Israelites did evil before God, and He gave them over to the Philistines for 40 years (v. 1). We're back at the beginning of another cycle with the Israelites of disobedience, punishment, deliverance through a judge, and restoration. When the judge died, the cycle began again. For example, we've traced this cycle through multiple judges, such as: Othniel (Judges 3:7–9), Ehud (Judges 3:12–15), Shamgar (Judges 3:31), Deborah (Judges 4:1–4), and Gideon (Judges 6:12). There was a man from the tribe of Dan whose wife was barren (v. 2). The Angel of the Lord appeared to the man Manoah's wife, and told her she would bear a child who would be a Nazarite to God from birth. Therefore, Manoah's wife couldn't drink wine or beer, nor eat anything unclean (vv. 3–5). And she could never cut the child's hair because he would begin to save Israel from the Philistines.

We believe that the Angel of the Lord was the pre-incarnate Christ. The Creator was standing before Manoah's wife telling her she would have a child and the implication is that the child would be created through Him (John 1:1–4; Colossians 1:15–16). There has been a pattern of the pre-incarnate Christ showing up in the Old Testament:

- Genesis 12:7—with Abraham
- Genesis 16—with Hagar
- Genesis 18—with Abraham and Sarah

- Genesis 21—with Hagar
- Genesis 22:11–14—intervened with Abraham and Isaac
- Genesis 24:7, 40—with Abraham's servant
- Genesis 31:11—in a dream to Jacob; Genesis 32:24–43–wrestled with Jacob
- Exodus 3:2–22—with Moses through the burning bush
- Exodus 13:21; 14:19; 23:20–23; 32:34; 33:2—went before Israel in a pillar of cloud/fire
- Exodus 24:9–11—appeared to the elders of Israel
- Exodus 33:9–23; 40:38—to Moses
- Numbers 22:22–35—through the donkey to Balaam
- Joshua 5:14—as Commander of the Lord's army
- Judges 2:1–3; 5:23—to Israel
- Judges 6:11–24—to Gideon

The pre-incarnate appearance of Christ shows up all through the Old Testament.

Judges 13:6–11: The woman told Manoah about a man who looked like "the awe-inspiring Angel of God" and what He had told her (vv. 6–7). How would they have known what the Angel of God looked like if others had not seen Him and talked about Him? In response to his wife's news, Manoah prayed, asking God to send the Angel of God back so He could teach them how to raise this child (v. 8). What a cool father prayer! Imagine if men of God embraced their role as fathers and looked to Lord to teach them what to do! God sent the Angel back to the woman who ran and got her husband (vv. 9–11a). God wants to listen and respond to us when we pray to Him (Psalm 145:18; Lamentations 3:57; James 4:8). Manoah asked if He was the man who had spoken to his wife (v. 11b). Manoah's prayer was for the Angel of the Lord to come back, a prayer I believe is prophetic for the prayers of believers being lifted from and for Israel today. Right now, Israel is a mess, and we need His help. This is the crazy thing—the Angel of the Lord will wait on us and is waiting for us to get a lot of people and bring them to Him.

Judges 13:12–18: Verse 12 reflects that God is a patient God because Manoah asked about what they had already been told. The Angel of the Lord replied that his wife already knew what to do, and then listed it again (vv. 13–14). Then, Manoah asked the Angel to stay with them while they prepared food for Him (v. 15). Manoah hadn't realized this was the Angel of the Lord, but he offered hospitality. Could this be what Hebrews 13:1 refers to—giving hospitality to unknown angels? The Angel refused the food but said Manoah could offer a burnt offering to God (v. 16). Manoah asked the Angel of the Lord's name, and He responded that His name "is wonderful" (v. 18). Isaiah 9:6 says, "He will be named Wonderful Counselor, Mighty God, Eternal Father, Prince of Peace." His name IS "wonderful."

Judges 13:19–24: Manoah took a goat and a grain offering and offered them to the Lord on a rock as a burnt offering (v. 19). When the flame from the offering rose to the sky, the Angel of the Lord went up its flame. Manoah and his wife knew then who the Angel of the Lord was, and they fell on their faces (v. 20). Many times, God is portrayed in the Old Testament as a consuming fire: Exodus 3:2–the angel in the burning bush; Exodus 14:19–the angel in the pillar of fire; Judges 6:21–Gideon with the meat and the fire.

The Angel of the Lord did not appear again to Manoah and his wife (v. 21). Manoah expected to die when he realized he had seen God (v. 22). His wife was able to speak reason and faith into his life (v. 23). And Manoah's wife gave birth to a son named Samson (which could possibly mean "little sun" or "sunny boy"[1]). The boy grew and was blessed by the Lord (v. 24). This sounds very much like Luke 2:52 as Jesus increased in wisdom, stature, and in faith. Samson was a foreshadowed picture of Christ. Wiersbe interprets Samson's name as "sunny" or "brightness," for "certainly he brought light and joy to Manoah and his wife . . . and he also began to bring light to Israel during the dark days of Philistine oppression."[2]

Judges 13:25: The Spirit of the Lord began to direct Samson's life.

Closing

There are four chapters in Judges dedicated to Samson. Tomorrow, we'll look at how he used his amazing strength and how he allowed his weakness for women to derail what he was doing for God.

Our takeaway from this lesson is from Hebrew 11:32, where Samson is listed in the Hebrews Hall of Faith even though his life was a mess. God can use any of us at any given time. He can use us as parents of a "Samson" or He can use us similar to "Samson." We have an opportunity to keep pointing people to Him.

---

[1] Thomas L. Constable, *Expository Notes of Dr. Thomas Constable: Judges*, 148, http://planobiblechapel.org/tcon/notes/pdf/judges.pdf.
[2] Warren W. Wiersbe, *Be Available: Accepting the Challenge to Confront the Enemy* (Colorado Springs: David C. Cook, 1994), 130–31.

The Daily Word

The Israelites once again did what was evil in the Lord's eyes, so the Lord handed them over to the Philistines for forty years. During that time, a man named Manoah and his wife were unable to conceive a baby. But then the Angel of the Lord appeared to his wife, telling her she would have a son and giving her clear instructions on how to raise the son as a Nazarite. The Angel of the Lord said to her, "This child will begin to save Israel from the power of the Philistines." When his wife shared everything the Angel of the Lord said, Manoah turned to the Lord, asking Him to confirm and teach them how to raise their baby. God answered Manoah's request and sent the Angel of the Lord to visit this couple. Soon after, the couple gave birth to Samson, the last judge.

Manoah turned to the Lord for confirmation and clarity. He heard the news and instructions from the angel through his wife and believed it, but he wanted more confirmation. When you know the Lord has called you to something but you still have questions, *turn to Him and ask for even more wisdom.* Sometimes you may want to turn to a media source, see what your friends are doing, or look to the latest book. Instead, ask the Lord. The Lord will answer you and will direct your path. He promises that if anyone asks Him for wisdom, He will give generously without judgment. He will counsel you even through the night and make known His plans for you, teaching you along the way. Then it's your turn to step out in faith and walk out what He is leading you to do.

Manoah prayed to the Lord and said, "Please Lord, let the man of God you sent come again to us and teach us what we should do for the boy who will be born." God listened to Manoah, and the Angel of God came again to the woman. —Judges 13:8–9

Further Scripture: Psalm 16:7–8; Psalm 25:4–5; James 1:5

Questions

1. The Lord instructed Manoah's wife not to drink any wine or strong drink because she would conceive and give birth to a son. Does anyone else come to mind that received similar instructions (Luke 1:15)? What is she told about this child (Numbers 6:1–8; Judges 13:4–5, 7)?

2. Why do you think the angel of the Lord only repeated the instructions he had already given to Manoah's wife (Judges 13:12–14) rather than answer Manoah's questions about the child's future?

3. Does it surprise you that God used Samson's disobedience of the law (Deuteronomy 7:3) to set up deliverance from the Philistines? Does God still bring good from our disobedience (Isaiah 61:3; Romans 8:28)?

4. In spite of his sinful choices, Samson is listed in Hebrews 11:32 as an example of a man of faith. Do you see God's grace in that? Are you able to see yourself as a man or woman of faith, despite sinful choices in your past?

5. A young lion came racing toward Samson to attack, and he tore him with his bare hands and killed him. How was he able to do this (Judges 14:6; 16:17)? Was Samson a foreshadowing of Christ, who defeats Satan, the roaring lion (Hebrews 2:14; 1 Peter 5:8; 1 John 3:8)?

6. What did the Holy Spirit highlight to you in Judges 13—14 through the reading or the teaching?

Lesson 20: Judges 15—16

Judge: The Strength of the Spirit

Teaching Notes

Intro

As we move into lesson 20, welcome to a world of chaos, to the world of Samson's life that looked good, but the reality was that he was causing a lot of issues for himself. Samson has been defined as a hero and a deliverer—even an avenger. However, the wrongs Samson tried to right were because of him. Charles Spurgeon said that Samson's "whole life is a scene of miracles and follies."[1]

Samson's problems began early. Samson found a Philistine woman to marry (Judges 14:1), a woman from a people who didn't follow Yahweh. When his parents tried to dissuade him, Samson demanded that they go get her for him. The statement, "I want her," literally means "she is right in my eyes."[2] This phrase was usually used to "describe a person or action that was right in the Lord's eyes"[3] (Psalm 25:13). If Samson's eyes had been on the Lord, this would not have been an issue. But Samson wanted the flesh, not the godly (Colossians 3:1–2).

Teaching

Judges 15:1–5: Samson took a young goat as a gift for his wife, but her father would not let him see her (v. 1). In this culture, the gift was given before sexual relations. Samson was doing the same thing Judah had done with Tamar (Genesis 38:17). The father said he had already given Samson's wife to someone else and offered Samson his younger daughter instead (v. 2). In return, Samson announced he would not be responsible for how he harmed the Philistines (v. 3). Block described Samson as "a man with a higher calling than any other deliverer in the book, but he spends his whole life doing his own thing."[4] I think people

---

[1] Quoted in Warren W. Wiersbe, *Be Available: Accepting the Challenge to Confront the Enemy* (Colorado Springs: David C. Cook, 1994), 139.

[2] Earl D. Radmacher, Ronald B. Allen, and H. Wayne House, *Nelson's New Illustrated Bible Commentary* (Nashville: Thomas Nelson, 1999), 328.

[3] Radmacher et al., 328.

[4] Radmacher et al., 306.

who walk with the Lord have an incredibly high calling, but many, like Samson, would prefer to do their own thing.

Samson went out and caught 300 "foxes." The Hebrew word for fox is also used for jackal. *Nelson's Commentary* states that foxes are solitary animals, while jackals run in packs, suggesting that jackals would have been easier to catch.[5] He then tied a torch to the tails of each pair of animals, lit the torches, and sent them into the Philistine fields of grain. As an avenger, Samson burned piles of grain, fields of grain, vineyards, and olive groves (vv. 4–5). Since he didn't get what he wanted, Samson acted like a spoiled child and burned everything the Philistines had. Samson was given the task of delivering the people *from* the Philistines, but judgement was clouded by his own desires. It had nothing to do with his calling from God, but his fleshly desire for revenge.

Judges 15:6–8: When the Philistines found out why Samson had burned their crops, they took the father and Samson's intended bride and burned them to death (v. 6). Samson swore vengeance on the Philistines, even though he started it (v. 7). He tore them from limb to limb "with a great slaughter" (v. 8). *Nelson's Commentary* states this meant Samson dismembered the Philistines.[6] Then, Samson went to a cave at the rock of Etam.

Judges 15:9–13: The Philistines came north and camped in the land of Judah, not their own land, and raided the town of Lehi. When the people of Judah asked why, the Philistines explained they had come to arrest Samson and take him back to Philistia (v. 9). So, the Israelite army of Judah (3,000 men) went to get Samson for the Philistines (vv. 11–12). Samson agreed but asked that the Israelites swear they wouldn't kill him. Scholars have debated why Samson felt it was necessary to ask for this guarantee. Possibly, he didn't want to have to attack his own people. The Israelites promised and took new ropes and tied up Samson (v. 13). "Ropes were made of leather, hair, or plant fibers . . . being new, these ropes were the strongest possible."[7]

Judges 15:14–20: The Israelites took Samson to Lehi (still in Judah), where the Philistines were waiting for him. They came out shouting, either in joy at his capture or anger. But the Spirit of the Lord took control of Samson and the ropes that bound his arms became like burnt flax (the weakest of all ropes).[8] Samson picked up a donkey's jawbone and used it to kill 1,000 Philistines (v. 15). Because

---

[5] Radmacher et al., 329.

[6] Radmacher et al., 329.

[7] Radmacher et al., 329.

[8] Radmacher et al., 329.

the jawbone was fresh, Samson was touching something unclean, breaking one of the requirements of his Nazarite status. However, since the Spirit of the Lord directed him, that probably didn't matter. Here are other times the Spirit of the Lord came upon a judge: Judges 3:10; 6:34; 11:29; 13:25; 14:6,19; 15:14. Romans 8:14 talks about the sons of God.

God used His Spirit to penetrate the darkness and the evil and the chaos through the judges. And He does the same thing with us.

Samson told what he had done with those he killed by the jawbone of a donkey—he piled the bodies in a heap (v. 16). Then, Samson threw away the jawbone and they named the place Ramath-lehi or Jawbone Hill (v. 17). Wiersbe emphasizes that "so often in Scripture, testing follows triumph."[9] Samson called out to the Lord that he was going to die of thirst without water (v. 18). God brought water from the ground for Samson. After Samson drank, he named the place En-hakkore, which means "Caller's Spring" because he had called to the Lord for water (1 Corinthians 10:4). We don't know what Samson knew about God's provision of water during the exodus, but he knew God was able to hear him call out and to provide for his needs (v.19). Samson judged Israel for 20 years (v.20).

Judges 16 tells of Samson's encounter with Delilah, another Philistine. He fell in love with her, and she used his feelings for her to try to get him to tell her the secret of his great strength. Twice, he lied to her, and each time she tried to have him bound and given over to the Philistines. Finally, she cried that if he loved her, he would tell her. So, he revealed that his uncut hair was the source of his strength. She cut his hair as he slept, and the Philistines arrested him. They gouged out his eyes and put him in a dungeon where he ground grain. In the dungeon, his hair began to grow back. The Philistines gathered together one day and were drinking heavily. When they became drunk, they had Samson brought before them, standing him between the pillars that held up the temple. Samson asked to be placed where he could feel the temple pillars since he was blind. Then, Samson asked God to give him strength one more time so he could get revenge on the Philistines for taking his eyesight. It is interesting that his eyesight was taken, since that's what got him in so much trouble. Samson pushed with all his might and the pillars fell in, killing more than 3,000 men and women. Verse 30 says Samson killed more people in his death than he did in life.

Closing

We are a lot like Samson. We go through the day and make mistakes. We have a calling, but we mess up. For us, we have water that will never run dry. John 7 says there is living water inside us. So, we have to depend on the Holy Spirit

---

[9] Warren W. Wiersbe, *The Bible Exposition Commentary: Joshua–Esther* (Colorado Springs: David C. Cook, 2003), 151.

moving in and through us. Samson forgot that and depended upon himself instead of depending on God all the time. Don't wait until the end of your life to walk out your calling. Start walking now.

The Daily Word

The Lord's hand was upon Samson's life. Even though the men of Judah were determined to hand him over to the Philistines, Samson's God-given strength brought him victory. He was a one-man army, killing one thousand men with the jawbone of a donkey. Even though Samson did not walk closely with the Lord, the Lord gave him victory in battle. After the victory, he was tired and thirsty. In that moment of weakness, he asked the Lord for water. The Lord provided the water, Samson drank, his strength returned, and he was revived. He went on to judge for twenty more years in the days of the Philistines.

The Lord waits for you to turn to Him, so He can strengthen you. No matter how far you've gone astray or how long you have done life on your own, God never leaves you. He has a plan for you, and He waits for you to turn to Him for help. You may be thirsty and weary from the weight of life. Turn to Him for refreshment. He is your source for strength and living water. He will restore your soul. He will revive you. *Just ask Him.*

He became very thirsty and called out to the Lord . . . So God split a hollow place in the ground at Lehi, and water came out of it. After Samson drank, his strength returned, and he revived. That is why he named it En-hakkore, which is in Lehi to this day. —Judges 15:18–19

Further Scripture: 2 Samuel 7:1; Psalm 119:93; John 7:38

Questions

1. How many foxes did Samson catch (Judges 15)? What was the purpose of him doing that?

2. What can you learn from both Samson and the Philistines regarding retaliation (Matthew 5:38–42; Romans 12:19)?

3. What three lies did Samson tell Delilah? Why do you think he finally told her the truth about how to make him weak?

4. Scripture speaks about guarding our heart. What are some ways that Samson did not guard his heart (Proverbs 4:23; Galatians 5:16)?

5. Where did Samson's strength come from? Why did Samson not know that the Lord departed from him? How are we assured that the Holy Spirit will never leave us (John 14:16; Ephesians 1:13–14)?

6. What did the Holy Spirit highlight to you in Judges 15—16 through the reading or the teaching?

Lesson 21: Judges 17—18

Judge: The Progression of Sin

Teaching Notes

Intro

Our word for the book of Judges is *Judge*, and Jesus serves as a *Judge* who comes in to save. As *Judge*, Jesus knows we deserve punishment and death, but He chose to save us instead. Over the 300-year period of Judges, judge after judge attempted to save the people of Israel and set them free. But their attempts could not complete the process. Judges 17 provides the story of Micah, who owned 1100 pieces of silver that he had taken from his mother. He returned the silver to his mother who had a carved image made and overlaid with silver. The silver image was placed in Micah's house as part of a shrine, and he installed one of his sons as his priest. Judges 17:6 says, "In those days there was no king in Israel; everyone did whatever he wanted." When a Levite traveled through Micah's area, Micah hired him to be his priest. This is the backdrop for chapter 18.

Teaching

The Danite tribe was "looking for territory to occupy." This is confusing, because the tribe of Dan was given choice, ideal land (Joshua 19:40–47), along with the other 11 tribes of Israel. Apparently, the tribe just wanted more land. We're going to walk through the sins of the tribe of Dan.

Judges 18:1–2: Covetousness. They wanted something else than what they had already been given. In Judges 1:34, the Amorites gave the Danites opposition in taking the land they were given, so they went elsewhere. Now, in Judges 18, they sent out scouts to explore the land. Only, they went into lands that had already been allotted to other tribes. They came to the house of Micah and found the Levite at Micah's home shrine. The spies stayed for the night.

Judges 18:3–6: Ungodly Counsel. While at Micah's house, they received what Wiersbe refers to as "ungodly counsel."[1] The spies recognized the Levite's dia-

---

[1] Warren W. Wiersbe, *Be Available: Accepting the Challenge to Confront the Enemy* (Colorado Springs: David C. Cook, 1994), 159.

lect and asked him why he was there (v. 3). After the Levite explained, they asked him to enquire of God if their journey would be successful (vv. 4–5). The spies unwisely accepted what the Levite told them, even though he was being paid by the other tribe (Proverbs 12:26; 16:16). Most commentators agree that this Levite was "Jonathan son of Gershom," the grandson of Moses (v. 30). Think of the ramifications—the grandson of Moses was being paid to be Micah's personal priest. This is treading on holy ground.

Judges 18:7–13: Violence and Murder—Part 1. The spies went to Laish, approximately 125 miles away from Micah's house, and 30 miles east of the Mediterranean Sea. There, they found the Sidonians, a "quiet and unsuspecting" people who seemed like easy prey (v. 7). In New Testament times, this was Tyre and Sidon in Phoenicia. The spies returned to Dan and told the people the land was good and would be easy to take (vv. 8–9). Remember that when the spies entered the land under Moses' leadership, the Danite spy was afraid and voted not to take the land. These spies told the people that "God has handed it over to you . . . a place where nothing on earth is lacking" (v. 10). Six hundred Danites left to go into a land that wasn't theirs (v. 11). At some point, there were many more soldiers than this in Dan (Numbers 1:38–39; 26:42–43). Possibly this was only a small army, or many of the soldiers had not survived. The army made its way to Micah's house (vv. 12–13). These verses set up the violence and murder that will be covered below.

Judges 18:14–26: Breaking and Entering, Robbery, and Intimidation. The spies told their brothers about all the idols and goods inside Micah's house so they made a detour to the house, while the Danite soldiers waited at the gated entrance (vv. 14–16). The spies went into the house and took the silver-covered image, the ephod covered in stones, and the household idols (v. 17). The Levite priest asked what they were doing (v. 18). They told him to be quiet and asked if he wouldn't rather be a priest for an entire tribe than for one person (v. 19). This was a legitimate question, because it questioned where his allegiance was. This was not a question about numbers. We have to be careful in America because we tend to evaluate the church's success by the number of people within the church.

The Levite agreed and took his ephod, idols, and the carved image with them (v. 20). Small children, livestock, and possessions were put in front of the soldiers for safety, "because any attacks would come from the rear."[2] What was happening with the tribe of Dan was exactly what Jacob's prediction was for the tribe of Dan (Genesis 49:17): "a snake by the road, a viper beside the path, that bites the

---

[2] Wiersbe, 160.

horses' heels so that its rider falls backward." In chapter 18, we're beginning to see this prophetically come about. When Micah returned home, he realized what had happened and he called the men in homes nearby to go after the Danites (v. 22). They caught up with the Danites who turned around and asked Micah why he was chasing them (v. 23). Micah asked why they had taken everything from his house (v. 24). The Danites told Micah not to raise his voice against them or they would attack him and his family would be killed (v. 25). The Danites continued on their way. Micah returned home because he realized the Danites were stronger than he was (v. 26).

Judges 18:27–29: Violence and Murder—Part 2. The Danites went on to Laish and killed the people and burned the city (v. 27). The people of Laish had no alliance with anyone so no one could help them (v. 28). The Danites rebuilt the city, named it Dan, and lived there (v. 29). They settled into an area they should never have been in. Wiersbe says there are only "three philosophies of life in today's world: (1) 'What's mine is mine, I'll keep it'; (2) 'What's yours is mine, I'll take it'; and (3) 'What's mine is yours, I'll share it.'[3] The tribe of Dan operated under the second philosophy. It started with the eyes—they wanted what they saw.

Judges 18:30–31: Idolatry. The Danites set up the carved image they had taken from Micah and worshiped it, while Jonathan son of Gershom and his sons served as priests for the Danites (vv. 30–31). Wiersbe states that "the tribe of Dan was the first tribe in Israel to officially adopt an idolatrous system of religion"[4] (1 Kings 12:25–33). MacArthur explains that "the ark of God was far away from [the Danites], so they justified their idolatry by their distance from the rest of Israel."[5]

Closing

In Revelation 7:5–8, the 144,000 are not any current religion today, but are Jewish evangelists who come from the tribes of Israel. Jews from the 12 tribes will evangelize for Jesus. When you read Revelation 7:5–8, where the breakdown of the 144,000 is listed from each tribe, you'll see that the tribe of Dan is NOT even listed. Can I prove that it's because the tribe of Dan instituted the first idolatrous religious system within Israel? No, but I think there's a good chance that is the case. It all started through coveting what others had. And, coveting leads to all kinds of other issues. I hope this encourages you to keep your eye on the Lord.

---

[3] Wiersbe, 161.

[4] Wiersbe, 161.

[5] John MacArthur, *The MacArthur Bible Commentary* (Nashville: Thomas Nelson, 2005), 286.

The Daily Word

The Danites sent five brave men out to scout the land and explore it. They came to the hill country of Ephraim near the home of Micah and spent the night there. During their scouting journey, they discovered idolatry, lies, and deception. The spies of Dan did not have their eyes on God as Joshua had commanded. But even in their waywardness, they knew the truth. They knew to inquire of God, and they knew God was watching over everything on their journey.

What would someone discover if he or she looked into your life? Do you appear to glorify the Lord but have hidden sins behind closed doors? Rest assured, no matter what is discovered in your life, the Lord will always watch over your journey. That's the beauty of the Lord. He is with you, and He loves you unconditionally. No matter how far you may stray, no matter how deep into other false gods and idols you may go, the Lord is with you and watching over you. The Danites knew the Lord was with them but continued in bondage to false idols. Don't live like a Danite. *Ask the Lord for freedom.* Ask Him to help you on your journey and set you free from the temptation to bow down to other gods and live in sin.

Then they said to him, "Please inquire of God so we will know if we will have a successful journey." The priest told them, "Go in peace. The Lord is watching over the journey you are going on." —Judges 18:5–6

Further Scripture: Exodus 20:23; Psalm 91:11; 3 John 1:6

Questions

1. In Judges 17:5, what does it mean that Micah had a house of gods? Micah also had several pieces made and consecrated one of his sons to be his priest. Where else do we see this same set-up (Exodus 39)? In this setting, do you think Micah was wrong? Why or why not?

2. Why do you think Micah asked the Levite to stay and be his priest (Judges 17:7–13)?

3. In Judges 18:11–21, why did the Levite stand aside while Micah's items were stolen? Why did the Levite leave with the warriors of Dan?

4. What did the Holy Spirit highlight to you in Judges 17—18 through the reading or the teaching?

Lesson 22: Judges 19—20

Judge: The Horrific Sin of Benjamin

Teaching Notes

Intro

As we move through the last two studies in Judges, the craziness is going to continue to get worse. Our one word for the Messiah in this book is *Judge*. The Messiah is the *Judge* who is coming to save! Let's review the words for our study of the Old Testament so far: Genesis—*Seed*, Exodus—*Deliverer*, Leviticus—*Atonement*, Numbers—*Rock*, Deuteronomy—*Prophet*, Joshua—*Commander*, Judges—*Judge*.

Teaching

Judges 19:1–4: Chapter 19 begins with the statement, "when there was no king in Israel." In Judges 17—18, we had a Levite from Bethlehem who traveled to the hill country of Ephraim. In Judges 19, an unnamed Levite from Ephraim was traveling to Bethlehem. This Levite priest had issues . . . he had no problem partying or with interacting with people he shouldn't have been with (vv. 9–14), and no problem with the way he treated the concubine. This event precipitated the civil war in Israel.

Look at the Levite priest more closely. Leviticus 21:7 states that a priest could marry, as long as it wasn't to a prostitute or a divorced woman. The priest was to marry a virgin from his own people (Leviticus 21:13–14). A concubine wife was acceptable culturally at that time, but it wasn't acceptable to God.[1]

The concubine was unfaithful to the Levite, left to live at her father's house for four months (v. 2). The Old Testament law required that the guilty parties of adultery be put to death (Leviticus 20:10). Instead of requiring the law to be carried out, the Levite let her leave and later, went after her "to speak kindly" (v. 3). He still loved her so much that he was willing to ignore her unfaithfulness. The concubine's father gladly welcomed the Levite into his home, possibly because the Levite had served as his daughter's deliverer (v. 4). For three days, the Levite stayed there, and they celebrated together.

---

[1] John MacArthur, *The MacArthur Bible Commentary* (Nashville: Thomas Nelson, 2005), 286.

Judges 19:5–13: After three days, the Levite tried to leave but the father stalled him, providing food and begging him to stay another night (vv. 5–7). On the fifth day, the Levite again tried to leave, but the father convinced him to stay to eat. Afternoon came and the father again tried to make him stay another night (vv. 8–9). The Levite refused to stay this time. He, his concubine, and his servant left.

The Levite, his concubine, and his servant left the area of Judah and entered the land of Benjamin (v. 10). The servant asked for them to stay in the Jebusite city of Jebus, but the Levite refused, and they continued to travel to Gibeah (vv. 11–13). The Jebusites were always a problem, because Israel never finished conquering the land and removing the pagans. The Levite refused to stay in Jebus because there were no Israelites there.

Judges 19:14–21: They continued until they arrived at Gibeah in the land of Benjamin (v. 14). They went into the city square (v. 14), where all the town's leaders would gather. The Levite went there, expecting to be given hospitality and a place to stay the night (v. 15). There was sin in this community. Genesis 4:7 says, "But if you do not do what is right, sin is crouching at the door." James 1:14 says, "But each person is tempted when he is drawn away and enticed by his own evil desires" (James 1:14–16). The people in Gibeah had no idea how close sin was to them. Finally, an old man from Ephraim (not a Benjaminite) saw the Levite at the square and asked where he had come from and where he was going (vv. 16–17). The Levite responded that they were going back to the house of the Lord (in Shiloh[2]). And, although they had all the provisions they needed, they had no safe place to stay (v. 18–19). The old man told them he would take care of everything for them, even a place to stay (v. 20). The old man took them home and showed them eastern hospitality—he washed their feet and fed them (v. 22).

Judges 19:22–28: But perverted men in the city demanded that the male visitor come out so they could have sex with him (v. 22). It was the Genesis 19:4–5 situation at Sodom and Gomorrah all over again. And it happened in the tribe of Benjamin, not with pagans. There was nothing of the Lord in this encounter. The old man talked to his "brothers"—he knew them personally—and begged them to not do this horrible thing—to have sex (homosexuality) with the man (v. 23). The old man said he would bring out his own virgin daughter and the Levite's concubine for them instead (v. 24). The old man would have rather seen his daughter be raped than the horrible sin of homosexuality. Either scenario is all wrong and all sin. When the men from Benjamin did not listen, the Levite

---

[2] MacArthur, 286.

priest took his concubine outside and gave her to them (v. 25). How could he in good conscious do that? The men raped and sexually abused her all night. The sin of homosexuality had led to rape and sexual abuse.

At daybreak, the men let the concubine go. She made her way back to the old man's house and collapsed (v. 26). Can you imagine being the husband who gave his wife over for this and then went back to sleep? The Levite did and prepared to leave to continue his journey. When he opened the door to leave, he found the concubine laying at the door (v. 27). He was leaving her behind! He told her to get up but there was no response, so he took her body home (v. 28).

Judges 19:29–30: At home, the Levite cut the concubine into 12 pieces and sent the pieces to all the territories of Israel (v. 29). In 1 Samuel 11:6–7, Saul did something similar when "the Spirit of God suddenly took control of him" and he took two oxen, cut them into pieces, and sent them throughout Israel. The terror of the Lord fell upon the people, and they followed Saul. When the tribes of Israel received the pieces of the concubine, the people talked about what they saw and what had happened. Nothing like this ever happened since the day the Israelites came out of Egypt (v. 30).

Judges 20: It's hard to accept the actions of the Levite, one of the priests of Israel. However, maybe it was a cry for help to the nation of Israel for the sin within them. In chapter 20, the other tribes of Israel were fired up against the tribe of Benjamin for what they had done. This was a call to the nations to come together and blot out the sin of the Benjaminites. So, "all the Israelites" (400,000 foot soldiers) came together before God at Mizpah (vv. 1–2). The Levite explained that his actions were because of the horrible shame in Israel (vv. 3–6). The gathered Israelites decided to take 10 men out of every 100 in each tribe, and 100 out of every 1,000, and 1,000 out of every 10,000 to collect provisions to send the army into Benjamin to punish them (v. 10). When the Israelite army arrived at Benjamin, they asked for the perverted men of Gibeah, but the Benjaminites refused, and went out and gathered their own army of 26,000 (vv. 13–15).

Closing

The Israelites (without Benjamin) numbered 400,000. They went to Bethel and asked God who should lead their army against the Benjaminites. The Lord answered, "Judah" (vv. 17–18). The battle took place and almost wiped out the tribe of Benjamin.

The Daily Word

A Levite traveling with his concubine sought hospitality in the city of Gibeah in Benjamin. When no one offered the Levite a place to stay, an older man took them in for the evening. But the Benjaminites of Gibeah surrounded the house and threatened the Levite. They took his concubine and raped her through the night. As a result of the abuse, she died. The Levite gruesomely cut her body up into twelve pieces and sent the pieces to each of the twelve tribes of Israel. This alerted the Israelites of the deep sin occurring in the tribe of Benjamin. The Israelites grieved and wept over how they had taken their eyes off the Lord. They knew they were in need of a judge to deliver them from the evil. The Lord gave them orders to fight because once again He would give them victory.

Lack of hospitality, homosexuality, rape, abuse, murder—you may find it difficult to read this list of sins from the Benjaminites as they took their eyes off the Lord. They did what was right in their own eyes, and it led to a corrupt, evil culture. Would you agree that the culture you live in today sounds alarmingly similar to the Benjaminites? Many in this generation have taken their eyes off Jesus and gone their own way. And yet hope remains because Christ's love remains. The same victory and saving grace for the Benjaminites is available to you and to all those around you. Jesus restores all who turn to Him. Today, pray for this generation to turn their eyes back to Jesus and walk in His victory!

Phinehas son of Eleazar, son of Aaron, was serving before it. The Israelites asked: "Should we again fight against our brothers the Benjaminites or should we stop?" The Lord answered: "Fight, because I will hand them over to you tomorrow." —Judges 20:28

Further Scripture: Psalm 44:6–8; Isaiah 40:28; James 4:9–10

Questions

1. When the Levite stopped in Gibeah, he could find no one to put him up for the night. While an older man provided for him, some townspeople wanted the old man to send his visitor out. Why did they want him to come out (Judges 19:22)? Where else did this behavior occur (Genesis 19:5)?

2. What happened to the man's concubine? What did the Levite do with her body? Why do you think he did that?

3. In Judges 20:13, why wouldn't the children of Benjamin release the men who abused the Levite's concubine? What was the result?

4. What did the Holy Spirit highlight to you in Judges 19—20 through the reading or the teaching?

Lesson 23: Judges 21

Judge: Under the Spirit of the Lord

Teaching Notes

Intro

Some people have referred to the time of the Judges as the Israelites' dark ages. This was a period of 300 years of pure evilness. The Lord would raise up judges to speak into the times and lead the people back to God for a while. God used each of the judges for a specific period of time. Mindi's painting is like a snapshot that shows what real life was like during the book of Judges. Each of the judges began when the Spirit of the Lord came over them. Each was called to deliver and to save God's people. Remember that our goal is to look at how each book of the Bible ultimately points to the coming of the Messiah—Jesus Christ. Because of our mess, we, too, need a *Deliverer*. In chapter 20, most of the Benjaminites were killed in battle. In chapter 21, the Israelites looked for wives to reestablish the tribe of Benjamin.

Teaching

Judges 21:1–4: When the oath (v. 1) was made is not recorded in Scripture, but the reason behind it is important—the Israelites didn't want the tribe of Benjamin to survive. However, the people of Israel gathered at Bethel and mourned together because of the absence of Benjamin (vv. 2–3). The people turned to the Lord in their grief, built an altar, and presented burnt offerings and fellowship offerings (v. 4). Burnt offerings were a sacrifice of atonement that acknowledged the sin nature and recognized a renewed relationship with God (Leviticus 1; 6:8–13). Fellowship offerings were a voluntary sacrifice given to thank God for His provision and deliverance (Leviticus 7:11–21). This provides a glimmer of hope that the Israelites were showing signs of returning to the Lord. However, God requires more than just the giving of sacrifices. Joel 2:12–13 says we are to rend our hearts, not our clothes. He was addressing grieving in the heart, more than outward signs of grief. Some outward expressions of dealing with the grief of sin: Genesis 37:34: Jacob tore his clothes and put on sackcloth; 2 Samuel 1:11: David tore his clothes in mourning; Job 1:20: Job tore his robe and shaved his head.

Listed are some expressions of inwardly dealing with the grief of sin:

- Hosea 6:6—God requires loyalty over sacrifice and knowledge of God over offerings.
- Psalm 51:17—God wants a broken spirit and a broken and humble heart.
- 2 Corinthians 7:10—God wants godly grief that produces repentance.

Judges 21:5–9: The Israelites grieved that the tribe of Benjamin was not with them, and that the oath they had taken called for any to be put to death that violated it (v. 5). In their grief, they found compassion and wanted to save the entire tribe of Benjamin from annihilation (vv. 6–7). They were concerned that they had made an oath not to allow their daughters to marry any men from Benjamin. They realized that no one from Jabesh-gilead had come to the assembly (vv. 8–9).

"The Gileadites were descended from Manasseh, the grandson of Rachel, and thus there was a blood-tie with the descendants of Benjamin, Rachel's son. In the subsequent history there was a very close link between the tribe of Benjamin and the men of Jabesh-gilead."[1]

Judges 21:10–18: The Israelites gathered together and sent 12,000 men to kill all the inhabitants of Jabesh-gilead (v. 10), except for women who were virgins (v. 11). They found 400 virgins and brought them to Shiloh (v. 12). There were 600 Benjaminite survivors from the battle (Judges 20:47), so 200 virgins were still needed for these survivors. The Israelites sent a message of peace to the Benjaminites who had survived the fight (v. 13). The tribe of Benjamin returned, and Israel gave the 400 virgins to them (v. 14). The people had compassion on the tribe of Benjamin and decided they would give more virgins to be brides of the Benjaminites so they would not be wiped out (vv. 15–17). But they could not give their own daughters because they had made an oath (v. 18).

Judges 21:19–22: The Israelites determined that an upcoming annual feast (possibly the Feast of Tabernacles or Passover) would give them the opportunity to fix the deficit number of women needed (v. 19). The Benjaminites were told to hide in the vineyards while they watched for young women of Shiloh to come out to dance. Then, they were to each catch one to be their wife and take them back to Benjamin (vv. 20–21). That way, when the fathers (or brothers) came looking for their daughters, the fathers could be told that they had not broken

---

[1] Arthur E. Cundall and Leon Morris, *Tyndale Old Testament Commentaries: Judges and Ruth*, v. 7 (Downer's Grove, IL: IVP Academic, 2015), 200.

their oath, but that the Benjaminites had need of more wives than what were available (v. 22).

Judges 21:23–25: The Benjaminites did as they were told. They took the women back to the land they had inherited and rebuilt their lives and families (v. 23). All the gathered Israelites returned home as well (v. 24). And, "in those days there was no king in Israel; everyone did whatever he wanted" (v. 25).

As we come to the end of this study, let's look at the big picture of the book of Judges. Judges 17:6; 18:1; 19:1; 21:25 all say the same thing: "In those days there was no king in Israel." Over and over again, because there was no king, the people did whatever they wanted. The men of Gibeah raped a woman all night. The men of Benjamin had no problem defending evil. In Israel, there were massacres of innocent people, kidnappings of innocent people, constant disobedience of the law, and taking their eyes off the Lord.

Closing

The reality is that we do the same thing. The difference is that they didn't have a king, and we do—King Jesus. In Judges, they wanted a king, and they kept looking for someone to come and save them. All of the judges were great people whom God used, but they fell short! Why? Because there is a real King who will come and set us free from all of this. The reality is that we're all in this evil period:

- Romans 3:23: "For all have sinned and fall short of the glory of God." Every one of us falls short.
- Romans 6:23: "For the wages of sin is death, but the gift of God is eternal life in Christ Jesus our Lord." Sin will always lead to death. It doesn't matter who you are or what you've done!
- Romans 5:8: "But God proves His own love for us in that while we were still sinners, Christ died for us"!
- Ephesians 2:8–9: "For you are saved by grace through faith, and this is not from yourselves; it is God's gift—not from works, so that no one can boast."
- Romans 10:9–10: "If you confess with your mouth, 'Jesus is Lord,' and believe in your heart that God raised Him from the dead, you will be saved. One believes with the heart, resulting in righteousness, and one confesses with the mouth, resulting in salvation."

There are people reading this who have never embraced the gift of God's love. They haven't embraced this gift from Christ Jesus who died on the cross for them so that this craziness and evil will end for them. When you have this faith in God's gift of Jesus Christ, it leads to life. When you believe in your heart that God raised Jesus from the dead, then you will be saved. When you confess out loud that Jesus is your Lord, you will experience salvation.

The cycle of sin and death in Judges was all they had. But we do not have that anymore—we have the love of Christ. One of the things I love about Mindi's painting is her depiction of the Holy Spirit. Scripture says that when you say yes to Jesus, He promises you the Holy Spirit will dwell inside you. Romans 8:14 says, "All those led by God's Spirit are God's sons." You are a child of God. That's what the book of Judges does. It gives us the hope of deliverance in Christ from the evil that ruled Israel.

If you've never told Jesus, you want Him to be in charge of your life, now is the time. Do it now! Just say these words out loud,

"Jesus, I want you to be Lord. Forgive me of the cycle of sin in my life. Jesus, I believe that You died on the cross, were buried, and came back alive so I could be saved. Jesus, I want You as my Savior. Amen."

If you've prayed this tonight, please go to www.reviveschool.org or www.timeto-revive.com so we can help you grow in this process.

The Daily Word

The Lord used judges to deliver and save the Israelites. It was only by God's hand that His people, the Israelites, were not wiped out. Four times in the book of Judges, Israel did what they wanted because there was no king in Israel. Because God had a plan, purpose, and promise for Israel, He continued to appoint a judge to step in and lead the nation. Even so, every judge fell short to the *One True King*: Jesus Christ—the King of kings and Lord of lords.

There's a good chance you have fallen a few times in life. Fallen back into that addiction to pornography. Fallen back to one more round of pain medication, promising this will be the last. Fallen into a pit of worry, anxiety, or self-pity. Fallen into the trap of gossip or deception. But just as God spared the tribe of Benjamin when He could have destroyed them for good, He sent Jesus to come and save you. Regardless of how far you have fallen, Jesus came to save you because He loves you. Give your life fully to Jesus saying, *"Jesus, take over my life. I surrender, and I want You to be the King of my life forever."*

In those days there was no king in Israel; everyone did whatever he wanted. —Judges 21:25

Further Scripture: John 18:37; Galatians 2:20; Revelation 17:14

Questions

1. In verse 1, why do you think the men of Israel swore to not give their daughters to the tribe of Benjamin in marriage?

2. In verse 5, why did the sons of Israel take an oath to kill any man who did not come up to Mizpah?

3. Do you think they were justified in taking the daughters of Shiloh by force to be their wives? Why or why not?

4. What was wrong with everyone doing what was right in their own eyes? How are things similar today (Jeremiah 17:9)?

5. What did the Holy Spirit highlight to you in Judges 21 through the reading or the teaching?

Lesson 24: Ruth 1—2

Kinsman Redeemer: Naomi and Ruth

Teaching Notes

Intro

How crazy is this? We are finally out of the book of Judges, except we're not! Why? The book of Ruth took place in the time period of the book of Judges. However, this is a story that has a good ending! Instead of one word, we have two words for Jesus in the book of Ruth, *Kinsman Redeemer.* A kinsman redeemer is a relative or family member who comes in and redeems an entire situation. This is what we will see in the book of Ruth.

Teaching

Ruth 1:1: Most scholars believe the author of the book of Ruth was Samuel. It was written during the times of Judges, which lasted for 300 years. Some speculate that Ruth came during the time period described in Judges 10:3–5. This book probably covers ten to twelve of those 300 years. In Ruth, the Moabites were Israel's enemy.

During a famine in Israel, a man with his family left the promised land to go to Moab. I do not tend to look at this and see disobedience; however, Wiersbe points out that Elimelech's sin was the same as Abraham's (Genesis 12).[1] Isaac and Jacob also left the land because of famine (Genesis 26; 46). Elimelech did not wait for God's instructions before he took his family to Moab.

Ruth 1:2: Elimelech, whose name means "My God is King" left with his wife Naomi, whose name means "pleasant," and their two sons, Mahlon, and Chilion. The family was from Bethlehem, the tribe of Judah. We know that Bethlehem was the birthplace of Christ. The Messiah was going to come from this little community of Ephrathites (Genesis 35:16; Micah 5:2). Elimelech and his family left Bethlehem because there was no food.

---

[1] Warren W. Wiersbe, *The Bible Exposition Commentary: Joshua–Esther* (Colorado Springs: David C. Cook, 2003), 180.

Ruth 1:3: Elimelech died in Moab. Wiersbe points out that all three of the men of the family died in Moab as a consequence of their disobedience and sin.[2] Oswald Chambers writes that we cannot run away from our problems: "The majority of us begin with the bigger problems outside and forget the one the inside. A man has to learn 'the plague of his own heart' before his own problems can be solved."[3]

Ruth 1:4–5: Living in Moab, Naomi's sons married Moabite women. Every time the Israelites took a wife from outside the tribe, it always caused problems! The Moabite women were named Orpah and Ruth. They lived in Moab for ten years before both of Naomi's sons died. Only the three women remained in the family, two Moabite women and Naomi who was the only one from the promised land.

Ruth 1:6–7: This is the verses many use to make the argument that Elimelech was disobedient. Back in Bethlehem, while Elimelech's family lived in Moab, the Lord had paid attention and provided food for His people. Because of this, the widow Naomi started to head home to the land of Judah. I think the point is that the people of Bethlehem stayed and relied on God, while it seems that Elimelech and His family ran away. Obviously, the famine had been broken, so there had to have been rain (Deuteronomy 11:14). The rain can come at any time (Job 5:10)!

Ruth 1:8–9: Naomi told both of her daughters-in-law to go home to their mothers. This was hard on Naomi to tell them to go back and worship their false gods. As a human, I think Naomi had good intentions for her daughters-in-law. The difference was her eyes were not on the Lord, her eyes were on man who could provide for them. In Naomi's mind, she was thinking out of the flesh.

Ruth 1:10–13: Neither of Naomi's daughters-in-law wanted to leave her, but Naomi insisted that they return home. Her main concern was that she had no sons to offer them for marriage. She claimed that her life was too bitter to share because the Lord had turned against her. Naomi's perspective was that there had been multiple mistakes made, and the Lord had removed Himself from her life. In these dark moments, we are supposed to turn to God! Naomi did the opposite. She was bitter (Psalm 100:5; 119:68; 86:15). God can redeem any situation (Romans 8:28). God can use anything for the good of those who love Him. God redeemed all of these situations (Isaiah 61:3).

---

[2] Wiersbe, 180.

[3] Oswald Chambers, *The Shadow of an Agony* (Grand Rapids: Discovery House, 1918, 1942), 76.

Ruth 1:14–15: Orpah returned to her family. Once again, Naomi tried to persuade Ruth to go home.

Ruth 1:16–18: In these verses, Ruth showed her loyalty not only to Naomi, but also the Lord. I think her loyalty is why Ruth is listed in Jesus' genealogy in Matthew 1:5. Ruth refused to go home and said, "Your people will be my people, Your God my God." Here was Ruth's conversion. Nothing was getting in the way of Ruth's relationship with Naomi. Naomi finally accepted that Ruth was determined to stay with her.

Ruth 1:19–20: After days of walking, Naomi and Ruth made it to Bethlehem. The whole town was excited to see Naomi return. Naomi told everyone to call her Mara because she was so bitter (Hebrews 12:15; Ephesians 4).

Ruth 1:21: Naomi said, "I went away full and I come back empty. The almighty has afflicted me." The reality of Naomi's situation was that there was a full harvest she was walking into. She had a daughter with her and a family in Bethlehem. Instead of focusing on the positives in her life, Naomi was filled with bitterness. When bitterness takes hold of our lives, we don't see anything positive. Naomi had taken her eyes off the Lord (Psalm 25:15).

Ruth 1:22: After a seven to ten day walk, Naomi and Ruth had arrived at the beginning of the barley harvest. Ruth was genuinely excited. She was in at all cost, but her mother-in-law didn't want anything to do with the current situation.

Closing

Let me sum up chapter 2 since we won't cover it in the next lesson.

Ruth 2:1–3: Boaz, a family member of Naomi, was introduced to Ruth.

Ruth 2:4–13: Boaz began to discover who Ruth really was. He wants to bless her for taking care of Naomi. He even says to Ruth, "may you receive a full reward from the Lord God" (v. 12).

Ruth 2:14–23: Boaz genuinely cared for Ruth and wanted to make sure she was being taken care of.

Ruth 2:20: Naomi tells Ruth, "The man is a close relative. He is one of our family redeemers." Ruth interacting with the family redeemer is our backdrop as we go into chapter 3.

The Daily Word

During the time of the judges, Naomi, a widow living in Moab, moved back to her native Bethlehem with her two widowed daughters-in-law. At Naomi's urging, one daughter-in-law returned to her own family, but Ruth was committed to staying with Naomi. Despite Naomi's negative and bitter attitude about her circumstances, Ruth made a commitment to go wherever Naomi went, live where she lived, and even serve Naomi's God. Ruth committed to the Lord, and she never turned back. The Lord honored Ruth's sincere commitment, and through her faith, He began to turn their circumstances around.

Have you made a commitment to the Lord? Have you told Him, "You have my life. You are my all. I will go wherever You lead me"? Where do you stand with that commitment? Today is the day to think through it. You may have wandered or gotten sidetracked, but Jesus is always there for you. May you be reminded of your first love in Jesus and your commitment to Him. Today, recommit yourself to Jesus. Tell Jesus you love Him and will have no other gods before Him. Tell Him that you will go wherever He leads you, and you will follow Him by putting others before yourself. The Lord your God will honor you for your commitment to Him.

But Ruth replied: Do not persuade me to leave you or go back and not follow you. For wherever you go, I will go, and wherever you live, I will live; your people will be my people, and your God will be my God. —Ruth 1:16

Further Scripture: Psalm 31:14; Zechariah 13:9; John 12:25–26

Questions

1. Do you think it was disobedient for Elimelech to leave the land of promise when he faced hardships? If so, do you think the death of the three men were a result of it (Genesis 12:10; 26:1–6; Ruth 1:1–3, 5)?
2. Why do you think Ruth would not leave her mother-in-law?
3. Why did Boaz show Ruth favor?
4. What made Ruth think she could go into someone else's field to harvest (Leviticus 19:9–10)?
5. What did the Holy Spirit highlight to you in Ruth 1—2 through the reading or the teaching?

Lesson 25: Ruth 3—4

Kinsman Redeemer: The Kinsman Redeemer

Teaching Notes

Intro

It sounds like we've been doing a lot of lessons, but it's really just two lessons in the book of Ruth. Yesterday we covered chapters one and two. Today, we are going to talk about the connection between Ruth and Boaz. Remember our phrase for Jesus in the book of Ruth is *Kinsman Redeemer.* After leaving Bethlehem for Moab, Naomi and Ruth were returning as widows. God redeemed this situation for Naomi and Ruth. How was God going to redeem them? He redeemed them through a kinsman redeemer.

Teaching

Ruth 3:1–2: Naomi was concerned about Ruth and wanted to find her security. She wanted to make sure that Ruth was taken care of. Naomi asked, "Isn't Boaz a relative?" Remember, Ruth had been working in Boaz's fields. Naomi knew that Boaz would be at the threshing floor because it was out in public. Therefore, everyone knew that Boaz went to the threshing floor at night.

Ruth 3:3–5: Naomi gave instructions to Ruth about how to approach Boaz. She instructed Ruth to clean herself up and put on her best dress. What I like about this picture is that we see what Wiersbe calls "the steps God's people must take if they want to enter into a deeper relationship with the Lord."[1] These five steps were used to prepare for a kinsman redeemer. For us, this is how we prepare for our *Kinsman Redeemer*, the Messiah.

1. *Wash* (Isaiah 1:16): As simple as this sounds, it was part of preparation (2 Corinthians 7:1–2).
2. *Anoint yourself* (1 John 2:20, 27): We have an anointing from the Spirit of God.

---

[1] Warren W. Wiersbe, *Be Available: Accepting the Challenge to Confront the Enemy* (Colorado Springs: David C. Cook, 1994), 48.

3. *Change clothes* (Isaiah 61:3; Luke 15:22): Picture the image of the wedding feast and having the right clothes. For us, it's the robe of righteousness.
4. *Learn how to present ourselves at the feet of the Lord of the harvest:* This is a complete surrender mentality, just laying at His feet.
5. *Promise to obey.* Ruth knew how to do all this because of Naomi. This is the 2 Timothy mentality of having an older person disciple a younger one.[2]

Ruth 3:6–7: Ruth did everything Naomi told her to do (v. 6). Once Boaz was in a good mood from drinking, Ruth secretly went in, uncovered his feet, and laid down there (v. 7). Let me walk through some cultural elements of this passage. Wiersbe explains that "to spread one's mantle over a person meant to claim that person for yourself (1 Kings 19:19; Ezekiel 16:8), particularly in marriage."[3] This action clearly communicated, "I want to get married." Boaz was a generation older than Ruth, but she honored culture and handled this whole situation very respectfully.

Ruth 3:8–9: At midnight, Boaz was startled and woke up to find Ruth at his feet. Ruth said to Boaz, "You are a family redeemer" (Ruth 2:12). The roles of the kinsman redeemer were[4]:

1. To purchase back any property that a family member had been forced to sell in order to keep it in the family.
2. To provide an heir for a deceased brother by marrying that brother's wife and producing a child with her.
3. To purchase back any family member who had been sold into slavery.
4. To avenge any family member had been murdered.

God is the ultimate redeemer who is going to take care of everyone (Isaiah 60:16).

Ruth 3:10–11: Boaz blessed Ruth, encouraged her not to be afraid, and reassured her he would do all she asked. The reason he was willing to be a family redeemer was because of Ruth's noble character (Proverbs 31:10).

Ruth 3:12–13: Boaz pointed out that while he was a family redeemer, there was another family redeemer who had to be approached first. Boaz had a plan of

---

[2] Wiersbe, 48–51.

[3] Wiersbe, 53.

[4] Alexander Maclaren, "Kinsman-Redeemer," *Expositions of Holy Scripture*, Bible Hub, https://biblehub.com/library/maclaren/expositions_of_holy_scripture_h/the_kinsman-redeemer.htm.

action. He told Ruth to stay with him that night and to go home in the morning. Then, he would see if another family member would be willing to redeem Ruth.

Ruth 3:14–15: Ruth laid down at his feet. In the morning, Ruth was up before the sun. Boaz shoveled six measures of barley in her shawl and sent Ruth home. Boaz poured out his generosity on her.

Ruth 3:16–17: Ruth returned to Naomi to give her the details from the night before. Ruth told her everything and gave her the barley that Boaz had sent back with her.

Ruth 3:18: Naomi informed Ruth that Boaz would want to have things figured out by the end of the day.

Ruth 4:1: A closer kinsman redeemer wanted the land but did not want to marry Ruth. He turned down the offer to be the kinsman redeemer.

Ruth 4:13: Boaz took Ruth, and she became his wife. They conceived a child, and she later gave birth to a son.

Closing

Ruth the Moabite was totally redeemed! The kinsman redeemer took on the death of a family member and redeemed the whole situation. Because of a kinsman redeemer, we have the genealogy of Christ. Ruth's son was Obed. Obed was the father of Jesse and Jesse was the father of David. It all goes back to Ruth saying to Naomi, "I will go where you go . . . Your God, my God.

How does Boaz, this kinsman redeemer, relate to Christ? Three requirements of a kinsman redeemer were:

1. *A blood relationship* (Leviticus 25:25; Deuteronomy 25:5–7): How does this get fulfilled through Christ? The redemption comes from Christ through our adoption as His sons and daughters (Galatians 4:3–5).
2. *The necessary resources* (1 Corinthians 6:20): We were bought with a price through Christ, who died on the cross in our place. The kinsman redeemer bought property; Christ bought us freedom.
3. *Must be willing* (Deuteronomy 25:7–9; 1 John 3:16): Jesus willingly gave up His life so you and I can be redeemed.

First Peter 1:18–19 is our key verse for a kinsman redeemer. We are redeemed from our empty way of life. Christ is our *Kinsman Redeemer*!

The Daily Word

After Ruth spent time in the fields working, Naomi encouraged her to find security for her future. Naomi understood Boaz's role in Ruth's life as her kinsman redeemer. According to the laws of the Pentateuch, a kinsman redeemer is one who redeems or rescues a person or property. Boaz was the male relative who had the privilege or responsibility to act on behalf of Ruth—his relative in need. Boaz showed honor and respect toward Ruth in this process. In time, Boaz and Ruth married and gave birth to a son, Obed. In God's sovereignty, Obed became the grandfather of David. David was not only a great king for Israel, but he was also a part of the genealogy of your New Testament redeemer, Jesus Christ.

This example of Boaz and Ruth serves as a reminder of God's plan to provide a kinsman redeemer for you through His Son. Jesus meets your needs and rescues you. Jesus encourages fellow believers to meet the needs of one another, just as Boaz helped meet the needs of Ruth. Jesus purchased the life of every believer through His blood on the Cross, paying a high cost. Jesus graciously showed you kindness, hope, and joy through redemption, something you cannot earn. *Redemption is Jesus loving you through grace.* Redemption is God's ultimate plan for His people. Today, give thanks for your life in Christ through redemption.

Boaz took Ruth and she became his wife. When he was intimate with her, the Lord enabled her to conceive, and she gave birth to a son. Then the women said to Naomi, "Praise the Lord, who has not left you without a family redeemer today. May his name become well known in Israel."
—Ruth 4:13–14

Further Scripture: Ruth 4:17; Galatians 4:4–5; Ephesians 1:7–8

Questions

1. Why do you think that Naomi instructed Ruth to lay at the feet of Boaz?

2. In Ruth 3:14, why do you think Boaz said, "Do not let it be known that the woman came to the threshing floor."?

3. Referring to Ruth 4:7, why was it a custom for a man to take off his sandal and give it to another (Deuteronomy 25:8–10)?

4. In the book of Ruth, who was Ruth's *Kinsman Redeemer* (Ruth 3:12–13)? What does that mean? Who is our *Kinsman Redeemer* (Psalm 82:4)?

5. What did the Holy Spirit highlight to you in Ruth 3—4 through the reading or the teaching?

Lesson 26: 1 Samuel 1—2

Anointed One: Hannah's Vow to God

Teaching Notes

Intro

This is the first lesson of 1 Samuel, the fourth book in the historical books of the Old Testament. We've already studied Joshua, Judges, Ruth, and now 1 Samuel. In the Old Testament, the book of Samuel is divided into two sections: 1 Samuel and 2 Samuel. In the original manuscript, it was one complete book. There are three major characters in 1 and 2 Samuel: Samuel, Saul, and David who are each the anointed one and point to the Messiah. Our phrase for the book of 1 Samuel is *Anointed One*.

We like to think the prophet Samuel wrote both books that bear his name. However, Samuel's death is recorded in 1 Samuel. While it is more accurate to say the writer is unknown, 1 Chronicles 29:29 explains the writers possibly included Nathan and Gad. First Samuel covers a period of 135 years. It's a book of transition between the chaos of Judges and Ruth where God moves from using priests, to judges, to the time of the prophets, and eventually kings. After this period came the division of Israel into two kingdoms—Israel to the north and Judah to the south. In the first chapters of 1 Samuel, Israel had a corrupt priesthood, a defiled tabernacle, and a stolen ark.[1] This dire situation will be reversed through His *Anointed One*.

There are four major themes in 1 and 2 Samuel[2]:

- *The Davidic Covenant* (1 Samuel 2:10; 2 Samuel 22:51)—the anointed kings would lead to the anointed Messiah.
- *The Sovereignty of God*—God was completely in control.
- *The Work of the Holy Spirit* (1 Samuel 10:10; 16:13)—the Spirit empowered people for divinely appointed tasks.

---

[1] Earl D. Radmacher, Ronald B. Allen, and H. Wayne House, eds., *Nelson's New Illustrated Bible Commentary* (Nashville: Thomas Nelson, 1999), 343.

[2] John MacArthur, *The MacArthur Bible Commentary* (Nashville: Thomas Nelson, 2005), 300–301.

- *The Personal and National Effects of Sin*—examples include: Eli and his sons, the lack of reverence for the ark of the covenant, and David's sin.

Teaching

1 Samuel 1:1–3: The name Elkanah means "God has created." Elkanah had two wives—Hannah, who was childless, and Peninnah, who had children (vv. 1–2). Most theologians stress that because Hannah was listed first, she was the first wife. However, because Hannah was childless, Elkanah married a second time. Hannah's name means "grace," and we'll see that it's an appropriate name because God poured out abundant grace on her. Every year, Elkanah made the journey to the tabernacle in Shiloh to worship the Lord and offer sacrifices (Joshua 18:1). Eli's sons Hophni and Phinehas served there as priests (v. 3).

1 Samuel 1:4–8: Elkanah gave Peninnah and her children portions of the meat to sacrifice (v. 4), but he gave Hannah a double portion as a sign of how greatly he loved her (v. 5). His action must have caused jealousy in Peninnah, who taunted Hannah every year because the Lord had not allowed her to have children (v. 6). The taunts bothered Hannah greatly, she wept and refused to eat anything (v. 7). Elkanah asked Hannah why she was so troubled, even if she had no children, she had his love (v. 8).

1 Samuel 1:9–28: In the presence of Eli the priest, Hannah prayed to the Lord, weeping as she prayed (vv. 9–10). Hannah asked the Lord to remember her barrenness and begged that He would allow her to have a son. She vowed that her son would spend his life in service to the Lord and promised his hair would never be cut (Nazarite vow) (v. 11). In her prayer, Hannah:

1. *Remembered God's works (v. 11)*—Hannah prayed to God because she remembered who God is and what He had done in the past. She knew the Lord had the power to intervene. She knew of Jericho and Gideon. Because God could do these things in the past, Hannah knew He could take care of her barrenness as well. She addressed Him as "Lord of Hosts" or the Commander of the Lord's Army (Joshua 5:14).
2. *Poured out her heart to Him (vv. 12–16)*—Although Hannah's lips were moving, she made no sound. Public prayers were made audibly, so Eli wondered if Hannah was drunk (v.13). Eli scolded her, telling her to get rid of the wine (v. 14). Hannah explained that she wasn't drunk, but had a broken heart and was pouring out her pain to the Lord (v. 15). It's okay to pour out our pain to God (Psalm 62:8; 142:1–3; Matthew 11:28; Philippians 4:6; 1 Peter 5:7).

3. *Received His peace (vv. 17–18)*—Eli told her to go in peace and added his blessing to her request (v. 17). When Hannah left, she no longer looked so despondent (v. 18) (John 14:27; Colossians 3:15).

4. *Trusted His timing (vv. 19–20)*—In her peace, Hannah was able to trust God's timing. "After some time," or as some translations say, "in due time," Hannah conceived and gave birth to Samuel whose name means "I requested him from the Lord" (v. 20). When we receive God's peace, we are able to walk out what He has told us to do.

5. *Worshipped Him in the victory (vv. 21–28)*—Elkanah took his family to Shiloh to worship the Lord for the gift of Samuel. Hannah and the child stayed behind because the child was not yet weaned and the time had not come to return him to the Lord. Once Samuel was weaned, Hannah took him to Shiloh along with the required sacrifices: a three-year-old bull, a half bushel of flour, and a jar of wine (Numbers 15:8–10). Hannah's sacrifices were above what was required (Psalm 95:2–3; 100:4–5).

Closing

When we trust in God's timing, we are able to worship the Lord in His victory. All of this leads to Hannah's prayer of thanksgiving and worship in 1 Samuel 2:1–10. Chapter 2 of 1 Samuel records how Samuel grew up under Eli's care and that Eli's sons were wicked men. As God began removing the corrupt priesthood, He was raising up a young boy named Samuel.

The Daily Word

Elkanah, a man from Ramathaim-zophim in Ephraim, had two wives: Peninnah and Hannah. Peninnah had children, but Hannah was childless. Elkanah loved Hannah despite her barrenness. Even so, Hannah longed for a child. She went to Eli, the priest at the Lord's Tabernacle. She made a vow to the Lord, and, with a broken heart, she prayed from the depth of her soul, requesting a child from the Lord. In God's timing, Hannah received the whom cried out for.

Have you ever desired something so deeply it broke your heart? Have you ever found yourself pouring your heart out to the Lord? Hannah exemplified this heart of brokenness and longing. When you are at the point of brokenness, remember who God is, and remember His faithful works. The Lord desires for you to pour out your heart to Him. He desires for you to make your requests known to Him. Ask Him for help, and receive the Lord's peace. Trust God's timing and worship Him.

"No, my lord," Hannah replied. "I am a woman with a broken heart. I haven't had any wine or beer; I've been pouring out my heart before the Lord. Don't think of me as a wicked woman; I've been praying from the depth of my anguish and resentment." —1 Samuel 1:15–16

Further Scripture: Psalm 62:8; John 14:27; Philippians 4:6

Questions

1. In 1 Samuel 1:1–8, there are two wives, including one who had no children. Where else in the Old Testament do we see the same scenario (Genesis 29)?

2. Why did Eli, the priest, think that Hannah was drunk (1 Samuel 1:13–14)?

3. In 1 Samuel 1:18, Hannah left no longer sad and she ate food. What do you think happened to change her? Have you prayed and known beyond a doubt that God heard you and granted your prayers? In what ways?

4. What vow did Hannah make to the Lord in 1 Samuel 1:11? Did she keep her vow (1 Samuel 1:24)? What did keeping that vow mean for her as a parent (1 Samuel 2:11)?

5. In 1 Samuel 2:20–21, Eli prayed for Hannah each year. What was his prayer? Did God grant it?

6. Eli, the priest, had two sons who served in the Temple and sinned greatly against God. In 1 Samuel 2:27, God sent a man to give Eli a message. What was the message? What was to become of him and his sons?

7. What did the Holy Spirit highlight to you in 1 Samuel 1—2 through the reading or the teaching?

Lesson 27: 1 Samuel 3—4

Anointed One: Seeing the Big Picture

Teaching Notes

Intro

Whenever we are in the Old Testament, 1 Corinthians 10:11 should be on our minds: "Now these things happened to them as examples, and they were written as a warning to us, on whom the ends of the ages have come." In revive-SCHOOL, we are looking at each of the 66 books of the Bible to see how Jesus is portrayed. One of the things I have become really convicted of is the need to step back from Scripture a bit so I can see "the big picture." Before we move into chapter 3, I want to explore "the big picture" of 1 Samuel.

How does the miracle of Samuel's birth speak to what God was doing during that time? From chapters 1–2, we've learned that the house of the Lord was out of order. Eli, the high priest, was old and blind. His sons, the natural heirs to the priesthood were vile. The questions to think about are: What would God do? What could God do? God used Hannah and Elkanah to bring about a "new order." Hannah just wanted a child; God needed a prophet. Hannah's bargain with God brings His plan into fruition. If Hannah had gotten pregnant in her own time frame, would we have had the miracle of Samuel's birth? This shows the timing and movement of God we need to pay attention to, because I believe God does the same thing today. We get upset when God does not answer in our timing, but God has a bigger picture we need to come into agreement with through an understanding of what God wants to do.

Teaching

1 Samuel 3:1–3: After Samuel was weaned, he was given to Eli. Samuel served God under Eli's supervision. "In those days the word of the Lord was rare and prophetic visions were not widespread" (v. 1). The King James Version says, "the word of the Lord was precious in those days; there was no open vision." Eli and Samuel lit the night lamp in the tabernacle, laid down, and rested until early in the morning (v. 3).

1 Samuel 3:4–14: While they were both sleeping, Samuel heard the voice of God. Thinking the voice was Eli's, Samuel went into his presence three times (vv. 5–6, 8). This reminds us that God can speak to children. Finally, Eli figured out that God was speaking to Samuel, giving him instructions (v. 8). Eli instructed Samuel to respond, "Speak, Lord, for Your servant is listening" (v. 9). Samuel did so and listened to what God had to say. God told Samuel He would judge Eli, because he had not stopped his sons from knowingly committing sins and defiling the sanctuary (vv. 12–14). God had already sent this word to Eli through a man (1 Samuel 2:27). God has ways of making His desires for Israel happen that we cannot comprehend.

1 Samuel 3:15–18: In the morning, Samuel tried to act normal, but Eli demanded to know what God had said. When Samuel told Eli of God's coming judgment, Eli confirmed that Samuel heard God correctly (1 Samuel 2:27–36). I believe Eli was aware of God's desire to speak and to be heard. However, He could no longer speak to Eli because of all that had happened in his family and what he had already heard from God.

I have to feel a little sorry for Eli. When you were born into the priesthood during this period, you had certain things you had to do. Eli's sons were required to follow him in the priesthood, but they were doing vile things and they were living completely in sin. Eli knew they were doing wrong, but found himself in a tough position. Eli responded to Samuel with, "He is the Lord. He will do what He thinks is good" (v. 18). In my opinion, I think Eli was hoping God's message would somehow release him from the responsibilities he had in the tabernacle. He was old and blind, so how was he supposed to carry all this out? These stories in the Bible show that there has to be an intervention and God will intervene in His timing. Eli could have felt shame and discouragement over his heirs and been concerned that he had not provided an heir to take his place; but God provided the heir. This brings us back to "the big picture," to step back far enough to see what God is doing, even when we're not able to take care of things ourselves. I want us to be able to step back far enough that we can see God has intervened.

This was a child who had been put in a place in which he waited on the Lord. He attended to the high priest, unlike the priest's sons. Eli seems to have rested in the knowledge that Samuel heard from God and was in the sight of God. Romans 12:1 says, "Therefore, brothers, by the mercies of God, I urge you to present your bodies as a living sacrifice, holy and pleasing to God; this is your spiritual worship." This is the New Testament picture of what Samuel was doing in the tabernacle.

1 Samuel 4:1–11: In chapter 4, Israel went into battle against the Philistines and was defeated (vv. 1–2). The people of Israel didn't understand why God would allow them to be defeated, so they brought the ark from Shiloh, thinking it might save them from further defeat by the Philistines (vv. 3–5). They thought God was present in the box, in the ark of the covenant of the Lord. The Philistines heard the great shout from the Israelite camp and realized their God had arrived (vv. 6–9). The Philistines panicked, but fought against the army of Israel (v. 10). The ark was captured and both of Eli's sons died, just as God had promised (v. 11).

1 Samuel 4:12–18: A messenger ran from the battle to Shiloh to tell Eli that the ark had been captured and Eli's sons were dead (vv. 12–17). When Eli heard the ark was taken, he fell off the chair, broke his neck, and died (v. 18). His deep grief was from the capture of the ark, not the death of his sons.

1 Samuel 4:19–22: When Phinehas' pregnant wife heard her husband and Eli had been killed and the ark had been captured; she collapsed into labor (v. 19). As she was dying, she was told she had given birth to a son whom she named Ichabod, meaning "The glory has departed from Israel" (vv. 20–22). They were now a nation without the presence of God.

Closing

What is "the big picture" from this passage for us today who are living in the last days? I believe that when we are living in dark days; God can raise up a passionate person who will be a deliverer for the kingdom of God and bring them into a position of anointing. God can speak through the young as well as the old, and they will be able to recognize the voice of God. God can bring an end to a covenant that has been made with those who have not submitted themselves to Him. God can bring the correction necessary to a system that is headed into peril.

We'll see in the chapters to come that even though the ark had been taken, God could still work things together for good (Romans 8:28). Here's my challenge: To look for those things that are written for my admonition and decipher those things that God is speaking to me. God what do you need me to do today so that I come into agreement with your plan?

The Daily Word

Samuel, Hannah and Elkanah's son, grew up in the presence of Eli the priest just as Hannah had promised he would in her vow to the Lord. While Samuel was lying down to rest in the Tabernacle of the Lord, the Lord spoke to him. However, it took a few times for Samuel to understand it was God, not Eli, speaking to him. At last, after the counsel of Eli, Samuel replied to the Lord, "Speak, for Your servant is listening!"

The Lord, your great Shepherd, speaks to those who believe in Him. His sheep know His voice. Are you at a place where you can hear the voice of the Lord? Today, take ten minutes to rest in the Lord. Say to Him, "*Speak, for Your servant is listening.*" You must be intentional to open your ears to hear His voice. Ask Him to show you a broader picture than you can see at the moment. Then, when you hear from the Lord, act on the things He says. The Lord gave Samuel a bold word to deliver to Eli, and Samuel obeyed. The Lord may want to speak to others through you. Don't get in the way of listening to His voice.

The Lord came, stood there, and called as before, "Samuel, Samuel!" Samuel responded, "Speak, for Your servant is listening." —1 Samuel 3:10

Further Scripture: John 10:27; 1 Corinthians 10:11; Revelation 3:20

Questions

1. Has there ever been a time in your life when the Lord was calling you and you didn't recognize His voice until later?

2. What long term consequences could we possibly face today for not disciplining our own children like Eli failed to do (1 Samuel 3:13)?

3. Do you think Eli knew judgment was coming to his family?

4. Referring to 1 Samuel 4:3, why do you think the Israelites thought they would be delivered from their enemies just because the ark of the covenant was in their presence? Was it wrong for them to take the ark in the first place (Leviticus 16:2)?

5. In 1 Samuel 4:13, why do you think Eli's heart trembled for the ark of God?

6. What did the Holy Spirit highlight to you in 1 Samuel 3—4 through the reading or the teaching?

Lesson 28: 1 Samuel 5—6

Anointed One: Ascribe God His Glory

Teaching Notes

Intro

I love 1 Samuel 3—4. How awesome is it to hear the voice of God calling you by name? We're seeing the process of God's anointing on special individuals, first on Samuel, then Saul and David. All of this points to the ultimate *Anointed One*, Jesus Christ. This becomes our phrase for the book of 1 Samuel, *Anointed One*. In 1 Samuel 1, we saw Hannah's prayer being fulfilled with the birth of Samuel. In 1 Samuel 2, Hannah prayed prophetically and Samuel was placed in the tabernacle to serve the Lord. In 1 Samuel 3, Samuel learned to hear God's voice. In 1 Samuel 4, the Israelites went to war against the Philistines, they lost the ark of the covenant, and God's judgment on Eli was fulfilled. The chapter ends with the birth of Ichabod, whose name means "The glory has departed from Israel." In chapter 5, the Philistines move the captured ark from city to city—from Ebenezer to Ashdod to Gath to Ekron. In each city, the people felt God's hand heavy against them. They cried out, asking that the ark be sent away from them. The chapter ends with this description: "The men who did not die were afflicted with tumors, and the outcry of the city went up to heaven" (v. 12).

Teaching

1 Samuel 6:1–6: After seven months, the Philistines summoned the priests and diviners to find out how they could take the ark of the covenant back to Israel (vv. 1–2). *Nelson's Commentary* explains that "diviners claimed to be able to predict the future and determine the will of their gods by observing such omens as the flight pattern of birds or the liver of a sacrificed animal."[1] The priests and diviners told them not to take the ark back without sending a restitution, trespass, or guilt offering with it if they wanted to be healed (v. 3). The Philistines asked what kind of offering they should give for restitution (v. 4a; Leviticus

---

[1] Earl D. Radmacher, Ronald B. Allen, and H. Wayne House, eds., *Nelson's New Illustrated Bible Commentary* (Nashville: Thomas Nelson, 1999), 354.

5:14–19). The priests responded that they should make five gold tumors and five gold mice to represent the plagues they had suffered for each of the Philistine rulers (vv. 4b–5). When we begin to see other nations and other religions cry out to the Lord, we know that is a precursor to the end. Scripture states that what the Philistines did will actually happen in the end times (Isaiah 45:23; Romans 14:11; Philippians 2:9–11; Revelation 5:13;). *Nelson's Commentary* states the Philistines recognized the power of God to bring that affliction upon them.[2] The priests reminded the Philistines what happened to the Egyptians when Pharaoh hardened his heart against Israel's God, the afflictions only got worse (v. 6).

1 Samuel 6:7–12: The Philistines were given further instructions, to build a new cart and get two milk cows that had never been yoked (v. 7). The calves were taken away from their mothers and put in a pen. They were then to pack the cart, hitch the cows, and send it off toward Israel (v. 8). If the cows went toward Israel (Beth-shemesh), it was the Lord of Israel who had caused their affliction. But if the cows went a different way, then the affliction came just by chance (v. 9). Beth-shemesh was a Levitical city with pasturelands (Joshua 21:16), so the priests there would be able to take care of the ark. The Philistines did what they were told, and the cows went straight to Beth-shemesh without straying to the right or the left (vv. 10–12).

How many people studying this passage are so thick-headed that you know exactly what God is asking you to do, but you are too stubborn to give in and do it? Maybe you've refused to humble yourself and acknowledge that God is calling you to do something. If we're not careful, we can be in the camp of the Philistines, refusing to listen to God and do what He wants us to do. But when we come before God in humility, even after seven months, He can forgive the situation and set up the next one (Psalm 139:9–10).

The cows were "lowing" as they went, crying for the calves they left behind. This is a picture of the tension that all who are called into ministry must face, as they try to balance their call to serve God and their love for their families.

1 Samuel 6:13–18: The people of Beth-shemesh were in the fields harvesting their wheat crop when they saw the ark approach. They were overjoyed to see the presence of God (v. 13). The cart stopped near a large rock. The people of Beth-shemesh chopped up the cart for wood and sacrificed the cows as a burnt offering to the Lord (v. 14). The Levites removed the ark and the gold offerings and placed them on a large rock while the men continued to make burnt offerings (v. 15). After the Philistine rulers saw what happened, they returned to Ekron (v. 16). Verses 17–18 summarize what happened.

---

[2] Radmacher et al., 354.

1 Samuel 6:19–21: However, God struck down the men of Beth-shemesh because they looked inside the ark (v. 19a). This is possibly because they showed no respect for the ark or because they were gloating that the ark had been returned. God demands respect, reverence, and awe. God struck down 70 men of the 50,000 who were there (v. 19b). God's message was to not repeat the mistakes from the past—do not take the presence of God lightly. The men of Beth-shemesh asked, "Who is able to stand in the presence of this holy LORD God? Who should the ark go to from here" (v. 20)? Then, they sent messengers to the people of Kiriath-jearim, telling them to come get the ark (v. 21). Kiriath-jearim was located ten miles from Jerusalem,[3] and the ark remained there until King David moved it into Jerusalem (2 Samuel 6:1–9).

Closing

All of us must ascribe to continually give God the glory He deserves. First Chronicles 16:28–30 says, "Ascribe to the LORD, families of the peoples, ascribe to the LORD glory and strength. Ascribe to Yahweh the glory of His name; bring an offering and come before Him. Worship the LORD in the splendor of His holiness; tremble before Him, all the earth. The world is firmly established; it cannot be shaken."

The Daily Word

After the Philistines captured the Ark of the Lord from Israel, the Philistines began to experience God's hand against them. They moved the Ark to Ashdod, then Gath, and then Ekron, and God's wrath followed. The Philistines experienced God's hand so strongly against them that the Ekronites called out to the Philistine rulers, "Send the ark of Israel's God away. It must return to its place so it won't kill us and our people!" They realized they were not within the will of God. They needed to get back to His will and original plan for the Ark of the Lord.

Have you ever had a season in which everything went wrong? You may have experienced strife or pain and exhausted every effort to fix the situation. Finally you realized the one thing left to do: turn the situation over to God and follow His ways. That's what happened to the Philistines. Maybe that's where you are today. You made a poor choice and kept on going, trying to fix it. Today, *stop running. Surrender* and lift your heart to the Lord, releasing the burden you have carried. Confess your wrongdoing, and if there is anything you need to do to make right, do it. In the Lord's will there is perfect peace. You are longing for

---

[3] Radmacher et al., 354.

that peace. So *turn around* and run into God's loving, gracious arms. Let His love wash over you.

The Ekronites called all the Philistine rulers together. They said, "Send the ark of Israel's God away. It must return to its place so it won't kill us and our people!" For the fear of death pervaded the city; God's hand was oppressing them. —1 Samuel 5:11

Further Scripture: Isaiah 26:3; Joel 2:13; Matthew 7:13–14

Questions

1. Why do you think the Philistines sent the ark to another city when "God's hand became heavy upon them" instead of just returning it to Israel (1 Samuel 5:6)?

2. In 1 Samuel 6:6, why would the Philistines continue to harden their hearts for seven months while they were being plagued (Hebrews 3:15–16)?

3. Based on what they did with the ark when it was returned to them, does it seem the Israelites didn't really understand God's Word (1 Samuel 6:18–19)?

4. According to God's law, where should the ark have been taken (Exodus 40:1–3)?

5. What did the Holy Spirit highlight to you in 1 Samuel 5—6 through the reading or the teaching?

Lesson 29: 1 Samuel 7—8

Anointed One: Struggling to Rely on God

Teaching Notes

Intro

Chapters 7—8 of 1 Samuel are a crux point, or a transition point, here in the middle of 1 Samuel. Many important things will take place in these two chapters.

Teaching

1 Samuel 7:1–4: The ark spent 20 years at the house of Abinadab, where his son Eleazar took care of it (vv. 1–2a). Can you imagine the ark of the covenant sitting in your living room? In this one verse, we've gone 20 years. Notice there is no mention of the tabernacle or the tent. The whole priesthood was in disarray since the deaths of Eli and his sons. Samuel is not mentioned either. Possibly he traveled for this period of 20 years as a prophet, teaching the people, tribe by tribe, and city by city. He was acknowledged as prophet from Dan (the most northern point in Israel) to Beersheba (the most southern point) (1 Samuel 3:20). "Then the whole house of Israel began to seek the LORD" (v. 2b).

When Time To Revive goes into a city, they look for three things in a community: unity (v. 2b), hunger (v. 2b), and humility (vv. 3–4). The "whole house of Israel" shows the unity. They were seeking the Lord and showing their hunger, a hunger Israel hadn't experienced for a long time. At Samuel's instructions, they removed the foreign gods in order to seek the Lord with their full hearts, showing their humility (vv. 3–4). In his instructions, Samuel outlined what was necessary to come before God in holy repentance:

- Their decision must be genuine—they were to "return to God with a whole heart." Their repentance would be difficult because it would fly in the face of the surrounding culture.
- Their decision must be tangible—they were to "get rid of the foreign gods and the Ashtoreths" that were in their homes and hearts. Ashtoreths were the consort of Ba'al, whose worship included fertility and sexual rites. Since these gods were represented in idol form, their actions must be concrete as they physically removed and destroyed the idols.

- Their decision must be to worship only Yahweh—they could not worship "Yahweh and" but "Yahweh only."

1 Samuel 7:5–6: The prophet Samuel wanted to address the entire house of Israel in Mizpah (v. 5). Mizpah means "watchtower" or a risen plateau. Scholars are unsure of the exact location of Mizpah. All the people came together without the tabernacle or the ark. There was still some tension between the people in the north and the people in the south. For example, the northern tribes didn't like the tribe of Judah because they were jealous of their perception that Judah had been treated better than the other tribes. However, Samuel was able to bring all these tribes together despite the tensions. Keep in mind that this north-south divide continued to simmer and ferment for the next 500 years.

In verse 6, Samuel led them to perform a water libation, in which they drew up water and poured it out before the Lord. Bergen suggests this was Israel's "confession that the Lord's favor was more important to them than life-sustaining water."[1] The people of Israel fasted and confessed their sins to God. "And Samuel judged the Israelites at Mizpah" (v. 6). This was the first time Samuel acted not only as a prophet, but also as a judge. Since Samuel was of the tribe of Levi, he was also a legitimate priest. Samuel became a bridge between the period of the judges and the period of the kings. Samuel was the last of the judges and was sent to all Israel, under the mantle of leadership. Samuel was also a king maker, but in our understanding of the *Anointed One,* Samuel was actually the royalty anointer. Samuel is a picture of the foreshadowing of the Messiah: priest, prophet, king, and anointer of royalty. Because of their confession and repentance, Samuel prayed. This was a great revival moment that the adversary did not like and he moved against Israel through the Philistines.

1 Samuel 7:7–11: The Philistines heard about the gathering at Mizpah and assumed Israel was getting ready to go to war. They recruited the largest Philistine army ever recorded (v. 7). Picture the entire nation of Israel, including wives and children, watching the huge army of Philistines marching on Mizpah, from a religious convocation on a high plateau. The Israelites had no weapons and were in terror. The Philistines knew the power of the ark from their experiences when they had captured it (1 Samuel 4). When they realized the ark was not with the Israelites, they felt they had an advantage (v. 7).

Something new was happening. Israel had gathered against spiritual warfare, not physical battles, and that was the key! Never was Israel better prepared to receive its enemy. As the lyrics from the Christian rock band, Petra, exclaim: "Get

---

[1] Robert Bergen, *New American Bible Commentary: 1, 2 Samuel,* v. 7 (Nashville: Broadman & Holman, 1996), 107.

on your knees and fight like a man." They asked Samuel to intervene for them with God (v. 8). Instead of trying to manipulate God with the ark as they had done in the past, Israel turned to God through intercession. They dared to ask for the seemingly ridiculous, invasive, and intrusive miracle. Samuel offered a burnt offering to the Lord, and the Lord answered him (v. 9). Samuel acted without a word because time was short. He even offered the entire animal as a burnt offering. At that moment of sacrifice, God thundered loudly and overthrew the Philistines (v. 10). The Philistines immediately turned in great disarray and pandemonium. Israel finally understood the God of angel armies was fighting for them, and they chased the Philistine army down below Beth-car (v. 11).

1 Samuel 7:12–17: Since they had been restored to God and then saved by God from the Philistine army, Samuel set up a memorial stone as a reminder of what God had done. He named the place Ebenezer, or stone of hope (v. 12). This is the same name as the site of Israel's earlier defeat, just at a different location. So the Philistines were subdued and did not invade Israel again (v. 13). Samuel judged Israel for 40 years (vv. 15–17). What about the ark? It is possible Samuel deliberately left the ark in Kiriath-Jearim to teach the Israelites to focus on the substance of faith, rather than the symbol of faith.

1 Samuel 8:1–5: Samuel grew old and appointed two of his sons as judges (v. 1). However, they did not walk in the Lord's ways (vv. 2–3). The elders of Israel told Samuel his sons could not lead in Samuel's place when he died. The elders had unity and hunger for an earthly king but not for God. They did not have humility either, as they told Samuel what he was to do (vv. 4–5). Keith Lannon explained chapter 8: "Don't confuse them with the facts. An account of when democracy gets it wrong—but God makes it turn out OK—even though people mess it up again later."[2] The elders wanted a king so they would be like the earthly rulers, and their argument was that Samuel's sons were unfit.

1 Samuel 8:6–9: Samuel knew this was an affront to God and to himself. Even though their request was self-centered, Samuel prayed to God. God told him to listen to them because "They have not rejected you; they have rejected Me as their king" (vv. 6–7). This demand of the people had been predicted 300 years earlier by Moses (Deuteronomy 17:14–20), and God promised both Abraham (Genesis 17:7–16) and Jacob (Genesis 35:11) that they would be fathers of kings. God told Samuel to listen to the voice of the people, warn them solemnly, and let them know the actions and deeds of the king (v. 9).

---

[2] Keith Lannon, "The People Know What They Want," *Samuel: The Last Judge—The First Prophet* (blog), September 2, 2013, https://lannononsamuel.wordpress.com/2013/09/02/the-people-know-what-they-want/.

1 Samuel 8:10–22: Samuel repeated God's words to the people. He did not tell them what a king ought to be, Samuel instead told them what God said the king would be like (vv. 10–18). Everything God said would come true in the rules of kings in both the north and the south of Israel. But the people refused to listen to Samuel (vv. 19–20). God told Samuel to appoint a king (v. 22).

Closing

In spite of their rejection, God still had a plan that He would bring to fruition.

The Daily Word

Samuel served the Israelites as judge throughout his life. However, the elders came to Samuel and said they were done with the season of judges. They were not satisfied with God as their heavenly King, and instead, they wanted an earthly king to rule their land. Samuel listened to their request, knowing it was sinful. Then he sought the Lord for counsel. The Lord told Samuel, "Listen to the people, everything they say to you." The Lord assured Samuel not to worry. The people were rejecting God, not Samuel.

It's so hard to see people walk in the ways of the world. You share truth with them, but they don't listen. They want what others have. Sometimes they have to learn the hard way, figuring it out for themselves. It can be difficult to stand by and watch. Sometimes God allows people to have the answer they think they want. Remember the truth that God has a plan, and His plan will prevail. You can't force people to follow God, but you are called to love them like Jesus. And give thanks for God's promise to work all things together for the good of those who trust in the Lord.

When they said, "Give us a king to judge us," Samuel considered their demand sinful, so he prayed to the Lord. But the Lord told him, "Listen to the people and everything they say to you. They have not rejected you; they have rejected Me as their king." —1 Samuel 8:6–7

Further Scripture: Psalm 81:11–12; Proverbs 1:29–31; Romans 8:28

Questions

1. Why do you think the Israelites left the ark of the Lord at Kiriath-jearim for twenty years? What caused Israel to turn back to the Lord and remove their false gods (1 Samuel 7:3–4)?

2. What does the name Ebenezer mean? Why did Samuel set up a stone and call it this? Where else in Scripture is the Lord referred to as a rock or stone (Genesis 49:24; Deuteronomy 32:4; 1 Samuel 2:2; Psalm 118:22; Isaiah 44:8; Acts 4:11; 1 Corinthians 10:4; 1 Peter 2:4)?

3. What reason or excuse did the Israelites use for requesting a king (1 Samuel 8:4–5)? Did they already have a king (1 Samuel 8:7)? What did the Lord tell Moses in Deuteronomy 17:14–16?

4. The Lord warned the Israelites about the customs or rights of the king they were requesting how (1 Samuel 8:11–18)?

5. What was the Israelites' response to this warning (1 Samuel 8:19–20)? Who had been fighting their battles (Exodus 14:13–14; Deuteronomy 1:30; 3:22; Joshua 23:3)? Why do you think they forgot or disregarded this fact? Do you think God's people today do the same thing?

6. What did the Holy Spirit highlight to you in 1 Samuel 7—8 through the reading or the teaching?

Lesson 30: 1 Samuel 9—10

Anointed One: The Anointing of King Saul

Teaching Notes

Intro

In 1 Samuel 7, Samuel led Israel into a time of revival and turning back to the Lord. But in chapter 8, the people rejected God and asked Samuel to give them a king. Samuel warned the nation that they would not be happy with the rules and deeds that went along with having a king over them. Chapter 9 introduces the young man Saul, who stood a head taller than anyone else in Israel (v. 2). He was sent to find donkeys that wandered off, but returned home before his father could worry about him (v. 5). He was told to look for a man of God in the city who would tell him what to do (v. 6). God also told Samuel to look for Saul to anoint as king (vv. 15–16). When Saul was told what would happen, he pointed out that he was from the smallest tribe but for Samuel this was confirmation because Saul was from the tribe of Benjamin (vv. 19–21). In the process of obeying his father by finding the donkeys, Saul found his calling as king (vv. 22–27). As Saul walked out his calling, so did Samuel. That's the backdrop of 1 Samuel 10 and the anointing of Israel's first king.

Teaching

Throughout chapter 10, we're going to see six key points.

First, a private call was given (v. 1). This wasn't in front of Israel or any of the tribes. The anointing was a symbol of God's presence in Saul's life, of God's calling on his life, and the Holy Spirit beginning to move in his life (Exodus 29:7; 40:14–15). In the Old Testament, the Holy Spirit did not dwell within, but would come upon people. The anointing for us never leaves (1 John 2:20, 27).

Second, expect confirmation (vv. 2–8). Saul would hear confirmation from two men at Rachel's grave at Zelzah (v. 2), from three men at Bethel (v. 3), and a group of prophets with music at the Hill of God (v. 5). The men in Bethel would have bread with them that was intended as an offering to be eaten by priests

(Numbers 18:8). The group of prophets would be prophesying, possibly of future events. Saul would prophesy as well and be changed into a different person when the Spirit of the Lord came upon him. In 1 Samuel 16:13–14, the Holy Spirit came upon David when he was anointed. Saul was told he would prophesy. First Corinthians 14:1 says, "Pursue love and desire spiritual gifts, and above all that you may prophesy." Prophesy can radically change lives today. Saul was told no matter what happened, he should do whatever was required because God was with him (v. 7). He then went ahead to Gilgal and waited for Samuel there (v. 8). Isn't it interesting that after Saul was told to walk out this confirmation, he was told to wait? If we're not careful in the church today, we'll get ahead of the Holy Spirit when He's telling us to wait. A. W. Tozer said, "If the Holy Spirit was withdrawn from the church today, 95 percent of what we do would go on and no one would know the difference." You should notice if the church is completely dead if the Holy Spirit is not there!

Third, expect empowerment (vv. 9–16). After every sign happened that day, the Spirit of the Lord took control of Saul and he prophesied. The people who knew him wondered what had happened and why he was among the prophets (vv. 9–12). Saul had been empowered. Empowerment is being given the power to walk out the calling. Saul's uncle asked where he had gone (v. 14). Saul responded he went for the donkeys and then to see Samuel, but he did not tell his uncle what Samuel had said to him (vv.15–16).

Fourth, a public call was given (vv. 17–24). Samuel summoned the people to hear Saul's calling and Saul let it happen because he was genuinely about the anointing (v. 17). Samuel delivered God's words that He should be their *King*, but since they had rejected Him, a king would be selected (vv. 18–19). The tribes were called forward and the selection process began. Saul was selected king, but he was not present because he was hiding in the supplies (vv. 20–22).

Fifth, expect support (vv. 25–26). When you are called, you will get the support you need. Saul was given brave men whose hearts God had touched to go with him as support (v. 26).

Sixth, expect opposition (v. 27). Wicked men despised and opposed Saul, but Saul said nothing.

Closing

Saul was anointed, privately called, and received confirmation in the process. He was empowered to be Israel's first king. Saul was surrounded by brave men but opposed by wicked men. This sure sounds like the life of Christ who received the anointing in Isaiah 61 and Luke 4, and had support, but encountered extreme opposition.

The Daily Word

The Lord revealed to Samuel that Saul, an unassuming yet impressive young man from the tribe of Benjamin, would be king over Israel. Samuel anointed Saul with oil for this specific calling. Then the Lord confirmed His choice by allowing Saul to experience the Spirit of God taking control of him, and he prophesied with the prophets. Later as Saul was presented to the people as their king, he walked in humility and let the Lord unfold the timing of His plan.

As a follower of Christ, you have an anointing on your life. Another meaning for the word *anointed* is "chosen one." Today, you are a chosen one for a specific purpose in furthering the kingdom of God. This means you have been enabled, entrusted, and empowered to accomplish God's will. Anointing is not just for Christian speakers or leaders. It is for every believer because of the Holy Spirit's dwelling within you. No matter the tasks your walk with Jesus brings, in humility, *walk in the power of your anointing*. You were chosen. Whether it's parenting or teaching the Word of God, managing a company or working at a factory, the Holy Spirit empowers you to further His kingdom. Praise the Lord for this mighty truth!

At this time tomorrow I will send you a man from the land of Benjamin. Anoint him ruler over My people Israel. He will save them from the hand of the Philistines because I have seen the affliction of My people, for their cry has come to Me. —1 Samuel 9:16

Further Scripture: 1 Samuel 10:16; 2 Corinthians 1:22–23; 1 John 2:27

Questions

1. Saul, son of Kish, is described as "a choice and handsome man, and there was not a more handsome person than he among the sons of Israel." Why do you think these details are recorded? Contrast that to Isaiah 53:2. From a worldly perspective, who would most people prefer as their king, according to these descriptions?

2. In 1 Samuel 9:16, the Lord told Samuel He would anoint Saul as prince (other translations: ruler, leader, commander, captain) over the Israelites. Why does it not say "anoint him as king"?

3. Saul's response to Samuel's comments in 1 Samuel 9:20 was to inform Samuel he was from the tribe of Benjamin. Look back at Judges 20 and 21. How might Saul have felt about his tribe?

4. Samuel anointed Saul's head with oil and declared him the ruler over the Lord's inheritance. Even so, how did the Lord view Israel's desire for a king (1 Samuel 10:17–19)?

5. In 1 Samuel 10:22, the Lord revealed to the people that Saul was hiding himself among the baggage. Have you or someone you know hidden out in their baggage rather than stepping into their calling?

6. At the end of 1 Samuel 10, some worthless men said, "How can this one deliver us?" and they despised Saul and did not bring him any gifts. Does this sound like the way the Israelites had seen and treated the Lord?

7. What did the Holy Spirit highlight to you in 1 Samuel 9—10 through the reading or the teaching?

Lesson 31: 1 Samuel 11—12

Anointed One: A Brand-New King

Teaching Notes

Intro

As we get started, I want to bring a little bit of understanding. First Samuel moves along so fast. By chapter 8, Samuel was old. What we have in Scripture are the highlights.

Teaching

1 Samuel 11:1: Nahash the Ammonite came against Israel. Who were the Ammonites? They descended from Lot's youngest daughter and an incestuous situation.

They came specifically against Jabesh-gilead and the tribe of Gad. Why would they come against Jabesh-gilead? If you go back to Judges 20—21, you'll see that the people of Jabesh-gilead were greatly diminished in numbers because they had not joined in the battle against Benjamin. This is important to understand, because the first thing we see in this chapter was that the men of Gad said, "Make a covenant with us." Why? They didn't have an army.

1 Samuel 11:2: The Ammonites wanted to cut out everyone's right eye before they would make a covenant. Why the right eye? A lot of scholars believe it was because the right eye was used to sight an arrow. The Ammonites wanted to do this to humiliate Israel.

1 Samuel 11:3: The leaders asked to wait for seven days, allowing time to see if Israel would defend them.

1 Samuel 11:4–5: Messengers went to Saul. In these verses, you start to see the idea of brotherhood. When the people heard about Gad's situation, they mourned. Saul was in the field when the message was first relayed. When he returned, he asked "Why is everyone weeping?" Then, Saul was told the story from the men of Jabesh-gilead.

1 Samuel 11:6–7: The spirit of God came upon Saul powerfully and "his anger burned furiously" (v. 6). Saul killed two oxen and cut them to pieces. He then sent men to carry them to each of the tribes along with a threat. The threat was if they did not come to march with Saul and Samuel to defend the brothers of Jabesh-gilead, their oxen would be slaughtered in the same way.

1 Samuel 11:8–11: 330,000 men promised to come and fight. The brotherhood was established! Saul developed a plan that worked, and Israel destroyed the Ammonites.

1 Samuel 11:12–13: This victory elevated Saul as king. Samuel saw the opportunity and stepped in to bring unity to the tribes again. God claimed victory by using Saul's spirit of godly anger and indignation. Suddenly, Saul was being lifted up. Saul was the one who said, "God did this." God used Samuel as a bridge from a corrupt priesthood to Saul as king but it was never God's intention for Israel to have a king.

1 Samuel 11:14: The people came together in unity at Gilgal. We talk about unity in the church, but will we battle together? Will we come together for the cause? Will we hold one another up? Will we say, "I don't want to rejoice in sin taking over your life. I want to come and be a rescue agent in your life?" God can build a community around the broken. It is easy to get caught up in what is going on in our own lives while those around us are struggling and get decimated in the battle. The Spirit of God can raise up a rescuer. All of us need to rally to Jabesh-gilead; we all have a cause. I believe there is something here to understand. Even though Samuel was disappointed, he released the people over to God.

1 Samuel 12:1–12: In chapter 12, Samuel reviewed his own performance. He had been very careful in his demeanor toward Israel. Why do you think he was asking these questions? He wanted to point out that he fulfilled the calling of what God asked him to do. Sadly, when the people received what they wanted, they seemed to forget about God.

1 Samuel 12:13–21: Samuel stated the problem. The Israelites had a king, but they had wanted a king of their choosing, not God's.

1 Samuel 12:22: This choice of Israel for a king was not without displeasure from God. Samuel called them to one truth, the Lord would not abandon His people.

1 Samuel 12:23–25: Samuel promised he would not go against the Lord by ceasing to pray for the Israelites. He was still dedicated to teaching them the good and right way. He instructed the Israelites to fear the Lord and worship Him with all their hearts. They were also to remember the great things God had done. Samuel warned the Israelites; they and their king would be swept away if they continued to do evil.

Closing

In the Old Testament, God judged the sinful behaviors of His people with death and destruction. Through this, we can understand how bad sin truly is and how the death of sin in our lives is essential (Romans 7:12–13). The Israelites knew God meant business. Sin will cause us to be an Eli that can't hear, or a King Saul who later couldn't hear and veered off track. We have to be careful to not deviate from God's plan by becoming caught up with things of the flesh. Let's walk righteously before God.

The Daily Word

After Saul and Samuel led the Israelites in a united battle against the Ammorite forces, the Israelites agreed Saul should be their king. Now was the time for Samuel to step down and for Saul, the requested king, to begin his reign as leader. In his final public speech, Samuel warned the Israelites to fear the Lord, worship Him faithfully with all their heart, and consider all the great things the Lord had done for them. Even though an earthly king was not God's plan for His people, the Lord promised to never abandon them.

Throughout the years, the Lord reminded His people to keep their eyes on Him. How about you? Are your eyes on Jesus, the King of kings and Lord of lords? Or are you living as ruler of your own life? The enemy creates schemes to sidetrack you. The world is full of distractions, and life brings battles. In the midst of these distractions and battles, God is always there. He will never abandon you. Even when you make decisions in your flesh, He will never abandon you. There is nothing you can do to drive God away. Today, *turn your eyes to Jesus the King*, and tell Him you love Him and Him alone. Don't wait to turn to Him only when fear or trials overcome you. Turn to Him today!

The Lord will not abandon His people, because of His great name and because He has determined to make you His own people. . . . Above all, fear the Lord and worship Him faithfully with all your heart; consider the great things He has done for you. —1 Samuel 12:22, 24

Further Scripture: Psalm 29:10; Hebrews 13:5; Revelation 15:3

Questions

1. What was the deal that Nahash gave to Jabesh-gilead? Why would the tribe of Gad even consider this deal?

2. What happened when the Spirit of God came upon Saul? How does the Holy Spirit help us accomplish His will (Luke 4:1; Romans 8:14)?

3. In 1 Samuel 11:15, why does it say the people made Saul king before the Lord when he had already been anointed as king (1 Samuel 10:1, 24)?

4. What did God point out to the people in 1 Samuel 12:13? What did God say would happen if they feared Him and obeyed Him? What would happen if they disobeyed Him?

5. Read 1 Samuel 12:23. Did you ever consider that not praying for someone is a sin against the Lord? Why would ceasing to pray for someone be considered a sin (Acts 6:4; Romans 1:9; Ephesians 6:17–18)?

6. What did the Holy Spirit highlight to you in 1 Samuel 11—12 through the reading or the teaching?

Lesson 32: 1 Samuel 13

Anointed One: Losing the Royal Dynasty

Teaching Notes

Intro

Our theme today in 1 Samuel 13 is timing. Will you understand and wait on the will of God? Will you breathe in and walk out the will of God? In this chapter, we have Samuel the prophet, priest, Levite, and anointer of kings. We also have Saul the king, who was especially popular among the northern tribes, possibly because he was from the tribe of Benjamin and not Judah. Even though Saul was God's appointed and anointed choice for king, he had issues with obedience. Some commentators suggest Saul was emblematic of God's chosen people. In chapter 13, Saul made some really bad choices. He didn't accidentally fall into disobedience, he chose his direction and acted on it. Saul recognized the coming danger, got nervous while waiting, and poorly chose to take matters into his own hands.

The backdrop of the story is found in 1 Samuel 10:8. Samuel anointed Saul's head with oil and pronounced Saul would be king. Then, Samuel sent Saul ahead to Gilgal to wait for him to offer burnt offerings and sacrifice fellowship offerings. Samuel told Saul to wait seven days for him to arrive, and he would show him what to do. These were prophetic words and were to be remembered. Scholars estimate that in chapter 13, three years had passed, and Saul was in Gilgal again. He knew it felt familiar and knew he was to wait for Samuel's arrival.

Teaching

1 Samuel 13:1–4: Know that trying to figure out how many years Saul reigned is difficult because the exact number of years are vague in the Hebrew text. Scholars agree chapter 13 took place early in Saul's reign, probably between year one and year three (v. 1). Saul began to enlist an army—2,000 men for himself and 1,000 with his son Jonathan (v. 2). Samuel had warned Israel about kings needing a standing army (1 Samuel 8:11–12), and this was the starting point. Possibly, these were like bodyguards and special forces for Saul that could inflict damage on the Philistines when needed. The 3,000 conscripted soldiers were not nearly enough if the Philistines declared war. This is the first mention of Jonathan, who Saul based in his own hometown.

Jonathan attacked the Philistines because they had blocked the pass in Geba and gave the credit to Saul (v. 3). In every biblical account of Jonathan, he is described as wise and honorable. Saul blowing the ram's horn, announced the victory in this battle and was possibly a rallying call for all the fighting men who had been sent home, to come back to the king's aid at Gilgal (v. 5). Gilgal was a rallying place and a holy place for the Israelites during Joshua's time and continued into Samuel's time (Hosea 4:15; 9:15; Amos 5:5). However, Gilgal was not a good defensive location for the Israelites.

1 Samuel 13:5–9: I need to make a correction from when I taught a few days ago on 1 Samuel 7—8. I said then that the Philistine forces gathered there were the largest ever, but I got ahead of myself. THIS force was the largest—3,000 chariots, 6,000 horsemen, and innumerable foot soldiers (v. 5). The chariot was the tank of the ancient world. The Israelites were so terrified at what they saw, they hid in caves and among rocks (v. 6). Saul waited in Gilgal seven days for Samuel to come (vv. 7–8). While he waited, troops were deserting, fear was growing, and tension was mounting. Saul knew he needed to wait for Samuel to come because the prophetic word spoken years before instructed him to. Yet this became a catastrophe for Saul and his army. This was the severest of tests for Saul and would have been the severest of tests for any king. On the seventh day, Saul could take the waiting no longer, his patience and faith snapped. Saul called for the burnt offerings and the fellowship offerings, and he offered them to God (v. 9). This was a fateful decision for Saul because the Levitical priests had the responsibility for offering sacrifices, not kings.

1 Samuel 13:10–12: Samuel arrived as Saul finished with the sacrifices (v. 10). Saul went to Samuel and told him what he had done (vv. 11–12). It is difficult to explain the gravity of the implications of this moment for Saul. Saul's actions might seem trivial to us, but they were grave and mammoth in their significance. Samuel's question "What have you done?" shook Saul and the pain of his guilt was suddenly revealed. He started lying to defend himself and cover up his actions. Saul explained his actions with a lot of "I" statements and said he forced himself to offer the burnt offering (vv. 11–12). Saul justified his actions with excuses and even blamed Samuel for his lateness in coming.

Samuel arrived at exactly the right time, not early and not late. Romans 5:6 says, "For while we were still helpless, at the appointed moment, Christ died for the ungodly." The NIV says, "at just the right time." Saul was helpless and Samuel arrived at exactly the right time. At exactly the right time, Christ died for us. Don't get anxious because Christ is coming at exactly the right moment.

How many times do we get impatient with God so we make the choices without waiting?

1 Samuel 13:13–14: Before the remnant of his trembling army, Saul was publicly shamed. The consequence of his unfaithful disobedience was the loss of his kingship and his dynasty. His kingdom and his line would not continue. Saul rejected God's command; God rejected Saul and sought a man after God's own heart (v. 14). King Saul was after the hearts of the people; King David was after the heart of God. No date or timing was given. Possibly this pronouncement was made even before David was born, which brings into focus David's statement in Psalm 139 that God knew him before he had even been born (Psalm 139:13–16).

God's plan will never be thwarted! It is not going to happen. If we, who have been given the opportunity to be a part of God's plan are disobedient, He will use someone else.

1 Samuel 13:15–22: Saul returned to Gibeah where his son Jonathan had been. By that point, Saul had only 600 men left with him (vv. 15–16). Jonathan had heard Samuel's pronouncement and knew he would never inherit Saul's throne. The Philistines deployed their troops in three large raiding parties to utterly destroy Saul (vv. 17–18). Saul's armies had no weapons because the Philistines did not allow blacksmiths to be in the land (v. 19). The army prepared their weapons of plows, mattocks, axes, and sickles to face the coming battle (vv. 20–22).

1 Samuel 13:23: In this last verse of chapter 13, the Philistines set up for battle.

Closing

When God does not meet your "reasonable" timetable, what do you do? Remember, God is never late, but sometimes He tests our loyalty and obedience by waiting until beyond the last minute (from our perspective) to act. Are you willing to wait? The choices we make can have incredible consequences. When tempted to take matters into your own hands, choose to obey the revealed will of God and trust Him for what comes next.

The Daily Word

Saul reigned as king over Israel for forty-two years. He formed a standing military presence and reigned from Gilgal. During this time, Saul's son Jonathan attacked a Philistine garrison in Geba that threatened Gilgal. In response, the Philistine army gathered again and was as numerous as sands on the seashore.

Remembering Samuel's prophetic words to wait seven days for the appointed time, Saul remained in Gilgal. Saul waited day after day, but Samuel didn't come. His troops were gripped with fear and began to desert him. Therefore Saul made the choice to go ahead and offer the burnt offerings without Samuel. And then Samuel showed up on the seventh day, just as Saul had anticipated. Saul lost hope in Samuel coming and didn't wait. He chose to take the situation into his own hands without seeking the Lord. He forced it, and, when Samuel arrived right on time, he called Saul foolish. As a result of Saul's lack of patience, Samuel told Saul that his reign as king would not endure.

Have you ever grown impatient waiting on the Lord for a new job, a new home, a child, or a relationship? Even though you knew the Lord wanted you to wait, you were afraid of what waiting would do, so you forced the situation. And then, suddenly, you knew you made the wrong choice. *Ugh.* If only you could go back and wait on the Lord. Today, take a deep breath. Remember to wait on the Lord and His timing. *Wait until you can respond in peace, not panic.* Believe the Lord's promise that He is for you, not against you. He has plans to prosper you, giving you hope and a future. Don't force the matter. Wait upon the Lord.

Samuel said to Saul, "You have been foolish. You have not kept the command which the Lord your God gave you. It was at this time that the Lord would have permanently established your reign over Israel." —1 Samuel 13:13

Further Scripture: 1 Samuel 13:10–11a; Psalm 27:14; Jeremiah 29:11

Questions

1. Why does it say in verse 4 that the Israelites had become an abomination to the Philistines? Who are we, as Christians, warring against today (Ephesians 6:12)?

2. How do you see the insecurity of Saul in verse 4? Who was the one who actually attacked a garrison?

3. Why were the men of Israel scattering? Why do you think Saul did not believe the promise of Samuel (1 Samuel 10:8)?

4. How was Saul being disobedient to the Lord in verse 13? What was his consequence? Do you think this was a harsh consequence or justified?

5. What kind of heart did God desire in a king for Israel (1 Samuel 13:14; Psalm 23:1; 78:72; Acts 13:22)?

6. What did the Holy Spirit highlight to you in 1 Samuel 13 through the reading or the teaching?

Lesson 33: 1 Samuel 14

Anointed One: The Victory Is God's

Teaching Notes

Intro

Remember the phrase for 1 Samuel is *Anointed One*. Saul's life will lead to David's life, and David's life will lead to the Messiah. In 1 Samuel 13, Jonathan led the Israelite army to its first victory under Saul. Then, in typical "Jonathan" fashion, Jonathan gave credit for the victory to Saul. Saul already showed signs of jealousy and pride. Jonathan was a mighty warrior (2 Samuel 1:22). Wiersbe describes Jonathan as, "a courageous warrior, a born leader, and a man of faith who sought to do the will of God."[1]

Teaching

1 Samuel 14:1–6: It seems Jonathan was afraid of nothing as he led his attendant, or armor-bearer, to cross over to the Philistine garrison (v. 1). Jonathan didn't tell his father, possibly because "Saul would have thought Jonathan's plan was reckless."[2] Saul was sitting under a pomegranate tree near Gibeah, Saul's home town, with 600 troops (v. 2). Ahijah was also there, wearing an ephod, the white garment of the Levitical priest (v. 3).[3] However, the troops did not know Jonathan had left.

The two sides of the pass Jonathan had to get through were named Borez, meaning slippery, and Seneh, meaning thorny (vv. 4–5),[4] communicating the danger in the journey. In verse 6, Jonathan stated why he was so brave, "Nothing can keep the LORD from saving, whether by many or by few." Jonathan had faith in the victory and was ready to walk that out (Deuteronomy 20:1; Judges 7:7). One of the issues in the church today is that people are sitting under the

---

[1] Warren W. Wiersbe, *Be Successful: Attaining Wealth That Money Can't Buy* (Colorado Springs: David C. Cook, 2001), 83.

[2] Earl D. Radmacher, Ronald B. Allen, and H. Wayne House, eds., *Nelson's New Illustrated Bible Commentary* (Nashville: Thomas Nelson, 1999), 363.

[3] John MacArthur, *The MacArthur Bible Commentary* (Nashville: Thomas Nelson, 2005), 323.

[4] MacArthur, 323.

pomegranate tree without enough faith to get up and go do what God's called them to do (1 Samuel 9:16; Psalm 147:10). Saul should have had this mentality to win this victory, but it always ended up being Jonathan who had the faith instead.

1 Samuel 14:7–14: Jonathan had the support of his armor-bearer (v. 7). The Apostle Paul had Barnabas, Timothy, Titus, and Silas to walk with him as well. God surrounds us with people to walk with us who are like-minded. Jonathan looked for a sign from God to determine God's will. He and his armor-bearer would allow the Philistines to see them approach. If they were told to wait for the Philistines to come to them, they would stop there. If the Philistines told them to come up to them, they would go up, "because the LORD has handed them over to us" (vv. 8–10). MacArthur points out this is similar to Gideon's request for signs from God (Judges 6:36–40).[5] The Philistine soldiers called them up, so Jonathan and his armor-bearer went up to them (vv. 11–12). God gave Jonathan the sign he had requested, so he struck down 20 men and his armor-bearer finished them off (v. 14).

1 Samuel 14:15–17: Terror spread through the Philistine camp. Even "the earth shook, and terror spread from God" (v. 15). MacArthur states, "The earthquake affirms the fact that divine intervention aided Jonathan and his armor-bearer in their raid . . . [which] caused a panic among the Philistines"[6] (Psalm 3:8; Proverbs 21:31). The soldiers saw Jonathan's leap of faith and the panicking Philistines (v. 16). Saul then took a roll call to see who was missing and found only Jonathan and his armor-bearer were gone (v. 17).

1 Samuel 14:18–23: MacArthur states Saul told Ahijah the priest to get the ark of God (or possibly the ephod instead) in order to conduct an "inquiry into the will of the Lord."[7] But while Saul was still speaking, the Philistines' panic increased so Saul told the priest not to bother (vv. 18–19). Saul led his army against the Philistines who were fighting each other in great confusion (v. 20). Even the soldiers who fled Saul's army to join the Philistines returned and attacked with the Israelites (v. 21). And the Israelites who had been hiding in fear, joined Saul's army as well because the victory was clearly won (v. 22). Everyone on the battlefield saw the power of God, and the Lord saved Israel (v. 23).

---

[5] MacArthur, 323.

[6] MacArthur, 323.

[7] MacArthur, 323.

1 Samuel 14:24–26: The soldiers returned from the battle worn out and hungry, but Saul failed to provide for their physical needs. Instead, Saul placed them under an oath that none would eat food before evening or they would be cursed (v. 24). Why would Saul put such a ridiculous curse on his own people? He was establishing his own control, not God's. The soldiers went into the woods and saw honey flowing on the ground (vv. 25–26a). How many times have we seen the Promised Land described as a land flowing with milk and honey? The honey was there before them, but the soldiers ate none of it because of Saul's curse (v. 26b). This is more evidence of Saul's lack of understanding of who God is. He withheld what God had provided, showing his lack of dependence upon God as well. Saul wanted the credit for the victory for himself, not for the Lord (Psalm 19:9; 81:16; 119:103; Ezekiel 3:3).

1 Samuel 14:27–33: Jonathan saw the honey and dipped into it. When he ate it, he received renewed strength (v. 27). Jonathan knew the Word of God and knew the honey came from the Lord. In order to experience God's will, we must know the Word of God. When the troops told Jonathan about his father's curse, Jonathan replied that Saul had brought trouble to the land by not allowing the troops to eat (vv. 28–30). The Israelites defeated the Philistines but were so exhausted they rushed to take the plunder of the animals, slaughtered them, and ate the meat with the blood still in it (vv. 31–33). The troops were so hungry they disobeyed God's Law (Leviticus 17:10–14), bringing sin to the Israelites. As Jonathan explained in verse 30, "How much better if the troops had eaten freely today from the plunder they took from their enemies!"

Closing

When you follow God's plan, there is freedom. When you follow man's plan, there is bondage. In order to experience freedom, you have to step out in faith. Jonathan believed the victory was his, and in the process, he was able to experience more of the presence of God.

The Daily Word

Though Jonathan and his father Saul were both aware of the Philistine garrison, Saul remained with his six hundred troops on the outskirts of Gibeah while Jonathan and his armor bearer, in contrast, stepped out in faith to pursue an attack against the Philistines as the Lord confirmed their actions. Jonathan didn't just talk about it. He said to his loyal armor bearer, "Come on, let's go!" Jonathan believed if God was in it, they would find victory. With God by their side, the two men stepped out in faith and found victory, striking down twenty men. Saul remained trapped in fear while Jonathan experienced freedom, walking in faith and obedience.

Is there an area in your life in which you need to step out in faith? Is that still, small voice saying, "Come on, let's go"? You believe in the power of the Lord, and now it's time for you to take a step of faith. While stepping out, ask the Lord to confirm your steps, one at a time. Just as He confirmed Jonathan's steps, *He will confirm yours*. Today is the day to get over the fear of the unknown. The choice is yours—step out in faith and experience freedom and even more than you can imagine or remain and only watch others experience the adventure of walking in faith.

Jonathan said to the attendant who carried his weapons, "Come on, let's cross over to the garrison of these uncircumcised men. Perhaps the Lord will help us. Nothing can keep the Lord from saving, whether by many or by few."
—1 Samuel 14:6

Further Scripture: Ephesians 3:20; Hebrews 11:1; James 2:14–17

Questions

1. While Saul was hesitating in unbelief (v. 2), how was Jonathan moving forward in trusting the Lord? Why do you think Jonathan didn't tell his father about his plan to attack the enemy?

2. How do you see Jonathan having the heart described in Romans 8:31? How does verse 6 compare to what God did through Gideon (Judges 7)?

3. What was the rash oath Saul made to the men of Israel? How do you see Saul's focus being wrong?

4. Even though Saul had called a fast, how did God provide for the army? Who was the only one who ate the honey? What happened to him after eating the honey?

5. What was Saul seeking the counsel of God for in verse 37? How do you see 1 Peter 5:5 being played out in the life of Saul and Jonathan?

6. What did the Holy Spirit highlight to you in 1 Samuel 14 through the reading or the teaching?

Lesson 34: 1 Samuel 15—16

Anointed One: God's Anointed King

Teaching Notes

Intro

The phrase for the Messiah in 1 Samuel is *Anointed One*. If there's any passage that clearly shows that, it would be 1 Samuel 16. Saul was the first anointed king of Israel, but he was letting his son Jonathan take the lead. We saw it in chapter 14 and now chapter 15 as well. In 1 Samuel 15:1–3, Saul was told to destroy all the Amalekites, including the women, children, and their livestock. But, in verses 4–9, Saul allowed King Agag and the best of the livestock to live. The Lord regretted making Saul king (vv. 10–15). Because of his disobedience, Saul was rejected by both the Lord and by Samuel (vv. 16–23). Saul pleaded with Samuel to forgive him, and when Samuel turned away, Saul grabbed his robe and tore it. Samuel said the kingship had been torn away from Saul as well (vv. 24–30). Verse 28 explains the kingship had already been given to Saul's neighbor, David. Samuel carried out God's judgment and hacked Agag to pieces. He never saw Saul again (vv. 32–35).

Teaching

1 Samuel 16:1: God sent Samuel to Jesse of Bethlehem to anoint a new king (v. 1). God did the choosing of the king of Israel. This new king was prophesied in Genesis 3:15 and Numbers 24:17. These are not the only prophecies in Scripture about the coming *King*, the coming Messiah. They all point to God's chosen *King* who would come from Israel. 1 Samuel 2:10 says, "Those who oppose the LORD will be shattered; He will thunder in the heavens against them. The LORD will judge the ends of the earth. He will give power to His king; He will lift up the horn of His anointed." We know that this anointing will come through the kingship of Israel. God clearly has a plan for His Son to become *King* (Psalm 2:1–4, 7–9). Ruth 4:12 and 22 also explain that the *King* would come from the tribe of Judah. If Samuel knew Scripture, he would have recognized this next king could be the one God promised (Genesis 49:10; Micah 5:2).

1 Samuel 16:2–5: Surprisingly, Samuel's first response was fear. Samuel was more afraid of Saul than he was of God (Proverbs 29:25). God told Samuel to take a young cow with him as a sacrifice and to invite Jesse to the sacrifice. Then, God would tell him what to do next (vv. 2–3). Read 1 Samuel 2:10 again. Samuel would have heard this prophesy given to his mother Hannah about what he would do. Imagine his walk to Bethlehem, knowing that he was fulfilling that prophesy! That is what makes his fear so surprising (2 Samuel 2:7; 5:3). When Samuel arrived, the elders were afraid of what he was there to do and asked him why he had come (v. 4). MacArthur suggests they had heard of what Samuel had done to Agag and questioned what he was there to do.[1] Samuel responded to the elders he had come in peace to offer a sacrifice to God, and he instructed them to consecration themselves and go with him. MacArthur explains that "worship of Yahweh was always preceded by cleansing or washing, both of the outward garments and the inner man"[2] (Exodus 19:10, 14; 1 John 1:9). Samuel consecrated Jesse and his sons and invited them to the sacrifice, without knowing there was a son who was absent (v. 5).

1 Samuel 16:6–13: When Samuel saw Jesse's son Eliab, whose name means "My God is Father," he thought the anointed one was before him (v. 6). But the Lord told Samuel not to look at the sons' appearances, but to look at their hearts (v. 7). MacArthur explains, "The Hebrew concept of heart embodies emotions, will, intellect, and desires. The life of the person will reflect his heart."[3] (Jeremiah 17:10; Matthew 12:34). In verses 8–10, each son was presented to Samuel, but God did not choose them. Samuel finally asked if there were other sons, and Jesse said his youngest son was out tending sheep. Samuel told Jesse to send for that son while they all waited for him to come before they ate (v. 11). When David arrived, God said "Anoint him, for he is the one" (v. 12). The anointed are exalted by God, not man. Samuel anointed David in the presence of his brothers and the "Spirit of the Lord took control of David from that day forward" (v. 13). Later, David would be anointed a second time before his tribe of Judah and a third time before the entire nation of Israel.

Jacob, Gideon, and Joseph were all the youngest sons in their families as well. David was described as the firstborn of Israel who began as a shepherd and became king (Psalm 78:70–72). David was a type of Christ. David was rejected by his own brothers who saw him as worthless; Jesus' family thought He had lost His mind (Mark 3:21).

---

[1] John MacArthur, *The MacArthur Bible Commentary* (Nashville: Thomas Nelson, 2005), 327.

[2] MacArthur, 327.

[3] MacArthur, 327.

The Old Testament has many examples of the Spirit of the Lord empowering people: Samuel/Saul—1 Samuel 10:6, 10; Saul—1 Samuel 11:6; Saul's agents—1 Samuel 19:20, 23; David—2 Samuel 23:2; Jahaziel—2 Chronicles 20:14; the Davidic king—Isaiah 61:1; Ezekiel—Ezekiel 11:5; 37:1. In the New Testament, the Spirit came upon Jesus at His baptism (Matthew 3:13–17) when He was anointed by the Father and empowered by the Spirit (Acts 1:8).

1 Samuel 16:14–22: When the Spirit of the Lord left Saul, God sent an evil spirit to torment him (v. 14). *Nelson's Commentary* suggests this affliction by an evil spirit has four possible sources: "(1) demon possession as divine punishment; (2) demonic attack or influence; (3) an evil messenger, like the one sent to entice Ahab; or (4) a spirit of discontent created by God in Saul's heart."[4] Whatever the cause, Saul's servants noticed (v. 15). They offered to find someone to play the lyre for him, to soothe him when he came under attack (vv. 16–18). David was sent with gifts from Jesse to the king (vv. 19–20). David became Saul's armor bearer, a sign of David's service in humility (vv. 21–22).

Closing

To close, David had all the components of a person anointed of God:

- He had a heart for God.
- He was rejected my man.
- He was exalted by God.
- He was empowered by the Spirit of God.
- He was a man of integrity.
- He was a man of faith.
- He walked in humility.

As David walked in humility, God positioned him for more.

The Daily Word

In a battle against the Amalekites, Saul sinned and disobeyed the Lord's complete instructions. Because of his disobedience, the Lord rejected Saul as king of Israel. In the midst of Samuel's mourning and grief over Saul's sin and rejection as king, the Lord instructed Samuel to prepare to anoint the new king of Israel. The Lord selected David, who attended sheep and was the youngest, unassuming son of

---

[4] Earl D. Radmacher, Ronald B. Allen, and H. Wayne House, eds., *Nelson's New Illustrated Bible Commentary* (Nashville: Thomas Nelson, 1999), 366.

Jesse. The Lord chose David because of what He saw underneath that humble identity—David's heart. Samuel obediently anointed David, and the Spirit of the Lord took control of David from that day forward.

The Lord saw something in David no one else saw. Whereas people look at the visible, *the Lord sees the heart.* Jesus said life comes from the heart, and those with pure hearts will see God. If all you do is worry about your outward appearance, you are missing the point. Beauty can come and go, but the Lord praises a person who fears Him. Real beauty comes from within. Child of God, like David, you are anointed for the kingdom of God. The Lord just wants your heart. May the Lord renew your heart today as you seek Him.

But the Lord said to Samuel, "Do not look at his appearance or his stature, because I have rejected him. Man does not see what the Lord sees, for man sees what is visible, but the Lord sees the heart." —1 Samuel 16:7

Further Scripture: Proverbs 4:23; Proverbs 31:30; Matthew 12:34

Questions

1. In 1 Samuel 15:3, why do you think the Lord commanded that every living thing had to be destroyed?

2. What ultimately happened when Saul disobeyed God and allowed the king and the choice livestock to live? Can you think of a time when you may have disobeyed God? What was the outcome?

3. In 1 Samuel 16, the Lord told Samuel to go to Bethlehem. Why didn't Samuel want to go? What purpose did he have for going?

4. When you read 1 Samuel 16:7, what does this speak to you about the Lord (Proverbs 21:2; 1 Peter 3:4)? Are we guilty of only looking at the outside sometimes (John 7:24; 2 Corinthians 10:7)?

5. What did the Holy Spirit highlight to you in 1 Samuel 15—16 through the reading or the teaching?

Lesson 35: 1 Samuel 17

Anointed One: On the Battle Lines

Teaching Notes

Intro

As we continue to move through 1 Samuel, it's amazing to see all these things coming together. In chapter 4, Hannah was told her son would one day anoint the king, and in chapter 16, Samuel did just that. Yesterday, we talked about the implications of the king coming from Jesse's lineage, the tribe of Judah, and Bethlehem. At this point, David was still tending sheep for his father and playing music for Saul whenever the evil spirit took over Saul.

The backdrop for chapter 17 is David had been anointed, but now he had to wait for God's timing to take on the role of king. Consider these who had to wait too. Noah waited for decades for the flood to come. Abraham waited 25 years for Isaac to come. Moses spent 40 years working as a shepherd before God led him to Egypt to deliver His people. During periods of waiting, God continues to refine people to be more like Him. It's all about embracing God's timing in your anointing. The church today has received life, but we are not walking it out (John 10:10). In 1 Samuel 17:1–16, we will see David walk out his anointing under the control of the Holy Spirit, even as the enemy mocked him. In the New Testament, the Holy Spirit never leaves us. We are all anointed and have been sealed with the Holy Spirit (2 Corinthians 1:21–22).

Teaching

1 Samuel 17:1–7: The army of the Philistines and the army of Israel lined up across the Valley of Elah in battle positions (vv. 1–2). The valley is not large, they would have been able to look across the valley and see the faces of their opponents. Both armies were atop hills (v. 3). Goliath, whose name meant "Conspicuous One," was nine-feet and nine-inches tall[1] (v. 4). Goliath's armor weighed 125 pounds. The iron point of his spear alone weighed 15 pounds (vv. 5–7a). Constable states, "This is an unusually long description of an individual for

---

[1] Earl D. Radmacher, Ronald B. Allen, and H. Wayne House, eds., *Nelson's New Illustrated Bible Commentary* (Nashville: Thomas Nelson, 1999), 367.

the Old Testament. The writer evidently wanted to impress Goliath's awesome power and apparent invulnerability on the readers."[2]

1 Samuel 17:8–11: Goliath shouted at the Israelites, goading them into sending out a champion to fight him. Goliath promised that if the Israelite champion won, the Philistines would be their servants. If Goliath killed the Israelite champion, the Israelites would serve the Philistines (vv. 8–10). The enemy is going to constantly pick us apart, tell us lies, and attack what we know to be true. When Saul and the Israelite army heard Goliath's words, they bought into the lies and were terrified (v. 11). When the church becomes okay with surviving in the world, when we don't engage in the battle, then we are buying into the enemy's lies as well.

1 Samuel 17:12–16: Jesse's three oldest sons followed Saul into war. David, the youngest, kept going back and forth between his chores as a shepherd and his responsibilities to King Saul (vv. 12–15). Meanwhile, every morning and evening for 40 days, Goliath came out and challenged the Israelites (v. 16). Notice how the enemy's lies can be relentless! When the enemy is mocking us, we have to stop staring at the enemy and listening to his lies. The church today is on the front lines, we are in a position to do something about the battle.

1 Samuel 17:17–19: In Bethlehem, Jesse pulled together supplies and instructed David to deliver them to the Israelite camp. Notice the ten loaves of bread Jesse included (v. 17). The name Bethlehem meant "house of bread." Jesse also sent cheese to the commander and told David to check on his brothers (v. 18). The brothers were with Saul "fighting with the Philistines" (v. 19). They weren't actually fighting, but were waiting on Israel's side of the battle lines. Sometimes, the church today thinks we're fighting, but we're not. We have to move off the front lines into the battle. That's the goal of Time to Revive and reviveSCHOOL! We tend to want revival, but we want God to use someone else to do it.

1 Samuel 17:20–29: Moving off the front line and into the battle takes preparation. David made preparation. He got up early in the morning and made sure the sheep were taken care of before he left Bethlehem with supplies. He arrived in time to see the armies head out in battle formation, facing each other (vv. 20–21). Because David had taken care of his responsibilities, he could leave his supplies, run to the battle, and check on his brothers (v. 22). Goliath came out again, shouting his challenge (v. 23), and the Israelites retreated (v. 24). David

---

[2] Thomas L. Constable, *Expository Notes of Dr. Thomas Constable: 1 Samuel*, 133, http://planobiblechapel.org/tcon/notes/pdf/1samuel.pdf.

asked what the reward was for killing Goliath (vv. 25–27). The rewards included wealth and a place in Saul's family through marriage to Saul's daughter. When we fight in the battle, there is a reward for us as well (Matthew 5:10–12; 6:20). But be prepared for opposition from within the camp. David's brother Eliab attacked David's integrity and sense of responsibility (Psalms 78:72; v. 28), making David question what he had done wrong (v. 29). Wiersbe says, "Whenever you step out by faith to fight the enemy, there's always somebody around to discourage you, and often it begins in your own home."[3]

1 Samuel 17:30–39: Because of his interest, David was taken to Saul (v. 31). God had already qualified David for the battle through protecting the sheep (vv. 32–36). David claimed the victory (v. 37). Saul's armor did not fit David, but David did not need it (vv. 38–39). He was confident in the Lord and he did not need fancy weapons. Wiersbe says, "Saul didn't have the faith to believe that God could do something new, so he suggested the old-fashioned time-honored method of warfare."[4] Five years after his anointing, 17-year-old David was ready to walk out his call.

1 Samuel 17:40–58: David chose five stones, and with his sling in his hand, he approached Goliath (v. 40). It is time for new wineskins (Acts 11:19–26) in the American church. We are not changing culture. Let us pray to find one little thing we can tweak or change to see how that can make a difference. Finally, David was able to engage in the battle (vv. 41–47). David knew the victory was the Lord's. As Goliath came forward, David ran toward him and defeated him with a stone and a sling (vv. 48–50). David used Goliath's own sword to cut off his head (v. 51). The army of Israel chased the Philistines down, killed them, and plundered their camps (vv. 52–53).

Closing

The Israelites had stood on the front lines for days, just staring at the enemy. But when David came and walked out his call, his anointing, they were able to experience life more abundantly.

1 John 2:20, 27: "But you have an anointing from the Holy One, and all of you have knowledge . . . The anointing you received from Him remains in you, and you don't need anyone to teach you. Instead, His anointing teaches you about all things and is true and is not a lie; just as He has taught you, remain in Him."

---

[3] Warren W. Wiersbe, *Be Successful: Attaining Wealth That Money Can't Buy* (Colorado Springs: David C. Cook, 2001), 107.

[4] Wiersbe, 108.

When we walk out the Holy Spirit anointing that we've been given, just like the Israelites, we can experience the fullness of God that He wants for you and me. The questions is: Do you want to be the soldiers who are staring or David who is walking out his calling?

The Daily Word

David had been anointed by Samuel to be the king of Israel, but he remained in the pasture tending the sheep. While bringing food to his brothers who served in the army, David heard about Goliath, and he saw the Israelites retreat in fear of him. However, David was not afraid of battling this giant warrior. David knew the same God who rescued him from the paw of a lion and the paw of a bear would rescue him from the hands of this Philistine. He walked in faith, he walked in his anointing, and he walked as God created him, trusting the Spirit of God to be with him. Using weapons he was familiar with—ones he had used for years while tending sheep, David found victory by defeating Goliath with just a sling-shot and a stone.

Like David, it's time to face your giants. What is the overwhelming concern, or giant, you face that seems to get more difficult as time passes? It's time to recognize the Lord is with you and the victory belongs to Him. You are anointed with the power of the Holy Spirit, and through His power, you are able to overcome your giants. Stop standing on the sidelines. Go after it. The battle belongs to the Lord.

"The Lord who rescued me from the paw of the lion and the paw of the bear will rescue me from the hand of this Philistine." Saul said to David, "Go, and may the Lord be with you." —1 Samuel 17:37

Further Scripture: 1 Samuel 17:45–47; Psalm 18:39; 1 John 2:27

Questions

1. David was going to feed his father's sheep (v. 15). Where in the New Testament, do we hear Jesus speak of feeding sheep (John 21:17)? What differences can you see between these sheep?

2. Why was Saul's army afraid of Goliath (vv. 4–7)? What does God say about fear (Joshua 1:9; Isaiah 41:10; 2 Tim 1:7)? Have you conquered a fear with God's help? How? (1 John 4:18)

3. Why did David's brother get angry with him (1 Corinthians 1:27–29; James 3:14, 16; 4:11)? Why do you think David responded the way he did to his brother Eliab (1 Samuel 17:29)?

4. Young David had so much confidence in God he went to battle against a giant with only a few rocks. What giants have you battled against with the help of God? How did they turn out?

5. What did the Holy Spirit highlight to you in 1 Samuel 17 through the reading or the teaching?

Lesson 36: 1 Samuel 18

Anointed One: The Lord Was with David

Teaching Notes

Intro

We've just finished the story David destroying Goliath, the Philistine champion, with one stone as he walked out his anointing as king. David was anointed in the privacy of his family at the age of 12, and at the age of 17, he faced and defeated Goliath. However, for more than ten years, David had to stay on the run as a fugitive from King Saul. Saul was clearly in charge during this period, but the people wanted David's leadership. Wiersbe points out that "during the ten years or so that David was a fugitive, the Lord not only thwarted Saul's plans repeatedly, but He even used the king's hostility to mature David and make him into a man of courage and faith. While Saul was guarding his throne, David was being prepared for his throne."[1]

Teaching

1 Samuel 18:1–4: Jonathan, Saul's son, committed himself to David rather than his father (v. 1). Jonathan and David were probably about 25 years apart in age. Jonathan was a seasoned warrior who had already had two major victories; David's only victory was at the age of 17 against Goliath. From that day, Saul kept David with him, not allowing him to return to his father's house (v. 2). Jonathan committed himself to David and made a covenant with him by cutting up an animal and they both walked through the pieces (v. 3). Jonathan should have followed his father as the next king, but through this covenant, Jonathan was expressing, "If I am unfaithful to my word in this covenant, may I end up in pieces as this animal."[2] Jonathan then gave David his own clothes: his robe, his military tunic, his sword, his bow, and his belt (v. 4). Davis explains that "clothes signify the person and the position—hence Jonathan renounces his position as

---

[1] Warren W. Wiersbe, *Be Successful: Attaining Wealth That Money Can't Buy* (Colorado Springs: David C. Cook, 2001), 115–16.

[2] Dale Ralph Davis, *1 Samuel: Looking on the Heart,* Focus on the Bible series (Ross-shire, Scotland: Christian Focus, 2000, reprinted 2017), 194.

crown prince and transfers, so far as his own will goes, the right of succession to David."[3] DeGraaf states, "This deed on his part was an act of faith. Only faith makes us willing to be the lesser. Faith causes us to surrender our rights that we pretend that we have over against Christ, who is truly Israel's king."[4]

1 Samuel 18:5–9: David marched with Saul's army and was successful in every assignment Saul gave him. The soldiers and Saul's servants were pleased with David being put in charge (v. 5; Proverbs 3:3–4). As the troops returned, the women met King Saul in celebration, singing that Saul had killed thousands, and David had killed tens of thousands (vv. 6–7). Saul was furious with resentment and jealousy that David was receiving the credit and the honor (v. 8). Puritan minister John Flavel said, "It is a dangerous crisis when a proud heart meets with flattering lips." From then on, Saul watched David jealously (v. 9).

1 Samuel 18:10–16: The next day, an evil spirit took control of Saul, and he began to rave or prophesy. David was playing the lyre for Saul and Saul took his spear and threw it at David. But David avoided him twice (vv. 10–11). Saul's emotions were running high—jealousy, anger, envy, and fear. Saul became afraid of David because the Lord was with David and not with him (v. 12). David continued to have success. Saul assigned David more than 1,000 men (v. 13). Wiersbe explains Saul's reasons for reassigning David: "If David was killed in battle, it was the enemy's fault; and if he lost a battle but lived, his popularity would wane. But the plan didn't work because David won all the battles!"[5] (vv. 14–16). Saul continued to scheme where David was concerned. Wiersbe writes, "Envy is a dangerous and insidious enemy, a cancer that slowly eats out our inner life and leads us to say and do terrible things. . . . Envy is the pain we feel within when somebody achieves or receives what we think belongs to us"[6] (Proverbs 14:30). Wiersbe goes on to say, "Envious people max out their credit cards to buy things they don't need just to impress people who really don't care!"[7] (Psalm 5:12).

1 Samuel 18:17–30: Remember, as part of his reward for defeating Goliath, David was promised Saul's daughter in marriage. Saul finally offered David his daughter Merab (v. 17). In humility, David turned her down so Saul married her to someone else (vv. 18–19). But Saul's daughter Michal loved David, and Saul

---

[3] Davis, 194.

[4] S. G. DeGraaf, *Promise and Deliverance* (St. Catharines, Ontario: Paideia, 1978), 2:116.

[5] Warren W. Wiersbe, *The Bible Exposition Commentary: Joshua–Esther* (Colorado Springs: David C. Cook, 2003), 257.

[6] Wiersbe, *Be Successful*, 117.

[7] Wiersbe, *Be Successful*, 118.

offered Michal to David in marriage (vv. 20–21). Saul also instructed the servants to tell David how he was pleased with David (v. 22). But David again responded in humility, and he recognized that he was too poor to pay the bridal price (v.23; Exodus 22:16). When the king heard David's reply, Saul asked for 100 Philistine foreskins for the bride-price, hoping the Philistines would kill David (vv. 24–25). David accepted Saul's terms, killed 200 Philistines, and married Michal (vv. 26–27). Saul realized how deeply God loved David and became even more frightened. Saul became David's enemy from then on (vv. 28–29). Despite all Saul tried to do, David was more successful than all other officers (v. 30).

Closing

Clearly the hand of God was on the life of David. Psalm 92:8–11 says, "But You, Lord, are exalted forever. For indeed, Lord, Your enemies—indeed, Your enemies will perish; all evildoers will be scattered. You have lifted up my horn like that of a wild ox; I have been anointed with oil. My eyes look down on my enemies; my ears hear evildoers when they attack me."

Romans 8:28 sums up David's life: "We know that all things work together for the good of those who love God: those who are called according to His purpose." In reality David is just walking out his anointing and God is saying, "I got this."

The Daily Word

Even though Saul was still king over the Israelites, he jealously watched David's success. This jealousy drove Saul's actions and decisions in dealing with David. He even attempted to kill David . . . not once but twice! Despite Saul's efforts, David continued to find success because the Lord's hand was upon him.

Envy is the pain you feel when someone achieves something you think belongs to you. Pause for a moment and think about that statement. Do a heart check for yourself for envy and jealousy. Is there someone in your life who, when you think about his or her situation, causes your heart to stir up with emotion? When you walk in the flesh, jealousy is a natural emotion. Confess this jealousy to the Lord. Let it go. Ask the Lord to fill you anew with His Spirit. As you walk in the power of the Spirit, the Spirit gives you the strength to overcome the flesh and experience freedom. Rather than experience jealousy, you experience joy for the other person and delight in others' success. *Lord, fill me anew with your Spirit, bringing me freedom to build up your kingdom.*

So Saul watched David jealously from that day forward. —1 Samuel 18:9

Further Scripture: Psalm 25:4–5; Galatians 5:16, 19–20, 22–23; James 3:16

Questions

1. Jonathan loved David as he loved himself. What might he have felt differently (1 Samuel 15:28)? Read Mark 12:31. Does this verse reflect what we see in Jonathan?

2. Jonathan made a covenant with David and gave David his robe and his armor. How can we see Christ in this lavish display of love (Isaiah 61:10; Luke 15:22; Ephesians 6:13–17)?

3. David was the new "anointed one" although he was not yet serving as king. How do his actions in chapter 18 remind us of Christ (1 Samuel 18:5, 10–13; Luke 2:52; John 8:29, 59; 10:39; 11:53–54)?

4. In chapter 18, what progression do you see in Saul's attitude toward David (1 Samuel 18:8–9, 12, 15, 25b, 29)?

5. Why was David not willing to marry the king's daughter when she was offered to him (1 Samuel 18:23–26)? Why did Saul want David to marry his daughter Michal (1 Samuel 18:21)?

6. What did the Holy Spirit highlight to you in 1 Samuel 18 through the reading or the teaching?

Lesson 37: 1 Samuel 19—20

Anointed One: Covenant Relationships

Teaching Notes

Intro

Our phrase for 1 Samuel is *Anointed One*. In 1 Samuel 19, things got crazier. Saul told his son Jonathan to kill David (v. 1), and Jonathan told David what Saul had told him to do (vv. 2–3). Jonathan went back to his father and spoke well of David, so Saul said he would not kill David. Jonathan returned David back to Saul, and David served Saul again (vv. 4–8). But the evil spirit returned to Saul, and Saul tried to pin David to a wall with a spear. David had to run for his life (vv. 9–10). Saul searched David's home for him, but his wife Michal helped David escape by placing a household idol in bed to look like David was lying there sick (vv. 11–14). Saul sent his servants to bring David from his bed, but they only found the idol (vv. 15–18). When Saul found out where David was, he sent his agents there, but they encountered a group of prophets and began to prophesy. This happened three times (vv. 19–21). Saul then went as well, and the Spirit of the Lord came on him and he too began to prophesy (vv. 22–23). Saul stripped off his clothes, collapsed, and laid naked all day and night (v. 24). The story continues in chapter 20.

Teaching

Dale Ralph Davis highlights four scenes that are acted out in this chapter.[1] *The first scene was before Jonathan.* The first step was to debate the danger (vv. 1–4). David fled to Ramah, found Jonathan, and questioned why Saul was trying to kill him (v. 1). Davis states that David could go to Jonathan because their covenant provided David recourse.[2] Jonathan said Saul had promised he would not kill David (v. 2). But David countered that Saul was withholding information from Jonathan (v. 3). Jonathan reaffirmed his covenant with

---

[1] Dale Ralph Davis, *1 Samuel: Looking on the Heart*, Focus on the Bible series (Ross-shire, Scotland: Christian Focus, 2000, reprinted 2017), 204–5.

[2] Davis, 205.

David (1 Samuel 18:1–5). "Whatever you say, I will do" (v. 4). The covenant was not just renewed, but extended.

The second scene was to prepare a test (vv. 5–7). David said that since the next night was the New Moon, the beginning of a religious festival, he would skip having dinner with the king and hide for three days (v. 5). The New Moon festival had a sacrificial meal when the family came together for a time of worship (Numbers 10:10). David was now a part of Saul's family and expected to attend. The test was to see if Saul would miss David's presence and how Saul would react to his absence (vv. 5–6). David put Jonathan in a position of having to lie to Saul. The test would show if Saul was good with David's absence or if he became angry and had evil intentions (v. 7).

Jonathan appealed to the covenant (vv. 8–9). David said that if he had done anything wrong, then Jonathan should kill him (v. 8). The phrase "deal faithfully" (*hesed*) can be understood as the deal kindly or deal faithfully. In the KJV, the word is translated 250 times as "mercy." Davis explains that the order of this process is: "love gives itself in covenant and gladly promises devoted love; the covenant partner then rests in security of that promise and may appeal to it, as David does here.[3] Jonathan refused David's suggestion. Jonathan remained loyal to David and let him know Saul's intentions (v. 9).

Jonathan reaffirmed covenant promises again (vv. 10–17). David and Jonathan went out to the field to set up a "dry run" for how they would communicate Saul's reactions. Jonathan promised to send David word about whether Saul was favorable toward David (vv. 12–13). The covenant provided a vehicle for uncommon faithfulness. Jonathan recognized that David was the king and what was to come. Jonathan took it even further when he asked David to be gracious to him and to his household after Jonathan's death (vv. 14–16). The tradition was that a new king would eliminate anyone and their households who posed a threat to the king's reign (1 Kings 15:29). Wiersbe points out that "David never had a coregent because Jonathan was killed in battle, and David rejected Saul's daughter Michal as his wife and she died childless. Had she borne any children, it would have brought confusion into the royal line."[4] Jonathan then swore his love and support to David again (v. 17).

Jonathan and David also had to determine necessary signals (vv. 18–23). Jonathan told David to hide by a great rock in the field. Jonathan would shoot three arrows toward the rock. Then, depending on the instructions Jonathan gave to the young man fetching the arrows (to look for them off to the right or beyond

---

[3] Davis, 207.

[4] Warren W. Wiersbe, *The Bible Exposition Commentary: Joshua–Esther* (Colorado Springs: David C. Cook, 2003), 262.

the rock), David would know whether it was safe to return. In verse 23, Jonathan reaffirmed their covenant once again.

The third scene was at Saul's table (vv. 24–34). David's place at Saul's table remained empty for two days. When Saul asked where David was on the second day, Jonathan told his lie about David going to Bethlehem (vv. 24–29). Saul responded in anger and threw insults at Jonathan (v. 30). Saul recognized that Jonathan's allegiance was with David and explained that Jonathan's allegiance to David would cost Jonathan his throne (v. 31). Wiersbe explains that "God had made it very clear that none of Saul's sons would ever inherit the throne, and David was the king of God's choice, so Saul was fighting the will of God and asking Jonathan to do the same thing."[5] When Jonathan responded to Saul's anger by asking what David had done to him, Saul threw a spear at his son, trying to kill him (vv. 32–33). Jonathan was grieved over "his father's shameful behavior toward David" (v. 33). Jonathan is a foreshadow of a disciple of Christ (Luke 14:26).

The fourth scene was in the field (vv. 35–40). Jonathan followed their plan precisely to get his message to David (vv. 35–40). David bowed to the ground. Then, he and Jonathan wept together because David had to flee (vv. 41–42). Jonathan told David to "go in assurance" or "go in peace" that the Lord has your back.

Closing

There is peace because of the covenant. We can find peace in Christ alone:

Romans 5:1, 3: "Therefore, since we have been declared righteous by faith, we have peace with God through our Lord Jesus Christ. . . . And not only that, but we also rejoice in our afflictions, because we know that affliction produces endurance."

John 16:33: "I have told you these things so that in Me you may have peace. You will have suffering in this world. Be courageous! I have conquered the world." You can have covenant with Christ and He alone will give you peace.

Colossians 3:15: "And let the peace of the Messiah, to which you were called in one body, control your hearts. Be thankful." Only your relationship, your peace with the Messiah will get you through life. This is the beauty of walking with the anointing.

---

[5] Wiersbe, 263.

The Daily Word

Saul repeatedly attacked David, attempting to end David's life. But the Lord spared David. Saul's own son, Jonathan, loved David like a brother and helped protect him, even though it put his own life and his relationship with his father in danger. Jonathan even devised a plan to help David flee from Saul. Before parting ways, Jonathan and David made a covenant to watch over each other, even their future generations. Jonathan told David to go with the assurance (literally: "go in peace") because the Lord was with them. The two would always be friends.

The Lord sends you out with that same peace. The Lord watches over you in peace because you are in a covenant with Him. No matter what comes your way, *Jesus will give you peace.* He has already conquered the world, so His sons and daughters may be strong and courageous, even in the midst of suffering. He loves you, and He wants you to walk in the assurance of His love. There is so much in this world that is uncertain, but in Christ, you have assurance, no matter what.

Jonathan then said to David, "Go in the assurance the two of us pledged in the name of the Lord when we said: The Lord will be a witness between you and me and between my offspring and your offspring forever." Then David left, and Jonathan went into the city. —1 Samuel 20:42

Further Scripture: John 16:33; Romans 5:1–3; Colossians 3:15

Questions

1. In 1 Samuel 19:5, Jonathan's words sound like they could be describing who (Luke 23:4)?

2. Who helped David escape by letting him down through a window? What did she tell her father when he questioned her about letting David go (1 Samuel 19:17)?

3. In 1 Samuel 19:13, a household idol was used in the deception. Why do you think there was an idol there? Whose house was this in?

4. When Saul sent messengers to bring David back from Naioth in Ramah, what happened each time (1 Samuel 19:20–21)? What happened when Saul himself went to Naioth (1 Samuel 19:22–24)? Have you ever observed or experienced a special anointing or power of God in certain environments? (1 Samuel 10:5–6)

5. Saul tried to kill David repeatedly in chapters 19 and 20. Did he know David had been anointed as king by Samuel? What seemed to be at the root of his motivation to kill David (1 Samuel 20:31)? Did Saul not believe what Samuel told him in 1 Samuel 15:28?

6. What did the Holy Spirit highlight to you in 1 Samuel 19—20 through the reading or the teaching?

Lesson 38: 1 Samuel 21—22

Anointed One: David's Journey
Through Israel

Teaching Notes

Intro

We're going to start with a summary of 1 Samuel 21. In verses 1–6, David fled to Ahimelech, the priest of Nab, who was probably located in the north. David was hungry and asked for the consecrated bread that had been set aside for the priest. While there, David asked for a weapon and was given Goliath's sword. One of Saul's servants, the chief of his shepherds, happened to be there and saw what happened (vv. 7–9). David fled from there and went to King Achish of Gath. David became fearful of Achish and pretended to be insane (vv. 10–15). What's important for us to take away from chapter 21 is Ahimelech provided David with two things—the consecrated bread and the sword of Goliath. Saul's servant, Doeg the Edomite, saw it all. Part of the story line in chapters 21—22 is David's journey. David was the anointed one, and the Spirit of God left Saul and came on to David.

Teaching

1 Samuel 22:1–2: David left Gath and hid in the cave of Adullam (v. 1a). For David, walking out his calling was a journey. We tend to think the anointing process is miraculous and the anointed one has it all together. The reality is, it's a journey and a process. David's family heard he was there and joined him (v.1b). Remember, there had been issues between the brothers, but they now all came together as a family. Some of you may have family members who are not walking with the Lord and cannot support your calling. With time, David's family came around, and yours can too.

The cave was located two miles south of the Valley of Elah, ten miles southeast of Gath, and ten miles northeast of Bethlehem. In the area are huge caves that could hold the 400 men who were "desperate, in debt, or discontented" and chose David for their leader (v. 2). Constable says of these 400 men, "David became leader of a group of people who, for various reasons, had become discontented with Saul's government and were passionate for change."[1] David wrote Psalms 57 and 142 in this context from within the cave. As David cried out to God, the Lord began to surround him with people to support him. These 400 men would later be called the "mighty men" (1 Chronicles 11:16–18).

Wiersbe points out that David was in a region that supported him and that men from the tribes of Judah and Benjamin came to fight for him.[2] When David became thirsty, three men from Judah risked their lives to bring him water from the well at Bethlehem. This was something David did not take lightly and could not accept. So, he poured the water out as a drink offering to God. David didn't take his team members for granted. Over time, David's 400 men increased to 600 (1 Samuel 23:13). This was a much smaller force than Saul had, but they were willing to walk this journey with David.

1 Samuel 22:3–5: David continued to Moab, the home of Ruth, David's great grandmother. David asked the king to allow his family to stay in Moab for their safety (v. 3). It is essential that we also take care and love our aging parents. In the height of David's calling, David made sure his parents were safe. The word "stronghold," or *mesuda* in Hebrew, mentioned in verses 4–5 means fortress. Some biblical scholars suggest it refers to Masada, located to the west of the Dead Sea. *Mesuda* can also refer to "natural hiding places in the wilderness."[3] Wherever this was, David stayed there while his family was in Moab. The prophet Gad came to David and told him to return to Judah. David left for Hereth or "thicket" (v. 5). Gad was a prophetic voice speaking into David's life throughout his reign (2 Samuel 24:11). The prophet told David to take the next step. Saul never had the guidance of a prophetic voice. Gad was the king's seer, and he "assisted David in setting up the musical ministry for the sanctuary of the Lord"[4] (2 Chronicles 29:25). Why was this prophetic voice so important to David? Dale Ralph Davis says, "Desperation is no fun, but desperation and silence are unbearable."[5] The prophetic word can only come from God through the Holy Spirit (2 Peter 1:19–21). If we're not open to the prophetic word, we may be missing what God is speaking to us.

1 Samuel 22:6–10: Saul heard about the men going to David and became frightened. He questioned if David, Jesse's son, was going to pay them to get their

---

[1] Thomas L. Constable, *Expository Notes of Dr. Thomas Constable: 1 Samuel*, 164, http://planobiblechapel.org/tcon/notes/pdf/1samuel.pdf.

[2] Warren W. Wiersbe, *The Bible Exposition Commentary: Joshua–Esther* (Colorado Springs: David C. Cook, 2003), 266.

[3] Wiersbe, 266.

[4] Wiersbe, 267.

[5] Dale Ralph Davis, *1 Samuel: Looking on the Heart*, Focus on the Bible series (Ross-shire, Scotland: Christian Focus, 2000, reprinted 2017), 223.

loyalty (vv. 6–8). Saul's servant Doeg reported what he had seen at Ahimelech when David was given the bread and the sword (vv. 9–10).

1 Samuel 22:11–23: Saul summoned the priest Ahimelech and his family, who were also priests, and asked why they conspired with David against him (vv. 11–13). This was the beginning of an illegal trial. Saul made false accusations against Ahimelech and Ahimelech denied the charges (vv. 14–15). Dale Ralph Davis points out that this was where "the veil slips away and Saul is seen for the antichrist figure he really is as he has Yahweh's priests summarily butchered," going against God's own priests.[6] Saul ordered his guards to kill the priests who had sided with David, but the servants would not execute God's priests (v. 17). So, Saul sent Doeg to execute the priests. Doeg killed 85 men in priestly garb, along with all the men, women, children, infants, and animals in the city of Nob (vv. 18–19). Only one of the priests escaped and he ran to tell David what had happened (v. 20). David took responsibility for the deaths because he had seen Doeg there when Ahimelech helped him, and he did not prevent Doeg from telling Saul what had happened (vv. 22–23).

Closing

David had a group called The Mighty Men. Within that group God continued to raise up a king named David, a prophet named Gad, and a priest named Ahimelech. God was clearly at work bringing a new wine skin to His people. Just as today he is preparing a remnant to carry on God's plan.

The Daily Word

Knowing Saul wanted to kill him, David began a journey of fleeing from Saul in order to save himself. The Lord used specific people to speak into his life and direct him to the next location as he traveled from Nob to Gath, to the cave of Adullam, and to the land of Judah. David had an anointing on his life to be the king, but it wasn't an automatic, straight walk to the throne. It was quite the journey.

Have you ever thought about your own journey? The Holy Spirit guides the anointed and the Lord uses people to speak into your life. The journey may not always look like you expect. It will be filled with interesting stops and detours along the way. Remember to keep your eyes on Jesus. He will lead you where He desires you to serve in His kingdom. Talk with Him and trust Him as you go!

---

[6] Davis, 226.

Then the prophet Gad said to David, "Don't stay in the stronghold. Leave and return to the land of Judah." So David left and went to the forest of Hereth. —1 Samuel 22:5

Further Scripture: Psalm 119:105; Proverbs 3:5–6; Hebrews 12:1–2a

Questions

1. Why would it be wrong to eat the consecrated bread if the young men hadn't kept themselves away from women (Leviticus 15:18)? Would it have been acceptable to eat the consecrated bread at all (Matthew 12:3–4)?

2. Why did David pretend to be mad before the king of Gath?

3. What do you think made the people with issues come to David (1 Samuel 22:2)? Do you have someone to go to when you are struggling with issues? Is he or she someone who walks in the anointing of the Lord? Why not take some time this week to call that person and say thanks?

4. Why did Saul kill Ahimelech and his family as well as the people of Nob (1 Samuel 2:30–33)?

5. What did the Holy Spirit highlight to you in 1 Samuel 21—22 through the reading or the teaching?

Lesson 39: 1 Samuel 23—24

Anointed One: Cutting Saul's Robe

Teaching Notes

Intro

As a reminder, our word for Jesus in 1 Samuel is *Anointed One.* The book started out with Saul being the anointed one, but then it moved from King Saul to David. Although David knew what was to come, he kept telling people not to say anything because it wasn't his time yet. That's the theme for chapters 23 through 24—it was not yet David's time. It shows an incredible picture of David as the precursor to Christ.

In chapter 23, David fought the Philistines (vv. 1–6). In verses 7–8, Saul took his army to Keilah to trap David there, but David used Abiathar's ephod to determine what Saul was up to. Based on what the Lord told David, he left Keilah and moved from place to place (vv. 9–14). In verses 15–18, David and Jonathan renewed their covenant again, and Jonathan assumed the position as David's second-in-command. However, some Ziphites told Saul where David was hiding. Saul chased David until the Philistines attacked. David escaped again (vv. 19–29).

Teaching

Wiersbe shares four experiences David had in chapter 24.[1]

First, David's Temptation (vv. 1–4). David's army of 600 men was being chased by Saul's army of 3,000 (that's a ratio of one to five) in the wilderness of Engedi (vv. 1–2). In the middle of the journey, Saul went to relieve himself in a cave. It happened that David and his men were hiding in the back of the same cave (v. 3). Saul's need to relieve himself created a situation in which David's maturity was seen.

The law of Moses was strict about what to do when someone had to relieve himself. The person was required to go outside the camp, dig a hole, take care of

---

[1] Warren W. Wiersbe, *The Bible Exposition Commentary: Joshua–Esther* (Colorado Springs: David C. Cook, 2003), 272–74.

business, and then cover up the hole again (Deuteronomy 23:12–13). The reason was that "the Lord your God walks throughout your camp to protect you and deliver your enemies to you; so your encampments must be holy" (Deuteronomy 23:14). Wiersbe points out that Saul became extremely vulnerable while he was outside the camp and on his own.[2] Either Saul's spies were incompetent or this encounter was under God's control. The word "relieve" meant to cover the feet, because a person in a robe had to crouch above the ground with the outer garment around his feet.[3] While Saul was relieving himself, David and his leaders were having a conversation about the possibility that this was the day God had given Saul to him. Nowhere in Scripture was this promise recorded. In verse 4, David snuck over to where Saul was and secretly cut off a corner of Saul's robe (Psalm 26:1).

Second, David's Conviction (vv. 5–7). David felt guilty for having humiliated Saul by cutting off part of his robe while Saul was in such a vulnerable position (v. 5). Wiersbe states that, "by cutting off a piece of the robe, David was declaring that the kingdom had been transferred to him," and that "David did not intend to kill the king"[4] (1 Samuel 15:27–28). Dale Ralph Davis questions whether David's actions were based on "providence or temptation."[5] David's conscience bothered him because he knew about the incident in 1 Samuel 15, when Saul tore Samuel's robe, and that he had shown disrespect to God's anointed one (Exodus 22:28). On some level, David had given in to temptation to take advantage of Saul, and from that temptation, David had to deal with the guilt of what he did to God's king presently on the throne. We know temptation does not come from God (James 1:13–15). David knew he crossed the line and would not let his men kill Saul (v. 7).

Third, David's Vindication (vv. 8–15). David got up and went out of the cave. He called out to Saul, "My Lord the king!" and bowed to the ground in respect (v. 8). In 1 Samuel, David used a variety of terms for Saul, all of which were used in respect: father (24:11), anointed (24:6, 10), my lord (24:6, 10), and king (24:8, 14). David explained that he had no plans to harm Saul (vv. 9–15). David had two more opportunities to kill Saul that he didn't take (1 Samuel 26:2, 7–12; Romans 13:1–2). How do we know David was doing what he needed to do?

---

[2] Wiersbe, 272.

[3] John MacArthur, *The MacArthur Bible Commentary* (Nashville: Thomas Nelson, 2005), 338.

[4] Wiersbe, 272.

[5] Dale Ralph Davis, *1 Samuel: Looking on the Heart*, Focus on the Bible series (Ross-shire, Scotland: Christian Focus, 2000, reprinted 2017), 247–48.

Because of the character he displayed (Matthew 7:16–20). David verbalized his vindication in Psalm 54:1.

Fourth, David's Affirmation (vv. 16–24). After David finished speaking, Saul wept. Wiersbe points out that Saul "manifested temporary emotional reactions like that before, but they never brought about repentance or a change of heart."[6] Saul even admits he recognized God's call on David (v. 20). David swore he would not hurt Saul and Saul went back home, while David went up to the stronghold (v. 21–22).

Closing

Here's the big picture. First Peter 2:23: "when He was reviled, He did not revile in return: when He was suffering, He did not threaten but entrusted Himself to the One who judges justly." David as the anointed one served as a type of the *Anointed One.*

Isaiah 53:7: "He was oppressed and afflicted, yet He did not open His mouth. Like a lamb led to the slaughter and like a sheep silent before her shearers, He did not open His mouth." This is the same mentality of David's lifestyle pointing to the *Anointed One* to come. The only difference is that Jesus never gave in to temptation and that should be our model.

The Daily Word

Saul and his men were in pursuit of David when Saul needed to relieve himself. In God's sovereignty, out of all the caves available, they stopped by the cave in which David and his men were hiding. While Saul was inside the cave without his guards, he never realized David was there as well. At the encouragement of his men, David went to Saul and secretly cut off a corner of his robe. However, as soon as David took this action, his conscience bothered him because he lifted his hand against the Lord's anointed. In response, David told the men not to rise up against Saul, even though the king was right there in front of them. Rather, after Saul left the cave, David went out to him and honestly shared with Saul what he had done. He cleared his conscience, and, for a time, Saul and David were at peace with each other.

The Lord instructs His followers to live with a clear conscience—meaning to live free of guilt, without any hindrance in your relationship with God or anyone else. Stop for a minute and ask the Lord if there are any actions or words you need to confess. Ask the Lord to reveal to you how to make a situation right.

---

[6] Warren W. Wiersbe, *Be Successful: Attaining Wealth That Money Can't Buy* (Colorado Springs: David C. Cook, 2001), 152.

He may lead you to go and ask for forgiveness. When you have the courage to clear your conscience, the Lord will relieve the weight you have been carrying. He brings freedom and has a way of working the situation out for good as you trust Him. God will meet you in that place of honesty with His unconditional love and grace.

Afterward, David's conscience bothered him because he had cut off the corner of Saul's robe. —1 Samuel 24:5

Further Scripture: Isaiah 53:7; 1 Peter 3:16; Acts 24:16

Questions

1. In 1 Samuel 23:9, what do you think the significance was of David asking Abiathar the priest to bring the Ephod to him (Exodus 28:30; Numbers 27:21)?

2. David and Jonathan make a covenant before the Lord in 1 Samuel 23:18. What do you think this covenant involved? Had Jonathan and David ever made a covenant between them before (1 Samuel 18:3; 20:16)?

3. In 1 Samuel 23:17, was Jonathan prophesying about David's future (1 Samuel 16:13)?

4. Why didn't David kill Saul when he had the chance (1 Samuel 24:4)? Why did David feel bad that he had cut off the edge of Saul's robe (1 Corinthians 16:22; Ps 105:15)?

5. What did the Holy Spirit highlight to you in 1 Samuel 23—24 through the reading or the teaching?

Lesson 40: 1 Samuel 25

Anointed One: Rejection, Retaliation, and Refocus

Teaching Notes

Intro

We're getting close to finishing our 13th study of another book of the Bible, and this is the 240th lesson since we've started. That means we're one-third of the way through this study of the Bible. This can feel like a duty, just another day of stuff to get though. Or we can approach it every day, asking God what He wants us to learn today. Our phrase for 1 Samuel is *Anointed One*. The *Anointed One* always steps in at an unlikely time.

Teaching

1 Samuel 25:1–3: Samuel died, and all of Israel was there to mourn and bury him at his home in Ramah (v. 1). Most of those who mourned Samuel didn't like him, disobeyed what he said, but honored him in death. David and his men moved about 100 miles south of Masada to the wilderness of Paran.[1] Verse 2 introduces Nabal who lived in Maon and had a business in Carmel nearby. He was a wealthy man who carried a good deal of cash with him as he went back and forth. Carmel may not have had the best reputation. It was where Saul built a monument to himself (1 Samuel 15:12), and it was where Samuel refused to go when he told Saul that ruling the kingdom of Israel would not remain in his family line (1 Samuel 15:26). The man was Nabal, and his wife was Abigail, a beautiful and intelligent woman, whose name means "My father is joy." Nabal, a Calebite, was harsh and evil (or surly and mean), and his name means "fool" (v. 3). Abigail plays the role here as the anointed one. In verse 25, Abigail described her husband Nabal as "this worthless man . . . [who] lives up to his name."

1 Samuel 25:4–8: David heard that Nabal was shearing his 3,000 sheep, so he sent ten young men to take greetings to Nabal (vv. 4–6). They were to tell Nabal

---

[1] Warren W. Wiersbe, *The Bible Exposition Commentary: Joshua–Esther* (Colorado Springs: David C. Cook, 2003), 275.

they knew he was shearing sheep, and that when his shepherds were with David, they were protected, not harassed (v. 7). Since it was a feast day, the young men were to ask for Nabal's generous support (v. 8).

1 Samuel 25:9–13: David's request was legitimate and worthy. The young men did as David had instructed them (v. 9). Nabal responded by suggesting that David, the anointed one of God, was a runaway slave (v. 10). Nabal had a spirit of arrogance and control that hindered his desire to give. Everybody knew David. Even Abigail knew David. Nabal was intentional in his insults of David.

In this process, David was *rejected* (vv. 10–12). When his men returned and told David what Nabal had said, David *retaliated* (vv. 12–13, 21–22). David responded in anger and armed 400 soldiers (v. 13). In verses 21–22, David repeated he was going to retaliate because he had been rejected.

David's reaction goes against everything he had done in the past:

- 1 Samuel 17:28—David was rejected by his brother Eliab.
- 1 Samuel 17:32–33—David was rejected by Saul who said he wasn't big enough or strong enough to fight Goliath.
- 1 Samuel 17:37—David responded to both rejections in faith . . ."The Lord delivered me."

Perhaps Nabal's rejection seemed different from these because it came when David was tired, hungry, and on the run. This was not how David usually responded. After Saul tried to kill David (1 Samuel 18:11), David refused to retaliate (1 Samuel 24:10). Rejection can take us by surprise and bring out the worst in us. Satan uses rejection as an opportunity to speak lies about who we are (1 Peter 5:8).

1 Samuel 25:14–19: One of Nabal's men told Abigail what had happened with Nabal and how well David's soldiers had protected them (vv. 14–16). The servant said that Nabal was "such a worthless fool nobody can talk to him!" (v. 17). "Worthless fool" can be understood as a scoundrel or a son of worthlessness.[2] In response, Abigail gathered a huge store of supplies and loaded them on donkeys (v. 18). She sent her servants on ahead, but told her husband nothing (v. 19).

1 Samuel 25:20–31: As she rode through a mountain pass, Abigail saw David and his men approaching at a distance (v. 20). David had just announced his plans for retaliation again when Abigail approached David and fell on her face before him (vv. 21–23). Through Abigail's actions of humility, of taking on the

---

[2] Earl D. Radmacher, Ronald B. Allen, and H. Wayne House, eds., *Nelson's New Illustrated Bible Commentary* (Nashville: Thomas Nelson, 1999), 377.

guilt that was not hers, David *refocused*. Abigail identified David as her "lord" 14 times in chapter 25. She recognized David was the anointed king, and she still asked to speak to him directly, much like Esther approaching the king without an invitation. The word "listen" is used 1,100 times in the Old Testament and means to hear or obey. MacArthur explains, "It implies the listener is giving his or her total attention to the one who is speaking."[3] David should have recognized that God had a bigger plan, rather than focusing on what Nabal wouldn't do (2 Corinthians 4:18). In verse 28, Abigail prophesied about David's dynasty that would be established through the Lord. She went on to describe the protection God would give David (vv. 30–31).

1 Samuel 25:32–35: David praised the Lord for sending Abigail to him. God used Abigail to change David's actions and save the lives of Nabal and his men (vv. 32–34). David then sent Abigail home in peace (v. 35). David recognized that God is the avenger, not him.

1 Samuel 25:36–44: When Nabal found out what Abigail did, he had a seizure, became paralyzed and died ten days later. Abigail went to David and they were married.

Closing

Jesus was *rejected*, but He never *retaliated*. He kept His mind on God. When we face rejection, we need to *refocus* back on God. We belong to the Lord because of what He has done, not what we have done.

The Daily Word

After Israel mourned the death of Samuel, David went down to the Wilderness of Paran where he met a rich businessman named Nabal, who was probably at the peak of his sheep-shearing season. Yet Nabal refused to bless and provide food for David and his men, even after they had been kind to Nabal's shepherds. Nabal completely rejected David's request. David reacted to Nabal's rejection by organizing his men in an effort to retaliate and attack Nabal. However, the Lord intervened through Nabal's wife, Abigail. The Lord used Abigail's wisdom and determination to refocus David's attention back on the Lord. The Lord reminded David of His faithfulness and provided for all of David's needs.

Have you ever felt the gut-wrenching feeling of *rejection*? It's upsetting. You may feel as though you need to *retaliate* to prove a point, make it right, or even give the person what they deserve. Next time you feel like this, take a deep breath

---

[3] John MacArthur, *The MacArthur Bible Commentary* (Nashville: Thomas Nelson, 2005), 340.

and *ask the Lord to help you refocus.* The Lord sees and knows the situation. He may send someone to help you or even turn the heart of the other person around. Instead of responding in anger and taking matters into your own hands, rest in the Lord, and peace will cover you as you wait. God has a way of working things out for good and not for evil when you wait upon Him. He will rescue you.

Then David said to Abigail, "Praise to the Lord God of Israel, who sent you to meet me today! Your discernment is blessed, and you are blessed. Today you kept me from participating in bloodshed and avenging myself by my own hand." —1 Samuel 25:32–33

Further Scripture: Proverbs 20:22; 1 Thessalonians 5:15; 1 Peter 3:9

Questions

1. Samuel's death seems to be a footnote. Why (1 Samuel 8:4–8)?

2. What do we know about Nabal from this chapter? According to 1 Samuel 25:10, did Nabal appear to sympathize with Saul or with David?

3. Was David right in his response to Nabal's rejection by setting out to attack and kill Nabal and all males belonging to him (1 Samuel 25:13, 22)? Was this consistent with David's usual response to those who are against him (1 Samuel 17:37; 24:10)? Have you ever allowed circumstances to cause you to react rather than respond to a situation?

4. Why did David bless Abigail in 1 Samuel 25:33–34? Has the Lord used a person to bring you correction or prevent you from sinning? If so, how did you respond (Proverbs 10:17; 12:1; James 5:19–20)?

5. What ultimate reward did Abigail receive from David for ministering to his needs and the needs of his men, and in the process, keeping him from sinning (1 Samuel 25:40–42)? How does this parallel Christ (Isaiah 61:10; 62:5; Rev 19:7; 21:9)?

6. Who dealt with Nabal for rejecting the anointed one (1 Samuel 25:38)? Similarly, how will the Lord deal with those who reject His Anointed One (John 3:18, 36; 12:48; Hebrews 10:31)?

7. What did the Holy Spirit highlight to you in 1 Samuel 25 through the reading or teaching?

Lesson 41: 1 Samuel 26—27

Anointed One: God Is Faithful

Teaching Notes

Intro

Yesterday, we learned how God used Abigail, the wife of Nabal, to intervene in David's life when he was so focused on retaliation that he had lost his way.

Teaching

1 Samuel 26:1–4: The Ziphites went to Saul a second time and told him where David was hiding (1 Samuel 23). Saul left with 3,000 men to search for David (vv. 1–2). In this case, David's enemy was telling Saul where David was. But God was also communicating with David and let David know Saul was nearby (v. 3). David sent out spies to find exactly where Saul was (v. 4). There had to be a sense for David that he was going down the same path with Saul again. His feelings about it were captured in Psalm 37.

1 Samuel 26:5–12: When David found out where Saul's camp was, he went there and found Saul asleep in the middle of a circle of his 3,000 soldiers (v. 5). David asked Ahimelech, the Hittite, and Joab's brother Abishai (David's nephew) if one of them would go with him into the camp. Abishai agreed to go (v. 6). That night, David and Abishai snuck into the camp where Saul was sleeping (v. 7). Abishai saw this as a chance for David to kill his enemy and offered to pin Saul to the ground with his own spear that was next to him (v. 8). David knew the spear because Saul tried to kill him with it. Yet again, David refused to lift his hand against God's anointed king. He realized the Lord would take care of Saul in time (vv. 9–10). Instead, David took the spear and the water jug next to Saul's head and they left the camp where everyone within it was under a deep sleep from the Lord (vv. 11–12; Luke 6:27–36).

1 Samuel 26:13–16: David crossed to the other side of the mountain and then shouted to Abner and the Philistine camp (v. 13). David first met Abner when Abner took him before Saul, while David was still holding the head of Goliath

(1 Samuel 17:55–57). He asked Abner if he was going to answer him (v. 14). Abner questioned what David was doing. David explained that because the night watchmen had been asleep, he was able to sneak into the camp to Saul's side without anyone knowing it. For proof, David told Abner to look for Saul's spear and water jug (vv. 15–16).

1 Samuel 26:17–21: Although Abner did not immediately recognize David's voice, Saul did (v. 17). Notice Saul referred to David as his son and David referred to Saul as his lord and king. David asked why Saul relentlessly continued to chase him. David asked that if he had done evil against God to tell him what that was so he could bring an offering to God, or if Saul was believing lies about David (vv. 18–19). David said to Saul that using an army of 3,000 men just to get to him was like chasing a flea or running after a partridge hiding in the mountains (v. 20). David was speaking truth into Saul, trying to get Saul to realize what he was doing. Saul confessed that he had sinned against David again (v. 21). This is not the first time Saul became convicted about his sin toward David. It happened after David cut a piece of the hem of Saul's robe instead of harming Saul. Even though Saul confessed, he never repented for what he had done (2 Corinthians 7:10).

1 Samuel 26:22–25: David told Saul to send one of his young men over to get his spear (v. 22). David reaffirmed that he saw Saul's life as valuable, and asked that Saul see David's life the same (v. 23–24).

Closing

Hebrews 10:23 emphasizes that God is always faithful to His promises. God was faithful to David and David was faithful to God. When David faced Goliath, God was faithful. When David was in the cave with Saul, God was faithful. When David encountered Nabal, God was faithful. We are God's anointed, and He has always been faithful to us and to deliver.

David had to walk out his calling, even when things didn't seem to be happening in his favor. Instead of trying to manipulate the situation or make something happen, David remained faithful.

How can David's life speak to us? How can we take the Nabals and Sauls in our lives and shift them into something that is positive and productive? How can we pray for our enemies? Do we listen for the word of God and walk into the enemy camp and trust that God will be there with us? Instead of running away from problems, how can we run toward them? What if we just keep showing up as we trust that God is moving in our midst?

What's going on in your life today? Maybe this wilderness experience is part of the journey. Just be faithful to whatever God has promised and called you to do!

The Daily Word

Once again David found himself in a situation in which he could kill Saul. David knew that if he eliminated Saul, he would immediately ascend as king over Israel. Even so, David chose not to take God's plan into his own hands. David told his men not to destroy Saul, displaying his trust in God because he believed God's plan would prevail in God's timing. However, David did take Saul's jug of water and spear, proving to Saul his life had been spared. In taking the high road, David's actions brought forth Saul's conviction and confession. In turn, Saul blessed and honored David.

What is the "Saul" in your life? Is there something you could force to happen, knowing then you'd see God's promise happen quickly? In the moment, it may seem easier to take matters into your own hands. However, the Lord has a plan and timing for your life. If there is any question in your heart, then pause. As you walk in integrity, your plans will succeed with the Lord. Seek Him for direction. If the Lord has given you a promise for what is to come, then He has a plan for good. *He will bring to it to pass.* The Lord will bless the integrity of your heart.

May the Lord repay every man for his righteousness and his loyalty. I wasn't willing to lift my hand against the Lord's anointed, even though the Lord handed you over to me today. Just as I considered your life valuable today, so may the Lord consider my life valuable and rescue me from all trouble. —1 Samuel 26:23–24

Further Scripture: Psalm 41:12; Proverbs 4:24–26; Hebrews 10:23

Questions

1. In 1 Samuel 26:11, David said he would not touch the Lord's anointed one. What do you think it means to be anointed of the Lord? Where else do we see this anointing (Acts 4:27; 10:38; Luke 4:18)?

2. After Saul realized David had been close to him and didn't hurt him, he told David to return to him and admitted he had sinned. Why do you think David did not return (1 Samuel 26:21–25)?

3. While David was in Gath, he attacked several lands and left no one alive. Why did he do this? Do you believe he was he hearing from the Lord at that time? Why or why not?

4. What did the Holy Spirit highlight to you in 1 Samuel 26—27 through the reading or the teaching?

Lesson 42: 1 Samuel 28—29

Anointed One: When Faced with a Dilemma

Teaching Notes

Intro

I want to break down 1 Samuel 27 in order to truly understand 1 Samuel 28. Dale Ralph Davis breaks up chapter 27 into four sections: David's plan (27:1–4); David's town (27:5–7); David's practice (27:8–12); and David's dilemma (28:1–2).[1]

David's Plan: In verses 1–4, David fled to the enemy land of the Philistines, thinking Saul wouldn't chase him there. David's 600 men and their families all went to the Philistine land of Gath. David had two wives with him: Ahinoam and Abigail (Nabal's widow). When Saul heard where David was, he stopped his search. At this point, it looked like David's plan worked, but he was in the enemy camp.

David's Town: Apparently, David (the anointed king) was willing to settle there, because he asked the Philistine king Achish to give him a town to live in. Achish gave David the city of Ziklag and David stayed there for a year and four months (vv. 5–7).

David's Practice: During that time, David's practice was to raid enemy towns and kill everyone, but take all the animals and clothing. Achish would ask, "Where did you raid today?" David killed the people in each town so they could not tell Saul what he was doing. David even invaded the south country of Judah. Achish believed David had made himself so detestable to the people of Israel that he would remain Achish's servant forever.

Teaching

1 Samuel 28:1–2: David's Dilemma came when Achish brought the army together to fight Israel and Achish expected David and his men to fight with

---

[1] Dale Ralph Davis, *1 Samuel: Looking on the Heart*, Focus on the Bible series (Ross-shire, Scotland: Christian Focus, 2000, reprinted 2017), 279.

them (v. 1). Achish had seen how David had raided towns of their enemies and expected David to fight with them against their ultimate enemy—Israel. David's response to Achish was ambiguous. He did not promise to fight but gave the impression he would (v. 2). David did not reveal his plan, or he may not have had a plan at the time.

1 Samuel 28:3: Saul also faced a dilemma. Saul heard the Philistines were coming, that Samuel had died, and all Israel had mourned him (v. 3). Saul removed the mediums and spiritists from the land (Deuteronomy 18:9–12). Saul knew the Word of God and he followed it. Constable explains, "Mediums and spiritists are people who try to communicate with the dead, but in reality communicate with evil spirits."[2] Wizards were part of the spiritists (Isaiah 8:19).

1 Samuel 28:4–8: The Philistines camped at Shunem, and Israel camped on the other side of the Jezreel Valley at Gilboa (v. 4). Saul looked on the Philistine camp and was afraid. He told his servants to go find a woman who was a medium he could consult with (v. 7a). His servants replied there was a medium in En-dor (v. 7b). Saul disguised himself by removing all regal clothing and left with his servants to make the ten-mile journey to En-dor, passing near the Philistine battle lines.[3] Saul even asked his servants to do his talking for him (v. 8). Saul took things in his own hands and went against the teachings he was supposed to obey. Scripture says when we give into sin and temptation, we will suffer death (James 1:13–15).

1 Samuel 28:9–14: The medium stated that they were setting a trap for her since she knew Saul had killed the mediums (v. 9). In response, Saul swore to her "by the Lord" that nothing would happen to her (v. 10). The Lord didn't want her to live, but Saul used His name to get her to do his bidding. Saul wanted her to get him in touch with Samuel (v. 11). When Samuel appeared, she screamed and asked why Saul had deceived her (v. 12). Saul promised she was in no danger and asked what Samuel looked like (v. 13a). She told him she saw a "spirit form" (v. 13b). This spirit being could be a divine being (an Elohim) or the judges of the Great Judge. Samuel was wearing a robe (v. 14), a reminder of Saul grabbing the hem and tearing Samuel's robe in 1 Samuel 15:27–28.

1 Samuel 28:15–25: Samuel asked why Saul had bothered him, and Saul explained that God had turned away from him (v. 15). This is an example that

[2] Thomas L. Constable, *Expository Notes of Dr. Thomas Constable: 1 Samuel*, 198, http://planobiblechapel.org/tcon/notes/pdf/1samuel.pdf.

[3] Warren W. Wiersbe, *The Bible Exposition Commentary: Joshua–Esther* (Colorado Springs: David C. Cook, 2003), 287.

God can use any means to fulfill His purposes. In this case, He used evil to release a prophetic word onto Saul. Samuel told Saul God had done what He said He would and that Saul and his sons would be killed by the Philistines on the next day (vv. 16–19). Saul fell on the ground, terrified and weak from lack of food (v. 20). The medium saw Saul's reaction, and offered him food (vv. 21–22). Although he first refused, the woman and his servants urged him to eat. She killed a fatted cow and served Saul his last dinner (vv. 23–25).

Closing

At the beginning of chapter 29, David was trying to figure out how to handle the Philistines, and Saul was trying to deal with the news that he and his sons would be killed the next day. Saul had no hope; he was separated from Christ. However, we're in the new covenant with Christ. We are no longer far away from God, and there is no sin too big that can keep us away from Him (Ephesians 2:12–13). Jesus set us free.

As far as the east is from the west, God has removed our sin from us when we recognize we've messed up (Psalm 103:12). We have to go from the state of Saul to the state of David. Saul kept thinking he didn't need God.

Are you listening to this right now and know there are things you are hiding from others—little things and big things? You've got the disguise on, and you don't think you'll ever be caught. If you confess your sins, God is faithful and righteous, and He will forgive your sins and cleanse you from all unrighteousness (1 John 1:9). God gives everyone of us a chance to come clean.

The Daily Word

The Philistines came together as one army to fight against Israel and King Saul. When Saul saw them, he trembled with fear and inquired of the Lord. But the Lord was quiet and didn't answer him. In his fear and distress, Saul continued to search for direction. He disguised himself and, in the middle of the night, visited the home of a medium. He knew it was against the Lord to seek a medium, but he did it anyway. And what he heard did not make him feel any better. It actually brought him into even greater despair.

There are times in life when the Lord allows for quietness and does not give immediate answers. Even in quietness, even in the stillness, the Lord is with you. He has something for you to learn through the quiet seasons. Trust the Lord's timing and continue to seek Him. Like Saul, you may be tempted to look elsewhere for answers. Resist this temptation by standing firm in the Lord. However, if you find yourself disguised in the middle of the night seeking something or someone other than the Lord, *it is time to take off your mask.* Confess to the Lord.

He will wash away every sin as far as the east is from the west. He will set you free. He is there to fight your battle because His love for you never ends. His mercies are new each morning.

When Saul saw the Philistine camp, he was afraid and trembled violently. He inquired of the Lord, but the Lord did not answer him in dreams or by the Urim or by the prophets. Saul then said to his servants, "Find me a woman who is a medium, so I can go and consult her." His servants replied, "There is a woman at En-dor who is a medium." Saul disguised himself by putting on different clothes and set out with two of his men. They came to the woman at night. —1 Samuel 28:5–8

Further Scripture: Lamentations 3:22–23; Psalm 103:12; James 1:14–15

Questions

1. In 1 Samuel 28:6, Saul inquired of the Lord, and he didn't get an answer. Why do you think he didn't hear from God (Proverbs 1:28–33)?
2. Why did Saul put the mediums and spiritists out of the land (Leviticus 19:31; 20:6; Deuteronomy 18:10–11)? After having done so, why do you think Saul would seek out a medium and visit her?
3. In 1 Samuel 29:4, why did the Philistine princes make David return to his camp?
4. What did the Holy Spirit highlight to you in 1 Samuel 28—29 through the reading or the teaching?

Lesson 43: 1 Samuel 30—31

Anointed One: The Shift in David's Leadership

Teaching Notes

Intro

In yesterday's study (1 Samuel 28), Saul had a medium call Samuel back from the dead, and Samuel had to take on the role of giving Saul the bad news that he and his sons would die the next day. Saul then knew the kingdom was being taken away from him and turned over to David. Meanwhile, David was put into a dilemma by being in the Philistine lands and being expected to fight with them against Israel, the nation he had been called to lead. In chapter 29, the Philistine commanders began to question what David and his men were doing as a part of their army. These commanders wanted David and his men to be dismissed so they wouldn't change sides and become adversaries during the battle (vv. 1–5). When King Achish heeded his commanders' warning and dismissed David and his men to return home, David asked what he had done to not be trusted (vv. 6–8). Achish said he knew David was like an angel of God, but he and his men would have to leave (vv. 9–11). This is where we begin in 1 Samuel 30.

Teaching

1 Samuel 30:1–4: As David and his men arrived back in Ziklag, they found that the Amalekites had burned the city and kidnapped everyone left within it (vv. 1–2). When David and his men found that all of their family members had been kidnapped, they wept until they had no more tears (vv. 3–4). David and his men had to have been upset at being dismissed by the Philistines before they found their city in ruins. Their loss was overwhelming to the point of having no strength left to continue to weep. This is a reminder that grief can take it out of us physically.

1 Samuel 30:5–6: Even though David's wives had been taken too, his troops talked of stoning him because their sons and daughters were gone (vv. 5–6a). David was in greater distress over the turning of his troops. Although the troops had no strength to grieve, their bitterness had given them the strength to want to stone David. "But David found strength in the LORD his God" (v. 6b).

1 Samuel 30:7–8: In this moment, David turned to the Lord and shifted the future for his men and his kingdom. David asked Abiathar the priest to bring him the ephod. David put on the ephod, literally clothing himself in prayer and worship. David used it to ask God what he should do about those who had raided Ziklag. God told him to pursue the raiders and rescue the people (vv. 7–8). God has created us for victory's sake, but the enemy can use things like bitterness to strengthen us for the wrong thing. David sought out the Lord, rather than the pain in his heart.

David, the anointed one, stepped in to stop the weeping and the bitterness by restoring the people back to their families. Although David was upset because his wives had been taken, David pursued the Lord, who sent him to overtake the raiders and rescue and restore the families.

Where in this passage can we see the *Anointed One*, Jesus? The Jews wept in bitterness for the long years of captivity they'd experienced—the Egyptians, the Assyrians, the Babylonians, the Romans—and they looked for someone to rescue and restore them. Jesus stepped into that scene and also wept as He tried to overtake, rescue, and restore all that had been taken from His Father. Jesus looks upon the church as His bride and He weeps over her too. The Jews had become hopeless during the long captivity. Hopelessness can crush people—their hopes, dreams, and ability to move on. Consider Jesus, at the Mount of Olives, sweating drops of blood, asking the Father, "Do I take this on? Is there another way?" Yet in that moment, Jesus is actually pursuing God.

1 Samuel 30:9–15: David left with his 600 men, but 200 men were too exhausted from all the emotions to go on and were left at the brook Besor (vv. 9–10). Remember the reason Saul lost his throne was because he disobeyed God and did not destroy the Amalekites. David was now dealing with this group who should not have been there. As they marched, they found an Egyptian who had not eaten in three days and was left for dead in a field. David's army fed the Egyptian, who was revived from the food (vv. 11–12). David found out that the Egyptian was a servant of an Amalekite who had been with them when they burned Ziklag (vv. 13–14). David asked the young man to lead them to the Amalekites, and he agreed if they promised not to kill him (v. 15).

1 Samuel 30:16–19: The young man took them to the Amalekites who were celebrating with drinking and dancing because of all the spoils they had taken from the lands of Philistia and Judah. David slaughtered them from "twilight until the evening of the next day" and killed all but 400 men on camels who were able to flee (vv. 16–17).

The phrase, "from twilight until the evening of the next day," brings attention back to Christ:

> *From twilight*—the last supper and Judas' betrayal of Jesus
> *Until*—the stations of the Cross
> *The evening of the next day*—His death on the Cross.

David, the anointed, *recovered ALL* and *rescued ALL* his family, which is a foreshadowing of Christ (v. 18). Verse 19 says, "But nothing of theirs was missing, whether small or great, sons or daughters, spoil or anything that they had taken for themselves; David brought it all back." This is a reminder of the finished work at the Cross. Nothing was left behind in the authority of the enemy (v. 20). Jesus restored everything, and even robbed the grave.

1 Samuel 30:21–31: When they returned, the 200 men at Besor came out to meet David and the people with them. David approached them and greeted them (v. 21). The wicked and worthless men among the 400 didn't want the 200 men who had been left behind to receive any of the recovered spoils except for their wives and children (v. 22). Notice the wicked, who were so filled with bitterness and anger that they could only act out of selfishness, were the first to speak up and give their opinion. David responded that the victory had come from the Lord, not from the actions of the men, so all would share alike (vv. 23–24). David also recognized that those who had stayed behind had fulfilled a mission—they had protected the army's supplies. Where did David get this understanding? From strengthening himself in the Lord. This was a critical moment in David's leadership—he saw the heart of God and led the people from his victory in prayer, not in war. Jesus taught on this concept in His parable of the laborers in the vineyard (Matthew 20:1–16). Verse 25 states that this philosophy of all receiving the same share became a statute and an ordinance for Israel. David was beginning to move Israel into the kind of nation who showed the heart of God in how they treated others (v. 25). Then David began to share the spoils with the elders of Judah and the other tribes in Israel (vv. 26–31).

Closing

At the same time David fought his battle in chapter 30, Saul and his sons were captured in battle with the Philistines (1 Samuel 31:3–4). Saul was severely wounded by arrows and asked his armor bearer to kill him with a sword. The armor bearer refused, so Saul fell on his own sword, killing himself. When we look at chapters 30—31, we can't help but notice the parallels between these chapters and Jesus' journey. On the day the enemy crucified Jesus, He fell on His sword too.

Jesus is the *Anointed One*. He pursued, recaptured, and restored everything lost to mankind in the Garden of Eden. What Jesus did is a free gift. Everyone has benefited from Jesus going to the Cross. David sought the Lord instead of letting the pain motivate him. David's victory in this situation catapulted him in his anointing. Everyone benefits when we walk in our calling.

The Daily Word

David and his men arrived in Ziklag to discover that the Amalekites had raided the Negev and attacked and burned down Ziklag. Not only was everything destroyed, but their wives, sons, and daughters had been kidnapped. David and his men wept until they had no strength left to weep anymore. In David's deep grief over his loss, David found strength in the Lord. He turned to the Lord for direction and wisdom on what to do next. The Lord was faithful to give David clear direction and the promise of victory and restoration.

As you read David's story of loss, there's a good chance you can feel the pain in these words because you have walked through similar pain and loss. You can recall a time you wept so loudly and for so long that you got to a point you had no more tears. You may be going through a season of intense pain right now. Even in your misery, turn to the Lord for strength. He promises to strengthen you in your weakness. He promises to be near to the brokenhearted. He will comfort those who mourn. Ask Him for direction. He will give you the steps to take. In Jesus, He promises victory and restoration. Lift your head up and seek His face.

But David found strength in the Lord his God. . . . and David asked the Lord: "Should I pursue these raiders? Will I overtake them?" The Lord replied to him, "Pursue them, for you will certainly overtake them and rescue the people." —1 Samuel 30:6, 8

Further Scripture: Psalm 23:4; Psalm 32:8; Psalm 73:26

Questions

1. We have an enemy that comes to steal, kill and destroy (1 Samuel 30:3; John 10:10). How can we take comfort knowing we have the same promise of victory David was given in verse 8 of 1 Samuel 30 (Mark 12:36; Luke 1:71)?

2. Where did David place his focus first when he was between the grief of his army losing their families and the army wanting to stone him? When you are in dire situations or circumstances, who or what do you seek out first? What

do you do in order to "encourage yourself" or find strength in times of your greatest discouragement or distress?

3. What are some things the Lord did for David to encourage him during his time of crisis (1 Samuel 30:10–20; Ps 37:5)?

4. What was the difference in what the wicked and worthless men said about the spoils they recovered and what David said about them? Are those who are left behind, not out on the front lines but supporting us from a distance (maybe financially, or in prayer, or just encouraging us), just as valuable as anyone else?

5. Saul's life came to a tragic end in 1 Samuel 31. What did Samuel tell Saul a day earlier about what would happen to him and his sons (1 Samuel 28:19)? If you knew you had one day left to live, what would you do? How would you honor the Lord?

6. What did the Holy Spirit highlight to you in 1 Samuel 30—31 through the reading or the teaching?

Lesson 44: 2 Samuel 1—2

Eternal Throne: David's Second Anointing

Teaching Notes

Intro

This is our first lesson in 2 Samuel, and it feels as though we could just roll into 2 Samuel as a continuing story from 1 Samuel. The reality is that 1 and 2 Samuel were originally written as one book. But since we are dealing with them separately, we need to treat this as both the continuation of 1 Samuel and as a separate book as well. The author of 2 Samuel was probably Samuel, but it was possibly written by three different people (Samuel, Nathan, and Gad) and named after Samuel (1 Chronicles 29:29). Samuel had already died at this point. Both books of Samuel cover a period of 135 years, with 2 Samuel covering about 35 years. Paul Van Gorder explains the book of 1 Samuel as one of transition: "It outlines the change from the theocracy established under Moses to the monarchy begun under [king] Saul. The book also marks the transition from priests to prophets as the central figure of God's dealing with Israel."[1] Mindi has combined two paintings for these two books into one complete image (in art is called a diptych). The phrase for 1 Samuel was *Anointed One*. The phrase for 2 Samuel is *Eternal Throne*.

In 1 Samuel 2, Hannah was told she would give birth to a son, Samuel. "He will give power to His king, He will lift up the horn of His anointed" (1 Samuel 2:10b). In 2 Samuel there are four themes that you will see as we go through this book:

1. *The Davidic Covenant and the coming King* (2 Samuel 7:11–13, 16): The anointed one (David) will actually walk into the *Eternal Throne* (of Jesus). Consider Luke 1:30–33 which states that His throne will come through David, and His kingdom will have no end. Here we will begin to see this unfold.

---

[1] Paul R. Van Gorder, *The Old Testament Presents . . . Reflections of Christ: 1 Samuel*, http://www.thebookwurm.com/ref-1sam.htm.

2. *Jerusalem* (2 Samuel 5): David captured the city and made it his capital. The only references we have to Jerusalem up to this point are found in Genesis 14 and Judges 1:8, when the Jebusites were not yet conquered (Psalm 48:1–2). Jerusalem was also known at this point as the City of David.

3. *The sin of David and its consequences* (2 Samuel 11—18)

4. *The future hope* (2 Samuel 23:5): David repents and the story does not end like Saul who consulted a medium.

Teaching

2 Samuel 1:1–10: After defeating the Amalekites, David returned and stayed at Ziklag (v. 1). On the third day in Ziklag, a man from Saul's camp came and paid homage to David (v. 2). The man could have been a lone survivor who had traveled 90 miles from Mount Gilboa to Ziklag to see David (v. 3). When David asked about the outcome of the battle, the Amalekite man told him many of the troops, as well as Saul and Jonathan, were dead (v. 4). David demanded to know how the man knew that information (v. 5). This man had been an eye-witness of Saul's death, telling how he saw Saul leaning on his own spear as the Philistine chariots and the cavalry closed in (vv. 6–8). Saul had asked the man to kill him since he was mortally wounded "but his life still linger[ed]," meaning Saul was in agony of death (v. 9). The man told David he had killed Saul, taken the crown and arm band (Saul's royal regalia), and then brought it to David (v. 10).

The man's account seemed to contradict the record of Saul's death in 1 Samuel. In 1 Samuel 31:1–3, the Philistine archers severely wounded Saul, and in verses 4–6, Saul's armor bearer refused to kill Saul and Saul fell on his own sword. Remember that the Amalekite man said Saul was leaning on his spear, so it could be—and this is possibly a stretch—the Amalekite came along at the just the right time to do for Saul what his armor bearer refused to do. Possibly, this shows a different perspective from the Amalekite.

2 Samuel 1:11–16: David tore his clothes in mourning and his men did the same (v. 11). They wept and fasted throughout the day for all those of Israel, not just Saul and Jonathan, who had died in battle (v. 12). This seems to me to be a sign of integrity on David's part. David had three opportunities to kill Saul . . . none of which he took. He knew he was the anointed king, waiting on his time to take the throne. But he still loved Saul and respected the role of Saul's office. He walked with integrity. David asked the man where he was from and found out he was an Amalekite (v. 13). In verse 14, David asked, "How is it that you were not afraid to lift your hand to destroy the Lord's anointed?" David couldn't understand how anyone could lift a hand to give the final blow against God's anointed, Israel's first king. David summoned a servant to execute the Amalekite

(v. 15) because his blood was on his own head (v. 16). David had been guilty over just touching the hem of Saul's robe, so his actions against the Amalekite weren't unconceivable.

2 Samuel 1:17–27: David sang a lament for Saul and Jonathan and required that all in Judah learn the song, The Song of the Bow (vv. 17–18). *Nelson's Commentary* describes the song as "highly poetic, intensely personal, and emotionally charged."[2] The song represented a national tragedy with the death of the king. Those in Israel recognized their kings were chosen and anointed by God and that God pours out His blessing on them. David's song is written in three stanzas.

The first stanza (vv. 19–24) described Saul and Jonathan as the splendor of Israel that had been slain. David didn't want the information shared with other groups outside Israel because he didn't want them to rejoice over Saul's death. And even with the problems between them over David, Saul and Jonathan loved each other and would not be parted from each other.

The second stanza (vv. 25–26) shifted to David's love for his brother and friend, Jonathan. The third stanza (v. 27) concluded a repetition of verses 19 and 25: "How the mighty have fallen and the weapons of war have perished!"

2 Samuel 2:1–4: These four verses point out that David's time had finally come. David sought out the Lord to know what to do next. He asked God if he should go to Kirjath Arba, or "Town of Four."[3] This referenced the little towns in the area. God told David to go to Hebron (v. 1). Hebron was the key city in which God had moved among the patriarchs and was located 20 miles south of Jerusalem. David went with his two wives, Ahinoam and Abigail (v. 2). David also brought his men and their households who settled in the towns near Hebron (v. 3). There the men of Judah came and anointed David as king of Judah— the second time David was anointed as king. The first time David was anointed was by Samuel (1 Samuel 16:13). He would later be anointed a third time (2 Samuel 5:3), when all Israel would be a part of that anointing. David's anointing as king of Judah came after he had honored Israel's first king, Saul.

Closing

David knows what it means to wait on the Lord. Psalm 37:34 says, "Wait for the LORD and keep His way, and He will exalt you to inherit the land. You will watch when the wicked are destroyed." This describes David's life. He waited on the Lord and in God's timing, not man's timing, it all unfolded. Psalm 21:7:

---

[2] Earl D. Radmacher, Ronald B. Allen, and H. Wayne House, eds., *Nelson's New Illustrated Bible Commentary* (Nashville: Thomas Nelson, 1999), 388.

[3] Radmacher et al., 389.

"For the king relies on the LORD; through the faithful love of the Most High he is not shaken." This was David challenge. When you wait on the Lord, you will not be shaken. David's *Eternal Throne* will not be shaken.

The Daily Word

After grieving, fasting, and mourning the death of Saul, even composing a song in his honor and teaching it to the Judahites, David went to Hebron as directed by the Lord. It was in Hebron that the men of Judah came to anoint David king over the house of Judah—over David's tribe only. Although David knew the Lord promised he would be king over all Israel, David waited with humility that honored Saul and trusted the Lord's timing for his appointed reign.

Waiting . . . no one likes to wait for anything. However, everything has a season. Every season has a purpose. The Lord doesn't waste the waiting season. *Growth happens when you wait.* You tend to want to rush or get immediate satisfaction. Yet the Lord's ways can often be slow and take time. Let the Lord's plan unfold in His way and in His time. Enjoy the process as you hold fast and trust His promises.

Therefore, be strong and courageous, for though Saul your lord is dead, the house of Judah has anointed me king over them. —2 Samuel 2:7

Further Scripture: Psalm 21:7; Psalm 27:14; Psalm 37:34

Questions

1. What was the problem with the messenger who reported Saul's death in 2 Samuel 1 (1 Samuel 31:1–6; 1 Chronicles 10:14)?

2. The messenger claimed to be an Amalekite. What had God commanded the Israelites to do with the Amalekites (Deuteronomy 25:17–19)? When David had him killed, was he just obedient to what the Lord had commanded and what Saul had failed to do (1 Samuel 15:8–9)?

3. What was the emphasis on The Song of the Bow? What did David tell the people to do with this song?

4. Where was David living after the death of Saul? How was David showing his faith in God at the beginning of 2 Samuel? Do you continually ask the Lord about the intimate details of your life?

5. Where did the people finally anoint David as king of the tribe of Judah? Who was also made king at the same time? Was this a deliberate disobedience to the Lord?

6. What did the Holy Spirit highlight to you in 2 Samuel 1—2 through the reading or the teaching?

Lesson 45: 2 Samuel 3—4

Eternal Throne: The Assassinations of Abner and Ish-bosheth

Teaching Notes

Intro

In 2 Samuel 1—2, David was anointed king over the tribe of Judah. The first time David was anointed as king, he was a young boy, and Samuel anointed him as God's chosen king of Israel. This was his second anointing as king of a portion of Israel.

Teaching

2 Samuel 3:1–5: A long war took place between the house of Saul and the house of David. Saul's house grew weaker while David's grew stronger (v. 1). In 2 Samuel 2:8, Abner made Saul's son Ish-bosheth king over the lands of Gilead, Asher, Jezreel, Ephraim, and Benjamin—identified as "all Israel." The war was over who would rule over Israel—Saul's family or David. This battle for the throne will continue through the next six chapters of 2 Samuel.

Why was David's house growing stronger while Saul's house grew weaker? At this point, David had added more wives and children to his household (vv. 2–5). God's hand was on David. In Saul's house was confusion and chaos (1 Samuel 13:14). David was a man after God's own heart and sought God's will, and he walked with courage and integrity. Saul, however, acted out of fear and control. It comes down to who was the wisest in how they led.

Solomon is considered to be the wisest of all Israel's kings. Where did his wisdom come from (James 3:13–18)? From his father, David. Solomon saw wisdom walked out through his father. That's why Solomon asked God for wisdom in understanding.

2 Samuel 3:6–11: As the war between Saul's house and David continued, Saul's uncle and his army commander Abner continued to grow in strength (v. 6). Ish-bosheth accused Abner of sleeping with one of Saul's concubines (v. 7). Abner took great offense and asked if he was a dog's head who belonged

to Judah. In the Old Testament, dogs always were mentioned in a bad connotation. Possibly, Abner was asking if it was thought he was a male prostitute
working for Israel. Abner took offense because he had been the one who'd been
looking after Ish-bosheth's kingdom (v. 8). Abner knew what God had promised David and had been fighting against David's rule. But, as a result of this
accusation, Abner's allegiance swung to David (vv. 9–10). And Ish-bosheth
became afraid of Abner (v. 11).

2 Samuel 3:12–16: Abner let David know he now supported David's claim to the
throne (v. 12). David agreed to Abner's plan with one exception—Abner had to
bring Saul's daughter, Michal, with him (v. 13). David sent word to Ish-bosheth
(son of Saul) to give him back Michal, whom he was engaged to marry when
Saul "sold her" to the first person who brought him 100 Philistine foreskins (v.
14). Ish-bosheth responded, taking Michal from her husband, Paltiel, son of
Laish. (vv. 15–16).

2 Samuel 3:17–21: Abner then met with the elders of Israel, presenting David
to them as the one God had anointed to be their king (vv. 17–18). Abner also
met with the Benjaminites, Saul's tribe, and told them that the rest of Israel had
agreed upon David as their next king (v. 19). Abner brought 20 men to David,
and David held a banquet for them and for his men (v. 20). Abner promised to
gather all Israel before David, and David sent Abner away in peace (v. 21). These
former enemies were now at peace.

2 Samuel 3:22–27: After Abner left, Joab and David's soldiers returned with
the spoils from a raid (v. 22). Joab was David's nephew, and Abner had killed
one of Joab's brothers (2 Samuel 2). When Joab found out that Abner and
David had found peace, Joab questioned David's decision with Abner. Joab
assumed Abner had come to spy on David (vv. 23–25). Without David's
knowledge, Joab sent messengers out to bring Abner back from the well of
Sirah (v. 26). Joab pulled Abner aside and stabbed him in the stomach to
avenge his brother's death (v. 27). Joab's actions were not done out of wisdom
but retaliation and selfishness.

2 Samuel 3:28–39: David responded to Joab differently than he had to others
who had spilled blood. David made sure all Israel knew he had nothing to do
with Abner's murder (vv. 28–29). David ordered Joab and those with him to
publicly mourn Abner's death, and David walked in the funeral procession (v.
30–31). David mourned Abner's death.

2 Samuel 4:1–12: After Abner's death, Ish-bosheth lost his courage and all of Israel was dismayed (v. 1). Yet Saul's son was still caught up in selfish ambition (v. 2). Two men who worked for Saul's son assassinated Ish-bosheth in his own home while he napped (vv. 5–7). The men cut off Ish-bosheth's head and took it to David (v. 8). David had these men killed and hung their bodies by the pool of Hebron for all to see. Ish-bosheth's head was buried in Abner's tomb (vv. 9–12).

Closing

The question that rises from this is why David had these men executed but let Joab go. Interestingly, Solomon would have to deal with Joab later. Throughout David's story, Joab plays a big role, selfish ambitions got in the way, and his taking of lives did not stop with Abner. Joab did not walk with the same heart David did. David walked with God's own heart.

What does this mean to us? We have to be careful as we walk out our calling and as we intersect with people who would lead us away from that calling. God has given us wisdom, but if we're in the wrong posture like Joab was, that wisdom will not save us. May we have a heart like David's that responded like God would—in peace and in truth. We are seeing God's *Eternal Throne* established through one who had God's heart.

The Daily Word

Joab killed Abner. Rechab and Baanah killed Ish-bosheth. Then the three of them approached David, expecting him to be grateful these men were dead and no longer served as threats to the king. Instead, David had the opposite reaction. He was not grateful, and he grieved over the shedding of innocent blood. David sensed their motives. He cursed Joab's house and ordered Rechab and Baanah to be killed.

Why did they choose to murder? David knew these men had heart wounds from previous experiences and hadn't sought the Lord to heal their hurt, nor did they seek David's counsel.

You may find people rub you the wrong way and even hurt your feelings. If someone hurts you, do not let your wounded heart go untended. If you had a physical scrape from falling down, you would be certain to clean it out, treat it, and ensure no infection would manifest or grow larger. The same is true when others wound your heart. If a heart wound is left untreated, envy and bitterness can build up like an infection. In Joab, Rechab, and Baanah's case, their festered hearts led to murder. The Lord's love can heal your pain and bring hope to any situation. Today, if you have a heart wound you haven't tended to, ask the Lord to help you heal.

How much more when wicked men kill a righteous man in his own house on his own bed! So now, should I not require his blood from your hands and wipe you off the earth? —2 Samuel 4:11

Further Scripture: 2 Chronicles 7:14–15; Jeremiah 33:6; James 3:14–16

Questions

1. In 2 Samuel 3:11, Ish-bosheth could not answer Abner because he feared him. What reason did Ish-bosheth have to fear him?

2. In 2 Samuel 3:9–10, how did Abner know the Lord had sworn to give David the kingdom? Was it because he realized the Lord was with David (1 Samuel 15:28; 18:14, 28), and that David also spared Saul's life twice (1 Samuel 24; 26)?

3. Why is Jonathan's crippled son mentioned in 2 Samuel 4:4, and what relevance does it have in this chapter (2 Samuel 9:3)?

4. What did the Holy Spirit highlight to you in 2 Samuel 3—4 through the reading or the teaching?

Lesson 46: 2 Samuel 5—6

Eternal Throne: Bringing the Ark to Jerusalem

Teaching Notes

Intro

In 1 Samuel 16:12–13, David was brought before Samuel and then chosen by God as the next king of Israel. Verse 13 states that "the Spirit of the LORD took control of David from that day forward." In the remainder of 1 Samuel, God began to bless David, preparing him to one day sit on Israel's throne. Yet David was in a constant struggle and tension between his anointing as the future king and Saul's anointing as the current king. In the first part of 2 Samuel, David was established as king of Judah, and in chapter 5, all the tribes of Israel came together to anoint David as king over Israel. The Lord told David that while he had been a shepherd of sheep, he would now shepherd His people and rule over Israel (2 Samuel 5:1–3).

Israel said to David, as the anointed one, that they were his own flesh and blood, foreshadowing the coming of Jesus as the *Anointed One*. Jesus became flesh and blood for us. There's also an interesting parallel between Saul as the first king and Adam as the first man, to David as the second king and Jesus as the second Adam.

Some of you have had prophetic words spoken over you, and there's probably been a tension in your life as you've walked through that calling. You may not have had the public anointing yet. But none of that should discredit the truth of that anointing for you. As David walked out his calling, he developed perseverance and integrity in the process. David was 30 years old when he became king. It's interesting that Jesus was 30 years old as well when He began His ministry. In the remainder of chapter 5, David led his troops to take over Jerusalem from the Jebusites. The Israelites were supposed to have taken care of the Jebusites when they fought for the Promised Land. Since that had not happened, David took this on in a strategic move. By establishing Jerusalem as the new capital, David created an alliance between northern and southern Israel. The Jebusites believed the city was so fortified that they put the blind and the lame on the fortifications to fight them. David and his men entered the city through the water shaft and took the city. This was David's first battle as king. When the

Philistines heard David was king, they went after him, planning to defeat him. However, God gave the Philistines to David as well.

Teaching

2 Samuel 6:1–5: David brought together 30,000 choice men to take the ark to Jerusalem (vv. 1–2). David and his troops went to get the ark where it had been left at Abinadab's house for 50 years. The Philistines had captured the ark in battle, but they began to develop physical tumors from having it in their presence (1 Samuel 6). They sent it back on a new cart to see if the ark had caused their ailments, and the cows pulled it back to Beth-shemesh. The people there did not treat the ark with reverence and God struck 70 men down. The ark was taken to Abinadab's house where it stayed (1 Samuel 7). Because the ark had been returned to them on a new cart, David and his troops placed the ark on another new cart (v. 3).

2 Samuel 6:6–11: As they proceeded with the cart and the ark, the oxen stumbled and the cart shook. Uzzah reached out to the ark so it wouldn't fall off the cart (v. 6). God's anger burned at Uzzah's lack of reverence, and He struck Uzzah dead on the spot (v. 7). Under Israel's law, people were to treat it with reverence and respect. The ark was not handled properly. David became angry and then fearful of God at what happened (vv. 8–9). The ark was taken to the house of Obed-edom, instead of Jerusalem, and while it stayed there for three months, Obed-edom's household was blessed (vv. 10–11). When the presence of God dwells in our midst, things begin to change and fruit comes out of it. There are times in my own life when I'm not seeing fruit produced in my ministry, and I have to stop and seek the Lord to figure out why.

2 Samuel 6:12–19: People reported to David that the Lord was blessing Obed-edom's family because of the presence of the ark, so David went to bring the ark up to Jerusalem with gladness (v. 12). When the Levites carried the ark six paces, which represented the six days of creative process of God, the ark was stopped and David sacrificed an ox and a fattened calf (v. 13). David was the king, and he also took on the posture of the priest by wearing the linen ephod and dancing in worship (v. 14). All of Israel came with David, shouting and blowing the ram's horn, as he brought the ark into the city (v. 15). Michal, David's wife and Saul's daughter, looked out the window and saw David dancing before the Lord, and "she despised him in her heart" (v. 16). I wonder if we are reluctant to worship God in abandon with our actions because we are concerned about what others will think of us. In this passage, I see Michal giving her opinion so much that it could have swayed David's response and reaction to God. The ark was placed inside the tent David had set up for it, and David offered burnt offerings and fellowship offerings to God (v. 18).

The burnt offering was the whole offering, which means the only part of the sacrificed animal not burned was the skin, which was given to the Levites. The peace offering was about recognizing the coming of God's peace to the individual or to the group. The peace offering was supposed to be eaten there as a part of the sacrifice, not taken home. Everyone, Israelite and outsider, received a part of the peace offering. This is a beautiful picture of the sacrifice of Christ Jesus, the peace that has come for all people. Interestingly, there was no sin offering or guilt offering involved in this process. After the offerings, David blessed the people in the Lord's name. David also gave a loaf of bread, a date cake, and a raisin cake to each person in the community of Israel, men and women alike, and they all departed for their own homes (v. 19). Then David went home to bless his own household, what is described in 1 Chronicles as ministering to his own family. David honored families, his own and those of his people.

2 Samuel 6:20–23: When David got home, Saul's daughter, Michal, chastised him for his actions and said he had exposed himself and acted vulgar (v. 20). David didn't accept Michal's chastisement and said he was dancing before the Lord who had chosen him over Michal's family to rule (v. 21a). Then he stated, "I will celebrate before the LORD, and I will humble myself even more and humiliate myself. I will be honored by the slave girls you spoke about" (vv. 21b–22). David was basically telling Michal he was done with her. And verse 23 confirms this, "And Saul's daughter Michal had no child to the day of her death."

Closing

David established a place in Jerusalem to be his capital. And he showed that, above all else, he wanted God to be the true King over Israel. David wanted God ruling over him, so he had to have the ark and God's presence in his capital. It's why we call God the King of kings and Lord of lords. David honored God's presence and put His presence in the correct place—above everything and everyone.

One last thought is about the theme of the *Eternal Throne*. When Israel placed the ark on a cart, someone died, so they came back and placed the ark on the shoulders of the Levites. Isaiah 9:6 says that "the government will rest upon his shoulders." Jesus said, "For My yoke is easy and My burden is light" (Matthew 11:30). God's presence should be resting upon us and causing us to be elevated from that place. I believe their putting the ark on their shoulders was a foreshadowing of Jesus carrying God's presence on His shoulders.

The Daily Word

David brought the Ark of the Covenant to Jerusalem. As the Levites carried the Ark on their shoulders, David and the whole house of Israel celebrated with songs, instruments, lyres, harps, tambourines, and cymbals. David danced before the Lord with all his might. David's wife, Michal, saw her husband dancing in the Lord's presence and judged him as being a vulgar person. But David was not ashamed of his celebration in the Lord's sight.

The Lord longs for you to worship Him, not concerning yourself with what others may think. The Lord says that in His presence is fullness of joy. If worshipping the Lord makes you want to pick up your feet and twirl around, then do it! Worship the Lord because He has turned your lamenting into dancing! Don't worry about what others may think. He is worthy of it all and worthy to be praised! Offer your life to the Lord because He has removed your sackcloth and clothed you with gladness! You can sing and not be silent! Today, freely worship the Lord!

David replied to Michal, "I was dancing before the Lord who chose me over your father and his whole family to appoint me ruler over the Lord's people Israel. I will celebrate before the Lord, and I will humble myself even more and humiliate myself. I will be honored by the slave girls you spoke about."
—2 Samuel 6:21–22

Further Scripture: Psalm 16:11; Psalm 30:11–12; 2 Corinthians 3:17

Questions

1. Do you think that sometimes we are like the Jebusites, believing we are secure because of earthly possessions, status, or knowledge, while there is a "water shaft" (2 Samuel 5:8) or place of vulnerability or weakness in our lives?

2. In 2 Samuel 5:13, do you think David was doing the same thing the Jebusites did in verse 6 (taking advantage of his position)?

3. Should David have put the ark of the covenant on a new cart rather than having it carried (Numbers 4:5–6, 15; 2 Samuel 6:3)? Where might he have gotten this idea (1 Samuel 6:7–8)? What can we learn from David's mistake of failing to seek the Lord and instead doing things in the way of the world?

4. In 2 Samuel 6:20, Michal was embarrassed about how David was dressed and how he danced before the Lord. What was her consequence (2 Samuel 6:23)? Have you ever disagreed with or judged others for how they express their worship? Have you ever been embarrassed to express yourself in a manner like David did, just because of what people might think? Why or why not?

5. What did the Holy Spirit highlight to you in 2 Samuel 5—6 through the reading or the teaching?

Lesson 47: 2 Samuel 7—8

Eternal Throne: David's Kingdom Is Forever

Teaching Notes

Intro

Second Samuel 7 is unique and one of the most important chapters of the Old Testament. At this point, David had stopped running and was settling into his new role as the anointed king of Israel. Chapter 7 focuses on how the *Eternal Throne* (our phrase for 2 Samuel) will be walked out.

Teaching

2 Samuel 7:1–3: David had settled into his palace in Jerusalem, and the Lord had put David's enemies to rest (Exodus 33:14). This rest was promised prophetically and can only be found in the Lord. Sometimes the reason we deal with burnout is because we have yet to find true rest in Him. Now, as king, David's desire was to honor God. He looked at his house of cedar and questioned why it was right for the Lord not to have a permanent dwelling. When David confronted the prophet Nathan about it, Nathan told him to do what was in his heart, for God was with him (Psalm 132:1–5).

The prophet Nathan was not a "yes man." In fact, in 2 Samuel 12, he was the one who confronted David with his sin. Nathan came in to speak God's Word into David. However, in here in chapter 7, Nathan spoke too soon and apparently didn't inquire of the Lord for guidance (v. 3). Dale Ralph Davis states, "Nathan knew what [David] was thinking. It was noble, rational, and right. One didn't need to think twice about it. Nathan urged David to 'just do it.'"[1]

2 Samuel 7:4–8: Nathan had quickly given David the go-ahead to build God a house, but God had another plan—the Davidic Covenant that pointed to the coming Messiah. Why did God say "no" to David? Constable gives three reasons God denied David's desire: "First, there was no pressing need to do so since the ark had resided in tents since the Exodus. . . . Second, God had not commanded His people to build Him a permanent temple. . . . Third,

---

[1] Dale Ralph Davis, *2 Samuel: Out of Every Adversity*, Focus on the Bible series (Ross-shire, Scotland: Christian Focus, 1999), 84.

David was an inappropriate person to build a temple since he had shed much blood."[2] In verse 4, God corrected the word Nathan spoke to David. In all the years since the Israelites had left Egypt, God had not asked for a house (vv. 5–7). Wiersbe explains God used the metaphor of a shepherd to show He had called David to be a leader to His people, not a builder of His temple (v. 8).[3] Yet, "God's servants must learn to accept the disappointments of life, for as A. T. Pierson used to say, 'Disappointments are His appointments.'"[4] Constable states it was not that "God was disciplining David or had rejected him that He prohibited David's good intention. God was simply redirecting His servant. He was to be a ruler, not a temple builder."[5] Likewise, there are times when God has to redirect us from doing something we think He needs us to do, to what He wants us to do. We must not get ahead of Him doing what we think needs to be done, but instead, we are to rest in Him, accepting that He has a plan that goes back to the Davidic Covenant.

2 Samuel 7:9–13: God said He would make David's name great (v. 9), reminding David that God was walking out the Abrahamic Covenant through him. One day, one of David's descendants would build a house for Him, and God would establish the throne of His kingdom forever (Psalm 89:4). We know that this son would be Solomon, the son of David and Bathsheba. God redeemed the situation of David and Bathsheba in the lineage of the Messiah (vv. 12–13).

2 Samuel 7:14–17: God said He would be a father to this descendant who would be a son to Him. He would discipline this son with a human rod but His love would never leave the son. David's house and kingdom would endure forever, and his throne would be established forever (vv. 14–16). Nathan spoke all these things to David (v. 17).

2 Samuel 7:18–29: David sat in God's presence and asked, "Who am I, Lord GOD, and what is my house that You have brought me this far?" (v. 18). The rest of the chapter is David's prayer of thanksgiving.

In the Davidic Covenant, God promised David a house, a kingdom, and a throne that would last forever. David is the lamp of Israel, and the flame will never go out (2 Samuel 21:17). *Nelson's Commentary* explains these promises:

---

[2] Thomas L. Constable, *Expository Notes of Dr. Thomas Constable: 2 Samuel*, 54, http://planobiblechapel.org/tcon/notes/pdf/2samuel.pdf.

[3] Warren W. Wiersbe, *Be Restored: Trusting God to See Us Through* (Colorado Springs: David C. Cook, 2002), 63.

[4] Wiersbe, 63.

[5] Charles R. Swindoll, *David: A Man of Passion and Destiny*, Great Lives from God's Word series (Dallas: Word Publishing, 1997), 162–68.

"(1) the line, or house, of David will always be the royal line; (2) the right to rule will always belong to David's offspring; (3) the right to a literal, earthly kingdom will never be taken from David's posterity."[6] This does not mean there were no pauses in this rule (Hosea 3:4–5).

The rule would always come through the Davidic kingdom (Luke 1:32–33). And, "the ultimate fulfillment of this promise will be realized at the Second Advent when Christ returns to reign over His people" (Revelation 20:1–6).[7] Second Samuel 7 points to Jesus' birth (Luke 1) and to His return (Revelation 20). Wiersbe divides David's prayer of thanksgiving into three sections.[8] First, David gave thanks for God's favor on his life in the *present* (vv. 18–21). Second, David gave thanks for what God had done for Israel in the *past* (vv. 22–24). Third, David gave thanks for what God had revealed about the *future* and asked God for the fulfillment of these promises (vv. 25–29).

Closing

Here are three interesting perspectives on this passage from pastor Jack Wellman[9]:

1. God sees the future (Isaiah 46:9–10).
2. God's ways are higher than ours (Psalm 33:11; Isaiah 55:8, 9).
3. We plan—God directs (Proverbs 10:9; 19:21; 20:24; Jeremiah 10:23).

In 2 Samuel 8, because David was resting in the Lord, David had victories: against the Philistines (v. 1), the Moabites (v. 2), the Arameans (v. 5), and the Edomites (v. 13). "So David reigned over all Israel, administering justice and righteousness for all his people" (v. 15). David began to walk out his calling because he allowed the Lord to speak in his life.

The Daily Word

While King David reigned over Israel, he enjoyed rest inside the palace walls and began to make his own plans. However, the Lord used the prophet Nathan to share a vision and speak a word of counsel to David. After David received the word from Nathan, he spent time in the Lord's presence, remembering God's faithfulness and giving thanks. David heeded the words and direction from the

---

[6] Earl D. Radmacher, Ronald B. Allen, and H. Wayne House, eds., *Nelson's New Illustrated Bible Commentary* (Nashville: Thomas Nelson, 1999), 399.

[7] Radmacher et al., 399.

[8] Wiersbe, 66.

[9] Jack Wellman, "3 Ways God's Plan Is Better Than Your Plan," Faith in the News, https://faithinthenews.com/3-ways-gods-plan-is-better-than-your-plan/.

Lord. He understood the eternal covenant with the Lord. Rather than pursuing his own plans, David followed the will of the Lord.

The Lord promises that when you trust in Him, He will direct your path. You may have an idea and begin to walk it out, but then God puts people or situations along your path to redirect or even postpone your plans. The Lord desires for you to be teachable and moldable. Don't be stubborn and set in your ways. Allow the Spirit of God to guide and direct you. And if you are questioning the change of plans, ask the Lord for confirmation. Then walk without wavering in confident faith. The Lord will determine your steps. His plans will prevail because His ways are higher than your ways, and His thoughts higher than your thoughts. Be assured through Christ you will have victory.

The Lord made David victorious wherever he went. So David reigned over all Israel, administering justice and righteousness for all his people. —2 Samuel 8:14–15

Further Scripture: Proverbs 16:9; Isaiah 55:8–9; James 1:6

Questions

1. Why did David want to build a house of cedar for the ark of God to dwell in? What was God's response? Have you ever found yourself putting God in some type of box? How?

2. In 2 Samuel 7:12–13 and 16, the Lord spoke of setting up a kingdom from David's descendants. Do you think this is pointing to Jesus and His eternal reign? Does Jesus come from the lineage of David (Matthew 1:1–17)?

3. How does God continue to keep His promises in 2 Samuel 8:3 (Genesis 15:18–21; 1 Chronicles 18:3)?

4. The Word of God has promised complete victory. As children of God, have we taken all the territory we have been promised, or is there some still occupied by the enemy (Galatians 5:13; Philippians 4:19)?

5. What did the Holy Spirit highlight to you in 2 Samuel 7—8 through the reading or the teaching?

Lesson 48: 2 Samuel 9—10

Eternal Throne: David's Grace to Mephibosheth

Teaching Notes

Intro

In 2 Samuel 7, we looked at the Davidic Covenant and God's promise that the house of David would reign forever through his descendant (Psalm 78:70–72). In Luke 1, that descendant is identified as Jesus, the Messiah. In 2 Samuel 8, God gave David victory over the Philistines, the Moabites, the Arameans, and the Edomites.

Teaching

Wiersbe divides this chapter into three actions for David: "Finding Mephibosheth" (vv. 1–4); "Calling Mephibosheth" (vv. 5–8); and "Enriching Mephibosheth" (vv. 9–13).[1]

2 Samuel 9:1–4: Jonathan and David had made a covenant in which David promised to care for Jonathan's family when he became king. After David became king, he asked if there were any surviving family members connected to his beloved friend, Jonathan (v. 1). This is another picture of David's integrity as a man of his word—he didn't wait for family members to come find him. Ziba, Saul's "estate manager,"[2] was summoned and David inquired who was left that he could show kindness to. Ziba shared that Jonathan's son who was injured in both feet had survived (vv. 2–3). Ziba gave the king instructions for how he could find Jonathan's son in Lo-debar (v. 4).

2 Samuel 9:5–8: David had Jonathan's son Mephibosheth brought to him (v. 5). Mephibosheth bowed down before David (v. 6). David had asked for *any* family member of Saul, and he found the son of Jonathan. Mephibosheth was five years

---

[1] Warren W. Wiersbe, *Be Restored: Trusting God to See Us Through* (Colorado Springs: David C. Cook, 2002), 72–74.

[2] Wiersbe, 73.

old when his father was killed in battle, and he wasn't born crippled. But, in a rush to flee after hearing of Jonathan's death, his nurse dropped him, and he was crippled (2 Samuel 4:4). Scholars estimate that Mephibosheth was about 20 years old when he was brought to David, and had a son named Mica (v. 12). Mephibosheth pledged himself as a servant of David, because "it was usual in the Middle East for founders of new dynasties to kill the children of former rulers to keep them from trying to regain the throne in the name of their families."[3] David told Mephibosheth not to be afraid because he was going to restore all of Saul's lands to Mephibosheth (v. 7a). Plus, David would treat Mephibosheth as family at his table (v. 7b). Mephibosheth wondered why David would show such generosity to "a dead dog" like him (v. 8). Dogs "were regarded as unclean scavengers, and were generally viewed with contempt," so using the expression shows Mephibosheth's "low self-image and his astonishment at the grace being shown him"[4] (Proverbs 26:11). Mephibosheth saw himself as worthless.

2 Samuel 9:9–13: David summoned Ziba and explained all he had restored to Mephibosheth (v. 9). David also told Ziba that he along with his fifteen sons, and his twenty servants would now work for Mephibosheth by tending the crops. Mephibosheth would be made part of David's family and would eat at David's table (vv. 10–11). The Gospel of Luke explains the importance of having a seat at the table (Luke 13:29–30; 14:12–24; 22:29–30). God has made a place for all people at His table. Verse 13 concludes the chapter with the statement that Mephibosheth ate all his meals at the king's table, so his inheritance went to his son.

Closing

Chuck Swindoll wrote, "It is, in my personal opinion, the greatest illustration of grace in all the Old Testament."[5] Think how Mephibosheth was raised. He had been lame for years, "was hiding in a place of barrenness, and was fearful of the king. . . . David took the initiative to seek out Mephibosheth in spite of his unloveliness, bring him into his house and presence, and adopt him as his own son"[6] (Psalm 23:6). Likewise, believers are truly blessed for nothing we have done ourselves. All of us are in a state of "Lo-debar" and can do *nothing*

---

[3] Earl D. Radmacher, Ronald B. Allen, and H. Wayne House, eds., *Nelson's New Illustrated Bible Commentary* (Nashville: Thomas Nelson, 1999), 402.

[4] Radmacher et al., 402.

[5] Charles R. Swindoll, *David: A Man of Passion and Destiny*, Great Lives from God's Word series (Dallas: Word Publishing, 1997), 169.

[6] Thomas L. Constable, *Expository Notes of Dr. Thomas Constable: 2 Samuel*, 76, http://planobiblechapel.org/tcon/notes/pdf/2samuel.pdf.

to help ourselves out. We are in a state of barrenness that can only be made whole through Christ. No other religion can make this claim because each one demands the follower's good outweigh the bad. That is not the case with Christ, who is calling us to Him:

- Romans 9:16: "So then it does not depend on human will or effort but on God who shows mercy." It's not about our own efforts.
- Galatians 5:2: "Take note! I, Paul, tell you that if you get yourselves circumcised, Christ will not benefit you at all." It's not about our works.
- Acts 13:39: "And everyone who believes in Him is justified from everything that you could not be justified from through the law of Moses." It's not about following all the laws.
- Galatians 2:16: "Know that no one is justified by the works of the law but by faith in Jesus Christ. And we have believed in Christ Jesus so that we might be justified by faith in Christ and not by the works of the law, because by the works of the law no human being will be justified." You don't find your worth in what you do.
- 2 Timothy 1:9: "He has saved us and called us with a holy calling, not according to our works, but according to His own purpose and grace, which was given to us in Christ Jesus before time began." It's not about our works.
- Titus 3:4–5: "But when the kindness of God our Savior and His love for mankind appeared, He saved us—not by works of righteousness that we had done, but according to His mercy, through the washing of regeneration and renewal by the Holy Spirit." It is all from the Lord and not from ourselves.

Mephibosheth received from David what we have received through Jesus Christ, "For you are saved by grace through faith, and this is not from yourselves; it is God's gift—not from works, so that no one can boast" (Ephesians 2:8–9). For us, though, it is an eternal gift. We have been given a seat at the table, "for we are His creation, created in Christ Jesus for good works, which God prepared ahead of time so that we should walk in them" (Ephesians 2:10).

Mephibosheth became the adopted son of King David, and he never knew want or loneliness again. Romans 8:15 says, "For you did not receive a spirit of slavery to fall back into fear, but you received the Spirit of adoption, by whom we cry out, 'Abba, Father!'"

The Daily Word

David wondered if anyone was left in Saul's family to show kindness to because of his dear friend Jonathan. Saul's servant, Ziba, remembered Saul's crippled grandson Mephibosheth, who lived far away in Lo-debar. David had Mephibosheth brought to him, and Mephibosheth arrived afraid of why David had requested his presence. David assured him to not be afraid and welcomed Mephibosheth to eat every meal at his table and promised to restore Saul's fields to him. These were unexpected and untypical gifts to give a crippled person like Mephibosheth.

David offered Mephibosheth unmerited favor—God's grace. Mephibosheth did nothing to deserve it, and yet David sought him out, lavishing upon him lovingkindness. Friends, the same is true for you. The Lord chased after you and drew you to His love. The Lord's love is not based on your good works but because God the Father sees you and calls you His child. You are freely and wholly adopted into His kingdom and welcomed at the Lord's table. *He loves you just as you are*, imperfections and all, and He will lavish upon you good and perfect gifts. Today, receive His grace. He has a seat ready for you at His table, just sit down and enjoy His presence day after day!

David said, "Mephibosheth!" "I am your servant," he replied. "Don't be afraid," David said to him, "since I intended to show you kindness because of your father Jonathan, I will restore to you all your grandfather Saul's fields, and you will always eat meals at my table." —2 Samuel 9:6–7

Further Scripture: Romans 8:15; Ephesians 1:5; Titus 3:4–5

Questions

1. Why was it important for David to show kindness to a descendant of Saul for Jonathan's sake (1 Samuel 18:1–4)?
2. Why did David tell Mephibosheth not to fear (2 Samuel 9:7)?
3. Why did David give Mephibosheth all the land belonging to Saul (Numbers 36:7)?
4. What could have been the reason that Hanun chose the method of shaving the beards and cutting off the garments to humiliate the Ammonites?
5. What did the Holy Spirit highlight to you in 2 Samuel 9—10 through the reading or the teaching?

Lesson 49: 2 Samuel 11—12

Eternal Throne: David's Progressive Slide into Sin

Teaching Notes

Intro

This is a week of studies of the big stories in 2 Samuel. First, we looked at the Davidic Covenant, and then we looked at how David fulfilled his covenant with Jonathan by adopting Jonathan's son Mephibosheth into his own family. Today's passage looks at the break with Israel through David's sin with Bathsheba. "Even though David had been faithful to Jonathan in keeping his covenant with him, he was not faithful to Jehovah in keeping His covenant with Israel."[1] Constable introduces his commentary on 2 Samuel 11 with this statement: "This chapter records perhaps the third most notorious sin in the Bible, after the Fall and Judas' betrayal of Jesus."[2] Even in this context, the Davidic Covenant still holds, and the *Eternal Throne* will still happen.

Teaching

2 Samuel 11:1–2: *Nelson's Commentary* explains, "Kings in the ancient Middle East went to battle in the spring of the year, when they could be assured of good weather and an abundance of food along the way."[3] However, David sent his commander and all his soldiers for war, but he remained in Jerusalem (v. 1). Wiersbe points to the issue of idleness in David's life and states, "Idleness isn't just the absence of activity . . . idleness is also activity to no purpose."[4] (Luke 9:62). David got out of the groove of what he was called to do. David rose from his bed and went out on the roof and, from a distance, saw that a very beautiful woman was bathing (v. 2). When we are idle, our imagination kicks in and we

---

[1] Thomas L. Constable, *Expository Notes of Dr. Thomas Constable: 2 Samuel*, 80, http://planobiblechapel.org/tcon/notes/pdf/2samuel.pdf.

[2] Constable, 80.

[3] Earl D. Radmacher, Ronald B. Allen, and H. Wayne House, eds., *Nelson's New Illustrated Bible Commentary* (Nashville: Thomas Nelson, 1999), 403–4.

[4] Warren W. Wiersbe, *Be Restored: Trusting God to See Us Through* (Colorado Springs: David C. Cook, 2002), 82.

tend to take our eyes off Jesus. Swindoll points out: "This king who took another man's wife already had a harem full of women. The simple fact is that the passion of sex is not satisfied by a full harem of women; it is increased. Having many women does not reduce a man's libido, it excites it . . . it stimulates it. . . . One of the lies of our secular society is that if you just satisfy this drive, then it'll be abated."[5] David created an environment that this happened. He needed to flee the scene (Matthew 5:27–28). He needed to go back inside or head to war with his men.

The year before, the Arameans and the Ammonites had fled from David's approaching army and the Ammonites had gone into the city of Rabbah for protection (2 Samuel 10:14). Joab returned with the army a year later to besiege the city of Rabbah. Swindoll writes, "Our most difficult times are not when things are going hard. Hard times create dependent people. You don't get proud when you're dependent on God. Survival keeps you humble. Pride is what happens when everything is swinging in your direction."[6]

2 Samuel 11:3–5: David found out the woman's identity was Bathsheba and sent messengers to bring her to him (vv. 3–4a). David was in the position of authority over her. David and Bathsheba had sexual relations, and then she returned home. When Bathsheba came to David, she had just gone through ritual purification after menstruation. Bathsheba became pregnant and let David know (vv. 4b–5). Under the law, their adultery was evil, and both should have been killed (Leviticus 20:10; Deuteronomy 22:22). That didn't happen, and David didn't repent, so his evilness and sin progressed. First John 1:9 explains that we are to confess our sins, no matter what we've done, and God will forgive us.

2 Samuel 11:6–13: To take care of his sin problem, David sent a message to Joab to send Uriah the Hittite, Bathsheba's husband, to him with news of how the war was going (v. 6). After receiving Uriah's report, David told him to go to his house and "wash his feet," meaning to sleep with his wife (vv. 7–8).[7] David even gave food to Uriah to take home. But Uriah did not go to his house, choosing instead to stay with his soldiers (v. 9). When David questioned Uriah about why he didn't go home, Uriah stated that the ark, Israel and Judah, Joab, and his soldiers were all dwelling in tents, so how could he possibly sleep in a bed with his wife (vv. 10–11)? Uriah had the same heart David had shown when he wanted to build God a temple to dwell in. David told Uriah to stay in Jerusalem until the

---

[5] Charles R. Swindoll, *David: A Man of Passion and Destiny*, Great Lives from God's Word series (Dallas: Word Publishing, 1997), 182.

[6] Swindoll, 183.

[7] Constable, 84.

next day and invited him to eat and drink with him that evening (vv. 12–13). David kept passing the cup to Uriah, hoping that if Uriah became drunk, he would return to his wife. Even drunk, Uriah held to his integrity.

2 Samuel 11:14–21: When all his manipulations of Uriah didn't work, David wrote Joab a letter, which he gave to Uriah to deliver (v. 14). In verse 15, David sent Uriah to deliver his own death sentence. David told Joab to put Uriah on the front lines of the worst fighting and then pull back so Uriah was left alone to face the enemy (Proverbs 6:23–33). Joab followed David's instructions, and Uriah died in battle (vv. 16–17). Notice that Joab did not follow David's instructions exactly, because his soldiers did not retreat and leave Uriah alone. Some of David's men also died in the battle. Joab sent word to David, anticipating David would question why his soldiers died in the battle. Joab told the messenger to tell David that Uriah died with the soldiers (vv. 18–21).

2 Samuel 11:22–27: The messenger delivered Joab's message, explaining the army had counterattacked and were shot down by archers, killing some soldiers and Uriah (vv. 22–24). David took the news as though the loss of life were no big deal (v. 25). Bathsheba mourned the death of her husband (v. 26). When the time of mourning was over, Bathsheba returned to David and became his eighth wife, and she bore him a son. "However, the LORD considered what David had done to be evil" (v. 27).

Despite the evilness David had done, God would redeem him. Matthew 1:6 records the lineage of Jesus: "Jesse fathered King David. Then David fathered Solomon by Uriah's wife." There was such respect for Uriah that he was listed in David's line. In Matthew 1, four women are listed: Tamar, Rahab, Ruth, and Uriah's wife (Bathsheba). Three of these were marked with sin.

Their presence in this list of male ancestors give evidence of "the principle of the sovereign grace of God, who not only is able to use the foreign (and perhaps even the disreputable) to accomplish his eternal purposes, but even seems to delight in doing so."[8]

Closing

I want to wrap this up by addressing sexual sin. David was not where he was supposed to be, and when confronted with Bathsheba, he didn't keep his eyes on the Lord. If he had, this story would be different. Constable provides several suggestions of how to protect ourselves from falling into sexual sin:[9]

---

[8] A. Carr, *The Gospel According to St. Matthew* (Cambridge: University Press, 1913), 81.
[9] Constable, 87–88.

1.   None of us are immune to sexual sin (Corinthians 10:12).

2.   We must focus daily on the Lord (Luke 22:46; Romans 6:12–13).

3.   We must develop intimacy in our marriages (Philippians 4:11).

4.   We must develop accountability with our spouses.

5.   We should expect sexual temptation, and evade it at all costs.

When you see temptation, run. David didn't.

The Daily Word

While David's men were in battle, David chose to remain in Jerusalem. He was away from his army, his team, and his routine. In this situation, David committed adultery with Bathsheba, Uriah's wife. As a result, Bathsheba conceived a child, causing David to devise plans to cover up his sin of adultery. However, those plans didn't work. So David plotted for Uriah to be killed on the front lines of battle. One sin led to another. David may have thought he had deceived those around him, as he ended up marrying Bathsheba and having a son, but the Lord saw it all. The Lord saw exactly what David was doing in secret, and although David's eternal covenant would not change with the Lord, David would face consequences of his sin.

Secret sin. You may think no one knows. You take a break from your regular routine, step away from your team, your group, your people . . . and temptation hits you. The enemy knows your weaknesses, and he wants to disarm your power in the kingdom. If you are in the middle of a secret sin, you need to know the Lord sees you. You may think you are hidden, but the Lord knows. However, despite your sin, He loves you. Just as He did not break covenant with David, He does not break covenant with you. However, *it is time to stop hiding*. God's grace is always available, and His mercies are new each morning. Allow light to shine in the secret places of your life. Confess to the Lord, then share with a trusted person in your life, and turn away from the wicked ways. Free yourself of secrets, and you will find an abundant life with Christ!

"You acted in secret, but I will do this before all Israel and in broad daylight." David responded to Nathan, "I have sinned against the Lord." Then Nathan replied to David, "The Lord has taken away your sin; you will not die." —2 Samuel 12:12–13

Further Scripture: Psalm 69:5; James 5:16a; 1 John 1:9

Questions

1. Instead of fulfilling his calling, David stayed back in Jerusalem rather than going to battle with his men. Do you believe he was walking in the flesh rather than following the Spirit (his calling)? Was there ever a time when you were tempted to follow the flesh rather than your calling?

2. In 2 Samuel 11:4, David sent his messengers to bring Bathsheba to him. Why would he do this knowing that she was Uriah's wife (Exodus 20:14, 17)?

3. In 2 Samuel 12:13, the Lord quickly forgave David of his sin (Psalm 51:4; 1 John 1:9). Why did the child still die? Can you think of a time in your life when you sought forgiveness for your sin, and knew God had forgiven you, but still had to face the lingering consequences? Might it be helpful to remember this the next time you are tempted to sin?

4. Why was it that when David sinned against the Lord (2 Samuel 12:14), it gave the enemies of the Lord great occasion to blaspheme (Romans 2:24)? How about when we sin?

5. In 2 Samuel 12:23, David said, "I will go to him, but he will not return to me." Where did David mean that the child would go? What kind of hope should this give us?

6. Referring to 2 Samuel 12:24–25, why did God send the prophet Nathan to David to announce that He loved Solomon, and why did the Lord name him Jedidiah?

7. What did the Holy Spirit highlight to you in 2 Samuel 11—12 through the reading or the teaching?

Lesson 50: 2 Samuel 13—14

Eternal Throne: The Sins of David's Sons

Teaching Notes

Intro

Second Samuel has felt like an ongoing drama series of David's life—drama, adventure, and a whole lot of sin. That's basically the gist of 2 Samuel. We see David in 1 Samuel as a representative of the *Anointed One* and his calling in 2 Samuel is with the *Eternal Throne*. But, in the middle of all that, David showed he was not perfect. The amazing part of all this is that the *Eternal Throne* was not dependent upon David's perfection. That's the same for us—nothing in our relationship with the Lord is based on our works.

We've studied the Davidic Covenant with God's promise that David's line would reign forever, and we've studied David's covenant with Jonathan, that he would look after Jonathan's descendants. We saw that lived out in David's grace to, and adoption of, Jonathan's son Mephibosheth. Yesterday, we looked at David's adulterous relationship with Bathsheba and his sin of murder.

2 Timothy 2:22 says, "Flee from youthful passions, and pursue righteousness, faith, love, and peace, along with those who call on the Lord from a pure heart." This verse is the framework for our study of 2 Samuel 13.

Teaching

2 Samuel 13:1–9: David had a lustful eye where Bathsheba was concerned, and his son Amnon had a lustful eye for his half-brother Absalom's sister, Tamar (v. 1). Absalom's mother (and Tamar's) was Maacah, the daughter of the king of Geshur, and Amnon's mother was Ahinoam.[1] The word "infatuated" indicates Amnon was obsessed and lustful toward Tamar. Amnon was David's firstborn, and Absalom was the third-born son.

Amnon was physically sick over his sister Tamar because she was a virgin (v. 2) (Leviticus 18:11). Amnon's friend and cousin Jonadab was shrewd and

---

[1] Earl D. Radmacher, Ronald B. Allen, and H. Wayne House, eds., *Nelson's New Illustrated Bible Commentary* (Nashville: Thomas Nelson, 1999), 407.

experienced and questioned why Amnon was miserable.[2] Amnon explained he was in love with his brother's sister (vv. 3–4). Jonadab offered a plan—Amnon was to pretend to be sick and ask David to send his sister Tamar to him to prepare food for him (v. 5). Amnon did as Jonadab suggested, and David did as Amnon asked (vv. 6–7). It feels as though David was also guilty in this scenario by handing his daughter over to Amnon. Tamar prepared food in Amnon's presence. When it was ready, Amnon sent everyone else away and went into his bedroom to be fed (vv. 8–9). We have to learn to *run from* youthful passions (Romans 6:12; 1 Corinthians 6:18–19; Colossians 3:5; 1 Peter 2:11).

2 Samuel 13:10–20: When Tamar brought food to Amnon, he grabbed her and told her to come sleep with him (vv. 10–11). She begged him not to humiliate her, "for such a thing should never be done in Israel" (v. 12). Tamar even suggested that Amnon talk to David about marrying her (v. 13). Recognize that what Amnon wanted was incest, and he got what he wanted by raping his half-sister (v. 14). Amnon forced her and humiliated her. He cared nothing for what Tamar felt or wanted.

Afterward, Scripture says Amnon hated Tamar and threw her out (v. 15). Tamar begged him not to throw her out, but he had the door bolted behind her (vv. 16–18a). Tamar was wearing the dress of the king's virgin daughters—a long-sleeved garment. She tore the garment, put ashes on her head, and walked away with her hand on her head as signs of mourning (vv. 18b–19) (Job 1:20; 2:12; Jeremiah 2:37). Absalom found out what happened and took Tamar into his house to avoid public shame (v. 20).

2 Samuel 13:20–29: When the king found out what Amnon had done to Tamar, he was furious but doesn't seem to do anything about it (v. 21). Absalom remained silent (v. 22). Both David and Absalom knew Tamar had been raped and took no immediate action. Two years later, Absalom invited David, his sons, and his servants to come see the new sheepshearers he hired (vv. 23–24). When David declined to bring them all, Absalom asked that Amnon be allowed to go (vv. 25–26a). David asked why Amnon should go, and Absalom begged, and David allowed it (vv. 26b–27). David seems to have been a passive father who chose not to deal with the problems within his family. David sent Amnon and all of his sons. Absalom took on the role of his father to take revenge on his brother and told his men to be ready to strike Amnon down when he told them to (v. 28). The young men did as Absalom commanded, and the rest of David's sons fled the scene (v. 29).

---

[2] Radmacher et al., 407.

2 Samuel 13:30–39: When word got to King David, he was told that *all* of his sons had been struck down, and he was overcome with grief (vv. 30–31). But Jonadab told David what really happened and explained Absalom had planned this since the day Tamar was raped (vv. 32–33). Jonadab, the former friend of Amnon, was doing a good job of working the system. Absalom fled, while his surviving brothers returned to David, just as Jonadab had said (vv. 34–35). David, his sons, and his servants wept over the loss of Amnon (v. 36). Absalom fled to the king of Geshur, while David continued to mourn for Amnon every day (v. 37). Absalom stayed in Geshur three years until David began to long for his son Absalom (vv. 38–39).

Closing

Because Amnon did not run from youthful passions, chaos consumed the family. When people fall into sin, they tend to forget the impact their sin will have on their families. Things get messy! We must *run from* these youthful passions. Instead, we must *run to* and pursue righteousness, faith, love, and peace. Because none of this happened, chaos followed. And we must make sure we choose to *run along* with those who call on the Lord from a pure heart.

The Daily Word

David's son, Amnon, had lustful desires for his half-sister, Tamar. Rather than seeking the counsel of someone who walked uprightly with the Lord, Amnon shared his feelings with his shrewd cousin, Jonadab. Then Jonadab devised a plan for Amnon to be alone with Tamar. The plan worked, enabling Amnon to act on his lustful feelings by raping his sister. As things unfolded, Amnon was later murdered by his brother Absalom in revenge. David's family found themselves in chaos. Rather than flee the temptation to sin, Amnon gave into it, and its effects cascaded through several families.

Believers are to stand firm and not give into temptation. You are instructed to *flee* from your fleshly desires. Fleeing involves speed and effort. You flee when a situation is dangerous and you need to get away quickly. Fleeing sexual immorality may mean quickly leaving a room to get away from someone you know may lead to lustful thoughts or actions. It may mean leaving your computer, TV, or phone if you have a temptation to view pornography. You resist the temptation. Then you align yourself with people who will encourage you to stand strong and seek the things of Christ. *The Lord has given you strength and power to stand strong, and His Spirit is great within you for help and guidance.* Call upon the name of the Lord. You will be stronger when you flee.

> When she brought them to him to eat, he grabbed her and said, "Come sleep with me, my sister!" —2 Samuel 13:11
>
> Further Scripture: 1 Corinthians 6:18; 2 Timothy 2:22; 1 Peter 2:11

Questions

1. What sin was Amnon blatantly disregarding toward Tamar (Leviticus 18:9–11; 20:17; Deuteronomy 27:22)? Do you believe his father's example with Bathsheba influenced him?

2. How should Amnon have reacted when he immediately started having feelings for Tamar (Genesis 39:9–10; Matthew 5:27–30; 2 Timothy 2:22)?

3. What did Tamar say to try and convince Amnon that what he was doing was evil and foolish? Why do you think he did not take her advice?

4. What was Absalom's plan for his servants against Amnon? How long after Tamar's rape did Absalom wait to implement his plan?

5. Did reconciliation happen for David and his son Absalom in 2 Samuel 14? Has there been a time in your life when you have made reconciliation with someone? Was it hard for you to do?

6. 2 Samuel 14:14b says, "Yet God does not take away life, but plans ways so that the banished one will not be cast out from Him." How would you describe this characteristic of God (2 Peter 3:9)?

7. What did the Holy Spirit highlight to you in 2 Samuel 13—14 through the reading or the teaching?

Lesson 51: 2 Samuel 15—16

Eternal Throne: Absalom's Rebellion Against the King

Teaching Notes

Intro

In 2 Samuel 13, David's son Amnon raped his half-sister, Tamar. Her brother, Absalom, waited two years before having his men kill Amnon in retribution. King David was distraught with grief and mourned Amnon's death daily. Absalom had to flee Israel and was gone three years before he and David were reconciled in chapter 14. In chapter 15, Absalom began to scheme against David's throne and even declared himself king (2 Samuel 15:10). As Absalom and his army approached Jerusalem, David fled with his servants, and the people of Jerusalem followed (2 Samuel 15:14). When Absalom and David's armies eventually face each other, 20,000 are killed (2 Samuel 18:6–8). That gives both the background on chapter 16 and a sense of where the conflict was heading.

Teaching

2 Samuel 16:1–4: After David fled Jerusalem from Absalom's approaching army, he was met by Mephibosheth's servant Ziba, who had supplies for David and his servants (vv. 1–2). David asked where Mephibosheth was. Ziba responded that Mephibosheth had stayed behind, anticipating that Saul's kingdom would be restored to him (v. 3). David then gave everything Mephibosheth owned to Ziba (v. 4). Although David accepted what Ziba said, there was a lie in it. Ziba was working on a set up to cover themselves.

2 Samuel 16:5–8: David went on to Bahurim. Shimei, son of Gera, a relative of Saul's, came out of a house and began cursing at David and throwing stones at David and the people—the servants, the people from Jerusalem, and even David's mighty soldiers (vv. 5–6). Shimei even accused David of being a murderer (2 Samuel 3:27–29; 4:1–12; 7:25–27) and told David that God had given his kingdom to Absalom (vv. 7–8). Shimei's words were obviously not from the Lord, but there was some truth there as well.

2 Samuel 16:9–14: Abishai, David's nephew, described Shimei as a "dead dog" and suggested David allow him to quiet Shimei by cutting his head off (v. 9). We saw the phrase "dead dog," which meant worthless and despised, applied to Mephibosheth as well in his situation before David found him. David stated that Shimei was bringing the Lord's word against him, and even his son Absalom was coming to kill him (v. 11). Instead of accepting Abishai's suggestion, David showed patience and restraint (v. 12). Shimei continued to follow David and his men, cursing David and throwing stones and dirt at him (v. 13). Shimei had become David's "thorn in the flesh," a constant irritation that didn't stop (2 Corinthians 12:7–10). The only way to handle this kind of attack is to find peace in the Lord. David and his servants were exhausted from this constant attack by the time they stopped for rest (v. 14).

2 Samuel 16:15–19: Meanwhile, Absalom and the Israelites who followed him arrived in Jerusalem. Ahithophel, one of David's counselors, who was considered to be an "oracle of God," was with him (v. 15). Possibly just as important is that Ahithophel was Bathsheba's grandfather.[1] In verse 16, David's friend Hushai appeared before Absalom, proclaiming, "Long live the King!" Absalom asked where Hushai's loyalty was (v. 17). Hushai responded that since he served the one the Lord had chosen, King David, Absalom's father, likewise he would serve the son (vv. 18–19).

2 Samuel 16:20–23: Absalom asked Ahithophel for advice for what to do next (v. 20). Ahithophel told Absalom to sleep with the ten concubines David left behind in Jerusalem so he would become repulsive to David (v. 21). By sleeping with David's concubines, or unofficial wives, Absalom would be asserting his right to David's throne.[2] Absalom had a tent pitched on the roof of the palace, and he took each of David's concubines, allowing all of Israel to see what was happening (v. 22). This was all prophesied by Nathan in 2 Samuel 12:11–12 in an announcement of David's sin. I wonder if some of Shimei's curses included a statement about Nathan's prophecy coming true. The advice Absalom received to take this action came from other family members. The chapter concludes with the statement that Ahithophel's advice was accepted as someone who was speaking God's word (v. 23).

---

[1] John MacArthur, *The MacArthur Bible Commentary* (Nashville: Thomas Nelson, 2005), 373.

[2] Earl D. Radmacher, Ronald B. Allen, and H. Wayne House, eds., *Nelson's New Illustrated Bible Commentary* (Nashville: Thomas Nelson, 1999), 414.

Closing

When the enemy comes at us with lies and accusations, do we respond in strength and faith? Here are three suggestions:

1. *Resist the lies of the enemy.* The enemy is a liar and the father of lies (John 8:44), who comes to steal, kill, and destroy (John 10:10). "Therefore, submit to God. But resist the Devil, and he will flee from you" (James 4:7).

2. *Know the Father's voice so you can distinguish it from the enemy's.* Followers of Christ know His voice (John 10:27), and continue in His word (John 8:31–32). And nothing can separate us from His love (Romans 8:12, 39).

3. *Walk confidently in your position in Christ!* We have been raised up with Christ and seated beside Him (Ephesians 2:6), who is above all rulers and authorities (Ephesians 1:20–21). He has rescued us from evil (Colossians 1:13–14; 2:14–15). Jesus took away the enemy's most valued and used weapon—accusation—and transformed us into His image (Romans 12:2).

Once you start to embrace the voice of the Holy Spirit in you life, you will begin to walk out that anointing in 1 John 2:20 with confidence. This is what David had to get to, to walk out his anointing regardless of what comes his way.

The Daily Word

As David and his men journeyed away from the palace, a man named Shimei, son of Gera, began to yell curses at David. He even threw stones and dirt at David. David and his men were exhausted from the journey and from the stress Shimei caused them, so they stopped to rest.

Can you imagine having stones and dirt thrown at you or curses yelled at you while on a journey? If you stop for a minute and think about it, you probably can relate. Think about your own walk with the Lord and the insults or the lies from the enemy that have come your way. These lies can beat you down to the point of exhaustion, leaving you with no strength to stand. However, the Lord promises that, in your weakness, you are made strong through His sufficient grace. So in the midst of any attack thrown at you, draw strength from the Lord and His truth. Remember your anointing from the Lord. When you embrace your anointing, no matter what comes your way, you will be able to stand strong. The Lord triumphs over the enemy and has the victory!

So David and his men proceeded along the road as Shimei was going along the ridge of the hill opposite him. As Shimei went, he cursed David, and

threw stones and dirt at him. Finally, the king and all the people with him arrived exhausted, so they rested there. —2 Samuel 16:13–14

Further Scripture: 2 Corinthians 12:7b–10; Colossians 2:15; 1 John 2:20

Questions

1. What was Absalom doing to get the people to fall in love with him? Was this tactic working? What was his end goal?

2. What are some similarities, having both been betrayed by people close to them, between how David dealt with Absalom and how Jesus dealt with Judas (2 Samuel 15:9–23; Matthew 26:36; John 13:27)?

3. How did God acknowledge David's faith in 2 Samuel 15:24–29?

4. What was the result of David praying what he did in 2 Samuel 15:31? David's heart was heavy at this point in his life (Psalm 41:9; 55:11–14). How do you think you would have prayed in that situation?

5. In 2 Samuel 16, what did Shimei blame David for? How did David handle the accusation (2 Samuel 15:26)? How did Shimei break the law by saying these things (Exodus 22:28)?

6. What did the Holy Spirit highlight to you in 2 Samuel 15—16 through the reading or the teaching?

Lesson 52: 2 Samuel 17—18

Eternal Throne: Absalom's Fall

Teaching Notes

Intro

Hushai and Ahithophel gave David different advice. When David didn't take Ahithophel's advice, Ahithophel hung himself. David's son, Absalom, decided to chase after David across the Jordan. While on the run, David gained some support.

Teaching

2 Samuel 18:1–3: In chapter 18, Joab becomes the dominant personality. Something had happened to David. After, the sin of Bathsheba, David became passive. It doesn't appear that he was walking out what his strengths normally were. Yet, he was a man after God's own heart. As David reviewed his troops, he broke them into thirds. One third was placed under the command of Joab, one third was placed under the command of Joab's brother Abishai, and the last third was placed under the command of Ittai. David expressed his intention to march out with the army, but the people begged him to stay behind to protect the city (vv. 2–3).

2 Samuel 18:4–5: David did as the people requested and encouraged the army as they went out. But David instructed Joab to take it easy on Absalom even though Absalom was the one behind the whole problem. And the army heard him!

2 Samuel 18:6–8: We don't know exactly where the forest of Ephraim was, but it was a dense forest where David's army marched out to encounter Israel's army that was under the command of Absalom. Absalom was out to kill his father, but his army was soundly defeated by David's army. The forest was so treacherous it claimed more lives than the sword in this battle. That had to be the Lord's hand!

2 Samuel 18:9: Absalom found himself dangling with his head caught in a tree. *Nelson's Commentary* outlined six characteristics of Absalom:

1. *Appearance*—"No man in all Israel was as handsome and highly praised as Absalom. From the sole of his foot to the top of his head, he did not have a single flaw. When he shaved his head—he shaved it every year because his hair got so heavy for him that he had to shave it off—he would weigh the hair from his head and it would be five pounds according to the royal standard" (2 Samuel 14:25–26). No one else in Scripture was ever described as flawless like Absalom was! Ironically, Absalom's hair probably got him stuck in the tree because he had not shaved it yet.

2. *Affluence*—Absalom was the son of a king, so he most likely owned his own palace at Baal Hazor. At the same time, Absalom employed sheep shearers.

3. *Advantage*—Absalom was in line as David's heir to the throne and had David's heart. David truly loved him. Even after Absalom killed Amnon, David mourned that Absalom was absent for three years.

4. *Anger*—Absalom took revenge on Amnon when Amnon raped his sister, Tamar.

5. *Ambition*—After two years of exile, Absalom began building a base of power without David knowing about it. He built a rebellion to get rid of David.

6. *Anguish*—His army was defeated by David's army, and he found himself stuck in a tree, hanging by his hair.[1]

Absalom didn't have to go this route. He was next in line for the throne! But when you don't wait on the Lord's timing, things don't always turn out well for you.

2 Samuel 18:10–15: One of David's men happened upon Absalom hanging in a tree and reported it to Joab. Joab wondered why the soldier didn't strike him down, but the soldier remembered David's exhortation that they were not to harm Absalom. Here, Joab stepped out of line. David wanted his commanders to be gentle to Absalom, but Joab took the first opportunity he had to kill him. Once Absalom was taken care of, the war would be ended, so Joab didn't want to mess around. Absalom died while hanging in a tree, which meant he died under a curse (Deuteronomy 21:22–23). Absalom didn't die on a tree because his enemies hung him there. It seems as though God orchestrated these events.

2 Samuel 18:16–17: Joab blew a horn to call off the attack. Since Absalom was dead, Joab knew the war was over. Even though he had been the king's son, Absalom's body was thrown into a pit. They piled stones on his body, which is

---

[1] Earl D. Radmacher, Ronald B. Allen, and H. Wayne House, eds., *Nelson's New Illustrated Bible Commentary* (Nashville: Thomas Nelson, 1999), 417.

a picture of stoning. In Old Testament law, rebellious sons were supposed to be executed by stoning. Absalom was the ultimate rebellious son.

2 Samuel 18:18–23: Two men wanted to run to tell the king the news about Absalom's death: Ahimaaz and the Cushite, who was probably an Ethiopian. In their minds, they were running to deliver the good news to the king that Absalom was dead and no longer a threat to the king. The Cushite chose a direct route through rugged terrain to get to the king. He was probably an experienced herald and a trained runner. Ahimaaz had taken messages to David before in Jerusalem and may have known the terrain better because he took a less direct route, but arrived first.

2 Samuel 18:24–33: David expected good news based on the fact that each of the runners were running alone. Ahimaaz arrived first and reported victory for David's army, but did not tell him about Absalom's fate. Ahimaaz might have had good intentions, but he didn't deliver the whole truth. He froze and didn't deliver the good news about David's rebellious son dying. David asked the Cushite about Absalom and the Cushite did not cushion the news about Absalom's death. The Cushite wished the same fate on every one of David's enemies. But David was still distraught at the news of Absalom's death.

Closing

David seemed to hope to the very end that Absalom would turn around. David loved his son in a way that reminds us of how God the Father truly loves us. David was ready to do whatever it took to draw his son back to him just as God the Father sent Jesus to bring us back to Him. Because of the death of Christ, we can embrace the good news that the Son has died because the Son came back to life.

First John 4:10 says, "Love consists in this: not that we loved God, but that He loved us and sent His Son to be the propitiation for our sins." God loves everyone in the world this way. John 3:16 says, "For God loved the world in this way: He gave His One and Only Son, so that everyone who believes in Him will not perish but have eternal life." God's plan always came back to His Son. Romans 8:3 says, "What the law could not do since it was limited by the flesh, God did. He condemned sin in the flesh by sending His own Son in flesh like ours under sin's domain, and as a sin offering."

Jesus, He died for us. That is the greatest news you will ever hear. The best part is, He came back to life. Because He came back to life, we can have life as well.

The Daily Word

Absalom, the son of King David, died in battle as David's troops pursued Israel. In response, Joab blew the ram's horn to assemble the troops, signaling the battle was over. Afterwards, the men gathered to discuss who would go and share the news with King David. Two men wanted to run to share the "good news." Each man ran a different route, arrived at different times, and conveyed the same "good news" but did so in different ways. Neither runner shared the "good news" directly or truthfully to King David. Although David's kingdom was restored because of the victory in battle, he was deeply grieved by the "good news" his son had died.

As followers of Christ, the Good News you carry is about the death of *the* Son. Even though Jesus' death grieved God the Father, it brings victory and hope as it covers the sins of those who believe. Will you deliver the good news directly and truthfully? The truth is God loved the world so much He gave His one and only Son so that everyone who believes in Him will not perish but have eternal life. This is the good news about the death of *the* Son you are called to deliver for the glory and honor of God's kingdom! Today, put on your running shoes and deliver the good news of the Gospel!

The watchman saw another man running. He called out to the gatekeeper, "Look! Another man is running alone!" "This one is also bringing good news," said the king. —2 Samuel 18:26

Further Scripture: John 3:16; Romans 10:15; 1 John 4:10

Questions

1. What was Ahithophel's counsel to Absalom about pursuing David? Compare this with the plot of Caiaphas in John 11:50 against the Son of David. What other part of this advice reminds us of the Messiah (2 Samuel 17:2b; Matthew 26:31)?

2. Two different men offer Absalom what sounds like good counsel. How did Absalom and the elders of Israel choose which advice to follow (2 Samuel 15:34; 17:14)? Have you ever been faced with opposing counsel and had to hear from the Lord to know what to do?

3. Machir the son of Ammiel from Lo-debar was one of the men who brought provisions to David and those with him. What else have we read about this man in 2 Samuel 9:4?

4. When David and those with him were on the run from Absalom, was there any planning or strategy involved (2 Samuel 18:1–3)? When we are under

attack from our enemy, where should we turn for an informed and strategic response (Romans 10:3–5; Ephesians 6:11–18; James 4:7–10; Jude 20–21)?

5. What seemed to be David's greatest concern when the troops were heading out to battle (2 Samuel 18:5, 29, 32–33)? Do you think this was appropriate?

6. What did the Holy Spirit highlight to you in 2 Samuel 17—18 through the reading or the teaching?

Lesson 53: 2 Samuel 19—20

Eternal Throne: Reasserting His Kingship

Teaching Notes

Intro

Second Samuel has been pretty graphic. The book started with David given a part in the *Eternal Throne* that points to the coming Messiah, Jesus. But after that, things got bad. David had his affair with Bathsheba and set up Bathsheba's husband to be killed. David's son Amnon raped his half-sister, Tamar. And Tamar's brother Absalom attempted to take over David's kingdom. After that, Joab and his men killed Absalom. When messengers from the battlefield told David about Absalom's death, David wept.

Teaching

2 Samuel 19:1–4: Twenty thousand troops died in the battle to defeat Absalom. Even though Absalom led an army against the king and the king's army won, the victory was turned into mourning because of how much David was mourning. Soldiers should not be grieving after such a big victory, but because David hadn't been able to get over the loss of Absalom, the soldiers went home feeling as though they had been defeated. David was in such despair he hid his face as he mourned.

2 Samuel 19:5–7: As the man who killed Absalom and took care of the problem, Joab came to David and pretty much told David to get over his grief. Joab stated David's mourning discredited all his soldiers had done for him and suggested David would have preferred for his own army to have died and for Absalom to have lived. David obviously needed the pep talk, but Joab's boldness could also have created a problem. David never sought the Lord or cried out to the Lord. In the past, David lamented the deaths of Saul and Jonathan to the Lord, but he didn't do that here. He was crying over his son without seeking God.

2 Samuel 19:8–10: When people were placed at the gate, they were positioned for authority. David sitting at the gate was a sign to his people that he was back and engaged. But the people were now unsure what they thought of the king. On one hand, David had delivered them from the Philistines. On the other, David had fled Absalom, and Absalom had been anointed king. The people were now unsure of who they were to follow. Would David rule only over Judah, over a section of the tribes, or the whole kingdom?

2 Samuel 19:11–13: David actually began to reinitiate his calling as king. He started to take active steps of restoring himself to the role of king. David knew how to play the game; he knew the political structure. This was similar to starting a campaign rally. David went to the elders of the tribe of Judah and made a familial appeal to begin the process of restoring his throne. His political strategy was in his promise to Amasa that Amasa would take Joab's place as commander of David's troops. David probably wanted to replace Joab with his arch-enemy Amasa because Joab had killed Absalom against David's wishes and then had been very forward with him afterwards. But David was also trying to secure the unity of the rebel army by promoting Amasa.

2 Samuel 19:14–15: David's political move and negotiating tactic worked. David could have been stuck in the grieving process over Absalom. He could have been stuck in the mistakes he made as a father or as a husband, but because Joab woke him up, he started to walk out his calling as God's anointed king again.

2 Samuel 19:16–20: Shimei was the man who had followed David around when he was exiled and threw rocks and hurled insults at David and his men. Now Shimei had second thoughts about what he had done, and he hurried down to meet the king, bringing a 1,000 men from Benjamin with him. This was a sign the old hostilities with Saul's family were coming to an end. Ziba, another servant in Saul's house, also came to meet the king. Ziba knew he had acted against the king's wishes when he neglected to take care of Mephibosheth. The whole group helped David cross the Jordan almost as a way of kissing up to the king. But Shimei made no excuses for his past conduct. He didn't try to shift blame, but he was ready to move forward as the first descendant from all of Joseph's family.

2 Samuel 19:21–23: Abishai didn't like Shimei from the first. When Shimei was insulting the king in 2 Samuel 16:9, Abishai asked David, "Why should this dead dog curse my lord the king? Let me go over and cut his head off!" Abishai wanted to kill Shimei in chapter 16, and he still wanted to kill him. David's response was basically, "Aren't I the king? I'm in charge of people who were on both sides." David made an oath to not kill Shimei, but he didn't promise anyone else wouldn't. In 1 Kings 2:8–9, David would tell Solomon, "Keep an eye on Shimei son of Gera . . . He uttered malicious curses against me the day I went to Mahanaim. But he came down to meet me at the Jordan River, and I swore to him by the LORD: 'I will never kill you with the sword.' So don't let him go unpunished, for you are a wise man. You know how to deal with him to bring his gray head down to Sheol with blood." David got the bigger picture. He was a man of integrity, but he knew how to work the system.

2 Samuel 19:24–30: Mephibosheth had not bathed or trimmed his hair since David left Jerusalem, possibly as a sign of mourning. Mephibosheth told David that Ziba left him behind and took his donkey. David wasn't sure who was telling him the truth, so David commanded Ziba and Mephibosheth to divide their property.

2 Samuel 19:31–39: Barzillai had taken care of David when he was on the other side of the Jordan. Now, David wanted Barzillai to come with him so he could return the favor. Barzillai refused because he was so old he wouldn't be able to enjoy all the nice things David offered. Instead, Barzillai asked David to take Chimham, who was probably Barzillai's son, and David agreed.

2 Samuel 19:40–43: As David began to walk out his calling, there was an argument between the men of Israel (the ten Northern tribes) and the men of Judah. The men of Israel wanted to know why Judah had crossed over the Jordan with David secretly. The bitterness between the two tribes would become a division when Solomon passed away, but they all came together at this point because of King David.

Closing

David eventually overcame his failures and his fears because he still pursued his calling as the king. Because David pursued his calling, the people of Israel came together. First Corinthians 7:17 says, "However, each one must live his life in the situation the Lord assigned when God called him." When David began to walk out his calling, everyone was impacted. Ephesians 4:1 says, "Therefore I, the prisoner of the Lord, urge you to walk worthy of the calling you have received." David had received a calling from the Lord and now he needed to walk it out.

The Daily Word

As David began to walk out his calling as king, not only was his kingdom restored, but so were his relationships. Joab, the commander of David's army, spoke truth into David, rebuking him in the midst of grief over the loss of his son. Then Shimei, son of Gera, apologized for the curses and insults he made. In humility, David showed forgiveness to both men. Mephibosheth, whom David believed had betrayed him, came forward and shed the light of truth onto the false reality portrayed by his own servant, Ziba. David showed Mephibosheth understanding. David showed appreciation toward an eighty-year-old man named Barzillai for his support. In all these interactions, David displayed grace and truth, bringing restoration to each relationship as he walked forward in his calling as king. The Lord blessed him for his obedience.

God is a God of restoration. He has restored you, a sinner, into a right relationship with His Son Jesus. As you walk into your calling as a child of God, an heir in the kingdom of God, who has been anointed for such a time as this, the Lord will restore those things in your life that were once broken. Walk out your calling with humility and love. Today, pause and ask the Lord for restoration in your own heart, in your relationships with others, or even in your relationship with Jesus. He will personally *restore, establish, and strengthen you.* May your life be a testimony of the Lord's restoration power of making all things new!

They forded the Jordan to bring the king's household across and do whatever the king desired. —2 Samuel 19:18

Further Scripture: Galatians 6:1; Ephesians 4:1; 1 Peter 5:10

Questions

1. How did David's men respond to David's weeping and mourning for Absalom (2 Samuel 19:3)? Why did they respond this way (2 Samuel 19:5–6)? Have you ever let emotion override wisdom in times of difficulty?

2. In 2 Samuel 19, the truth about Mephibosheth came out (2 Samuel 16:1–4). How did the king bring justice to the situation? Or did he? According to Deuteronomy 19:18–19, what should Ziba's punishment as a false witness have been?

3. We sometimes read about a wicked man who used his influence to turn the people in a wrong direction, like Sheba did in 2 Samuel 20:1–2. Why do you think people listen to the voice of rebels and follow them (Deuteronomy 13:13; 1 Samuel 30:22; Matthew 27:20; Acts 14:2; 21:27–30)? How can we guard ourselves against being led astray (Psalm 1:1–2; 86:11; 119:11, 105; 143:8; 1 Corinthians 16:13–14)?

4. Was Sheba's argument that the Israelites had no portion in David true (2 Samuel 20:1)? What became of Sheba? In 2 Samuel 20:22, what was the description of the woman who influenced the city's response? How would you contrast the way these two people, Sheba and the woman in Abel Beth-maacah, influenced those around them (Proverbs 1:7; 6:12–19)?

5. What did the Holy Spirit highlight to you in 2 Samuel 19—20 through the reading or the teaching?

Lesson 54: 2 Samuel 21—22

Eternal Throne: God Answered David's Prayers

Teaching Notes

Intro

This week, we'll finish 2 Samuel and jump into 1 Kings. Second Samuel has had one big moment after another. In chapter 7, we looked at the Davidic Covenant and the *Eternal Throne*. David's sin life after this anointing proves that we can't lose our anointing, regardless of what we do. As David messed up (2 Samuel 11) in an adulterous relationship with Bathsheba which led to murder, and the chaos that spread through his family in the years afterwards, the Davidic Covenant stayed in place. In today's study, things in David's kingdom will get even messier than what we've seen so far in 2 Samuel. In 2 Samuel 9, David showed kindness to Mephibosheth, the son of his best friend Jonathan. Between this show of kindness and the encounter with Shimei (2 Samuel 16) was a period of three years. This period of time is detailed in 2 Samuel 21, not in its chronological position.

Teaching

2 Samuel 21:1–2: During this three-year period, Israel experienced a famine. When David asked God why, he was told it was because Saul and his family had shed the blood of the Gibeonites (v. 1). MacArthur explains that, by attempting to clear the Promised Land of the non-Israelites as God had instructed, "Saul had broken a covenant that had been made 400 years before between Joshua and the Gibeonites, who were in the land when Israel took possession of it" (Joshua 9:3–27; 2 Samuel 21:2).[1] This brings up the question of why God allows people to suffer, and why God lets bad things happen to good people. In his suffering, David sought the Lord (Psalm 50:15).

Romans 8:28 says, "We know that all things work together for the good of those who love God: those who are called according to his purpose." John Piper has shared five purposes for suffering:

---

[1] John MacArthur, *The MacArthur Bible Commentary* (Nashville: Thomas Nelson, 2005), 380.

1. *Repentance.* Our suffering is a call for us to turn away from anything that gets in the way of our relationship with God so we can turn back to Him (Luke 13:4–5).

2. *Reliance.* Our suffering calls us back to trusting in God for our subsistence (2 Corinthians 1:8–9). Pastor Gordy said to us one day as we were driving around that we have to give God the space to work in the moment.

3. *Righteousness.* Our suffering teaches us God's discipline so we can learn to dwell in His righteousness and holiness (Hebrews 12:6, 10–11). Our suffering makes us look more like Him.

4. *Reward.* Our suffering helps prepare us for our reward in heaven (2 Corinthians 4:17).

5. *Reminder.* Our suffering helps us remember how Jesus suffered for us so we would not suffer from God's condemnation (Philippians 3:10).[2]

What David did in the face of the famine pointed to the coming Messiah.

2 Samuel 21:3–9: After hearing from the Lord, David summoned the Gibeonites to find out how he could make atonement for Saul's actions to them (v. 3). The Gibeonites did not want money, but asked that seven of Saul's male descendants be given to them to hang in the presence of the Lord. David agreed (vv. 4–6). David spared Jonathan's son Mephibosheth because of his oath with Jonathan, but handed over seven other descendants (including another family member named Mephibosheth) (vv. 7–8). The seven were hanged on a hill on the first days of the barley harvest (v. 9).

2 Samuel 21:10–14: Two of Rizpah's sons were among the seven hanged, so she went out to the hill and spread sackcloth out for herself so she could protect the bodies from birds and wild animals. While she was there, the rain poured down upon the bodies. The famine had ended because David did what God had commanded (v. 10). When David heard what Rizpah had done, he got the bones of Saul and Jonathan from Jabesh-gilead and brought them to where Rizpah was. They gathered the bones of the seven descendants who had been hung, and buried them all in the tomb of Saul's father Kish (vv. 11–14). And, God answered the prayers for the land.

---

[2] John Piper, "Five Purposes for Suffering," Desiring God, January 31, 2012, https://www.desiringgod.org/articles/five-purposes-for-suffering.

Closing

In the church today, we tend to try to sweep things under the rug and not confront or deal with them. But the Lord demanded that the broken covenant be addressed—it had to be dealt with and made right. The amazing thing is that we don't have to hang seven people to make something right, because Jesus has already hung on the cross for us. Yet, all of us who do not depend upon the Lord are in a season of famine. Praise the Lord that when we come to the cross, we will receive life!

Because David sought after the Lord, He answered David's prayers. And, the Lord wants to do that for us as well. But it can only happen through a relationship with Christ.

The Daily Word

For three years during David's reign, Israel experienced famine. David inquired of the Lord as to why they had to endure this season of suffering. The Lord explained it was because Saul and his family killed the Gibeonites. In response, David humbly went to the Gibeonites, asking what he could do to make the situation right. David agreed to do what the Gibeonites requested. After this act of atonement from David, the Lord answered David's prayer for the land, and the famine ended.

Have you ever asked the Lord why you are experiencing a season of suffering? Or why a loved one is enduring such pain? Or why your child has to walk a particularly difficult road? The key to remember during times of suffering is to ask the Lord for guidance and help *immediately*. Jesus promises to work all things together for the good of those who place their trust in Him. When you turn to the Lord, He will help you and give you the strength to endure. He may lead you to repent or to rely more on Him and not on yourself, but He will always be there to help you. If you are facing a time of suffering today, may you hold on to the hope that the Lord is with you and that you are not alone in your suffering.

During David's reign there was a famine for three successive years, so David inquired of the Lord. The Lord answered, "It is because of the blood shed by Saul and his family when he killed the Gibeonites." —2 Samuel 21:1

Further Scripture: 2 Corinthians 1:8–9; Philippians 3:10; Hebrews 12:7a, 11

Questions

1. In 2 Samuel 21:1–14, what reason did the Lord give David for the famine? What did David do about it?

2. In verse 17 of 2 Samuel 21, why did the men of David's army tell him that he could no longer go with them into battle (2 Samuel 18:3)? Do you believe this was a good decision on their part? Why?

3. How does 2 Samuel 22:29 point to Jesus (Psalm 27:1; 119:105; Isaiah 9:2; 60:1; John 8:12; 12:36–37)?

4. What did the Holy Spirit highlight to you in 2 Samuel 21–22 through the reading or the teaching?

Lesson 55: 2 Samuel 23—24

Eternal Throne: David's Anointed Mighty Men

Teaching Notes

Intro

Today we finish out 2 Samuel. We've learned a lot in the study of 1 and 2 Samuel. There are principles in these books that are easily transferrable to today. Second Samuel 23 records David's last words (vv. 1–7). David was older and looking back on his life. The rest of the chapter is about the Mighty Men of David (vv. 8–39).

Teaching

2 Samuel 23:8–12: David's mighty men were also listed in 1 Chronicles 11 and may use different names but the lists are consistent. The first listed was the chief of the officers, Josheb-basshebeth the Tahchemonite, who killed 800 men at one time with his spear (v. 8).

The next was Eleazar, one of three warriors with David, who attacked the Philistines with such vengeance that his hand "clave to the sword" (KJV). God brought great victory to Israel that day (v. 10).

Third was Shammah son of Agee the Hararite. Shammah defended a field of lentils against the Philistines. "So the Lord brought about a great victory" (v. 11–12).

2 Samuel 23:13–17: David recognized these three, because of their great exploits and their lack of fear. When he wanted something done that involved blood, he knew he could depend upon them to get it done. These three came to David who was at the cave of Adullam (v. 13). David was extremely thirsty and said what he really wanted was water from the well at Bethlehem, where a Philistine garrison was quartered (vv. 14–15). In response, these three Mighty Men broke through the Philistine lines, drew water from the well, and brought it to David. But David refused to drink it, and poured it on the ground as a drink offering to the Lord (v. 16). David said the water was "the blood of men who risked their lives" to get it for him (v. 17).

2 Samuel 23:18–23: In verse 18, Abishai, Joab's brother, is listed as the leader of the three (v. 18), and Asahel, another of Joab's brothers, was listed among the Mighty Men (v. 24). Joab was the commander of David's army. All three were sons of Zeruiah, David's sister (1 Chronicles 2:13–16). As nephews, these men would have been around David in his younger years. David's sister would have known about Samuel's anointing of David as the future king of Israel.

God has a master plan of the *Anointed One* that we see woven through the books of Samuel and is evidenced in the New Testament through Christ. To get to this evidence, we see God work through all these other people and events, despite the ravage of evil and the issues of jealousy and pride.

2 Samuel 23:24–39: In chapter 23 is a listing of the names of all the Mighty Men—many of the names are never referenced anywhere else in Scripture. These were men who had brought great victory to David the warrior. It is important for us to recognize the anointing was *the plan of God*. Asahel was described as being able to run as fast as a deer (2 Samuel 2:18). Joab had the leadership skills to be the commander. Each of the Mighty Men brought something different. God's plan was working through each of these through their anointing. The anointing is not purposeless, but is done to put each of the people God will use into His plan.

The Mighty Men, these 37 men, were *the equipment of God*. Each was important. Notice in verse 39 the last man named—Uriah the Hittite. Uriah, Bathsheba's husband, would not walk away from his anointed duty to David's army to go home to his wife while they were in battle, so David had him killed to cover up his own sin. God positioned these men in places to carry out His plan. These 37 men were named because each was part of God's plan in David's life. David didn't secure his kingdom by himself. What happened in David's life as the *Anointed One* was not about David but about God's plan coming into fulfillment. It's not about our personalities, our successes, our gifts—it's all about being anointed into God's plan. It's not about us. These 37 recognized the anointing of David, and would do whatever it took for David—even breaking through Philistine lines to bring him water. Imagine if we took our anointing as part of God's plan as seriously.

God's plan was to establish the kingdom of Israel through David (Matthew 1:1). Jesus' lineage covers multiple generations and the one thing that runs through it all is the plan of God. The gospel of God is the plan of God (Romans 1:1–4). The anointing of David through his kingship represents God's kingdom which would be fulfilled through Jesus Christ. In the kingdom, we see God's plan through *the product of God*. The anointing is never about us. What we should look for in determining who to connect our lives to is how the anointing is lived out in their lives. We should be looking for the anointing of God to become one of His Mighty Men. Let's get rid of the personalities that draw attention to themselves, and make it about God. Let's put aside all the discussions of what we should do when we worship Him, and just worship Him.

2 Samuel 24:1–17: 1 Chronicles 21:1 presents this same event, but possibly more clearly: "Satan stood up against Israel and incited David to count the people of Israel." One of the things we can draw comfort from is that there are times when we all will fail to hear clearly. David was nearing the end of his life. Why would he want to number the people of Israel? Possibly David was looking for a way to measure how his life had counted—his legacy. Joab questioned why David wanted to take a census (v. 3). As commander of David's army, Joab had seen more violence and bloodshed than anyone else in Israel. The counting took more than nine months (v. 8) and was detestable to Joab (1 Chronicles 21:6). They counted the troops and registered 800,000 men from Israel and 500,000 from Judah (v. 9). David wanted to know how many valiant soldiers were available to him. Joab recognized that they had never had to rely on large numbers of troops because the Lord gave them the victories.

Once again, this became an attitude adjustment for David. David realized his sin and asked God to take away his guilt (v. 10). But 70,000 of David's soldiers would die through a plague God sent onto Israel (v. 15). The consequences of David's sin were again great.

We will either walk in the anointing of God, or we will have thoughts of taking care of things for ourselves. Which way we choose to walk can have disastrous results when we're outside of God's anointing. We need to grab hold of this daily . . . to recognize every day how awesome God is and that the only thing that matters in our lives is walking out the anointing of God.

Closing

Even in the Old Testament, Romans 8:28 is still true, "And we know that all things work together for good to them that love God, to them who are the called according to his purpose" (KJV). We will either walk in the anointing of God, or we will have thoughts of taking care of things for ourselves. Which way we choose to walk can have disastrous results when we're outside of God's anointing. We need to grab hold of this daily . . . to recognize every day how awesome God is and that the only thing that matters in our lives is walking out the anointing of God. We are nothing and have nothing without the anointing of God flowing through our lives with God's equipment around us so we focus on the purposes of God.

In 2 Samuel 24:24, David turns down the gift of a place to offer burnt offerings, because he would not offer anything to God that cost him nothing. There is a cost to godliness. Let's ask God to teach us how to walk in the anointing and in humility.

The Daily Word

David was safe and surrounded by his thirty-seven mighty men. He was older in years, and he had found victory in battle. Yet for some reason David foolishly gave into the temptation to take a census of all people in Israel and Judah. This brought about God's anger, and David knew it. David's conscience troubled him, and he had great anxiety. In response, David went before the Lord in repentance, asking how to make things right again. As a consequence, the Lord brought about a nationwide plague that killed seventy thousand people. In the end, the Lord finally answered David's request, and the plague ended.

Have you ever had that feeling that you knew something just wasn't right? Are you overcome with anxiety or having a hard time sleeping at night? Are you replaying the same situation in your mind over and over? Stop and seek the Lord. Ask the Lord if you have you gone astray and have troubled Him. If so, the Holy Spirit will convict you of your sin. Your sense of conviction won't go away until you repent. However, the Lord is all-knowing and all-loving. Turn to the Lord to make things right and ask for forgiveness. He will clear your mind from the heaviness you feel and lighten your load. Today, give thanks for His forgiveness and mercy. And remember, nothing will ever separate you from His love.

David's conscience troubled him after he had taken a census of the troops. He said to the Lord, "I have sinned greatly in what I've done. Now, Lord, because I've been very foolish, please take away Your servant's guilt."
—2 Samuel 24:10

Further Scripture: Romans 9:1; Ephesians 2:4–5; 1 Peter 3:16

Questions

1. After stating that he is craving water (2 Samuel 23:15), why did David not drink the water that his mighty men brought to him (v. 16–17)? Has there ever been a time in your life that you asked for something from another person or even God and then didn't accept it? Why?

2. What could be the significance of naming all 37 of David's mighty men (Matthew 26:6–13)?

3. Second Samuel 24:1 records that the anger of the Lord burned against Israel. What do you think caused this anger? Do you think David handled it correctly (Proverbs 16:18; Luke 12:16–21)?

4. Second Samuel 24:15 states that 70,000 men died through the consequences of David's sin. How often do you consider who else is affected because of your sin?

5. How often do you offer something to God that doesn't cost you anything (2 Samuel 24:24)?

6. What did the Holy Spirit highlight to you in 2 Samuel 23—24 through the reading or the teaching?

Lesson 56: 1 Kings 1

Something Greater: Solomon's Anointed Reign

Teaching Notes

Intro

We're still in study of the 12 historical books. So far, we've covered five. Just like 1 and 2 Samuel, Mindi has combined two paintings for these two books into one complete image (called a diptych). Our phrase for 1 Kings is *Something Greater*. We'll be comparing Solomon's life to Jesus' to see how Christ is greater than Solomon. At the end of 2 Samuel, David was preparing Solomon to inherit his throne. First Kings shows this time of major leadership transition. The Davidic Covenant from 2 Samuel 7 was now being passed on to Solomon.

Originally, 1 and 2 Kings was one book. Before that, these books were the third and the fourth parts of the book of Samuel. The book was written between 561–538 BC. The historical information in the book was from the book of the acts of Solomon, the Chronicles of the kings of Israel (1 Kings 14:19), and the Chronicles of the kings of Judah (1 Kings 14:29). There are also references in Isaiah and Jeremiah to 1 Kings. MacArthur proposes that a single, inspired author, living in Babylon during the exile, used these pre-exilic source materials.[1]

First Kings 1—11 covers Solomon's reign and the uniting of Israel and Judah. In 1 Kings 12, this united kingdom began to struggle and there was division in the northern and southern kingdoms. In 2 Kings, the history of Judah, the southern kingdom, is outlined. MacArthur explains that "the Book of Kings is not only accurate history, but interpreted history. The author . . . wished to communicate the lessons of Israel's history to the exiles . . . why the Lord's judgment of exile had come."[2] Bottom line: The writer wanted to make sure the exiles understood that since the Mosaic Law required that Israel be obedient to God, disobedience led to punishment and being exiled.[3] The common theme that runs through 1 Kings is about the kings of both Israel and Judah, they "did evil in the sight of the Lord." Therefore, God sent His prophets to confront the kings to turn their

---

[1] John MacArthur, *The MacArthur Bible Commentary* (Nashville: Thomas Nelson, 2005), 387.

[2] MacArthur, 388.

[3] MacArthur, 388.

nations back to God. When they rejected God's prophets and their warnings, prophets declared both kingdoms would be exiled.

Geographically, Israel would have included all the land from Dan in the north to Beersheba in the south. The pattern at the beginning of the book is one new king after another was introduced with information about each, the date of succession in comparison to the contemporary ruler in the other kingdom, the age of the king when he took the throne, and the length and the place of his reign. In the Judah line of kings, the mother's name was given. Other information given was a spiritual appraisal of each king's reign (whether he did evil or good). Finally, at the end of the king's reign, citation of historical documents that verified the information was given, as well as notice or death and burial, and the identification of the successor.[4]

MacArthur presents three theological themes for 1 Kings: (1) "the Lord judged Israel and Judah because of their disobedience to His Law," (2) "the word of the true prophets came to pass," and (3) "the Lord remembered His promise to David."[5] With this background, let us dig into 1 Kings 1.

Teaching

1 Kings 1:1–10: David was around 70 years old when he became ill and he could not get warm. (v. 1). His servants suggested that a virgin be found who could attend to David as his caregiver (v. 2). Early church historian Josephus noted that "using a healthy person's body warmth to care for a sick person" was a medical treatment referenced in the second century.[6] The servants found Abishag the Shunammite, a beautiful girl to attend David. No intimate relations took place (v. 4). David's fourth-born son Adonijah, his oldest surviving son, claimed he would be king. He had chariots, cavalry, and men run ahead of him (v. 5). Adonijah exalted himself (Luke 14:11). David showed his passivity and never reprimanded Adonijah for his actions (v. 6). Adonijah conspired with David's army commander, his nephew Joab, and Abiathar. They agreed to support his claim to the throne (v. 7). However, Zadok the priest, Nathan the prophet, and David's other warriors did not support Adonijah (v. 8). Note: Shimei mentioned in verse 8 was not the man who hurled curses and threw stones at David (1 Kings 2:8–9; 2 Kings 4:7,18). Adonijah sacrificed animals and invited his royal brothers, the men of Judah, and the servants of Solomon to come. He did not invite those who had not sided with him (vv. 9–10). He was working to take the throne from Solomon.

---

[4] MacArthur, 389.

[5] MacArthur, 389.

[6] Earl D. Radmacher, Ronald B. Allen, and H. Wayne House, eds., *Nelson's New Illustrated Bible Commentary* (Nashville: Thomas Nelson, 1999), 428.

1 Kings 1:11–31: Nathan told Bathsheba about what was happening and she went to King David asking about Solomon's inheritance to be king, and explained how Adonijah was trying to take the inheritance from Solomon. She asked David to tell Israel who was to sit on the throne after him (vv. 11–20). Then, Nathan came into David and confirmed what Bathsheba had told him and explained that Adonijah was working behind David's back and not including him or the prophet (vv. 21–27). David called Bathsheba before him and swore again that Solomon was his rightful heir (vv. 28–31).

1 Kings 1:32–40: David called for Zadok the priest, Nathan the prophet, and Benaiah. When they came before him, he instructed them to place Solomon on David's mule and take him to Gihon to anoint Solomon as king over Israel (vv. 32–37). Solomon riding on David's mule would show Israel that David was passing his throne to Solomon (Zechariah 9:9). The men did as David had instructed, they took Solomon on David's mule to Gihon and anointed him with oil from the tabernacle. They blew the ram's horn and the people declared Solomon as their king (John 12:13). Then, they followed him with "such a great joy that the earth split open from the sound" (vv. 38–40).

1 Kings 1:41–53: Adonijah received word of what had happened (vv. 41–48). Adonijah and his guests trembled in fear from the news (v. 49). Adonijah was so afraid of Solomon that he took hold of the horns of the altar (v. 50). His action meant he was asking for mercy and refuge from those who would commit unintentional crimes (Leviticus 4; Exodus 21:12–14). Solomon received word that Adonijah was holding onto the horns of the altar, asking for Solomon to swear that he would not kill him (v. 51). Solomon agreed as long as no evil was found in Adonijah (v. 52). Solomon had Adonijah brought before him. Adonijah paid homage to King Solomon and sent Adonijah home, basically with a pardon (v. 53).

Closing

What we're going to see in 1 Kings, especially in the first eleven chapters, is that even though Solomon was an amazing man of God, Jesus is greater (Matthew 12:42).

The Daily Word

King David was confined to his room due to old age. It was here the prophet Nathan and Bathsheba visited him to share the news about Adonijah, David's son, who was exalting himself as David's successor and conspiring and gathering people to support him as king. Without hesitating, King David swore an oath that it was Solomon who would become king after him. He ordered Nathan and Zadok the priest to anoint Solomon. The people celebrated Solomon, their new king, as he rode through town on David's mule. That is, everyone celebrated but Adonijah, who now feared for his own life. However, Solomon granted mercy and forgiveness towards Adonijah for the prideful actions taken against him. The Lord's hand was upon Solomon.

In many ways, Solomon can be compared to Jesus. Solomon was celebrated while riding on a mule, was anointed as king, had great wisdom, and showed mercy and forgiveness. Even so, Jesus is *greater* than Solomon. Jesus came riding on a donkey as the people shouted, "Hosanna." Jesus, the Anointed One, forgives all your sins, offering grace, mercy, and eternal life. Jesus is the King of kings and the Lord of lords. Today, worship the Lord. Bow down before Him. Step away from the things of this world and pour your heart out to the one who saved you from death. He is worthy of your praise. He is the Almighty One!

The king swore an oath and said, "As the Lord lives, who has redeemed my life from every difficulty, just as I swore to you by the Lord God of Israel: Your son Solomon is to become king after me, and he is the one who is to sit on my throne in my place, that is exactly what I will do this very day."
—1 Kings 1:29–30

Further Scripture: Matthew 12:42; John 14:12; 1 Timothy 6:15–16

Questions

1. Why did Adonijah take it upon himself to seek the throne (2 Samuel 15:1–12; 1 Kings 1:6)? Does this show that the 'sins of the fathers' passed on to him (Exodus 20:5; Deuteronomy 5:9)?

2. Why do you think that David chose Solomon, over his other sons, to be his successor to the throne?

3. In verse 13, what could be the reason that Nathan told Bathsheba to go into David before him instead of just telling him about Adonijah's plan himself?

4. In verse 50, Adonijah "took hold of the horns of the altar." Why do you think he did this? Was there another time in the Bible that this was mentioned (Exodus 21:14; 1 Kings 2:28–29)?

5. What did the Holy Spirit highlight to you in 1 Kings 1 through the reading or the teaching?

Lesson 57: 1 Kings 2

Something Greater: David's Last Words

Teaching Notes

Intro

We already saw David's last words to the people in 2 Samuel 23. These verses were the last words David had for his son Solomon as he took over as king. What we see throughout scripture and especially in these verses is actions have consequences, forgiveness is required, and trust is earned. You will be surprised by the amount of grace shown in this chapter. Today, we are going to see how all the pieces of this chapter fit together, from David to Solomon.

Teaching

1 Kings 2:1–3: The first four verses from David were a *spiritual charge* for Solomon, urging him to obey God's word.[1] These were key verses for Solomon. David's encouragement was for Solomon to keep what the Lord required. Why was this important? Because obedience leads to blessing. There is no substitute for a lifestyle of obedience to God's Word. The same is true for us. Jesus said, "Everyone who hears these words of Mine and acts on them will be like a sensible man who built his house on the rock" (Matthew 7:24).

1 Kings 2:4: Solomon was David's son and God had promised David an everlasting kingdom (2 Samuel 7:14–16). But this everlasting kingdom continually depended on obedience to God's word. It has often been debated whether this promise to David was conditional or unconditional. There is a tension raised that only Jesus Christ can resolve. Solomon, like his father and other kings to come, would fail. Yet, God would keep His promise in Jesus Christ.

---

[1] Tony Merida, *Christ-Centered Exposition Commentary: Exalting Jesus in 1 & 2 Kings* (Nashville: Broadman & Holman, 2015), Kindle line 434.

1 Kings 2:5–9: These verses served as a *political charge* to Solomon.[2] There were serious threats to the kingdom. David had unfinished business. Consider these individuals mentioned here:

Joab was full of contradictions—victories and grief, and a lack of self-control.

- Joab was David's nephew (1 Chronicles 2:13–17).
- He murdered Abner out of revenge for killing Joab's brother . . . but after Abner made a pledge to David and received forgiveness (2 Samuel 2).
- He killed Absalom in disobedience to David's orders (2 Samuel 18).
- He treacherously murdered Amasa, his own cousin (2 Samuel 20).
- He gave good advice against David's sin (2 Samuel 24).
- He was a conspiracy member with Adonijah (1 Kings 1).
- David instructed that there was to be no peace for Joab (v.6).

Brazillai was loyal. He was to be given *royal pension*, which meant he was to eat at the king's table (v.7). Brazillai's decedents were mentioned in the books of Ezra and Nehemiah.

Shimei was a man David wanted Solomon to keep an eye on, because Shimei had cursed David but later asked for mercy. The question is, did David really give him mercy? Shimei was wicked and went unpunished, but David wanted Solomon to punish him. Shimei was from the tribe of Benjamin.

1 Kings 2:10: David died. David's tomb is located on modern, not historical, Mount Zion in Jerusalem. Most historians and archeologists do not consider this tomb David's actual resting place. We don't know where he was buried, but we know he was with his fathers.

1 Kings 2:11–12: 1 Kings 1—4 described the golden age of Israel. David had ruled for 40 years and Solomon ruled for 40 years. We are now in the middle of the golden age. Solomon carried out David's instructions in verses 13–46.

1 Kings 2:13: Solomon had hardly begun his own tenure as king when Adonijah visited Bathsheba with a shady proposal. Remember, Adonijah had attempted a coup to make himself king in 1 Kings 1 and Bathsheba was Solomon's mother.

1 Kings 2:14–18: Adonijah went to Bathsheba and asked for her daughter Abishag's hand in marriage. She was stunningly beautiful. Adonijah wanted to

---

[2] Merida, Kindle line 434.

marry the newly widowed Abishag, and he asked Bathsheba to convince Solomon that it was a good idea. Bathsheba agreed to help him.

1 Kings 2:19–22: When Bathsheba presented Solomon with Adonijah's request, Solomon refused. When a king died, all his possessions (including his wives and concubines) belonged to the heir to the throne. In 2 Samuel 16:20–22, Absalom slept with his father's concubines in full view for all to see his rebellion and his attempt to claim the throne. Adonijah taking Abishag as his wife would have amounted to a claim on the throne.

1 Kings 2:23–24: Solomon determined that Adonijah would have to die. First Kings 1:52 states, "Then Solomon said, 'If he is a man of character, not a single hair of his will fall to the ground, but if evil is found in him, he dies.'" This was the last mention of Bathsheba, other than in Psalm, "David's sin with her . . ." This was also the last mention of Abishag. Some have suggested, since she was a Shunammite, Abishag was the Shulamite of the Song of Solomon (Song of Solomon 6:13), but this is unlikely. What a bizarre love triangle!

1 Kings 2:25: Adonijah was killed by one of Solomon's servants.

1 Kings 2:26–27: Abiathar the priest, another fascinating character, was dealt with. His issue was conspiracy. He was loyal to David against Saul, and David against Absalom—but sided with Adonijah in his conspiracy. He served as a joint high priest functioning under David with Zadok. Solomon banished him.

1 Kings 2:28–46: Joab heard of Solomon's action and fled to the horns of the alter wanting to be saved. Because Joab was not innocent, salvation did not come and he was killed. Actions have consequences. Shimei was given grace only if he stayed in Israel. He left and then came back, and was killed for his disobedience.

Closing

Debate about this passage continues. Did Solomon act justly or unjustly? We don't know. The writer of Kings simply tells the events without saying whether these actions were necessary or even condoned. The writer does say that Solomon was King and that these rivals had been eliminated. Tony Merida wrote, "Perhaps this is a story of mixed motives, much like the story of our lives. This doesn't justify injustice, but it does highlight human weakness in leadership and the need for a perfectly just King and a better kingdom. Thankfully, God, by His grace, made good on His promise and gave us the Ruler we need in Christ."[3]

---

[3] Merida, Kindle line 514.

The Daily Word

In King David's final days, he gave Solomon instructions as king from the Law of Moses: "Be strong and courageous, keep your obligation to the Lord, walk in His ways, and keep His statutes, commands, ordinances, and decrees. If you follow the Law of Moses, you will have success in everything you do and wherever you turn." Then David gave an account of a few men and their past actions towards him, instructing Solomon to keep an eye on them. After David died, Solomon heeded his father's words, walking in authority and wisdom as king while keeping his heart set the Lord.

Like Solomon and the Israelites, you know the Word of God. You know His truth and His instructions to walk in the ways of the Lord. And now, through believing in Jesus, you have eternal life. You have received His grace, and you are able to walk daily in the power of the Holy Spirit who is inside you. Are you walking in His Truth? At times, it can be easy to let the truth go in one ear and out the other. But before you know it, you have conformed to the ways of the world. Slowly, other gods become more important than the one true God, your Messiah, Jesus Christ. Your Heavenly Father has instructed you, like David did to Solomon—*walk in His ways.*

As for me, I am going the way of all of the earth. Be strong and be courageous like a man, and keep your obligation to the Lord your God to walk in His ways and to keep His statutes, commands, ordinances, and decrees. This is written in the Law of Moses, so that you will have success in everything you do and wherever you turn. —1 Kings 2:2–3

Further Scripture: Psalm 119:1; Proverbs 23:26; Romans 12:2

Questions

1. In 1 Kings 2:2–4, David spoke of his approaching death. What did he instruct Solomon to do? What two commandments sum up all that David listed (Matthew 22:37–40)?

2. As David instructed Solomon, he declared Solomon's wisdom twice (1 Kings 2:6, 9). Do you think he was calling it into being, had observed this trait in his son, or both (Romans 4:17b, 2 Corinthians 5:7, Hebrews 11:1, 3)?

3. David encouraged Solomon to bring justice to several situations which had not been dealt with. Why had David not dealt with them? In these situations, do you see any mercy displayed by this newly anointed king (1 Kings 2:26, 36–38)? How does this combination of justice and mercy remind you of the Christ (Matthew 12:17–21, John 3:16–18, Romans 5:8–9)?

4. Abiathar was not killed for his part in Adonijah's taking over the throne, but he was sent home, no longer to serve as priest. What prophecy did this fulfill concerning the house of Eli in Shiloh (1 Samuel 2:30)?

5. In Kings 2, Multiple references were made to Solomon's kingdom being firmly established (1 Kings 2:12, 24, 45–46). What helps establish it (Proverbs 25:5)?

6. What did the Holy Spirit highlight to you in 1 Kings 2 through the reading or the teaching?

Lesson 58: 1 Kings 3—4

Something Greater: Solomon's Wisdom

Teaching Notes

Intro

I think as we keep going through historical books, everything we've studied can sometimes seem to run together. I feel like looking at the paintings can help remind us exactly what each book was about. I want us to continue to see the Messiah in all of our studies. He is even in the book of 1 Kings. As we go through these chapters, I want you to consider how they point us to the coming Messiah.

Teaching

1 Kings 3:1: This verse is a great summary of Solomon's life. Solomon made an alliance with Pharaoh, the king of Egypt, by marrying his daughter. She came to the city of David, where Solomon was building his palace, God's temple, and a wall around Jerusalem.

1 Kings 3:2: During this period, people had been making sacrifices on the high places because there had been no temple (1 Kings 1:7–13). After the new temple was completed, sacrifices in the high places were condemned.

1 Kings 3:3–4: Solomon went to one of the high places, made sacrifices, and burned incense. He then traveled to Gibeon because it was the most famous high place in Israel. There, he offered 1,000 burnt offerings. Gibeon was seven miles northwest of Jerusalem, and was the same place where Moses' tabernacle and the bronze altar was originally constructed.

1 Kings 3:5: At Gibeon, the Lord appeared to Solomon at night in a dream. God instructed Solomon, "Ask. What should I give you?" God uses dreams and visions to speak to us. Do not discredit your own dreams. If you have a dream you think could be from the Lord, write it down, pray about what the dream could mean, and share it with someone to see what they think. Joel 2:28–28 and Acts 2:17 both say dreams and visions are going to happen in the last days.

1 Kings 3:6–7: Before Solomon asked for anything, he gave thanks to God. Many believe Solomon was roughly 20 years old at this time. He understood the big picture and God's promises, but he also realized he was still very young (1 Timothy 4:12). He recognized he needed God's help.

1 Kings 3:8: It is believed Solomon served as king over 4,000,000 people. The author of 2 Samuel 24:9 wrote that in Israel, there were 800,000 fighting men, and in Judah there were 500,000 fighting men. Add women, children, the elderly, and men unable to fight, and that's a lot of people. Solomon desired to honor the promises he made to God and his father.

1 Kings 3:9: Solomon asked for an obedient heart to judge God's people and to discern between good and evil. Solomon wrote Proverbs 4:5–7. He saw the value of wisdom and wanted to be able to walk out his call (1 Corinthians 1:24; James 1:5).

1 Kings 3:11–13: It pleased the Lord that Solomon requested an obedient heart, so the Lord granted Solomon's request. The Lord gave Solomon a wise and understanding heart. Solomon was divinely unique. Because of Solomon's selfless request, God blessed him with riches and honor as well. No kingdom would ever equal Solomon's.

1 Kings 3:14: God told Solomon that if he kept His ways and commands the way his father, King David did, he would have a long life (Psalm 90:10). David died before the age 70 and Solomon died around the age of 70.

1 Kings 3:15: Solomon woke and realized he had experienced a dream. He traveled back to Jerusalem and brought offerings before the ark of the Lord's covenant. Then, he gave a feast.

1 Kings 3:16–22: In the middle of the feast, two prostitutes came and presented a situation that required Solomon's judgment. These two women lived in the same house and had both recently given birth. One woman claimed that during the night, the other woman's baby died. That woman then got up, took the other woman's child, and proclaimed it was her own. As this information was presented to Solomon, the other woman spoke up and said, "No, it is your son who is dead." The women began to argue in front of the king.

1 Kings 3:23–25: Solomon asked for his sword. He told the women that he would cut the living boy in two and they would each receive one half of the child.

1 Kings 3:26–27: The real mother was filled with anguish and compassion. She would rather give her baby up than see him killed. The other woman told the king to go ahead and cut the baby in half. Solomon then gave the baby to the first woman—the baby's real mother.

1 Kings 3:28: All Israel heard about Solomon's wisdom and stood in awe. They realized God's wisdom was with him.

Closing

When Solomon could have asked for anything, he requested wisdom. Through that wisdom, Solomon's reign was also one of peace. Biblical scholar Paul van Gorder gives five reasons Solomon's reign was notable:

1. *Wisdom* (1 Kings 3:9–12; 4:29–4): In Matthew 12:42, Queen Sheba came to hear Solomon's great wisdom. What she discovered was there was *Something Greater* than Solomon in Israel, the presence of the Lord. The wisdom in 1 Kings 3:9–12 points to Jesus and Isaiah 11:2–4. Isaiah had prophesized about Jesus. Both Solomon and Jesus would have wisdom, but Jesus' wisdom would be greater.
2. *Peace and Prosperity* (1 Kings 4:25): This was an unusual time of peace and prosperity in a torn apart country (1 Kings 4:25; Micah 4:3–4). The *Something Greater* than Solomon was the Messiah.
3. *The Building of the Temple* (1 Kings 5—7): This was the highpoint of Solomon's reign (Ezekiel 40—49; 2 Thessalonians 2:3–4; Revelation 11:1–2). When the Messiah returns, we will have a third temple.
4. *God Enters the Temple* (1 Kings 8): The structure of the Temple was completed and dedicated (Micah 4:2).
5. *Visit from Queen Sheba* (1 Kings 10): The nations will come and worship Him (Zechariah 14:8–9, 16). Everything about Solomon points to *Something Greater*. In Matthew 12:42 Jesus says, "something greater than Solomon is here!"[1]

The Daily Word

The Lord appeared to Solomon in a dream and said, "Ask. What should I give you?" Solomon asked for wisdom, explaining he desired to have an obedient heart to judge the people and to discern between good and evil. The Lord was

---

[1] Paul R. Van Gorder, *The Old Testament Presents . . . Reflections of Christ: 1 Kings*, http://www.thebookwurm.com/ref-1kin.htm.

pleased with Solomon's request. As Solomon walked out his calling as king, it became evident to all Israel that the Lord gave him the wisdom he requested. Because he humbly asked for wisdom, the Lord also granted Solomon riches and honor and blessed him abundantly.

Today, if you could ask God for anything, what would you ask for? A new house? A mended relationship? Healing from a disease? The possibilities could go on and on. But have you ever asked the Lord for wisdom? Start today. As you approach the moments of your day, ask the Lord for wisdom in making decisions both large and small. From what to eat, where to work, how to parent your teenager, what to say to a friend in a troubled marriage, or who to share the Gospel with—*ask Him.* The Lord wants to bless you generously with wisdom.

So give Your servant an obedient heart to judge Your people and to discern between good and evil. For who is able to judge this great people of Yours? —1 Kings 3:9

Further Scripture: Proverbs 4:6–7; James 1:5; James 3:17

Questions

1. When the Lord appeared to Solomon in a dream asking what he wished the Lord to give him, what does Solomon request? How did Solomon demonstrate humility (1 Kings 3:6–9)?

2. What things did the Lord promise to Solomon in addition to what he asked for (1 Kings 3:13–14)? How did this point to the theme for 1 Kings: *Something Greater* (1 Kings 1:47; Hebrews 1:8–9)?

3. After Solomon's judgement between the two prostitutes, all Israel heard and feared the king because they saw the wisdom of God was in him to administer justice. Why would this cause fear (Job 12:22; Psalm 72:4–5; Proverbs 15:12; 21:15; 2 Corinthians 5:10)?

4. First Kings 4:20 states Judah and Israel were as the grains of sand on the seashore in abundance. This it the fulfillment of what promise (Genesis 22:17)? Does this bring confidence that God will continue to fulfill His promises (2 Corinthians 1:20a)?

5. Solomon's wisdom surpassed the wisdom of all the sons of the east and all the wisdom of Egypt. How is he a type of Christ (Matthew 12:42; 1 Corinthians 1:30; Colossians 2:2–3)?

6. What did the Holy Spirit highlight to you in 1 Kings 3—4 through the reading or the teaching?

Lesson 59: 1 Kings 5—6

Something Greater: Solomon's Temple

Teaching Notes

Intro

We are running through the book of 1 Kings. It can be easy to get lost in the rhythm of ancient history. It can be tempting to skim over these stories and names. However, I believe there are seasons of the Christian life that are benefited by studying these stories. I want to encourage you to not skip over them. There are a number of perspectives we can gain from Scripture. In this passage, we will study the building of Solomon's temple.

Teaching

1 Kings 5:1: When the word had come that Solomon was the anointed king, Hiram, the king of Tyre, sent his servants to Solomon. Hiram had been a good friend of David. I believe Solomon learned a sense of kingdom rule and the importance of the alliances from his father David.

1 Kings 5:2–5: Solomon responded to Hiram, explaining his father was not able to build a temple because of the wars around him. Solomon also shared that because he had been experiencing peace, he planned to build his father's temple. In 2 Samuel 7:2, David had been the one who proposed that he build a house of God. I believe David was using natural reasoning, comparing how he lived to where the presence of the Lord had been dwelling and he concluded he would build a temple. The Lord told Nathan to go to David and tell him that it was not the time for him to build a temple. The building of the temple would happen in God's timing not David's. It is easy to insert personal preferences in what we believe is godly. The question is, how does God want to be worshipped versus how we want to worship?

1 Kings 5:6–9: Solomon told Hiram that Tyre had the best kind of trees and that Hiram's people were the most qualified to cut them. Solomon then asked Hiram for his support of the building project through providing the trees and manpower. Solomon promised to pay for the trees, the work of the men, and he pledged his own servants to help with the project. When Hiram heard Solomon's proposal, he rejoiced.

1 Kings 5:10–12: Solomon sent Hiram 125,000 bushels of wheat and 1,160 gallons of oil every year as the work continued. Because of the wisdom the Lord gave Solomon, there was peace and an alliance between Solomon and Hiram. God trained Solomon as a peacekeeper.

1 Kings 6:1–6: The temple for the Lord was not built until 480 years after the Israelites came out of Egypt. The temple was 125 feet long, 42 feet wide, and 62 feet high (25-inch cubit). Though we are used to big churches, it is difficult to really understand the size and ornate detail of the Solomon's temple.

1 Kings 6:7: The stones used to build the outer walls of the temple were pre-cut so no noise (axe or hammer) would be made in the house of the Lord. When someone viewed the temple, they would see stone on the outside and gold on the inside.

1 Kings 6:14–38: The inside was built with cedars and other building materials fitting seamlessly together, and was covered with pure gold so that no rough wood or other materials were seen individually (vv.21–22).

Verse 23 describes in detail the ornateness of the inside of the temple. There were two cherubim built in the holy of holies that were 10 cubits high and wide (21 feet high and 21 feet wide). Where were the cherubim before in Scripture? Originally there were two cherubim that sat on the top of the ark roughly 5 feet tall. The new cherubim's wings spread over the holy of holies, their outside wings touched the outside walls, and their inside wings touched the wings of the other cherubim. The idea was the mercy seat was where God came to dwell, but Solomon was trying to build a building for the glory of God to dwell (2 Samuel 7).

1 Kings 6:11: Let's jump back to verse 11. In the middle of the description of all this beauty in the temple, the Lord spoke to Solomon, saying, "I will dwell in this place if you follow my ordinances." He didn't say I would dwell in the temple because it was so nice. God said He would come because of Solomon's obedience. Sometimes we want to dress up our own ways and ideas. But God blesses one thing—our obedience. I wonder if I try to fit God into my own preferences? Solomon's temple was the first permanent dwelling place for God.

Closing

As we close, let's look at the New Testament and who we are today (1 Corinthians 3:16–17). Paul was talking to all of us who have received the Spirit of God. We are now the temples where God dwells. Through the Holy Spirit, God can move and direct us (Acts 7:44–50). I wonder if at times we try to put God back into a temple or in pretty box when we try to put our ideas and preferences above God's desire? My prayer has been that the Lord would help me not to make something that contains and strains, but that worships and satisfies.

The Daily Word

When a season of rest came for King Solomon and Israel, he began to build a temple so the presence of God could have a permanent dwelling place. Solomon used craftsmen and a gifted work force to create the temple. In the midst of construction, the word of the Lord came to Solomon, reaffirming the Lord's desire: "If you walk in My statutes, observe My ordinances, and keep all My commands by walking with them, then I will fulfill My promises to you." God did not say only that if the temple had ornate paneling and gold floors, then He would keep His promises. No, the Lord reaffirmed that His desire was for Solomon to walk in His ways.

The Lord said your body is now the temple of the Holy Spirit. The Spirit of God dwells within you. The Lord has not asked you to fix yourself up beautifully on the outside to be pleasing to Him. The Lord asks you to follow His ways. True beauty comes from within. Today, ask yourself, *"Am I focusing more on the construction on the outside of my temple or on following the Spirit of God who resides on the inside?"* As you walk in His ways, beauty from the inside will shine to the outside.

The word of the Lord came to Solomon: "As for this temple you are building—if you walk in My statutes, observe My ordinances, and keep all My commands by walking in them, I will fulfill My promise to you, which I made to your father David. I will live among the Israelites and not abandon My people Israel." —1 Kings 6:11–13

Further Scripture: Isaiah 66:2; 1 Corinthians 3:16; 1 Corinthians 6:19–20

Questions

1. How did Hiram show he always loved David (2 Samuel 5:11; 2 Chronicles 2:3)? How was the relationship between Hiram and David a benefit to Solomon?

2. Why was David not able to build the temple during his reign as king (1 Chronicles 22:8)? Why was Solomon able to build the temple during his reign (1 Kings 4:24)?

3. According to David's census, how many men were available to help build the temple (2 Samuel 24:9)? How many Israelite men did Solomon use?

4. Why is it significant that both Jews and Gentiles assisted in the construction of the temple (Isaiah 49:6; 56:6–7; Matthew 21:13; Ephesians 2:11–22)?

5. Why do you think the Lord spoke to Solomon during the building of the temple (1 Kings 6:11–13)? What is most important to the Lord when serving Him (Ephesians 6:6)?

6. What did the Holy Spirit highlight to you in 1 Kings 5—6 through the reading or the teaching?

Lesson 60: 1 Kings 7

Something Greater: Extravagant Disobedience

Teaching Notes

Intro

The focus for the beginning of this chapter was building structures. Moses' instructions for Israel's king said: "However, he must not acquire many horses for himself or send the people back to Egypt to acquire many horses, for the LORD has told you, 'You are never to go back that way again.' He must not acquire many wives for himself so that his heart won't go astray. He must not acquire very large amounts of silver and gold for himself" (Deuteronomy 17:16–17). These instructions have a connection in the next several chapters.

Teaching

1 Kings 6:38—7:1: The study of 1 Kings 7 begins with 1 Kings 6:38. The temple was completed with every detail in seven years, during the 11th year of Solomon's reign. It took Solomon 13 years, nearly twice as long to complete his own palace complex (1 Kings 7:1).

The complex was more than just one house. It included the private residence for Solomon and was the administrative center for the kingdom. There is a jarring transition between 1 Kings 6:38 and 1 Kings 7:1; an interruption that appears to be out of sequence chronologically. We are not sure how these two were built, if work took place on one through completion and then on the other, or if work would move back and forth between the two. These passages: 1 Kings 9:1 and 1 Kings 9:10 list the temple work and then the palace. In 1 Kings 3:1, the order is presented as palace first and then the temple. The writer wanted to make sure the reader saw the contrast; 13 years for the palace and seven years for the temple.

1 Kings 7:2–12: The details of the building, and the size and number of cedar beams and pillars, were extraordinary. The house was designed with many windows and doors, a long portico, and a canopy with pillars (vv. 2–6). Solomon created the hall of the throne where he would judge cases and fully covered it with paneling of cedar (v. 7). Famous decisions, such as the judgment about the baby claimed by two mothers, and receptions, such as when the Queen of Sheba arrived, were all held in this hall. Note the Queen of Sheba would not have seen the inside of the temple. When she talked about Solomon and all his glory; she was referring to his palace. The cedar smelled good and stood up well to insect damage, but it was very flammable as we will see at the end of Kings. Solomon had a similar house built for his wife, who was Pharaoh's daughter. Other homes and apartments were built as well, all with expensive materials and costly stones (vv. 8–12).

Twelve verses describe the palace complex that took 13 years to build. The writer of 1 Kings did not seem to consider these buildings as important as the temple. The building of the temple was described in part of chapter 5, all of chapter 6, part of chapter 7, and its dedication was yet to come. How important was the palace to Solomon? Was the palace in danger of becoming the main thing? Did Solomon want something greater for himself than for God?

A comparison list in 'Lesson 62: 1 Kings 9—10' gives the difference between the greatness of King Jesus compared to that of King Solomon. When these two building projects are compared, it seems to suggest that priorities were out of order. It is unclear from the text whether this extravagance in the palace complex was positive as an example of God's blessing or negative as an example of Solomon's self-indulgence and divided heart. The New Testament emphasizes that indulgence can be sinful (Luke 12:17–21), but in some cases can be acceptable, such as the woman who anointed Jesus' head (Mark 14:3–9). The bottom line is God is after the heart, not just what you build. Keep these things in mind as you move forward in 1 Kings: (1) Solomon used conscripted labor in both building projects (1 Kings 5:13–18). (2) Solomon used slave labor, enslaving non-Israelites who had remained in Israel (1 Kings 9:20–22). (3) In its final form, the use of forced labor will arouse great anger in the nation (1 Kings 12). All this came from a group of people who, 480 years before, had come out of slavery.

1 Kings 7:13–51: This section covers the final stages of the temple construction and temple furnishings. The author seems to relish in the minute details of the temple, possibly to emphasize the use of technical and artistic skills that were used to the glorify God. As you read this section, consider if you are using God-given gifts to create things for glory for your Creator. All the accessories described had a meaning, an influence, a testimony, or served as a visual aid. One of these craftsmen was Hiram, from Tyre, who was a bronze craftsman (vv. 13–14). He cast two hollow bronze pillars that were each 27 feet high and 18 feet in circumference. Hiram also created capitals to go atop the pillars that were seven-and-a-half feet high. Both the capitals and the pillars were covered with latticework gratings and wreaths of chain work (vv. 15–20).

The pillars were set up in the portico and given names—Jachin for the right pillar and Boaz for the left (vv. 21–22). The names of the pillars were important. The name Jachin meant, "He will establish," and was used to reinforce God's promise to establish David's throne and God's strength to accomplish it (2 Samuel 7:12–16). The name Boaz meant, "in Him is strength." Psalm 21:1 and 13 begins and ends with the word Boaz, and also include this picture of strength. Putting this together means He will establish the promise of God to establish David's throne and in Him is strength, the power of God exalted to accomplish it.

Verse 26 describes the water reservoir placed on golden calves (which they were not told to do). The 11,000 gallons of water show God's focus on cleansing. Notice inside the temple was seven menorahs, also not called for. Solomon had gilded the lily on his own. Take special notice of all these details as you read this chapter.

In verse 51, the temple was completed and King Solomon brought into the temple the consecrated things of his father. But then, Solomon waited 11 months to dedicate the temple in the holiest month of the year when Rosh Hashanah (New Year), Yom Kippur (Day of Atonement), and Sukkoth (Feast of Tabernacles) were all celebrated. He waited for *Something Greater*. The temple is now ready for the ark to come.

Closing

The glory of Solomon's temple was intended to leave us breathless. Herod's temple will put it to shame when it's built. Gary Inrig wrote, "Followers of Christ need to remember this glory as we ponder that we, both as congregations and as individuals, are described as 'God's temple'" (1 Corinthians 3:1–17, 6:19–20).[2] What God desires from His people isn't a building, but rather obedience. The nation of Israel later believed that the presence of the temple assured them of God's favor. In fact, some of the prophet Jeremiah's harshest sermons were directed against that false belief.

The readers of 1 Kings knew the temple didn't protect them from God's divine judgment because they were reading and hearing these words for the first time while in captivity in Babylon. The temple was in ruins. That is one of the reasons Kings was written—to answer the question for the Jews in exile in Babylon: How did we get here? The takeaway here is that any time we use a substitute for obedience to God, God allows judgment.

---

[2] Gary Inrig, *Holman Old Testament Commentary: 1 & 2 Kings* (Nashville: Broadman & Holman, 2003), 43.

The Daily Word

Not only did Solomon spend seven years building the Temple, he also took thirteen years building an elaborate palace complex for himself and his family. In the middle of discussing the details of the Temple, the resting place for the presence of the Lord, details of the palace complex are intricately described. And then the final details of the Temple are outlined and the construction was completed. Solomon was assigned by God to build a Temple for the presence of the Lord to reside, and then, in the midst of Temple construction, he built an even larger and extensive palace complex.

Do you ever get sidetracked while in the presence of the Lord? You may be having prayer time or reading His Word, when suddenly you click on social media or you find yourself dreaming about where to go shopping or wondering who won the latest football game? The world has so many things to distract you that it can be hard to stay focused on the Lord. The Lord says to set your mind on things above, not on earthly things. Seek first the kingdom of God and His righteousness, and then all these things will be added to you. As you rest and focus in His presence, you will experience the fullness of joy. You may look to the things that sidetrack you for peace, but when it comes down to it, *it's only when you focus your mind on Christ that He will keep you in perfect peace.* Today, stay focused on Christ.

Solomon completed his entire palace complex after 13 years of construction. —1 Kings 7:1

Further Scripture: Proverbs 5:1–2; Isaiah 26:3; Colossians 3:1–2

Questions

1. How long did it take Solomon to build the temple? How long did it take him to build his own house? What does this show about desiring comfort and luxury in his own life?

2. What were the names of the two pillars of bronze? What do these two names mean? How does this relate to the character of God?

3. What was the significance of the showbread in 1 Kings 7:48 (Leviticus 24:5–8)?

4. The temple was impressive even by today's standards. What goes through your mind to know that the same man that helped build this beautiful temple for the Lord was the same one, because of his sins, that brought judgment to Israel (1 Kings 11:6)?

5. What did the Holy Spirit highlight to you in 1 Kings 7 through the reading or the teaching?

Lesson 61: 1 Kings 8

Something Greater: The Dedication of the House of God

Teaching Notes

Intro

We're continuing through the historical books of the Old Testament. Constable states that 1 Kings 8 is "the most detailed account of a dedication service in the Bible. It is also one of the most theologically significant texts in 1 and 2 Kings."[1] This is going to give us the best picture of Israel's House of God. As Solomon built the temple, he was building *Something Greater*. Jesus is greater than that. This chapter is also one of the longest—sixty-six verses long. Wiersbe divides the chapter this way: a house of God (vv. 1–11); a house of testimony (vv. 12–21); a house of prayer (vv. 22–53); a house of praise (vv. 54–61); and a house of fellowship (vv. 62–66).[2]

Teaching

1 Kings 8:1–11: A House of God. Solomon brought together the elders of Israel—"the tribal heads and the ancestral leaders" were the "oldest living males within each extended family unit."[3] God's presence had been in the tabernacle but was going to be moved to a much better place in Jerusalem. God's presence was being moved from a portable place to a permanent home (v. 1). They gathered in the seventh month, the most holy month and the festival of the tabernacles or the festival of booths, which happened 11 months after the completion of the temple (v. 2). All males of Israel were required to attend. The priests and Levites brought the ark, the tabernacle tent, and the worship utensils to Jerusalem (vv. 3–4). Meanwhile, Solomon and the people of Israel sacrificed more sheep and cattle than could be counted (v. 5). The priests placed the ark below

---

[1] Thomas L. Constable, *Expository Notes of Dr. Thomas Constable: 1 Kings*, 54, http://planobiblechapel.org/tcon/notes/pdf/1kings.pdf.

[2] Warren W. Wiersbe, *Be Responsible: Being Good Stewards of God's Gifts* (Colorado Springs: David C. Cook, 2002), 64–76.

[3] John MacArthur, *The MacArthur Bible Commentary* (Nashville: Thomas Nelson, 2005), 404.

the cherubim in the most holy place in the temple (vv. 6–8). The only things in the ark were Moses' stone tablets with the Ten Commandments, and these were the only things that were not new in the temple (v. 9). When the priests came out, the shekinah glory of the Lord came down and filled the temple (vv. 10–11).

1 Kings 8:12–21: A House of Testimony (Solomon gave testimony about God's presence coming into the temple (vv. 12–13). This mentality shows the dependence Israel had on being able to come to God's presence. But God has never been limited to being inside a building, or a tent, or any other place. Solomon continued before the congregation while they all stood (v. 14). Solomon reminded them of God's goodness and faithfulness to and through King David, and now, through him (vv. 15–21).

In 2 Samuel 7, God made a covenant with David, promising He would work through David (vv. 12–16). Solomon had built the temple for God that his father had wanted to build. God kept His promises. Ultimately, though God's covenants with Abraham and David, they would be fulfilled in Jesus (Jeremiah 31:31–34).

1 Kings 8:22–53: A House of Prayer. (Solomon's testimony became a time of prayer. He prayed with his hands stretched out toward heaven (v. 22), a normal posture of individual prayer (Exodus 9:29). It seems Solomon prayed out of the understanding that God fulfills His promises (vv. 23–24). Think about this—God's promise to David would not have been fulfilled if Solomon hadn't acted. Then, Solomon asked the Lord for His presence and His protection (vv. 25–30).

There's so much in Scripture about extraordinary prayers: Moses' prayer for Israel (Exodus 32:8–14); David's prayer for pardon and confession (Psalm 51); Hezekiah's petitions for deliverance and healing (2 Kings 19:14–19; 20:1–7); David's prayer of surrender (Psalm 139); the prayer of Jabez (1 Chronicles 4:10); the Lord's Prayer (Matthew 6:9–13); Jonah's prayer for salvation (Jonah 2:29); David's prayer for deliverance (Psalm 3); Hannah's prayer (1 Samuel 2:1–10); Nehemiah's prayer for success (Nehemiah 1:1—2:9); and Jesus' prayer of submission (Luke 22:37–46). There are so many examples of people in Scripture coming before the Lord in the power of prayer. In verse 30, Solomon acknowledged that the people of Israel prayed toward Jerusalem from wherever they were, which continues today as well.

Wiersbe identified seven petitions Solomon asked of God:

1. *For justice in the land* (vv. 31–32; 2 Chronicles 6:22–23). Solomon asked that "the Lord would judge between the wicked and the righteous."

2. *For military defeat* (vv. 33–34; 2 Chronicles 6:24–25). Solomon asked that "the Lord would forgive the sins that had caused defeat in battle."

3. *For drought in the land* (vv. 35–36; 2 Chronicles 6:26–27). Solomon asked God for forgiveness of sin that had brought a drought on the land.

4. *For other natural calamities* (vv. 37–40; 2 Chronicles 6:28–31). Solomon asked God's forgiveness of sin that had brought calamities upon the nation in response to the prayers directed toward Jerusalem.

5. *For foreigners who came to pray* (vv. 41–43; 2 Chronicles 6:32–33). Solomon asked God for mercy on foreigners who feared God and prayed toward Jerusalem.

6. *For armies in battle* (vv. 44–45; 2 Chronicles 6:34–35). Solomon prayed God would make the armies victorious in battle when they prayed in the direction of Jerusalem.

7. *For defeat and captivity* (vv. 46–53; 2 Chronicles 6:36–39). Solomon asked God to "bring about restoration after captivity" when they prayed in the direction of Jerusalem.[4]

1 Kings 8:54–61: A House of Praise. Solomon's hands remained lifted toward heaven through the entire prayer. Verse 56 records, "Not one of all the good promises He made through His servant Moses has failed."

1 Kings 8:62–66: A House of Fellowship. Solomon and the people offered fellowship offerings to the Lord of 22,000 cattle and 120,000 sheep. On the 15th day, Solomon sent the people of Israel home. They left "rejoicing and with joyful hearts for all the goodness that the Lord had done for His servant and for His people Israel" (v. 66).

Closing

All of this happened because from the beginning of chapter 8, the people of Israel came together to dedicate the temple to God. Constable states, "This was the biggest event in Israel, in terms of its theological significance, since God gave Israel the Law at Mount Sinai. Israel was finally in the Promised Land with her God 'enthroned' in a place of great honor. Now Israel was in position to fulfill her calling as a nation in the world as never before in her history"[5] (Exodus 19:5–6). First Kings 8 launches the prophetic word given in 2 Samuel 7.

---

[4] The seven petitions are from Wiersbe, 70–73. The supporting statements after each petition are from MacArthur, 405.

[5] Constable, 59.

The Daily Word

Solomon dedicated the newly constructed Temple to the Lord. On his knees, Solomon testified and praised the Lord for His faithfulness and petitioned for the Lord to restore His people. With his hands spread out toward heaven, Solomon stood before the Lord, blessed the Temple, and experienced fellowship in the Lord's presence.

As you come before the Lord in prayer, think about your posture. It is okay to physically kneel or physically stand, expressing your devotion to the Lord. Today, take a minute to kneel or bow your head to the ground in adoration. Perhaps you feel led to walk outside and look at His mighty creation with your hands stretched toward heaven. Thank Him for His faithful promises in your life. Just as there are times when you need to get down on the floor to talk with small children, something happens in your heart when you lower yourself before the Lord and talk with Him. Don't worry about what others may think. Enjoy this fellowship with your Heavenly Father.

When Solomon finished praying this entire prayer and petition to the Lord, he got up from kneeling before the altar of the Lord, with his hands spread out toward heaven, and he stood and blessed the whole congregation of Israel with a loud voice: "May the Lord be praised! He has given rest to His people Israel according to all He has said. Not one of all the good promises He made through His servant Moses has failed." —1 Kings 8:54–56

Further Scripture: Psalm 134:1–2; Daniel 6:10; Revelation 7:11

Questions

1. What was Solomon's first act of dedication for the ark? How did Solomon follow in his father David's footsteps (2 Samuel 6:17)?

2. What are some things Solomon highlighted in his prayer? Are you praying specifically in your own prayer life?

3. What was the distinguishing mark of the nation of Israel (Exodus 33:13–23; 1 Kings 8:10–11; Romans 9:4)?

4. What did it mean when Solomon knelt and spread out his hands toward heaven to pray (Exodus 9:29, 33; 1 Kings 8:22, 54; 2 Chronicles 6:13; Psalm 63:4; Ezra 9:5; 1 Timothy 2:8)?

5. How do you see the goodness and faithfulness of God in verses 15–21 (2 Samuel 7:2, 12–13, 25)? Why did God do these things and fulfill His promises?

6. What did the Holy Spirit highlight to you in 1 Kings 8 through the reading or the teaching?

Lesson 62: 1 Kings 9—10

Something Greater: Jesus Is Greater Than Solomon

Teaching Notes

Intro

Yesterday, we talked about Solomon's prayer at the dedication of the temple. After the prayer, Solomon sacrificed 22,000 cattle and 120,000 sheep in offering to the Lord. Israel was in a good season of peace.

Teaching

1 Kings 9:1–9: Solomon had finished the temple, the royal palace, and everything on his to-do list. The Lord appeared to Solomon a second time and instructed Solomon to walk as David had (vv. 2–4). God promised He would establish Solomon's royal throne over Israel forever as long as Solomon kept His commands, but He would cut off the line if Solomon or his sons turned away from Him (vv. 5–9).

1 Kings 9:10–14: Solomon gave 20 cities in Israel to King Hiram in return for Hiram's gold, but Hiram was not satisfied with the towns and called them the Land of Cabul (vv. 10–14).

1Kings 9:15–23: The rebuilding of storage cities with forced labor is outlined.

1 Kings 9:24–28: Here is a report some of Solomon's other activities—his wife moved to his palace, he offered sacrifices on the Lord's altar three times a year, and he built a fleet of ships. Wiersbe describes Solomon as "a great entrepreneur. He made trade agreements with many nations, built a navy, and hired Hiram's expert seaman to manage it for him."[1] Solomon was an importer of goods, an international figure, and a witness to the Gentiles about his God. He managed a massive budget and possibly even had a zoo (Ecclesiastes 2:4–9).

---

[1] Warren W. Wiersbe, *Be Responsible: Being Good Stewards of God's Gifts* (Colorado Springs: David C. Cook, 2002), 89.

1 Kings 10:1–22: People throughout the world knew of Solomon. Despite Solomon's greatness, Jesus said there was "something greater than Solomon" (Matthew 12:42). I want to take the conversation between Solomon and the Queen of Sheba to prove how Jesus is *Something Greater*. Sheba was located in the Arabian Desert (what is considered Yemen today). The queen would have traveled somewhere between 1,200 and 1,500 miles on her journey to Jerusalem.

How is Jesus *Something Greater* than Solomon?

- *Solomon*: The queen heard about Solomon and came to see for herself (v. 1a).
- *Jesus*: The crowds came to Jesus because of who He is and what He was doing (John 12:9, 12).
- *Solomon*: She came to test Solomon with difficult questions (v. 1b).
- *Jesus*: The religious leaders came to test Jesus (Matthew 22:12, 23, 34–35, 46).
- *Solomon*: Nothing was too difficult for Solomon to explain to her (v. 3).
- *Jesus*: Jesus knows all things! (John 16:30; 21:17b)
- *Solomon*: Solomon's wisdom took her breath away (v. 5).
- *Jesus*: Everyone was in awe and astounded; awestruck (Matthew 9:8; Luke 5:25–26).
- *Solomon*: She didn't believe what she heard until she came and saw (vv. 6–7a).
- *Jesus*: No eye has seen . . . what God has prepared for those who love Him (1 Corinthians 2:9).
- *Solomon*: Solomon's wisdom and prosperity far exceeded what she had heard (v. 7b).
- *Jesus*: All wisdom is hidden in Jesus (Isaiah 11:2; Colossians 2:3).
- *Solomon*: Solomon's servants were happy (v. 8).
- *Jesus*: There will be no more tears/pain (Revelation 21:4).
- *Solomon*: She gave Solomon gifts (v. 10).
- *Jesus*: Wise men brought gifts. Nations will bring wealth to Israel again (Isaiah 60; Matthew 2:11).
- *Solomon*: Solomon granted the queen's every desire (v. 13).
- *Jesus*: Jesus gives us the desires of our hearts (Psalm 37:3; Matthew 21:22).
- *Solomon*: Solomon amassed great wealth (vv. 14–22).
- *Jesus*: All things belong to Jesus and He became poor for our sakes (Psalm 50:10–11; 2 Corinthians 8:9).

1 Kings 10:23–29: Solomon had great wisdom, and everyone in the world wanted to hear his wisdom (v. 24). Kue (v. 28) was probably the city of Que. An inscription found in the 9th century in Asia Minor mentioned the city. This was one of the places from which Solomon obtained horses. His collection of horses brought Solomon perilously close to actually violating the prohibition of acquiring a great number of horses (Deuteronomy 17:16). Solomon had even become a horse trader (v. 29). While Solomon was enormously rich, Jesus' wealth is greater (Psalm 50:10–11; 2 Corinthians 8:9).

Closing

Jesus is *Something Greater* than Solomon. Jesus is the ultimate King!

- Philippians 2:9–11: "For this reason God highly exalted Him and gave Him the name that is above every name, so that at the name of Jesus every knee will bow—of those who are in heaven and on earth and under the earth—and every tongue should confess that Jesus Christ is Lord, to the glory of God the Father."
- Revelation 5:12–13: "They said with a loud voice: 'The Lamb who was slaughtered is worthy to receive power and riches and wisdom and strength and honor and glory and blessing! I heard every creature in heaven, on earth, under the earth, on the sea, and everything in them say: Blessing and honor and glory and dominion to the One seated on the throne, and to the Lamb, forever and ever!'"

Through the Queen of Sheba meeting Solomon, it ultimately points to the one who is greater than even Solomon. Jesus is always *Something Greater*!

The Daily Word

The Temple and King Solomon's palace were completed and dedicated. Now Solomon grew his kingdom with wisdom from the Lord. He so surpassed all the kings of the world in riches and wisdom that the Queen of Sheba came to confirm that what she had heard about King Solomon was true. Solomon's kingdom took her breath away because, yes, the things she had heard were true. Solomon's kingdom was great indeed, and even his servants were happy.

What if you received a visit from someone to see if the things said about you were true? Would their visit make you nervous or would you be free to say, "Come on in!"? The Lord desires for you to live your life with integrity and a clear conscience so when a surprise visit happens, your life will reflect the words of your mouth. But what if the "surprise visitor" finds something you'd rather he or she not know about? Take a deep breath. It's okay. Because someone greater has come since King Solomon—someone named Jesus. Yes, Jesus knows everything about your life. He knows where you struggle, and He is there to walk with you. He loves you through it. When you surrender your life to Christ, He provides the grace you need to press on and keep walking. Rest in His greatness today. There is no reason to strive in your own power for perfection in this world because His grace is great within you!

She said to the king, "The report I heard in my own country about your words and about your wisdom is true. But I didn't believe the reports until I came and saw with my own eyes. Indeed, I was not even told half. Your wisdom and prosperity far exceed the report I heard. How happy are your men."
—1 Kings 10:6–8

Further Scripture: Matthew 12:42; 2 Corinthians 8:9; 1 John 4:4

Questions

1. In 1 Kings 9:2, the Lord appeared to Solomon a second time. When was the first time and why (1 Kings 3:5)?

2. In 1 Kings 9:12, why do you think Hiram was not pleased with the cities that Solomon had given him? What does Cabul mean (1 Kings 9:13)?

3. If Solomon was the wisest man who ever lived, why do you suppose he was marrying foreign women and multiplying horses (Deuteronomy 7:3–4; 17:16–17; 1 Kings 9:16; 10:26)?

4. 1 Kings 10:9 (NKJV) says, "Blessed be the LORD your God, who delighted in you, setting you on the throne of Israel! Because the LORD has loved Israel forever, therefore He made you king, to do justice and righteousness." Is it possible the Queen of Sheba realized through the beauty of all of Solomon's kingdom that his God was the one true God (Matthew 12:38–42)?

5. How does Solomon's earthly kingdom compare to the kingdom of heaven (1 Kings 10:18–20; Revelation 21:10–21)?

6. What did the Holy Spirit highlight to you in 1 Kings 9—10 through the reading or the teaching?

Lesson 63: 1 Kings 11—12

Something Greater: Solomon Sinned Against God

Teaching Notes

Intro

Yesterday, we looked at how wealthy Solomon had become in both wisdom and money. Even the Queen of Sheba was made breathless when she saw his wisdom in person, but that all changed in 1 Kings 11 as the chapter describes the sad close to his brilliant reign. Solomon's life was taken over by the sin of having many wives. He faced adversaries, things that had not been an issue earlier in his life, but became a problem later on. Wiersbe outlined chapter 11 with these divisions: "Solomon disobeyed God's Word (vv. 1–8); Solomon ignored God's warning (vv. 9–13); Solomon resisted God's discipline (vv. 14–25); Solomon opposed God's servant (vv. 26–43)."[1] Today, we will continue to look at *Something Greater* than Solomon.

Teaching

1 Kings 11:1–8: Solomon Disobeyed God's Word. Solomon loved many foreign women, and he knew what he did went against God's instructions (Deuteronomy 7:1–3). His love of these women turned his heart from God, a warning God gave in Deuteronomy 17:17 (Proverbs 19:3). Besides the number of wives, Solomon married foreign women who worshipped other gods. Scripture is clear about not marrying unbelievers—do not yoke yourself with a nonbeliever. By marrying foreign women, Solomon went back into bondage of the world. Wiersbe states, "First, he was friendly with the world (James 4:4), then spotted by the world (James 1:27), and then he came to love the world (1 John 2:15–17) and conformed to the world (Romans 12:2)."[2] This is a slippery slope that a lot of us can slide down if we don't keep our eyes on the Lord (vv. 1–3). When Solomon was old, he allowed his many wives to seduce him into worshipping

---

[1] Warren W. Wiersbe, *Be Responsible: Being Good Stewards of God's Gifts* (Colorado Springs: David C. Cook, 2002), 97–103.

[2] Wiersbe, 100.

other gods—gods whose worship included unspeakably violent and/or sexual acts (vv. 4–8).

1 Kings 11:9–13: Solomon Ignored God's Warning. When we conform to the world, God always gives us another chance. Solomon ignored God's warning and anger, and continued with his sin. Therefore, God said He would tear the kingdom away from Solomon's son, leaving him only the tribe of Judah and the city of Jerusalem to continue the Davidic covenant. The rest of Israel would be given to His servant, Jeroboam.

1 Kings 11:14–15: Solomon Resisted God's Discipline. The Lord raised enemies against Solomon. First, God raised up Hadad the Edomite. In 2 Samuel 8:13–14, David had his commander, Joab, kill every male in Edom. But Hadad had fled to Egypt as a small boy. Later, Pharaoh gave his wife's sister to Hadad as his bride. When Hadad heard that both David and Joab were dead, he was ready to return to his own country (vv. 14–22). Then, the Lord raised up Rezon of Damascus as another enemy. Rezon had also fled from his master, the king of Zobah, and gathered an army. Rezon hated Israel and was Solomon's enemy (vv. 23–25).

1 Kings 11:26–43: Solomon Opposed God's Servant. Solomon saw Jeroboam was capable and put him in charge of all the laborers in the house of Joseph. Wiersbe explains Jeroboam was an Ephraimite and was placed over forced laborers who were from the tribes of Ephraim and Manasseh, while the people of Israel tired of Solomon's forcing laborers, especially Jews, to do his work.[3] During that time, the prophet Ahijah came to Jeroboam on the road. Ahijah took the new cloak he was wearing and tore it into twelve pieces. Ahijah told Jeroboam to take ten pieces and explained God was going to tear the kingdom out of Solomon's hands and give ten tribes to Jeroboam to rule (vv. 26–33). The prophet was releasing the word to Jeroboam that Solomon would lose his kingdom because Solomon had become friendly with the world. God explained Solomon's son would keep part of the kingdom, a sign of His mercy for and promise to David (vv. 34–37). God then made the same promise to Jeroboam. If he walked in God's ways, God would remain with him and his house would become a great dynasty (vv. 38–39).

Solomon didn't like Jeroboam and tried to kill him. Jeroboam fled to Egypt and stayed until Solomon died. The last verses (vv. 41–43) give the closing data on Solomon's reign. Solomon's son Rehoboam became king after his father died. At the death of Solomon, his kingdom was split into two kingdoms:

---

[3] Wiersbe, 103.

Judah, the Southern Kingdom (the tribe of Judah and city of Jerusalem) under King Rehoboam

Israel, the Northern Kingdom (the ten tribes located in the north) under King Jeroboam

This all came to be because Solomon disobeyed the Lord.

Closing

Why was Solomon's kingdom split up? Moses gave clear instructions to Jewish kings:

1. The king must not acquire many horses (Deuteronomy 17:16). Solomon had 1,400 chariots and 12,000 horsemen (1 Kings 10:26).

2. The king must not acquire many wives (Deuteronomy 17:17a). Solomon had 700 wives and 300 concubines (1 Kings 11:3).

3. The king must not acquire excessive silver and gold (Deuteronomy 17:17b). Solomon had excessive amounts of gold, even gold drinking vessels and utensils, but no silver since it was worthless in comparison (1 Kings 10:21).

The Lord was angry with Solomon (1 Kings 11:9–11), so Solomon was not the one. Jesus, however, is the One:

1. Jesus did not have excessive silver and gold. He gave it all up so we might be rich (2 Corinthians 8:9).

2. Jesus did not have many horses, but used a borrowed donkey (John 12:14).

3. Jesus did not have many wives, but only had one bride—the Church (Ephesians 5:25–27).

Zechariah 9:9 puts this all together of *Something Greater:* "Rejoice greatly, Daughter Zion! Shout in triumph, Daughter Jerusalem! Look, your King is coming to you; He is righteous and victorious, humble and riding on a donkey, on a colt, the foal of a donkey." All of this is describing the coming King—Jesus!

The Daily Word

Solomon appeared to be at the peak of his reign. He had more wisdom and riches than anyone else in the world. But then his heart got sidetracked, and he willingly disobeyed the Lord. He accumulated seven hundred wives and three hundred concubines who seduced Solomon to follow other gods and turned his heart away from the Lord. Solomon did evil in the Lord's eyes, and the Lord became angry with him. Solomon's kingdom began to fall apart. The Lord asked Solomon to keep his eyes on Him alone, but as time went on, Solomon strayed, wanting more and more of that which wasn't of the Lord.

The things of this world will seduce you into wanting more. But it doesn't just happen overnight. Daily, small choices you make against the Lord's way will sidetrack your heart. Before you know it, you have built your own kingdom, your own ways, and your own people. Be careful! Allow Solomon's life to be a warning to you. The gate leading to life is narrow and difficult. In order to keep walking through the narrow gate, renew your mind in Christ. Meditate on His Word. Find fellowship with other believers. Remember, you are anointed to walk in the truth, not the lies of this world. Jesus is enough to satisfy your soul.

He had 700 wives who were princesses and 300 concubines, and they turned his heart away from the Lord. When Solomon was old, his wives seduced him to follow other gods. He was not completely devoted to Yahweh his God, as his father David had been. —1 Kings 11:3–4

Further Scripture: Matthew 7:13–14; Romans 12:2; 1 John 2:27

Questions

1. In 1 Kings 11:14, God began to raise up adversaries against Solomon. Do you believe God raises up adversaries against us when we seek other gods in our own lives? If so, can you think of a time when this happened to you?

2. In 1 Kings 11:31–32, why did God save one tribe for the sake of David (2 Samuel 7:12–13; Matthew 1:1–17)?

3. Why do you think King Rehoboam asked for advice from the elders and then didn't follow it? Has there ever been a time when you asked for advice and didn't follow it? If so, why not?

4. What would make Jeroboam think the people of Israel would kill him just because they went to the house of the Lord in Jerusalem to worship (1 Kings 12:26–27)?

5. 1 Kings 12:28–31 speaks of Jeroboam returning to idol worship. Why do you believe he did this? Do we still do this today? Who and/or what are the idols in your life?

6. In 1 Kings 12:33, do you think there was any significance to the date Jeroboam instituted a feast for the sons of Israel or in that he "devised it in his own heart? (Jeremiah 17:9; Matthew 12:34)

7. What did the Holy Spirit highlight to you in 1 Kings 11—12 through the reading or the teaching?

Lesson 64: 1 Kings 13—14

Something Greater: The Deception of the Man of God

Teaching Notes

Intro

As we move into the study of 1 Kings 13—14, we are also moving into chaos. This study will feel a little like the lessons in the book of Judges with evil and killing. In 1 Kings 11—12, we saw the death of Solomon and the division of the kingdom with two new kings: Jeroboam as king over the ten tribes of Israel in the northern kingdom and Rehoboam, Solomon's son, as king over the tribe of Judah in the southern kingdom. Jeroboam was a servant of Solomon's, but a prophet told him he would become king over ten tribes when Solomon died. While 1 Kings 11 was all about Solomon's problems and sins, 1 Kings 13 is about Jeroboam's problems and sins.

Teaching

Wiersbe divided chapter 13 into these sections:[1]

1 Kings 13:1–2: The Message. A man of God heard from the Lord through a revelation to go to Bethel with a message for Jeroboam while Jeroboam was getting ready to burn incense on the altar (v. 1). Jeroboam was already taking on the place of the king and the role of the priest—both would have been bad. A king was never to take on the role of the priest until the coming Messiah (2 Chronicles 26:16–23). The man of God proclaimed Josiah, from the house of David, would become king and would root out the evil in the kingdom (v. 2). Josiah's reign would come 300 years later when he would burn the high places, slaughter the illegitimate priests, burn the Asherah, destroy the altars, and burn human bones that defiled the altars (2 Kings 23:15–20). Bethel was a community where many came to learn about being a prophet. The man of God completed God's

---

[1] Warren W. Wiersbe, *Be Responsible: Being Good Stewards of God's Gifts* (Colorado Springs: David C. Cook, 2002), 133–34.

message to Jeroboam by explaining the altar would be destroyed and the ashes poured out (v. 3).

1 Kings 13:4–6: The Miracles. King Jeroboam stretched out his hand, pointed to the man of God, and told his guard to arrest the man. His hand withered as he spoke and it did not go back to normal (v. 4). Then, the man of God's statement came true—the altar ripped apart and the ashes poured from the altar (v. 5). The king asked the man to pray for God's favor to restore his hand. The man did, and the king's hand was restored completely (v. 6).

1 Kings 13:7–10: The Maneuver. The king invited the man of God to come to his home so he could be refreshed and rewarded (v. 7). Wiersbe suggests that Jeroboam "was a clever man and tried to trap the prophet by inviting him to the palace for a meal."[2] The man replied he would not even accept half of Jeroboam's house, his food, or his water because the Lord had specifically told him not to (vv. 8–9). If the man of God had eaten a meal with Jeroboam after just releasing God's message about Jeroboam's sin, his actions would have "wiped out the effectiveness of his witness and ministry."[3] The man of God followed God's instructions completely, even returning home a different way from the way he had come (v. 10).

1 Kings 13:11–34: The Mistake. In Bethel, Jeroboam was leading the people in worship of idols. An old prophet was living in this town where the things of God were no longer taking place (v. 11a). The old prophet's sons told him what had happened when the man of God released God's message in Bethel (v. 11b). The prophet asked which way the man of God had gone and his sons told him (v. 12). He told his sons to saddle his donkey for him, and he rode after the man of God (v. 13). The prophet found the man of God under an oak tree. The prophet asked if he was the man of God and invited him to come home with him for a meal (vv. 14–15). The man of God explained that God told him not to eat or drink there or return home the same way (vv. 16–17). The prophet told the man of God he had been told to invite him back by an angel (v.18). The old prophet lied to the man of God, and the man of God failed to discern the old man's deceit (v. 19). Why did the old prophet lie? MacArthur suggests, "It may be that his own sons were worshipers at Bethel or perhaps priests, and this man wanted to gain favor with the king by showing up the man of God as an imposter who acted contrary to his own claim to have heard from God"[4] (Jeremiah 23:16; Ezekiel 13:2, 7).

---

[2] Wiersbe, 134.

[3] Wiersbe, 134.

[4] John MacArthur, *The MacArthur Bible Commentary* (Nashville: Thomas Nelson, 2005), 414.

While they were dining, the word of the Lord came to the prophet who had lied to the man of God. The prophet told the man of God that since he had disobeyed God's commands to him, his bones would not reach the grave of his ancestors (vv. 20–22). The Israelites buried their dead with the bones of their ancestors in a common grave (Judges 8:32; 2 Samuel 2:32). This indicated a disgrace. The old prophet saddled his donkey for the man of God (v. 23). On his way home, the man of God was attacked and killed by a lion on the road. The donkey and the lion stood beside the corpse (v. 24). This is not a natural response of a lion and a donkey to the man's corpse. *Nelson's Commentary* states, "The way the lion stood by both the man of God and his donkey shows that the lion did not kill for food but was God's executioner."[5] Men who passed by the corpse went back to Bethel and told what they had seen (v. 25). When the old prophet recognized that the man of God suffered God's punishment, he went and recovered the man's corpse, mourned his death, and buried his body in his own family grave (vv. 26–30). Then the old prophet instructed his sons to bury his body next to the bones of the man of God, who had carried God's message (vv. 31–32). After this, Jeroboam still did not repent or hear God's word. He did not turn from his sin, and his house would be annihilated because of it (vv. 33–34).

Closing

We must trust the voice of God in our lives, not others speaking "for Him." God must be our primary source. Everything else must filter through that (1 John 2:26–27). How can we be sure of God's voice?

Greg Simas offers 10 Ways to Confirm God's Voice:

1. Does it agree with the Bible? (Psalm 119:105; 2 Timothy 3:16)

2. Will it make me more like Christ? (Romans 8:29)

3. Do my spouse and family confirm it? (Proverbs 11:14; Amos 3:3; Ephesians 5:21)

4. Do spiritually mature believers confirm it? (Proverbs 11:14; 15:22; Ephesians 3:10)

5. Is it consistent with how God made me? (Romans 12:6; 1 Peter 4:10)

6. Does it line up with prophetic words spoken over me? (1 Timothy 4:14)

7. Does it move me? (Romans 12:11)

8. Will it stretch me? (2 Corinthians 12:9; Philippians 3:13–14)

---

[5] Earl D. Radmacher, Ronald B. Allen, and H. Wayne House, eds., *Nelson's New Illustrated Bible Commentary* (Nashville: Thomas Nelson, 1999), 447.

9. Will it require faith? (Romans 10:17; 2 Corinthians 5:7; Hebrews 11:6)
10. Do I have peace about it? (Philippians 4:7)[6]

After you go through this list confirming it is God's voice in your life, do not take five months to make a decision. This list is not to delay your process, it is to confirm what you are hearing is from the Lord. The man of God heard clearly from the Lord and knew what to do, yet he disobeyed because he gave in to the old prophet who deceived him. Stick to what you hear, do not add to it.

The Daily Word

During Jeroboam's reign as king, a man of God came to Jeroboam with a revelation from the Lord. When this word actually happened, King Jeroboam invited the man of God to his home, offering the man refreshment and a reward. However, the man of God refused because God told him not to eat bread or drink water. In this instance, the man of God was obedient to the Lord's specific direction and was steadfast in his walk. But later, when an old prophet went after the man of God and also asked him to come back with him for bread and drink, the man of God returned. At this point, he disobeyed the voice of the Lord, and as a result, he faced deadly consequences.

As you walk with the Lord, you need to trust His voice in your life and stick to it. Jesus says, "My sheep hear Me and know My voice." Others may speak into your life, *but if you know what you heard from the Lord, don't be easily persuaded by others*. If someone tells you to do something or has a word for you, listen to it. But before you react or respond, take some time to ask the Lord to confirm it through His Word, through others, and by giving you peace. If it goes against what the Lord is saying to you, don't compromise or let it persuade you. The Lord will honor your obedience to His voice in your life.

But he answered, "I cannot go back with you, eat bread, or drink water with you in this place, for a message came to me by the word of the Lord: 'You must not eat bread or drink water there or go back by the way you came.'"
—1 Kings 13:16–17

Further Scripture: Isaiah 30:21; John 10:27; Galatians 5:7–8

---

[6] Greg Simas, "10 Ways to Confirm God's Voice in Your Life," Greg Simas, January 3, 2022, www.gregsimas.org/p/10-ways-to-confirm-gods-voice.

Questions

1. In 1 Kings 13:18, why do you think the old prophet lied to the man of God? In your opinion, what should the man of God have done (1 John 4:1)?

2. Why do you think the lion killed the man of God and left him uneaten? Is this an example of the animals obeying the Word of the Lord (Psalm 148:7)?

3. In 1 Kings 13:33, Jeroboam made priests out of every people group/class. Why was this a sin (Numbers 8:16–18)? What was the price he would pay for these sins (1 Kings 14)?

4. What did the Holy Spirit highlight to you in 1 Kings 13—14 through the reading or the teaching?

Lesson 65: 1 Kings 15—16

Something Greater: Good or Evil in God's Sight

Teaching Notes

Intro

My goal for reviveSCHOOL is to take each of you deeper into the Word. There is so much meat in these historical books we've been studying. Read the Word like it is brand new to you and ask the Lord what He wants you to hear. I want us to know the Word inside and out so we will be ready to release God's Word to others.

In the past couple of days, we saw the nation of Israel divided into two kingdoms because of King Solomon's sin of disobedience. However, because of the Davidic covenant, we know these kingdoms will come back together and that the house of David will always be on the throne in Israel. The Kingdom of Israel (the northern part) experienced nine different dynasties that lasted for 250 years. The Kingdom of Judah (the southern part) contained the tribe of Judah and the house of David that lasted 350 years. First Kings 15 covers the kings of both Judah and Israel from 913 to 885 BC.[1] The southern kingdom and the house of David would point to one thing—*Something Greater*, it pointed to Jesus.

To keep the royal lineage in mind, here were the kings of each kingdom after Solomon's death through 1 Kings 15:

Judah (southern kingdom*)	*Israel (northern kingdom)*
Rehoboam (evil king)	Jeroboam (evil king)
Abijam/Abijah (evil king)	Nadab (evil king)
Asa (good king)	Baasha (evil king)

*The southern kingdom maintained the lineage of David and the Davidic Covenant.

Teaching

1 Kings 15:1–8: In the 18th year of King Jeroboam's reign of Israel (the northern kingdom), Abijam followed Rehoboam and became king of Judah (the

---

[1] John MacArthur, *The MacArthur Bible Commentary* (Nashville: Thomas Nelson, 2005), 415.

southern kingdom) and reigned three years (vv. 1–2). Abijah's name was a mixture of the Hebrew word for "father" with the Hebrew word for "sea," usually used for a Canaanite god. Possibly, "This name reflects the Canaanite influence that had come even into the royal family this early in Judah's reign."[2] Abijam continued in all the sins his father Rehoboam had committed and was not devoted to the Lord as David had been (v. 3). Rehoboam had at least 18 wives, but because of God's covenant with David, He used David's son to establish Jerusalem (v. 4). David had been obedient to God, except in how he dealt with Uriah the Hittite (v. 5). Rehoboam and Jeroboam had been at war throughout Rehoboam's life (v. 6). Abijam and Jeroboam were also at war, but Abijam trusted God and was victorious (2 Chronicles 13:2–20). The pattern of recording obituaries is provided for Abijam in verses 7–8.

1 Kings 15:9–15: Asa followed Abijam and reigned 41 years (vv. 9–10). Asa had a good reign and did what was right in God's sight (v. 11). Asa banished male cult prostitutes, moved all the idols his fathers had made, removed his grandmother Maacah as queen mother because she had an obscene image of Asherah. King Asa chopped down his grandmother's obscene image and burned it (vv. 12–13). MacArthur describes the queen mother as "corrupt," who had created an obscene image, an idol that was "a horrible, repulsive thing," possibly something that was "sexually explicit."[3] Asa did not get rid of the high places of worship (v.14) because they could have been used for the worship of God, his heart was completely devoted to God for his entire life (1 Kings 8:61; 2 Chronicles 14:4; Matthew 22:37–38). Asa also brought things to the Lord's temple that he and his father had consecrated to the Lord (v. 16).

1 Kings 15:16–22: Asa, the good king, was constantly at war against Baasha, the king of Israel (v. 16). Sadly, of all 19 kings of Israel and Judah, only eight of them did right in the eyes of the Lord. Asa is an important king for us to study. Baasha built Ramah to cut off access to Asa (v. 17). Asa made a treaty with one of Baasha's supporters and then attacked the cities of Israel. Baasha finally quit building Ramah and returned home. King Asa commanded everyone in Judah to remove the stones and timbers of Ramah so it could not be built again.

1 Kings 15:25–31: Nadab's evil reign.

---

[2] Earl D. Radmacher, Ronald B. Allen, and H. Wayne House, eds., *Nelson's New Illustrated Bible Commentary* (Nashville: Thomas Nelson, 1999), 449.

[3] MacArthur, 415.

Closing

Asa addressed the sin in his own family's life and removed his grandmother from his palace. He removed the idols and unholy things from the land. The questions for us to consider are:

1. What things need to be removed from our lives?
2. What unholy things exist?
3. What idols have we created or do we hold in a place of primary importance?

What do you need to remove from your life in order to bless somebody else? Asa probably offended family by removing the evil of his grandmother's doing, but he didn't let it stay so that his family could be a blessing to the Lord.

The Daily Word

Following the reign of several kings who did what was evil in the eyes of the Lord, King Asa took the throne. King Asa reigned for forty-one years and did what was right in the Lord's sight. He banished male cultic prostitutes, removed all idols, and even dealt with generational sin by removing his grandmother as queen mother, by chopping and burning down her obscene images. In other words, King Asa removed anything not pleasing to God, except for the high places. King Asa's heart was devoted to God his entire life.

King Asa went into his grandmother's home and found obscene images. Would the King of kings find anything in your home that needs to be removed? As you reflect, think about items or activities that may have become idols in your life: a TV show, gaming for long hours, an app on your phone, or clothes in your closet. Maybe there is an activity you partake in because all the generations of your family have, but you know it is evil in the eyes of the Lord. Ask the Lord today: "*Is there anything in my home I need to remove in order to keep my heart completely devoted to You?*" Then, in obedience, remove whatever the Lord reveals to you.

Asa did what was right in the Lord's eyes, as his ancestor David had done. —1 Kings 15:11

Further Scripture: Romans 6:1–2; Matthew 6:21; 1 Corinthians 8:5–6

Questions

1. In 1 Kings 15:3–4, why did God continue to let evil kings rule (2 Samuel 7:8–9)?

2. In 1 Kings 15:28–30, Baasha became king and slaughtered all of King Jeroboam's descendants. Did he do this because the Lord told him to, or did God use an evil king to carry out His promise? Why do you think that?

3. Ahab became king and did evil in the sight of the Lord, even more than any king before him. In what ways was Ahab worse?

4. What did the Holy Spirit highlight to you in 1 Kings 15—16 through the reading or the teaching?

Lesson 66: 1 Kings 17—18

Something Greater: The Coming of Revival

Teaching Notes

Intro

1 Kings 18 takes me back to my time of study at Gordon Cornwall Theological Seminary under Dr. Robert Coleman, who, in my opinion, is one of the most gifted and insightful teachers on revival, outreach, and discipleship. After three years under Dr. Coleman, I had to write a doctoral dissertation on this passage. Walt Kaiser wrote a book titled, *Revive Us Again*, a book that shaped Time to Revive. Kaiser wrote about an incredible number of revivals in both the Old and New Testaments, including one based on today's passage, which he called, "It's Time to Let God Be God." First Kings 18 could be called Time to Revive's chapter, because the heart within it is the need for national revival and for God to show up. We too have to give God space to be God—to direct how He wants to revive our nation and our lives.

In 1 Kings 17—18, Israel had become divided, and two new kingdoms, Israel in the north and Judah in the south, were created. Both kingdoms experienced several kings, and all but one was evil in God's sight. At this point, 58 years had passed since the kingdoms were divided (931 BC). In the northern kingdom, the kings did evil that is documented in 1 Kings: *Jeroboam* created two golden calves for his people to worship (1 Kings 12:28–32); *Nadab*, his son, continued the idol worship his father started (1 Kings 15:26); *Baasha* murdered King Nadab to take the throne (1 Kings 15:27); *Elah*, Baasha's son, was a drunkard and a murderer (1 Kings 16:8–9); *Zimri* committed treason against Elah and took the throne (1 Kings 16:20); Omri led his people into idol worship (1 Kings 16:25–26); and *Ahab*, son of Omri, married Jezebel and did more evil than any of the kings who had gone before him (1 Kings 16:30–31).

Teaching

1 Kings 17: There was pure evilness in the northern kingdom. In this backdrop, God sent Elijah the Tishbite to announce the coming drought that God was going to hold over the land (v. 1). After his pronouncement, Elijah had to hide for three years in the Wadi Cherith (vv. 2–7) and then with a widow in Zarephath (vv. 8–24). As we walk through 1 Kings 18, I'm going to use three statements from Kaiser as we consider letting God be God.[1]

1 Kings 18:1–6: He Makes us Courageous. After three years of hiding from Ahab, God sent Elijah to appear before Ahab with the message that the rain was coming (vv. 1–2). We need to be courageous and step up to deliver God's Word (Deuteronomy 31:6; Joshua 1:9; 1 Chronicles 28:20). Ahab called for Obadiah (not the prophet, but his name meant "servant of the Lord"), who was in charge of Ahab's household and feared the Lord. Obadiah hid 100 of God's prophets in two caves and provided them with food and water while Jezebel had all the other prophets slaughtered (vv. 3–4). Obadiah was sent one way throughout the land to feed the horses, mules and cattle to prevent them from dying of starvation, while King Ahab went the other direction (vv. 5–6).

1 Kings 18:7–20: While Obadiah was walking, Elijah "suddenly met him." Obadiah recognized him immediately (v. 7) and Elijah sent Obadiah to tell Ahab he was back (v. 8). Obadiah asked Elijah why he would send him back to be killed by Ahab when he delivered his message, especially since he already risked his life taking care of God's prophets (vv. 9–14). Obadiah obeyed and Ahab met Elijah, calling him a troubler (vv. 15–17). Elijah proclaimed that Ahab and his father had destroyed Israel by ignoring God's commands and worshipping idols (v. 18). Elijah told Ahab to meet him on Mount Carmel along with all the prophets of Baal and Asherah (vv. 19–20).

The theological discussions about this Obadiah are fascinating. Many propose that Obadiah compromised his relationship with the Lord as a servant of Ahab. While Kaiser doesn't accept this as a compromise, he does note inconsistencies in Obadiah's behavior:

- He gave no evidence of delight in seeing a fellow follower of God.
- He resented being told to go tell Ahab that Elijah had returned.
- He was self-centered and concerned only for his own protection, not the welfare of God's kingdom.
- He distrusted Yahweh's words and didn't fear the Lord.
- He was overly defensive about his actions from his youth.

1 Kings 18:21–29: He Shows Us His Power. Elijah asked the people how long they were going to go back and forth between Yahweh and the other gods. The people

---

[1] Walter C. Kaiser Jr., *Revive Us Again*, rev. ed. (Ross–shire, Scotland: Christian Focus, 2013), 77–87.

couldn't even answer (Revelation 3:15–16). Elijah declared he was the only prophet of the Lord, even though there were other prophets at the time (v. 22). He was probably "focused on the fact that he alone stood ready to confront the 450 prophets of Baal."[2] In verses 23–25, Elijah challenged the prophets of Baal to see whose God would reign down fire on a sacrificed bull (Psalm 71:18; 147:4–5; Jeremiah 10:12–13). The prophets of Baal did what Elijah told them, prepared the sacrifice, and then spent hours calling down their god Baal (v. 26). At noon, Elijah mocked them for their actions, and they worked even harder (vv. 27–29). No god answered.

1 Kings 18:30–39: Elijah drew the people before him, rebuilt the Lord's altar that had been destroyed, took twelve stones, and made a trench around it that could hold four gallons of water (vv. 30–32). Next, Elijah prepared the sacrifice and then called for four full water pots to be poured over the offering and the wood that was to be burned (v. 33). Elijah directed them to do that two more times (v. 34) and fill the trench with water (v. 35). Elijah began the evening sacrifice and called on the God of Abraham, Isaac, and Israel (or Jacob), tapping into the history of God's promises to the people of Israel (v. 36). *Nelson's Commentary* breaks up Elijah's prayer (v. 37) into two parts: "First, he wished that the Lord would demonstrate clearly to the people that He alone is the living God. Second, he prayed for the full revival of God's people."[3] Yahweh's fire fell and consumed the wood, the stones, the dust, and the water in the trench (v. 38). The people watching recognized the power had come from their God, Yahweh (v. 39).

1 Kings 18:40–46: He Answers Our Prayers. Elijah told the people of Israel to slaughter the prophets of Baal (v. 40), and he told Ahab to go eat and drink because rain was coming (v. 41). While Ahab ate, Elijah went atop Carmel and bowed in prayer (v. 42). Then, Elijah told his servant seven times to go look at the sea to see if rain was on its way (vv. 43–44a). On the seventh time, the servant saw a tiny cloud on the horizon, so Elijah told the servant to tell Ahab to get in his chariot and get off the mountain before the rains came (vv. 44b–45). As Ahab started down the mountain in the rain and headed to Jezreel, the power of the Lord was on Elijah. He ran ahead of Ahab the 13 miles to Jezreel (vv. 45–46).

---

[2] Earl D. Radmacher, Ronald B. Allen, and H. Wayne House, eds., *Nelson's New Illustrated Bible Commentary* (Nashville: Thomas Nelson, 1999), 454.

[3] Radmacher et al., 454.

Closing

God wants each of us to be courageous. He wants us to pray for "the rain to come down." Do you have enough faith and courage to pray that kind of prayer (James 5:16–18)? We can pray like Elijah, and God wants to respond. Do you believe that? When you believe this, revival can actually come.

The Daily Word

After three years of hiding during a famine, the Lord sent Elijah to present himself to Ahab, saying God would finally send the rain. Before King Ahab and all the people of Israel, Elijah courageously prayed to the God of Abraham, Isaac, and Jacob to send rain so the people would know Yahweh was God. First the people prayed to Baal for it to rain, but Baal did not answer. The Lord, however, answered in a mighty way. Yahweh sent fire to fall and consume the burnt offering. When the people saw this, they exclaimed, "Yahweh, He is God! Yahweh, He is God!" And then, after Elijah bowed before the Lord on his knees, the Lord answered with a downpour of rain throughout the land! After three years, water returned, and the people witnessed a mighty act from Yahweh!

The Lord calls you to live courageously and boldly for Him. He desires for you to live with His power, not in your own strength, but instead fully relying on God. This begins with prayer. It begins with asking the Lord to show His power in your life. *What are you praying boldly about today?* You can ask God because you know God hears you. Be courageous and believe the Lord will answer your prayer. And when He answers your God-sized prayer, testify to others how great God is in your life! There is no other God like your God.

Then Yahweh's fire fell and consumed the burnt offering, the wood, the stones, and the dust, and it licked up the water that was in the trench. When all the people saw it, they fell facedown and said, "Yahweh, He is God! Yahweh, He is God!" —1 Kings 18:38–39

Further Scripture: Isaiah 45:5–6a; Micah 7:7; 1 John 5:14–15

Questions

1. Elijah entered the story in 1 Kings 17:1 when he declared there would be no dew or rain except by his word. Who in the future will have this same power (Revelation 11:6)? What type of man does James 5:17 say Elijah was? How should this verse bolster our confidence in how the Lord sees us (James 5:16)?

2. The Lord instructed Elijah to go to Zarephath to be provided for by a widow there. What reason did Jesus give for Elijah being sent there in Luke 4:24–26?

3. When Elijah met the widow, why did she expect both herself and her son to die soon (1 Kings 17:12)? She saw the miraculous provision from the Lord. Why, then, did she say in 1 Kings 17:24, "Now I know that you are a man of God and that the word of the Lord in your mouth is truth"?

4. The fear Obadiah voiced in 1 Kings 18:12 seems to be based on the Spirit of the Lord doing something "unsafe." Have you ever felt "unsafe" letting the Holy Spirit be in charge?

5. The prophets of Baal and Elijah started their prayer by asking their gods to answer (1 Kings 18:26, 37). How long did the prophets of Baal wait for an answer? What was the people's immediate response when the Lord answered with fire?

6. What did the Holy Spirit highlight to you in 1 Kings 17—18 through the reading or the teaching?

Lesson 67: 1 Kings 19—20

Something Greater: Hearing God's Whisper

Teaching Notes

Intro

We're nearing the end of 1 Kings, and I love this passage on Elijah. We have all experienced that feeling of letdown after having had an amazing time in God's presence. For example, after we finished 50 days of evangelizing in revive-TEXAS, there was mental and emotional fatigue. That is where Elijah was. He had just seen God rain fire down from heaven and then bring rain to Israel. But then, Ahab told Jezebel what Elijah had done, although we don't know if everything he told her was truth. James 5:17 states Elijah had "a nature like ours." Wiersbe points out the Bible "describes the warts and wrinkles of even the greatest," and that in 1 Kings 18—19, "we see Elijah at his highest and at his lowest."[4] This passage shows Elijah's humanity after he'd poured himself out in ministry (Psalm 39:5).

Teaching

Wiersbe divides chapter 19 into four sections, which we will follow in this study: "The enemy's message of danger," "The angel's message of grace," "The Creator's message of power," and "The Lord's message of hope."[5]

1 Kings 19:1–4: The Enemy's Message of Danger. Ahab told Jezebel everything and she sent a message to Elijah, promising she would take his life (vv. 1–2). It's interesting that the message didn't come from Ahab, the king, but the queen. Wiersbe suggests, "If Jezebel transformed the prophet into a martyr, he might influence people more by his death than by his life."[6] Jezebel seemed to have had a plan, which is typical for "Jezebels." They are looking for what any

---

[4] Warren W. Wiersbe, *The Exposition Bible Commentary: Joshua–Esther* (Colorado Springs: David C. Cook, 2003), 173.

[5] Wiersbe, 174–82.

[6] Wiersbe, 175.

situation will do for them personally—not someone you want in your life or your ministry.

Elijah received Jezebel's message and was afraid. He ran south to Beersheba and then left his servant there to go into the desert (vv. 3–4a). "Charles Spurgeon said that Elijah 'retreated before a beaten enemy.'"[7] Elijah ran from the enemy he had already defeated. "God had answered [Elijah's] prayer (1 Kings 18:36–37) and God's hand had been upon him in the storm (1 Kings 18:46), but now he was walking by sight and not by faith."[8] Elijah "was running ahead of the Lord in order to save his own life."[9] Elijah journeyed an entire day into the wilderness and then sat under a broom tree and prayed God would take his life (v. 4b).

1 Kings 19:5–8: The Angel's Message of Grace. The tone of the passage changes in verse 5. While Elijah slept under the tree, an angel touched him and told him to get up and eat (v. 5). Vance Havner would say, "If we didn't come apart and rest, we'd come apart."[10] This was not the only time angels came to someone in the Old and New Testaments (Acts 12:7). When he looked, Elijah found bread that had been baked over hot stones and a jug of water (v. 6). Remember angels come to minister to us (Hebrews 1:14; Psalm 91:11). In verse 7, the angel is referred to as "the angel of the Lord," which I believe indicates this was the preincarnate Christ (Genesis 16:10; Exodus 3:1–6; Judges 2:1–4). Christ showed up to one of the greatest prophets, woke him a second time, and fed him so Elijah could continue the journey. Elijah ate and drink and then, on the strength of that food, walked 40 days and nights, a distance of about 200 miles, to the mountain of God at Mount Horeb (or Mount Sinai) (v. 8).

1 Kings 19:9–14: The Creator's Message of Power. Elijah entered a cave and stayed the night (v. 9a). *Nelson's Commentary* states that the way "the cave" was written in Hebrew suggests "this was 'the cave' in which Moses had hidden when he experienced the presence of Yahweh on the mountain of God (Exodus 45)."[11] God asked why Elijah had come to the cave (v. 9b). Elijah explained that even with all he had done, the people had abandoned God and ignored His prophets (v. 10). The Lord told Elijah to stand outside the cave in God's presence. The Lord passed by, and a mighty wind whipped at the mountain and shattered the cliffs, and an earthquake rumbled, but the Lord was not found in either the

---

[7] Wiersbe, 175.

[8] Wiersbe, 175.

[9] Wiersbe, 175.

[10] Wiersbe, 177.

[11] Earl D. Radmacher, Ronald B. Allen, and H. Wayne House, eds., *Nelson's New Illustrated Bible Commentary* (Nashville: Thomas Nelson, 1999), 455.

wind or the quaking (v. 11). Although we see God show up in the wind in Acts 2:2–3 and in an earthquake in Zechariah 14:4–5, that was not the case with Elijah. Next came fire (Exodus 40:38), but God was not in the fire. Finally, there was a soft whisper, which was the voice of God (v. 12). *Nelson's Commentary* points out that "Elijah had called for lightning, and he had called for fire and national revival. What Elijah did not see was that God was at work in the lives of many people."[12] In the quiet and the stillness, God was working in the lives of everyday people. But Elijah was looking for the fire and the lightening and for revival.

Elijah recognized the voice, so he wrapped his face in his mantel and stood at the entrance of the cave (v. 13a). The voice asked again what Elijah was doing there (v. 13b). *Nelson's Commentary* states that the Lord's question implied "it is time to be elsewhere, serving God both in the normal routine of life and in accordance with His special commissions."[13] At God's question, Elijah repeated what he first said in verse 10, "I alone am left, and they're looking for me to take my life" (v. 14).

1 Kings 19:15–21: The Lord's Message of Hope. The Lord sent Elijah back the way he came to anoint Hazael as king over Aram (v. 15). Notice God didn't give up on Elijah, and he doesn't give up on us, even when we are complaining or running from what He wants us to do. Instead, God sent Elijah in a new direction in which to walk out his anointing (Psalm 103:11–14). Then Elijah was to go anoint Jehu as king over Israel and Elisha as the prophet to take his place (v. 16). Jehu, Hazael, and Elisha would be used as God's instruments (v. 17). God pointed out that there were 7,000 people who remained loyal to their God, *Yahweh* (v. 18). *Nelson's Commentary* describes them as "a community of God among everyday people whose lives are not spectacular but who live faithfully for God."[14] Elijah responded obediently and found Elisha in the fields working and threw his mantle over him (v. 19). Elijah overcame everything he had been thinking and feeling because God still had a purpose in his life. Elisha asked for time to say goodbye to his family, and then he obediently and faithfully followed Elijah (vv. 20–21).

Closing

Elijah experienced God, not through God's power, but through God's soft voice. It was not flashy or crazy, but was the whisper of the God Elijah heard in his everyday life. As a result, Elijah could pass on his mantle to Elisha. No matter

---

[12] Radmacher et al., 455.

[13] Radmacher et al., 455.

[14] Radmacher et al., 455.

what state you are in right now, there is hope for you—God can continue to work through your life!

The Daily Word

Though the prophet Elijah saw the Lord move in a miraculous, powerful way when it finally rained after three years of drought, the enemy was able to discourage him. He became afraid and ran for his life. Elijah journeyed to the wilderness alone, sat under a tree, and prayed he would just die. He said to the Lord, "I have had enough!" But then an angel showed up and told him, "Get up and eat or the journey will be too much for you." The angel provided food and water for Elijah to eat and drink. Elijah regained strength and began the new journey the Lord called him to.

Have you ever found yourself at the point in your ministry, your job, your family, or your marriage where you've said, "I have had enough!" When you do, here's the promise to remember: Even when you think you are at the end and the enemy has convinced you there's no way out, *do not give up. There is always hope.* In Elijah's weakness, the Lord provided truth, food, water, and an angel to say, "Get up!" Today, you may need to hear these words: *Get Up!* Or maybe, you need to say those words to a friend who is in despair. The Lord will provide even when you think you are at the end of your rope. Don't lose hope. The Lord will lift you up and help you regain your strength to stand strong again. You can do this through Christ who gives you strength.

But he went on a day's journey into the wilderness. He sat down under a broom tree and prayed that he might die. He said, "I have had enough! Lord, take my life, for I'm no better than my fathers." Then he lay down and slept under the broom tree. Suddenly, an angel touched him. The angel told him, "Get up and eat." —1 Kings 19:4–5

Further Scripture: Psalm 28:7; Psalm 73:26; Isaiah 40:31

Questions

1. In 1 Kings 19:2, Jezebel vowed to take Elijah's life by the next day. Why did Elijah become fearful and run for his life after such a demonstration of the Lord's power? Does it remind you of Peter in Matthew 14:20–31? Why?

2. An angel had Elijah eat bread baked on hot stones and drink water. How do each of these elements (bread, stones, and water) point to Christ (John 4:14, 6:35; 1 Corinthians 10:4)?

3. God called Elijah to stand on the mountain before Him. What phenomena took place while the Lord was passing by (1 Kings 19:11–13)? When the Lord speaks throughout Scripture, how is it described (1 Samuel 3:6; Psalms 29:3–8; 68:33; Jeremiah 10:13; Ezekiel 43:2; Revelation 1:10, 15)?

4. What three charges did Elijah bring against the sons of Israel in 1 Kings 19:10, 14?

5. In 1 Kings 20, men came to Ahab several times with a message from the Lord in regard to fighting the Arameans. Why do you think Ahab listened, even though we know he was not serving the Lord and had no respect for Him (1 Kings 18:18)? Why did the Lord deliver Israel from the Arameans (1 Kings 20:13, 28)?

6. What did the Holy Spirit highlight to you in 1 Kings 19—20 through the reading or the teaching?

Lesson 68: 1 Kings 21—22

Something Greater: The Death of Ahab

Teaching Notes

Intro

Our phrase for the book of 1 Kings is *Something Greater* and was demonstrated clearly through the first 11 chapters about Solomon. The rest of the book feels more like a study of Judges as kings fight against kings and nations fight against each other. Solomon's reign brought unification. After his death; however, Israel became the divided kingdom and was thrown into chaos.

In 1 Kings 21, Jezebel had Naboth the Jezreelite killed (vv. 1–14), Ahab took Naboth's vineyard (vv. 15–16), and Elijah came in and pronounced God's judgment on Ahab (vv. 17–29). That's the backdrop to the last chapter of 1 Kings. Chapter 22 continues the story of Jezebel and Ahab, as well as King Jehoshaphat, another good king in Judah. Judah experienced a period of peace under Jehoshaphat. *Nelson's Commentary* points out that, "Faced with the rising threat of Assyria, Ahab had failed to press his advantage of three years before. He had not reoccupied the strategic highlands of Ramoth in Gilead."[1] As you read through these notes, watch for the italicized statements that emphasize He is *Something Greater*.

Teaching

1 Kings 22:1–5: Wiersbe explains, "After three years, Ben-hadad hadn't kept his agreement to give Israel back the cities his father took, [so] Ahab decided it was time to fight Syria and take them back."[2] After three years of no war, Jehoshaphat, king of Judah, visited Ahab, king of Israel (vv. 1–2), who was also his son's father-in-law. Ahab asked Jehoshaphat to help him fight for Ramoth-gilead (v. 3). Jehoshaphat had fought with Ahab in the past, and he accepted Ahab's request (v. 4). Jehoshaphat did stop to seek God's will (v. 5). The problem with

---

[1] Earl D. Radmacher, Ronald B. Allen, and H. Wayne House, eds., *Nelson's New Illustrated Bible Commentary* (Nashville: Thomas Nelson, 1999), 458.

[2] Warren W. Wiersbe, *The Exposition Bible Commentary: Joshua–Esther* (Colorado Springs: David C. Cook, 2003), 488.

this is the order—Jehoshaphat made a decision first and *then* asked the Lord what he should do.

We must be careful who we align ourselves with! Jehoshaphat compromised what he knew should be done by allowing his son to marry Ahab's daughter. We cannot become unequally yoked (Proverbs 4:14–17). Ahab and Jezebel were evil, and yet Jehoshaphat allowed his son to marry into the family and he chose to align himself and his nation as an ally of Israel. Things got complicated when he became unequally yoked by making alliance with those who had an evil heart.

1 Kings 22:6–12: Ahab called on his prophets, about 400 men, and asked if he should go to war. They all told Ahab what he wanted to hear and told him to go (v. 6). Jehoshaphat realized that none were prophets of Yahweh and asked where are Yahweh's prophets (v. 7). Ahab responded there was one left that he hated because he never prophesied good things to him (v. 8). Jehoshaphat asked to see that prophet—Micaiah, son of Imiah. While Micaiah was sent for, Ahab's other prophets promised him a great victory (vv. 11–12). *We must listen to right counsel and seek God's will!*

1 Kings 22:13–28: The messenger told the prophet Micaiah that he should join the other prophets in declaring that Ahab's war would be victorious (v. 13). Micaiah refused to say anything except what God told him to say (v. 14). *We must not conform, but to seek to please God, not man!* When asked, and prompted by the king to speak truthfully (2 Chronicles 18:14–15), Micaiah told King Ahab to go ahead in war, and Yahweh would hand over victory to "the king" (v. 15). The king asked Micaiah again, not trusting him, and Micaiah told him two visions. In the first vision, Micaiah said Israel would be scattered without a leader (vv. 16–17). Visions will happen until the Messiah returns, so we too can experience visions (Joel 2; Acts 2). This pointed to common imagery (Matthew 9:36) that people were everywhere and no one was taking care of them. Ahab understood the vision and complained that Micaiah only gave visions of defeat (v. 18). Micaiah responded with a second vision: God was on His throne surrounded by the heavenly host and asked who would trick Ahab into marching on Ramoth-gilead, and a spirit agreed to go as "a lying spirit in the mouth of all his prophets" (vv. 19–22). *Nelson's Commentary* shares, "These prophets prophesied under the influences of evil, but their false predictions were just what Ahab wanted to hear."[3] Jehoshaphat explained God had put that lying spirit into Ahab's prophets (v. 23). For other examples of God using evil (Job 1—2; John 13:21–30).

Zedekiah, one of Ahab's prophets, hit Micaiah in the face and asked if the spirit of the Lord had left him to go to Micaiah (v. 24). *We must expect opposition.*

---

[3] Radmacher et al., 458.

Micaiah told Zedekiah that the day would come when he would know Micaiah had been right (v. 25). Ahab sent Micaiah back to prison with instructions he was only to be fed bread and water until his safe return (vv. 26–27). Micaiah replied that if Ahab returned safely, then God had not spoken to him (v. 28). *Once we release God's word, we must remain confident and stand firm!*

1 Kings 22:29–40: The kings led their armies up Ramoth-gilead (v. 29). Ahab disguised himself but had Jehoshaphat wear his royal garments (v. 30). Ahab was trying to avoid Micaiah's prophecy from coming true. The king of Aram ordered his 32 chariot commanders to only fight the king of Israel (v. 31). When they charged Jehoshaphat in his royal garments, they turned toward him, but Jehoshaphat cried out in fear (v. 32). The chariots turned away from Jehoshaphat (v. 33). Someone shot an arrow randomly into the air and it struck Ahab, the king of Israel, between the breastplate and his lower armor (v. 34). Ahab told his charioteer to take him from the battle (v. 35). Ahab was propped up in his chariot, and he watched the rest of the battle rage on while he bled to death (vv. 36). As the sun set, Micaiah's prophecy came true, and each man was sent to his own city or land (v. 37). Ahab was buried in Samaria (v. 37). The chariot was washed at the pool of Samaria, the dogs licked up the blood that remained in it, and prostitutes bathed in it, as God has promised (v. 38). Ahab rested with his fathers, and his son Ahaziah became the next king of Israel (v. 40).

1 Kings 22:41–50: Jehoshaphat made three major compromises, each one outside God's will:

- *A bride compromise*: He compromised when he chose his son's bride and married him to the daughter of Ahab and Jezebel.
- *A battle compromise*: He became entangled in the affairs of his son's father-in-law, King Ahab, when Israel attacked Aram, and he almost lost his own life.
- *A boat compromise*: He agreed to a commercial enterprise with Ahaziah, Ahab's son and Jehoshaphat's sons' brother-in-law, which were destroyed through God's displeasure.

Closing

What can we learn from this? Keep walking in the sweet spot of God's will. Be careful who you align yourself with. Seek God's will. Listen to the right counsel in the process. As you are listening, do not conform to false truth, do not give in to evil. You can expect opposition, but as you do this, one thing I want to learn myself is to stand firm and remain confident in what you've heard from the

Lord. In Jude, it talks about all these seemingly 'truths' that will start coming at us, but they are false. We have the absolute truth and our job is to hold firm to this truth and inquire of the Lord as we go. We can hold on to the truth because Jesus is *Something Greater* than any of these kings we've talked about!

The Daily Word

Judah's King Jehoshaphat walked in the ways of his father King Asa and did what was right in the eyes of the Lord. However there were times when Jehoshaphat would make a decision on his own and then include the Lord in His plan. When facing battle, King Jehoshaphat first aligned with King Ahab, who was not a man of God and then, afterwards, sought the Lord for direction. King Jehoshaphat lacked care in determining with whom to align himself, ultimately compromising what he believed.

As you walk with Christ, the enemy wants to distract you and entice you to walk away from the Lord. Be careful with whom you align yourself. When you align yourself with people who are not seeking the Lord, they can distract you and point you away from Christ. However, when you take the time and align yourself with like-minded believers, you sharpen one another. Today, take a minute to think about the people in your life you turn to for counsel. Are they walking with the Lord or walking in their own ways? If you are walking with Christ, be sure to hold on to His truth and His ways.

The king of Israel said to Jehoshaphat, "There is still one man who can ask Yahweh, but I hate him because he never prophesies good about me, but only disaster. He is Micaiah son of Imlah." "The king shouldn't say that!" Jehoshaphat replied. —1 Kings 22:8

Further Scripture: Proverbs 27:17; 2 Corinthians 6:14; 1 John 4:1

Questions

1. In 1 Kings 21:3, what was the inheritance of their fathers, and why was it so important (Numbers 36:9–12)? What is our inheritance in the kingdom (Ephesians 1:14, 18; Hebrews 9:15; 1 Peter 1:4)? How can we hold on to it without "selling or trading" it?

2. Jezebel arranged for two men to falsely accuse Naboth in order to have him killed. How does this point to Christ (Matthew 26:59; Mark 14:55)?

3. Jezebel used the king's authority to initiate Naboth's death, and King Ahab allowed it to happen. Did the Lord hold him responsible (1 Kings 21:18–19)? Does this remind you of Adam in Genesis 3:6; 3:17?

4. Ahab humbled himself after hearing the Lord's judgment on him and his family. How did the Lord respond (1 Kings 21:28–29)? What does this tell us about the character of the Lord (Exodus 34:6–7; Ezekiel 18:23)?

5. In 1 Kings 22, how many prophecies do you see fulfilled (1 Kings 22:34, 38)? Have you ever had a prophetic word spoken to you and experienced its fulfillment?

6. What did the Holy Spirit highlight to you in 1 Kings 21—22 through the reading or the teaching?

Lesson 69: 2 Kings 1—2

Surviving Seed: Passing the Mantle

Teaching Notes

Intro

The writing in 2 Kings might sound familiar, because 1 and 2 Kings were written as one book. Jewish tradition holds that Jeremiah wrote 2 Kings. That doesn't make sense because Jeremiah was never in Babylon. So, we are not completely sure who wrote the books of 1 and 2 Kings. These books are an accurate and interpreted historical account, meaning that the author wrote these books so Israel could learn from their mistakes. Paul Van Gorder wrote, "[2 Kings is] perhaps the saddest book of all Jewish history."[1] Why? Because 2 Kings is a recording of the Israelites being taken into captivity.

The book of 2 Kings is divided into two divisions. Chapters 1 through 17 cover Israel and Judah until the fall of Samaria. Then, chapters 18 through 25 cover the history of Judah up to the destruction of Jerusalem. Despite the brokenness and chaos of the kingdom, God had a plan. Remember *Something Greater* was coming. Amidst the fighting, brokenness, and division, God allowed a *Surviving Seed* that points to Christ. As we study the book of 2 Kings, we will see a picture of Christ—Christ and the believer (2:1–22), Christ and the world (4:38–41), and Christ and the sinner (5:1–14).[2] In 2 Kings 1, Moab rebelled against Israel (v. 1), Elijah rebuked Ahaziah (vv. 2–16), Ahaziah king of Israel died, and Joram succeeded Ahaziah as king (v. 17). The phrase for the Messiah in 2 Kings is *Surviving Seed*.

Teaching

2 Kings 2:1: Remember that Elijah was the prophet who asked for the fire to fall on Mount Carmel, and he was also the one who ran ahead of Ahab. The Lord would take Elijah up to heaven in a whirlwind. A whirlwind was a specific storm that involved lightning and thunder (Job 38:1; 40:6; Jeremiah 23:19; Zechariah 9:14). This storm was from the Lord; His presence was in the storm.

---

[1] Paul R. Van Gorder, *The Old Testament Presents . . . Reflections of Christ: 2 Kings*, https://www.thebookwurm.com/ref-2kin.htm.

[2] Van Gorder, https://www.thebookwurm.com/ref-2kin.htm.

2 Kings 2:2: Elijah and Elisha were both prophets. Elijah said to Elisha, "Stay here; the Lord is sending me on to Bethel." Elisha replied, "I will not leave you." Bethel was six to eight miles north of Jerusalem and had a bad reputation because of the false worship centers that were located there.

2 Kings 2:3: They arrived in Bethel, and the sons of the prophets came to meet them. John MacArthur explains that the sons of the prophets were "an association of prophets that met and possibly lived together for study, encouragement, and service."[3] They said to Elisha, "Do you know that the Lord will take your master away from you today?" To which he replied, "Yes, I know. Be quiet."

2 Kings 2:4: Again, Elijah tried to get Elisha to stay because the Lord was sending him to Jericho. Again, Elisha replied, "I will not leave you." Jericho was fourteen miles southeast of Bethel.

2 Kings 2:5: When the two men arrived in Jericho, the sons of the prophets again came out and told Elisha, "Do you know that the Lord will take your master away from you today?" To which he replied, "Yes, I know. Be quiet." He wanted to make the most of his time with his mentor.

2 Kings 2:6–8: For the third time, Elijah told Elisha to stay behind. For the third time, Elisha said, "I will not leave you." So, the two of them went to the Jordan. At the Jordan River, the two men faced fifty sons of prophets on the other side. Elijah took his mantle (cloak) rolled it up and struck the river with it. Instantly the river parted. The two men crossed over on dry ground. This is mind blowing! Elijah was a miracle worker!

2 Kings 2:9–10: Elijah asked Elisha what he could do for him before he was taken away. Elisha replied, "Please, let me inherit two shares of your spirit." He wanted to function and walk in that power. He wanted a double blessing, or as MacArthur wrote, "a double share of God's spirit."[4] Elisha did not want material blessings; he wanted to be blessed so he could advance God's purpose. Elijah pointed out that what Elisha asked for was something difficult. It would essentially be up to God if Elisha's request would be granted.

In our own lives, we need to consider, what does it mean to receive the double portion of the Spirit of God?

2 Kings 2:11: As the two men walked and talked, a chariot of fire pulled by horses of fire came from the sky and separated the two. Then Elijah was taken up to

---

[3] John MacArthur, *The MacArthur Bible Commentary* (Nashville: Thomas Nelson, 2005), 424.

[4] MacArthur, 432.

heaven. Elijah did not die; he was carried up to heaven (Genesis 5:24). There are not many instances of God plucking someone up to heaven.

2 Kings 2:12–15: Elisha cried out and tore his clothes. Then he picked up Elijah's cloak and struck the water. When he did this, the waters parted. Where did he learn that? You can learn from those who go before you. When the sons of prophets saw him, they bowed down. They had seen the anointing of Elisha.

2 Kings 2:16–18: The fifty other prophets wanted to go and search for Elijah's body, just in case Elijah's body had been separated from his spirit and placed somewhere else. Elisha knew they would not find anything, but after much urging, he let the men go. They searched for three days and couldn't find Elijah. When they returned to Elisha in Jericho, he said, "Didn't I tell you not to go?"

2 Kings 2:19–21: The men of the city complained to Elisha that the land and water was cursed. Remember Joshua put a curse on Jericho (Joshua 6:26). Then in 1 Kings 16:34, Jericho was reestablished at the cost of the king's sons. Elisha asked the local men to bring him a bowl with salt in it. He went to the river, threw salt in the water, and the water was healed. It remains healthy to this very day. I love this story. This story shows that God's presence was with Elisha.

2 Kings 2:22–25: Some young boys harassed Elisha because he was bald. He turned around and cursed them. Then, two female bears came out and killed forty-two of the children. Don't mess with Elisha!

Closing

We are always to persevere. As you pursue more, pick up the mantle that God has given you. We have all received an anointing from God (1 John 2:20–27).

The Daily Word

Elisha never left the side of his mentor Elijah. Even when Elijah told him over and over to "stay here," Elisha remained by his side, traveling with him. Finally Elijah looked at Elisha and said, "Tell me what I can do for you before I am taken from you?" Elisha could have asked for anything from Elijah, and he asked for a double portion of God's power that was evident in Elijah. After the Lord took Elijah to heaven in a whirlwind, Elisha picked up his predecessor's mantle and began walking out the miraculous power of God. It became evident the Lord answered Elisha's request.

Everyone who believes in Jesus has received His mantle—the full anointing of the Holy Spirit. As you walk by Jesus' side daily, remember you are anointed for the kingdom of God, and *His power resides in you.* When you hunger and thirst for righteousness, *the Lord promises you will be filled.* As you are filled up with Him, your life will display His power. Walk out His power with confident trust in the Lord.

After they had crossed over, Elijah said to Elisha, "Tell me what I can do for you before I am taken from you." So Elisha answered, "Please, let me inherit two shares of your spirit." —2 Kings 2:9

Further Scripture: Psalm 63:1; Matthew 5:6; 1 John 2:20

Questions

1. Do you think Elijah's answer to the messengers would have been different if they would have inquired of God and not Baal-zebub (2 Kings 1:3–4)? If so, why?

2. What might have been the intention of King Ahaziah when he sent out the groups of fifty to Elijah (2 Kings 1:9, 11, 13)?

3. In 2 Kings 2, why did Elijah keep telling Elisha to stay, and why didn't Elisha listen to him?

4. Why did Elijah say to Elisha in 2 Kings 2:9, "Tell me what I can do for you before I am taken from you"?

5. In your opinion, why didn't Elisha just tell the sons of the prophets who were at Jericho (2 Kings 2:16) what happened to Elijah?

6. In 2 Kings 2:19–22, the water was bad and the land unfruitful. What might the new jar (or bowl) Elisha asked for point to (2 Corinthians 4:7; 5:17)? What do you think the salt, which purified the water and healed the land of its unfruitfulness, represents (Matthew 5:13a)?

7. What did the Holy Spirit highlight to you in 2 Kings 1—2 through the reading or the teaching?

Lesson 70: 2 Kings 3

Surviving Seed: Flood of Victory

Teaching Notes

Intro

In today's lesson, we'll see a picture of God's provision for the kings of Israel, Judah, and Edom through God's Word delivered by Elisha. Wiersbe states, "Elisha's miracles were primarily revelations of God's grace and mercy."[1] Elisha's life points to the coming Messiah as the *Surviving Seed*.

Teaching

2 Kings 3:1–3: Ahab was king over Israel, and Jezebel was his queen. Ahab and Jezebel had two sons: Ahaziah and Joram. Ahaziah had been king before Joram, but he only ruled for two years (1 Kings 22:51).

2 Kings 3:4–5: King Mesha of Moab rebelled against King Ahaziah. King Ahaziah accepted Mesha's rebellion and did nothing to force Mesha to continue to pay tribute from Moab. But when Ahaziah's brother Joram became king, he decided to force Moab to start paying the tribute again.

2 Kings 3:6–9: King Joram from the northern kingdom asked King Jehoshaphat from the southern kingdom to join him against Moab. His request was based on the family relationship between them—Jehoram, one of the sons of Jehoshaphat, was married to Joram's sister, Athaliah. Jehoshaphat, who had defeated the Moabites the year before with God's help, agreed.

The kings of Israel and Judah approached Moab from the back way, which would have been the more indirect route to attack. King Mesha would not have been expecting an attack to come from this direction. As they traveled through Edom, the king of Edom also joined them to fight against Moab. It was a good plan, but Joram and Jehoshaphat didn't take the availability of supplies into account. They must have thought they would eventually run across a river or

---

[1] Warren W. Wiersbe, *Be Distinct: Standing Firmly Against the World's Tides* (Colorado Springs: David C. Cook, 2002), 35.

stream, but after seven days, they had not come across water, and their supplies were exhausted.

2 Kings 3:10–12: Jehoshaphat suggested they seek the prophet Elisha to hear what God wanted them to do. Joram didn't like Elisha because Elisha never had anything good to say about him, but Joram listened to Jehoshaphat's advice to go talk to Elisha. Joram seemed to be one of those guys who defaulted to a worst-case scenario mindset. When they didn't have any supplies, he immediately concluded God had brought them together only to have the Moabites defeat them.

2 Kings 3:13–14: Elisha initially told Joram to go talk to the prophets of his mother and his father. Joram's parents were King Ahab and Queen Jezebel, with whom Elijah had many dealings. Joram was probably one of the worst kings in either of the kingdoms of Israel or Judah, being just a tad bit better than Ahab or Jehu. Jehoshaphat was on the other end of the spectrum. Jehoshaphat wasn't quite as good as David, but he was still a righteous king who served the Lord. Elisha served as a buffer here. He tried to reign things in and keep the kings on track.

2 Kings 3:15: Elisha's request of a musician was reminiscent of when David played the harp to calm Saul: "Now the Spirit of the Lord had left Saul, and an evil spirit sent from the Lord began to torment him, so Saul's servants said to him, 'You see that an evil spirit from God is tormenting you. Let our lord command your servants here in your presence to look for someone who knows how to play the lyre. Whenever the evil spirit from God troubles you, that person can play the lyre, and you will feel better.' Then Saul commanded his servants, 'Find me someone who plays well and bring him to me.' One of the young men answered, 'I have seen a son of Jesse of Bethlehem who knows how to play the lyre. He is also a valiant man, a warrior, eloquent, handsome, and the Lord is with him.' . . . Whenever the spirit from God troubled Saul, David would pick up his lyre and play, and Saul would then be relieved, feel better, and the evil spirit would leave him" (1 Samuel 16:14–18, 23). There is something about the playing of a melody on the ear that can affect the spirit.

2 Kings 3:16–20: Elisha instructed the kings to dig trenches and proclaimed that God would fill the trenches with water to provide for their immediate need by quenching their thirst. But God would also go one step further by giving the Moabites into their hands. We don't know how severe this drought was for the armies, but without God intervening through Elisha they could have been facing death.

2 Kings 3:21–23: Moab's army may have gone over to Judah's camp without their armor or weapons because they didn't think there was an oncoming battle. They thought the three kings in Judah's camp had turned on one another, and they were simply going to gather the spoils of battle.

2 Kings 3:24–26: The king of Edom may have been somewhat neutral in the battle, which led the king of Moab to take seven hundred swordsmen to break through the lines to him. Edom and Moab were neighbors, so they may have had a good relationship. The Moabites were probably peace-loving people. They were known for herding sheep, and you don't think of shepherds as being war-makers.

2 Kings 3:27: When the king of Moab sacrificed his firstborn son as a burnt offering, it's almost as though the other kings asked one another in disgust, "What's he doing?" and went home. The New English Bible reads, "The Israelites were filled with such consternation at this sight, that they struck camp and returned to their own land."

Closing

Joram, the king of Israel, was another evil king who did evil in God's sight. Yet, God allowed him a victory of sorts over the Moabites because Jehoshaphat, the king of Judah, was with him. Once again, God preserved the lineage of David through the kings of Judah.

The Daily Word

Elisha walked with the Lord and was therefore ready with a Word when called upon by the kings of Judah, Israel, and Edom as they headed into battle with Moab. The Lord's hand came on Elisha, and he spoke out confidently. However, the armies did not listen to the Word from the Lord completely. As a result, not only did they not receive the complete benefit, but the Lord chose to show His wrath to them.

Are you walking with the Lord so that when you need to make a decision or talk with someone about Jesus, you are ready to proclaim the truth? Like Elisha, the Lord's hand will be on you. He is always with you, and His power is within you. In Christ, you are to be alert at all times. Today, take the time to spend with the Lord and read His Word so you will be ready. Then, be confident as the Lord guides you and opens opportunities for you to speak for Him.

But Jehoshaphat said, "Isn't there a prophet of the Lord here? Let's inquire of Yahweh through him." One of the servants of the king of Israel answered,

---

**"Elisha son of Shaphat, who used to pour water on Elijah's hands, is here."
Jehoshaphat affirmed, "The Lord's words are with him." So the king of Israel
and Jehoshaphat and the king of Edom went to him. —2 Kings 3:11–12**

Further Scripture: Isaiah 64:8; Luke 21:36; 1 Peter 3:15

Questions

1. In 2 Kings 3:3, what sins did the verse refer to when it said Jehoram clung to
   the sins of Jeroboam the son of Nebat (1 Kings 12:28–31)?
2. In verse 15, why did Elisha call for a musician (1 Chronicles 25:1)?
3. What do you think possessed the king of Moab to offer his son as a burnt
   sacrifice when he realized he could not break through to the king of Edom?
   What did he think this would accomplish (2 Kings 3:27)?
4. What did the Holy Spirit highlight to you in 2 Kings 3 through the reading
   or the teaching?

Lesson 71: 2 Kings 4

Surviving Seed: Limited Only by Faith

Teaching Notes

Intro

The phrase for 1 Kings was *Something Greater*, and the phrase for 2 Kings is *Surviving Seed*. All we've looked at in both books is fulfilled in Christ. The failure of the prophets, priests, and kings of God's people points to the necessity of Christ. Christ was the ideal combination of these three offices. As a Prophet, Christ's word far surpasses that of the great prophet Elijah (Matthew 17:1–5; Hebrews 1:1–2). Christ is a Priest superior to any of those recorded in Kings (Hebrews 7:22–27). And 2 Kings vividly illustrates the need for Christ as our reigning King. When asked if He was King of the Jews, Jesus affirmed He was (Matthew 27:11). Christ is a King greater than their greatest king. The reign of each of the twenty-six rulers came to an end, but Christ will reign on the throne of David forever (1 Chronicles 17:14; Isaiah 9:6–7). He is "KING OF KINGS AND LORD OF LORDS" (Revelation 19:11–16). Consider that Christ has given gifts to be used in the church (Ephesians 4:7–8, 11–16) for the equipping of the saints for the work of ministry, for the edifying, the building up of the body of Christ. Christ gives these because He is the fullness of all five gifts, so some are: apostles, prophets, evangelists, pastors, and teachers.

One other picture from 1 and 2 Kings is that of fathers of the faith. Elijah mentored Elisha, like Moses mentored Joshua, and Paul mentored Timothy. We need fathers and mothers in the church!

Teaching

Chapter 4 contains four miracles: the refilling of the widow's oil, raising the Shunammite's son, purifying the pot of stew, and the feeding of one hundred men.

2 Kings 4:1–7: One of the wives of the sons of the prophets cried out to Elisha for help in saving her sons from slavery (v. 1). Josephus said the woman was the widow of the prophet Obadiah. Elisha asked what he could do for her and what she had in the house. She had only a jar of oil (v. 2). Elisha told her to collect empty jars from all the neighbors (v. 3). Notice how God used people around her to help her. Wiersbe points out, "God often begins with what we already have"[2] (Exodus 4:2; Luke 5; John 6).

John Maxwell says, "There's something about 'nothing' that moves God's hand. He loves leading us to empty places where we can lean on nothing except His provision."[3] The woman did as Elisha said, and she filled all the borrowed vessels with oil (vv. 4–5). The oil stopped flowing when there were no more empty vessels (v. 6). Bellett said, "The vessels were the measure of the oil. In other words, divine power waited on faith—faith measured the active resources of God on the occasion."[4] The amount of oil she received was limited to the number of vessels she had, and that was controlled by her faith (2 Kings 13:18–19). Maybe we need to dream bigger and believe for more. Maybe God will fill to the measure what we've believed and prepared for (Romans 4:17)! *Nelson's Commentary* explains, "Elisha met not only her immediate needs but the long-range ones as well."[5] This is a foreshadow of Christ who gave it all to pay our debt so we can live.

2 Kings 4:8–26: Elisha met the Shunammite woman who gave him a place to stay, and he prophesied that she would have a son. Later, her son died, and she ran to find Elisha to help her.

2 Kings 4:27: Although Elisha had heard numerous times from the Lord, the Lord hid from him what the woman needed (v. 27). In the New Testament, we are encouraged to earnestly desire spiritual gifts (1 Corinthians 14:1). God does not want only to be studied but to be experienced. Practice listening to and hearing the voice of the Lord. Take chances in public, and then come back to the Lord in private. Keep walking it out as you learn, grow, develop, and pursue Him.

Closing

We need to know the voice of the Lord through His Word, but we also need to "hear" the voice of the Lord. Not everything is written in Scripture. In Matthew 28, the disciples were told to go and make disciples. That means we need to be

---

[2] Warren W. Wiersbe, *Be Distinct: Standing Firmly Against the World's Tides* (Colorado Springs: David C. Cook, 2002), 40.

[3] John C. Maxwell, *The Maxwell Leadership Bible, 3rd ed. (Nashville: Thomas Nelson, 2018)*, 449.

[4] John Gifford Bellett, *Short Meditations on Elisha* (New York: Loizeaux Brothers, n.d.), 17.

[5] Earl D. Radmacher, Ronald B. Allen, and H. Wayne House, eds., *Nelson's New Illustrated Bible Commentary* (Nashville: Thomas Nelson, 1999), 466.

ready for the person we meet on aisle 4 at Walmart to make disciples as we listen to the Lord.

The Daily Word

The Lord used the prophet Elisha to display His miraculous power. The Lord filled jar after jar after jar of oil, delivering a miraculous provision for the widowed woman and her sons. The Lord recognized the hospitality of the Shunammite woman, allowing her and her older husband to conceive their first son. And even when the son died, Elisha called upon the Lord to breathe life back into the boy and raise him from the dead. Then through God's power, Elisha turned a deadly stew into a healthy, life-giving stew. Through the Lord, Elisha multiplied bread for one hundred men to eat and even had leftovers. In all of these situations, the Lord provided when there seemed to be no way.

God is a God of miracles—yesterday, today, and tomorrow. Believers are able to call upon His name and believe for His power to work in ways you cannot imagine, in His time and in His way. Hold fast to the faith and believe He is at work, even if you don't see evidence of it. Maybe today, you need to hear this truth so your hope remains steadfast. Continue to press in and believe that He is able to heal, provide, comfort, and strengthen you. He promises He will never leave you, so keep on holding on to Him by faith.

The woman conceived and gave birth to a son at the same time the following year, as Elisha had promised her. —2 Kings 4:17

Further Scripture: Jeremiah 32:27; Matthew 17:20; Acts 3:16

Questions

1. In 2 Kings 4:1–7, the oil played a huge part in saving this woman's family. Where else do we find the use of oil in great ways (Exodus 27:20; Psalm 45:7)? Do you think the oil represents the Holy Spirit? Why or why not (Acts 10:38)?

2. How was the hospitality that the rich woman gave to Elisha rewarded (2 Kings 4:16)? Where else do we see hospitality shown (Leviticus 19:33–34; Matthew 25:34–36)?

3. On two different occasions, the Shunammite woman said it was fine or it would be all right. Why do you think she said this (Proverbs 18:21; Mark 11:23)?

4. How does what Elisha did to her son (2 Kings 4:34–35) point to Jesus (Mark 5:22–43; Luke 7:11–15; John 11:1–44)?

5. In 2 Kings 4:42–44, Elisha told his servant to feed the people the sack of grain and loaves of bread. The servant said that it was not enough food, but they all ate. Where else do we see this miracle (Matthew 14:13–21; Mark 8:1–8)?

6. What did the Holy Spirit highlight to you in 2 Kings 4 through the reading or the teaching?

Lesson 72: 2 Kings 5—6

Surviving Seed: Radical Transformation

Teaching Notes

Intro

The stories in 2 Kings depict a cycle of someone new coming in, thinking that things would get better, and how God intervened all the time. We'll see that again today in 2 Kings 5 through the intervention of a little girl.

Teaching

2 Kings 5:1: Naaman was the commander and frontrunner for the king of Aram. Naaman always paved the way for the king. Naaman was the man in charge and was not someone you would want to cross. But Naaman developed a big problem in the form of a skin disease. Most think the disease was leprosy, but it isn't specifically named in the passage. We do know it was degenerative and would eventually lead to Naaman's death. In Israel, lepers had to be separated from the rest of society, but Naaman was able to continue in his duties to this point. Eventually, Naaman's disease would isolate him and destroy him. In this way, Naaman's skin disease was like sin.

2 Kings 5:2–3: This little Israeli girl in verse 2 would have been Naaman's enemy. Naaman had raided her home and taken her into captivity. She was Naaman's opposite in almost every way. Naaman was a powerful man; she was a servant girl. Naaman was in charge of lots of people; she served Naaman's wife. But this girl's encouragement to Naaman's wife for Naaman to go visit the prophet in Samaria is evidence of her radical faith. The servant girl wanted Naaman, the man who should have been her enemy, to be healed.

2 Kings 5:4–10: Naaman began to move from needing the Lord to seeking the Lord.[1] Naaman sought the king's permission to visit Samaria. The king agreed to send Naaman with a letter, along with gold, silver, and changes of clothing.

---

[1] Warren W. Wiersbe, *The Exposition Bible Commentary: Joshua–Esther* (Colorado Springs: David C. Cook, 2003), 521.

All the gifts were probably an attempt to buy a favor from the king of Israel to have Naaman healed.

When Joram, the king of Israel, received the king of Aram's letter, he must have thought it was a political trick. He tore his clothes and wondered why he had been given the task of healing Naaman of his skin disease. Elisha heard about the king's predicament and sent word to have Naaman sent to him. Elisha demonstrated radical confidence in God by saying that when Naaman came to him, Naaman would know there was a prophet in Israel. Elisha walked out his calling like he actually had the answer. He walked like he had a double anointing. He demonstrated confidence in God's power to save. As Naaman sought the Lord, Elisha knew he had the answer. Naaman brought all of his horses and chariots to Elisha's house to show the wealth and power he was bringing to the table as he sought healing. But Elisha didn't even go to the door to answer Naaman. Instead, Elisha sent a servant. Elisha might have acted this way because the Law prohibited Israelites from being near an unclean person (Numbers 5:1–4). Elisha may also have been sending a message to Naaman to humble himself. Elisha's message was just one sentence: wash in the Jordan seven times. This probably meant Naaman was to walk into the river, get himself all wet, get out of the river, then do it all again seven times. How humiliating for Naaman!

2 Kings 5:11–12: After Naaman started seeking the Lord, he began to resist the Lord.[2] Elisha's instructions were easy, but they would make Naaman look foolish. Naaman needed to be humbled (1 Peter 5:5). No horses, messengers, or chariots would be needed. Those things would not cleanse him, nor would they make him righteous before God. We have not been saved based on what we have done or what we have brought to the table. Titus 3:5 says, *"He saved us, not by works of righteousness that we had done, but according to His mercy, through the washing of regeneration and renewal by the Holy Spirit."* All Naaman needed to do was to humble himself and listen to Elisha. Amazingly, no one in Scripture had been healed of leprosy to this point. Naaman had the nerve to hear Elisha's instructions on how he could be healed—how he could be the *first* person to be healed from leprosy—and he got mad because he didn't like Elisha's answer. Naaman had his own game plan. If he continued to resist the Lord, Naaman would discover that his spiritual standing before God would mirror his leprosy. Naaman's physical condition would continue to degrade to the point that his disease would kill him—much like his spirit would degrade because of sin, and he would die spiritually separated from God.

---

[2] Wiersbe, 522.

2 Kings 5:13–14: Naaman began to trust the Lord. Most of the time when a king or a commander began to resist the Lord, they continued to resist the Lord. But Naaman's story was different, and it began to change because of one of his servants. The servant pointed out that Naaman would have done what the prophet said if the prophet had told him to do something that he wanted to do. The servant convinced Naaman to be humble and do the small thing the prophet told him to do. After Naaman washed himself seven times in the Jordan, his skin was healed. He was clean. His radical, childlike faith saved him (Matthew 18:3). If Naaman had stayed thick-headed and prideful, he wouldn't have been healed. But because he exercised childlike faith and listened to his servant, he was saved.

Jesus referred to 2 Kings in Luke 4:23–29. Jesus' hearers were enraged because a Gentile had come to know the Lord. But it was a little Israelite girl who helped Naaman come to know the Lord.

2 Kings 5:15–19a: Naaman wanted to offer a gift to the Lord, but Elisha resisted because Naaman's healing was not for sale. Elisha was a man of God who functioned solely out of obedience. Naaman then asked for soil from Israel so he could put it under his knees when he was forced to bow down in the temple of a false God. Naaman wanted his foundation to be on the Lord. Even though he was in the world, he knew his foundation was Yahweh. Naaman, a Gentile, came to know the Lord because an Israelite helped him.

2 Kings 519b–24: Gehazi, Elisha's attendant, wanted to use his position to gain something from the Lord. He came up with a story about someone coming to visit Elisha and made a request for money and clothing. Naaman, eager to help, gave Gehazi twice as much money as he asked for along with the clothes and two servants to carry everything. When they arrived, Gehazi hid everything and sent the servants back.

2 Kings 5:25–27: Gehazi was more about himself than advancing the kingdom of God. He used his work as a way to further his own agenda, then he lied to Elisha about it. As a result, Gehazi was cursed with the very skin disease Naaman had just been healed of.

Closing

The simple faith of an Israeli girl, who took a chance to tell her master about the Lord, resulted in the salvation of a Gentile. To whom is the Lord sending you?

The Daily Word

Naaman, the commander of the army for King Aram and a brave warrior, had a skin disease. In faith, Naaman's wife's Israelite servant girl boldly spoke up and shared about a prophet in Samaria who could heal Naaman. So Naaman traveled to see this prophet named Elisha. Elisha instructed Naaman, "Go wash seven times in the Jordan and your flesh will be clean." After refusing to follow Elisha's instructions at first, Naaman humbled himself, got over his pride, and walked in obedient faith. In doing so, he was completely healed. Elisha told him to go in peace. Naaman didn't have to pay Elisha for the healing; he only had to walk in humble obedience.

Are there any areas in your life where you need to swallow your pride, walk in humility, and obey the Lord? Today, you may need to hear, "Humble yourself and just do it." Whatever you feel the Lord asking you to do, walk it out in faith. It may not be hard, heroic, or complicated. *The Lord doesn't ask you to be fancy, He just asks for humble obedience.* When you walk in faith and in obedience to the Lord, His peace will wash over you, and He will receive the glory.

But his servants approached and said to him, "My father, if the prophet had told you to do some great thing, would you not have done it? How much more should you do it when he tells you: 'Wash and be clean'?" So Naaman went down and dipped himself in the Jordan seven times, according to the command of the man of God. Then his skin was restored and became like the skin of a small boy, and he was clean. —2 Kings 5:13–14

Further Scripture: Psalm 25:8–9; Psalm 115:1; Micah 6:8

Questions

1. In 2 Kings 5:11, why did Naaman get angry when the servant came out and told him what to do to be free of leprosy (Proverbs 26:12)?

2. In 2 Kings 6:16–17, when Elisha prayed to have his servant's eyes opened, Elisha told the servant, "Don't be afraid, for those who are with us outnumber those who are with them." What does this say about God (Psalm 46:1–2; Romans 8:31)?

3. In 2 Kings 6:22–23, how did Elisha portray Jesus in his actions (Matthew 5:39; 14:13–21)?

4. In 2 Kings 6:26–29, a woman cried out to the king for help, saying they had eaten her son and the other woman was now hiding her son to prevent him from being eaten as well. Where and who predicted this would happen if the people turned their backs on God (Deuteronomy 28:53–57)?

5. What did the Holy Spirit highlight to you in 2 Kings 5—6 through the reading or the teaching?

Lesson 73: 2 Kings 7—8

Surviving Seed: The Sin of Disobedience

Teaching Notes

Intro

We continue our study today with 2 Kings 7. To paint the backdrop for this lesson, remember 2 Kings 6 records that Samaria was under siege, and they were without food. A woman had called out to the king in desperation because another woman had wanted to kill her own son so they would have food for that day and promised they would eat her son the next. The women ate the first son, but then the mother of the second child hid her son away (vv. 28–29). The king was mortified by what happened and put on sackcloth to show his grief (v. 30). This is the backdrop for chapter 7.

Teaching

2 Kings 7:1–20: We could title this section, "Elisha to the Rescue" because once again, Elisha jumped in and did some saving. Elisha proclaimed that the Lord promised food would be sold the next day at the gate of Samaria (v. 1). But the royal officer, whom the king relied on, doubted Elisha's word (v. 2a). Elisha responded that the officer would see the food but not eat it (v. 2b). Four men with leprosy sat outside of the city, knowing they couldn't go inside the city, and would die where they were. They went to the camp of the Arameans, hoping the Arameans would provide for them (vv. 3–4). However, they found the camp deserted because the Arameans had fled (vv. 5–13). When the king received the news, the people went out and plundered the camp (v. 14–16). The king appointed the royal officer who had doubted Elisha's word to take charge of the gate, but in their haste to get to food, the people trampled him, and he died (vv. 17–20).

As Christians, this is our story. We were those sinful lepers. We were sick and starving outside the camp of God's provision. Deserving death for our rebellion against God, we humbly stumbled into the presence of God. Instead of death and bondage, we found grace. We found life. We ate and drank of the goodness of God. We discovered great treasures and riches and have taken them and hidden them in our hearts (Psalm 34:8). We have the way to salvation within us (Revelation 3:17). I invite you to come out of your walls. Come out of safety. Leave what is comfortable, and you will find life.

2 Kings 8:1–6: Remember the son of the Shunammite woman who died, and Elisha brought back to life (2 Kings 4)? Elisha spoke to the woman again and warned her a famine was coming (v. 1). To pack up everything you own and move away because of the coming famine would have taken a degree of humility and faith. However, this woman had a long-term relationship with Elisha. He stayed in her upper room when he traveled through the area. He told her of the coming birth of her son and then restored him back to life. She trusted him and went to the land of the Philistines for seven years (v. 2). At the end of seven years, she returned home (v. 3a). Isn't it interesting, how God used these cycles of seven years of famine over and over to test His people (Genesis 41:17–30)? Seven years indicated completion. Possibly in this case God used the famine for discipline or cleansing.

The woman had to go to the king to ask for her house and her field to be returned to her (v. 3b). When she came before the king, he was in conversation with Elisha's servant Gehazi, asking what great things Elisha had done (v. 4). It is interesting that the king of Israel would be asking to hear what Elisha had done. As Gehazi responded, the woman appeared, and Gehazi explained how Elisha had restored her son to life (v. 5). Was this a coincidence or by divine appointment? Personally, I don't believe in coincidences. The king heard her story and restored everything she had left behind (v. 6).

2 Kings 8:7–15: The king of Aram was sick. When he heard Elisha was nearby, he sent his servant Hazael, with forty camels loaded with gifts, to find out if he would recover from the sickness (vv. 7–9). Elisha promised the king would survive the illness, but he would still die (v. 10). Then Elisha fixed his eyes on Hazael, and Elisha wept (v. 11). Elisha said Hazael would become king of Aram and would do horrific things to the people of Israel (vv. 12–13). This is another example of God using a lying spirit (1 Kings 22:20). Is it possible this prophecy from Elisha enticed Hazael to murder his master, the king? When Hazael returned to the king, he only told him half of what Elisha said (v. 14). The next day, Hazael murdered the king (v. 15).

2 Kings 8:16–24: In the fifth year of Joram's reign as king of Israel, Jehoram, the son of Jehoshaphat, became the king of Judah (v. 16). Jehoram was thirty-two at the time, reigned eight years, married the daughter of King Ahab and Queen Jezebel, and was an evil king in the sight of the Lord (vv. 1–18). Jezebel was the daughter of the King of Sidon. The picture created is that the King of Sidon was reaching all the way through Israel and into Judah, so his influence was powerful (Deuteronomy 7:3–4; 2 Corinthians 6:14). At this point, Jezebel was still alive. Yet, God was unwilling to punish Judah because of the Davidic covenant (v. 19). Edom revolted against Jehoram, and then Libnah revolted (vv. 20–23). Jehoram died and was buried in the city of David with his fathers. His son Ahaziah became king (v. 24).

2 Kings 8:25–29: Ahaziah was twenty-two years old when he became king and reigned only one year (vv. 25–26). He too did evil in the sight of the Lord (v. 27). He went to war with his uncle, King Joram, against Hazael, the king of Aram. Joram was wounded and was taken to Jezreel (where Jezebel lived) to be healed (vv. 28–29a). Ahaziah followed Joram to Jezreel (v. 29b).

Closing

The battle between good and evil, and godly leadership versus evil leadership, plagued both Israel and Judah. Those kings who chose to walk in obedience to the Lord were few and far between. Those who refused to walk obediently continued to damage their countries from a national perspective and the people within their nations as well.

The Daily Word

Four lepers sat outside the wall of Samaria during a time of great famine. They recognized they had no option but to die. However, they had an idea and said, "Why just sit here until we die? If we say, 'Let's go into the city,' we will die there because the famine is in the city, but if we sit here, we will also die. So now, come on. Let's go to the Arameans' camp. If they let us live, we will live; if they kill us, we will die." And so they went to the Arameans' camp, and to their surprise, the Lord had caused the Arameans to flee in fear, leaving all kinds of treasure and provisions. The lepers hid what they found until their consciences caught up with them. They ultimately decided to go and tell the king's household the good news, so they too could reap the benefits!

This is a story of salvation. You are dead in your sins. Without Christ, you face hopelessness and death. You have a choice to sit and die in your sin, or get up and go discover the riches of grace, hope, love, and eternal life found in Jesus. To receive Jesus' grace, *you have to get up from the place of normalcy and go see what the Lord has for you.* When you believe what you have found in Jesus, you will become alive, made whole, and be healed. This good news is not just for you to receive but is for others as well. Go and tell others about these powerful riches found in Jesus alone.

Then they said to each other, "We're not doing what is right. Today is a day of good news. If we are silent and wait until morning light, our sin will catch up with us. Let's go tell the king's household." —2 Kings 7:9

Further Scripture: Mark 16:15; Romans 6:23; Ephesians 2:7

Questions

1. At the beginning of 2 Kings 7, what was Elisha saying would happen? Whom was he speaking to, and what did he say would happen? Did this eventually happen (2 Kings 7:16)?

2. Why were the lepers at the entrance of the city gates (Leviticus 13:36, 45–46)?

3. Which of the five senses did God use to defeat the Moabites (2 Kings 3:21–23)? How did God defeat the Arameans?

4. What was happening when the mother and the boy walked in to make her appeal to the king? Can you think of a time God did something for you that could only have been done by His perfect timing?

5. Why did Elisha respond the way he did to the question of whether or not the king would die? What did the Lord show Elisha? How was it carried out?

6. What did the Holy Spirit highlight to you in 2 Kings 7—8 through the reading or the teaching?

Lesson 74: 2 Kings 9—10

Surviving Seed: Not Having a Complete
Heart for God

Teaching Notes

Intro

Today's lesson, as Kyle would say, is a bit of a humdinger. Let's start with the background of this passage that's found in chapter 8. Second Kings covers a three-hundred-year span from the reign of Ahaziah (the ninth king of Israel) around 863 BC through the fall of Israel to Assyria in 722 BC and on through the fall of Jerusalem and Judah to Babylon in 586 BC. This was a difficult time in the history of God's people.

It's easy to get confused in looking at these kings because there were two King Ahaziahs and two King Jehorams, one of each in each kingdom. Both Ahaziahs reigned only one year each, but their reigns did not overlap. The reign of the two Jehorams did overlap. Ahaziah of Israel reigned eleven years earlier than Ahaziah of Judah. In Judah, Jehoram (853–841 BC) preceded Ahaziah (841 BC), but in Israel, Ahaziah (853–852 BC) preceded Jehoram (852–841 BC).

Teaching

2 Kings 9:1–10: Elisha sent a prophet to anoint Jehu, the commander of King Joram (also known as Jehoram), as the new king to clean house in Israel (vv. 1–4). The prophet risked his own life to do so. According to the Bible, "Jehu is the only king of Israel who was anointed by an appointed servant of the Lord."[1] The anointing of Jehu as king fulfilled Elijah's prophecy given some 20 years earlier (1 Kings 19:15–16). There's so much prophecy fulfilled in these two chapters because evil could only be stored up for so long. In the anointing, Jehu was told to strike down all of the house of Ahab and Jezebel (vv. 7–10).

---

[1] Warren W. Wiersbe, *The Exposition Bible Commentary: Joshua–Esther* (Colorado Springs: David C. Cook, 2003), 538.

2 Kings 9:11–13: When his men asked what happened, Jehu tried not to answer but finally admitted that the Lord had anointed him king over Israel (vv. 11–12). The men proclaimed Jehu as king (v. 13).

2 Kings 9:14–16: Jehu lost no time in planning the assassination of the king (v. 14–16). Joram, the current king of Israel, who was son to Ahab and Jezebel, had been injured in battle and gone to Jezreel to recover. Ahaziah, king of Judah, had also gone to Jezreel (2 Kings 8:28–29). Jehu ordered his commanders not to let anyone escape from Jezreel, located about 25 miles away, and his order included both the king of Israel and the king of Judah.

2 Kings 9:17–29: A watchman on the wall of Jezreel announced that Jehu's troops were approaching, so Joram sent a rider out to ask if they came in peace (v. 17). However, the messenger didn't return and joined Jehu's army instead (v. 18). Joram sent out another rider with the same question, but he also joined Jehu's army (vv. 19–20).

The kings of Israel and Judah went out to meet Jehu and asked him if he came in peace (vv. 21–22a). They met Jehu on the property of Naboth, where Naboth was murdered, so Ahab could have his vineyard (1 Kings 21:1–16). *Nelson's Commentary* says, "To his credit, the battled weakened king came out and faced his possible opponent. He may have feared a military attack from his hot-headed captain. Perhaps he wanted to get him to realize that his plans would be acts of sedition against the legally constituted king."[2] Jehu responded that there could be no peace because of the acts of Jezebel (v. 22b). "Jezebel's spiritual adultery had brought heinous demonic practices into the kingdom and sealed its doom. As God had threatened, such activities would surely bring about the nation's demise"[3] (Deuteronomy 28:15, 25–26).

This shows the principle of reaping and sowing—what is planted is what will grow, whether godly or worldly. As Joram tried to escape, Jehu shot him with an arrow and Joram died (v. 24). Jehu had Joram's body thrown into Naboth's field, fulfilling Elijah's prophecy from God in 1 Kings 21. King Ahaziah also fled but was shot, and he died in Megiddo (v. 27). Wiersbe suggests that Ahaziah tried to hide in Megiddo, but Jehu's men tracked him down there and killed him. Ahaziah's body was returned to Jerusalem where he was buried with the Davidic kings.[4] "Had he not compromised with Joram, worshiped Baal, and followed his mother

---

[2] Earl D. Radmacher, Ronald B. Allen, and H. Wayne House, eds., *Nelson's New Illustrated Bible Commentary* (Nashville: Thomas Nelson, 1999), 472.

[3] Radmacher et al., 472.

[4] Wiersbe, 539.

Athaliah's, counsel, he would have been spared all this shame and defeat."[5] Sin always leads to death but Jesus came to get us out of that cycle.

2 Kings 9:30–37: Jezebel heard what happened, so she painted her eyes and adorned her hair, remaining defiant to the end (v. 30). When Jehu showed up, she taunted him, calling him Zimri, the name of a traitor who killed his master to seize his throne (v. 31) (1 Kings 16:11–12). When Jehu found support in some of the eunuchs, he ordered them to throw Jezebel out of the window. Her blood was splattered on the wall and on the horses, and Jehu rode over her (vv. 32–33). This fulfilled another prophecy (1 Kings 21:22–23). Her body was thrown into a field and treated as garbage (v. 37).

2 Kings 10: Jehu continued to remove the house of Ahab. He killed Ahab's seventy sons (vv. 1–11), Ahaziah's forty-two brothers (vv. 12–14), the rest of Ahab's family (vv. 15–17), and worshippers of Baal (vv. 18–27). Jehu was proud of his zeal for the Lord (v. 16). But Jehu didn't walk in God's ways (vv. 29–31). *Nelson's Commentary* says, "Jehu's destruction of Baal worship was a political act. His continuing the state worship policies established by Jeroboam 1 clearly shows his disregard for true spiritual revival in Israel."[6]

Closing

Jesus came to set us free from sin. The only way to find this freedom is to make Jesus the Lord of our life—that means we give him everything. Jehu did not get rid of his idols, and it hurt his legacy. For us today, our time on earth is so short. It is a blink compared to eternity. I encourage you, give it all for the Lord. There is nothing on this earth, no deception or type of sin that is worth hanging onto. Walk in total freedom with the Lord and let Him use you.

The Daily Word

Elisha anointed Jehu as king of Israel. After killing King Joram, King Ahaziah, and Jezebel, King Jehu went on to kill the entire house of Ahab and all the Baal worshippers. Although King Jehu said he was zealous for the Lord and succeeded in killing and eliminating much of the evil, he never fully removed one sin—worshipping the golden calves. This sin remained in Israel.

Jesus came to set us free from the bondage of sin. He longs for you to surrender your whole life to Him. The Lord's grace covers you, and His love can't be separated from you. However, when you hang onto a pocket of sin, you miss

---

[5] Wiersbe, 539.

[6] Radmacher et al., 474.

out on the complete freedom in Christ. Because of Christ, there really is no sin worth hanging on to. What do you need to eliminate completely from your life today? Say, *"Lord, have it all."* Receive His grace, walk in the Spirit moment-by-moment, and you will not carry out the deeds of your flesh.

Jehu eliminated Baal worship from Israel, but he did not turn away from the sins that Jeroboam son of Nebat had caused Israel to commit—worshiping the gold calves that were in Bethel and Dan. —2 Kings 10:28–29

Further Scripture: John 3:36; John 8:36; Galatians 5:1

Questions

1. Whom did God originally tell to anoint Jehu (1 Kings 19:16)? What did anointing someone mean (Exodus 40:9; 1 Samuel 10:1; Luke 4:18–19)?

2. Why was Jehu asked to destroy the family of Ahab (1 Kings 21:21–24)? Did he obey this word from the Lord (2 Kings 10:17)?

3. In 2 Kings 9:11, Jehu's fellow officers called the young prophet a madman. Can you think of other places in Scripture where a believer was accused of madness (1 Samuel 21:12–14; Mark 3:20–21; John 10:20; Acts 26:24; 2 Corinthians 5:13)? Have you ever been accused of being crazy for the gospel?

4. What made Jezebel so evil in the sight of God (1 Kings 16:31; 18:19)? What do you need to do to drastically get rid of the "Jezebel's" in your own life?

5. How did God reward Jehu for the work that he had done? If Jehu had done well, how do you take into account Hosea 1:4 (2 Kings 9:15)? Was Jehu compromising the word of God?

6. What did the Holy Spirit highlight to you in 2 Kings 9—10 through the reading or the teaching?

Lesson 75: 2 Kings 11—12

Surviving Seed: Waiting on the Lord's Timing

Teaching Notes

Intro

We've all heard of road rage and how one action behind the wheel from someone else can set off another driver until the situation escalates out of control. When we talk about returning evil for evil, it's easy to say we would never do such a thing. But it's possible when anger spirals out of control. Jehu, the king of Israel, had killed Ahaziah, the king of Judah. His mother Athaliah would take over her son's throne by killing off all the heirs to the throne. But this is also the story of the *Surviving Seed*.

Teaching

2 Kings 11:1–3: When Athaliah, King Ahaziah's mother, found out her son was dead, she had all the royal heirs killed (v. 1). But Jehosheba, Ahaziah's sister, rescued Ahaziah's baby son Joash and hid him and his nurse from Ahaziah's mother (v. 2). Joash remained in hiding for six years while his grandmother Athaliah ruled Judah (v. 3). Wiersbe describes Joash's hiding places as "a room where old bedding was stored and then in a room in the temple."[1] This next king of Judah had to wait upon the Lord's timing.

2 Kings 11:4–16: Jehosheba was the wife of Jehoiada, the high priest. In the seventh year of Athaliah's reign, Jehoiada brought together five commanders, who were over a hundred men each, and the five temple guards. He presented the young king to them and swore them to an oath to protect Joash.

Jehoiada gave this group of 510 men instructions for how to continually protect the life of Joash (vv. 4–8). He instructed three divisions of one hundred men each to each be stationed at the entrances around the king's palace. The other two divisions were to be stationed at the gates of the temple. The divisions were to

---

[1] Warren W. Wiersbe, *Be Distinct: Standing Firmly Against the World's Tides* (Colorado Springs: David C. Cook, 2002), 107.

be rotated at the palace and the temple. They were also told to keep the soldiers armed and to instruct them to kill anyone who approached the king.

The commanders did everything Jehoiada commanded (v. 9). The commanders gave out the spears and shields of King David that had been dedicated and stored in the temple to use in protecting Joash (vv. 10–11). These weapons had been dedicated to the temple after the campaign against Hadadezer (2 Samuel 8:11). Then Jehoiada brought out Joash, put a crown on him, and proclaimed him as king (v. 12) (Hebrews 6:12).

When the queen heard the noise from the temple, she went out to see what was going on (v. 13). She looked into the temple and saw the newly crowned king standing by the pillar according to the custom (v. 14). Although Athaliah screamed that it was treason, Jehoiada ordered the commanders to arrest her, take her out of the temple, and to kill anyone who followed her (v. 15). She was put to death outside the king's palace (v. 16).

2 Kings 11:17–21: Jehoiada then made a covenant between the Lord, the king, and the people, and another between the king and the people, renewing the covenant that had been broken (v. 17). The people tore down the temple of Baal and broke all the altars and images (v. 18). And King Joash was placed upon the king's throne in the palace (v. 19). The Davidic covenant was reestablished, and the people rejoiced (v. 20). Joash became king at the age of seven (v. 21).

Closing

The group that Jehoiada brought together was a remnant who believed in the promises of God. Their actions brought about revival in Judah. Wiersbe wrote, "Revival is simply obeying God's Word and doing what He commanded our fathers to do. We don't need the novelties of the present; we need the realities of the past."[2]

The Daily Word

When Ahaziah's mother Athaliah discovered her son was dead, she killed all other heirs in line for the royal throne. Then she seized the throne for herself and served as queen of Judah for six years. However, a brave woman named Jehosheba secretly rescued and hid the young boy Joash, one of Ahaziah's sons. In the seventh year, the high priest Jehoiada revealed the secret that David's seed had survived—seven-year-old Joash was alive! They crowned and anointed Joash as king, and he took his rightful place on the throne. All the people rejoiced, and Athaliah was put to death.

[2] Wiersbe, 110.

For seven years, Joash remained hidden from the people of Judah. If he had not had this time in hiding, he may never have been crowned king of Judah. *Have you ever been through a season of hiddenness?* Maybe today, you know the Lord has called you to something, but you can sense the time has not yet come. You are in a place of hiding, a place of waiting, a quiet season. From the outside, no one may see or understand, but inside your heart, you know the Lord is preparing you for what lies ahead. Rest in Him. Don't force it. Don't push it. Trust God is at work in the hiddenness. As you wait, draw near to God, and He will draw near to you.

Joash was in hiding with Jehosheba in the Lord's temple six years while Athaliah ruled over the land. —2 Kings 11:3

Further Scripture: Ecclesiastes 3:11; Lamentations 3:25–27; Hebrews 6:12

Questions

1. Do you think Athaliah destroyed the entire family so she would be queen since her son was dead? Why did Jehosheba steal away Joash (2 Kings 11:1–3)?

2. In 2 Kings 12:6, the repairs had not yet been made to the temple. Why do you think they hadn't been done?

3. In 2 Kings 12:17–18, why did Joash take all the hallowed things found in the treasury and send them to King Hazael?

4. What did the Holy Spirit highlight to you in 2 Kings 11—12 through the reading or the teaching?

Lesson 76: 2 Kings 13—14

Surviving Seed: Walking Out Limited Faith

Teaching Notes

Intro

We're in the seventh book in the Old Testament, and every one of these books points to the coming Messiah. Our phrase for 2 Kings is *Surviving Seed*. In chapter 11, we looked at a small group of people who believed in the Davidic covenant and a seven-year-old boy named Joash who became the king of Judah, and a surviving seed.

Teaching

2 Kings 13:1–3: In the 23rd year of Joash's reign as king of Judah, Jehoahaz, son of Jehu, became the king of Israel (v. 1). And, as with all the kings of Israel, Jehoahaz did evil in the Lord's sight and continued the sins that Jeroboam had first committed (v. 2a). You would think that Jehoahaz would have some idea of the consequences of following the sins of Jeroboam, but "he did not turn away from them" (v. 2b). Notice the phrase, "the sins that Jeroboam . . . had caused Israel to commit." The same phrase in used to describe other kings in 2 Kings 10:29, 31; 13:6, 11; 15:9. At least 17 times, this phrase was used in 2 Kings. Imagine if the model of how to act had been David and not evil King Jeroboam? Sadly, this was the only pattern Jehoahaz knew.

John MacArthur suggests that 2 Kings 13 reflects the cycle outlined in the book of Judges[1]:

1. Jehoahaz did evil in the sight of the Lord (v. 2; Judges 2:11–13; 3:7).
2. God was angry at Israel and delivered them to their enemies (v. 3; Judges 2:14–15; 3:8).
3. Jehoahaz cried out for God to intervene with his enemies (v. 4; Judges 2:18; 3:9).
4. God called a deliverer to rescue Israel (v. 5; Judges 2:16, 18; 3:9).

---

[1] John MacArthur, *The MacArthur Bible Commentary* (Nashville: Thomas Nelson, 2005), 450.

5. After being delivered, Israel went back to their evil ways and the cycle began again (v. 6; Judges 2:19; 3:12–14).

Nelson's Commentary explains that God's anger can be slow in coming but can be incited into exercising His judgment (Deuteronomy 4:24–25; Psalm 103:8). God is also compassionate, but "His wrath is reserved for those who break His covenant" (Deuteronomy 13:17; 29:25– 27; Joshua 23:16; Judges 2:20), and "God's wrath is righteous, while human anger is evaluated in negative terms" (Genesis 49:6; Proverbs 14:17).[2]

2 Kings 13:4–9: Jehoahaz called out to the Lord who heard him and sent Israel a deliverer. Israel escaped the power of the Arameans (vv. 4–5a). The people went back to their tents, but they continued following Jeroboam's sin (vv. 5b–6). They continued the pattern of committing sin, experiencing God's judgment, crying out for help, being delivered, and then going back to sin. Jehoahaz walked with them in sin. Even the Asherah pole, "a sacred tree or pole that was perceived perhaps as some sexually-oriented symbol of the fertility religion of Canaan," was left standing.[3] Meanwhile, Jehoahaz had no army left and very few soldiers (v. 7). Jehoahaz died and was buried in Samaria. His son Jehoash became king (vv. 8–9).

2 Kings 13:10–13: King Joash was in his 37th year on the throne when Jehoash became king over Israel and reigned 16 years (v. 10). Jehoash also did evil in the sight of the Lord and walked in the sins of Jeroboam (v. 11). Jehoash waged war against Judah's king, Amaziah. When Jehoash died, he was buried in Samaria with the other kings of Israel (vv. 12–13).

2 Kings 13:14–21: No mention was made of Elisha for more than 40 years, and at this point, he had served 70 years. Elisha became sick and later died from that illness (v. 14a). Jehoash, the king of Israel, wept over Elisha who was lying ill in bed (v. 14b). Elisha told Jehoash to get his bow and arrows, and Elisha joined his hands to the king's hands on the bow, symbolizing that "Jehoash would exert power against the Syrians that came from the Lord through His prophet"[4] (vv. 15–16). Elisha told Jehoash to open the east window and then shoot the arrow out of the window (v. 17a). When Jehoash shot, Elisha told him that was the arrow of victory over Aram (v. 17b).

---

[2] Earl D. Radmacher, Ronald B. Allen, and H. Wayne House, eds., *Nelson's New Illustrated Bible Commentary* (Nashville: Thomas Nelson, 1999), 477.

[3] Radmacher et al., 477.

[4] MacArthur, 451.

Elisha told Jehoash to take the rest of the arrows and strike the ground. Jehoash struck the ground three times (v. 18). Elisha was angry that Jehoash had only struck the ground three times instead of five or six and gave the prophetic word that Jehoash would strike down Aram only three times, not enough to put an end to them (v. 19). Then Elisha died and was buried (v. 20). When Moabite raiders came into the land in the spring, the Israelites, who were about to bury a man, instead threw the body into Elisha's tomb. When the body touched Elisha's bones, the man was revived and stood up (v. 21). God did the work, not Elisha's bones (Ezekiel 37:4; Matthew 27:52)!

2 Kings 13:22–25: Hazael, the king of Aram, oppressed Israel throughout Jehoahaz's entire reign (v. 22). But God still had compassion on them because of His covenant with Abraham, Isaac, and Jacob (v. 23). When King Hazael died, his son Ben-hadad was made king of Aram. Jehoash waged war against Ben-hadad and took back the cities that Hazael had taken from King Jehoahaz, Jehoash's father. Jehoash defeated Ben-hadad exactly *three times* (vv. 24–25), as prophesied by Elisha.

Closing

Jehoash only had a partial victory over Aram and Ben-hadad, because he only walked out what he had faith in. That goes for us as well, in all areas of our life.

The Daily Word

Elisha was God's chosen prophet who had been given a double portion of the power that was within Elijah. Anointed for his calling, Elisha had God's great power within Him in miraculous ways. When Elisha passed away, his body was buried. In the spring of that year, the Israelites were burying a man but were caught off guard by a Moab raiding party, so they just threw the dead body into Elisha's tomb. When the dead body touched the bones of Elisha, the man was revived and stood up! The Lord had one more miracle that displayed His power and strength through the life and death of Elisha!

The Lord promises to wake up the things that are dead—to wake up the dry bones. As a follower of Christ, you have this same resurrection power inside you. What if someone bumped into you? Would they even know you are alive in Christ? Jesus came to bring *life* to all who will receive it. Today, live bursting with the love of Jesus and let it be contagious to those who bump into you as you live out your day. May today be a day of awakening the dry bones all around us!

Once, as the Israelites were burying a man, suddenly they saw a raiding party, so they threw the man into Elisha's tomb. When he touched Elisha's bones, the man revived and stood up! —2 Kings 13:21

Further Scripture: Job 33:4; Ezekiel 37:5; John 5:21

Questions

1. What did the arrow represent in 2 Kings 13:17? Why was the man of God angry at the king of Israel in verse 19?

2. In 2 Kings 13:23, God was gracious and merciful because of His covenant. What covenant was that (Genesis 15:18–21; 26:2–5; 28:13–15)?

3. In 2 Kings 14:3, Amaziah did what was pleasing in God's eyes, but not fully. He followed in his father's footsteps instead of his ancestor David's. Can you think of a time or circumstance that you followed after God, but not fully? In what ways? Did you regret it? Why or why not?

4. What did the Holy Spirit highlight to you in 2 Kings 13—14 through the reading or the teaching?

Lesson 77: 2 Kings 15—16

Surviving Seed: Defiling the Temple

Teaching Notes

Intro

As we look at the crazy genealogy of 2 Kings, we can praise the Lord that we have the *Surviving Seed*. Most of the kings for both the northern kingdom of Israel and the southern kingdom of Judah were evil in God's sight. Occasionally in Judah, a king would do what was right in God's sight. Chapter 15 jumps between kings in both kingdoms, but their reigns were shortened because they all followed in the sin of King Jeroboam. In verse 32, Jotham is introduced as the king of Judah.

Teaching

2 Kings 16:1–4: In the seventeenth year of Pekah's reign in Israel, Ahaz became king of Judah at the age of 20 (vv. 1–2). Ahaz also chose to walk in the way of Jeroboam, instead of King David. During this time, two new prophets entered Judah: Isaiah and Micah. Not sure how this all worked out, but Ahaz's father, King Jotham, was still alive at this point. Ahaz sacrificed his son in the fire to the god Molech (v. 3) (Leviticus 18:21). Ahaz also sacrificed and burned incense throughout the nation (v. 4).

2 Kings 16:5–9: Aram's King Rezin and Israel's King Pekah joined forces to wage war against Jerusalem and King Ahaz. They besieged the city but could not conquer it (v. 5). According to 2 Chronicles 28:5–8, Ahaz was handed over to the king of Israel because of his sin. King Ahaz' son was killed in the process, and many others were also killed and captured. Sin constantly leads to consequences. Meanwhile the king of Aram took back Elath, an important port town that was essential to Judah's economy, and expelled the Judahites from it (v. 6). Ahaz sent messengers to the king of Assyria asking him for help against the king of Aram and the king of Israel and swearing allegiance to him (v. 7). Ahaz also sent the king of Assyria the silver and the gold from the temple and the palace as a tribute to Assyria (v. 8). Assyria marched in to help, deported the people of Aram, and killed King Rezin (v. 9).

2 Kings 16:10–18: Ahaz went to meet the king of Assyria. There he saw the altar of Damascus and sent a model of the altar and building plans to Uriah the priest (v. 10). "The serious iniquity in this was meddling with and changing, according to personal taste, the furnishings of the temple, the design for which had been given by God"[1] (Exodus 25:40; 26:30; 27:1–8; 1 Chronicles 28:19). Ahaz's action showed his desire to please the Assyrian king instead of his own God.[2]

We must avoid trying to make friends with the world instead of staying obedient to God. Ahaz sought to be friendly with the world (James 4:4), he became stained by the world (James 1:27), he came to love the world (1 John 2:15–17), and he chose to become conformed to the world (Romans 12:2). Is the church today becoming more like the world?

Priest Uriah followed Ahaz's instructions for the altar rather than staying obedient to God (v. 11). When Ahaz returned, he worshipped and sacrificed at the new altar (vv. 12–13). Then Ahaz moved the bronze altar God wanted off to the side (v. 14). Ahaz commanded Uriah to make all offerings on the new altar, and only the king would sacrifice at the bronze altar so he could seek God's guidance (v. 15). Uriah, God's priest, complied (v. 16). Ahaz then altered the water carts and the bronze basins at the temple and removed the Sabbath canopy from the temple, all to satisfy the king of Assyria (vv. 17–18). Wiersbe writes, "Ahaz thought that the Lord would be pleased with sacrifices offered on this magnificent new altar, but he was wrong. The Lord doesn't want sacrifice; He wants obedience."[3]

Dale Ralph Davis points out that Ahaz made four major changes. Ahaz (1) created new altars (vv. 10–11); (2) made new arrangements (vv. 12–14); (3) developed new regulations (vv. 15–16); and (4) brought new rationale (vv. 17–18).[4] Scripture describes four major changes that Ahaz brought to the temple in Jerusalem:

1. He removed the side panels and basins from the portable stands (1 Kings 7:27–29, 38).

2. He removed the large ornate reservoir, called the "sea" from atop the twelve bronze bulls to a new stone base (1 Kings 7:23–26).

---

[1] John MacArthur, *The MacArthur Bible Commentary* (Nashville: Thomas Nelson, 2005), 458.

[2] MacArthur, 458.

[3] Warren W. Wiersbe, *The Exposition Bible Commentary: Joshua–Esther* (Colorado Springs: David C. Cook, 2003), 566.

[4] Dale Ralph Davis, *2 Kings: The Power and the Fury*, Focus on the Bible series (Ross-shire, Scotland: Christian Focus, 2011), n.p.

3. He removed the Sabbath canopy used by the king on Sabbath.
4. He removed the king's outer entrance, a special entrance to the temple used by the king on Sabbath and feast days.

These changes removed the options that covered the king when he came into the presence of the Lord. Ahaz didn't want those because he coveted the approval of the king of Assyria. Ahaz turned his back on the Lord.

Closing

I want to close with these words from Wiersbe: "Once we allow worldliness to get into the church fellowship, it will quietly grow, pollute the fellowship and eventually take over. It was not until the reign of his son Hezekiah that the temple Ahaz defiled was reopened and sanctified for ministry (2 Chronicles 29:1–29)."[5]

1 Corinthians 5:6 makes me think of King Ahaz: "Your boasting is not good. Don't you know that a little yeast permeates the whole batch of dough?"

The Daily Word

Years before King Ahaz ruled Judah, the Lord instructed King Solomon on the specifics for His Temple—the permanent place for Yahweh's presence to dwell and where the people could go and worship Him. Even so, King Ahaz aligned himself with the king of Assyria and began to make changes to the Temple. He disregarded the previous instructions from the Lord. He removed side paneling, removed a reservoir, removed the Sabbath canopy, and removed the king's outer entrance. King Ahaz wanted to satisfy the king of Assyria more than Yahweh God.

When you seek to satisfy the world, you will begin changing things about yourself. The world will try to allure you, tempt you, and distract you from focusing on the Lord. You may slowly begin to remove parts of your life that represent Christ. The changes may seem small at first, but what you begin to do on the outside reflects the inside condition of your heart. If you remove things representing Christ, then you are most likely replacing them with things that are not of Christ. Today, ask yourself: *Are you living to satisfy the world's standards or walking in the ways pleasing to the Lord?*

To satisfy the king of Assyria, he removed from the Lord's temple the Sabbath canopy they had built in the palace, and he closed the outer entrance for the king. —2 Kings 16:18

Further Scripture: Psalm 84:10; Galatians 1:10; 1 Thessalonians 2:4

---

[5] Wiersbe, 566.

Questions

1. In 2 Kings 15:19, the current king of Israel paid the king of Assyria 1,000 talents of silver to gain his support. Where did this silver come from?

2. How did all but two of the kings of Israel mentioned in 2 Kings 15 die? What does this tell us about the condition of this kingdom (Romans 1:28–32)?

3. King Ahaz of Judah had his son "walk through the fire." What does this mean (Leviticus 20:2–3; Deuteronomy 18:9–10; Ezekiel 16:21)?

4. When meeting with the king of Assyria, King Ahaz saw his altar and had one made just like it for worship in Jerusalem. Do you think the Lord was okay with this (Exodus 39:32, 39, 42–43)? What changes did King Ahaz make to how the people worshiped at the temple (2 Kings 16:14–18)? Is this a portrayal of how mankind designs his own way to worship rather than obedience to the instruction of the Lord?

5. What did the Holy Spirit highlight to you in 2 Kings 15—16 through the reading or the teaching?

Lesson 78: 2 Kings 17—18

Surviving Seed: Doing Evil in God's Sight

Teaching Notes

Intro

Today, we're going to continue to see more of the evil practices we've been studying all week. King Hezekiah is coming, but not yet. In chapter 17, we're getting to the last of the kings. The *Surviving Seed* will come from the line of Judah, not Israel.

Teaching

2 Kings 17:1–6: King Ahaz of Judah was an evil king. During the twelfth year of his reign, Hoshea became king over Israel (v. 1). Hoshea did evil in God's sight but was not as bad as the other kings of Israel (v. 2). Shalmaneser, the king of Assyria, attacked Israel. In return, Hoshea became Shalmaneser's vassal and paid him tribute for protection (v. 3). Hoshea had sent envoys to King So of Egypt, looking for help against Assyria. When Shalmaneser found out, he arrested Hoshea and put him in prison (v. 4). The king of Assyria besieged the entire land for three years (v. 5). Israel had lost its last king. Then the land of Samaria was taken from Israel and the Israelites were deported to Assyria and resettled there (v. 6).

2 Kings 17:7–20: Israel was beginning to be punished because of their disobedience against the Lord (v. 7). God had redeemed His people, yet they chose to worship other gods. Dale Ralph Davis states that the sin of the Israelites was actually ingratitude.[1]

Half the battle in life is overcoming situations by giving God thanks. Because the Israelites had stopped giving thanks, they wanted more. They lived according to the customs of other nations that the kings of Israel had brought them (v. 8). Davis suggests that the Israelites were constantly looking for the

---

[1] Dale Ralph Davis, *2 Kings: The Power and the Fury*, Focus on the Bible series (Ross-shire, Scotland: Christian Focus, 2011), n.p.

next great thing they could embrace that had nothing to do with the Lord.[2] They not only embraced the cultures, but they expanded the worship of the pagan gods on every hill and under every green tree (vv. 9–11). They were doing exactly what the people they had driven out of the Promised Land had done (v. 12). The Lord sent prophets and seers to warn His people of their evil ways (v. 13) (Hebrews 12:25).

The people refused to listen to God's warning (v. 14). They became obstinate and ended up in exile in Assyria. The Israelites were guilty of ten actions of disobedience—what Davis calls "200 years of infidelity"[3]:

1. They rejected His statutes and covenants (v. 15).
2. They pursued worthless idols (v. 15).
3. They abandoned God's commands (v. 16).
4. The made cast images for themselves (v. 16).
5. They made an Asherah pole (which had to do with sexual immorality) (v. 16).
6. They worshipped the heavenly host (v. 16).
7. They served Baal (v. 16).
8. They made their sons and daughters pass through the fire (v. 17).
9. They practiced divination and interpreted omens (v. 17).
10. They devoted themselves to doing evil in the Lord's sight (they provoked Him) (v. 17).

The Lord was "very angry with Israel" because of their complete disobedience, so "He removed them from His presence. Only the tribe of Judah remained" (v. 18). The *Surviving Seed* was only in Judah, even though Judah had also disobeyed and lived like the Israelites (v. 19). The Lord rejected ALL Israel, removed them, and banished them from His presence (v. 20).

2 Kings 17:21–23: Verses 21–23 provide a summary of Israel's history, of their disobedience which led them into exile. The beginning of this path of disobedience goes back to the dividing of the kingdom of Israel into two nations and Jeroboam, the king of Israel, who intentionally led the northern kingdom away from following the Lord (v. 21). Even after Jeroboam was dead, the Israelites persisted in these sins (v. 22). Finally, because of their complete disobedience, God had them exiled to Assyria (v. 23).

---

[2] Davis, n.p.

[3] Davis, n.p.

Closing

Many of us are in bondage right now, and we must look to Judah for hope. If not, we will remain in bondage. My prayer is simple, "Lord, what are the areas where we are in bondage? Show us where we are rejecting you and pursuing worthless idols. Holy Spirit speak to us."

Jesus came to set the captives free. We can experience this freedom if we will release the things that are holding us back.

The Daily Word

Israel became obstinate and did not believe in the Lord their God. They rejected His covenant, pursued worthless idols, abandoned His Word, worshiped heavenly hosts, served Baal, made cast images for themselves, and practiced divination, among other things. Ultimately, they devoted themselves to what was evil in the Lord's sight and provoked the Lord to anger. At last, the Lord had enough. In His anger, the Lord removed Israel from His presence. Only the tribe of Judah remained as the surviving seed for the coming Messiah.

Are you different from Israel? The people took their eyes completely off the Lord, His ways, His Word, His commands. They did whatever they wanted and found themselves back in bondage. *Are you any different?* Jesus came to set the captives free. Jesus came to bring you hope and a future. Jesus came to break you from bondage and give you freedom. Jesus came to offer you life and not death. *Where have you taken your eyes off the Lord?* Be honest with yourself and ask the Lord to reveal any area where you have gone astray. Surrender and confess it to the Lord. Then ask Him to set you free. He will bring you freedom just as He promises. He is such a faithful God!

They devoted themselves to do what was evil in the Lord's sight and provoked Him. Therefore, the Lord was very angry with Israel, and He removed them from His presence. Only the tribe of Judah remained. —2 Kings 17:17–18

Questions

1. 2 Kings 17 describes how the kingdom of Israel was captured and taken into captivity. According to 2 Kings 17:7–23, why did this happen (Deuteronomy 31:16–18; Joshua 24:20; Romans 1:21–25)?

2. Because those who were brought to settle in the cities of Samaria did not fear the Lord, what did the Lord do (2 Kings 17:25)? How did they try to appease Israel's God (2 Kings 17:27–28)? After a priest came to teach them how to fear the Lord, did they get it right (2 Kings 17:33, 41)?

3. What did King Hezekiah destroy (broke into pieces) that Moses had made (Numbers 21:9)? What did the bronze snake point to (John 3:14–15; 12:32)? How did they misuse it?

4. Read the description of King Hezekiah in 2 Kings 18:5–6. Does anything stand out to you in this description? Is he a "type" of Christ?

5. In 2 Kings 18:22, the king of Assyria's men stated that King Hezekiah tore down the Lord's high places and took away His altars. Was this accurate (2 Kings 18:3–4)?

6. Do you believe the king of Assyria was really sent by the Lord against Judah (2 Kings 18:25)? What tactic was he using by speaking to the people in Judah, telling them the Lord would not deliver them (2 Kings 18:32b)? Was anything he said in 2 Kings 18:27–35 true (2 Kings 19:6)? Does the enemy use this kind of strategy (lies and fear) to defeat you?

7. What did the Holy Spirit highlight to you in 2 Kings 17—18 through the reading or the teaching?

Lesson 79: 2 Kings 19—20

Surviving Seed: God Gave Hezekiah a
Second Chance

Teaching Notes

Intro

This whole week, the message has been about the disobedience of the kings of
Israel. God finally sent the Israelites into exile in Assyria. Today, we move back
to the Judah lineage.

Teaching

2 Kings 20:1–3: King Hezekiah became terminally ill. The prophet Isaiah told
the king to put his affairs in order because he would not survive (v. 1). Hezekiah
became king at the age of 25 and reigned for 29 years (2 Kings 18:1–2). His son
Manasseh would eventually become king in 687 BC at the age of 22. Manasseh
was seven years old when Isaiah told his father he was about to die.[1] Hezekiah's
first response to Isaiah's announcement was to turn to God in prayer (vv. 2–3).
(Read Isaiah 38:2 for Hezekiah's prayer and Isaiah 38:10–20 for his poem about
this experience.) Hezekiah seemed to model Solomon's prayer. (Read 2 Chronicles 6:16–17 for part of Solomon's prayer.)

2 Kings 20:4–11: Something changed after God heard Hezekiah's prayer. God
responded immediately and stopped Isaiah before he left the courtyard (v. 4).
God sent Isaiah back to Hezekiah with news that He would heal him. In return,
Hezekiah was told to go to the temple on the third day (v. 5). God also promised
to give Hezekiah another 15 years of life and defend the city of Jerusalem (v. 6).
Prayer can radically change things! Isaiah asked for pressed figs, which he used
to treat Hezekiah's infected skin. Hezekiah recovered fully (v. 7).

Hezekiah asked Isaiah for a sign that he would be healed completely (v. 8).
Isaiah replied, "Should the shadow go ahead 10 steps or go back 10 steps?" (v.
9). Isaiah's question was whether Hezekiah wanted to see the shadow divinely

---

[1] Warren W. Wiersbe, *The Exposition Bible Commentary: Joshua–Esther* (Colorado Springs:
David C. Cook, 2003), 574.

lengthen or shorten. Hezekiah answered to let the shadow go back 10 steps (shorten) (v. 10). Isaiah told the Lord the sign that Hezekiah wanted, and God brought the shadow back ten steps (v. 11). Theologians question whether God reversed the orbit of the planet or stopped the rotation of the orbit to make this happen, but obviously, no one knows.

2 Kings 20:12–19: Hezekiah received a visit from the son of the king of Babylon who brought letters and gifts since Hezekiah had been sick (v. 12). Hezekiah returned the hospitality by showing the king's son everything he had—everything in his treasure house and his armory (v. 13). When Isaiah found that strangers had visited Hezekiah, he questioned where the men had come from. Hezekiah answered that they were from Babylon (v. 14). Then Isaiah asked what the men had been shown in the palace, and Hezekiah told Isaiah he had shown them everything (v. 15).

Isaiah then delivered the word of the Lord that eventually everything Judah had would be carried off to Babylon (v. 17). Further, some of Hezekiah's descendants would be taken off as well (v. 18). However, his son Manasseh would be carried off to Babylon even before the fall of Jerusalem in 586 BC.[2]

Hezekiah was excited to show what he had because of his pride. *Nelson's Commentary* states the "remarkable feature of the Bible is that it does not gloss over the faults of its best heroes and heroines. The foolishness of Hezekiah follows immediately on the narrative of his trust in the Lord."[3] Wiersbe points out that "pride makes us rob God of the glory that belongs to Him alone. Pride gives us a feeling of false security and this leads us into sin and defeat."[4] It was pride that caused Satan to rebel against God. The enemy (the serpent) comes to deceive us—and the lion to devour us.

2 Kings 20:20–21: Verse 20 highlights Hezekiah's significant achievements as king. He had a tunnel dug that ran between the spring of Gishon, located outside the walls of Jerusalem, and the pool of Siloam, which was located inside the walls. The tunnel helped the people within the city survive during a siege. The tunnel, still in existence and called Hezekiah's Tunnel, was a remarkable engineering feat.[5]

---

[2] Earl D. Radmacher, Ronald B. Allen, and H. Wayne House, eds., *Nelson's New Illustrated Bible Commentary* (Nashville: Thomas Nelson, 1999), 487.

[3] Radmacher et al., 487.

[4] Wiersbe, 576.

[5] Radmacher et al., 487.

Closing

Hezekiah was one of the kings of Judah who did what was right in the sight of the Lord. His tunnel alone shows the wisdom and foresight he had as king. But his pride ultimately led to the fall of Judah.

The Daily Word

King Hezekiah became terminally ill. The prophet Isaiah told Hezekiah to get his affairs in order because he would not survive the illness. In this moment, Hezekiah turned to the Lord. He wept bitterly and asked the Lord to remember him and his faithful walk through life. Soon after this prayer, the Lord changed the course for Hezekiah's life. The word of the Lord came to Isaiah saying Hezekiah would be healed in three days. However, the Lord granted Hezekiah fifteen more years of life, allowing him to see victory in Assyria. The Lord heard Hezekiah's prayers and answered him. Has there been a time in your life when you were hit with a difficult life circumstance and you sought the Lord in prayer? A surprise health report? A loss of a job? Unexpected news about your child? The Lord sees your tears. He hears your prayers. He is able to work in ways you can't imagine. Today, *seek the Lord in prayer*. He wants you to cry out to Him, and His ears are always open. No matter how big or little the need may be, if it is important to you, it's important to the Lord. He is there to lift you up and rescue you. The Lord came to redeem and is the God of second chances.

Then Hezekiah turned his face to the wall and prayed to the Lord, "Please Lord, remember how I have walked before You faithfully and wholeheartedly and have done what pleases You." And Hezekiah wept bitterly.
—2 Kings 20:2–3

Further Scripture: Psalm 66:17–18; 1 Peter 3:11b–12; 1 John 5:14

Questions

1. What was the report King Hezekiah heard? What were the responses from Hezekiah? Were these good responses?

2. What did King Hezekiah realize about the people of Judah (2 Kings 19:4, 30)?

3. Why did it seem that the King of Assyria had zero fear of the Lord? Why did he think that God would not help Hezekiah?

4. What was Hezekiah's reaction and response after reading the letter that had been sent to him? What was the Lord's response to Hezekiah's prayer? When have you seen God fight for you as a response to your prayers?

5. Why do you think God relented about what He said to Hezekiah regarding his death (2 Kings 20:1, 5–6)? Where do you see this kind of mercy from God with other people in Scripture (Exodus 32:9–14; Jonah 3:10; Romans 5:8)?

6. What did the Holy Spirit highlight to you in 2 Kings 19—20 through the reading or the teaching?

Lesson 80: 2 Kings 21—22

Surviving Seed: The Beginning of Revival

Teaching Notes

Intro

As we've worked through the book of 2 Kings, one theme seems to be common—most kings did evil in the sight of the Lord. Every once in a while, a king would be sprinkled into the mix that did good in God's sight, but there weren't many. In 2 Kings 21, Hezekiah's son, Manasseh, became king at the age of 12. According to verse 1, he was the most wicked king of them all. Things got so bad in Judah that when Manasseh's son Amon became king, he was so wicked that his servants killed him and put Amon's son Josiah on the throne as king (v. 26).

In total, there were 20 kings (including Queen Athaliah) over Judah. Of these 20, eight did good in God's sight: Asa, Jehoshaphat, Joash, Amaziah, Uzziah, Jotham, Hezekiah, and Josiah. These kings were pointing to the *Surviving Seed*.

Teaching

2 Kings 22:1–2: Josiah was only eight years old when he became king and reigned 31 years. Josiah did what was right in the Lord's sight and he walked in the ways of King David (vv. 1–2). Chapter 22 records Josiah's good efforts for the Lord.

2 Kings 22: 3–7: The temple was repaired (vv. 3–7): In the 18 year of his reign (at age 26), Josiah sent his secretary to the temple to the high priest Hilkiah with instructions about repairing the damage King Ahaz had done to the temple (vv. 3–6). Josiah trusted Hilkiah to oversee the funds with no accounting because the workers worked with integrity (v. 7). *Nelson's Commentary* describes Hilkiah as "a major figure in the revival of the true religion that young Josiah accomplished."[1]

2 Kings 22: 8–20: The Book of the Law was discovered (vv. 8–20): During the repair of the temple, the Book of the Law was found (v. 8). *Nelson's Commentary*

---

[1] Earl D. Radmacher, Ronald B. Allen, and H. Wayne House, eds., *Nelson's New Illustrated Bible Commentary* (Nashville: Thomas Nelson, 1999), 488.

states the Book of the Law could have included "parts or all of the Pentateuch" and suggests it "may have been lost, set aside, or hidden during the wicked reigns of Manasseh and Amon."[2] Constable states, "It seems probable that Manasseh or Amon had destroyed existing copies of Israel's covenant constitution since there is every reason to believe that Hezekiah knew the Mosaic Law. This would not have been difficult because in ancient times there were few copies of even official documents."[3] Hilkiah passed the Book of the Law to Josiah's secretary Shaphan, who read it himself and then to Josiah (vv. 9–10).

Theologians like to discuss what part of the Book of the Law Shaphan read to Josiah. Many feel it must have been from the book of Deuteronomy, such as: how wicked the people of Israel had become (Deuteronomy 4—13); what Israel had not done that God had asked of them (Deuteronomy 14—18); or the warning of what God would do (Deuteronomy 27–30).[4] For Josiah, this was the first time he had heard Scripture, and it brought him into distress. He tore his clothes to show genuine remorse (v. 11).

Josiah desired a prophetic insight from the Lord, so he commissioned five men to go inquire of the Lord for him: Hilkiah the priest, his secretary Shaphan, Shaphan's son Ahikam, Micaiah's son Achbor, and Josiah's servant Asaiah (vv. 12–13). Shaphan played a unique role in this, and his family (except for one son) had been involved in preserving and sharing God's Word for many years (1 Kings 22:12–28; Jeremiah 26:16–24; 29:1–23; 36:11ff; Ezekiel 8:11–12).[5] The men went to the prophetess Huldah and explained what had happened (v. 14). Note that there were other prophetesses in Scripture, such as Miriam (Exodus 15:20) and Deborah (Judges 4:4).

Huldah delivered God's message with prophetic clarity. The message was divided into two parts, each addressed to Josiah as "the man who sent you" (vv. 15–17) and "the king of Judah who sent you" (vv. 18–20). In verses 15–17, God said to tell the man who had sent them that He was about to bring disaster to Judah because of the people's disobedience. *Nelson's Commentary* suggests, "The threat of calamity for apostasy that the king heard may have been intended to reinforce the message of the parts of the Book of the Law that were found when the temple was being repaired and read to the king."[6] In verses 18–20, God said to tell the king that because he had humbled himself and shown genuine remorse

---

[2] Radmacher et al., 488–89.

[3] Thomas L. Constable, *Expository Notes of Dr. Thomas Constable: 2 Kings*, 86, http://planobiblechapel.org/tcon/notes/pdf/2kings.pdf.

[4] Warren W. Wiersbe, *The Exposition Bible Commentary: Joshua–Esther* (Colorado Springs: David C. Cook, 2003), 587.

[5] Wiersbe, 587.

[6] Radmacher et al., 489.

when he heard the Book of the Law, no disaster would happen to Judah during his reign. Josiah was promised peace when he died.

Closing

Where is the revival in this chapter? It's seen in the response of Josiah's heart. It's seen in embracing the Word of God. It's seen in pursuing God's direction. And it's begun in humility to want to know more. Second Timothy 3:16–17 says, "All Scripture is inspired by God and is profitable for teaching, for rebuking, for correcting, for training in righteousness, so that the man of God may be complete, equipped for every good work." Josiah did all of this, with humbleness and humility, by embracing God's Word (Psalm 119:105).

The Daily Word

Josiah was eight years old when he became king, and he reigned for thirty-one years. King Josiah did what was right in the Lord's sight and did not turn to the right or to the left. During Josiah's reign as king, as repairs were being made to the Temple, the Book of the Law was discovered and read in the presence of the king. When King Josiah heard the words of the Lord, he humbled himself and asked the Lord for help in understanding. Josiah longed to know more about the Lord's heart for His people, and his desire to follow the Book of the Law impacted an entire nation.

The Word of God is living and effective. It is used for teaching, rebuking, correcting, and training in righteousness so that you may be complete and equipped for *every* good work. The Word of God is a light to your feet and a lamp to your path. Most likely, you have the Word of God at your disposal wherever and whenever you want. *And yet, why is it so hard to read each day?* Today, open the Word of God and read His words. Be aware of the enemy's plans and schemes to keep you from reading the Word of God. Fight through the schemes and take time to open the Word of God. Your life will be transformed.

Go and inquire of the Lord for me, the people, and all Judah about the instruction in this book that has been found. For great is the Lord's wrath that is kindled against us because our ancestors have not obeyed the words of this book in order to do everything written about us. —2 Kings 22:13

Further Scripture: Psalm 119:105; 2 Timothy 3:16–17; Hebrews 4:12

Questions

1. What were some things that Manasseh did that were evil in the Lord's sight (Deuteronomy 12:31; 17:3; 18:10)? What was God's judgment because of this evil?

2. God promises to never abandon His people (Leviticus 26:11; 1 Samuel 12:22). What was He saying in 2 Kings 21:14 (2 Samuel 7:14; Proverbs 3:12; Hebrews 12:6)?

3. According to 2 Chronicles 33:11–13, what did Manasseh do at the end of his life? Does this give you hope and encouragement that God wants to save everyone, even those family and friends of yours who are far from the Lord (2 Samuel 14:14; 2 Chronicles 7:14; 2 Peter 3:9)?

4. What are some steps that King Josiah took to indicate that he was desiring to obey God?

5. What did the Holy Spirit highlight to you in 2 Kings 21—22 through the reading or the teaching?

Lesson 81: 2 Kings 23

Surviving Seed: The Spirit of Revival

Teaching Notes

Intro

Everything we do at Time to Revive and reviveSchool is about revival. Scripture says we need to wake up to the truth that is inside of us in order to find transformation. In 2 Kings, under the leading of King Josiah, Judah was finally facing revival and the chance to renew their covenant with the Lord. Josiah had been suddenly awakened to the truth that his fathers knew from the Book of the Law that he had received. Are we ready to be revived through what we have been given (Hebrews 4:12)? It is time for revival!

Teaching

In chapter 23, we'll walk through Josiah's religious reforms in Judah.

2 Kings 23:1–3: First, Josiah entered into a new covenant with the Lord. When he realized he had the Book of the Law, Josiah gathered the people of Jerusalem and Judah at the temple (v. 1). Then Josiah took them into the temple and read about the covenant God had made with Israel (v. 2). Josiah then stood by the pillar in the temple and made a new covenant in the presence of the Lord, reading aloud the commands, decrees, and statutes God had given them (v. 3a) (Joshua 8:34; 1 Samuel 7:2). All the people agreed to the covenant (v. 3b). When you have a heart that is humble and grateful, you have a recipe for revival.

2 Kings 23:4–20: Second, Josiah instituted religious reforms throughout the land. Once revival begins to break out, change occurs—there's a desire to learn, to be in the presence of other believers, to have a new level of excitement about their faith, and a desire to share the Lord with others. Josiah responded to the revival by bringing about religious reforms:

- Josiah commanded the removal of all things inside the temple that honored pagan gods and he burned them outside of Jerusalem (v. 4). The ashes were then carried ten miles to Bethel to desecrate the site where Jeroboam had established his own pagan worship center (1 Kings 12:28–33).

- Josiah got rid of all the priests who had burned incense to Baal and others at the high places (v. 5).
- Josiah removed the Asherah pole from inside the Lord's temple, burned it in the Kidron Valley, and threw the ashes on the graves of the common people there to show their disobedience (v. 6).
- Josiah tore down all the houses or booths of the male cult prostitutes and of the women who wove tapestries for Asherah that were inside the Lord's temple (v. 7).
- Josiah had all of Judah's priests defile the high places throughout Judah that had honored pagan gods (v. 8). The priests of the high places did not come to Jerusalem but ate unleavened bread with other priests (v. 9).
- Josiah had Topheth defiled so there could no longer be child sacrifices offered to Molech (v. 10).
- Josiah did away with the horses that were dedicated to the sun by former kings of Judah and burned the chariots (v. 11).
- Josiah destroyed all the altars on the palace roof and courtyards of the temple that had been built by evil kings (v. 12). They were smashed to pieces and thrown into the Kidron Valley.
- Josiah destroyed all the high places King Solomon built to honor the gods of his wives (v. 13).
- Josiah destroyed the sacred pagan pillars and Asherah poles and filled the places with human bones to defile the area so it could never be used for worship again (v. 14).
- Josiah destroyed Jeroboam's altar and high place in Bethel, burned the bones of the priests buried there, and scattered the ashes to defile the whole area (vv. 15–16) (1 Kings 3:2).
- Josiah destroyed the altars and slaughtered the priests of the high places in Samaria and defiled them with human bones (vv. 19–20a).

Josiah found the monument to the man of God who had prophesied that these things would happen and left it alone (vv. 17–18). When Josiah had finished cleansing Judah of all non-Levitical priests, he returned to Jerusalem (v. 20b).

2 Kings 23:21–23: Third, Josiah reinstituted the Passover celebration. Hezekiah had led the people in a lavish Passover celebration (2 Chronicles 30). But Josiah offered two times the number of sacrifices Hezekiah had. Wiersbe says, "At least

37,000 small animals were offered, plus 3,800 bulls. The priests and Levites were cleansed and sanctified, ready to serve, and there were many Levites who sang praises to the Lord and played instruments."[7]

2 Kings 23:24: Fourth, Josiah continued his reforms. Josiah went on to remove mediums, spiritists, household idols, images, and anything left in Judah and Jerusalem that were not of God (v. 24).

2 Kings 23:25–27: Verse 25 says no other king had turned to the Lord "with all his mind and with all his heart and with all his strength according to all the law of Moses, and no one like him arose after him." Here you see the surviving seed carrying out all that God wanted done. Yet, all Josiah did could not make up for the years of Judah's disobedience against the Lord (vv. 26–27).

Closing

Dale Ralph Davis describes what Josiah did as "Josiah's 12-step 'de-Manasseh-fi-cation' Program." Based on the Word of God, Josiah had to remove everything Manasseh and Amon and the other evil kings had brought to Judah. Likewise, we need to remove everything in our churches and our lives that do not honor our Lord. Let us keep our focus on Jesus.

The Daily Word

After Josiah read the Word of the Lord, it changed his life and prompted him to take action. He gathered all the elders, priests, prophets, and people from young to old, and he read to them all the words of the book of the covenant that had been found in the Temple. Then King Josiah made a covenant to follow the Lord and keep His commands, decrees, and statues with all his mind and all his heart. He vowed to carry out the words in the covenant, and all the people agreed! Following this commitment, King Josiah began removing, cleaning, burning, smashing, slaughtering, and tearing down anything that defiled God. The Word of God truly transformed this community!

It is time. It is time for revival in the nation, in the world, in your community, in your family, and in your life. Let the Word of God radically transform your life. As you read the Word and follow the Lord's way, think about what idols, images, or things in your life that need to be removed and torn down. Take action, and do the work. Purify yourself. May you live in the same boldness as

---

[7] Warren W. Wiersbe, *Be Distinct: Standing Firmly Against the World's Tides* (Colorado Springs: David C. Cook, 2002), 203.

King Josiah. *Do not hold back.* Start reviving your heart today through the Word of God, and take action!

In addition, Josiah removed the mediums, the spiritists, household idols, images, and all the detestable things that were seen in the land of Judah and in Jerusalem. He did this in order to carry out the words of the law that were written in the book that Hilkiah the priest found in the Lord's temple. Before him there was no king like him who turned to the Lord with all his mind and with all his heart and with all his strength according to all the law of Moses, and no one like him arose after him. —2 Kings 23:24–25

Further Scripture: Acts 28:31; 1 John 5:21; Revelation 21:27

Questions

1. What did Josiah do after hearing the impending judgment that God was going to bring? Who did he call in to be a part of renewing the covenant?

2. What is significant about the fact that all the people pledged themselves to the covenant? Do you see a moving of the Holy Spirit among the people? Where else in Scripture did the Holy Spirit move among a group of people (Acts 2:4; 4:31; 10:44)?

3. What were some things Josiah did to restore things back to honoring God? Are there some things in your own life that need to be immediately dealt with and repented of?

4. In many respects, whose example was Josiah following, including the celebration of Passover (2 Kings 18:3–6; 2 Chronicles 30:1)? Why was Josiah's celebration of Passover so significant (2 Chronicles 35:18–19)?

5. Why was God still angry with Judah despite Josiah's godly leadership (2 Kings 21:11–13; 22:15–17)?

6. It took nearly 300 years to fulfill the prophecy about King Josiah (1 Kings 13:2). How do you handle waiting on the Lord when you know He has promised you something, but you have been waiting for months or even years (Psalm 27:14; 2 Corinthians 1:20)?

7. What did the Holy Spirit highlight to you in 2 Kings 23 through the reading or the teaching?

Lesson 82: 2 Kings 24—25

Surviving Seed: The Last Kings of Israel

Teaching Notes

Intro

Today, we are going to look at the last kings of Israel. God had a strong covenant with these people, but these were hard days with Israel. In the previous chapters, God brought great revival through Josiah. Josiah was just a child when he was made king. Yet there were things about him that we will see in king after king. How many righteous kings did Israel have? Zero. How many righteous kings did Judah have? Eight.

Israel and Judah came from the same seed and the same covenant, and yet Israel didn't have even one of those commendations. Judah had Josiah, who had done what was right with the Lord. God commended him over and over because he had thrown out the things that caused sin. There was a revival with king Josiah. He was king for 31 years, and he reigned in righteousness. After 31 years, Josiah was killed in battle. His son Jehoahaz was brought into kingship. But then Eliakim, whose name was changed to Jehoiakim, replaced him shortly into his reign. Both kings did what was evil in the sight of the Lord. As we come into these chapters, I want us to understand how God views sin.

Teaching

2 Kings 24:1: As we start this chapter, I want you to understand who the contemporaries were during this time (Jeremiah 25:1–7). We are going to see how God was working. Despite warnings from the prophets, the Israelites failed to listen and were overtaken by Babylon. I think this shows that we don't serve well and that we forget God in times of great prosperity. I want us to see the pattern of humanity. I also want us to see the mercy of God to send prophets (Daniel 1:1–7). Who are the people that can give us understanding?

2 Kings 24:2–4: Look at 2 Kings 21:1–7. These verses give the history of the sins of Manasseh. What I want us to understand is, you can have a Manasseh and then you can have a Josiah. With his 31 years of being a faithful king, you would think Josiah would deliver a reprieve for the sins of Manasseh. But God is God. Sin is sin. The question is, how does God regard sin in us? There are consequences for sin. We must be careful. God will forgive our sin, but there are still consequences. Manasseh did horrible things and Judah was judged for those sins, even though there was a Josiah who ruled in righteousness.

2 Kings 24:5–20: The king of Babylon had taken so much territory that the king of Egypt could no longer come to wreak havoc. Jehoiakim's son Jehoiachin became king at the age of 18 (v. 8). He also did evil in the sight of the Lord, and Jerusalem was overrun by Babylon. Jehoiachin reigned for eight years before he was taken as a prisoner to Babylon (v. 15). The Babylonians carried off all the treasures of the house of the Lord from the Temple and the king's house. They cut many of the treasures into pieces and carried away the powerful and influential people of the land and put them in captivity.

We still battle in warfare and if we don't regard spiritual counsel, if we have hard places in our hearts and are not willing to change, it will lead to destruction. We have to be ready and willing to hear, slow to speak, and swift to respond. God continues to warn His people, even to this day.

When I hear of the Israelites' things being carried away and broken down, it tells me that this was not only a black day for the kings and Judah but also a black day in the sight of God. His plan was always for the Israelites to prosper. The very last king was named Zedekiah. Once again, the nation did its own thing and worshiped idols instead of the Lord.

What is the house of the Lord today? Where is the temple of the Lord? The truth is we are the temple of God. It is convenient to associate the church building as the house of the God, but it is not His true house. Anything that would defile the house of God, the presence of God, or the law of God is something that needs to be brought out of the temple. It is easy for us to dress up the building but dress down the temple. I look at this captivity and I mourn, realizing how much God wanted His people to flourish. God wants us to flourish, but are we living in ways that will allow that to come to pass?

2 Kings 25: While Zedekiah was king, Babylon brought full siege against Jerusalem. The Babylonian army cut off all trade and all roads in and out of the city. On the ninth day, the city ran out of food. The city fell apart and focused on survival and preservation (Jeremiah 27:12). Jeremiah understood there would be a Manasseh, and even though there would be a Josiah, Israel would be punished. Jeremiah said, "Don't fight it, live and God will restore us." Yet the people would not listen to Jeremiah. They only listened to the prophets who told them good things.

Closing

Oh, that we would have ears to hear what the Holy Spirit is saying to the church today. Oh, that we would hear those who speak for God. Oh, that we would understand the day we are in—days of mercy or days of prosperity. We can learn from the pattern of the kings of Israel and say, "God help us to walk righteously in this day and not repeat their mistakes."

The Daily Word

King Nebuchadnezzar of Babylon entered Jerusalem and destroyed everything—the Lord's Temple, the king's house, all the great houses, and the wall of Jerusalem. Everything the Lord instructed King Solomon to build during the Davidic covenant came to an end. *Everything.* Year after year, the kings had done what was evil in the Lord's eyes by welcoming activities into the Temple that were not of the Lord. As a result, everything man built ended in complete destruction, and the Jewish captives were exiled to live and serve in Babylon.

As a follower of Christ, holy and beloved, your body is the temple of the Lord. His presence abides inside you, and you are to present your bodies as a living sacrifice to Him. *What are you allowing into your temple?* The Lord says to dwell on whatever is true, honorable, just, pure, lovely, commendable, and of moral excellence. Because the Lord desires you to flourish, He instructs you to put to death the things that defile your temple, such as sexual immorality, impurity, lust, evil desire, and greed. Be aware of these things! Over time, if allowed in your temple, these activities will bring destruction in your life. In the moment, what you give up may seem like a sacrifice, but it is your act of worship to the Lord and is well worth the discipline. May the Lord bless you abundantly as you preserve your body, the temple of the Lord!

Indeed, this happened to Judah at the Lord's command to remove them from His sight. It was because of the sins of Manasseh, according to all he had done. —2 Kings 24:3

Further Scripture: Romans 12:1; 1 Corinthians 3:16–17; Colossians 3:5

Questions

1. In 2 Kings 24:1, what do you think made Jehoiakim rebel against Nebuchadnezzar after three years (2 Chronicles 36:6)?
2. In 2 Kings 24:14, why were the poorest people not taken captive?

3. How does the pattern of the kings continuously doing evil in the sight of the Lord relate to the leaders and people of our time? Are the consequences similar today?

4. How did King Evil-merodach's release and provision of Jehoiachin reflect King Jesus' grace toward us as believers (2 Kings 25:27–30; Luke 4:18)?

5. What did the Holy Spirit highlight to you in 2 Kings 24—25 through the reading or the teaching?

Lesson 83: 1 Chronicles 1

Son of David: Christ's Genealogy

Teaching Notes

Intro

The book of 1 Chronicles is a list of names. I feel like the Lord will give us a fresh perspective on this. When you see a genealogy list, please don't shut your Bible and go to sleep. I know it can be a lot. I'll admit that while studying 1 Chronicles, my head was swimming. We will be seeing names we've already studied. Don't be discouraged! Repetition helps us to learn. There are 54 verses of names—hard names—but we can do this!

Teaching

Background: Just like the books of 1 and 2 Kings and the two books of Samuel, 1 and 2 Chronicles was originally one book. The word "Chronicles" means "the annals of the days," essentially the events or happenings of the days. In Jerome's Latin Vulgate, these verses were first called Chronicles. J. Vernon McGee wrote, "Greek translators gave Chronicles the title of 'Things Omitted'—there is more here that does not occur in the other historical books."[1] Fifty-five percent of Chronicles is not in the books of Kings or Samuel, yet they all overlap. It's similar to the gospels, how John has stories not in Matthew or Luke, but they all point towards the same thing.

Chronicles partners with the book of 2 Samuel. In 2 Samuel, we reference Jesus as the *Eternal Throne* (2 Samuel 7:16). First Chronicles is about Jesus, the *Son of David*. The coming Messiah was going to come through the lineage of David. What you should see in these first nine chapters is a whole lot of names. But it is important to see where David is positioned in all of these names. How do we see this genealogy point to Christ? We see this through the lineage of Judah, in the southern part of the kingdom. We are going to see how David came through the line of Judah.

---

[1] J. Vernon McGee. "1 Chronicles, 2 Chronicles: Notes and Outlines," Thru the Bible, https://www.ttb.org/docs/default-source/notes-and-outlines_2022/no12_1-2-chronicles.pdf?sfvrsn=105d1816_2.

There is no direct statement regarding who authored 1 Chronicles. Jewish traditions favor Ezra the priest as the writer of Chronicles (Ezra 7:1–6). We ended in 2 Kings talking about how the Israelites were sent to Syria, and the people from Judah were sent to Babylon. At the end of 2 Chronicles, the Israelites have been released from captivity. Here in 1 Chronicles, the Israelites are in captivity and do not get released until the end of 2 Chronicles. What we are going to see is a factual account of them saying, "How did we get here?" Zerubbabel, Ezra, and Nehemiah all wrote about what the Israelites needed to do to get back to where God wanted them to be.

John MacArthur wrote, "The Jews had returned from their seventy years of captivity (538 BC) to a land that was markedly different from the one once ruled by King David and King Solomon."[2] MacArthur provides seven areas that were different for the Jewish people when they returned: (1) The Persian government ruled, rather than a Hebrew king (Ezra 6:2, 6); (2) The wall of Jerusalem had been destroyed, so the city had no security wall (Nehemiah 1—7); (3) The temple had been destroyed, and Zerubbabel had to reconstruct a pitiful resemblance of Solomon's glory (Ezra 3); (4) Jews were no longer powerful and had to live on the defensive (Ezra 4; Nehemiah 4); (5) The Jews faced hardship and difficulties on their return, instead of divine blessings; (6) The Jews returned with little, having lost their wealth when they were removed; and (7) Without the Temple, God's divine presence was no longer in Jerusalem (Ezra 8:11).[3]

Despite all MacArthur points out, God was still with the Israelites. We know God had a bigger picture in store for the Israelites—the *Son of David*. The promise of the *Son of David* was not conditional; it was based on God's covenant with His people.

Second Kings 25 ends with the dispersion of the people of Judah to Babylon. At the end of 2 Chronicles 26, the Jews began to experience release from Persia to go back to Jerusalem. Remember, 55 percent of Chronicles is unique.

Here is the outline for 1 and 2 Chronicles:

1. Genealogical history of Israel (1 Chronicles 1—9)
2. Israel's united kingdom under:
   a. Saul (1 Chronicles 10)
   b. David (1 Chronicles 11—29)
   c. Solomon (2 Chronicles 1—9)
3. Divided kingdom (2 Chronicles 10—36:21)
4. Judah's release from seventy years captivity (2 Chronicles 36:22–23)

---

[2] John MacArthur, *The MacArthur Bible Commentary* (Nashville: Thomas Nelson, 2005), 478.

[3] MacArthur, 478.

1 Chronicles 1:1–27: By covering the descendants of Adam, we will see the tie to the coming Messiah. I think this is a really powerful picture! We are going to tie the coming Messiah back to Adam. Verses 4–27 literally walk through the sons of Noah and his descendants. Let's look at Ham, Noah's son, from whom Scripture said would come great nations. This impact came through Ham's son's whom we can see have influenced the nations of Cush (Ethiopians), Mizraim (Egypt), and Canaan (Canaanites).

The sons of Shem are listed beginning in verse 17. Shem was considered the favored one of Noah's sons (Genesis 9:25–27). Shem's great grandson, Eber, was an ancestor of Abraham, Isaac, and Jacob. The name "Hebrew" is possibly a derivative of Eber's name, and is applied to the Israelites. Eber became a central place in the genealogies of Abraham in Genesis. First Chronicles 1:24–27 suggests a connection between Hebrew and Eber. Hebrew could refer to an "Eberite" (Genesis 10:21; 11:10–26). Eber's son Peleg (which means divided) was around when the earth was divided at the tower of Babel (Genesis 11:1–9).

1 Chronicles 1:28–37: Here the descendants of Abraham are listed. Isaac is blessed above Abraham's other son, Ishmael by Hagar. As the chosen one, Isaac fathers Jacob from whom come the 12 tribes of Israel.

1 Chronicles 1:38–50: These verses cover the descendants of Esau, who were the kings of Edom. The Edomites were ruled by kings before the Israelites. All throughout Chronicles you see the words "son of." MacArthur explains that the word "son" means "to build." "The ancient Hebrews considered their children the 'builders' of the future generations."[4] So what we see is that every generation was building upon each other to point to the *Son of David*.

Closing

Christ built upon what David was doing on earth, from an earthly standpoint. I think that is a pretty cool picture. Paul Van Gorder gives three reasons why 1 Chronicles 1—9 is profitable:

- First, they were of great benefit to the Jews who returned from captivity in Babylon. During this time of confusion, the Israelites were in danger of losing their family and tribal identities. The lists helped them maintain their distinctive [lineage].

- Second, the genealogies impressed the Jews with the unity of God. As they returned from captivity, the Israelites saw in the genealogies that the God who had restored them was the "one true God" of their fathers.

---

[4] MacArthur, 483.

- Third, the genealogies were a demonstration of the divine purpose being worked out until Christ's coming. They helped complete the Bible story of our Savior, who was the *Son of David*, the son of Judah, the son of Abraham, and the son of Adam. He took their humanity, "yet without sin." (emphasis added)[5]

This book demonstrates identity in the family (you're a child of God), identity in the Father, and identity in the Son. Why Chronicles? Because it actually helps you find who you are in the Lord.

The Daily Word

As the people of Israel returned to Jerusalem after exile in Babylon, they reconnected with their identity as the people of God's family. The genealogical review reminded them of their history and how God's hand had been on every single person through each generation. Each name in the lineage of Jesus, the Son of David, carries the significance of God's faithfulness, redemption, and calling. Whether they sought the Lord or rejected His ways, the Lord used their lives to carry on the seed of Christ.

Today, take a minute to reflect on your family heritage. As you reflect, you may feel a pit in your stomach, thinking of difficult times, or you may have all warm, cozy memories. Either way, the Lord used your family line to get you where you are today. The Lord is a God of restoration. The Lord is calling you to an identity in Him. As you trust Him, you are His. No matter what your family line may say, you are a child of God, and He is your Heavenly Father. He is writing your story. He has plans for your life and a purpose for *you*. Give thanks for the past and walk in your identity as God's chosen child.

Adam, Seth, Enosh, Kenan, Mahalalel, Jared, Enoch, Methuselah, Lamech, Noah, Noah's sons: Shem, Ham, and Japheth. —1 Chronicles 1:1–4

Further Scripture: John 1:12; 2 Corinthians 6:18; Galatians 3:26

Questions

1. In 1 Chronicles 1:10, Nimrod is mentioned as an ancestor of Cush. What was Nimrod known for (Genesis 10:8–9)? What did God do to the people groups at the tower of Babel? Why (Genesis 11:1–4)?

---

[5] Paul R. Van Gorder, *The Old Testament Presents . . . Reflections of Christ: 1 Chronicles*, https://www.thebookwurm.com/ref-1chr.htm.

2. In 1 Chronicles 1:13, the lineage of Canaan is given. What happened to these people groups (Deuteronomy 7:1–6)? Why did God say they were to be destroyed?

3. One of Eber's sons was named Peleg, whose name meant division or days of earth divided (1 Chronicles 1:19). It is believed God confused the language at the tower of Babel during Peleg's life. Do you think Peleg's parents ever realized his name was a prophetic view of things to come?

4. There are two women mentioned in the lineage of 1 Chronicles 1. Who were they? Where else do we see women listed in a lineage (Matthew 1:1–17)? Who were they and what were they known for?

5. What did the Holy Spirit highlight to you in 1 Chronicles 1 through the reading or the teaching?

Lesson 84: 1 Chronicles 2

Son of David: What's Your Role?

Teaching Notes

Intro

First Chronicles builds on what we've studied in the other historical books and points to the genealogy of Christ by linking Jesus to Old Testament key figures. Jesus' ministry was built on Adam, Noah, Abraham, Moses, David, Solomon, and the remaining kings. This chapter is a transition from the descendants of Abraham to the descendants of Israel (that is, Jacob).

Teaching

1 Chronicles 2:1–2: The 12 sons of Israel are listed in verses 1 and 2. They were linked first to Adam, then to Noah, then to Abraham, and now to Jacob, who was also called Israel. Before Jacob died, he gathered his sons and spoke prophetically over them: "Then Jacob called his sons and said, 'Gather around, and I will tell you what will happen to you in the days to come. Come together and listen, sons of Jacob; listen to your father Israel: Reuben, you are my firstborn, my strength and the firstfruits of my virility, excelling in prominence, excelling in power. Turbulent as water, you will no longer excel, because you got into your father's bed and you defiled it—he got into my bed'" (Genesis 49:1–4).

Since Reuben was the oldest, it would make sense for him to be listed first in this genealogy, but Judah was listed first. Reuben slept with his father's concubine Bilhah (Genesis 35:22) and lost that place of prominence. Judah wasn't even the second oldest. He was the fourth, but the first three sons all messed up.

1 Chronicles 2:3: Er is one of the first people 1 Chronicles describes as evil. The chronicler, probably Ezra, went out of his way to link generations together by naming parents. Parents played an important role in 1 Chronicles when the author described the sons of David.

1 Chronicles 2:4: Tamar was Israel's (also known as Jacob) daughter-in-law. Even though she might have felt as though she didn't have any importance in her family, the author mentioned her role in serving the *Son of David*.

1 Chronicles 2:5–8: The author moved from Judah to Hezron. Judah's family will take a prominent role in 1 Chronicles from now through chapter 5. The other tribes will get their own genealogies later. Each tribe played an important part in the coming of the *Son of David*.

1 Chronicles 2:9–12: The author moved from the descendants of Judah to the descendants of Hezron. These verses transition into the descendants of Ram. Even though Ram was listed as the second son of Hezron, God chose his family line to be in the line of the coming Messiah. The chronicler listed Boaz in verse 11. This was the same Boaz from the book of Ruth that took place in the time of the judges.

1 Chronicles 2:13–17: The chronicler proceeds to list seven sons of Jesse with David being the seventh. Other texts list David as the eighth son. Then when Jesse's sons were listed in 1 Chronicles 27:18, David was back in the eighth position with Elihu being added in at seventh. Why would the chronicler not list Elihu in this passage when he would be listed later? It may not have been his focus for some reason in this context.

1 Chronicles 2:18–24: The chronicler next listed the sons of Caleb. This was not the Caleb from the Book of Joshua, but Caleb from Genesis. These descendants of Caleb were actually broken up three times: twice here and once in 1 Chronicles 4. Bezalel, mentioned in verse 20, was the same Bezalel who was a craftsman (Exodus 31:2–5). Bezalel's job was to serve the coming king because of his identity in his father and his identity in the line of the *Son of David*.

1 Chronicles 2:25–41: Here the chronicler listed the descendants of Jerahmeel. None of the names in verses 25–41 are mentioned anywhere else in the Old Testament except in this passage. However, they were listed together as a people group in 1 Samuel 27:10 and again in 1 Samuel 30:29. The Jerahmeelites were not in the lineage of the *Son of David*, but they were included so that we can see the bigger picture of the entire lineage.

1 Chronicles 2:42–54: The chronicler returned to the second group of Caleb's descendants. Caleb's daughter was Achsah, who was mentioned in Judges 1:12–23. She married Othniel, who was one of Israel's first judges.

1 Chronicles 2:55: Even scribes were mentioned! Although they were not included in the lineage of the *Son of David*, they had an important role to play in pointing others to Him.

Closing

All throughout this chapter, we have seen people playing different roles. We've seen parents, sisters, scribes, and more, all playing a role in pointing others to the *Son of David*. Regardless of the role you play in pointing others to the *Son of David*, Romans 12:11 contains two great reminders: "Do not lack diligence; be fervent in spirit; serve the Lord." Diligence means being dedicated to a task. Being fervent in spirit means being passionate about serving the Lord and blessing others without overlooking anyone. We are to serve others with passion and without stopping, as we point them to the *Son of David*.

Pastor Steven Cole pointed out four concepts for us to remember as we serve the Lord:

1. All believers are called to serve. There are no exceptions.

2. We are to serve the Lord as His slaves, not as His volunteers. If we want our lives to point to the *Son of David*, we have to be sold out to Him. Jesus taught, "Which one of you having a slave tending sheep or plowing will say to him when he comes in from the field, 'Come at once and sit down to eat'? Instead, will he not tell him, 'Prepare something for me to eat, get ready, and serve me while I eat and drink; later you can eat and drink'? Does he thank that slave because he did what was commanded? In the same way, when you have done all that you were commanded, you should say, 'We are good-for-nothing slaves; we've only done our duty'" (Luke 17:7–10).

3. We are serving the Lord, not serving ourselves. When we begin to understand this and work where He wants us, people will be pointed to the *Son of David*.

Serving the Lord means we are not primarily serving others. Paul put it this way, "For am I now trying to win the favor of people, or God? Or am I striving to please people? If I were still trying to please people, I would not be a slave of Christ" (Galatians 1:10). When you are serving others, you are not serving to please them. You are serving because you are God's child and Christ's slave.[1]

No matter how you serve, remember that what you are doing could be building on a foundation for the next generation. However you serve, you could be ushering in the King.

---

[1] Steven J. Cole, "Lesson 82: How to Serve the Lord (Romans 12:11)," Bible.org. https://bible.org/seriespage/lesson-82-how-serve-lord-romans-1211.

The Daily Word

The list of names in the genealogy continues, remembering Israel's sons and Judah's descendants. Each name represents a family: a daughter, a son, a mother, a father. Each name represents a person in the Israelites' rich history. By listing the names, the chronicler confirmed the importance of reflecting on the families, making them known to the Israelites as they came out of exile. From Reuben to Perez to Caleb, each family and person pointed to the coming Messiah.

Just like each person recalled to the Israelites after their exile, *you too are important*. You may need to hear that today. You are a brother, a sister, a wife, a husband, a mother, a father. You build, you teach, you operate technology, you research, you do laundry, and you are important to the Lord and to His kingdom. Many have gone before you, playing a role in the kingdom of God. But *now* it's your time. Don't believe the lie that you are not important to the Lord. He created you. He loves you. He believes in you. So stand up tall and do the thing He called you to. The King, the Messiah, is coming back, and you have a role in ushering Him in as you live your life for Him and Him alone!

These were Israel's sons: Reuben, Simeon, Levi, Judah, Issachar, Zebulun, Dan, Joseph, Benjamin, Naphtali, Gad, and Asher. —1 Chronicles 2:1–2

Further Scripture: Isaiah 43:1–2; Romans 12:11–12; Hebrews 9:28

Questions

1. On what tribe does the genealogy in 1 Chronicles 2 focus? Why do you think the writer did this?

2. Who was Achan, son of Carmi, the troubler of Israel (Joshua 7:1, 24–25)?

3. Is it confusing that David is listed as Jesse's seventh son (1 Samuel 16:10–11)? Bible scholars believe the reason David is listed as the seventh son is that one of his brothers died with no heir. Do you think this is a plausible explanation? Is the number seven significant in Scripture? If so, what does it represent?

4. What did the Holy Spirit highlight to you in 1 Chronicles 2 through the reading or the teaching?

Lesson 85: 1 Chronicles 3

Son of David: David's Descendants

Teaching Notes

Intro

This is one of the more exciting chapters in 1 Chronicles. This whole chapter is about the genealogy of David. Remember the word for Genesis is *Seed*. It is important for the chronicler to show the *Seed* from David back to the Promise Land. These genealogies express the line of the promise of God. Every name has so many stories and connections. It's our job to highlight the line that leads to the *Son of David*.

Teaching

The Direct Descendants of David (1 Chronicles 3:1–9):

1 Chronicles 3:1–2: David ruled for seven years in Hebron and had six sons. David had a lot of sons and a lot of wives. Each of the first six sons listed were with different wives. Amnon, David's firstborn, raped his half-sister Tamar (2 Samuel 13). While David was furious, he took no action against Amnon, but Absalom, Amnon's brother, killed him in revenge and fled. David's second born was Daniel, also referred to as Chileab or Kileab, which means "like his father." There are lots of name variations in these genealogies. Rabbinic literature says the two names were because of circumstances of the relationship between David and Abigail. Abigail was the wife of Nabal, who refused to assist David's men, and was later struck by the Lord and died (1 Samuel 25:2–42). Abigail befriended David and he later married her. These first four sons were not positioned in the line of the *Seed*. There was rebellion, rape, and death.

1 Chronicles 3:3: While Eglah and Ithream did not fit into the line, some Jewish scholars think Eglah was actually Michal. Michal was Saul's daughter, whom some say was David's only legal wife. But most point out that Michal, David's first wife, was not represented. In fact, the relationship between the two was strained. Second Samuel 6:23 states Michal was "childless unto the day of her death." I mention this because of the importance of the *Seed* and carrying of the *Seed*. The *Seed* carried on to David's other wives.

1 Chronicles 3:4–5: David ruled 33 years in Jerusalem. In those 33 years, he married Bath-shua, an alternative pronunciation for Bathsheba—a wife who bore four sons! The first thing you'll notice is that the son who died was not mentioned nor was the sin David committed with Bath-shua (2 Samuel 11—12) mentioned. The details were not important to the chronicler, but only where the *Seed* came through the line. We all know Solomon, but I don't want you to forget Nathan. Nathan's claim to fame is he is in the genealogy of Jesus (Luke 3:31). Nathan's heirs led to Mary, the mother of Jesus. Solomon was listed last as the son who followed David as king.

1 Chronicles 3:6–8: David's other sons were listed and there were many. I want you to notice that the name Eliphelet was listed twice. This name could be repeated because there might have been a child who died in infancy and his name was passed on as a way to preserve the memory. The chronicler was making sure we understood that all were David's sons.

1 Chronicles 3:9: Tamar probably wasn't David's only daughter. Women were not normally named in a genealogy unless they had an impact on history. Tamar had an impact on history. We don't know how many concubines David had. He had at least ten (2 Samuel 15:16; 20:3). We know there were a number of concubines who dishonored David with his son Absalom (2 Samuel 16:22). Again, the focus on David's line is the *Seed*. The chief reason for such detailed genealogies is that they affirmed the line of Christ from Adam (Luke 3:38) and through Abraham to David (Matthew 1:1), thus emphasizing the kingdom intentions of God in Christ.

Sometimes it is easy for us to lose track of the fact that these were real people. God uses amazingly flawed people for His purpose. David's "family" was an unhealthy situation due to the consequences of sin. But God still used it (for example, Solomon, the son of Bathsheba, wife of Urriah the Hittite = line of Messiah). God also used these sins in the spiritual growth and formation of David. For example, David wrote the Psalms in the midst of turmoil and chaos, from a soul that could not find rest or peace but for the faithfulness of God. In the midst of his sin, David turned to God.

The Line of David (through Solomon) until Judah's Exile (1 Chronicles 3:10–16):
1 Chronicles 3:10–12: The chronicler made sure we saw the line of King Solomon, and that it was important. We've already looked at Solomon in the Book of 1 Kings. We saw the line of the kings of Judah. I confess, I sometimes find the names a tedious task. But these were real people God used to carry on the *Seed*. We swung back and forth between studying good kings and bad kings. Solomon's son Rehoboam sealed the split of the kingdom. Then we moved to

Solomon's other sons. Remember there were so many name variations in these lists and with accounts elsewhere that it can be difficult to track sometimes. Carefully studying these allows us to see how the *Seed* was passed on time and time again.

1 Chronicles 3:3–14: In Solomon's sons, Hezekiah and Manasseh, there was a crazy swing from wicked to good and back to wicked—father to son to grandson. Amnon was very evil, while Josiah was a very good king. Josiah's sons are listed.

1 Chronicles 3:15–16: In verse 15, this whole sequence of the sons of Josiah had a crazy ending. Jehoiakim reined as king for 11 years and died in Jerusalem. His son Jehoiachin reined for three months. Jehoiachin was cursed by God and produced no royal descendants (Jeremiah 22:24–30). Even though Jeconiah was in the line of Christ, the Messiah was not a physical child of that line, thus affirming the curse. His blood birthright came through Mary, who traced her line to David through his son Nathan, not Solomon (Luke 3:31). The line of kingship came through Solomon. Both Mary and Joseph came from David, the line of Judah.

The lines will merge with Shealtiel and Zerubbabel in Luke and in Matthew. Jeconiah (also known as Jehoiachin) was captured and led to Babylon. His uncle, Zedekiah took over the throne but was eventually blinded and taken into captivity by Babylon. Sin and idolatry ruined the kingdom of Judah and desolated the temple of God.

The line of David After Judah's Exile (1 Chronicles 3:17–19):
1 Chronicles 3:17–18: The names listed here were the descendants of the line of David born after the fall of Judah. They carried on the royal line of David.

1 Chronicles 3:19: The lineage continued through Zerubbabel. He led the first captives back to Jerusalem and would attempt to rebuild the altar to the Lord and a temple. But there is a problem here. According to 1 Chronicles 3:19, Zerubbabel was the son of Pedaiah. However, according to Ezra 3:2, Zerubbabel was the son of Shealtiel. Which is the correct genealogical relationship?

There are two options that both fit in the Pentateuch and the historical books. Option A is Zerubbabel was the son of Pedaiah and the nephew of Shealtiel, Pedaiah's older brother. Although the Bible does not record the death of Pedaiah, it is reasonable to assume he died shortly after Shimei was born, and Shealtiel, the oldest of the sons of Jeconiah, adopted Zerubbabel as his own son. Option B is that Shealtiel died without a son. Accordingly, Pedaiah, his brother married his widow and gave birth to Zerubbabel. A Levirate marriage

(Deuteronomy 25:5–10) was to maintain the dead husband's line. Hence, Zerubbabel was legally the son of Shealtiel. Why is this important? The genealogical lists of Jesus (Matthew 1:1–16; Luke 3:23–38) find common ground in Shealtiel and Zerubbabel (Matthew 1:12–13; Luke 3:27).

1 Chronicles 3:20–24 contain a lot of other names. They might be obscure but they were real people. And the chronicler was making sure we understand that they all fit together and that the line continues.

Closing

The list ends with Anani, born at the end of the fifth century BC at the close of the Old Testament Canon. As the family of David was the most considerable of any of the tribes of Judah, the genealogy of his descendants was preserved with great care and exactness. We know how messed up David's own home life was, and Solomon's marriage indiscretions have become as legendary as his wisdom. Furthermore, these kings were frequently either not intelligent or evil—or both. Yet the seed and the promise moved from generation to generation. David's line was, by the promise, to be continued forever in the *Son of David*, who yet was David's Lord. This chapter points to Christ—in such a complex and wild route that only by God's hand could it have come together!

The Daily Word

Recalling the genealogy to the Israelites continues with David's descendants and Judah's kings. The names continue to point to the line of Christ and the seed preserved through the family of David and the tribe of Judah. Each person listed is a real person with a real story and real sin issues. However, they are not remembered by their sin but by preserving the seed of the Messiah.

You are not defined by your sin. Yes, the Lord hates sin, but Jesus came to free you from the bondage of sin and death and to give you life and a future. As you look at the family line of David, remember the seed of Jesus was preserved through the son of David. That is the key. God's hand was upon this family, just as the Lord's hand is upon you as His child. You may fall into sin. However, as you seek Jesus and turn away from sin, you receive His forgiveness. In Christ, you will find hope and freedom from sin. Don't dwell on the sin of your past; instead, allow the beautiful redemptive story of Jesus to shine through your life. God promises to work all things together for His good. He promises to bring beauty from ashes. *He promises redemption.* Let your name tell the story of redeeming love for His glory!

Six sons were born to David in Hebron, where he ruled seven years and six months, and he ruled in Jerusalem 33 years. These sons were born to him in Jerusalem: Shimea, Shobab, Nathan, and Solomon. These four were born to him by Bath-shua daughter of Ammiel. —1 Chronicles 3:4–5

Further Scripture: Ephesians 1:7–8; Philippians 3:13–14; 1 John 1:9

Questions

1. According to 1 Chronicles 3:5, how many children did Bathsheba bear David? Does this surprise you? Why do you think we know nothing of these other sons?

2. Does the statement in 1 Chronicles 3:9 indicate the sons of David's concubines had less importance and recognition?

3. Why do you think the writer of 1 Chronicles was recording this genealogy, and specifically, the details of David's lineage?

4. What did the Holy Spirit highlight to you in 1 Chronicles 3 through the reading or the teaching?

Lesson 86: 1 Chronicles 4

Son of David: The Prayer of Jabez

Teaching Notes

Intro

With the end goal of Chronicles being the *Eternal Throne* (2 Samuel), remember the focus of 1 Chronicles is the *Son of David*. To this point, Chronicles names the descendants of the tribe of Judah. Now the chronicler transitions into the remaining tribes.

Teaching

1 Chronicles 4:1–24: The list of Judah's descendants continues.

1 Chronicles 4:24–43: The chronicler lists Simeon's descendants. Simeon's land was located in the middle of Judah: "The second lot came out for Simeon, for the tribe of his descendants by their clans, but their inheritance was within the portion of Judah's descendants. . . . The inheritance of Simeon's descendants was within the territory of Judah's descendants, because the share for Judah's descendants was too large for them" (Joshua 19:1, 9). Simeon was included in Judah's land to help support Judah. Judah and Simeon worked together to drive out the people who lived in their inheritances: "Judah said to his brother Simeon, 'Come with me to my territory, and let us fight against the Canaanites. I will also go with you to your territory.' So Simeon went with him" (Judges 1:3).

Through verse 28 and beyond, the chronicler highlighted the geography of the genealogy. They lived in all of these places "until David became king" (v. 31). They served a purpose in these places as they ushered in the king.

1 Chronicles 4:34–43: The chronicler highlighted territorial expansions. As the people continued to grow, they needed more space. The land they found was "rich," and had "good pasture," and was "broad, peaceful, and quiet" (v. 40). In short, the land was everything the people had wanted.

The Hamites and the Meunites (v. 41) were among the people groups who descended from Ham. They were some of the people that the Lord told the Israelites to drive out of the land.

Now, let's go back and focus on the prayer of Jabez, found earlier in this chapter.

1 Chronicles 4:9–10: This short section of Scripture became a nationwide phenomenon in the early 2000s in the book, *The Prayer of Jabez*.

The prayer Elijah prayed when he confronted the prophets of Baal is another example of a powerful Old Testament prayer: "At the time for offering the evening sacrifice, Elijah the prophet approached the altar and said, 'Yahweh, God of Abraham, Isaac, and Israel, today let it be known that You are God in Israel and I am Your servant, and that at Your word I have done all these things. Answer me, Lord! Answer me so that this people will know that You, Yahweh, are God and that You have turned their hearts back.' Then Yahweh's fire fell and consumed the burnt offering, the wood, the stones, and the dust, and it licked up the water that was in the trench . . . So, Ahab went to eat and drink, but Elijah went up to the summit of Carmel. He bowed down on the ground and put his face between his knees. Then he said to his servant, 'Go up and look toward the sea.' So, he went up, looked, and said, 'There's nothing.' Seven times Elijah said, 'Go back.' On the seventh time, he reported, 'There's a cloud as small as a man's hand coming from the sea.' Then Elijah said, 'Go and tell Ahab, 'Get your chariot ready and go down so the rain doesn't stop you." In a little while, the sky grew dark with clouds and wind, and there was a downpour. So, Ahab got in his chariot and went to Jezreel" (1 Kings 18:36–38, 42–45).

Elijah was a radical man of God who believed that God wanted to show up in his life. Through his prayer, fire physically fell on the altar and the wood and completely consumed everything. James described Elijah as "a man with a nature like ours; yet he prayed earnestly that it would not rain, and for three years and six months it did not rain on the land. Then he prayed again, and the sky gave rain and the land produced its fruit" (James 5:17–18). If Elijah was a man "with a nature like ours," then we can pray the same way he did. Some have said Old Testament prayers like Elijah's and Jabez's are not prayers that New Testament believers should pray and expect God to answer; they were for a specific time and a specific purpose. But James wrote that Elijah's nature was like ours, and we could also put Jabez's name there as having a nature like ours. Commentator Richard Pratt said, "Jabez's prayer related directly to the needs of the Chronicler's original readers in at least three ways":

1. The readers had experienced a lot of pain during and after the exile.
2. Jabez's prayer related to the now returned Israelites' desire to expand their territory after the exile.

3. Jabez was an example of how to gain relief from pain and the work of territorial expansion.[1]

Jabez's name actually means "pain." Jabez's mother gave him this name because she experienced a lot of pain when she gave birth to him in keeping with the curse given in the garden of Eden: "He said to the woman: 'I will intensify your labor pains: you will bear children in anguish. Your desire will be for your husband, yet he will rule over you'" (Genesis 3:16). Jabez just wanted relief from life. Jabez called out to the God of Israel in verse 10 and asked God in faith to intervene in his life. Without faith it is impossible to please God. Jeremiah 33:3 says, "Call to Me and I will answer you and tell you great and incomprehensible things you do not know." Jesus said that His followers would do greater things than He did (John 14:12), so we should be asking God to show us the greater things He wants us to do.

Jabez asked God to bless him. There was nothing wrong with this request! God promised to bless Abraham so that Abraham would be a blessing (Genesis 12:2–3). Jabez fell into the lineage of Abraham, so his request for God to bless him shows his understanding of God's promise to Abraham. We have been blessed with every spiritual blessing in Christ (Ephesians 1:3), so it's not bad for us to ask God to give us those blessings.

Jabez also asked for God to extend his border. His request for more was so that others could experience more of God. Jabez asked for land out of practicality. It was not the equivalent of asking for a nice car or a million dollars.

Jabez asked to experience God's presence: "let your hand be with me."

Jabez prayed, "Keep me from harm, so that I will not cause any pain." Jabez's request was for God's protection.

Closing

Just because the prayer of Jabez is in the Old Testament doesn't mean we can't pray a similar prayer. Jabez was in the lineage of David. He was talking to God and wanted to experience God's presence, provision, and care. We are co-heirs with Christ and have the exact same right as Jabez to pray big prayers. We only need to have childlike faith, come to him, and trust in His timing.

---

[1] Richard L. Pratt, "The Identity, Privileges and Responsibilities of God's People: 1 Chronicles 1:1—9:34," *Reformed Perspectives Magazine*, March 8, 1999, http://reformedperspectives. org/magazine/article.asp/link/http:%5E%5Ereformedperspectives.org%5Earticles%5Eric_ pratt%5EOT.Pratt.Chronicles.1.2.html/at/The%20Identity,%20Privileges%20and%20 Responsibilities%20of%20God's%20People%20(1%20Chr.%201:1-9:34),%20part%202.

The Daily Word

Jabez lived as an honorable man and prayed in faith as he called out to the God of Israel. In his prayer, Jabez asked the Lord to bless him and extend his borders. He asked for God's hand to be upon him to experience even more of the Lord's presence in his life. He asked for protection. Jabez talked to the Lord because he wanted to experience more of God in his life.

How do you pray? *Do you pray in faith and ask for more of the Lord's presence in your life?* Jabez's prayer isn't a formula. Rather, it is an honest man seeking more of the Lord's presence in his life. *Isn't that what you want?* Today, call out to the Lord. Ask Him to bless you and expand the borders in your life. Ask the Lord for protection. The Lord says He is your refuge and your stronghold. He will shelter you in His wings. The Lord says to call upon Him. He will answer you in His timing, so *trust him* as you cry out!

Jabez called out to the God of Israel: "If only You would bless me, extend my border, let Your hand be with me, and keep me from harm, so that I will not cause any pain." And God granted his request. —1 Chronicles 4:10

Further Scripture: Psalm 37:23; Isaiah 54:2; Jeremiah 33:3

Questions

1. Why did Jabez's mother give him this name (1 Chronicles 4:9)? Read his prayer in 1 Chronicles 4:10. What four things did he pray for? God granted what he requested. Describe what that might have looked like.

2. Shelah's offspring were called "linen workers" in 1 Chronicles 4:21. Why would they be important? Who was Shelah (Genesis 38:11–14)?

3. Some of the tribe of Simeon were looking for pasture for their flocks. They found rich and good pasture that was quiet and peaceful. What two groups of people did they destroy to take this land (1 Chronicles 4:40–43)?

4. Of the people groups that the Simeonites destroyed, who were the Hamites (Genesis 9:22, 25)? What had the Lord told Moses to write concerning the Amalekites in Exodus 17:14 (Deuteronomy 25:17–19)?

5. What did the Holy Spirit highlight to you in 1 Chronicles 4 through the reading or the teaching?

Lesson 87: 1 Chronicles 5

Son of David: The Descendants of Reuben, Gad, and Manasseh

Teaching Notes

Intro

This is an interesting chapter in several ways. We'll be discussing the lineage of the 12 sons of Jacob, who was renamed Israel. We'll start with the lineage of Rueben. But first, let's look at the big picture—the plan—from Adam to Noah to Abraham to Jacob to the twelve sons all the way down to the kings of Israel and Judah. The lineage tells the whole story of God's plan through Israel's history. All of it points to the *Son of David*, Jesus. This chapter tells the story of Rueben, Gad, and the half the tribe of Manasseh.

Teaching

1 Chronicles 5:1: Rueben was Jacob's firstborn son, born to Leah, but he defiled his father's bed so his birthright was given to the sons of Joseph. Deuteronomy 21:15–17 explains that Rueben was the firstborn even though his mother wasn't Jacob's beloved. As the firstborn, he should have received the birthright—a double portion. Since Jacob had 12 sons, he divided his wealth into 13 shares, the firstborn traditionally received two of those shares, while the other sons should have each received one share. However, Rueben forfeited his birthright, not because he was the son of the unloved wife (Leah), but because he defiled his father's bed. Genesis 35:19–22 describes Rachel's burial. Rachel died giving birth to Benjamin, Jacob's twelfth and last son. While Jacob's family dwelt in the land of Eder, Rueben lay with Jacob's concubine Bilhah, and Jacob (Israel) heard about it. Bilhah was Rachel's servant, who now belonged to Israel. So, Rueben lay with one of the mothers of Israel's 12 sons. This act violated the law of God. Therefore, Rueben defiled God's plan by laying with Bilhah, and consequently lost his birthright.

1 Chronicles 5:2–6: These verses listed a portion of the genealogy of Rueben, but does not give the connection between Joel and Rueben. A little research shows

"Joel" is named four or five times in Chronicles, so how do we keep this straight? Joel's relationship with Rueben is unstated. Suggestions include that Joel was the son of Carmi, or that he was the son of Hanoch because Hanoch was listed first. Because Scripture doesn't give Joel's connection to Rueben, any conclusion we reach will be conjecture. The only thing we can know is that, down through the generations, Beerah was Joel's descendant who was taken captive by Tiglath-pilesar, the king of Assyria.

1 Chronicles 5:7–10: Rueben's descendants (Jeiel, Bela, and Shema, the son of Joel) settled in Aroer and toward the desert east to the Euphrates. During the days of Saul, they warred against the Hagrites and dwelt throughout the region of Gilead. Rueben, Gad, and half the tribe of Manasseh dwelled east of the Jordan while the remaining tribes crossed the Jordan into Canaan. These two and half tribes lived in the expanded territory where they faced more of the enemies from the east and the north.

1 Chronicles 5:11–17: The children of Gad, another of Israel's sons, lived in Bashan, which is modern-day Syria and the Golan Heights. The generations of Gad were listed, with Joel (descendant of Gad, not the previously mentioned Joel who was of Rueben) as their chief. Many of the people in this genealogy are not listed anywhere else in Scripture. At some point in time, Jotham, the king of Judah, did a genealogy, which preserved the names of these descendants of Israel. Jeroboam, the king of Israel, also completed a genealogy to preserve the lineage of all the tribes of Israel.

1 Chronicles 5:18–22: The men of Rueben and Gad and the half tribe of Manasseh numbered 44,760. These men were trained for war and waged war against Israel's enemies. The Hagrites were the descendants of Hagar (handmaid of Abraham's wife, Sarah). Jetur, Naphish, and Nodab were sons of Ishmael. This describes the conflict between the Israelites and the Ishmaelites. The Israelites cried to God in battle, and they defeated the Hagrites and captured their livestock. Because it was God's battle, the Hagrites were defeated and the tribes of Rueben and Gad lived in this land until the exile.

1 Chronicles 5:23–26: The descendants of half of the tribe of Manasseh settled east of the Jordan in the land of Bashan to Mount Hermon. Although they were known as mighty men and were famous in their day, we know nothing else about them because they transgressed against God and chased after the gods of foreign nations. As a result, God delivered them into the hands of Tiglath-pileser, the king of Assyria, who carried them into exile. Second Kings 15—16 provides more details about Tiglath-pileser's campaign against Israel. Although

Rueben didn't inherit his birthright because he violated his father's bed, this passage describes a time when his descendants cried out to God and defeated their enemies (1Chronicles 5:18–20). But when they turned from God, they were defeated by the king of Assyria (vv. 25–26).

There will be times in our life when we know we have things that aren't pleasing in the sight of God. Yet God's promises are established in our lives, therefore, violations do not remove us from the blessings of God. We need repentance in our lives. We need to stand firm in our journey for the things of God and His plans.

Rueben lost a great deal because of the major sin in his life that brought shame to his father and to God. His birthright was given to Joseph's two sons, Manasseh and Ephraim. But when the time came to take the land—the Land of Promise that God had assigned to the Israelites through Moses and Joshua, they could take it because God had promised it to them. God kept His promises to Israel even though there was sin in the nation.

We can draw four principles from these events:

1. There is one big plan. We can understand that God has one big plan with many players. While we don't know anything about the majority of the people in Israel, God worked to bring His plan to completion.
2. God always rewards faithfulness. God loves those who consistently follow Him even if they mess up from time to time.
3. God blesses integrity. Rueben made a big mistake, and he lost the birthright. He didn't walk away from God, but remained faithful to God. He didn't walk away from the promise God made to him and his people.
4. The promises are for everyone. There were people living in this time who walked with God, so they inherited what God promised to Israel. We may not know their names, but we know they lived in the Promised Land as God had promised.

Closing

The promises of God are for everyone who will receive the word of God. We walk it out in faithfulness and integrity, cooperating in the big plan of God, so His plans are honored above our own. God's promises for us today mean God never leaves us; He never forsakes us. He will honor His word, even though we transgress. We must honor Him in our obedience. God doesn't give up on us. If He calls us to repentance, He will bring us back and honor His promise to us. Once we see the promise(s) of God come into our lives, we need to take stock of where we are with Him and let Him be the Lord of our lives, and then watch how He will bless us and walk us through. Integrity and faithfulness always cooperate with the big plan of God.

The Daily Word

As the chronicler continued to remember the past generations, he wrote about Jacob's oldest son, Reuben, who lost his birthright after defiling his father's bed. Although he certainly sinned against God, Reuben's past did not define him, and the Lord didn't give up on him or his descendants. Later the sons of Reuben, Gad, and half of Manasseh waged war against the Hagrites, Jetur, Naphish and Nodab. During this battle, they received help from God because they cried out to Him. They found victory in the battle because they presented their requests to God and trusted Him.

Every day your spiritual enemy, the devil, wages war against you as you follow Jesus. *Do you ever wonder how to fight the battle?* Follow the example of the tribes of Reuben, Gad, and Manasseh, and *cry out to the Lord in battle.* Humble yourself before the Lord, admitting you don't have the strength to fight. Ask God to come to your side, and He will deliver you. He promises you will have victory in Him. Just go to Him. Don't let the sins of your past define you or keep you from asking the Lord for help. He loves you and nothing separates you from His great love. Allow Jesus to be Lord of your life, and He will give you victory in your battles.

They received help against these enemies because they cried out to God in battle, and the Hagrites and all their allies were handed over to them. He granted their request because they trusted in Him. —1 Chronicles 5:20

Further Scripture: Psalm 20:7; Psalm 34:4; 1 Corinthians 15:57

Questions

1. Reuben was the oldest son of Israel. Why was Reuben not listed as the first-born in the genealogical records? To whom did the birthright belong?

2. What prophecy did Jacob speak over Judah? How was this prophecy fulfilled (Genesis 49:8–10; Micah 5:2; Matthew 2:6)?

3. What was the response of the armies of Reuben, Gad, and the half-tribe of Manasseh when they were in battle (2 Chronicles 14:11–13; Psalm 9:10)? Is the Lord the first one you call upon when you are in a tough battle?

4. What caused God to use a nonbelieving king to invade the land and take His own people captive?

5. What did the Holy Spirit highlight to you in 1 Chronicles 5 through the reading or the teaching?

Lesson 88: 1 Chronicles 6

Son of David: The Descendants of Levi

Teaching Notes

Intro

We've studied the genealogy of the tribes of Israel in 1 Chronicles. Chapter 6 focuses on the tribe of Levi—the tribe that points to Christ, to the living God. Everything about the Levite's ministry points to the living God.

Teaching

1 Chronicles 6:1: Levi had three sons: Gershon, Kohath, and Merari. This tribe had a wide range of characters, like Moses and Samuel. There were also the not-so-great characters, like the sons of Aaron, the sons of Eli, and the sons of Samuel. Levi's three sons became the head of three clans. Aaron was from the tribe of Kohath, and he became the first high priest. All three of the tribes had general temple duties. From those three tribes came the musicians. Because of the function of the tabernacle and the roles assigned to the Levites, understanding this tribe is important.

1 Chronicles 6:2–15: In this passage, the descendants of Kohath provided the lineage of the line of priests. From Kohath came Amram, whose son Aaron was designated as the high priest when the tabernacle was first erected. Zadok was the priest when the first temple was erected. And we have the priest who saw the temple destroyed—Jehozadak. Amram's children were Moses, Aaron, and Miriam. Only Aaron's descendants were allowed to serve as priests. Aaron was the father of Nadab, Abihu, Eleazar, and Ithamar. When Nadab and Abihu offered strange fire to the Lord, they died without any descendants. Eleazar's descendants became the high priests, but that duty passed to descendants of Ithamar at some point in time. Notably, the high priest Eli, who raised and trained Samuel, is not mentioned in this genealogy at all. After his service, the line of high priests passed to the sons of Ithamar so that when we get to the time of King David, Abiathar and Zadok served as co-high priests. Abiathar sided with Adonijah in his bid for kingship while Zadok remained loyal to David and Solomon.

In response, Solomon deposed Abiathar as high priest, leaving Zadok as the sole high priest and reestablishing the priesthood in the lineage of Eleazar.[1] The priesthood never left the family of Aaron.

In verse 10, the chronicler emphasized that Azariah was the high priest of Solomon's temple. In 2 Chronicles 26:16–21, Azariah was the priest who defied King Uzziah when the king attempted to assume the office of priest and burn incense in the temple. King Uzziah was struck with leprosy and never again entered the temple. The chronicler celebrated Azariah for protecting the purity of the priesthood and the temple.

Another priest that stands out is Hilkiah in verse 13. He is the high priest who found the book of the law and brought it to King Josiah. While King Josiah is the one who acted on it, Hilkiah was the priest who found it. Verse 14 names Seraiah, who was the high priest during the reign of King Zedekiah, the last of the kings. He was sent as a prisoner to Babylon and killed by King Nebuchadnezzar. His son, Jehozadak, was taken captive when Babylon conquered Judah and Jerusalem. This was a momentary end of the line of the high priests. Israel's actions had consequences, so even the chronicler emphasized that the Lord had carried them off into exile.

This element of genealogy has importance even today. Scientists have found DNA that can be traced back to Aaron so they can identify people today who are from the priestly line.[2] Genealogy has importance because it points to the holiness of God, the consistency of God, and the promises of God.

1 Chronicles 6:17–28: These verses listed many obscure names, but the name Elkanah appeared several times. In verse 27, this Elkanah was the father of Samuel, the prophet. Although Samuel wasn't named as a son, verse 28 listed Samuel's sons Joel and Abijah. According to 1 Samuel 8, Samuel's sons were unfaithful to the Lord. They were corrupt and accepted bribes. They became the excuse the people of Israel used to demand the earthly king they wanted. Although these men were unfaithful, Joel's son would later play an important role.

1 Chronicles 6:31–43: This passage lists the men David put in charge of the music in the Lord's temple. This is one of the unique elements recorded in Chronicles. David included the musicians as an important part of pointing toward the holiness of God. Heman the singer, one of the chief musicians (v. 33), was the son of Joel and grandson of Samuel. Psalm 88 was attributed to him. Verse 39 named

---

[1] Ralph F. Wilson, "The Genealogy of the Priesthood in David's Time," Jesus Walk, 2012, http://www.jesuswalk.com/david/genealogy_of_the_priesthood_in_davids_time.htm.

[2] Adam Eliyahu Berkowitz, "DNA Studies Trace Jewish Priestly Lineage from Biblical Times," Israel 365, September 30, 2015, https://www.israel365news.com/301195/dna-studies-prove-existence-of-biblical-priestly-class-health-and-science/.

Heman's relative (some translations say brother) Asaph, as "his right hand." Asaph wrote Psalm 50 and 73—83. Asaph was also chief of the ceremony when David led Israel to bring the ark of the covenant to the tabernacle in Jerusalem (1 Chronicles 16:1–6).

1 Chronicles 6:44–47: These verses list the descendants of Merari, who served as musicians alongside the sons of Kohath. Ethan (v. 44) was also known as Jeduthun. While he didn't write any of the Psalms, three Psalms (39; 62; 77) were written to the choir director, Jeduthun. Two were written by David and one by Asaph. This arrangement of chief singers, one from each of the three clans from Levi, remained unbroken until Josiah's reign (2 Chronicles 35:15).

1 Chronicles 6:48–53: Aaron's relatives, the Levites, were assigned to all the service of the tabernacle. Their work supported the work of the priests and their efforts pointed to the holiness of God and the *Son of David*, Jesus.

1 Chronicles 6:54–81: To fulfill their duties, the Levites were spread throughout the land to minister to the people and to point toward the holiness of God. This goes back to Genesis 34, which said that the tribes of Simeon and Levi were cursed because they had led the massacre of the men at Shechem. Because of their lack of faithfulness, the tribe of Simeon was effectively dissolved and absorbed into the tribe of Judah. The Levites, because of their faithfulness during the rebellion of the golden calf, were scattered as a blessing throughout the whole nation of Israel. Simeon was scattered as a curse; Levi was scattered as a blessing.

The Levites were assigned to different regions. The Kohathites received the cities in the south, covering the tribes of Judah, Benjamin, and Ephraim. The Gershomites were in the north, covering the tribes of Issachar, Asher, Naphtali, and Manasseh (v. 62). The Merarites were on the east side of the Jordan River, covering the tribes of Rueben, Gad, and Zebulun (v. 63). Though they weren't in Jerusalem at the tabernacle, their ministry and commissioning remained the same—to make sure God's law was still present and obeyed in those areas. Second Chronicles 17 explains that some of the Levites had a distinct teaching ministry—they actually taught the common people.

Closing

This was the tribe of Levi, and there are so many names and locations where they were placed in cities throughout the land. Notice that here among the chosen people was a consecrated tribe. Aaron's family formed the priesthood. The whole tribe pointed to the Messiah. A provision was made, from beginning unto the end, for worship and sacrifice. They modeled for us devotion to God. Some did it well, others did not. But as we look at this entire family, the heartbeat of Ezra was to reestablish them where they needed to be, because the worship of God, pointing to all that God is, was so incredibly important. Notice they had priests, those doing temple duty, musicians, and those teaching throughout the land. There was uniqueness to their calling, which they modeled for us. The Levites came alongside the king pointing to the glory of God. If we miss that, then we've missed something for us. We are the hands, feet, and mouth of our Lord Jesus Christ. We may not be Levites, but we're called to the same call that they received—to give glory to the Most High King—to give praise to Jesus, the *Son of David*.

The Daily Word

As the chronicler continued reminding the Israelites of their past, the different roles of the Levites and Aaron's descendants were highlighted. Some were tabernacle service workers, some were priests, and some were musicians—each had a role. The chronicler reestablished truth for the Israelites about the different settlements for the Levites, assigning them to specific territories.

It is important to remember God's heartbeat is to point to the coming Messiah. Today, each follower of Christ has a unique role in specific territories. The Lord has given you a territory—a home, a workplace, a community, an organization. In your territory, you shine the light and love of Christ to those around you. In addition, He has called you to a unique role. So sing and make music, clean toilets, teach Scripture, cook, write the business plan, train up your children in the way they should go—ultimately, lead others to worship Jesus, the one true Savior and Son of God. Jesus says, "*Just worship Me.*" Do the thing you do, in the place you do it, for the glory of God.

Their relatives, the Levites, were assigned to all the service of the tabernacle, God's temple. But Aaron and his sons did all the work of the most holy place. . . . These were the places assigned to Aaron's sons from the Kohathite family for their settlements in their territory, because the first lot was for them.
—1 Chronicles 6:48–49, 54

Further Scripture: Psalm 100:2–3; Romans 12:4; Ephesians 2:10

Questions

1. What special role were the Levites given? Were all the Levites priests?
2. Why were the tribes of Levi and Simeon both cursed to be scattered (Genesis 34:24–30; 49:5–7)? Why was the tribe of Levi scattered as a blessing to Israel (Exodus 32:26–29)?

3. How was worshipping God through music shown to be important (2 Samuel 6:5; 1 Chronicles 15:16–17; 2 Chronicles 5:11–14; 7:6)?

4. What kind of man was Heman shown to be in Psalm 88?

5. According to 1 Chronicles 6:48, how can we know that every service to God is important? Do you tend to measure a certain service to God as better than another?

6. What did the Holy Spirit highlight to you in 1 Chronicles 6 through the reading or the teaching?

Lesson 89: 1 Chronicles 7

Son of David: Recognizing the Importance of Unity

Teaching Notes

Intro

We've been working through the historical books of the Bible. Chronicles isn't as exciting a study as some of the other historical books, but its importance is found in tracing the lineage of David from its beginning and toward its promised fulfillment in the Messiah. That explains our theme for 1 Chronicles—*Son of David*. The people of Israel were in captivity in Assyria and the people of Judah were in captivity in Babylon. After seventy years, the people of Judah were released, and 1 Chronicles gave the explanation of all they had gone through that led them to captivity and exile from their own country. The end goal is that the tribes of Israel would come together in unity (Ezekiel 37:15–28).

Teaching

1 Chronicles 7:1–5: The Descendants of Issachar. These verses support Genesis 46:13 and Numbers 26:23–24 by listing Issachar's four sons as Tola, Puah, Jashub, and Shimron (v. 1). Verse 2 names the heads of the ancestral families. Tola was one of the judges from the period of the judges. From Tola alone came 22,600 warriors. The descendants of Uzzi, Tola's son, numbered 36,000 battle troops, and from their tribesmen came 87,000 battle troops (vv. 4–5). These numbers probably came from a military census David took. While these descendants were not part of the lineage of David, they were actively involved in fighting for and protecting the nation. They were important to the future of the nation, which would continue to face threats and warfare after they returned from exile (Ezra 4:1–6; 5:3; Nehemiah 2:7, 9–10, 19). Even though they had been set free, the battle to come would be real. The nation needed to rebuild its military might. In the spiritual realm, it's important to recognize that just because we've been set free, doesn't mean our battles are over or the enemy will not come back after us.

1 Chronicles 7:6–12: The Descendants of Benjamin. The process we looked at in the first five verses continued for the tribe of Benjamin, once again focusing on the number of fighting men the tribe had produced.

1 Chronicles 7:13: The Descendants of Naphtali. Naphtali's sons were listed, but no other details were listed about their fighting men in the past. They were included because they were important to the unity of the nation.

1 Chronicles 7:14–19: The Descendants of Manasseh. Manasseh's list included sons *and* daughters. There is an interesting focus on women in this section, specifically the daughters of Manasseh's descendant Zelophehad. Numbers 27:1–11 gives a detailed account of these five women.

1 Chronicles 7:20–29: The Descendants of Ephraim. As these lists continue, the chronicler makes one statement again and again—although the Messiah would come through David and the tribe of Judah, all the tribes of Israel and Judah were important in the future of the country. Women were also included in the lineage of Ephraim, indicating that both men and women were important in the future of Israel (v. 24). The lineage also included Joshua of Nun who led the people into the Promised Land (v. 27).

1 Chronicles 7:30–40: The Descendants of Asher. Asher's genealogy included "the heads of their ancestral houses, chosen men, warriors, and chiefs among the leaders" (v. 40). The number who had served in the military was 26,000.

Closing

I asked God what we should do with this information. On one level, chapter 7 presents a long list of names that are difficult to pronounce. On another level, chapter 7 is a reminder that the battle has to be fought together. I'm afraid what has happened today is that we keep trying to fight the battle by ourselves—alone and without support. In the American church, we tend to pick our own hills that we're willing to go to war over, and it's not about a united front. We have to get over our own concerns and our own battles and recognize that the war is on a spiritual level. The principalities of Satan are trying to defeat us, and the only way we will be victorious over him is when we come together, united against our common enemy. Romans 8:38–39 says, "For I am persuaded that not even death or life, angels or rulers, things present or things to come, hostile powers, height or depth, or any other created thing will have the power to separate us from the love of God that is in Christ Jesus our Lord!"

The Daily Word

The chronicler brings attention to the powerful number of warriors in the tribes of Issachar, Benjamin, and Asher as they continue to specifically list out the genealogy. The tribes trained several warriors in preparation for battle.

The Lord calls you, as a follower of Christ, as a warrior in the battle you face each day. The word *warrior* means "a person engaged or experienced in warfare; a soldier; a person who shows or has shown great vigor, courage, or aggressiveness; one who is brave." You can wake up each day saying, "*I am a warrior for the Lord! I am ready for battle.*" Remember, greater is He who is in you, than He who is in the world. Do not be afraid of what your days may hold because you are equipped with the armor of God, the power of God, and the grace of God. God clothes you in strength and subdues your enemies beneath you. Take heart, mighty warrior! No weapon formed against you will prosper. Today, walk in this powerful truth, and you will have victory in Jesus' name.

During David's reign, 22,600 descendants of Tola were recorded as warriors in their genealogies. —1 Chronicles 7:2

Further Scripture: Psalm 18:39; Isaiah 54:17; 1 John 4:4

Questions

1. In 1 Chronicles 7, the writer records the numbers of fighting men in his genealogical account. What might have been the reason for including this detail in chapter 7 but not in earlier chapters?

2. How many tribes were written about in 1 Chronicles 7? Why do you think these are such brief accounts but others are much more detailed?

3. What did the Holy Spirit highlight to you in 1 Chronicles 7 through the reading or the teaching?

Lesson 90: 1 Chronicles 8

Son of David: The Tribe of Benjamin

Teaching Notes

Intro

We are about to go through the eighth chapter of names. In 1 Chronicles 7, we talked about six tribes, including Benjamin. Why are we going to talk about Benjamin again? It can seem daunting and repetitive, but there is a bigger picture here. When we slow down and study, we should ask God to show us what He wants us to see (1 John 2:20, 27). We need to position ourselves to go deeper into the word; move from the milk to the meat (Hebrews 5:13—6:12). We should be able to teach this stuff! We have literally gone over and over these names, because, for some reason, the writer needed us to learn something deeper.

The tribe of Benjamin was broken up into two groups. When the northern tribes broke away from Judah (922 BC), the tribe of Benjamin split its allegiance. After Rehoboam's foolishness and Solomon turned away from the Lord, Ahijah prophesied that God would split the kingdom of Israel: "For this is what the LORD God of Israel says: 'I am about to tear the kingdom out of Solomon's hand. I will give you ten tribes, but one tribe will remain his because of my servant David and because of Jerusalem, the city I chose out of all the tribes of Israel'" (1 Kings 11:31–32). But when the kingdom did divide, some Benjaminites remained loyal to Judah: "When Rehoboam arrived in Jerusalem, he mobilized 180,000 choice warriors from the entire house of Judah and the tribe of Benjamin to fight against the house of Israel to restore the kingdom to Rehoboam son of Solomon" (1 Kings 12:21).

Teaching

1 Chronicles 8:1–7: The Benjaminites were on the level of Judah and Levi. They were part of the returning remnant into the settlements. Ehud was a well-known Israelite judge who helped bring victory over the Moabite king (Judges 3:12–30). Geba (v. 6) was a Levitical city on the southern border of Benjamin, about six miles north-northeast of Jerusalem. King Asa fortified Geba during his reign but the city was repossessed by the Israelites during the early exile period (Ezra 2:26).

1 Chronicles 8:8–13: Several other locations were named: Moab (v. 8), Ono and Lod (v. 12), and Gath (v. 13).

1 Chronicles 8:14–28: The heads of families and chief Benjaminites set up their homes in Jerusalem. Their identity was in their family name and where they were from. Some of the remaining Benjaminites went north while others went south. They had messed up family lines and misplaced identity. We need to place our identity in the *Son of David*—Jesus, and not in our own name or lineage.

1 Chronicles 8:29–40: This family lived in Gibeon, which was near Jerusalem. Constable explains, "Gibeon was where the central sanctuary stood during most of Saul's reign."[1] Gibeon wasn't God's choice for a sanctuary. God's choice was Jerusalem. Saul wasn't the chosen leader. David was.

The tribe of Benjamin is representative of the struggle between the flesh and the spirit. Some went north and some went south. Some stayed in Jerusalem while some stayed around in Gibeon. They could not decide what they wanted to do.

The Benjaminites were always on the fence. Civil war started in Israel because of the Benjaminites. Judges 19—21 describes the account of the horrific death of a Levite's concubine. The Benjaminites were the only tribe that didn't see a problem with it. The other tribes united against Benjamin and almost completely wiped them out because of the Benjaminites' refusal to turn in the perpetrators. After the small civil war, only six hundred Benjaminites were left. The Benjaminites were a great example of giving in to the flesh, of those who were going to do whatever was right in their own eyes. Jacob's prophecy of Benjamin certainly came true: "Benjamin is a wolf; he tears his prey. In the morning he devours the prey, and in the evening he divides the plunder" (Genesis 49:27). This verse describes three sets of two things:

1. Time frames: morning and evening
2. Actions: dividing and devouring
3. Outcomes: prey and spoil[2]

The Benjaminites didn't know who they were. They weren't from the north or the south. They weren't from Jerusalem or Gibeon. James 1:5–8 could have described the Benjaminites: "Now if any of you lacks wisdom, he should ask

---

[1] Thomas L. Constable, *Expository Notes of Dr. Thomas Constable: 1 Chronicles*, 28, http://planobiblechapel.org/tcon/notes/pdf/1Chronicles.pdf.

[2] "What Should We Learn from the Tribe of Benjamin?," Gotquestions.org, https://www.gotquestions.org/tribe-of-Benjamin.html.

God, who gives to all generously and without criticizing, and it will be given to him. But let him ask in faith without doubting. For the doubter is like the surging sea, driven and tossed by the wind. That person should not expect to receive anything from the Lord. An indecisive man is unstable in all his ways." The Benjaminites who remained with Judah saw the hope of the future.

Closing

Just because you come from an unstable family doesn't mean your identity is found there. You can be part of something bigger. Revelation 7:4–8 describes 144,000 slaves (servants) who all will come together, and Benjamin could be a part of this since this passage mentions "every tribe of the Israelites." The Benjaminites will also have their name inscribed on one of the gates of the new Jerusalem (Revelation 21:12–13). This will only be possible because of the small remnant of the tribe of Benjamin who remained faithful to the Lord and pointed others to the *Son of David*.

The Daily Word

As you read through Benjamin's descendants, you review who they were, who their fathers were, and where they came from. The tribe of Benjamin included King Saul, the first anointed king of Israel. However, the tribe of Judah anointed King David, which ultimately led to the throne of Jesus. Pause for a minute and think about the contrast between the tribe of Benjamin and the tribe of Judah. Think about David and Saul, both anointed as kings over God's people. King Saul chose to walk in evil ways, whereas King David walked in the ways of the Lord.

As anointed children of God, you have a choice to walk in the Spirit or walk in the flesh. Walking in the Spirit bears the fruit of the Spirit: love, joy, peace, patience, kindness, goodness, faithfulness, gentleness, and self-control. Walking in the flesh may lead to works of the flesh like lust, pride, idolatry, outbursts of anger, selfish ambition, envy, and drunkenness. *How are you walking?* The Lord says to remain in Him. As you spend time with Christ, praying and reading God's Word, you will begin to bear the fruit of the Spirit. Ultimately, the world will know you are a follower of Christ by your love as you remain in Christ. The Lord promises when you walk in the Spirit, you will not give way to the temptations of the flesh.

Ner fathered Kish, Kish fathered Saul, and Saul fathered Jonathan, Malchishua, Abinadab, and Esh-baal. —1 Chronicles 8:33

Further Scripture: Galatians 5:19–21a, 22–23a; 1 John 2:6

Questions

1. In all the genealogical accounts in 1 Chronicles 1—9, there is no mention of any of the kings of Israel after they defected from the house of David. Why do you think that is?

2. Although God had rejected Saul as king, we read a detailed account of Saul's family in 1 Chronicles 8. In verses 33–40, it records Saul's sons, then only Jonathan's lineage. Why might that be (1 Samuel 20:14–17, 42)?

3. What did the Holy Spirit highlight to you in 1 Chronicles 8 through the reading or the teaching?

Lesson 91: 1 Chronicles 9

Son of David: The Service of the Nethinim

Teaching Notes

Intro

We've seen that the tribe of Benjamin created a civil war and were almost wiped out. Only six hundred from the tribe survived. Remember the crazy passage we studied when they were given wives to marry so the tribe could continue? Some of the Benjaminites dwelled in the northern kingdom and some in the southern. MacArthur points out, "Even though the northern kingdom of Israel never returned from dispersion in 722 BC, many from the ten tribes which made up that kingdom migrated south after the division in 931 BC."[1] That possibly means all of Israel's original twelve tribes were represented in Judah. However, Judah was not what it could have been because of its unfaithfulness to God.

Teaching

1 Chronicles 9:1–34: "All Israel" refers to the remnants of each tribe who returned to Judah (v. 1). The chronicler then moves on to document who returned to Judah. The people were coming back to Jerusalem and Judah and resettling there. Verse 2 identifies four groups:

1. *The Israelites* (not all): People from four tribes—Judah, Benjamin, Ephraim, and Manasseh—resettled in Jerusalem, 956 were Benjaminites (vv. 3–9).

2. *The Priests*: The priests were mentioned by name and were accompanied by 1,760 relatives (vv. 10–12). They are described as "capable men employed in the ministry of God's temple" (v. 13). These priests had more of a job description than you'll ever see given to a pastor in the New Testament.

3. *The Levites*: The Levites supported the work of the priests, and they too were listed by name (vv. 13–16). The fact that the priests and the Levites were among the first groups to resettle is important. Judah had been punished because of their unfaithfulness. For Israel to start over as a faithful nation,

---

[1] John MacArthur, *The MacArthur Bible Commentary* (Nashville: Thomas Nelson, 2005), 483.

those who led worship, oversaw sacrifices, and took care of the temple were essential. They pointed the people back to God.

4. *The Temple Servants*: In verse 17, this group was identified more specifically as gatekeepers. The gatekeepers were identified by name according to their assignments:

- Guards of the entrances (vv. 19–25): They tended the gates, opened and closed them in the morning and at night, and made sure the city was safe. Gatekeepers were given authority over who came in and out of the city.
- Guards of the treasury (vv. 26–27): Four chief gatekeepers, who were Levites, were given the responsibility to oversee the rooms and treasures in the temple. They were responsible for the money in the temple.
- Service in the temple (vv. 28–32): They had responsibility for the temple utensils, furnishings, and supplies used in worship.
- Leading in music within the temple (vv. 33–34): Some were exempt from these other duties because their responsibility was to be available to sing and worship within the temple.

The temple servants described in verse 2 had another name—Nethinim—which means those who were given (Numbers 31:30). One out of every 50 people was given to the Levites to serve in whatever capacity was needed (Ezra 2:58). They were given menial tasks within the temple, such as carrying firewood or cleaning. The names of the Nethinim were not Hebrew but Gentile, possibly indicating these were people who had been conquered by the Israelites. Yet they were appointed by David and other leaders to serve the Levites and the Jews (Ezra 8:20). David and the leaders recognized that the Nethinim had a role to serve, and that was a direct foreshadowing of what was to come (Romans 15:25–27). Because we have experienced the presence of the living God, Yeshua (that is, Jesus), we are "obligated to minister to Jews in material needs" (Romans 15:27). Nehemiah 3:26 records that when the Nethinim first returned to Jerusalem, they worked to repair the wall and the tower near the Water Gate in the city wall. They couldn't yet work as temple servants, so they found something else to do because they understood the bigger picture. Nehemiah 10:28–29 shows that the Nethinim were faithful to their calling because they kept their eyes on God and His law.

Closing

When we come to terms with the fact that all of us have been called as servants to do whatever needs to be done, then people can experience the presence of God in our work. Being a servant should help us realize that there is a bigger picture that relies on the work of everyone to be completed. When I reflect on the Nethinim, I automatically go to the big picture. We received the spiritual benefit and giftings as followers of Christ, and we have the responsibility to minister to those whom God chose as His chosen people.

Ephesians 4:11–13 explains, "And He personally gave some to be apostles, some prophets, some evangelists, some pastors and teachers, for the training of the saints in the work of ministry, to build up the body of Christ, until we all reach unity in the faith and in the knowledge of God's Son, growing into a mature man with a stature measured by Christ's fullness." When all the servants embrace their roles and work together in unity it will point people to the *Son of David.*

The Daily Word

The kingdoms of Judah and Israel were no longer divided. They returned to Jerusalem after the seventy-year exile in Babylon to rebuild the temple. The first to return to live in towns on their own property were the Israelites, the priests, the Levites, and the temple servants. The chronicler outlines each role used to rebuild the temple—a distinct calling and act of obedience for this time in history.

As a follower of Christ in the kingdom of God, you have a specific role. In His body, He has chosen some to be apostles, teachers, evangelists, shepherds, and prophets for the training up of the saints for the work of the ministry. Each role serves one another as they work together in unity to build up the body of Christ. Today, *embrace the role you have been asked to do with humility.* Serve one another—no matter the task and no matter the role. Whether you are seen or unseen, work with all your heart as though working for the Lord, not for people. When you embrace what you have been asked to do for the Lord with a selfless attitude, you will experience the Lord's presence in your life and abundant joy and peace.

The first to live in their towns on their own property again were Israelites, priests, Levites, and temple servants. —1 Chronicles 9:2

Further Scripture: Romans 15:25; Ephesians 4:11–12; Colossians 3:23

Questions

1. First Chronicles 9:1 reminds the readers why Judah was carried into exile. Why did the writer mention this?

2. There was a tent set up so that those returning from exile could worship the LORD. How did the Levites determine who would serve in each role (1 Chronicles 9:22)?

3. How important does it appear that the role of the singers were to the Israelites at this time (1 Chronicles 9:33)? Explain the parallel between this verse and Revelation 4:8. How important is music to you as part of your worship of God?

4. There is a repeat of 1 Chronicles 8:29–38 in 9:35–44. Some think this was an error on the part of the transcriber of the text. What do you think? If so, in your opinion, does this detract from God's Word or make it unreliable?

5. One of the groups mentioned in 1 Chronicles 9:2 were the temple servants, also called the Nethinim. Who were they (Numbers 31:30; Joshua 9:27; Ezra 2:43–58)? How do you see yourself in this role for the service of God?

6. What did the Holy Spirit highlight to you in 1 Chronicles 9 through the reading or the teaching?

Lesson 92: 1 Chronicles 10

Son of David: Reasons to Fast

Teaching Notes

Intro

I find it humbling that you have allowed reviveSCHOOL to enter your life every day. We're now three-fourths of the way through the first year of this study. I have a request for you. Would you take a picture of where you study, where you watch the video or listen to the audio, and send it to us at info@reviveSchool. org? Our team would love to see that. You don't have to say anything. I'm always intrigued to see where people spend time with the Lord. Chronicles has been a tough study for us as well, so your pictures would also encourage us.

Let's briefly review. The nation of Judah had sinned against God. The nation was conquered and the people exiled to Babylon. In Chronicles, the people had finally been freed from captivity and were returning to Judah and Jerusalem. In the first nine chapters of 1 Chronicles, the genealogies of the twelve tribes were recorded—to remind the people of their sin and demonstrate that God's plan was still intact and His promises would be fulfilled. Yesterday, we looked at how the people were returning in groups (the Israelites, the priests, the Levites, and the temple servants) to reinstate where they were in the Lord.

Teaching

1 Chronicles 10:1–6: Verse 1 describes the massacre of Israel's men on Mount Gilboa. In the massacre, Saul and his sons Jonathan, Abinadab, and Malchishua were all killed (v. 2). In 1 Chronicles 8, we read that Saul had four sons. The fourth son (Esh-baal) is listed in 1 Chronicles 9:39. In 2 Samuel 2:8, the fourth son is called Ish-bosheth, meaning "man of shame," which was possibly changed since Esh-baal didn't die in battle.

Saul was severely wounded by an arrow, so he asked his armor-bearer to use his sword to kill him before the Philistines could finish his death (vv. 3–4a). However, when his armor-bearer refused, Saul fell on the sword and killed himself (v. 4b). When the armor-bearer saw Saul die, he killed himself with the same sword (v. 5). In verse 6, the chronicler proclaimed that Saul's whole house died.

Did Saul really trust the Lord if he felt he had to take his own life? MacArthur stated, "Saul's suicide is the ultimate expression of his faithlessness towards God at this moment in his life."[1] Suicide was a rare occurrence in the Old Testament (2 Samuel 17:23; 1 Kings 16:18). God can always redeem us from anything we've experienced. Suicide is not of God. We always have hope!

1 Chronicles 10:7–10: When those in the valley below the battle heard that Saul and his sons were dead, they fled from their cities. The Philistines then moved into the cities and settled there (v. 7). The Philistines found the bodies of Saul and his sons (v. 8). They stripped Saul, cut off his head, and sent news throughout the land that they had conquered the Israelites (v. 9). They placed his armor in the temple of their gods and hung his skull in the temple of the god Dagon (v. 10). The temple of Dagon was where the Philistines had placed the ark of the covenant they stole from the Israelites one hundred years earlier.[2]

1 Chronicles 10:11–12: The brave men of Jabesh-gilead heard what had happened to the bodies of Saul and his sons, so they went and retrieved the bodies. They buried the bones under an oak tree and then fasted for seven days to mourn their deaths (1 Samuel 31:12–13).

1 Chronicles 10:1314: Saul died because he had been unfaithful to the Lord. He had even consulted a medium, an act that was punishable by death (Leviticus 20:27) and hadn't consulted the Lord. At his death, Saul's kingdom was turned over to David. God allowed Saul to kill himself for his disobedience and unfaithfulness. Because of Saul's actions, God turned His ear and would not listen to the cries of Saul (Jeremiah 7:13–16). Remember, Saul was under the old covenant, but, praise God, we are under the new covenant. It doesn't matter if we've consulted a medium or been disobedient because we can repent and find forgiveness of sin through Jesus Christ.

Closing

Blogger Kristen Feole gives three reasons why believers don't fast: (1) fear, (2) ignorance, and (3) rebellion. But she emphasizes, "Fasting prepares you for the work God has ordained for you."[3] What are reasons to fast?

---

[1] John MacArthur, *The MacArthur Bible Commentary* (Nashville: Thomas Nelson, 2005), 347.

[2] Earl D. Radmacher, Ronald B. Allen, and H. Wayne House, eds., *Nelson's New Illustrated Bible Commentary* (Nashville: Thomas Nelson, 1999), 506.

[3] Kristen Feole, *Why Should I Fast? Seven Examples of Fasting in the Bible*, Faith Gateway, https://www.faithgateway.com/why-should-i-fast-7-examples-fasting-bible/#.W6qPW34pBPM.

1. To prepare for ministry (Matthew 4:1–17; Mark 1:12–13)
2. To seek God's wisdom (Acts 14:23)
3. To show grief (Nehemiah 1:1–4)
4. To seek deliverance or protection (Ezra 8:21–23)
5. To repent (Jonah 3:6–10)
6. To gain victory (Judges 20:26)
7. To worship God (Luke 2:36–38)

Bill Bright (founder of Campus Crusade Ministries) has fasted often in his life. He says that fasting restores him to his first love of Jesus Christ even while it humbles him and reveals his true spiritual condition. He says it quickens God's Word in his heart, increases his prayer life, and brings about personal revival.[4] Fasting costs nothing, and yet it costs everything. When the Israelites were waiting for their new king, they fasted. I believe this is a prophetic word for us as well.

The Daily Word

In just a few sentences, the chronicler summarizes King Saul's life for the people of Israel. It's like they wrote a eulogy of Saul's life.

As you read this summary of Saul's life, think about what your eulogy would be. If your life ended tomorrow, how would people describe you in a few sentences? Are you living your life the way you hope to be remembered? Live your life with no regrets. Don't hold back. Don't wait for tomorrow. Be who the Lord created you to be. Go and do the thing on your heart you've wanted to do but just haven't yet. Reach out to that friend. Forgive that person. Have that party. Go after that career change. Stop the busy schedule, and spend your day in solitude with Jesus. Just do it! As you do, trust in the Lord with all your heart, and follow Him. Let go of the fear, and live in faith. Walk humbly with your God. Jesus will hold you in His loving hands. Go for it!

Saul died for his unfaithfulness to the Lord because he did not keep the Lord's word. He even consulted a medium for guidance, but he did not inquire of the Lord. So the Lord put him to death and turned the kingdom over to David son of Jesse. —1 Chronicles 10:13–14

Further Scripture: Psalm 118:24; Psalm 119:73–74; Micah 6:8

---

[4] Bill Bright, *7 Basic Steps to Successful Fasting & Prayer* (Wayne, NJ: New Life Publications, 1995), n.p.

Questions

1. What was the name of Saul's son who was not killed along with his brothers (1 Chronicles 8:33)? How was he killed (2 Samuel 4:5–7)?

2. What happened with the Israelites when King Saul was killed? Do you see a comparison with this act and when Jesus was arrested and killed (Mark 14:27)?

3. What were some of Saul's sins? How many people, if any, were affected by Saul's sins? Do you ever think about how your sin effects more than just you?

4. Why did the mighty men of Jabesh-Gilead treat Saul's body with honor (1 Samuel 11:1–11)?

5. What did the Holy Spirit highlight to you in 1 Chronicles 10 through the reading or the teaching?

Lesson 93: 1 Chronicles 11—12

Son of David: Being a Mighty Man

Teaching Notes

Intro

I love this chapter of Scripture because it allows us to look at David's mighty men and learn what it means for us to be mighty men for God. David Livingstone was a missionary and an incredible man of God. When people asked if Livingstone had found a good road into his area so they could send men to work under and learn from him, Livingstone replied, "If you have men who will come only if they know there is a good road, I don't want them." A mighty man of God is not looking for a paved road or attractive path. Instead, a mighty man of God will create his own path, unconcerned for his own safety, because he knows God has called him to the path.

Teaching

1 Chronicles 11:1–3: David's Anointing. All Israel (the remnant) came to David at Hebron. They recognized how he had led them in battle and how God had anointed him to rule over Israel (vv. 1–2; Psalm 78:70–72). The representatives of the remaining tribes came together and made a covenant with David in God's presence, making David the king over all Israel, not just Judah (v. 3). These verses state the fulfillment of God's anointing of David found in 1 Samuel 16 (2 Samuel 5:1–3).

1 Chronicles 11:4–9: David's Conquest of Jerusalem. David led Israel to march in the city of Jerusalem (also called Jebus). Although the residents there thought David would never be able to enter Jerusalem, he captured the city (vv. 4–5). As they entered the city, David said that whoever was mighty enough to first kill one of the inhabitants of the city would become his chief commander. Joab was the first and became the chief (v. 6). In this process, David released the anointing, the covering, in his life so people could walk in it. Joab walked into what David had been called to do. Joab aligned himself with that anointing, by walking beside David. It makes us wonder how that motivation for Joab was passed on to others. Interestingly, Joab was the son of Zeruiah, David's sister (1 Chronicles 2:15), so Joab was David's nephew. The city of David was located along the Kidron Valley, below Mount Moriah where the temple was later built (2 Chronicles 3:1). Zion referred to the entire area of Jerusalem—the city of David, the temple mount, and the entire city of Jerusalem (Isaiah 28:16). It was also the site of the Jebusite citadel located on the southeastern hill (v. 7). Note that these terms: city of David, Jerusalem, and Zion, were used interchangeably. David built up around the city, and Joab restored the rest of it (v. 8). As David grew in power, the Lord was with him (v. 9).

1 Chronicles 11:10–47: David's Mighty Men. The Hebrew word for "mighty" means strong or mighty and emphasizes excellence or unusual quality. In verse 10, David's mighty men were introduced. Throughout the Old Testament, the term "mighty" was used to express excellence: for the strength of a lion (Proverbs 30:30); for good and bad men (1 Chronicles 19:8); for "giants" (Genesis 6:4); for angels (Psalm 103:20), and for God (Deuteronomy 10:17). Beginning in verse 11, the mighty men were introduced, and their accomplishments were recorded—Joab was the commander, and Jashobeam was the chief of the 30 mighty men who killed 300 men at one time (v. 11). Three specific warriors worked together for David—Eleazar (v. 12), Josheb-basshebeth (2 Samuel 23:8), and Shammah (2 Samuel 23:11–12). Verses 13–14 explain that David and Eleazar fought together against the Philistines and were given a great victory.

I think David was given mighty men because he fought in the field beside them. Leaders have to be willing to jump in and do whatever it takes to be victorious. And can you imagine the relationship between David and Eleazar after they fought together against the Philistine army?

These three of the 30 chief men went to David at the rock of the cave of Adullam while the Philistines were in Bethlehem (vv. 15–16). David was thirsty for water from the well in Bethlehem, so the three mighty men snuck into Bethlehem to get water for him (vv. 17–18a). But David refused to drink the water and, instead, poured it out for the Lord (v. 18b). David's reason for doing this is found in verse 19; he could not accept that refreshment because his men had risked their lives solely for his comfort.

Abishai, Joab's brother, was listed as the commander of the 30 mighty men (vv. 20–21). Benaiah was then listed with his mighty exploits (vv. 22–24). Benaiah was then identified as the most honored of the 30 who was set over David's bodyguard (v. 25). In verses 26–47, the rest of the mighty men were listed, including Bathsheba's husband, Uriah the Hittite (v. 41).

Closing

What would it take to be a mighty man (or woman) for God? Stephen Cole suggests five characteristics David's mighty men shared.[1] These principles can be applied to all of us today—men and women.

1. A commitment to God so strong to be able to overcome any odds with faith (2 Samuel 23:8–12, 18, 21).
2. A commitment to God so strong to be able to endure exhaustion (2 Samuel 23:8, 10).
3. A commitment to God so strong to be able to ignore the opinion of the majority and stand alone in order to fulfill the role God has given (2 Samuel 23:10).
4. A commitment to God so strong to have the strength and wisdom to take the initiative (2 Samuel 23:9–12).
5. A commitment to God so strong to be able to risk one's own life for the cause (Matthew 10:38–39).

The mighty men of David surrounded him, protected him, fought with him, and helped him fulfill his calling. Jesus had His mighty men as well—the 12 disciples, even though one of them lost his way. The Apostle Paul had his as well—Timothy, Barnabas, John Mark, Silas, Erastus, and Luke.

The question for us is whether we are so committed that we're ready to take on any odds, to continue on past exhaustion, to be able to ignore other opinions to follow God, to have the strength and wisdom to take the initiative, and to be willing to risk our own lives for God's call (Matthew 10:38).

The Daily Word

When David ruled as king, not only was he anointed, but he also surrounded himself with thirty mighty men. These men allowed David to grow more powerful in his calling as king. These mighty men stood apart from others as formidable warriors. They overcame the odds by faith and their commitment to endure tiredness. For example, Benaiah killed a lion in the snow, and Jashobeam wielded his spear against three hundred, killing them at one time! These mighty men were committed to take the initiative, show loyalty, and selflessly serve their king, regardless of the cost. For instance, three men went out to the frontlines to get water for a thirsty King David, risking their lives for his needs.

---

[1] Stephen J. Cole, "God's Mighty Men (2 Samuel 28:8–39)," Bible.org, September 10, 2013, https://bible.org/seriespage/lesson-14-god-s-mighty-men-2-samuel-238-39.

Like the mighty men, you are called to full devotion to the Lord, the King of kings. The Lord doesn't ask you to follow Him because of a tradition or because it will get you something. Rather, *you follow Jesus out of a wholehearted love for Him.* He asks you to deny yourself, pick up your cross, and follow Him. Love Jesus with all your heart, soul, and mind. You may look different from the crowd. You may stand alone. You may have to overcome great odds. You may grow weary. But . . . the Lord promises you can do anything through Christ who gives you strength.

The following were the chiefs of David's warriors who, together with all Israel, strongly supported him in his reign to make him king according to the Lord's word about Israel. —1 Chronicles 11:10

Further Scripture: 1 Kings 8:61; Matthew 16:24; Philippians 4:13

Questions

1. What did Joab have to do to become the commander of David's armies? What should this say about us fulfilling our calling?

2. How long was David the king of Judah before becoming the king of all Israel (2 Samuel 5:4–5)? What were some things the people of Israel spoke to David about why he was the one that should be their king? Obviously, they knew the prophetic word that had been spoken over David's life. Why do you think it took them so long to conform to it?

3. Who were the three mightiest warriors among David's men? Why were they considered to be the mightiest?

4. Why did David refuse to drink the water from the well after mentioning he wanted some? Is there a longing that you have that, if received, you would give up as an offering to the Lord?

5. Describe David's coronation as king in 1 Chronicles 12. What feast are we, as believers, looking forward to, and what will happen (Isaiah 51:11; Revelation 7:17; 19:7–10; 21:4; 22:3–5)?

6. What did the Holy Spirit highlight to you in 1 Chronicles 11–12 through the reading or the teaching?

Lesson 94: 1 Chronicles 13—14

Son of David: Taking God Lightly

Teaching Notes

Intro

As we've worked through 1 Chronicles, we're beginning to see a transition as David was about to encounter the Lord. Constable explains the chronicler wanted to make sure his readers understood, "Yahweh is holy and His people should not take His presence among them lightly."[2] In a weird way, I think we can use that quote to understand why the Israelites were in their present condition. They didn't recognize Yahweh's presence, and they didn't value, honor, and fear who He is. They took Him lightly. David, the Israelites, and David's mighty men were all learning in a new way to work through this process. But not everyone held the same honor and value David had for the Lord.

Teaching

1 Chronicles 13:1–4: As David was getting ready to move the ark, he sought counsel with his leaders and commanders (v. 1). Both King Jehoshaphat (2 Chronicles 20:17) and King Hezekiah (2 Chronicles 30:2, 4, 12, 23) sought counsel from their men as well. It's good to seek wise counsel (Proverbs 11:14; 12:15; 15:31–33). David said that if he understood the message from God, they were to call all the people together (v. 2) so they could bring back God's ark (v. 3). The whole assembly agreed to move the ark (v. 4).

Remember that the ark, which contained the Ten Commandments, had been stolen from the Philistines who had captured it in battle. When the ark returned to Israel, Saul didn't ask God what He wanted them to do with it. David wanted to unify the people by establishing Jerusalem as his capital and reinstating the relationship with God they (Israel) had first fallen in love with. This could be classified as a time of revival. In Exodus 35—40, the presence of God was in the tabernacle. In 2 Chronicles 7:14–16, God proclaimed the temple of Solomon as His dwelling place. Saul in Gibeon was man's plan; David in Jerusalem was God's

---

[2] Thomas L. Constable, *Expository Notes of Dr. Thomas Constable: 1 Chronicles*, 38, http://planobiblechapel.org/tcon/notes/pdf/1Chronicles.pdf.

plan. David led the people to seek the Lord (Isaiah 55:6–7; Jeremiah 29:13–14). Just as Adam and Eve had experienced God's love, forgiveness, and provision (Genesis 3:15, 21; 4:26; 5:24), David wanted to lead his people to draw near and experience God's love, forgiveness, and provision personally. In the New Testament there are other passages that focus on drawing near to God (James 4:8–10), seeking God first (Matthew 6:33), returning back to God the Father (Luke 15:11–32), and having fellowship with God.

1 Chronicles 13:5–8: David pulled all the people together, from Shihor, a river in Egypt that flowed into the Mediterranean Sea and formed Israel's southern border, to Hamath, located on the northern border.[3] David called all the people to Kiriath-jearim, in Judah, to get the ark and move it to Jerusalem (vv. 5–6). They put the ark on a new cart to transport it (v. 7). The Philistines had also used a cart to transport the ark, but Old Testament law required that the ark be carried (not carted) by the sons of Kohath (Numbers 3:30–31). It is a possibility that Uzzah and Ahio (who drove the cart) were grandsons of Kohath. As they moved along, David and the people celebrated that God was near by singing songs and playing musical instruments (v. 8).

1 Chronicles 13:9–10: As they moved, the oxen stumbled on the uneven threshing floor and Uzzah reached out to steady the ark and keep it from falling (v. 9). God became angry at Uzzah's disobedience and struck him dead (v. 10). Not only were they not to touch the ark, but they were also to use poles to carry it (Exodus 25:12–15). No matter how innocently the act was done, touching the ark was in direct violation of God's law and resulted in death (Numbers 4:15). It's one thing to get God's confirmation about doing something, but it's another thing to find out how it should be done. God had given them instructions for how to move the ark, but they clearly chose not to follow those instructions here.

1 Chronicles 13:11–14: Uzzah died because David took God's instructions lightly. In response, David was angry with God's action, so he named the place "Outburst Against Uzzah" (v. 11). David also feared God and was afraid to continue to take the ark to Jerusalem. He took it instead to the house of Obed-edom the Gittite, where it remained for three months (vv. 13–14a). God blessed Obed-edom, his family, and all he had (v. 14b). As a Gittite, Obed-edom was a Levite from the Levitical city of Gath-rimmon (Joshua 21:24–25). The ark was in the presence of a Levite who didn't take God's presence lightly.

---

[3] John MacArthur, *The MacArthur Bible Commentary* (Nashville: Thomas Nelson, 2005), 484.

Closing

I don't know where you are in your walk with the Lord right now. Are you taking the presence of God in your life lightly? Or do you realize what God through Christ has done for you? When you do, you will be blessed because you can experience His presence.

The Daily Word

David faced his enemy the Philistines with confidence that the Lord had established him as the king over Israel. Even though David heard the Philistines had searched for him, he faced them boldly. Then David inquired of the Lord about going to war with the Philistines. The Lord said, "Go, and I will hand them over to you."

Like David, God has established you. He made you, called you, equipped you, and empowered you to face your enemy. Fear may say to back down, go hide, or let someone else face it, but confident faith in the Lord speaks truth into your soul. As a child of God, you are more than able to face your enemy. Ask the Lord to replace each lie with a truth from His Word. You are more than able because He will abundantly do more than you can even dream or imagine. The same power that raised Jesus from the dead is in you. You are perfectly and wonderfully made. In Jesus, there is victory. Pray at all times as you walk this out with confidence in the Lord. He will hand your enemy over to you in Jesus' mighty name!

When the Philistines heard that David had been anointed king over all Israel, they all went in search of David; when David heard of this, he went out to face them. —1 Chronicles 14:8

Further Scripture: Proverbs 16:7; Acts 4:13; Romans 8:11

Questions

1. In 1 Chronicles 13:10, why did God strike Uzzah dead? What was wrong with him steadying the ark to keep it from falling (Numbers 4:15)?

2. In 1 Chronicles 13:7, the ark of the covenant was placed on a cart. Did this act violate God's command on moving it (Exodus 25:12–15; Numbers 7:9)? Why?

3. How were they commanded to travel with the ark (Numbers 4:5–15)?

4. Where did the ark end up? Why (1 Chronicles 13:12–13)? What were the results for Obed-edom?

5. In 1 Chronicles 14, David asked the Lord several times if he should do something. In your own life, have you found yourself asking God for directions before you go forward or after you've gone? Have you noticed in your own life that God does not always give the same answer even though circumstances might be similar? What should this convict us to do?

6. What did the Holy Spirit highlight to you in 1 Chronicles 13—14 through the reading or the teaching?

Lesson 95: 1 Chronicles 15—16

Son of David: David Danced Before the Lord

Teaching Notes

Intro

In 1 Chronicles 13, we talked about David and the ark, where one minor mistake—not doing what the Word of God said—resulted in Uzzah's death. The house of Obed-edom experienced the blessings of God because the ark remained at his house for three months. In 1 Chronicles 15, the ark will be moved from the house of Obed-edom to a tent David erects in Jerusalem.

Teaching

1 Chronicles 15:27: David and the Levites carrying the ark were dressed in fine linen. This time, the Levites were carrying the ark in obedience to God's instructions. In Exodus 25:14, God gave instructions for how the ark should be carried. David, the Levites, and the singers gathered the people of Israel to worship God. It appears that David, wearing a linen ephod, was playing the role of the priest. Remember, our phrase for 1 Chronicles is *Son of David*. When you see David starting to play the role of king and priest, even for a season, you know he was pointing to Jesus, the coming Messiah.

1 Chronicles 15:28–29: The Israelites embraced that "God was back," meaning they were reunited with Him. David joined in the celebration by dancing with the people in worship, while Saul's daughter Michal watched and despised him in her heart. Why did she despise David? Michal came from "the old guard," and she didn't like how David embraced the ark. The word "despise" describes her anger at David. Perhaps she felt this was not how someone in authority should act. Maybe she believed David, as the anointed one, should not behave in such a way.

King Saul gave his daughter Michal to David after David killed Goliath. Over time, a great distance grew between her and David. David had other wives and was completely different from her father Saul. Michal's mentality is similar to the Pharisees in their regard for Jesus. In Matthew 23:13–16, 23–32, Jesus pronounced woes against the Pharisees for "locking up the kingdom of heaven" by not going in themselves or allowing others to go in. Here, the Pharisees' response was similar to Saul's actions in the Old Testament, by neglecting the experiential nearness and presence of God in the lives of His people, and replacing it with a cold and distant form of worship. Under a religious spirit, the way to control a relationship with God is to not invite people into His presence. Michal was upset because her father had done everything to prevent the people from experiencing this while David invited them to join in the worship experience.

As we unpack 1 Chronicles 16, think of the spirit of control in Michal. She didn't like what David did because they had never done it that way—dancing and clapping as they came into the presence of God. Why was David so excited that he celebrated by dancing before the Lord? Because he experienced the presence of the Lord.

1 Chronicles 16:1–2: They brought the ark of God to the tent and offered the burnt offerings and fellowship offerings in God's presence, and then David blessed the people. Remember back in 1 Chronicles 13, when the ark rested in the house of Obed-edom for three months and the Lord blessed his family? When you are in the presence of God, you're blessed. When you have freedom in Christ, you're not looking out the window; you're the one dancing in the streets.

1 Chronicles 16:3: David distributed to each Israelite a loaf of bread, a date cake, and a raisin cake. When Jesus interacted with people in the New Testament and they experienced the presence of God, it seems as though there was always a miracle with food. He fed the 4,000 and the 5,000, and He ate a meal with the people, which seemed to usher in God's provision and presence. When you begin to understand Acts 2:46–48 to see how God designed us to have fellowship together with food, then this begins to make sense. God wants to bless those with the spirit of religion and break them from it so they can experience a relationship with Him.

Three times when David celebrated the presence of God, food was involved. In 1 Chronicles 12:39, they spent three days eating and drinking with David. Food was involved in this celebration in 1 Chronicles 16:3. Then look at 1 Chronicles 29:22, when David invited the people to contribute to the building of the temple, "They ate and drank with great joy in the Lord's presence that day." When David's family experienced God's presence, they did it with food.

1 Chronicles 16:4–7: David was so excited that he began to turn this experience into a Psalm. In verses 4–7, David appointed the Levites as directed by God. Compare his actions this time with the previous time in 1 Chronicles 13. Even though he was excited and rejoicing in God's presence, he put the proper things in place. He appointed the Levites to be ministers before the Lord and to give thanks and praise to God. He named Asaph as the leader because David didn't need to do this himself. He also appointed several other people to play the harp and lyre while Asaph sounded the cymbals.

The people were genuinely excited about the presence of God because they felt like they were starting all over again, encountering the living God anew. When you realize that you're tapping into your first love, going back to Christ, falling in love with Him and embracing who He is, you will rejoice because of what He has done for you. David released the people to do these things. A spirit of religion will always control; a spirit of relationship with the Father will always empower.

According to verse 7, "David decreed for the first time that thanks be given to the Lord by Asaph and his relatives." David appointed these Levites to be in charge and officially approved this song for worship of the Lord.

1 Chronicles 16:8–36: In verses 8–22, David recited Psalm 105:1–15. Verses 23–33 are reflected in Psalm 96:1–13. Next, you will see Psalm 106:1, 47, 48 as David decreed these songs for Asaph to make sure the people would never forget who God is and what He had done (vv. 34–36). The chronicler reminds us: "Give thanks to the LORD, for He is good; His faithful love endures forever" (v. 34). Why is this message so important? To those coming out of exile, they needed to remember all God had done. David encouraged them to praise God for everything He did for them.

Closing

Where are you personally? Are you willing to dance? Or are you sitting at the window? When you can decide that you're free to dance, then you've understood what this means. If you can't quite get there, ask the Lord to free you from this bondage that is not designed from the Lord.

The Daily Word

Three months after David's first attempt to move the Ark of the Covenant to Jerusalem, he attempted the move again. This time David inquired of the Lord and prepared a place for the Ark. As the people walked through the streets, they danced, celebrated, and worshipped the Lord. At the same time, Michal, David's wife and Saul's daughter, sat near her window and looked down on King David celebrating in the streets. As they moved the Ark, she despised David in her heart.

The presence of God moves when His people seek Him. You can either jump in and be a part of it or sit on the sidelines. Where are you? Do you judge those walking with the Lord in the fullness of joy? Do you watch others enjoy their lives with Jesus as they walk in faith, while you drown in fear and bitterness? It's never too late to make the choice to come to Jesus and enjoy His presence. Jesus loves you. Let go of control. Let go of fear. Let go of pride. As you release these things, allow Him to fill you up with His great love, peace, and joy. Walk in humility and seek the Lord. When you seek Him, you will find Him, so seek Him with all your heart.

As the ark of the covenant of the Lord was entering the city of David, Saul's daughter Michal looked down from the window and saw King David dancing and celebrating, and she despised him in her heart. —1 Chronicles 15:29

Further Scripture: Psalm 16:11; Jeremiah 29:13; John 3:17

Questions

1. In 1 Chronicles 15, David prepared to move the ark again. What were the differences between this trip and the first time they tried to move it in 1 Chronicles 13:6–11?

2. Michal, who loved David in 1 Samuel 18:20, felt contempt for him in 1 Chronicles 15:29. Why do you think her feelings changed? Could it be because David had her taken from her husband in 2 Samuel 3:13–16 (2 Samuel 6:20)?

3. David appointed the Levites to worship before the ark in 1 Chronicles 16:4. Was this according to God's commands in Numbers 3:6–7?

4. In 1 Chronicles 16:11, we see David singing about seeking the Lord. Where else do we see verses like this (Deuteronomy 4:29; Jeremiah 29:13; Matthew 7:7–8)?

5. First Chronicles 16:34 and Psalm 136:1 read virtually the same. What does this verse mean to you?

6. What did the Holy Spirit highlight to you in 1 Chronicles 15–16 through the reading or the teaching?

Lesson 96: 1 Chronicles 17—18

Son of David: The Lord's Covenant with David

Teaching Notes

Intro

First Chronicles 17 is going to feel like a repeat of 2 Samuel 7. When you compare the texts of the two chapters, they are almost identical. Remember, our phrase for 1 Chronicles is *Son of David*. This is a key chapter in the Old Testament. Even though we've looked at this account before, today we'll look at it from a different perspective. We'll focus on the Davidic covenant.

Teaching

1 Chronicles 17:1–3: Wolfgang Roth said, "David completed what Joshua had begun: the taking possession of Canaan."[1] Living in such an incredible house implied David was living in wealth and comfort. David told Nathan he was troubled because he lived in wealth while God lived in a tent. Psalm 132:1–5 records David's desire and commitment to find a dwelling place "for the Mighty One of Jacob." Nathan immediately told David to do what was on his heart. But as a prophet, a mighty man of God, when someone asks you for counsel, always remember to be slow to speak a prophetic word. In this case, Nathan spoke quickly, without consulting the Lord. Later that night, the Lord came to Nathan to correct him. James 1:19 urges believers to be quick to hear and slow to speak. This instruction counters our natural inclination to just spit out an answer without first asking God what He wants us to say. Sometimes this gets us in trouble. When we hear people releasing a word from God, sometimes we have to wonder if they really inquired of the Lord before speaking. This is why people don't trust prophetic words today. In this case, David had no reason to doubt Nathan's word.

---

[1] Wolfgang Roth, *The Deuteronomic Rest Theology*, 8; quoted in *The Expositor's Bible Commentary: 1 Samuel—2 Kings*, ed. Tremper Longman III and David E. Garland (Grand Rapids: Zondervan, 2005), 381.

1 Chronicles 17:3: Thankfully, Nathan was open to God's correction. After coming to terms with God's correction, Nathan humbled himself and returned to David with God's instructions. This is the kind of leadership people want to be under—the leadership of someone who can say, "I messed up, and I need to correct this because this is what God showed me."

1 Chronicles 17:4–6: God gave Nathan a timeline and pointed out He had moved from tent to tent and tabernacle to tabernacle, since He had brought Israel out of Egypt. God moved from the tent of meeting to the Mosaic tabernacle and eventually to David's tabernacle. In all those moves, God never once spoke to anyone about where He should dwell. Likewise, what did Jesus do in the New Testament? He lived as a nomad, a man who didn't have a place to call home. Why is it so important to understand this about God? To understand we can't put God in a box. God was never in one place, but our mentality is to put God in a temple or church, so we understand the role we have to play. But when God is constantly on the move and present, everywhere we go, then we might have to act like it. This is what makes it so hard to follow the Lord. God wanted to honor David's desire to build a house for Him, but it wouldn't happen the way David wanted.

1 Chronicles 17:7–10a: God said He took David from a shepherd and made him king over Israel. Remember God delivered this word because Nathan humbled himself to listen; humility can lead to revival. God was with David and destroyed his enemies. God promised to establish a place for Israel to live where they would not be disturbed. Again, God shows He is in control, always directing and guiding and leading His people.

1 Chronicles 17:10b–15: Catch this: a house will be built. God promised to build a house for David. God promised that when David died, He would bring forth a descendant, one of his sons, and establish his kingdom (v. 11). Several things can be seen in this prophetic word. One, God would raise up a son from David—Solomon. In 1 Chronicles 22:6–10, David tells his son, Solomon, to build a house for the Lord. David wanted to do this, but God wouldn't allow it because David had shed much blood, as a man of war. Comparing these passages, we learn God told Nathan that David's son would build a house for Him (1 Chronicles 22:11–13). Not only would God establish a kingdom for David's son, but the son would build a house for God. The word for "house" can also mean "dynasty." God promised to establish his throne forever. Our phrase for 2 Samuel is *Eternal Throne*. The *Eternal Throne* would come through the *Son of David*—Jesus. Compare this promise to 2 Samuel 7:16—you might as well be reading the same verse. This is an awesome picture of the *Son of David* who will establish God's house and rule from an *Eternal Throne*. God promised He would never take His faithful love away from this Son. The lineage of David constantly points to the coming king—the *Son of David*, the King of kings Himself— Jesus! God promised this would happen—it could not fail! It was not conditional on anything David did except his complete reliance on God's promise.

This Davidic covenant was described seven times in 1 and 2 Chronicles.

- God spoke to Nathan, and then Nathan spoke to David (1 Chronicles 17).
- David spoke to Solomon (1 Chronicles 22).
- David again spoke to Solomon (1 Chronicles 28).
- Solomon spoke to the nation of Israel (2 Chronicles 6).
- God spoke to Solomon (2 Chronicles 7).
- Abijah spoke to Jeroboam (2 Chronicles 13).
- The chronicler commented on the Davidic covenant (2 Chronicles 21).

When God releases a word, it will stick.

1 Chronicles 17:16–19: After David heard this, he sat in God's presence and wondered who he was that God would do this. As Warren Wiersbe said, this became David's prayer of thanksgiving for present favor.[2] David recognized God had spoken about his house in the distant future (v. 17) and that God had made all of these great promises according to His will. As Nathan spoke the prophetic word, David received it because he recognized it was according to God's will. God made many promises regarding Judah. In Genesis 49:10, Jacob blessed his son Judah, by saying, "The scepter will not depart from Judah or the staff from between his feet." This meant Judah's rule (favor) would last forever—the scepter would not depart from Judah because of the *Son of David*—by Solomon, and ultimately, through Jesus, the Messiah.

1 Chronicles 17:20–22: David continued to praise God: "There is no one like You, and there is no God besides You" (v. 20). Wiersbe pointed out that David shifted from thanksgiving in the present to praising God for what He had done in the past.[3]

---

[2] Warren W. Wiersbe, *The Wiersbe Bible Commentary: Old Testament* (Colorado Springs: David C. Cook, 2007), 566.

[3] Wiersbe, 566.

1 Chronicles 17:23–27: David shifted again, now making a petition for God's future fulfillment of His promises.[4] David pleaded with God to make the things He promised come true. Once David heard the word, he went to God in prayer. *Nelson's Commentary* said the house of David would always be in the royal line and the right to rule would always belong to David's offspring. This promise would last forever, even when they messed up.[5]

Closing

How do you receive a word from God? What can we learn from David?[6] First, record it and then listen to it. When we talk about prophetic words today, we're not talking about new Scripture but about words believers speak to each other (1 Corinthians 14:3). Ask God what He meant by that prophetic word. Ask what your part is and what God's part is. The key step is testing the prophetic word to see if it aligns with Scripture. Second Timothy 3:16 explains why we have to test things with Scripture. First Thessalonians 5:19–21a tells us to be open to what God is speaking into our lives but to test all things. Our job is to test the word of God that comes into our lives by making sure it aligns with Scripture, then hold on to what is good and stay away from evil (1 Thessalonians 5:21b–22).

In Philippians 4:8, we're told to keep our eyes on things that are right, honorable, and true. Prophetic words can be from the Lord. We know the words David heard were accurate because Luke 1:31–33 tells us Jesus was given the throne of His father David. Jesus was the *Son of David*. And because of Jesus, we can receive spiritual blessings. Jesus promised a spiritual kingdom was coming through Him. All of these things align with what David heard in 2 Samuel 7 and 1 Chronicles 17. The common theme here is the *Son of David* is fulfilled through Jesus Christ.

The Daily Word

David desired to build a permanent home for the Lord to dwell in. However, through a word given to the prophet, Nathan, God shared a different plan for David and for who would build His permanent dwelling place. After King David heard the word, he *went and sat in the Lord's presence* where he thanked and

---

[4] Wiersbe, 566.

[5] Earl D. Radmacher, Ronald B. Allen, and H. Wayne House, eds., *Nelson's New Illustrated Bible Commentary* (Nashville: Thomas Nelson, 1999), 517.

[6] Jeffrey Hardwick, "What Do You Do When You Receive A Prophecy?," A Transforming Word, August 22, 2017, https://atwministries.com/2017/08/when-you-receive-a-prophecy.

worshipped the Lord. Then David petitioned the Lord for further fulfillment of His promises.

When you hear from the Lord, however He speaks to you, take the time to *go and sit* in His presence. Maybe you have a favorite chair or a prayer closet. Maybe you need to sit in your car a little longer before walking into the house or office. Maybe you need to go for a walk alone. Wherever the place, abide and rest in Him. Today, if you have a burden, a decision to make, or the Lord has redirected the desires of your heart, *go and sit* in the Lord's presence. As you sit, give thanks to the Lord, praise His name, and then ask Him to fulfill His promises in your life.

Then King David went in, sat in the Lord's presence, and said, Who am I, Lord God, and what is my house that You have brought me this far? —1 Chronicles 17:16

Further Scripture: Psalm 103:1–2; Mark 6:31; John 15:5

Questions

1. David wanted to build a house for the ark of the covenant, but God told him no. Do you think David was out of line or do you think he had pure intentions? Why or why not? Have you ever been overzealous for the Lord and He told you no, or not yet? In what ways?

2. Read 1 Chronicles 17:26–27 carefully. David sat before the Lord in awe and full of thanksgiving. Do you think society, as a whole, neglects to give God praise? What more could you do or say in your time with the Lord to be like David? Do you feel you give God your all when you pray/praise? Why or why not?

3. Where else have we seen God go before someone and give them victory over their enemies (Joshua 8:1–2; 2 Chronicles 20:27)?

4. What did the Holy Spirit highlight to you in 1 Chronicles 17—18 through the reading or the teaching?

Lesson 97: 1 Chronicles 19—20

Son of David: David Expands and Establishes His Kingdom

Teaching Notes

Intro

In 1 Chronicles 18, David conquered the Philistines and took control of Gath. He conquered the Moabites and established his kingdom in Moab. Then he went down the Euphrates River where he conquered other nations to establish his kingdom across the land. In Genesis, God promised Abraham that his descendants would possess the land; now we see David taking possession of the land. David reigned over all Israel, administering justice to all his people (1 Chronicles 18:14).

Teaching

1 Chronicles 19:1: Nahash, king of the Ammonites, died, and his son became king over Ammon. In 1 Samuel 11:1–6, Nahash had attacked Israel at Jabesh-gilead until they asked to make a treaty with Nahash. Nashash placed one condition on the treaty—that he would gouge out everyone's right eye just to humiliate Israel. Not only did Nahash want to conquer Israel, but he also wanted to make a mockery of them. The elders of Jabesh asked for seven days to send messengers throughout Israel. When Saul heard about the threat, the Spirit of God came upon him and he became furious with Nahash. Why was Saul so angry about the threat to Jabesh-gilead? The answer may be found in Judges 21 when Israel attacked the city of Jabesh-gilead and killed all the inhabitants, except the four hundred virgins who were given as wives to men from the tribe of Benjamin. Saul was from the tribe of Benjamin, so he got fired up when Nahash threatened the town. Saul raised up an army and attacked the Ammonites, leaving very few survivors.

1 Chronicles 19:2: David decided to show kindness to Hanun, Nahash's son, because Nahash had shown kindness to David. Acts 13:21 says Saul was king for 40 years but reading the account of his reign leaves some scholars to suggest his actual reign was anywhere from 12–20 years. The conflict between Saul and Nahash happened at the beginning of his reign. When David came on the scene, he lived in exile because Saul hunted David and tried to kill him. During the time when David was running from Saul, Nahash probably showed kindness to David. Although the Ammonites were enemies of Israel, David's heart was the heart of a peacemaker. So, when Nahash died, David sent comforters to mourn his death.

1 Chronicles 19:3–5: David's act of kindness was rejected, and Hanun ordered the messengers' beards shaved off and their clothing cut off at the hips. In ancient times, the beard was a symbol of masculinity and an important aspect of an Israelite's culture and religion. So even though David showed kindness, Hanun responded with evil. Hanun's actions started a war that cost many men their lives. When David heard what had been done to his men, he encouraged them to remain in Jericho until their beards grew back.

1 Chronicles 19:6–7: The Ammonites knew the consequences of this action, so they used their silver to hire the Arameans, with their chariots and horses, to help them battle Israel. The Ammonites and Arameans gathered for battle in the valley of Medeba.

1 Chronicles 19:8–13: David sent Joab and the entire army to meet the Ammonite army. When Joab saw the army arrayed against him, he knew he was outnumbered. Joab divided his forces between himself and his brother Abishai. Joab's forces battled the Arameans while Abishai's forces battled the Ammonites, with each helping the other when necessary to win the battle. Joab urged the army to "Be strong!" His words echoed Moses' words to Joshua. He encouraged his troops to trust God and what He had said. Though Joab divided his army to fight their enemies (divide and conquer), they were also instructed to provide support to each other when one group was struggling.

The body of Christ is on the same team. We're each fighting our own battles, but we need to be willing to support those who are starting to lose the battle. We need to pour into others when they need us and to allow others to pour into us when we need help.

1 Chronicles 19:14–16: The Arameans fled from Joab, and the Ammonites fled from Abishai. Joab and Abishai entered the city of Jerusalem. The Arameans, seeing their defeat, sent messengers across the Euphrates to call for reinforcements.

1 Chronicles 19:17–19: When David saw what they were doing, he gathered Israel and crossed the Jordan River. With the entire army of Israel lined up against them, the Arameans fled from Israel. David killed 7,000 charioteers, 40,000 soldiers, and the commander of their army. Soundly defeated, the Arameans made peace with Israel and became David's subjects. They never helped the Ammonites again.

Although David had taken the enemy's land, the enemy always retaliated and tried to take it back. We saw this in the Ammonites, Nahash's son, and the Arameans. Israel today is still in chaos because people are constantly trying to retake what God said is Israel's. The enemies are still fighting, but Israel and Jerusalem are still there.

1 Chronicles 20:1–3: Although the Arameans had given up, the Ammonites had not. In the spring, Joab led the army of Israel against Ammon at Rabbah and demolished it. But David stayed in Jerusalem. Remember what happened when David stayed in Jerusalem? This was the time when David sinned with Bathsheba (2 Samuel 11) and he called Uriah off the battlefield. Joab was fighting against Rabbah and captured its water supply (2 Samuel 12:26). Historically, in this age, capturing a city's water supply meant certain defeat; they could not survive without water. Joab sent a message to David, "It's time for you to show up and capture the city." Joab was calling David to take up his rightful place in the battle instead of remaining back in the city of Jerusalem. When David came to the battlefield, Israel conquered Ammon. Even in the process of David's sin with Bathsheba and Uriah, God restored David and his authority.

Sometimes we read over these stories without processing everything. In reviveSCHOOL, we're trying to bring Scripture together and see how it all fits in the bigger picture.

1 Chronicles 20:4–8: As this chapter concludes, David leads Israel to kill the remaining Philistine giants. We see God's sovereign plan, no matter what the enemy did. Even though David and his mighty men didn't do everything right, David's heart was to serve God. God showed up and delivered. Their enemies fled before them, and they continued to conquer the land and occupy it.

Closing

No matter what is going on in your life today, you can continue to trust the Lord. No matter who your enemies are or what you're up against today, like David, you can trust that God will be faithful to His promises.

The Daily Word

The Arameans lined up in battle formation in front of Joab, the commander of the Israelite army. And then Joab noticed the Ammonites were lined up in battle behind him as well. He chose some men to fight the Arameans in front and placed the rest of the forces under the command of his brother to engage the Ammonites coming from behind the army. He told his brother, "Be strong! If the battle gets too much for me, *then you'll be my help,* and if the battle is too much for you, then *I'll help you!*" The Lord brought them victory in this battle.

As believers in Christ, the Lord promises you will face spiritual battles. Through these battles, you may feel exhausted or even angry with the Lord and feel as though you have no strength to keep going. In these moments, remember you are never alone. The Lord is always with you, and you have brothers and sisters in Christ to help you fight the battle, to pray for you, to strengthen you with words of encouragement, and to remind you of Truth. Whatever you face today, humble yourself and reach out to a friend. Share with them if the battle is too much for you alone, and *ask for help.* Be strong in the Lord, and trust He will bring you victory.

"If the Arameans are too strong for me," Joab said, "then you'll be my help. However, if the Ammonites are too strong for you, I'll help you. Be strong! We must prove ourselves strong for our people and for the cities of our God. May the Lord's will be done." —1 Chronicles 19:12–13

Further Scripture: Isaiah 43:2; Galatians 6:10; Philippians 2:4

Questions

1. Why did Hanun treat David's men so badly in 1 Chronicles 19:1–5? Why do you think they were so ashamed? When David sent them to Jericho to wait until their beards grew, was this a punishment? Why or why not?

2. In 1 Chronicles 19:14, the Syrians fled before Joab and his men. Where else have we seen the enemy fleeing (Deuteronomy 32:30; James 4:7)?

3. Several descendants of giants were killed by David's army in 1 Chronicles 20:4–8. This was not the first encounter with giants we have seen. Where else were they defeated (1 Samuel 17:32–50)?

4. What did the Holy Spirit highlight to you in 1 Chronicles 19—20 through the reading or the teaching?

Lesson 98: 1 Chronicles 21—22

Son of David: The Price of Pride

Teaching Notes

Intro

This lesson continues to build on the theme for 1 Chronicles: the *Son of David*. While many people believe that David's "classic sin" was his sin with Bathsheba, chapter 21 describes another of David's sins. Though people don't often talk about this sin, it nearly destroyed the city of Jerusalem. This story was also told in 2 Samuel 24, but we're going to talk about it again.

Teaching

1 Chronicles 21:1: The word for "Satan" also means "adversary." In Zechariah 3:1–2, Zechariah saw Satan standing before the Angel of the Lord to accuse Joshua the high priest. Satan "incited" David—he persuaded and convinced David—to count the people of Israel. While God had instructed Moses to take a census of Israel at certain times, David's decision to count was based on his pride. According to John MacArthur, by counting Israel, David was beginning to take credit for what he had done and to establish more trust in his own work and men than in God.[1] If Satan could tap into David's pride, then maybe he could cause David to fall.

But 2 Samuel 24:1 says, "The Lord's anger burned against Israel again, and He stirred up David against them." Did the Lord or Satan tell David to count the people? Remember that whatever Satan does, God allows him to do it. Satan did not do this without permission from the Lord. This could be compared to the Lord allowing Satan to torment Job. So, God could have allowed Satan to test David.

John MacArthur clearly identified some of Satan's roles. One of Satan's roles is to judge the sinners (Mark 4:15).[2] (Just to clarify the statement that Satan judges the sinners: Ultimately, Jesus judges sinners, but Jesus (God) allows Satan to come in and grab hold of those sinners.) Another of Satan's roles is to refine

---

[1] John MacArthur, *The MacArthur Bible Commentary* (Nashville: Thomas Nelson, 2005), 487.

[2] MacArthur, 487.

the saints (Luke 22:31–32).[3] Note that Satan asked God, "Can I sift Simon?" Part of the role of Satan is to refine believers. God can actually use Satan to make us stronger in Him. In David's case, however, his faith failed and there was no refining in this instance. Satan is also used to discipline those in the church.[4] In 1 Corinthians 5:1–5, Paul turned an immoral man over to Satan to destroy his flesh so his spirit might be saved. In 2 Corinthians 12:7, Paul said Satan tormented him so he wouldn't exalt himself. Satan's end goal in this encounter with David was to steal, kill, and destroy.

1 Chronicles 21:2–4: David ordered Joab to count Israel from Beer-sheba in the south to Dan in the north. But Joab protested, asking David why he would want to bring guilt on Israel by doing this. Joab knew this was not God's timing. But David's orders prevailed. Joab traveled through Israel counting the troops, knowing the whole time it was against God's will.

1 Chronicles 21:5–7: Compare the count in this story with the count in 2 Samuel 24. John MacArthur gives a really good perspective on this. While there were 800,000 seasoned soldiers, there could have been another 300,000 men of military age in the military reserve. The difference in the 470,000 versus 500,000 men from Judah could have been 30,000 men from the tribe of Benjamin.[5] Note: Joab did not count the Levites or men from the tribe of Benjamin in 1 Chronicles 21:6. What David did was considered evil in God's sight, so He afflicted Israel. Sin will always bring wrath.

1 Chronicles 21:8–13: When David sinned, there was always genuine repentance. David knew he sinned, and he repented. Great men and women of God always acknowledge when they sin. The guilt of sin weighs on people. God sent Gad, the seer, to tell David to choose one of three options for his punishment. This is the only time in Scripture where God did this. Of the three choices, David chose to fall into God's hands because of His mercy rather than into human hands. David knew the punishment would not be good, but he chose to trust God's mercy even in the midst of His wrath. He realized God's mercies are new every morning.

1 Chronicles 21:14–15: God sent a plague on Israel, and 70,000 men died. Then God sent an angel to destroy Jerusalem. But at the moment of destruction, God instructed the angel to withdraw his hand. This could be the angel of the Lord

---

[3] MacArthur, 487.

[4] MacArthur, 487.

[5] MacArthur, 487.

who visited Abraham, Gideon, and Samson's parents. This could even be the angel with the spirit of death at Passover. This could even be Christ Himself, showing up at Jerusalem with His sword drawn. Ornan was about to receive the wrath of God because of David's sin. The same thing could happen to us. Because of the sin of one man—Adam—we have to deal with the wrath of God as well.

1 Chronicles 21:16–22: When David saw the angel of the Lord with his hand stretched out over Jerusalem, he and the elders fell down before God. David knew that because of his sin, Israel now faced God's wrath. David confessed he was the one who sinned and pleaded that "these sheep," the innocent people, not suffer for his sins. The angel of the Lord ordered Gad to tell David to set up an altar on the threshing floor of Ornan, the Jebusite. Ornan was threshing wheat when he turned and saw the angel (v. 20). David offered Ornan full price to buy the threshing floor. This place, Mt. Moriah, was the same place where Abraham had been willing to sacrifice Isaac.

1 Chronicles 21:23–30: Ornan offered to give the land to David, as well as the oxen and the wheat for the offerings. Ornan intervened on behalf of the people, giving up everything needed for the sacrifice. But David insisted on paying full price. This account says 15 pounds of gold, which was the total cost of everything used in the sacrifice. David then built the altar and offered burnt offerings and fellowship offerings. This site in Jerusalem is where the Al-Aqsa Mosque, the Dome of the Rock, stands today. Just on the other side is the Golden Gate, which leads to the Mount of Olives. One day Jesus will come through that gate and reestablish Himself as King on this land. It's like God really has a purpose for this land. He has a plan to save and redeem His people. When David made his offering and called on the Lord, God answered with fire from heaven. We typically think of fire from heaven in the account of Elijah on Mt. Carmel. It happened at the threshing floor of Ornan, too. Because of His mercy, God spared the city . . . and David trusted God to do that. David remained there in the presence of God.

Closing

We will face times when we ignore others and radically mess up. But when we come before God with a heart of repentance (2 Chronicles 7:14), God will respond. When we repent and turn back to God, we can know that God will respond. Even though we deserve God's wrath, we can be forgiven because of what Christ did on the Cross.

The Daily Word

David was victorious in battle and accumulated more troops. During this season of success, Satan tempted him with the desire to count the people of Israel. The Lord never commanded David to count the people, and it was evil in His eyes. Although God's great mercies ultimately saved Israel, the sin of pride still impacted the nation, and seventy thousand Israelite men died. After this, David continued serving the Lord in humility and obedience because of God's forgiving love and mercy.

Pride often presents itself as a hidden, private sin. It can show up in different ways—too proud to ask for help, too good to do certain tasks, being critical of others, disregarding the advice of others, or being preoccupied with your physical appearance. Just as David's pride affected and almost destroyed a nation, your pride has the ability to greatly impact the lives of others. However, there is still hope. As you walk with Jesus, He desires for you to make every effort to live humbly and unselfishly. *Ask the Lord if you have any prideful areas in your heart.* Then confess this sin and ask for forgiveness. As you allow His grace and mercy to infiltrate your life, the Lord will create in you a clean heart filled with grace and love for others.

Satan stood up against Israel and incited David to count the people of Israel. So David said to Joab and the commanders of the troops, "Go and count Israel from Beer-sheba to Dan and bring a report to me so I can know their number." . . . David said to God, "I have sinned greatly because I have done this thing. Now, please take away Your servant's guilt, for I've been very foolish." —1 Chronicles 21:1–2, 8

Further Scripture: Philippians 2:3; James 4:6; 1 John 1:9

Questions

1. In 1 Chronicles 21:1 Satan was behind David ordering a census of the fighting men. Why do you think 2 Samuel 24:1 made it sound like God incited David to do it?

2. Should the story of David's sin, taking the census and the Lord inflicting punishment on Israel, teach us something about those in leadership over God's people (James 3:1)? How do you see a similar cause and effect in Adam's sin and the consequences on all of humanity?

3. Do you think it was significant that David had foreigners provide many things for the house that would be built for the Lord? If so, how was it significant?

4. According to 1 Chronicles 22:9, who chose the name "Solomon" for David's son? What does this name mean? How does Jesus also bear a name that means peace (Isaiah 9:6)?

5. Read 1 Chronicles 22:10. Who besides Solomon was often referred to as the *Son of David* (Matthew 1:1; Mark 10:47; Luke 18:38)? How did Jesus fulfill this verse?

6. What did the Holy Spirit highlight to you in 1 Chronicles 21—22 through the reading or the teaching?

Lesson 99: 1 Chronicles 23—24

Son of David: The Power of a Plan

Teaching Notes

Intro

I would strongly suggest looking at Mindi's painting for this chapter. It is one of my favorites. There are many different aspects to this painting. It is a picture of an olive tree. At the base, she's used the roots to represent growing sin. Mindi has also used 12 branches that represent the 12 tribes, seven trumpets that represent the priesthood, the harp that represents David's lifestyle of worship, a bird singing to the Lord, the crown of glory, and the scrolls at the bottom that represent the blueprints of the plans for God's people. Today I want to focus on the tribe of Levi.

Teaching

1 Chronicles 23:1: The phrase "old and full of day" describes David as a righteous man. The only other people described that way were Abraham, Isaac, Job, and Moses. Solomon was anointed as king before David passed away. First Kings 3:13–14 contains the promise that was passed down from David to King Solomon. This was the inheritance; this was the blessing. This was the result of King David's righteousness (Deuteronomy 5:33) and an example of a long life well lived.

1 Chronicles 23:2: The leaders of Israel were David's sons, the princes of Israel. First Chronicles 3:1–9 shows David's lineage. David called his sons together, who were still living, to talk about his last days.

1 Chronicles 23:3–4: At this point, the Levitical men totaled 38,000. Why did they count the men who were 30 years or older (Numbers 4:3)? On a practical level, these men were seasoned and mature. Of the 38,000 men, 24,000 were given the task of building the temple, another 6,000 were chosen to be officers and judges.

1 Chronicles 23:5: Also, 4,000 men were chosen to be gatekeepers and 4,000 were chosen to be instrumentalists. King David was a cool inventor. He made many musical instruments like the lyre. What is so cool is that you can see a parallel between the Old and New Testaments in Ephesians 4:11 (1 Corinthians 12:27–31). It is not about being a popular apostle or pastor; it is about being the body of Christ!

As I look at this chapter, what I see coming into play is that they needed 24,000 builders. They needed instrumentalists and judges. Everyone was needed. We are all equal in the body of Christ. Yes, there is an authority structure, but we are all equal. What King David was doing was unfolding the power of the plan—laying out the blueprint. His plan determined who was going to do which tasks and assignments. Because of the confusion in the land at the time, David called his sons to make sure they completely understood their roles.

1 Chronicles 23:6: David divided the 38,000 men into divisions according to Levi's sons. David's logic in dividing the men, according to which son of Levi they descended from, was because he understood that the family ties were strong.

1 Chronicles 23:7–12: As David set up the plan, he worked through family by family, level by level, and name by name.

1 Chronicles 23:13: This was evidence of the everlasting consecration of Moses and Aaron (1 Peter 2:4–10). What Moses had sown years ago was coming to fruition in 1 Peter. What you sow is what you are going to reap. What you do now will affect future generations. In this idea of the royal priesthood, Tersteegen wrote,

> The race of God's anointed priests
> Shall never pass away;
> Before his glorious face they stand,
> And serve Him night and day.
> Though reason raves, and unbelief
> Flows on, a mighty flood,
> They are, and shall be, till the end
> The hidden priests of God.
>
> His chosen souls, their earthly dross
> Consumed in sacred fire,
> To God's own heart their hearts ascend
> In flame of deep desire;
> The incense of their worship fills

His Temple's holiest place;
Their song with wonder fills the heavens,
The glad new song of grace.[1]

We get to participate in the royal priesthood. As Peter said, we are the living stones being formed together—we are the body of Christ. We are the blueprint. We are a part of the plan, the living stones of the Holy Spirit.

1 Chronicles 23:25–26: Remember the book of Judges was a little crazy! Israel was enjoying a level of peace against their previous adversaries. The ark of the covenant would now be safely kept in a new palatial structure. David's tabernacle would be a permanent structure, the center of worship for all Israel and beyond. What made this a holy place wasn't the gold or the precious stones. What made this place holy was that this was where the Holy One was.

1 Chronicles 23:27: Unfortunately, holy places do not always stay holy. When we start to worship structures and buildings more than God, He removes His presence. God's presence did not reside in this new temple forever. The temple spoken of here is no longer in Jerusalem, and this is what happens when we kick God out of the building.

Closing

David, under the anointing of God Himself, set the stage for what would be built. He committed the plan to the Lord. We'll see in the coming chapters how this plan plays out. Spoiler alert: It succeeds! This planning phase spills over into chapter 24. Layer upon layer, brick by brick, King David was building his life-long dream—to build for the Lord a house worthy of Him. David was putting his affairs in order so that the transition to Solomon's reign was seamless and efficient. The blueprint was in place and we begin to see the power of this plan.

The Daily Word

King David outlined the Levite's specific assignments and roles for the temple, a permanent home for the presence of the Lord. The Levites received new assignments because transporting the tabernacle was no longer needed. In the temple, they would assist the sons of Aaron with the service. Specifically, it was important

---

[1] Gerhard Tersteegen (1697–1769), "The Race of God's Anointed Priests," trans. Emma F. Bevan (1827–1909), Hymn Time, http://www.hymntime.com/tch/htm/r/a/c/e/racegods.htm.

to have regular temple music. Therefore, every morning and evening, they were instructed to stand and give thanks and praise to the Lord.

As New Testament believers, the Lord's presence is with you always. He promises to never leave you. The Lord delights when you praise and give Him thanks. He tells you, "In everything give thanks." Today, be intentional! Make it a priority to stand up in the morning and give thanks and praise to the Lord! Then do it again in the evening. Perhaps before you eat dinner, take five minutes to stand up and tell the Lord why you are thankful for the day and give Him praise! Sometimes life can get mundane. Sometimes life is just plain hard. But through it all, the Lord's presence remains with you. So *stop, stand up, and give Him praise!* Today is going to be a great day in the presence of the Lord!

They are also to stand every morning to give thanks and praise to the Lord, and likewise in the evening. —1 Chronicles 23:30

Further Scripture: Psalm 9:1; Psalm 95:2–3; Matthew 28:20b

Questions

1. In 1 Chronicles 23:3, why was the census taken only on the Levites who were 30 years of age or older (Numbers 4:1–4)?

2. The Levites were ordered by God to take care of the temple. Where do you think David got the idea to put specific families in charge of specific duties? Do you think this was inspired?

3. In 1 Chronicles 24:2, Nadab and Abihu died before their father. How did they die and why (Leviticus 10:1–2)?

4. What did the Holy Spirit highlight to you in 1 Chronicles 23—24 through the reading or the teaching?

Lesson 100: 1 Chronicles 25—26

Son of David: Receiving God's Blessing

Teaching Notes

Intro

This is a time to celebrate. This is lesson 100, and you've almost made it through the entire first year of study. That's an accomplishment! As we continue through the historical books, we're nearing the end of the study of 1 Chronicles. First Chronicles 25 covers the Levitical musicians and Chapter 26 looks at the gatekeepers and their families.

Chapter 26 looks at the gatekeepers who played an important role, but they mostly went unrecognized. When they were noticed, it was because someone needed something from them. Two of the three Levitical families served as gatekeepers—the Korahites and the Merarites, but not the Gershonites. Verses 1–11 look at the families of the gatekeepers, and verses 12–19 look at the roles assigned to the gatekeepers. We're going to unpack chapter 26 and then look specifically at one gatekeeper.

Teaching

1 Chronicles 26:1–11: The Korahites were listed in verses 1–9. Obed-edom, listed in verse 4, was described as the blessed (2 Samuel 6:10–11; 1 Chronicles 13:13–14). This Levite house was where David placed the ark for three months. God blessed Obed-edom with eight sons (vv. 4–5). Obed-edom's grandsons were proof of the fulfillment of this prophecy. Sixty-two capable men were descended from Obed-edom (vv. 6–8). Children are a blessing from the Lord. In verses 10–11, the sons of the Merarites are named. The total number of descendants was 93, and two-thirds of those listed were from Obed-edom (vv. 1–11).

1 Chronicles 26:12–19: From *Nelson's Commentary*, we learn about the division of duties and the roles the Korahites and Merarites filled, as gatekeepers:

- Guarded the temple gates (1 Chronicles 26:16b).
- In charge of equipment (1 Chronicles 9:23).

- Responsible for the temple treasuries (1 Chronicles 9:26).
- Oversaw the contributions to the temple (2 Kings 12:9; 22:4; 2 Chronicles 31:14).
- Took care of the articles for temple services (1 Chronicles 9:28).
- Took care of the furnishings, oil, and spices in the temple (1 Chronicles 9:29).
- Mixed the spices for sacrifices (1 Chronicles 9:30).
- Baked the bread for offerings (1 Chronicles 9:31).
- Set the bread out for the Sabbath (1 Chronicles 9:32).
- Provided the music (1 Chronicles 9:33).
- Oversaw the chambers and supply rooms (1 Chronicles 23:28; 26:20–29).
- Prepared the baked goods (Exodus 25:30).
- Oversaw the supplies and furnishings (1 Chronicles 28:13–18).[2]

Obed-edom was assigned to the south gate, and his sons oversaw the storehouses (v. 15).

1 Chronicles 26:20–32: Some of the Levites were assigned to be in charge of the treasuries and other official positions.

The first time we looked at Obed-edom, we didn't get to explore what it means to be "blessed." As I was reading this chapter, it was clear that Obed-edom was blessed significantly beyond his brothers. I want to look at what it means to be "blessed."

The word "Targum" refers to spoken paraphrases, explanations, and expansions of the Jewish Scripture that a rabbi would give in the common language of the listeners, often Aramaic. For example, when the Amish have church every other Sunday, they use the Pennsylvania Dutch language in their service. But when the service is completed, people can comment on the teaching in English. The Targum was when Scripture was delivered in one language and then discussed in their own language. It's a translation or an interpretation of the Scripture.[3] There was a Targum written on 1 Chronicles 13:13–14, about what it means to be blessed. The Targum says at the end of 1 Chronicles 13, although it is NOT Scripture itself: "And the Word of the Lord blessed Obed-edom, and his children, and his grand-children; and his wife conceived, and his eight daughters-in-law, and each brought forth eight at one birth, insomuch that in one day

---

[2] Earl D. Radmacher, Ronald B. Allen, and H. Wayne House, eds., *Nelson's New Illustrated Bible Commentary* (Nashville: Thomas Nelson, 1999), 526–27.

[3] George Knopper, *The Anchor Bible Dictionary: 1 Chronicles* (New Haven, CT: Yale University Press, 2004), n.p.

there were found of fathers and children fourscore and one; and He blessed and increased greatly all that belonged to him."[4] (Psalm 127:3–5)

Obed-edom got to this point because for three months he was surrounded with the presence of the Lord. The ark is a sign of the covenant God made with His people, a record of God's dealings with their rebellions, and an instrument of communion between God and His people. God's presence and the tablets of God's law were in Obed-edom's house (Deuteronomy 6:1–9).

Closing

In 1 Chronicles 26 is one man who was faithful enough to receive the ark and to use that time for his family. Don't miss this time as the opportunity to pour into your family so they too can receive God's blessing. Luke 11:28 proclaims those who hear the Word of God will be blessed.

The Daily Word

The chronicler remembered Obed-edom, recalling how God had *blessed him*. Obed-edom, a gatekeeper by profession, joined the musicians as they carried the Ark of the Covenant to Jerusalem. This gatekeeper/musician had eight sons, and the chronicler recorded sixty-two *capable men* as descending from Obed-edom.

Children are a gift from the Lord, a heritage, and a reward. The Lord delights in the concept of family, and as followers of Christ, He calls you His son or daughter. Perhaps the concept of family stirs up difficult emotions, and you feel pain or recall hurt. Today, ask the Lord to begin to heal this area of your life and bring about reconciliation. On the other hand, perhaps you have children, and you need to pause today and thank the Lord for the gift of children. Maybe you need to ask the Lord for fresh wisdom in parenting and in training them up in the Word of God. Through all the emotions the idea of family and children bring, you are called to give thanks and rejoice. *The Lord sees you and will bless you as you depend upon Him* entirely for the needs of your children and even for your deepest pain. He is working, even when you can't see Him. His love is everlasting.

Obed-edom also had sons: Shemaiah the firstborn, Jehozabad the second, Joah the third, Sachar the fourth, Nethanel the fifth, Ammiel the sixth, Issachar the seventh, and Peullethai the eighth, for God blessed him.
—1 Chronicles 26:4–5

Further Scripture: Psalm 127:3–5; Matthew 5:3; Romans 12:18

---

[4] Adam Clark, *Adam Clark's Bible Commentary: 1 Chronicles* (Nashville: Abingdon, 2004), n.p.

Questions

1. In 1 Chronicles 25:1, Asaph and Heman were mentioned. Where else in the Bible can we find these men (1 Chronicles 15:19; Psalm 50; 73—83; 88)?

2. Why do you think the practice of casting lots was used to assign duties in the temple (Leviticus 16:8; 1 Samuel 14:41; Proverbs 16:33)?

3. In your opinion, what was the purpose of David appointing the Hebronites as head over the two-and-a-half tribes West of the Jordan?

4. What did the Holy Spirit highlight to you in 1 Chronicles 25—26 through the reading or the teaching?

Lesson 101: 1 Chronicles 27—28

Son of David: Passing On the Plans of the Temple

Teaching Notes

Intro

Our hope is that your time spent studying the Bible has been fruitful, even when it's difficult to understand. The important thing is to keep studying, because the more you know about God's Word, the more it will come out of you. As we move to the end of 1 Chronicles, there's still a lot for us to learn.

Teaching

1 Chronicles 28:1–10: David brought together the leaders of Israel—all the officers of the tribes, commanders, captains of the army, the stewards that took care of everything David had, the officials, the valiant men, and his mighty men of valor (v. 1). David told them that while his heart wanted to build a temple for God, God had told him that was not His plan (vv. 2–3). Rather, God promised David's desire would be fulfilled through his son, Solomon (vv. 4–6). David was still the person with whom God had made His covenant. Meanwhile, God chose Solomon as the next king to sit on the throne of Israel (v. 5). As king, Solomon would build God's Temple (vv. 6–7). God reveals to us what He plans. In verse 7, God's revealed promise to David was still in effect . . . David's lineage would pass through Solomon all the way to Christ.

The Davidic covenant God established with David would continue through his son, Solomon, and would end in the ministry of Jesus (2 Samuel 7:12–16). Jesus will be the one that sits on the throne eternally. God does not do anything without revealing it first to His people (Amos 3:7). God instructed David to seek and obey His commands so His promise would come to pass (v. 8). Then in verse 10, God told Solomon he had to know the God of his father and serve Him through the establishment of God's temple so He could dwell among His followers (John 3:16). Most importantly, Solomon was not to forsake God as His God.

1 Chronicles 28:11–19: David gave the complete plans of the temple to Solomon (vv. 11–12). The plans also included how the priests and the Levites were to complete the work and serve the Lord in the Temple (v. 13). The plans also included how much gold and silver was needed to complete the temple and create the furnishings (vv. 14–18). David explained all the details were written with God's hand upon him (v. 19).

1 Chronicles 28:20–21: David told Solomon to be strong and courageous because God would be with him and would direct his leadership in the building of the temple.

Closing

The temple was extraordinarily ornate. It was one of the ancient wonders of the world. But the temple itself, rather than God who dwelled there, became the target for the people. We have to be careful and make sure we don't put all our energy into buildings but rather into the people. We are to be a kingdom of priests, not caretakers.

The Daily Word

King David gathered the leaders, commanders, officials in charge of all the property and cattle, the court officials, the fighting men, and the brave warriors. When they were all together, King David rose and humbly shared his heart. He talked honestly and vulnerably. He explained how it was on his heart to build the temple, but God said He had a different plan. Therefore, David yielded to the Lord and His plans for the temple.

Have you ever been so burdened *in your heart* to do something and yet the Lord suddenly redirected your plans? You may have been passionately moving along in one direction, and then you have a "but God said to me" moment like David. Therefore you yielded to God's new plan and accepted it. It may not have made any sense. It may have even seemed goofy to those on the outside. But you knew the Lord was redirecting you, and you couldn't delay responding to His leading and guidance. You dropped the pride. You stopped worrying what others might think. And you obediently followed His voice. This may even be what you need to do today. Remember, He will not fail you when you follow Him. Trust Him with all your heart, and don't depend on your own understanding. He will direct your path as you walk humbly, depending on the Lord.

Then King David rose to his feet and said, "Listen to me, my brothers and my people. It was in my heart to build a house as a resting place for the ark of the Lord's covenant and as a footstool for our God. I had made preparations

to build, but God said to me, 'You are not to build a house for My name because you are a man of war and have shed blood.'" —1 Chronicles 28:2–3

Further Scripture: Proverbs 3:5–6; Proverbs 16:9; Romans 12:2

Questions

1. Why did each division of the army serve only one month out of the year?

2. Benaiah was the commander of the third division. Why was he considered a great hero in Israel (2 Samuel 23:20–21)?

3. Whom did David summon to give instructions? What was David doing in Chapter 28 that made him a great leader?

4. What was the message David gave to all Israel? What was the message he gave to his son Solomon? How many times did David tell Solomon to be strong (1 Chronicles 22:13; 28:20)?

5. David exhorted Solomon to "know the God of your father intimately." How can you personally come to know Jesus more intimately (John 14:21–24)?

6. What did the Holy Spirit highlight to you in 1 Chronicles 27—28 through the reading or the teaching?

Lesson 102: 1 Chronicles 29

Son of David: Finding Delight in the Lord

Teaching Notes

Intro

This is the final study in 1 Chronicles. This is, for all intents and purposes, King David's final address to the people. In the past couple of chapters, we've looked at how God gave David the specifics for what the temple would be like. In this chapter, the responsibility for the construction of the temple was passed on to Solomon.

The underlying theme in this entire chapter is finding *delight* in God (Psalm 119:16, 47). The word "delight" can be understood as taking great pleasure in something or to revel or glory in something. David had a heart for worship, seen throughout his entire life.

Teaching

1 Chronicles 29:1–9: There had been a fight over who would take David's throne, and two of David's sons died in the fight. Therefore, David called the people together to make sure they understood God chose Solomon as the next king (v. 1). Solomon was around 20 years old, but he was seen as young and inexperienced. Therefore, Solomon would be surrounded by teachers and fathers who would support and help him (1 Corinthians 4:15). Further, David had gathered the provisions for building the temple—gold, silver, bronze, precious stones, and marble (v. 2).

These materials created a great mosaic within the temple, providing another foreshadowing of the spiritual kingdom to come in the New Jerusalem (Revelation 21:1–2, 10–12, 18–20). The 12 stones mentioned in Revelation point to the future and the coming of the new temple that is within us, a mosaic of living stones (1 Corinthians 3:16–17; 6:19). We are a sanctuary for the living God; we are no longer our own (1 Peter 2:4–5).

David also gave his personal treasures of gold and silver for the building of the temple (vv. 3–4a). The British Museum has established that a talent weighs 66.5 pounds. Therefore, based on today's economy, David's personal gifts would be valued at more than $1,267,000,000 or $1.26 billion. Remember that David was unwilling to give anything to God that cost him nothing (1 Chronicles 21:24). After telling what he gave, David asked those in the assembly to give to the work of the temple as well (v. 5b). He asked them to consecrate themselves by declaring what they had as sacred and was dedicated for use in a divine purpose. The leaders and officials gave willingly with delight (2 Corinthians 9:7). They gave cheerfully and radically. They have gold, silver, bronze, and iron that today would be worth approximately $2,268,000,000—almost twice what David personally gave (v. 7). The people, along with King David, rejoiced and took delight in what the leaders gave, and David also rejoiced in delight (vv. 8–9).

1 Chronicles 29:10–18: David led the people in prayer, praising God as being eternal (v. 10), reminiscent of the line that's been added to the Lord's Prayer in Matthew: "For thine is the kingdom, and the power, and the glory, forever and ever." David praised in delight. David's prayer described God's greatness and power, His glory and splendor and majesty, as the creator of everything, and the owner and provider of everything (vv. 11–13). David worshipped with delight (Psalm 100:4). David acknowledged everything that had been given to God belonged to God already (Psalm 24:1–2; Haggai 2:8). Everything belongs to God (vv. 14, 16).

In verse 15, David gave a prophetic word, acknowledging that "our days on earth are like a shadow, without hope." David stated that the people had given joyfully, with delight, because of who God is and what He had done (vv. 17–18).

1 Chronicles 29:19–25: Then David asked God to help Solomon keep his heart fully focused on Him in carrying out His commands (v. 19). David's prayer set Solomon up for success. It shows the power of a father's prayer and blessing, which we too can give to our children. David led the people in worship, and they bowed down and gave homage with delight to the Lord (v. 20). The next day, offerings were made to the Lord, and they ate and drank with great joy and delight in God's presence (vv. 21–22a). Afterwards, they anointed Solomon as king a second time, making it abundantly clear Solomon was God's chosen heir to the throne (v. 22b). Solomon took the throne, and all the leaders and David's mighty men, and all of the remaining sons of David, pledged their allegiance to King Solomon (vv. 23–24). The Lord exalted Solomon, and his reign prospered (v. 25).

1 Chronicles 29:26–30: The remaining verses give the summary of David's reign. As king over Israel, David reigned 40 years: reigning at Hebron for seven years and 33 years in Jerusalem (vv. 26–27). David died "at a ripe old age, full of days, riches, and honor" (v. 28). This is a sign of a life well lived, a sign of a man full of faith just like Moses, Abraham, and Isaac, who had gone before him (vv. 28–30).

Closing

Verse 25 says God bestowed on Solomon "such royal majesty as had not been bestowed on any king over Israel before him." Why? Because Solomon had the blessing of his father, David. Because Solomon delighted in the Lord as his father David had, he received everything David originally wanted. When we *delight* in God, He gives us the desires of our hearts.

The Daily Word

Before the temple building began, King David spoke to the assembly and explained the task was great because it was for the Lord, not man. King David provided for the expenses as best he could but also approached the leaders and asked them to set money aside as well. As people who worshipped and delighted in the Lord, they answered David's plea for resources. Then the people rejoiced and worshipped the Lord together because of their willingness to give with a whole heart.

Every good and perfect gift comes from the Lord. One way God calls you to worship Him is through the giving of your resources. But remember, giving to the Lord is not meant to be a drag. God doesn't want you to give because of tradition, obligation, or peer pressure. The Lord desires for you to give with a cheerful heart. In the Greek, this means "hilarious giving." In other words, it means to give up of yourself even beyond the point it makes sense, and yet you give out of obedience to the Lord. If the Spirit leads you to give a specific amount and it seems *hilarious*, trust the Lord because it will make sense in His economy. God will grant you abundant grace, and you will have everything you need for the work He has called you to! *Is the Lord asking you to give hilariously for His work today?* Respond in obedience as an act of worship.

Moreover, because of my delight in the house of my God, I now give my personal treasures of gold and silver for the house of my God over and above all that I've provided for the holy house . . . Now who will volunteer to consecrate himself to the Lord today? —1 Chronicles 29:3, 5

Further Scripture: 1 Chronicles 29:6, 9; Psalm 37:4; 2 Corinthians 9:7–8

Questions

1. Why did David give all of his private treasures to the building of the temple? What are you so passionate about that you would give everything toward the cause (Matthew 6:21)? Is your passion toward worldly things or Godly things?

2. How did the leaders respond to David's plea for giving toward the temple of God (2 Corinthians 9:7)? In the context of this Scripture, what does the word "cheerful" mean? When was the last time you gave in that manner to the Lord or His work?

3. How do you see a similarity between how David started his prayer of praise in verse 10 and the Lord's Prayer (Matthew 6:9–13)?

4. What do you see as David's most important prayer request concerning Solomon (1 Chronicles 29:19; Psalm 72:1)?

5. What do you think the difference is between the anointing of Solomon the first time (1 Kings 1:38–39) and 1 Chronicles 29:21–25?

6. What did the Holy Spirit highlight to you in 1 Chronicles 29 through the reading or the teaching?

Lesson 103: 2 Chronicles 1—2

Royal Throne: Preparing to Build the Temple

Teaching Notes

Intro

Today we start our study of 2 Chronicles. Originally, Chronicles was written as one book, and it wasn't until later the book was made into 1 and 2 Chronicles. Our phrase for 1 Chronicles is *Son of David* because the book constantly points to the coming Messiah, the *Son of David*. Our phrase for 2 Chronicles is *Royal Throne*, because it focuses mainly on the kings of Judah, not Israel, who were also tied to David. Mindi's paintings for 1 and 2 Chronicles is a diptych (two separate paintings that create one picture when placed together), and you'll see that the trumpets from the first painting carry across to the second.

Chronicles means "the annals or happenings of the days," and it was written to the Jews after they returned from their captivity in Babylon. At one point, the book was titled, "The Things Omitted," because it contained so much material not included anywhere else in Scripture. Tradition holds that Ezra was the chronicler (Ezra 7:1–6). The exiles returned to Jerusalem after 70 years in captivity in three phases with: (1) Zerubbabel (Ezra 1—6); (2) Ezra (Ezra 7—10); and (3) Nehemiah (Nehemiah 1—13).

MacArthur explains that the exiles returned to a city in ruins with no Hebrew king, no security, no temple, no dominant region to dwell in, few divine blessings, little of the kingdom's former wealth, and no presence of God in Jerusalem.[1] Fifty-five percent of Chronicles is new material.

Second Chronicles 1 records Solomon's succession to the throne of David. God told Solomon to ask for whatever he wanted, and he requested wisdom. David asked for wisdom too (1 Chronicles 22:12). God granted Solomon's request with great wealth and wisdom.

Chapters 2—9 cover Solomon's reign, and chapter 10 records the rebellion of ten tribes in which the kingdom became divided. Chapters 11—36 cover the kings of Judah: Asa's renovation of the altar (2 Chronicles 15), Jehoshaphat's establishment of missions (chapter 18); Joash's repair of the Temple (2 Chronicles

---

[1] John MacArthur, *The MacArthur Bible Commentary* (Nashville: Thomas Nelson, 2005), 478.

23—24); Hezekiah's opening of the Temple (chapters 29—31); and Josiah's discovery of the "book of the law" (2 Chronicles 34—35). In these chapters, renewal, revival, and reformation took place. Captivity is covered in 2 Chronicles 36:15–23. Amidst all this, the *Royal Throne* is established.

Teaching

2 Chronicles 2:1–10: Walking out his father David's desire, Solomon was ready to build the temple for the name of Yahweh (Hebrew name for God meaning the LORD), and a palace for himself (v. 1). He didn't build a cage for God but rather a temple in God's name to honor Him. Solomon assigned tasks to men as porters, stonecutters, and supervisors (v. 2). Solomon then asked for help from King Hiram of Tyre, asking for cedars to build the temple to worship Yahweh (vv. 3–4). The temple would be for the one great God who cannot be contained by heaven or earth (vv. 5–6). Solomon requested a craftsman who could engrave and work with yarn to work with the craftsmen from Judah appointed by David (v. 7). King Solomon also asked for logs from Lebanon and promised his craftsmen would help Hiram's workers to cut and prepare the logs (vv. 8–9). Then he promised to pay the workers with an abundance of food supplies (v. 10).

2 Chronicles 2:11–16: Hiram replied to Solomon's request by praising the God of Israel who gave King David's son such wisdom (vv. 11–12). He sent an engraver, Huram-abi, to work with Solomon's craftsmen on the choice metal and stones for the temple (vv. 13–14). Hiram then asked the king to send the food supplies he had promised, and Hiram's men would begin to cut the cedar trees down and transport them to the port of Joppa in Israel (vv. 15–16). Solomon was given everything he asked for.

2 Chronicles 2:17–18: Solomon took a census of all the foreigners (non-Israelites) in the land and found 153,600. Then, he put the men to work: 70,000 as porters, 80,000 as stonecutters, and 3,600 as supervisors.

Closing

Solomon's temple was the first of three temples that are discussed in Scripture. Solomon's temple took seven-and-a-half years to build. However, Solomon's temple was destroyed in 586 BC. Zerubbabel rebuilt the second temple, a much more modest temple, upon returning to Jerusalem after the exile. Then King Herod expanded this temple in 20 BC that was destroyed by the Romans in AD 70. Herod's temple was the one Jesus visited. There is no physical temple today.

However, Hosea 3:4–5 explains, "The Israelites must live many days without king or prince, without sacrifice or sacred pillar, and without ephod or household idols. Afterward, the people of Israel will return and seek the LORD their God and David their king. They will come with awe to the LORD and to His goodness in the last days."

Ezekiel 37:27–28 states God will dwell among them and His sanctuary will be with them forever after the reunification of Israel. Jesus talked about a third temple (Matthew 24:15–21). In the last days, we will see the evil one standing in the holy place (2 Thessalonians 2:1–4), so there has to be a temple then.

On the Temple Mount today in Jerusalem are two Muslim holy places. It's the place where Abraham met Melchizedek (Genesis 14), where Abraham came to sacrifice his son Isaac (Genesis 22), where David bought Ornan's threshing floor to build an altar to God's (1 Chronicles 21), and it's the place where Solomon built the first temple. There's discussion of where the third temple will be built in the last days. In Revelation 11:1–2, the temple of God is measured.

All this is to say, I believe there will be a physical third temple built in Jerusalem. When it's completed, we'll be that much closer to the return of Christ.

The Daily Word

In preparing the temple, God had to first prepare Solomon. The chronicler describes Solomon as a leader and a king—a man not competent out of his own power but rather a man the Lord highly exalted and was with. When the Lord gave Solomon the opportunity to request one thing, Solomon asked for wisdom. And with wisdom from the Lord, he also received wealth, riches, and glory.

The New Testament describes wisdom from the Lord as pure, peace-loving, gentle, compliant, full of mercy and good fruits, and without favoritism or hypocrisy. As a follower of Christ, Paul wrote you are to pay attention to how you walk, not as unwise but as wise because the days you live in are hard. *How will today be different from yesterday if in every situation you pause and ask the Lord for wisdom?* You are promised that when you call upon the Lord, He will answer you and tell you great things you do not know. Today, pause in every situation and seek the Lord for wisdom, believe He will hear you, and look for His answer. Fear the Lord because He wants to do great things in your life today!

Now grant me wisdom and knowledge so that I may lead these people, for who can judge this great people of Yours? —2 Chronicles 1:10

Further Scripture: Jeremiah 33:3; Ephesians 5:15–16; James 3:17

Questions

1. What was the incredible way for Solomon to begin his reign as king and show he was a godly leader?

2. What was the purpose of going to the tent of meeting? When you go to church, do you sometimes catch yourself desiring to meet more with people or with God?

3. Although Solomon had wealth, health, and fame, why does that not necessarily mean he was satisfied or content (Ecclesiastes 2:1–9, 11)? How does a believer experience joy in the Lord (Psalm 16:11; John 15:9–11; Philippians 4:4)?

4. What were some things King Solomon asked King Hiram for to help build the temple? What was King Hiram's reaction to the request?

5. How does the concept of a sacred space where God meets with His people point to Jesus, the Holy Spirit, and the Church (John 1:14; 1 Corinthians 6:19; Ephesians 2:21)?

6. What did the Holy Spirit highlight to you in 2 Chronicles 1—2 through the reading or the teaching?

Lesson 104: 2 Chronicles 3—4

Royal Throne: "Then He Made"

Teaching Notes

Intro

Our theme for 2 Chronicles is *Royal Throne*. In 2 Chronicles, the son of David (Solomon) was able to walk out what David had been promised—the building of the temple for God in Jerusalem. In chapters 1—2, Solomon asked for help from King Hiram of Tyre in working together to build the temple. Remember this was written to explain to those returning from Babylonian exile what had happened in the past. One of those returning exiles, Zerubbabel, rebuilt the temple after he returned, so these specifics would have been important to him (Zechariah 4:10).

Teaching

2 Chronicles 3:1–4: The Sanctuary Foundation. Solomon began building the temple on Mount Moriah (now known as the temple mount and located across the Kidron Valley from the Mount of Olives) in the place David had prepared on the threshing floor of Ornan (v.1). It was the same place where Abraham met Melchizedek (Genesis 14), and where Abraham came to sacrifice his son Isaac (Genesis 22). Land in Israel is always important. This was the place where the Lord showed up to David and Ornan. The building began on the second day of the second month of the fourth year of Solomon's reign, which, according to MacArthur, would have been in April or May of 966 BC.[1] The project was completed in seven-and-a-half years. The temple was 90 feet long and 30 feet wide (v. 3), with a portico that added another 30 feet and was overlaid with pure gold (v. 4). It was not a huge building and is smaller than most church buildings today. The craftsman leading the work was Huram-abi from Tyre (2 Chronicles 2:13).

2 Chronicles 3:5–7: The Main Sanctuary. The chronicler continues with detailed descriptions, these for the main room of the sanctuary. It included palm trees, possibly as an image of the tree of life, and chains, possibly created using buds

---

[1] John MacArthur, *The MacArthur Bible Commentary* (Nashville: Thomas Nelson, 2005), 496.

and flowers to represent the Garden of Eden (v. 5).[2] The term "gold of Parvaim" is not understood by scholars, but the assumption is that it was a purer and more valuable type of gold (v. 6). Most everything in the temple was covered with gold; and cherubim were carved into the wood (v.7).

2 Chronicles 3:8–14: The Holy of Holies. This would become the permanent dwelling of the ark and God's presence. The sacredness of the Holy of Holies is seen in the 45,000 pounds (23 tons) of gold that was used. Solomon's attention to the details is staggering.

The statement "then he made" used throughout this chapter reflects that the work was done by Solomon (v. 8). Martin Selman states Solomon was faithful to the plans God gave him.[3] The plan came to fruition because Solomon walked it out. Gary Linten writes, "God is not looking for perfect people, He is simply searching for those who are devoted to Him."[4] If you're praying for revival, you should walk it out!

What does the Bible say about faithfulness?

- 1 Samuel 26:23: David was faithful to God and waited on God to fulfill his calling to be king.
- 2 Chronicles 16:9: God is looking for those whose hearts are completely His.
- Psalm 12:1: God is looking for the faithful.
- Proverbs 20:6: Who can find a trustworthy man?
- Proverbs 28:20: A faithful man will have many blessings.
- Matthew 25:21: Well done, you good and faithful servant.
- Luke 16:10, 12: Those who are faithful with little are also faithful with much; those who are unfaithful will lose what they have.
- 1 Corinthians 4:1–2: We are managers of God's mysteries.
- Revelation 2:10: Be faithful until death.

Many of us do not realize we've been given the blueprints to God's plans because we haven't been faithful in our lives. We see the level of Solomon's faithfulness

[2] Earl D. Radmacher, Ronald B. Allen, and H. Wayne House, eds., *Nelson's New Illustrated Bible Commentary* (Nashville: Thomas Nelson, 1999), 538.

[3] Martin Selman, *2 Chronicles*, Tyndale Old Testament Commentary (Downer's Grove, IL: InterVarsity, 1994), 304.

[4] Gary Linten, "12 Scriptures on Being Faithful to God," Ministrymaker, April 7, 2022, https://www.ministrymaker.com/12-scriptures-on-being-faithful-to-god#:~:text=Scriptures%20on%20Being%20Faithful%20to%20God%201%20Samuel,of%20Israel%2C%20had%20been%20trying%20to%20kill%20David.

because he built the porch and the foundation of the temple well. He built the sanctuary well. He built the Holy of Holies extremely well. He handled rightly the tasks God gave him to do. He did it well.

2 Chronicles 3:14: *The Temple Veil.* Solomon used the same colors for the veil in the temple as was used for the veil of the tabernacle. Cherubim were woven into it.

2 Chronicles 3:15–17: *The Entrance Pillars.* Two free-standing pillars that were 27 feet high were placed in the entrance to the temple. More chainwork was made in the inner sanctuary and placed on the pillars (1 Kings 7:17–20).

2 Chronicles 4: The furnishings and the lampstands are described in chapter 4.

Closing

Selman recorded that the responses to the temple were conflicting. Some recognized the temple would bring God near to the people and give them great joy (Psalm 27:4–6), and attending the temple provided the people a way to come into God's presence (2 Samuel 22:7; Jonah 2:7). On the other hand, the actual design and layout of the temple emphasized how difficult it was to get to God. The only Israelites who were allowed into the temple were the Levites and the priests. Only the high priest could enter the Holy of Holies, and then only once each year. Therefore, the people never saw any of what is described in this chapter. "To most Israelites, therefore, the temple was an unseen world. God had drawn near to them, but the way to him was hedged around with many restrictions."[5]

The presence of God was unseen and untouchable by the majority of the people. The temple was beautifully built, but no one could get in it to come to God. But, at the death of Christ, the veil in the sanctuary was split from top to bottom so everyone, even us ordinary people, could have access to God (Matthew 27:51; Hebrews 10:19–20). Solomon's faithfulness in building the temple is a shadow of what is in heaven (Hebrews 8:5).

The Daily Word

After Solomon's coronation as king, he didn't waste any time getting started on the temple. Early in the fourth year of his reign, he completed the foundation—the first step in the building project. King Solomon believed God would establish the plans and provide the strength necessary to walk it out

---

[5] Selman, 304.

in faith. The Lord remained faithful, and Solomon remained obedient to the plans given by the Lord.

God calls you to live obediently as He leads you. Is there anything you know God has asked you to do, but you are just blowing it off? It could be sending a letter, giving to a person in need, seeking reconciliation, or even cleaning your house or car. *The Lord desires to see your faithfulness even in the small things entrusted to you.* So today, stop procrastinating, write it down, ask the Lord for wisdom, and then do it! Just as Solomon started with the foundation of the temple, put the first "block" into whatever the Lord has asked you to do. The Lord will be faithful as you walk obediently. Just get started!

Then Solomon began to build the Lord's temple in Jerusalem on Mount Moriah where the Lord had appeared to his father David, at the site David had prepared on the threshing floor of Ornan the Jebusite. He began to build on the second day of the second month in the fourth year of his reign. These are Solomon's foundations for building God's temple. —2 Chronicles 3:1–3

Further Scripture: Psalm 119:60; Matthew 25:21; Romans 1:5

Questions

1. Where else do we see Mount Moriah mentioned (Genesis 22:2)? What significant event occurred there? What was the outcome?

2. Solomon began building the house of the Lord on the threshing floor of Ornan the Jebusite. Why this place? What took place there involving his father David (2 Samuel 24:16)? What led up to this happening (2 Samuel 24)?

3. In 2 Chronicles 3—4, the temple was being built. Where else do we find some of these specifications (Exodus 36—38)? What are some of the differences between the two?

4. What did the Holy Spirit highlight to you in 2 Chronicles 3—4 through the reading or the teaching?

Lesson 105: 2 Chronicles 5—6

Royal Throne: Praising God in One Voice

Teaching Notes

Intro

I've enjoyed this study, but I didn't expect to. After all we've gone through with the historical books, 2 Chronicles seemed like a big mess. But the Word of God is alive and active. When we open it up, God can show us something powerful within it. In 2 Chronicles so far, we've been looking at how Solomon fulfilled David's desire to build a temple for the Lord.

MacArthur explains that building the temple took seven-and-a-half years to complete and was finished in the eleventh year of Solomon's reign. The dedication took place 11 months later so it could take place along with the celebration of the Feast of Tabernacles.[1] The temple pointed to the coming of the Messiah and served five important functions for the people of Israel:

1. It served as the center of worship that represented righteous beliefs and worship over many generations.
2. It symbolized God's presence among His people
3. It symbolized God's forgiveness, grace, and mercy, while emphasizing the seriousness of sin.
4. It prepared the way for the coming Messiah, who, as the Lamb of God, would take away sin.
5. It functioned as a place of prayer (2 Chronicles 7:12–17).[2]

Teaching

2 Chronicles 5:1–3: Solomon brought all the things David had set aside from the tabernacle and put them in the treasuries of the temple (v. 1) Then Solomon brought together the elders of Israel so they could bring the ark into the temple,

---

[1] John MacArthur, *The MacArthur Bible Commentary* (Nashville: Thomas Nelson, 2005), 497.

[2] MacArthur, 497.

which, at this time, was in a temporary tent in Jerusalem (2 Samuel 6:17).[3] The men assembled during the festival—the Feast of Tabernacles or Booths (v. 3). The feast celebrated the years of wandering in the wilderness, while worshipping in the tabernacle (which was a tent), so this was an appropriate occasion to relocate the ark to God's permanent dwelling place (Leviticus 23:39–43).

2 Chronicles 5:4–6: This time, the Israelites followed God's instructions. The Levites carried the Ark (v. 4), and the priests and the Levites brought up the holy utensils that had been in the tent (v. 5). Solomon and the congregation of Israel gathered to sacrifice innumerable sheep and cattle (v. 6). Notice Solomon was acting in the role as both priest and king and exercised the privileges of his office by offering sacrifices[4] (1 Chronicles 16:1–3).

2 Chronicles 5:7–10: The ark was placed in the Most Holy Place or Holy of Holies in the temple. There the wings of the cherubim formed a cover above the ark (vv. 7–8). Verse 9 speaks of long poles, about 30 feet in length, and they allowed the priests to minister in the Holy of Holies (like guardrails that guided the high priest to stay in line before God) (Exodus 25:12–15; 1 Kings 8:8). The poles also helped the Levites move the ark into place. The exiles who returned saw no poles because all had been destroyed. *Nelson's Commentary* states that recognizing the poles were missing, charged the returning Jews with emotion since King Nebuchadnezzar's army had destroyed the temple and everything in it.[5] Only the tablets God gave to Moses were in the ark (v. 10).

We have "poles" today to keep us in line with God—His Word and the Holy Spirit. Without these poles, people choose what to accept and what to reject. When we don't function with these poles, our lives become chaotic.

2 Chronicles 5:11–14: The priests, who had been consecrated, came out of the holy place and were met by the Levitical singers and musicians and 120 priests blowing trumpets. The people had never had a temple before, so they continued to celebrate the dedication of the temple (vv. 11–12a). The main families of the Levites were represented as their sons and relatives participated (v. 12b). Everyone joined together to praise and thank God with one voice (v. 13). The temple was filled with the cloud of God's presence, and the glory of the Lord filled the temple (v. 14)

---

[3] Earl D. Radmacher, Ronald B. Allen, and H. Wayne House, eds., *Nelson's New Illustrated Bible Commentary* (Nashville: Thomas Nelson, 1999), 539.

[4] Radmacher et al., 540.

[5] Radmacher et al., 540.

Closing

We are called to come together with one voice in unity and praise:

- Psalm 133:1–3: It is good and pleasant to come together in one voice.
- 2 Chronicles 30:12: It is good to have unity of mind.
- Ephesians 4:1–6: We are to be one in unity.
- Ephesians 4:11–13: We are called to continue together until we all reach unity.
- 1 Corinthians 1:10: We all called together, not in divisions, but perfectly united in mind.
- Colossians 3:12–14: We are to be bound together in unity.
- 1 Corinthians 12:4–6: We've been given different gifts but only one Spirit.
- Romans 15:4–6: We are to be united in mind and voice.
- Romans 15:7–13: We are called to glorify God together . . . in unity.

Second Chronicles 5:14 states the glory of the Lord filled God's temple. When we have one voice, we get to experience God's glory.

The Daily Word

The construction for the temple was completed, and the priests carried the Ark of the Covenant to its proper place in the inner sanctuary. Once in place, King Solomon, along with all the priests and Levitical musicians, regardless of their division or role, *gathered to worship the Lord in one voice*. At this point, the Lord's glory came and filled the temple as a great cloud. The people united together and focused on God alone.

Those who had been divided came together with one voice. Unity happened. God's glory came. *Did you catch it?* Did you see what brings God glory? *Unity in the body of Christ.* What will it take for the church to stop arguing over differences and become *one?* The Lord instructs believers to walk in humility and gentleness, with patience, accepting each other in love, diligently keeping unity of the spirit with the bonds of peace. That peace is Jesus Christ. Worship the Lord in unity because of the love of Christ. Focus on the Lord, not on man. When you have *one* voice, the Lord will reveal His glory. And then others will want to know the love binding you together. Gather together as *one* voice, and expect God's glory!

The trumpeters and singers joined together to praise and thank the Lord with one voice. They raised their voices, accompanied by trumpets, cymbals, and musical instruments, in praise to the Lord: For He is good; His faithful love endures forever. The temple, the Lord's temple, was filled with a cloud. —2 Chronicles 5:13

Further Scripture: John 17:23; Romans 15:6–7; Ephesians 4:1–3

Questions

1. Second Chronicles 5:10 states the only thing in the ark was the Ten Commandments. But in Hebrews 9:4, Paul wrote the pot of manna and Aaron's rod were also in the ark. What do you think happened to them? Any ideas on who would have taken them or why?

2. In 2 Chronicles 5:14, the people gathered and with one voice worshipped God. The house was filled with a cloud. Where else do we see this happening (Exodus 40:34–35)?

3. Throughout time, we have seen that when God's people gather as "one people" and "one voice," mighty things can happen. What is an example (Genesis 11:1–9)? What about during Jesus' time (Acts 2:1–4)? What could we accomplish if we came together with one voice as one people? Could we change a nation?

4. In 2 Chronicles 6:2, Solomon said he built a house for the Lord to reside forever. Is this still true? Why or why not (Acts 17:24–25)? Where does God reside now (John 14:23; 1 Corinthians 3:16)?

5. What did the Holy Spirit highlight to you in 2 Chronicles 5—6 through the reading or the teaching?

Lesson 106: 2 Chronicles 7—8

Royal Throne: "If My People . . ."

Teaching Notes

Intro

Yesterday, we looked at the dedication of the temple after it was completed by Solomon. The people and leaders came together and dedicated the temple in *one voice*. For a season, the people—all of the tribes of Israel—were united in one voice. Chapter 6 contains Solomon's prayer at the dedication. Chapter 7 works through the ceremonies that took place during the dedication. The most recognized verse in 2 Chronicles comes from chapter 7: "And My people who are called by My name humble themselves, pray and seek My face, and turn from their evil ways, then I will hear from heaven, forgive their sin, and heal their land" (v. 14). That's where we're headed in our study of chapter 7 (Luke 2:25).

Teaching

2 Chronicles 7:1–7: After Solomon's prayer, fire came down from heaven and consumed the offering and sacrifices, and God's glory filled the temple (v. 1). This was not the only time fire came from heaven (Leviticus 9:23–24; Judges 6:21; 1 Kings 18:38). God can reveal Himself through fire and through our earnest prayers (James 5:16–18). Both Elijah and Solomon modeled how we should pray. This is important. There are layers of how to pray and what that looks like in 2 Chronicles 7:14. You and I have every right to come before the throne and pray like this.

God's glory so filled (overflowed) the temple that the priests were unable to enter it (v. 2). All the Israelites who gathered saw the fire and God's glory and they responded in homage (v. 3). The people responded with offerings, and Solomon offered 22,000 cattle and 120,000 sheep (vv. 4–5). Selman suggests that to accomplish this, an animal would have to have been sacrificed every three seconds for ten hours for 12 days.[1] These were peace offerings (Leviticus 3:1–17; 7:11–12; 1 Kings 8:62).

---

[1] Martin J. Selman, *2 Chronicles*, Tyndale Old Testament Commentaries (Downer's Grove, IL: InterVarsity, 1994), 351.

Solomon brought the Levites and their musical instruments, and the priests and their trumpets, into the celebration as well "for His faithful love endures forever" (v. 6). That phrase, "for His faithful love endures forever," is the reason behind 1 and 2 Chronicles. No matter what the returning exiles had to face, they could be assured God's faithful love endures forever. There were so many sacrifices the altar couldn't handle it, so Solomon consecrated the courtyard to use as a place of offerings and sacrifices (v. 7).

2 Chronicles 7:8–11: All Israel, from the northern borders of Hamath to the southern borders at the Brook of Egypt, worshipped together for seven days (v. 8). The Feast of the Tabernacles had lasted seven days, and the dedication of the temple lasted seven days. On the eighth day, the Israelites held a sacred assembly to dedicate the altar, and then the people were sent back to their tents (homes), "Rejoicing and with happy hearts for the goodness the LORD had done for David, for Solomon, and for the people of Israel" (vv. 9–10). Solomon finished the temple and the royal palace, which took 22 years to accomplish (v. 11). This verse places the timing of all this as about halfway through Solomon's reign.

2 Chronicles 7:12–22: After all this was completed, the Lord "appeared" to Solomon because He had heard Solomon's prayers (v. 12). Was the appearance through an angel, in a dream, in a vision? This was important for those coming out of exile to be reminded God chose to dwell in the temple in this place (vv. 12–13). God emphasized His power over all the earth and then reminded the Israelites of the conditions of His covenant with them—they were to pray and seek Him and to turn away from their evil ways (v. 14).

This verse was a catalyst for revival for the people of Israel to turn to the Lord (Daniel 9:3–19). Was it meant for the United States? No. But, we can take these conditions and principles and apply them to our own lives. Israel is in the covenant relationship with God, America is not. It makes all the difference.

In verses 15–18, God confirms His covenant with the generations of Israel, a *Royal Throne* that had been established to reign forever. God called them to live as He instructed in verse 14. However, God promised that if Israel did not live that way, if they turned away from Him again, He would uproot the people, destroy the temple, and banish the people (vv. 19–22). Remember that this was exactly what had happened to Israel when they were exiled to Babylon.

Closing

Verse 14 was given as the antidote for the people returning from exile. They could choose to walk in God's ways, or they could face what had happened to Israel when the Babylonian banishment had taken place. Walter C. Kaiser Jr., identifies four conditions for revival to take place that are presented in 2 Chronicles 7:14:[2]

1. *If My people humble themselves*: God's people are called to be humble and to deny themselves, just as Jesus was humble and died Himself on our behalf (Matthew 16:24; Philippians 2:8).
2. *If My people will pray*: God's people are to intercede with God through prayer (1 Samuel 12:23). We participate with God through prayer—through petition, communion, and intercession—in the conflict between Him and Satan. God gives us weapons for the battle—the sword of the Spirit and the power of prayers of intercession (Ephesians 6:17–18).
3. *If My people will seek My face*: Seeking God's "face" is searching for "the joy and benefits that come from experiencing his presence, his approval, and his communion with the likes of humanity."[3] We seek His face by drawing near to Him, by knowing Him, and by experiencing Him.
4. *If My people will turn from their wicked ways*: God's people must turn away from the sin in their lives and repent.

Ephesians 4:27 says not to give Satan a foothold in our lives. If we do these things, Satan cannot get a foothold in our lives. We have only to look to God in the process.

The Daily Word

All King Solomon desired to do for the Lord's temple and his own palace succeeded. After the dedication ceremonies, the Lord responded to Solomon at night, confirming everything Solomon had prayed. The Lord told Solomon that *even if* God's covenant people turn away from Him, if they then *humble themselves, pray and seek His face, and turn from their evil ways*, God would hear them from heaven, forgive their sin, and heal their land.

The principles in this promise from the Lord still hold true today. The Lord remains a forgiving and healing God to the person with a humbled, repentant heart who seeks His face and turns from their wicked ways. The world desperately needs the Lord's gracious, redeeming love. With this in mind, take a moment to pray: "*May we, as God's people, humble ourselves, pray, seek the face of the Lord, and turn from our evil ways. And may God hear our prayers from heaven, forgive our sin*

---

[2] Walter C. Kaiser Jr., "Revival on God's Terms," LifeCoach4God, April 23, 2012, https://verticallivingministries.com/tag/an-exposition-of-2-Chronicles-714-by-dr-walter-kaiser/.

[3] Kaiser.

and heal our land." May you begin with humbling yourself, praying, seeking the face of the Lord, and turning from your evil ways. The time is now.

And My people who are called by My name humble themselves, pray and seek My face, and turn from their evil ways, then I will hear from heaven, forgive their sin, and heal their land. —2 Chronicles 7:14

Further Scripture: Proverbs 8:17; Psalm 34:14; 1 Peter 5:6

Questions

1. In your opinion, what prevented the priests from entering the temple when the glory of the Lord filled the house (2 Chronicles 7:1–3)? What is this presence of God commonly referred to today, and what does it mean?
2. How long do you think the process of sacrificing the 22,000 oxen and 120,000 sheep actually took (2 Chronicles 7:5)? How were the type and number of animals determined (Leviticus 11)?
3. What feast were they celebrating during the time the Temple was being dedicated (Leviticus 23:33–34)?
4. What was God's promise and warning to Solomon for the people and to him personally (2 Chronicles 7:12–14, 17–20)?
5. In 2 Chronicles 7:14, God said to Solomon, "And my people who are called by My name humble themselves and pray and seek My face and turn from their wicked ways, then I will hear from heaven, forgive their sin and will heal their land" (NASB). Do you think this still applies to today?
6. What did the Holy Spirit highlight to you in 2 Chronicles 7—8 through the reading or the teaching?

Lesson 107: 2 Chronicles 9—10

Royal Throne: The Fulfillment of Prophecy
in Jeroboam

Teaching Notes

Intro

Second Chronicles can feel as though we're reading the same book over and over.
I encourage you to stay with it and allow God to teach us something new out
of the repetition. Second Chronicles is a continuation of 1 Chronicles and has
moved to the theme for the book as *Royal Throne* (2 Chronicles 7:18). What was
promised to David was walked out by his son, Solomon. In 2 Chronicles 9, the
Queen of Sheba visited Solomon (vv. 1–12); Solomon built a shipping fleet (vv.
10–11, 21); and Solomon gained wealth and reputation (vv. 13–28). However, in
verses 30 and 31, Solomon died, and Rehoboam succeeded him as king (v. 31).
Regardless of what happened through the kings of Israel, the *Royal Throne* continued. The *Royal Throne* of Judah (south) had passed from David to Solomon to
Rehoboam. At this point, the kings of Israel (north) were not yet in the picture.

Teaching

2 Chronicles 10:1–7: Solomon's son Rehoboam was made the king at Shechem
(Genesis 12:6–7; 35:4; Joshua 24). Jeroboam had fled from Solomon because of a
prophetic word (1 Kings 11:26–40), but he felt released to return after Solomon's
death (v. 2). Rehoboam summoned Jeroboam and all Israel to Shechem (v. 3).
Jeroboam spoke for the northern tribes and told Rehoboam that if he lightened
the heavy yoke King Solomon had placed on them, they would accept Rehoboam
as their king (v. 4). That heavy yoke included required labor and high taxes.[1] This
was an opportunity for reconciliation. Rehoboam told them to come back in
three days for his answer (v. 5). Rehoboam consulted the elders—advisors who
had served Solomon—for their advice (vv. 6–7). Seeking counsel was a good
thing to do. Other kings who sought counsel: David (1 Chronicles 13:1–9),
Jehoshaphat (2 Chronicles 20:21), and Hezekiah (2 Chronicles 30:2; 32:3).

---

[1] John MacArthur, *The MacArthur Bible Commentary* (Nashville: Thomas Nelson, 2005), 411.

2 Chronicles 10:8–15: But Rehoboam chose not to listen to their counsel to be kind to the northern tribes, and instead turned to the young men who had grown up with him, probably those about the age of 40 who served as his "yes men"[2] (vv. 8–9). These young, inexperienced men told Rehoboam to increase the burden of the northern tribes, punishing them with a heavier burden and the threat of barbed whips (vv. 10–11). *Nelson's Commentary* describes Rehoboam's whip as a scourge that had bits of metal inserted into the leather strands that would rip flesh away from the body of the one being beaten, causing severe pain.[3] In three days, when the people of Israel returned, Rehoboam told them his decision (vv. 12–14). Verse 15 explains Solomon tried to kill Jeroboam because the prophetic word said all that Rehoboam had decided had been spoken before (v. 15). The prophecy said God would take ten tribes away from Solomon's son and give those to Jeroboam to rule as king (1 Kings 11:28–38). MacArthur states, "God sovereignly used the foolishness of Rehoboam to fulfill Ahijah's prophecy."[4] Judah was humbled by losing ten of the tribes to the new nation of Israel, but God promised their humiliation would not last forever (1 Kings 11:39).

2 Chronicles 10:16–19: The people of Israel (the ten tribes) realized from Rehoboam's response that they had no inheritance from David and they would have to go their own way (vv. 16–17). Remember when we talked about everyone singing in one voice? In a short time, that unity was destroyed and the kingdom became divided. Rehoboam tried to follow through with his threat against the people of Israel and sent Hadoram, the man who oversaw the forced labor, to the north. When the people of Israel stoned Hadoram to death, Rehoboam fled and returned safely to Jerusalem (v. 18). The people of Israel remained in rebellion against Rehoboam and Judah (v. 19). Rehoboam had the opportunity to keep the unity in the kingdom, but he allowed greed and pride to influence his actions.

Martin Selman describes what this division looked like:

1. Rehoboam was so focused on the people within Judah that he allowed the majority of the tribes, "all Israel," to leave the kingdom (v. 16c).
2. The phrase "the Israelites" was used to refer to all the people of Judah and Israel, which kept an over-arching unity of the people (v. 17).
3. The division into two nations referred to the people of Israel versus the house of David (vv. 16, 19).

---

[2] MacArthur, 411.

[3] Earl D. Radmacher, Ronald B. Allen, and H. Wayne House, eds. *Nelson's New Illustrated Bible Commentary* (Nashville: Thomas Nelson, 1999), 545.

[4] MacArthur, 411.

4. The call for the people of Israel to become a new nation was in complete opposition of the support the people of Israel had given to King David (v. 16).

5. "The addition of 'each (of you)' before 'to your tents' (v. 16) invites every individual in the north to separate from David's dynasty."[5]

In this, Rehoboam had lost his structure and his guidelines. He surrounded himself with bad company, and "bad company corrupts good morals" (1 Corinthians 15:33). Rehoboam no longer listened for God's guidance and instead trusted a group of young "fools" (Proverbs 13:20). Proverbs 18:24 says, "A man with many friends may be harmed, but there is a friend who stays closer than a brother."

Closing

How do you know when the advice given to you is of God or not? Debbie McDaniel suggests "Five Ways to Recognize a Wolf in Sheep's Clothing":

1. *Watch Out* (Matthew 7:15; 1 Corinthians 16:13): Be on guard for those around you.

2. *Know the real, and you'll know the fake too* (Matthew 7:16; 1 Corinthians 4:5): You will know who is real and who is fake by their fruit.

3. *Know God's Word, and you'll know when it's being twisted and manipulated* (Psalm 199:11; 2 Corinthians 11:14–15): If you don't know what God's Word says, it will be easy for someone to twist or manipulate it to say something God did not intend.

4. *Trust the discernment and wisdom of God's Spirit living through your life* (Matthew 24:23–25; John 16:13): You can depend upon the Holy Spirit to help you discern what is of God and what is not.

5. *Surround yourself with other believers you know and trust* (Proverbs 11:14; 2 Peter 3:3): Make sure those you're willing to listen to are people you trust to offer biblical guidance and speak into your life.[6]

Bad company almost always corrupts good morals and good character. Rehoboam lost sight of process God established. Because he listened to a group of young guys who wanted to usurp power over the Israelites, the tribes were dispersed and unity was lost. We deal with this even today.

---

[5] Martin J. Selman, *2 Chronicles*, Tyndale Old Testament Commentary (Downer's Grove, IL: InterVarsity, 1994), 364. 23

[6] Debbie McDaniel, "Five Ways to Recognize 'A Wolf in Sheep's Clothing,'" Crosswalk, May 14, 2020, https://www.crosswalk.com/faith/spiritual-life/5-ways-to-recognize-a-wolf-in-sheep-s-clothing.html.

The Daily Word

Rehoboam took over as king of Israel after Solomon's forty-year reign. With a new king in place, the people requested the harsh service and heavy yoke be lightened. King Rehoboam took three days to seek counsel in making this decision. First he sought the advice of the elders who served his father. Then he consulted the younger men, his peers. In the end, he listened to the younger men and made a poor decision, which divided the nation of Israel in two.

When you have a decision to make, what do you do? Remember, slow down, take your time, and seek the Lord. He promises to be your helper as you delight in Him day and night. Oftentimes, the Lord will lead you to seek counsel. However, be careful who you turn to for counsel. Find someone with a pure heart who faithfully serves the Lord. Some people will offer you advice, but they may have selfish or prideful motives. Others may just go along with whatever you say, not really offering sound advice. *Seek the Lord for discernment as you listen to counsel and make your decision.* In all things, the Lord promises to work all things together for the good of those who trust Him. He hears you when you cry for help, and He will never leave you.

Then the king answered them harshly. King Rehoboam rejected the elders' advice and spoke to them according to the young men's advice, saying, "My father made your yoke heavy, but I will add to it; my father disciplined you with whips, but I, with barbed whips." —2 Chronicles 10:13–14

Further Scripture: Psalm 1:1–2; Proverbs 11:14; 1 John 4:1

Questions

1. In what ways do you find yourself like the Queen of Sheba when it comes to your faith (2 Chronicles 9:5–6)?

2. What are some other similarities between King Solomon and King Jesus?

3. The number 666 is mentioned in 2 Chronicles 9:13 as the weight of gold that came to Solomon in one year. Where else is this number mentioned in the Bible, and do you think there is a correlation between the two verses (Revelation 13:16–18)?

4. Second Chronicles 10:15 talks about a turn of events from God, which He spoke to Ahijah. What was this verse referring to (1 Kings 11:9–13)?

5. What did the Holy Spirit highlight to you in 2 Chronicles 9—10 through the reading or the teaching?

Lesson 108: 2 Chronicles 11—12

Royal Throne: Shishak's Invasion, Rehoboam's
Last Days

Teaching Notes

Intro

In 2 Samuel 7, David was told he would have an *Eternal Throne*, an eternal
kingdom, and that the Messiah would come through him. David's desire was
to build a temple for God, but God said no to David and yes to Solomon. In 2
Chronicles 1—9, Solomon built the temple and reigned over Israel for 40 years.
After the death of King Solomon, the kingdom was divided with Rehoboam
as king over one side (Judah) and Jeroboam as king over the other side (Israel).

Teaching

2 Chronicles 11: Rehoboam was discouraged from fighting against the other
ten tribes ("your brothers," v. 4). So, Rehoboam fortifies Judah (v. 5), and
the priests and Levites side with Rehoboam (v. 13). But in verse 15, we learn
Jeroboam led his people (the ten tribes of Israel) into idolatry. At this point,
with the kingdom divided and trouble on both sides, it's not looking so good
for the promises made to David in 2 Samuel 7 to come true. Over time,
Rehoboam married, and he appointed his son, Abijah, as chief because he
intended to make him king (vv. 18–22).

2 Chronicles 12:1–4: During his reign, Rehoboam abandoned the Law (v. 1) and
was unfaithful to the Lord (v. 2). Shishak, king of Egypt, went to war against
Judah. Some of the people who came with him were the Libyans, the Sukkiim
(the desert tribes), and the Cushites (most people say this was the Ethiopians).
Rehoboam was being overtaken by the Egyptians who were seizing fortified
cities of Judah along the way.

2 Chronicles 12:5–7: The prophet Shemaiah told Rehoboam and the leaders of
Jerusalem that God had abandoned them into the hands of Shishak because
they had first abandoned God and the Law. Since they were no longer faithful

to God and the Law, God would no longer dwell among them. In 2 Chronicles 7:13–14, God gave Solomon the remedy for this situation. So, the prophet released a word to Rehoboam that he and the people needed to humble themselves, seek God, and turn from their evil ways. In 2 Chronicles 12:6, the king and all the leaders humbled themselves. They did exactly what they should have done. When God saw this, He told Shemaiah that He would not destroy them but would grant them "a little deliverance" (v. 7). We'll come back to talk about "a little deliverance" after we walk through this story. Because of sin, there will be "little deliverance" or there will be consequences. The consequences might not be as bad as if you didn't turn back, but you still have to deal with the consequences of your sin. (We will walk through some instances later how this applies.) When people commit sins but never get caught, they begin to believe there are no consequences. But there is always a consequence. Sin always catches up with you.

2 Chronicles 12:8–12: In this instance, God didn't pour out His full wrath, but He allowed them to become servants of Shishak so they would learn the difference between serving God and serving other nations (v. 8). King Shishak took everything valuable from them (v. 9). With the gold shields stolen, Rehoboam made shields of bronze and gave them to his captains to guard the palace—but they had already lost to Shishak. This was the first major military encounter with Egypt since the Exodus hundreds of years before. Now they have to taste slavery again. "If the Jews would forsake true worship of God, they would also lose His protective hand of blessing."[1] Even though Rehoboam humbled himself, he still had to deal with the consequences of losing everything—he lost the treasury. "Besides that, conditions were good in Judah" (v. 12).

2 Chronicles 12:13–14: Rehoboam reigned as king in Jerusalem for 17 years. His mother was Naamah the Ammonite (v. 13), and he did evil by not seeking the Lord (v. 14). Look back at 2 Chronicles 7:14. Rehoboam may have humbled himself, but he did not seek God, and he did not turn from his evil ways. As Rehoboam dealt with his sin, he was only partially obedient—just enough to get by—and then continued to do what he wanted to do. Even though God showed up, Rehoboam did not continue to seek the Lord. Rehoboam knew the part he had to play to get through this battle, but then he went back to his evil ways. When we do this with the Lord, it's a slap in Christ's face—almost like we're saying what the cross did for us is not worth it. So how are we going to walk out this faith? In this story, Rehoboam was like a halfway believer. He

---

[1] John MacArthur, *The MacArthur Bible Commentary* (Nashville: Thomas Nelson, 2005), 502.

humbled himself for the immediate need but he had no intention of following the Lord.

2 Chronicles 12:15–16: The events in Rehoboam's reign, along with the genealogies, were recorded. Rehoboam and Jeroboam remained at war as long as they both reigned. When Rehoboam died, the kingdom passed to his son Abijah. In 1 Kings 15:3, Abijah was described as a great sinner.[2] None of them deserved to be labeled in the lineage of the *Royal Throne*, but that's the beauty of the way God works. God works despite our inadequacies, our sins, our abandoning the Law and being unfaithful to the Lord. Even if we are called a great sinner, God can still use us for His glory.

Let's back up to David and walk through the consequences of sin. We always paint David as some perfect guy, but he was far from it. In fact, David was labeled as an adulterer (affair with Bathsheba), and a murderer (he murdered Uriah the Hittite, one of his mighty men). In 2 Samuel 7, David described the man in Nathan's story as one who deserved to die. But in 2 Samuel 12:13, Nathan said God had taken away David's sin so David would not die. But there was a consequence: the son born from the affair with Bathsheba would die (v. 14). There are consequences for the sins we commit.

Derek Hill gave a list of the consequences of sin.[3] *First,* when you sin, it leads to separation from God. Isaiah 59:2 says our sin builds a barrier between us and God. Romans 3:23 says all have sinned and fall short of the glory of God. Sin separates us from God.

Second, sin is just flat-out harmful to you. In Genesis 19, when God judged Sodom and Gomorrah, the angels clearly told Lot and his family not to look back as they ran from the city. But Lot's wife looked back at the city, so she was turned into a pillar of salt (Genesis 19:26).

Third, sin can bring harm to others. In Matthew 2:16, King Herod, in a rage because he had been outwitted by the wise men, ordered the massacre of all the baby boys in Bethlehem. Other people had to deal with the consequences of Herod's sin. When Rehoboam refused to listen to the advice of the elders, the tribes of Israel split. When Rehoboam abandoned the Law and was unfaithful to God, the people became slaves to Shishak.

Fourth, sin serves as a catalyst for more sin. One sin leads to another because you're never satisfied because you think something is better on the other side of the road. Ultimately, sin leads to eternal death. Romans 6:23 says the wages of sin is death. Sin creates major issues. But there is no sin too big that God can't

---

[2] MacArthur, 411.

[3] Derek Hill, "5 Biblical Consequences of Sin," What Christians Want to Know, https://www.whatchristianswanttoknow.com/5-biblical-consequences-of-sin/.

overcome it, that God can't forgive it. Romans 6:23 proves the gift of God is eternal life in Christ Jesus. Although sin leads to death, Jesus took our sin upon Him and, through His death on the cross, offers us eternal life. Through His death, Jesus takes away all the consequences of sin: the separation, the harm to self and others, the catalyst for more sin, the eternal death. When we believe in Jesus and follow Him with everything we have, we can receive this free gift.

Closing

What do you do when you've sinned? Second Chronicles 7:14 gives the Old Testament mentality. The New Testament mentality says to confess these things to the Lord so you can be forgiven. Charles Stanley described a process for this:[4]

1. Assume responsibility for your sin.
2. Confess and repent of the sin.
3. Don't complain about the consequences. Hebrews 12:6 says God loves those He disciplines.
4. Ask God to help you discover the weakness that has crept into your life.
5. Recognize that God wants to use adversity (the hard stuff) in your life. Learn from this so you don't go back to it.
6. Thank God for revealing your sin.

Rehoboam only went halfway, maybe a third. Our challenge is to go all the way. Let's turn from our sin and seek God so that we look more like Him each and every day.

The Daily Word

When King Rehoboam and the leaders heard the Lord was abandoning them because they were unfaithful and had forsaken the law, they humbled themselves before Him. However, they did not pray, seek God's face, or turn from their wicked ways as the Lord had previously instructed His people. Therefore the Lord granted them just a *little deliverance*. Later the chronicler recorded that Rehoboam did what was evil. He may have humbled himself for a bit, but he never fully devoted himself to the Lord, turning his heart from evil. As a result, King Rehoboam faced the consequences for his sin.

God sees everything, and He knows your heart. He asks you to confess *all* your sin. And He promised to forgive *all* of it. Don't go halfway or you will only

---

[4] Charles Stanley, "The Consequences of Sin," available from https://www.intouch.org/Read/the-consequences-of-sin.

experience a *little deliverance* and will likely fall back into your old ways. The Lord says pray and seek Him with *all* your heart. Give the Lord your heart, your temptations, your fears, your joys, and your dreams. Surrender all of it to Him. Trust Him. Turn away from the things not from the Lord. Begin to walk with Jesus, and He will make your path straight, leading you through full deliverance and complete freedom in Christ.

When the Lord saw that they had humbled themselves, the Lord's message came to Shemaiah: "They have humbled themselves; I will not destroy them but will grant them a little deliverance. My wrath will not be poured out on Jerusalem through Shishak." —2 Chronicles 12:7

Further Scripture: 2 Chronicles 7:14; Proverbs 28:13; Romans 10:9

Questions

1. King Rehoboam set out to fight against Israel to restore his kingdom, which was divided due to his foolish choices. How did the Lord keep this from happening (2 Chronicles 11:4)? What causes us to fight with our brothers and sisters in Christ (James 3:16; 4:1–2)? What does Jesus say about our relationship with other believers (John 13:34–35)?

2. Because of the division between the ten tribes and Judah, along with Benjamin, what did King Rehoboam do for protection (2 Chronicles 11:5, 11–12)? What kind of defenses do we put up against one another for protection?

3. How many years did King Rehoboam and Judah walk in the ways of David and Solomon (2 Chronicles 11:17)? When did they forsake the law of the Lord (2 Chronicles 12:1)? How did the Lord respond?

4. Read 2 Chronicles 12:8. What, in your opinion, is the difference between serving the Lord and serving other "kings" (Romans 7:6; Galatians 5:13; Colossians 3:23–24; 1 Thessalonians 1:9–10)?

5. King Jeroboam excluded the Levites from serving as priests to the Lord, so they gave up their pasturelands and property and moved to Judah. Why was this so important that they would walk away from everything they had? When and how have you given up things to fulfill your calling?

6. What did the Holy Spirit highlight to you in 2 Chronicles 11—12 through the reading or the teaching?

Lesson 109: 2 Chronicles 13—14

Royal Throne: God Fights for Us

Teaching Notes

Intro

This is our 308th day together studying the Word of God. So far in 2 Chronicles, we've been studying the kings: David, Solomon, Rehoboam of Judah, and Jeroboam of Israel. Rehoboam was unfaithful to the Lord, which led to the divided kingdom. Judah lost ten of the tribes from its land, and those ten tribes became the kingdom of Israel. Chapter 13 covers King Abijah. In verses 2–22, Abijah fought Jeroboam, and Abijah died in verse 1 of chapter 14. Today's study from chapter 14 will cover the reign of King Asa. Both Abijah and Asa were kings over Judah.

Teaching

2 Chronicles 14:1–7: Asa was king for 41 years, and for a period of ten years, there was peace in the land, because Asa did what was right in God's sight (vv. 1–2). Beginning in verse 3, the chronicler recorded the things Asa did that were right: King Asa removed the pagan altars and high places that probably dated back to Solomon and his foreign wives, shattered the sacred pillars, and chopped down the Asherah poles (v. 3).[1] Either Asa had not eliminated *all* the pagan worship sites, or more were built in the years to come (Deuteronomy 12:2–3; 1 Kings 15:14; 2 Chronicles 15:17). Asa then instructed the people of Judah to seek God and to follow His instructions, just like we have read in 2 Chronicles 7:14 (v. 4). Asa continued with cleansing Judah of pagan worship by removing the incense altars (v. 5).

This cleansing brought peace to the land, giving Asa time to build new fortified cities in Judah. Without war, Judah experienced rest, also understood as blessing (vv. 6–7a). They built and succeeded in what they did (v. 7b). Asa sought the Lord, then followed God's leading and entered a new covenant with Him (2 Chronicles 15:12). However, in the thirty-ninth year of his reign, Asa developed a disease in his feet that cause him tremendous pain. In this case, he didn't seek the Lord but only went to physicians (2 Chronicles 16:12).

---

[1] John MacArthur, *The MacArthur Bible Commentary* (Nashville: Thomas Nelson, 2005), 503.

2 Chronicles 14:8–15: In verse 8, the peace ended. Asa had an army of 300,000 men from Judah and 280,000 from Benjamin, all brave warriors with shields and spears or bows. Zerah brought the Cushite army of one million men and 300 chariots against Asa. The Cushite army marched as far north as Maresha, one of the fortified cities Asa built. Asa led his men to line up for battle. Zerah lined up his men opposite Asa's army in battle formation (vv. 9–10). Asa's army was facing a much greater force for battle, but Asa cried out to the Lord, acknowledging God's omnipotence and reputation (v. 11).

Asa demonstrated his great faith in what God would do. The Lord led Asa's army to route the Cushites, who fled for their lives (v. 12). Asa and his army pursued the Cushites and killed all the soldiers and carried off a great supply of loot (v. 13). Asa had so much faith that he put his men in battle lines, expecting God's help in battle. Asa's army also attacked the cities around Gerar and plundered those cities (v. 14) and the tents of the herdsmen and returned to Jerusalem with their sheep and camels (v. 15).

Asa testified in front of his soldiers that he knew no mere mortals could stand against God. In his prayer (v. 11), Asa declared his confidence in the supremacy of God and asked God to help them in their weakness, emphasizing that they relied upon Him. Finally, Asa pointed out that God should help him instead of letting men prevail against him (v. 14).

Closing

Asa expected God to fight for the army of Judah. Debbie McDaniel gives nine reminders that God fights for us:

1. Deuteronomy 20:4: The Lord goes with us.
2. Romans 8:31: If God is with us, who can possibly be against us?
3. Joshua 1:9: Always be strong and courageous.
4. Psalms 44:5: God will push back our adversaries.
5. Matthew 10:23: Do not fear.
6. John 10:10: God comes to give us life.
7. Deuteronomy 3:22: Don't be afraid, because God fights for you.
8. Isaiah 40:31: We are to wait for the Lord to give us strength.
9. Joshua 23:10: God fights for us.[2]

---

[2] Debbie McDaniel, "When Life Is Hard: 9 Reminders that 'The Lord Fights for You,'" Crosswalk, August 18, 2016, https://www.crosswalk.com/blogs/debbie-mcdaniel/when-life-is-hard-9-reminders-that-god-fights-for-us.html.

God is our advocate refuge and strength. He will be with us in the battle:

- 1 Corinthians 15:57: "But thanks be to God, who gives us the victory through our Lord Jesus Christ!"
- Romans 8:37: "No, in all these things we are more than victorious through Him who loved us."

We have already won the battle; walk like we walk in victory. This was Asa's mindset that God is the one who does the work and wins the battle. In a new covenant mentality, it is what Jesus Christ did on the cross that won the battle and we need to walk in this victory.

The Daily Word

King Asa of Judah did what was good and right in the sight of the Lord. Even when the Cushite army, which was double the size of King Asa's army, came against Judah, Asa remained confident in the Lord. Asa walked in faith, marching out against his enemy and lining up in battle formation. At that moment, he cried out to the Lord: "There is no one besides You to help the mighty and those without strength. Help us, Lord, for *we depend on You.*" The Lord brought King Asa's army complete victory in the battle, plus a bonus of provision for the people's needs!

What battle do you need the Lord to fight for you today? Do you feel weak or unsure about how today will turn out? Take a moment and intentionally depend upon the Lord. Humble yourself, submit to His ways, and turn from evil. Believe that even in your weakness, the Lord is strong with you. He will fight your battle. It may require you to walk out in faith and step up to the battle line—but believe the Lord *will show up.* In God, you have victory. In God, you are a conqueror. In God, you are not alone. God will even trample your enemies and bring you *life* in abundance. Today, do not be afraid of the battle before you. Walk it out in faith, for the Lord is mighty within you!

Then Asa cried out to the Lord his God: "Lord, there is no one besides You to help the mighty and those without strength. Help us, Lord our God, for we depend on You, and in Your name we have come against this large army. Yahweh, You are our God. Do not let a mere mortal hinder You."
—2 Chronicles 14:11

Further Scripture: Deuteronomy 20:4; Psalm 44:5; 1 Corinthians 15:57

Questions

1. In 2 Chronicles 13:5, King Abijah reminded King Jeroboam that David's throne was eternal. What was Abijah's purpose?

2. In 2 Chronicles 13:9, Jeroboam was reminded that he drove out the priests of the Lord and became like the people of the other lands. What had the Lord foretold would happen if the Israelites became like the nations they were to drive out (Deuteronomy 18:9; 28:14–68; Joshua 23:15–16)?

3. Why were King Abijah and his men victorious against Israel? How can you ensure victory in your battles against our common foe (2 Chronicles 13:18; Proverbs 3:5; Isaiah 12:2; Jeremiah 17:7)?

4. Asa was a great grandson of Solomon. How do you see Asa walking in wisdom? Where does wisdom come from (2 Chronicles 9:23; Job 28—31; Psalm 111:10; Proverbs 2:6; Colossians 2:2b–3)?

5. What did the Holy Spirit highlight to you in 2 Chronicles 13—14 through the reading or the teaching?

Lesson 110: 2 Chronicles 15—16

Royal Throne: Revival Under King Asa

Teaching Notes

Intro

Every one of the books of the Bible, even the historical books, point to the coming Messiah. Our phrase for 1 Chronicles was *Son of David*. For 2 Chronicles, our phrase is *Royal Throne*. In 2 Chronicles 10, we saw the nation of Israel broken into the northern tribes and the southern tribes. The rest of 2 Chronicles points toward the kings of Judah. Today, we'll be looking at King Asa.

Teaching

2 Chronicles 15:1–2: God's Spirit came on Azariah, who then delivered God's word to King Asa. *Nelson's Commentary* noted that much of what Azariah said to King Asa could be said of the era of the judges.[1] So what Azariah said would sound like much of what was said in the book of Judges—the question was how the person who heard his prophetic words would respond. Would Asa respond like the judges of the past, or would he respond by doing what the Lord wanted him to do?

Remember that in the period of the Old Testament, the Spirit of God came upon people for a time. This was different than both New Testament times and today because the Spirit dwells within those who trust in Jesus Christ to guide, lead, direct, comfort, and speak through them.

Azariah told Asa and the people of Judah and Benjamin, "The Lord is with you when you are with Him" (v. 2). King Asa would rule for 41 years, and he had to choose whether to walk with the Lord or go his own way. The phrases, "When you are with Him" and "If you seek Him," remind us of 2 Chronicles 7:13–14.

2 Chronicles 15:3–4: For years, Israel had been without God, without a teaching priest, and without instruction. The chronicler, who may have been Ezra, was writing for those coming back from exile who needed to know they could get

---

[1] Earl D. Radmacher, Ronald B. Allen, and H. Wayne House, eds., *Nelson's New Illustrated Bible Commentary* (Nashville: Thomas Nelson, 1999), 547.

back to the point where they could experience God. So just like in the time of Asa, they could turn to the Lord and seek Him to experience all He had for them. But if they failed to seek the Lord, He would not be with them.

2 Chronicles 15:5–7: *Nelson's Commentary* said the Israelites were constantly in danger of war and being robbed; they experienced crime and were plagued by other nations.[2] Azariah's message was similar to Judges 5:6–7, in which Israel faced a similar time until Deborah stepped up, and then they experienced a revival. All it took was for someone like Deborah or King Asa to lead people back to the Lord. Unfortunately, we often wait for others to step up rather than stepping up ourselves. Azariah gave the simple solution—seek the Lord.

2 Chronicles 15:8–9: Asa found strength in these words and removed the detestable idols from the whole land. Over the course of years, the kings had let things go, so Asa had to renovate the land and altar the previous kings did not care about. We are really seeing what looks like what we might call a 'modern-day' revival. When Asa led Judah and Benjamin to seek God, people defected from Israel to join Judah because they saw God was with them.

In his book, *Experiencing God*, Henry Blackaby encouraged people to watch to see where God was working and then join Him there.[3] When we have a passionate longing to experience God, other people will want that, too. Is your faith so attractive others want to join you because they see the spirit God in your life? Our passion and zeal for God can draw people to the Lord (Isaiah 60:3). In Matthew 5:14–16, Jesus said we are the light of the world. When we let that light shine, people will give glory to God. Acts 13:47 says we are a light for the Gentiles to bring salvation to all. Isaiah mentions God has called us for a righteous purpose—to be a light for the nations (Isaiah 42:6). Deuteronomy 32:21 implied that when Israel fell away to worship idols, God would make them jealous of other nations. In Romans 11:11–12, Paul said that when Israel stumbled, salvation came to the Gentiles to make Israel jealous.

Rick Thomas offered some questions to determine if our lives can attract other people to God: "Can people actually relate to you?" "Do people want to relate to you?" "Do people who are different desire to be around you?"[4] So how do we create a spirit of jealousy in others so they want to know God as we know Him? In 1 Corinthians 11:1, Paul urged believers to "imitate me, as I also imitate

---

[2] Radmacher et al., 547.

[3] Henry Blackaby, Richard Blackaby, and Claude King, *Experiencing God* (Nashville: B & H Publishing, 2008), 69.

[4] Rick Thomas, "How to Relate to People Through Ministry, Music, and Mentoring," https://rickthomas.net/how-to-relate-to-people-through-ministry-music-and-mentoring/.

Christ." Here in the Old Testament, Asa was a model for this. People were attracted to Asa because God was working in his life. As he cleansed his life and cleansed the land, others were drawn to God, who was working in his life.

By looking at Hebrews 10:22, we can see how this could happen in our lives. First, we need to have a true heart, a pure heart, and an undivided heart. Psalm 24:3–4 says people with clean hands and a pure heart can approach the Lord. Next, we have to have a confident faith. We know God is big enough that when we remove the idols from our life, He will fill their absence with His presence. Then our hearts have to be cleansed so we have a clear conscience. When Asa cleaned house by destroying the idols throughout the land, he was freed from guilt. When we are cleansed and freed from guilt, we will have a clear conscience that others will notice. Lastly, we have to have a clean body. John 13:10 says when we enter into a relationship with Christ, we have been cleansed. When we have been cleansed, light shines from us and people will either be attracted by Christ in us—or they will be repelled by His light. First John 1:6–7 says when we walk in the light of Christ, then we begin to have fellowship with others. That's when we begin to see true unity.

Closing

King Asa is a model for what we need to do. We need to clean house so the light can permeate us so that people can truly be drawn to Jesus. Asa led the people to gather in Jerusalem and make offerings to the Lord and then enter into a covenant to seek the Lord God with all of their minds and all of their hearts (2 Chronicles 15:12). A prophet spoke truth to a king who decided to do something about it. He changed the culture, the environment, of his nation by removing the idols. His bold actions led others to seek the Lord. When we do this, it will carry over to those around us.

The Daily Word

Over time, the people abandoned the Lord's ways, filling the temple with idols. However, when King Asa heard the Word of the Lord through the prophet Azariah, he courageously removed the idols from the whole land of Judah and Benjamin. King Asa cleaned up the temple and even gathered the people to seek the Lord with all their minds and hearts. King Asa lived boldly for the Lord before all the people, and they recognized *Yahweh was with him.*

Ask yourself whether or not people recognize Jesus is with you. When King Asa cleaned up the temple, the people recognized *Yahweh was with him.* It may be time to clean up an area of your life so you too reflect Jesus. Today, look at your life and "clean your temple" where needed. Start with just one area the Lord puts on your heart. Gossip? Materialism? Addictions? Sports teams? Rid your life of any idols interfering with your reflection of Jesus. The time to love the Lord with *all* of your heart, soul, and mind, authentically reflecting Jesus, is *now*. If you want to see change in your community, it can begin with shining the love of Jesus to those around you. May they want the Jesus who is *with you*.

Then he gathered all Judah and Benjamin, as well as those from the tribes of Ephraim, Manasseh, and Simeon who had settled among them, for they had defected to him from Israel in great numbers when they saw that Yahweh his God was with him. —2 Chronicles 15:9

Further Scripture: Deuteronomy 32:21; Isaiah 42:6; Acts 13:47

Questions

1. Second Chronicles 15:1 stated that "the Spirit of God came on Azariah." What did this mean? Do you still think this happens today? Has the Lord ever spoken to you through someone else?

2. Second Chronicles 15:13 said the people who would not seek the Lord would be put to death. Do you think this was a just punishment? Why or why not?

3. In verse 16, "King Asa also removed Maacah, his grandmother, from being queen mother because she had made an obscene image of Asherah." What do you think this says about how seriously he took the covenant he made with the people of Judah?

4. In your opinion, why did Asa decide to make a treaty with Ben-hadad, king of Aram, instead of seeking the Lord to help when Baasha, king of Israel, come up against Judah (2 Chronicles 16:1–3)? What were the consequences for not seeking the Lord (2 Chronicles 16:7, 9)?

5. Read 2 Chronicles 15:9. Why were people defecting from Israel and coming to Judah? When have you seen people drawn to the eternal in you or someone you know (Ecclesiastes 3:11)?

6. What did the Holy Spirit highlight to you in 2 Chronicles 15—16 through the reading or the teaching?

Lesson 111: 2 Chronicles 17—18

Royal Throne: Hearing the Word of the Lord

Teaching Notes

Intro

We are continuing our study in 2 Chronicles, specifically chapters 17—18. There's so much here that can speak into us today.

Teaching

2 Chronicles 17:1–9: In chapter 15, King Asa heard from the prophet Azariah, and Asa returned to the Lord, began to cleanse the house, and led the nation in a time of revival. At Asa's death, his son Jehoshaphat began to reign (v. 1). Jehoshaphat strengthened the nation of Judah and placed forces throughout the walled cities of Judah (v. 2). The Lord was with Jehoshaphat because he walked in the ways of David (vv. 3–4). All Judah brought Jehoshaphat presents as the reigning king, and Jehoshaphat responded by clearing out the high places and pagan groves in Judah (vv. 5–6). In the third year of his reign, Jehoshaphat sent his officials and the Levites into all the cities of Judah to teach the book of the law to the people (vv. 7–9).

2 Chronicles 17:10–18: The Word of God always brings into focus Jesus Christ. The people of Judah didn't know Christ, but they did understand they were seeing a revelation of God in their times through the following of the Word of the Lord. But it's not just a reading of the Word, it is doing what it says, for "man shall not live by bread alone" (Deuteronomy 8:1–3; Matthew 4:1–4).

We're going to see a huge contrast between Jehoshaphat in chapter 17 and in chapter 18. Look at the progression. Asa told his son to walk in the Lord. As Jehoshaphat walked out the Word of the Lord, he made sure the people of Judah had access to it as well. God's Word began to transform the people of Judah. "And the fear of the Lord fell upon the kingdoms of the lands that were round about Judah, so that they made no war against Jehoshaphat" (v. 10 KJV). Other nations also sent tributes, allowing Jehoshaphat to be even more successful in leading his country in a building program (vv. 11–18). This shows how confidence in the Lord impacts others around us and even other nations.

As we get ready to contrast Jehoshaphat in his territory of Judah in chapter 18 with him in chapter 17, transferring him into the place of king of Israel who had all bad kings. Jehoshaphat was one of the good kings of Judah who led the people to revival. Israel had never experienced revival.

2 Chronicles 18:1–7: Jehoshaphat continued to walk in confidence and made an affiliation with King Ahab, one of the evil kings of Israel (v. 1). After several years, Jehoshaphat traveled to see Ahab in Samaria. Ahab had a great celebration when Jehoshaphat arrived and then persuaded Jehoshaphat to join him in battle against Ramoth-gilead. Jehoshaphat agreed to Ahab's proposal (vv. 2–3). But Jehoshaphat requested that they seek God's direction before they left (v. 4). Ahab called 400 prophets together and asked them whether they should go to Ramoth-gilead. The prophets told them God would deliver Ramoth-gilead to them (v 5). Jehoshaphat was not satisfied with what the 400 prophets said and asked if there was not another prophet of the Lord they could ask (v. 6). Ahab told him there was one more prophet named Micaiah, but that the king hated him because he never prophesied what Ahab wanted to hear (v. 7). Notice Jehoshaphat was unafraid of the Word of the Lord, and Ahab had built his own group of prophets who would tell him what he wanted to hear.

2 Chronicles 18:8–11: Ahab sent for Micaiah the prophet (v. 8). The kings of Israel and Judah (Ahab and Jehoshaphat) sat in their royal robes at the gate of Samaria and watched as the 400 prophets of Ahab's choice delivered their message (v. 9). One prophet made horns of iron and prophesied Ahab would push Syria into oblivion (v. 10). Ahab's prophets were in agreement with the thought that the Lord would deliver Ahab's enemy to him (v. 11).

2 Chronicles 18:12–14: Ahab sent a messenger to get Micaiah and tell him that all the other prophets had been in agreement, so his prophecy should be the same as theirs (v. 12). Micaiah replied he would speak whatever his God told him to speak (v. 13). Before King Ahab, Micaiah repeated the same thing the other 400 prophets had said (v. 14).

In the anointing of a king, the Spirit of God was supposed to be a part of that anointing in the life of a king, not just the king's prophet. There should have been something divine in the life of the king that let him know when something was of God or not. Jehoshaphat was in that place of being able to discern God's truth; Ahab was not.

2 Chronicles 18:15–22: King Jehoshaphat told Micaiah he should not repeat what the others said but to tell him the truth (v. 15). Micaiah said that "he did see," which was the role of the prophet/seer. Micaiah said he saw all Israel scattered on the mountains with no master and that God had sent them all home (v. 16). Ahab responded that Micaiah always had a negative response for him (v. 17).

Micaiah then responded with a vision of God on his throne asking the host of heaven who would entice Ahab to go against Ramoth-gilead so he would be defeated (vv. 18–20). In the vision, answered the Lord saying he would go and become a "lying spirit in the mouth of all his (Ahab's) prophets" to convince the king to go into battle, and God sent the spirit out (vv. 21–22).

2 Chronicles 18:23–27: After Micaiah spoke, one of the prophets of Ahab slapped Micaiah on the cheek and accused Micaiah of the one in which the lying spirit resided (v. 23). Micaiah responded that all of Ahab's prophets would see the truth in time (v. 24). King Ahab told his servants to put Micaiah in prison and feed him only bread of affliction and water of affliction (vv. 25–26). Before he was taken away, Micaiah declared that if Ahab returned safely from the battle, only then would he know that Micaiah had not spoken God's truth (v. 27).

2 Chronicles 18:28–34: Ahab and Jehoshaphat went to Ramoth-gilead, and Ahab decided to disguise himself while Jehoshaphat wore the royal robes (vv. 28–29). The king of Syria told his army to not worry about the soldiers against them but only to find the king of Israel (v. 30). However, when the soldiers of Syria saw Jehoshaphat in his robes, they assumed he was king of Israel and surround him. Jehoshaphat cried out to the Lord who saved him (v. 31). The soldiers turned away from Jehoshaphat. One of them shot an arrow, which wounded Ahab by chance (vv. 32–33) and Ahab died in battle (v. 34).

Closing

John 8:31–32 states, "If you continue in My word, you really are My disciples. You will know the truth, and the truth will set you free." What does the truth set us free from? Jesus explained we are slaves to sin, but the Son can set us free. What are we hearing today that we can establish ourselves in and say *this* is the Word of the Lord? That's the reason for reviveSCHOOL!

The Daily Word

King Ahab of Israel disguised himself during the battle in Ramoth-gilead. In contrast, King Jehoshaphat of Judah clothed himself with his royal robes. King Jehoshaphat walked out his calling with confidence in the Lord, not himself. When the enemies attacked, King Jehoshaphat cried out to the Lord for help, and God drew the enemy away, saving King Jehoshaphat. On the other hand, King Ahab, in his disguised identity, was killed when an unintentional arrow hit a weakness in his armor.

In fear, King Ahab attempted to manipulate a situation. In confidence, King Jehosephat walked by faith in the Lord. As you face your own battles, you have a choice: *take control and manipulate* or *have faith in the Lord and walk with integrity*. Remember, you are called as a chosen child of the King. You are loved. You are part of a royal priesthood. You don't need to hide or even blend into your surroundings. Walk confidently in Christ. King Jehoshaphat studied God's Word and drew strength from the truth. As a believer, God calls you to live on His bread alone to fight the battles. Don't try to be who you are not. Let go of control and walk in your identity in Christ. God is fighting your battles!

But the king of Israel said to Jehoshaphat, "I will disguise myself and go into battle, but you wear your royal attire." So the king of Israel disguised himself, and they went into battle. —2 Chronicles 18:29

Further Scripture: Matthew 4:4; Ephesians 3:12; 1 Peter 2:9

Questions

1. How is what King Jehoshaphat did in 2 Chronicles 17:7–9 like what Moses did in Deuteronomy 4:5?

2. What other king in the Old Testament does King Jehoshaphat remind you of (1 Kings 4:21–28)?

3. What reason could King Jehoshaphat have had to join himself in alliance with such an evil king as King Ahab (2 Chronicles 18:1)?

4. Why did King Ahab have the prophet Micaiah thrown into prison (2 Chronicles 18:7, 18–22)?

5. Do you think it was an accident that the king of Israel was "struck by a bow at random" (2 Chronicles 18:29, 33)?

6. What did the Holy Spirit highlight to you in 2 Chronicles 17—18 through the reading or the teaching?

Lesson 112: 2 Chronicles 19—20

Royal Throne: Jehoshaphat's Prayer

Teaching Notes

Intro

God used the prophets to speak into the lives of the kings of Israel and Judah, and they responded. Even in the midst of troubling times, if you're open to hearing what the LORD wants to say to you in that time, He will get you through it. There are times, however, when we shut the door to hearing because we say, "God, you've gotten me through those previous things, but I don't need you now." The promise of 2 Chronicles 7:14 is that God will hear us when we humble ourselves and pray, seek His face, and turn from our wicked ways.

Teaching

2 Chronicles 19: Jehu rebukes King Jehoshaphat (vv. 1–3). The rest of chapter 19 describes the reforms Jehoshaphat put into place to lead Judah back to the Lord. In this process, troubled times were coming in chapter 20.

2 Chronicles 20:1–4: The Moabites, Ammonites, and Meunites (from Edom) came to fight against Jehoshaphat. A vast number of enemies were already in the land of Judah. Jehoshaphat's first emotion was fear. But right away, he quickly sought the Lord and proclaimed a fast for all of Judah. The fast would turn their focus from the enemy's strength to the Lord's strength. They followed the command in 1 Chronicles 16:11 to find their strength in the Lord. Psalm 14:2 says God looks down from heaven to see who seeks Him. They determined to seek God until He showed Himself in this situation (Hosea 10:12). Jehoshaphat has now gone from fear to faith. The people follow what Jehoshaphat modeled: they came from all the cities of Judah to fast, pray, and seek God.

2 Chronicles 20:5–9: Jehoshaphat began his prayer by reminding himself, his people, and God, that God alone rules over all the kingdoms of the world, so no one could stand against Him. In that prayer, Jehoshaphat shifted from fear to faith. He remembered that when Joshua came into the land, God cleared out the people (v. 7). Like the people before him, Jehoshaphat stood before the temple crying out to God who would hear and deliver them (v. 9). This was similar to the message to Solomon in 2 Chronicles 7:13–14.

2 Chronicles 20:10–12: Jehoshaphat reminded God that He had not allowed Israel to invade the lands of the Ammonites, Moabites, and Mount Seir when they came out of Egypt. It's as if Jehoshaphat was saying, "Won't You judge them now that they're fighting against us?"

Jehoshaphat cried out to God that this was His problem to handle. Then Jehoshaphat admitted they didn't know what to do, so they looked to God for help. This is an incredible definition of faith.

2 Chronicles 20:13–17: All of Judah (men, women, and children) stood before God. Then the Spirit of the Lord came on Jahaziel, a Levite, who said: "Listen carefully . . . [to] what the LORD says: 'Do not be afraid or discouraged.'" Jahaziel called them to go from fear to faith. Israel didn't have to worry about this fight; it was God's fight. He told them where to take up their position so they could stand and watch God fight for them. Notice that Israel actually had to move into a place of acting in faith in God. Psalm 46 says, "Stop your fighting—and know that I am God, exalted among the nations, exalted on the earth." Jehoshaphat and Israel, by faith, could see the salvation of the LORD.

2 Chronicles 20:18–19: Jehoshaphat continued to respond in faith (not fear). He and all Judah worshipped God while the Levites, Kohathites, and Korahites praised God with loud voice.

2 Chronicles 20:20–23: Early in the morning, Jehoshaphat led the people out to the wilderness and challenged them to believe in God to see victory. He surrounded himself with godly counsel and appointed some to sing praises to God. When they began to shout praises, God ambushed and destroyed their enemies. God's game plan, from the very beginning, was, "Trust Me!" When we walk in fear, nothing will change. But when we walk in faith, God shows up. To get to this position of faith, seek the Lord. In this case, God caused Jehoshaphat's enemies to turn against each other until all were destroyed.

2 Chronicles 20:24–26: When Judah looked for the enemy armies, they saw nothing but corpses. Jehoshaphat and his people gathered plunder from their enemies for three days until they could carry no more. On the fourth day, they gathered in the Valley of Beracah and praised the Lord.

2 Chronicles 20:27–28: Jehoshaphat and the men of Judah returned to Jerusalem and worshipped the Lord in the temple.

All throughout Scripture, God asked people to do ridiculous things. Joshua led the Israelites to march around the city in the conquest at Jericho (Joshua 6:1–5). Naaman washed in the Jordan River seven times to be healed of his leprosy (2 Kings 5:1–19). When we walk by faith, God shows up. Jesus told Peter he would find the coin to pay taxes in the mouth of a fish (Matthew 17:27). The disciples fed 5,000 men with a little boy's lunch (John 6:1–15). Walking with the Lord is the most radical, ridiculous adventure you will ever find in your life. Do you trust that He'll show up as you walk? When you move from fear to faith in seeking the Lord, things don't have to make sense.

Closing

An article called "Strange Bible Instructions"[1] says when you walk by faith, God doesn't have to make sense; you simply have to obey the instructions. We have to realize that when God's plan makes no sense to us, then it's His plan. Further, we don't have to understand what God's asking us to do. We have to realize that God is God, and we are human. When we move from fear to faith, when we don't know what to do but look to God, then God shows up. So please, walk by faith, and let God show up in the impossible.

The Daily Word

A vast number of Moabites, Ammonites, and Meunites came together to fight against King Jehoshaphat. Facing the battle afraid, King Jehoshaphat sought the Lord, proclaiming a fast for all of Judah. *King Jehoshaphat did not know what to do; he only knew to seek the Lord.* So the people praised the Lord, they remembered His promises, and they believed He would fight their battle. The Lord answered them, saying, "Tomorrow, go down against them . . . you do not have to fight this battle. Position yourselves, stand still, and see the salvation of the Lord." The people went out and believed in Yahweh their God. And the Lord brought them victory in the battle.

Are you afraid of something today? Take a deep breath and seek the Lord. Have a radical trust that says, "I do not know what to do, but I look to You, God." Believe the Lord will provide. Believe the Lord is faithful. Believe the Lord will guide you. Believe the Lord will turn your enemy around. Just as the Lord instructed Jehoshaphat in battle, today, you need to get up, go face your battle,

---

[1] Hook Publications, "Strange Bible Instructions," April 8, 2011, http://www.hookpublications.com/truth/strange-bible-instructions.

and believe in the Lord your God. He says, "Be still. I will fight for you." Give thanks to the Lord for His faithful love that endures forever.

Our God, will You not judge them? For we are powerless before this vast number that comes to fight against us. We do not know what to do, but we look to You. —2 Chronicles 20:12

Further Scripture: 2 Chronicles 20:20; Psalm 46:10; Psalm 136:1

Questions

1. How do you see God's grace and mercy in Jehoshaphat's safe arrival home in 2 Chronicles 19:1 (2 Chronicles 18:1, 28–31)? Contrast the fate of Ahab with Jehoshaphat.

2. What was one similarity between King Jehoshaphat and King Asa (2 Chronicles 16:7)?

3. What two things did Jehoshaphat do when he heard the news about the armies declaring war against him? Who else in 2 Chronicles sought the Lord (2 Chronicles 11:16; 14:2–4; 15:10–13; 31:21; 34:3)?

4. Whom did the Spirit of the Lord come upon to speak over the people? What was his message? How was the message received?

5. Whom did King Jehoshaphat appoint to lead the army into battle? What was the result of listening to the Lord and acting by faith (Hebrews 11:6)?

6. What did the Holy Spirit highlight to you in 2 Chronicles 19—20 through the reading or the teaching?

Lesson 113: 2 Chronicles 21—22

Royal Throne: God Is the Keeper of Promises

Teaching Notes

Intro

In the chapters we study today, things change and go in a different direction from the past few chapters. The change begins in 2 Chronicles 21.

Teaching

2 Chronicles 21:1–4: Jehoshaphat did amazing things for Judah as he walked out his reign in the Lord. When he died, his son Jehoram became king (v. 1). Jehoshaphat was a godly king, but in his attempt to bring Judah and Israel together through a marriage alliance brought trouble. Interestingly, Jehoram who was king of Israel, was a different man. Jehoram's brothers are listed in verse 2. Jehoshaphat brought in one of Ahab's daughters to marry Jehoram. Jehoshaphat had been generous with all his children, but Jehoram received the kingdom as the first born (v. 3). Jehoram strengthened his position by killing all his brothers as well as some of the princes of Israel (v. 4).

Every time there is a revival, Satan comes in to try to destroy what is happening. Jehoshaphat had trained his son Jehoram to walk in the ways of the Lord, but evil entered the kingdom when Jehoram murdered his brothers and other potential heirs.

2 Chronicles 21:5–7: Jehoram married Athaliah, the daughter of Ahab and Jezebel of Israel. But the bad influence of Ahab entered Judah. In fact, the chronicler had nothing good to say about Jehoram. The chronicler focuses on the spiritual health of Judah and noted how Jehoram pursued the same practices and policies that Israel followed (vv. 5–6). Even though Jehoram was doing exactly what the depraved kings of Israel were doing, he had one thing going for him the kings of Israel didn't have—he was a descendant of the house of David. In spite of Jehoram's disobedience to God, the Lord would not eliminate his entire family (v. 7). God had promised David that a descendant of Solomon's would always be on the throne (1 Chronicles 17:14), which kept Jehoram's family from obliteration, although it came very close.

2 Chronicles 21:8–11: During Jehoram's reign the nation of Edom rebelled against Judah and chose their own king (v. 8). Jehoram crossed into Edom, and the king of Edom and his officers barely escaped (2 Kings 8:21). The Levites who lived in Libnah also rebelled against Judah because Jehoram had abandoned the Lord. In verse 10, the reason for Libnah's rebellion is more than likely due to Jehoram's idolatry (Joshua 21:13). None of this dissuaded Jehoram, who was under the influence of his wife! Jehoram built pagan places of worship, taking an active role in leading the people to betray God and prostitute themselves.

2 Chronicles 21:12–15: Elijah was the prophet who was Ahab and Jezebel's opponent in the northern kingdom. He sent a letter to Jehoram, their son-in-law, and offered three charges and two punishments (v. 12). The charges included: (1) Jehoram had not walked in the ways of his father Jehoshaphat, but in the ways of the kings of Israel; (2) Jehoram had caused Judah and the inhabitants of Jerusalem to prostitute themselves like Ahab's house did; and (3) Jehoram killed his brothers in cold blood (v. 13). Therefore, Jehoram would be punished. First, his entire family and all his possessions would be struck down with a horrible affliction. Second, Jehoram himself would be struck down with many illnesses, including a disease of the intestines, until his intestines came out day after day (vv. 14–15). Usually, prophecies were given verbally, but Elijah chose to put it in writing—a bold move!

2 Chronicles 21:16–20: God put it in the mind of the Philistines and the Arabs to attack Jehoram (v. 16). They went to war with Judah and carried off everything Jehoram had, including his sons and wives, leaving only one son, Jehoahaz, behind (v. 17). They also missed one of the wives, who was not mentioned at this time. Then the Lord afflicted Jehoram with disease in his intestines. Jehoram suffered for two years until his intestines indeed came out of his body, and he died at the age of 40 after eight years as king. His people did nothing to honor the death of their king (vv. 19–20). Jehoram was not allowed to be buried in the same site as his predecessors. Sadly, the evil influence in Judah did not die with him.

2 Chronicles 22:1–12: The people of Jerusalem made Jehoram's only surviving son Ahaziah king (v. 1). He was 22 years old when he was made king and was the son of Athaliah (v. 2). Ahaziah followed his mother's influence, which came from her grandparents, evil king Ahab and queen Jezebel. She guided Ahaziah into the ways of pagan worship (vv. 3–4). Ahaziah joined King Joram (also Jehoram) who was the son of Ahab to fight the king of Aram in Ramoth-gilead (v. 5). King Joram was wounded in battle and returned home to Jezreel to recover (v. 6). Ahaziah went to Jezreel to see Joram (v. 6). When he arrived, he went with Joram to meet Jehu, whom God had sent to destroy the house of Ahab

(v. 7). Jehu executed judgment on the house of Ahab, killing Ahaziah's family members serving Ahab. Ahaziah was also executed, so that no one from the house of Ahaziah had the strength to rule the kingdom (vv. 8–9).

Since Ahaziah was executed, his mother Athaliah (which means "Afflicted of the Lord") seized the throne for herself and ruthlessly eliminated anyone who posed a threat to her reign (v. 10). Athaliah purged anyone who could be identified with the house of David, including her grandchildren. Her attempt to wipe out the line of David failed when Jehoshabeath, Athaliah's sister, rescued one of the king's sons, the baby Joash, and hid him in a bedroom (v. 11). God promised the line of David would continue until the coming of the Messiah (2 Samuel 7:16), and it came only one infant away from extinction. Athaliah was not a legitimate ruler, she was not of the house of David, and she was a worshipper of Baal. She managed to rule six years (v. 12). In this six-year period, it felt as though God was gone and evil had won.

Closing

Until Joash had sons, all the promises of God—the promise given to Eve in the garden, the covenant made with Abraham and renewed with Isaac and Jacob, the vow to David—rested in his young body. If Joash had been killed, God would have been proven fallible.

"But God was not nervous. He was not only the maker of promises but the keeper of promises."[1] Consider also the hidden presence of King Joash. Athaliah was on the throne, but the real king was still present. Doesn't this remind you of our day? People are on thrones, but the real *King*, Jesus, is present!

The Daily Word

Judah's leadership style changed following King Jehoshaphat's reign. Jehoshaphat's son, Jehoram, succeeded as king after strengthening his position by killing his six brothers. Just as the prophet Elijah prophesied, King Jehoram was struck by an intestinal disease because he did not walk in the ways of the Lord like his father had. Jehoram died without honor to no one's regret.

As a follower of Christ, Jesus commands you to go and make disciples. He encourages you to invest into people's lives, depositing the love of Christ. Consequently, when the Lord calls you home, the love of Christ you invested into others will be carried on long after your own life. Think about this: if you died tomorrow, would anyone regret it? Would they miss the love of Jesus alive in you? God's grace is abundant. Jesus poured out His love for you, just as you are.

---

[1] Don Finto, *Your People Shall Be My People: How Israel, the Jews and the Christian Church Will Come Together in the Last Days* (Bloomington, MN: Chosen Book, 2001, 2016), 67–68.

Believe you are worthy to receive His love. And as you receive Christ's love into your own life by faith, go deposit Jesus' love into someone else. The love of Jesus can impact someone for eternity.

But his people did not hold a fire in his honor like the fire in honor of his fathers. Jehoram was 32 years old when he became king; he reigned eight years in Jerusalem. He died to no one's regret and was buried in the city of David but not in the tombs of the kings. —2 Chronicles 21:19–20

Further Scripture: Matthew 28:19–20; 1 Timothy 1:16; 1 John 4:19

Questions

1. What blessings did Jehoshaphat give to his sons? Why did he designate Jehoram to be the next king?

2. Why did God withhold immediate and definitive punishment upon the house of Jehoram (2 Chronicles 6:16)?

3. What are some things that were happening because Jehoram had abandoned the Lord? What message did Elijah give to him regarding his evil reign?

4. What did God decide would be Ahaziah's downfall? Why did another king not follow after Ahaziah?

5. What evil did Queen Athaliah do after the death of her son Ahaziah? How did God intervene to save the line of David and keep His covenant promise?

6. What did the Holy Spirit highlight to you in 2 Chronicles 21—22 through the reading or the teaching?

Lesson 114: 2 Chronicles 23—24

Royal Throne: Joash Repairs the Temple

Teaching Notes

Intro

Our phrase for 1 Chronicles was *Son of David*, and our phrase for 2 Chronicles is *Royal Throne*. Together these phrases point to the lineage of Jesus. Today we'll see that lineage continued through a seven-year-old king, a child God protected for this purpose.

Teaching

2 Chronicles 23:1–11: Joash was crowned king of Judah.

2 Chronicles 23:12–15: Athaliah was executed.

2 Chronicles 23:16–21: Jehoiada made reforms throughout the land.

2 Chronicles 24:1–3: Joash was only seven years old when he was crowned king, and he reigned 40 years in Jerusalem. He actually had someone who helped him grow and who led him in the discipleship process. This was an incredible model of discipleship. The end goal for Jehoiada, as he walked with Joash, was that Joash would grow to become a godly king. For as long as Jehoiada was priest, Joash did what was right in the sight of the Lord. Unfortunately, after Jehoiada died, Joash listened to the rulers of Judah and abandoned the temple of Yahweh (the Lord) and served the Asherah poles and idols (2 Chronicles 24:17–18). Surely Jehoiada would have been greatly saddened to know that as soon as he died, Joash turned away from the Lord as though nothing he had learned from Jehoiada mattered.

2 Chronicles 24:4–5: Joash decided to renovate the Lord's temple. Joash followed in the footsteps of some of the good kings of Judah. He sent the priests and Levites throughout Judah to collect money to repair the temple. Though Joash said, "Do it quickly," the Levites did not hurry. In 2 Kings 12:6, we learn that 23 years of King Joash's reign had passed, yet the priests had not repaired the temple. Since Joash was seven when he became king, this means he was 30 before the priests began to listen to him. This first collection failed. It would have been easy for Joash to quit at this point.

2 Chronicles 24:6–7: Failure doesn't mean you're a failure. It just means that your efforts didn't work the first time. God might have a different plan. But if you stay in this position of failure, living as a victim, then you won't experience the victory of faith.

In this case, the Levites were disobedient to King Joash's instructions because they had no desire to be obedient. So, the king called Jehoiada the high priest, his mentor and teacher, and asked why he hadn't required the Levites to collect the tax imposed by Moses. The king's question pointed out that Jehoiada was also disobedient because he had failed to make the Levites do what the king instructed. In Exodus 30:11–16, Moses established the temple tax as directed by the Lord. Every man 20 years old or more was required to give half a shekel as atonement money to serve the tent of meeting. So Joash was only asking the Levites to do what God had directed through Moses. This was one way they received money for the temple. The second way was money received from individuals who made vows and the third way was voluntary offerings (2 Kings 12:4–5). This money was needed because the sons of wicked Athaliah had broken into the Lord's temple and even used the Lord's sacred things for the Baals (v. 7).

2 Chronicles 24:8–12: King Joash had a chest made and put it outside the gate of the Lord's temple. He then issued a proclamation that the people bring the tax imposed by Moses to the temple. The leaders and the people rejoiced and brought the tax to the temple. The Levites had controlled how the people worshipped the Lord by refusing to collect the tax, but now the people were able to worship again. The Levites had actually limited how God could work among His people. Now that Joash had gone around the Levites by building the chest for the collection, the people rejoiced and filled the chest because they knew the money would go toward God's kingdom work. Every day the people gave so much money the Levites had to deliver the chest to the king's secretary and the high priest's deputy and then return the empty chest to its place before the temple. They gathered money in abundance. The king and high priest gave the money to those in charge of the labor on the Lord's temple, who hired the stonecutters, carpenters, blacksmiths, and coppersmiths to make repairs. Everybody got to do their part—the people gave, the workmen worked—so that, in the end, everybody was able to experience the presence of God.

2 Chronicles 24:13–14: The workmen restored the temple to its specifications and reinforced it. When they finished, they gave the remaining money to the king and Jehoiada the high priest, who made articles for the temple with it. Then the people regularly offered burnt offerings in the Lord's temple throughout Jehoiada's life.

Let's talk about abundance and how God meets needs. Joash made the call, but the Levites didn't do it. Therefore, the people missed out on the blessing of experiencing God for 23 years. But then Joash followed through and sent a proclamation throughout Judah because he knew God had asked him to do this. In the process, people gladly brought their contributions so that the chest was literally full. The offerings were so large the chest had to be emptied every single day. When God calls you to something, He will meet your needs in abundance. These everyday Israelites constantly gave in gladness and joy so everyone got to enjoy the presence of God.

Second Corinthians 9:6–8 says those who sow sparingly will reap sparingly while the person who sows generously will reap generously. Each person should give according to his heart, for God loves a cheerful giver. The people experienced a true revival because they gave from an abundant heart. What would have happened if Joash had given up after the first 23 years? But Joash persisted, and God showed up through generous givers.

Proverbs 3:9–10 tells us to honor the Lord with our possessions, and then our barns will be filled. Luke 6:38 tells us to give, and in return, it will be given to us. We cannot out give God. The more you pour out, the more the Lord will pour in. It's important to remember it's not ours anyway; it already belongs to Him. It's important to give generously to the church and its ministry so the Lord can use that to advance the kingdom of God. Never shortchange the Lord when He asks you to do it. You could actually be holding back the next move of God, as the Levites did for 23 years.

Closing

Bible.org did a quick picture about God's abundant provision.[1]

God always provides abundantly for our needs— materially, emotionally, and spiritually; God will meet our needs.

1. God provides for our needs in His timing.
2. God provides in ways we would never expect.
3. God provides for us through grace, not merit.

---

[1] Steven J. Cole, "Lesson 75: God's Abundant Provision," Bible.org, https://bible.org/seriespage/lesson-75-god-s-abundant-provision-genesis-4516-28.

His abundance comes because of His grace, not because of what we do. As far as merit goes, God pours out to you because He knows you're going to do something with it, not because you're doing something. This is how God works. Don't be a stingy Levite but be a generous Israelite who is constantly pouring into the kingdom of God so that more people can experience His presence.

The Daily Word

When Joash became king, the Lord burdened his heart with the task to renovate the temple. King Joash gathered the Levites, instructed them to collect money, and told them to do so quickly. However, the Levites did not hurry. Therefore Joash took a different approach. He made a chest and positioned it outside the gate of the Lord's temple. In response, the people of Judah and Jerusalem gave generously and obediently. Money was collected daily, enabling the temple's complete restoration.

When God calls you to something, He will provide. Keep in mind, you may have to press in and continue seeking the Lord for His plan and His timing. You never know exactly how the Lord will move in the hearts of His people. When plans don't go the way you imagined or in your expected time frame, don't give up. Don't get frustrated. Press in and seek the Lord for wisdom in the situation. Be open minded, willing to make an adjustment. Sometimes the Lord will use frustrating moments to get to the sweet spot of God's will. Seek the Lord and your plans will succeed. Remain focused on God's will through a situation, and it will work out as *He* planned.

So he gathered the priests and Levites and said, "Go out to the cities of Judah and collect money from all Israel to repair the temple of your God as needed year by year, and do it quickly." However, the Levites did not hurry.
—2 Chronicles 24:5

Further Scripture: Psalm 84:11; Psalm 105:4; Proverbs 16:3

Questions

1. Why do you think Jehoiada the priest waited six years to take action against Athaliah and reestablish the kingdom with David's descendant?

2. What seems to be the reason King Joash started off doing what was right in the sight of the Lord (2 Chronicles 24:2, 17)? What got him off track?

3. Second Chronicles 24:19 said the Lord sent prophets to King Joash and the officials to bring them back to the Lord, but they would not listen. How have people responded to you when you have shared the gospel with them?

4. How does the dying prayer of Zechariah in 2 Chronicles 24:22 differ from Jesus' dying prayer in Luke 23:34?

5. In Luke 11:51, Jesus referred to the murders of Zechariah and others. Whom did He charge with those murders? Why?

6. What did the Holy Spirit highlight to you in 2 Chronicles 23—24 through the reading or the teaching?

Lesson 115: 2 Chronicles 25—27

Royal Throne: Becoming Desensitized to God's Word

Teaching Notes

Intro

I hope as we continue to study the historical books, you will see it is profitable to look at and review the kings and prophets in Scripture. We have saw the deceit and conspiracy, and yet there are those whom God still used to bring light to the kingdom. The theme of 2 Chronicles is *Royal Throne* and refers to the establishment of God's kingdom on earth through Jesus Christ. We continue to work on the establishment of His kingdom today through faith. In our study of 2 Chronicles 25—27, we'll study three kings: Amaziah, Uzziah, and Jotham.

Teaching

2 Chronicles 25:1–8: King Amaziah, the son of Joash, began his reign at the age of 25, and he reigned 29 years (v. 1). Amaziah did right in the sight of the Lord, but he did not have a perfect heart—he did not have complete belief in God and lacked the passion to walk out his calling completely (v. 2). Amaziah killed his father's servants who took his father's life (v. 3), however, based on the book of Moses, he did not kill their children. He knew the principles of his faith (v. 4). Amaziah then organized the men of Judah into groups and counted those who were 20 years or older, finding 300,000 choice soldiers (v. 5). Amaziah also hired 100,000 men from Israel, the northern kingdom (v. 6). Scripture does not state whether or not Amaziah made a political alliance with Israel, but a man of God (a prophet) told Amaziah God was not with Israel, and he would lose in battle if he took the Israelite soldiers with him (vv. 7–8).

What is God's part in how all this played out? "God has the power to help" and the power "to make one stumble" (v. 8). What happens lies in the difference of obedience (or not) to what God has spoken.

2 Chronicles 25:9–27: Amaziah pointed out he already paid for the Israelite soldiers, but the man of God stated that God would give much more support than his paid army (v. 9). Therefore, Amaziah separated out the Israelite soldiers that sent them home, however they were angry with the nation of Judah because they would not receive the spoils from the war (v. 10). Amaziah led his army against Seir to victory (v. 11). Amaziah wanted to be obedient to God, but he, also, brought back the gods of the Seirites and worshipped them (v. 14). God's anger was kindled by Amaziah's actions and the declining faith in Judah (something we'll see in all three of these chapters). God sent a prophet to ask Amaziah why he was seeking out the pagan gods who had no power when God gave them the victory (v. 15).

In anger and pride, Amaziah took advice (from his counselors, not God's prophets) and called for King Jehoash of Israel to meet with him (vv. 16–17). Amaziah tried to form an alliance with Jehoash which was rejected. This led to war, the defeat of Judah and Amaziah's capture. He was eventually killed in Lachish (vv. 18–27).

2 Chronicles 26:1–23: Amaziah's son Uzziah became the next king at the age of 16 and restored Judah, reigning 52 years (vv. 1–3). Uzziah did right in God's sight, seeking God (v. 4). In spite of the fact Uzziah was a good king, there seemed to be a desensitizing of the people of what God expected. Uzziah sought God through Zechariah (not the prophet who has a book in the Old Testament); Uzziah prospered as long as he sought God's will (vv. 5–6). When he became successful, Uzziah also became arrogant and went into the temple and burned incense (v. 16). The priests told Uzziah he had no right to offer incense to the Lord because he was not a priest (vv. 17–18). Uzziah was angry, and leprosy struck him at that moment while he was still in the temple (vv. 19). God needs cooperation and obedience, not arrogance and pride. As a leper, Uzziah was removed from Jerusalem and lived out his days in quarantine (vv. 20–23).

2 Chronicles 27:1–14: Uzziah's son Jotham became the next king at the age of 25 and reigned 16 years (v. 1). Jotham did what was right in the Lord and did not enter the temple as his father had done, yet the people acted corruptly (v. 2). He did right, but what was his normal? We have to have a baseline in the Word of God as a moral compass to know how to draw lines and be in balance with God. However, we too can become desensitized to God's Word and His calling. We're fooling ourselves if we believe we are not living in a desensitized world.

Closing

There was continual work of the kings that demonstrated a level of power. How that power was handled was significant. Power can lead to pride, idolatry, self-reliance and self-governance, lack of honor for leadership, and corruption in people.

John 10:10 states, "A thief comes only to steal and to kill and to destroy. I have come so that they may have life and have it in abundance." We have to decide to whom we will be devoted and consecrated. The enemy continues to work. Who will you follow?

The Daily Word

The Lord made King Uzziah of Judah very powerful, and his fame spread as far as Egypt. King Uzziah tore down walls, built cities, found victory in battle, and led a mighty army. A marvelous and strong leadership evolved into King Uzziah becoming arrogant. Consequently, he acted unfaithfully against God, which led to his own destruction. King Uzziah stopped depending on the Lord as he became strong in himself. His leadership crumbled, ultimately leading to his death.

From the moment you said yes to Jesus as your Savior and Lord, you were saved through faith, not by any works of your own. As you go through life with your eyes on Christ, your strength, success, and accomplishments come from the Lord alone. Although some people trust in the things of this world, as a follower of Christ, *you trust only in the name of the Lord your God*. The Lord says if you remain humble, He will lift you up in due time. Therefore, you do not need to exalt yourself. Don't even waste time giving yourself credit. Honor the Lord and give thanks for His great faithfulness, strength, and might! No matter how powerful you become from the world's perspective, may the Lord receive all the glory!

He made skillfully designed devices in Jerusalem to shoot arrows and catapult large stones for use on the towers and on the corners. So his fame spread even to distant places, for he was marvelously helped until he became strong. But when he became strong, he grew arrogant and it led to his own destruction. He acted unfaithfully against the Lord his God by going into the Lord's sanctuary to burn incense on the incense altar. —2 Chronicles 26:15–16

Further Scripture: Proverbs 16:5; Ephesians 2:8–9; 1 Peter 5:6

Questions

1. Amaziah started out doing right, but after defeating the Edomites, he brought their gods back, set them up as his gods, bowed down to them, and burned incense to them. Why do you think he forsook the Lord and worshipped these gods? Have you witnessed people in your life forsake the Lord and turn to other "gods"? If so, what did you do?

2. What was Amaziah's response to the prophet the Lord sent to him (2 Chronicles 25:15–16)? Have you ever avoided being confronted with your sin because you weren't willing to change? If so, what was the outcome?

3. 2 Chronicles 26:5b says, as long as he sought the Lord, God prospered him. Do you think this verse could support someone with a "works-based" belief system? How would you refute that idea with other Scripture passages?

4. King Uzziah's pride caused him to act corruptly and be unfaithful to the Lord. What was the outcome of his unfaithfulness (2 Chronicles 26:19)? Are consequences for unfaithfulness meant to punish us, or do they serve another purpose? What Scripture passage would you use to support your answer?

5. What did the Holy Spirit highlight to you in 2 Chronicles 25—27 through the reading or the teaching?

Lesson 116: 2 Chronicles 28—29

Royal Throne: From Evil Leadership to Godly

Teaching Notes

Intro

We've been studying the kings of Judah, some good in the sight of the Lord, and some bad. Today, we go from bad, to worse, to revival. Jotham's son Ahaz found a way of committing every conceivable act of idolatry. Our theme for 2 Chronicles is *Royal Throne*. The question for you today is, who do you put on the *Royal Throne*? This was the major question for our two protagonists in chapters 28 and 29.

Teaching

2 Chronicles 28:1–8: Ahaz become king at the age of 20 and reigned for 16 years (v. 1). Remember that Chronicles focuses on the temple and what led to spiritual captivity of the exiles in Babylon. As king, Ahaz committed every conceivable act of idolatry, even sacrificing and burning his own children. This was something the evil kings of Israel had never done (vv. 2–3). The place where the children were sacrificed to the Canaanite god Moloch led to the valley called Gehenna— the word for hell. He personally participated in worship in the high places (v. 4). Few men in the Bible were as strongly opposed to God as King Ahaz of Judah.

Between verses 4 and 5, God demonstrated to Ahaz that he could rely on God (Isaiah 7:1–17). He declined Isaiah's invitation to believe the Word of God with false piety, saying he would not put the Lord to the test (Isaiah 7:12). God still gave a sign—the prophecy of the virgin birth who would be called Immanuel (Isaiah 7:14). This was a future prophecy for Christ as well as prophecy of the coming Assyrian invasion. God handed evil Ahaz over to the king of Aram who took Judean captives to Damascus and gave Ahaz to the king of Israel. The king of Israel struck Ahaz soundly (v. 5).

Commentator Winfried Corduan wrote, "Abandonment of God inevitably led to abandonment by God."[1] In verses 5b–8, the armies of Israel killed hun-

---

[1] Winfried Corduan, *Holman Old Testament Commentary: 1 and 2 Chronicles* (Nashville: Holman Reference Publishers, 2004), 324.

dreds of thousands of Judah's men and killed Masseiah, Ahaz's son; Azikam, the governor of the palace; and Elkanah, Ahaz's second son. The Israelites also took 200,000 captives (including women and children), and plunder to Samaria. God used not only the Arameans to serve His punishment of Judah, but he also used the army of Israel from the idolatrous northern kingdom to defeat them as well.

2 Chronicles 28:9–15: Verse 9 begins an interesting interlude. Oded, an ultra-minor prophet of the Lord, went out to meet the Israelite army that came to Samaria and told them they were pushing their luck against God. God used them to punish Judah, but that didn't give them license to do as they pleased, so they had to take the hostages back to Judah (vv. 9–11). In response, the leaders of the Ephraimites said the captives and the plunder must go back to Judah so the Israelites' guilt wouldn't be brought upon the tribe of Ephraim (vv. 12–13). The men of Ephraim cared for the captives, gave clothes and sandals to those who needed them (some of whom were naked), fed them, dressed their wounds, and provided donkeys for all the feeble. Then they took the Judeans back to Jericho (vv. 14–15). They went above and beyond to minimize the captives' suffering on the return trip. The people of Israel listened to Obed's warning and responded.

2 Chronicles 28:16–27: Judah continued to deteriorate under Ahaz's reign. Ahaz next asked the king of Assyria for help (v. 16). In response, the Edomites and the Philistines attacked Judah, took captives, and took over their villages, and the Assyrians attacked as well (vv. 17–18, 20). "For the LORD humbled Judah because of King Ahaz of Judah, who threw off restraint in Judah and was faithful to the Lord" (v. 19). Ahaz had even plundered the Lord's temple to try to buy off the Assyrians, but they would not help him (v. 21). Ahaz then became even more unfaithful to the LORD and sacrificed to the gods of Damascus hoping they would help him (vv. 22–23a). "But they were the downfall of him and all Israel" (v. 23b).

Instead of turning back to Yahweh the Lord, Ahaz continued to try to connect to other countries by worshipping their foreign gods to get support for Judah. For Ahaz, a return to the worship of God was unthinkable, but the hybrid religion of Aram in Damascus, combining Canaanite deities with some of their own gods, seemed right to him. Then Ahaz cut up the utensils of God's temple, shut the temple up, made altars on every street corner in Jerusalem, and created high places in every city of Judah (v. 24). Ahaz wanted to supplant the worship of God throughout his kingdom. The good news is that Hezekiah, the son of King Ahaz, became king in his place (vv. 26–27). *The Davidic line still held despite this awful king.*

The state of faith in Judah was as bad as it could get. There is a similar time in American history, in 1790, when the Church seemed at its weakest and college students wouldn't even acknowledge their belief in Jesus. It was at this time the second Great Awakening began as a prayer movement of five students at Yale University in New Haven, Connecticut. That prayer movement led to revival at Yale, and an exploding move of the Holy Spirit across our nation.

2 Chronicles 29:1–19: Hezekiah was 25 years old when he became king, and he reigned 29 years. "He did what was right in the LORD's sight just as his ancestor David had done" (vv. 1–2). Hezekiah's name means, "My father is Jehovah" or "The Will of God." His mother's name was Abijah (a name we've often seen used for men) and was a daughter of Zechariah (not the prophet). The chronicler gave Hezekiah the highest possible praise by comparing his conduct to his ancestor David. Hezekiah's story was so significant it was told three times in the Old Testament: 2 Kings, 2 Chronicles, and Isaiah.

Hezekiah never saw himself as a victim of his father's disastrous reign, but instead he enthusiastically and deliberately went to work to undo the damage his father caused. Hezekiah began with the reclamation of the temple. He instructed the priests and Levites to cleanse themselves and then reestablished the temple (vv. 3–11). His speech was possibly based on Solomon's dedication prayer for the temple 250 years earlier (2 Chronicles 6:14–42). Hezekiah also initiated a paradigm shift for the kingdom of Judah by committing himself to a new covenant. The Levites resuming their duties would also signal a fresh relationship between God and His people. The Levites and the temple musicians stood up and embraced the new project with enthusiasm (vv.12–14). They consecrated themselves and went to work according to the king's command and the words of the Lord (vv. 15–19). This decontamination took two weeks.

2 Chronicles 29:20–36: Hezekiah led in rededicating the temple with a variation on the annual Feast of Atonement (Leviticus 16:18) and the sin offering (Leviticus 4), except that they used more animals than would normally be the case. Notice the symbolism as the king laid hands on the sacrifices, not to usurp the role of the priest but to demonstrate the need of the people. He used it correctly by the Law (vv. 20–24). In the celebration and dedication, they sang the psalms of David, finally bringing the worship of God again to Jerusalem (vv. 25–26). Verses 27–33 talks about the sacrifices brought before the Lord. And a total of 600 bulls and 3,000 sheep and goats were consecrated. Then, Hezekiah invited others to bring their sacrifices. The number of sacrifices and offerings was huge—to the point there weren't enough priests to handle the sacrifices because a number of priests hadn't finished their ritual cleansing (Leviticus 8:136).

Since there weren't enough priests, the Levites helped. They had been more conscientious to consecrate themselves than the priests (v. 34). After the sacrifices and offerings, Hezekiah and the people rejoiced over how God had prepared the people because it had happened in only one month (vv. 35–36). In the first month of Hezekiah's reign (2 Chronicles 29:3), Judah had moved from a nation mired in Ahaz's national idolatry to a renewed relationship with the Lord.

Closing

What, by God's power, is He calling you to in service for Him? What is God prompting you to do in relationship to God? Change comes about, not by our strength, but the Lord's. What is going on around you? It might be your family. King Hezekiah knew that changes needed to be made, he had work to do. Who are you going to put on the *Royal Throne*? Who are you going to call alongside of you in this work? Are you going to do this for the Lord? He is the one on the *Royal Throne*. He deserves it all!

The Daily Word

After the ungodly reign of King Ahaz, his son Hezekiah took over the throne. In contrast to his father, Hezekiah began turning things around for the Lord. In the first month in the first year of his reign, twenty-five-year-old Hezekiah didn't hesitate or waste time doing what was right in the Lord's sight, just as his ancestor David had done. King Hezekiah followed the desire the Lord placed on his heart to make a covenant with Yahweh and began cleansing the Temple. He repaired the broken things and removed anything impure from the holy place. After this, King Hezekiah and those around him sang praises with rejoicing, bowing down in worship to the Lord. A sudden revival occurred in Jerusalem, and it was good!

Is it time to turn things around in your life? Your past and the generations of sin before you do not define who you are. Is it on your heart to repair, heal, or remove the "junk" from your life? It can happen. Allow the love of Jesus to cleanse you from all unrighteousness. His grace covers all, and His mercy is new day by day. Surround yourself with others to love and support you through this time. You will rejoice again. You will make music again. You will live in the freedom of Christ's love. *The hard work and effort to restore all things will be worth it.* If it's in your heart to turn around, then start walking it out in faith.

It is in my heart now to make a covenant with Yahweh, the God of Israel so that His burning anger may turn away from us. My sons, don't be negligent

now, for the Lord has chosen you to stand in His presence, to serve Him, and to be His ministers and burners of incense. —2 Chronicles 29:10–11

Further Scripture: Titus 3:3–5; 1 Peter 2:1–3; 1 John 1:9

Questions

1. King Ahaz sinned greatly in the eyes of God. In 2 Chronicles 28:3, he burned his children in the fire. Where else do we find child sacrifice (2 Kings 21:6; Jeremiah 32:35a)? What was God's response to this (Leviticus 20:2–5; Jeremiah 32:35b)?

2. In 2 Chronicles 28:15, the people were caring for the captives. How does this model what Jesus taught (Matthew 25:34, 40)?

3. King Hezekiah did what was good in the sight of God. What did God grant him (2 Kings 20:1–6)? Why?

4. King Hezekiah started to rectify the wrongdoings of his father. What steps did he take in 2 Chronicles 29 to accomplish this?

5. Why did the priests need more help in 2 Chronicles 29:34? From where did they draw their help? In your opinion, was this in line with God's Word? Why or why not?

6. What did the Holy Spirit highlight to you in 2 Chronicles 28—29 through the reading or the teaching?

Lesson 117: 2 Chronicles 30—31

Royal Throne: The Call for Revival

Teaching Notes

Intro

We've now done 316 lessons in reviveSCHOOL, and this week, we'll finish up our study of 2 Chronicles. Our last three studies in 2 Chronicles will build to a climax like nothing we've ever studied before. We are going to see King Hezekiah walk out goodness.

MacArthur states, "Hezekiah reached back to restore the Feast of Unleavened Bread and the Passover which apparently had not been properly and regularly observed in some time, perhaps since the division of the kingdom 215 years earlier."[1] Hezekiah reestablished the Word of God that had been long forgotten back into their culture. *Nelson's Commentary* states, "Hezekiah never lost sight of the fact that God's covenant was made with all twelve tribes and that His promises included them all."[2]

Teaching

2 Chronicles 30:1–9: Hezekiah and his officials and the people of Jerusalem decided to celebrate the Passover in the second month (they had missed the Passover at the normal time), and sent word to all Israel and all Judah, and to those of Ephraim and Manasseh to come participate with them (vv. 1–3). Putting it off a month allowed them to finish the work in the temple, consecrate enough priests, and have time for the people to come to Jerusalem. Everyone was satisfied with the proposal and spread the message all over Israel from the northernmost city (Dan) to the southernmost (Beer-sheba) (vv. 4–5). The king sent handwritten notes by couriers throughout both kingdoms, calling the people to revival—"Return to Yahweh" (v. 6). These couriers acted as ambassadors for the king throughout both lands. Just as Hezekiah appealed through his couriers, God appeals through us as well (Acts 1:8). It's a picture of what revival

---

[1] John MacArthur, *The MacArthur Bible Commentary* (Nashville: Thomas Nelson, 2005), 512.

[2] Earl D. Radmacher, Ronald B. Allen, and H. Wayne House, eds., *Nelson's New Illustrated Bible Commentary* (Nashville: Thomas Nelson, 1999), 559.

could look like today. Hezekiah's message was that, through the Passover lamb, the people could return to the Lord, just as we can through Jesus, the Lamb of God. Notice the couriers' names were not recorded, but that didn't stop them from delivering the king's message. We have been given the authority to be "letter-bearers" and "message-bearers" to God's redemptive message as well (Acts 10—11).

Richard L. Pratt Jr., points out eight exhortations in the king's messages recorded in 2 Chronicles 30:6–9:

1. Return (v. 6a), a guiding principle.
2. Don't be like your fathers (v. 7a), a negative requirement.
3. Don't be stiff-necked, or obstinate (v. 8a), a negative requirement.
4. Submit (v. 8b), a positive requirement.
5. Come (v. 8c), a positive requirement.
6. Serve (v. 8c), a positive requirement.
7. If you return (v. 9a), a guiding principle.
8. If you return (v. 9b), a guiding principle.[3]

The thing that Hezekiah wrote to the people of Israel and Judah is the same message that is needed for the church today to experience revival—we have to *return* to God!

2 Chronicles 30:10–15: Many of the inhabitants refused to hear Hezekiah's message and laughed at the couriers (v. 10). But Asher, Manasseh, and Zebulon humbled themselves, received the message and came to Jerusalem (vv. 11–12). And a very large assembly of people gathered in Jerusalem to observe the festival (v.13). Where there is humility there can be unity.

2 Chronicles 30:16–27: The celebration went so well the people wanted more and continued to worship for another seven days (v. 23).

Closing

When the people experience the presence of God, they will want more and revival breaks out!

---

[3] Richard L. Pratt Jr., "The Reunited Kingdom, part 4," Reformed Perspectives, May 15-21, 2000, http://reformedperspectives.org/article.asp/link/http:%5E%5Ereformedperspectives. org%5Earticles%5Eric_pratt%5EOT.Pratt.2Chr.30.1-12.html/at/The%20Reunited%20 Kingdom,%20part%204.

The Daily Word

King Hezekiah sent word throughout all Israel and Judah for the people to gather at the Lord's Temple in Jerusalem to observe the Passover of Yahweh, the God of Israel, which hadn't been observed in quite some time. He wrote letters and sent couriers to spread the message: "*It is time to return to Yahweh, the God of Abraham, Isaac, and Israel, so that He may return to those of you who remain.*" Upon hearing the message, some laughed and mocked the couriers, but others humbled themselves and traveled to Jerusalem. God's power united them all, and King Hezekiah was the tool through which the Lord's power worked.

Sometimes you may need to walk obediently as the Lord's messenger in someone's life, understanding that God's power goes before you. Today, take a minute to ask the Lord if there is someone in your life who needs to *return to the Lord*. Don't worry. If they chose not to listen, or if they laugh and mock you, they are rejecting Jesus, not you. However, you may hear a humble response and witness them turn their heart back to the Lord. The Lord's mercy covers all those who return to Him. So go send that text, write that email, or pick up the phone and call! *Be the tool that can help change begin in someone's life and* allow God's grace to flow.

So the couriers went throughout Israel and Judah with letters from the hand of the king and his officials, and according to the king's command, saying, "Israelites, return to Yahweh, the God of Abraham, Isaac, and Israel so that He may return to those of you who remain, who have escaped from the grasp of the kings of Assyria." —2 Chronicles 30:6

Further Scripture: Jeremiah 15:19; Joel 2:13; 1 Corinthians 15:1–3

Questions

1. Why did King Hezekiah change the dates for the Passover? What is the meaning of Passover? Where did God give instructions for Passover (Exodus 12:11–14)?

2. In 2 Chronicles 30:18, many of the people were not clean, and yet they ate anyway. What were the proper procedures at that time for Passover (Deuteronomy 16:1–8)? What happened when Hezekiah prayed for them?

3. The people brought their firstfruits in 2 Chronicles 31:5–6. Where else do we see God giving this directive (Deuteronomy 26:2; Proverbs 3:9)?

4. In 2 Chronicles 31:10–21, King Hezekiah had a storehouse built. Why? Where do we see the promises of God on giving (Malachi 3:10; Matthew 6:33)? Can a person out-give God? Why or why not?

5. What did the Holy Spirit highlight to you in 2 Chronicles 30—31 through the reading or the teaching?

Lesson 118: 2 Chronicles 32—33

Royal Throne: God Is Our Warrior

Teaching Notes

Intro

We are so close to the end of 2 Chronicles. The phrase for 1 Chronicles is *Son of David* and for 2 Chronicles is *Royal Throne*. Hezekiah just called the people to be renewed in God. Hezekiah, from the lineage of David, points to the coming of the *Royal Throne* through the ultimate *King*, Jesus Christ. In 2 Chronicles 32, however, we will see Satan coming in and trying to destroy it all. Notice both God and Satan can use rulers anywhere in the world, one for God's glory and the other in an attempt to destroy. Ultimately, God is in charge and can use even bad rulers for His good (Proverbs 21:1). When we see revival such as that brought on by Hezekiah, we should always expect Satan to try to ruin it.

Teaching

2 Chronicles 32:1–8: After Hezekiah's reforms, Sennacherib, the king of Assyria, entered Judah and laid siege to the fortified cities (v. 1). Second Kings 18:13 says Sennacherib took all 46 of the fortified cities. Hezekiah realized Sennacherib planned war on Jerusalem (v. 2). Solomon was the king who built these cities and settled people into them (2 Chronicles 8:2–6). Hezekiah consulted his officials and warriors about stopping up the spring waters outside the city, and they helped him (v. 3). Hezekiah worked out three ways to stop Sennacherib's attack.

First, he (and his officials) stopped up the springs outside the city walls of Jerusalem so Sennacherib and his army would not find water (vv. 3–4). Hezekiah then built a tunnel that went from the Gihon Springs to the Pool of Siloam so the city of Jerusalem would have plenty of water. *Second,* Hezekiah had the entire broken section of the wall rebuilt and the watchtowers heightened (v. 5a). *Third,* Hezekiah reorganized and reequipped his army (vv. 5b–6c). Are we equipped and ready for battle like Hezekiah and Judah (Ephesians 6:10–18)? Hezekiah encouraged the people of Jerusalem to be strong and courageous rather than afraid or discouraged before the king of Assyria (v. 7a). Hezekiah pointed out there were more of them in Jerusalem than Sennacherib had in his army (v. 7b). This king prepared for war by fortifying the water supply, the walls, and equipping the warriors. Are we ready for the battle? Is the Church ready for a battle (Ephesians 6:10–18)?

King Hezekiah sought godly council and he prepared for war. Some would say Hezekiah should have just depended upon God alone without taking other action. I see divine wisdom in the actions Hezekiah took to prepare the city. I wonder if Hezekiah knew the "horses and chariots of fire" were all around (2 Kings 6:16–17). In verse 8, Hezekiah stated Sennacherib only had human strength while the people of Judah had God's strength to fight their battles. Hezekiah trusted in the Lord, regardless of the improvements they had made. (For the opposite of trusting God, see Isaiah 22:8–11.) Martin Selman has pulled out multiple examples of trusting God:

- Deuteronomy 31:7–8, 23: Moses called the people to be strong and courageous. Do not be afraid or discouraged.
- Joshua 1:6–9: Joshua called the people to be strong and courageous!
- 1 Chronicles 22:13: David called the people to be strong and courageous! Don't be afraid or discouraged.

In the first 8 verses, Hezekiah prepared to defend his people against attack because he saw "the present struggle as a battle not just between nations but also between competing religious systems and ideologies."[1] Hezekiah was ready to depend upon Yahweh as the warrior.

Because Hezekiah brought the people back to God, he and his people became a threat to Satan. If you're not bringing people to God, then you are no threat to Satan!

2 Chronicles 32:9–19: Sennacherib and his forces besieged the city of Lachish, which was located west of Jerusalem (v. 9). Capturing Lachish would have cut Jerusalem off from the west and from the sea.[2] Then Sennacherib questioned why the people were willing to stay in Jerusalem while under siege, especially since they must be hungry and thirsty (vv. 10–11). Sennacherib mocked all Hezekiah had done to remove the high places and altars, while requiring all Israelites to worship at the one altar at the temple (v. 12). This king of Assyria then questioned why people thought they could stop him since he and his fathers had a history of having successfully battled the cities of Judah (vv. 13–14). Sennacherib was basically undermining Hezekiah's beliefs and his reforms. Imagine

---

[1] Earl D. Radmacher, Ronald B. Allen, and H. Wayne House, eds., *Nelson's New Illustrated Bible Commentary* (Nashville: Thomas Nelson, 1999), 561.

[2] Radmacher et al., 561.

how devastating his threats could be to someone who did not trust the Lord. Sennacherib was bragging that no god of any nation was strong enough to be victorious over him (v. 15) and his servants said even more against God and Hezekiah (v. 16). Sennacherib wrote mocking letters about the Lord with these same lies (v. 17) and eventually his servants even spoke in Hebrew to frighten the Israelites. The lies, threats, and accusations continued through verses 18–19.

2 Chronicles 32:20–23: But Hezekiah and the prophet Isaiah, son of Amoz, cried out to the Lord who sent an angel to annihilate every warrior, leader, and commander in Sennacherib's camp (vv. 20–21a). Sennacherib returned home in disgrace and his own children killed him (v. 21b). The Lord saved His people from Sennacherib of Assyria and from all others, giving His people rest and peace (v. 22). Many brought offerings to Hezekiah and he became exalted in the eyes of all nations (v. 23). Hezekiah got everything ready, but the Lord fought the battle for them.

Closing

John 8:31–32 states, "If you continue in My word, you really are My disciples. You will know the truth, and the truth will set you free." What does the truth set us free from? Jesus explained we are slaves to sin, but the Son can set us free. What are we hearing today that we can establish ourselves in and say, *this* is the Word of the Lord? That's the reason for reviveSCHOOL!

The Daily Word

After King Hezekiah's faithfulness in leading the people to return to Yahweh, Sennacherib, king of Assyria, entered Judah with the intention to break into the fortified cities. King Hezekiah saw the enemy approaching, recognized he was in battle, and immediately sought counsel. Then he gathered the people together and encouraged them: "Be strong and courageous . . . Sennacherib has only human strength, but we have Yahweh our God to help us and to fight our battles." The Lord brought the victory and saved King Hezekiah along with all Jerusalem, giving them rest on every side.

Many times, after a season of great faithfulness to the Lord, the enemy comes in to steal, kill, and destroy. Be aware of the battle raging around you as you live your life boldly for the Lord. But do not be afraid. Just as the Lord said to Moses, Joshua, David, and Hezekiah as they led the people, the Lord tells you to be ready for battle. Be strengthened by the Lord. Put on the full armor of God so you can stand against the tactics of the devil. Pray in the Spirit at all times. Stay alert. The Lord your God is with you to fight your battle, so continue to speak boldly about the mystery of the Gospel. Others only have human strength, but you have the Lord on your side. Walk by faith and do not fear.

"Be strong and courageous! Don't be afraid or discouraged before the king of Assyria or before the large army that is with him, for there are more with us than with him. He has only human strength, but we have Yahweh our God to help us and to fight our battles." So the people relied on the words of King Hezekiah of Judah. —2 Chronicles 32:7–8

Further Scripture: Deuteronomy 31:7–8; Joshua 1:7; Ephesians 6:10–11

Questions

1. Hezekiah was telling his people to be strong and courageous in 2 Chronicles 32:7–8. In your opinion, can we lose if we have God on our side fighting for us? Where else are we told to be strong, courageous and not to fear (Deuteronomy 31:6; Joshua 1:9)?

2. The Lord sent an angel to fight Sennacherib and his army in 2 Chronicles 32:21. How many men were cut down (2 Kings 19:35)? What later befell Sennacherib and by whom?

3. What sign did the Lord give to Hezekiah that he was heard and healed (2 Kings 20:8–11)?

4. In chapter 33, Manasseh was ruling and doing evil in the sight of the Lord. What happened that made him change his ways? Even though he changed his behavior and started following God, where was he buried compared to his father?

5. What did the Holy Spirit highlight to you in 2 Chronicles 32—33 through the reading or the teaching?

Lesson 119: 2 Chronicles 34—36

Royal Throne: Doing Evil in God's Sight

Teaching Notes

Intro

We wrap up our study in 2 Chronicles with chapters 34—36. Remember, all of Chronicles and the entire Bible points to Jesus as the coming Messiah. The theme for 2 Chronicles is *Royal Throne*. In chapter 34, King Josiah begins with his religious reforms and makes a new covenant with God. In chapter 35, King Josiah keeps the Passover feast, focusing on the blood of the lamb. At the end of the chapter, Josiah is killed by Egyptian arrows. While the situation seems dire, the book ends in hope!

Teaching

2 Chronicles 36:1–4: Jehoahaz, Josiah's son, was made king in Jerusalem in 609 BC (2 Kings 23:31–33), the exact period in which Jeremiah prophesied he would rule (Jeremiah 1:3). Jehoahaz was 23 years old and reigned only three months (vv. 1–2). The king of Egypt deposed Jehoahaz and fined Judah 7,500 pounds of silver and 75 pounds of gold (v. 3). How quickly things can change! The king of Egypt made Jehoahaz's brother Eliakim king of Judah, renaming him to Jehoiakim, and had Jehoahaz imprisoned in Egypt (v. 4).

2 Chronicles 36:5–8: Jehoiakim reigned for 11 years (609–597 BC), and did evil in God's sight (2 Kings 23:34—24:7) (v. 1). God sent His message to Jehoiakim through the prophet Jeremiah. Jehoiakim destroyed the message as it was read, showing his complete disdain for God. And then King Nebuchadnezzar of Babylon attacked and had Jehoiakim taken to Babylon in shackles, along with the temple's utensils (vv. 6–7). During this same period, in 605 BC, Daniel was taken captive to Babylon. Jeremiah continued to prophesy during this time.

2 Chronicles 36:9–10: Jehoiakim's son, Jehoiachin, became the next king, reigned three months, and did evil in God's sight (Jeremiah 22:24–30). Jehoiachin reigned in 597 BC (2 Kings 24:8–16). Note that Ezekiel was taken captive to Babylon in 597 BC as well.

2 Chronicles 36:11–21: King Nebuchadnezzar made Jehoiachin's brother Zedekiah the next king of Judah, and he reigned in Jerusalem (v. 11). Zedekiah reigned 11 years (597–586 BC) and did evil in God's sight (2 Kings 24:17—25:21; Jeremiah 32:4–27). Jeremiah wrote the book of Lamentations to mourn the destruction of Jerusalem and the temple that took place in 586 BC Ezekiel received his commission as a prophet during Zedekiah's reign and prophesied from 592–560 BC (Ezekiel 1:1). Zedekiah rebelled against Nebuchadnezzar of Babylon and against Yahweh (v. 13). The leaders of the priests and the people left behind in Jerusalem followed Zedekiah's example and defiled the temple and followed pagan practices (v. 14). God kept sending His messengers to bring them back to Him, but they wouldn't listen (vv. 15–16).

Remember Chronicles was written to explain to those who had just been released from this same captivity in Babylon what had happened that put them in captivity in the first place.

The Lord brought the king of the Chaldeans against them. The Chaldeans killed the choice young men of Judah in the temple and took everyone, men and women, young and old, into captivity to Babylon (v. 17). The Chaldeans also took all the treasures of the temple, the king, and his officials to Babylon (v. 18). Finally, the Chaldeans burned the temple and the palaces in Jerusalem, tore down the city wall, and destroyed everything in the city (v. 19). Everyone left in Judah was taken as servants to the Chaldeans (v. 20). This fulfilled God's Word to Jeremiah and the land rested for 70 years during "the days of the desolation" (Jeremiah 25:8–12).

Closing

For 70 years the land 'rested' and the people began returning back to their land before going into captivity. God called King Cyrus to finance the building of a new temple in Jerusalem and to free all the captives in Persia (2 Chronicles 36:22–23). As God's people returned, they began rebuilding their city and the temple.

The Daily Word

The people of Israel multiplied their unfaithful deeds, imitated all the detestable practices of the nations around them, and defiled the Lord's temple. Because of God's compassion, He offered them opportunities to repent, but they kept ridiculing God's messengers, despising His words, and scoffing at His prophets. Finally the Lord sent Nebuchadnezzar to carry the people from Jerusalem to exile in Babylon for seventy years. Later the Lord used Cyrus, the pagan king of Persia, to issue a decree for the Israelites to return to their homeland and rebuild the temple of the Lord. The Lord allowed yet another opportunity for His people to return to His presence, fulfilling His promises.

The Lord longs for you to be near Him. He is the God of second, third, and fourth chances. He will never give up on pursuing you. His love is wide. His love is deep. His love is high. You may feel like you have been banned from God's presence. You may feel like you have lost your way. You may feel like there is no way back to the Lord. But today, rest in knowing there is nowhere to escape from His Spirit. He desires for you to return to Him. *It is time to seek Him with all your heart.* He is your good Father, and He loves you.

For He had compassion on His people and on His dwelling place. But they kept ridiculing God's messengers, despising His words, and scoffing at His prophets, until the Lord's wrath was so stirred up against His people that there was no remedy. —2 Chronicles 36:15–16

Further Scripture: Psalm 139:7–10; Jeremiah 29:13–14; Ephesians 3:17–18

Questions

1. In 2 Chronicles 34:3, King Josiah began to seek the God of his father David. How do you think he would have gone about "seeking" God? How long after this did he start purging the land of its idolatry?

2. To what length did King Josiah go to see the land cleansed of its defilement? To what length are you willing to go to see your own life and that of your family cleansed from any ungodliness of the past?

3. The Book of the Law wasn't found until after King Josiah traveled through Judah and some of Israel, purging the land. Without the Book of the Law, how did he know to cleanse the land? How did he respond to what he heard when it was read (2 Chronicles 34:19–21)?

4. What was God's response to King Josiah in 2 Chronicles 34:26–28? What does this reveal about God? How did King Josiah walk out his devotion to the Lord?

5. Near the end of 2 Chronicles, how did the Lord show mercy to His people (2 Chronicles 36:15)? What became of each of the kings sitting on the *Royal Throne* in this last chapter? Where do you see hope in the text?

6. What did the Holy Spirit highlight to you in 2 Chronicles 34—36 through the reading or the teaching?

Lesson 120: Ezra 1—2

Promise Keeper: The Release of the Captives

Teaching Notes

Intro

Today we begin the next historical book—Ezra. At the end of Chronicles, we saw the four kings in Judah whose reigns followed King Josiah, and all the evil they did in the Lord's sight. All four ended up imprisoned, and the temple and the city of Jerusalem were destroyed. God's word through Jeremiah was fulfilled through King Cyrus of Persia. The people stayed in captivity for 70 years. In the book of Ezra, God kept His promises to His people (Genesis 12:1–3). God used Ezra to reinstate His temple in Jerusalem. Interestingly, the book of Ezra is never quoted in the New Testament.

Ezra's name doesn't appear in the book until Ezra 7:1, and in Ezra 7:5 he is identified as coming from the priestly lineage of Aaron. The name Ezra means "Jehovah helps." Jewish tradition accepts Ezra, the prophet, as this book's author as well as the author of the book of Nehemiah. Possibly, the books of Ezra and Nehemiah were written as one book and were divided later.[1] In the first six chapters, the book of Ezra was written in the third person and then it moves to the first person in chapters 7—10. Ezra is also believed to be the author of Chronicles. Jewish tradition holds that "Ezra was the founder of the Great Synagogue, where the complete Old Testament canon was first formally recognized."[2] The timeline for Ezra and Nehemiah looks like this[3]:

- 586 BC The destruction of the temple and Jerusalem and the final exile.
- 538 BC Ezra 1—6; Zerubbabel and Joshua (or Jeshua) enter as leaders under the rule of King Cyrus of Persia.
- 458 BC Ezra 7—10; Ezra was the Jewish priest under King Artaxerxes.
- 445 BC Nehemiah 1—13; Nehemiah was the Jewish leader under King Artaxerxes.

---

[1] John MacArthur, *The MacArthur Bible Commentary* (Nashville: Thomas Nelson, 2005), 518.

[2] MacArthur, 519.

[3] MacArthur, 518.

The first temple in Jerusalem was known as Solomon's temple. In Ezra, the second temple was known as Zerubbabel's temple. The third temple was known as Herod's temple and it was the temple in the New Testament. The fourth temple is still to come in preparation for the end times. The people being released from captivity and returning home somewhat mirrors the people being released from Egypt and coming into the Promised Land. God reestablished His covenant with the returning captives from Babylon.

Teaching

Ezra 1:1–4: God used King Cyrus of Persia, in his first year on the throne, to fulfill His promise that He revealed to Jeremiah (v. 1). This was at the end of the 70 years of captivity. God put a thought into Cyrus' mind to give a proclamation that he would free the captives of Judah and allow them to return to Jerusalem to rebuild God's temple. Cyrus put the proclamation in writing (vv. 2–4) (Jeremiah 25:8–12). The prophecy in Jeremiah 25:11 was fulfilled in the book of Ezra. God was in control (Proverbs 21:1). Wiersbe states that 50,000 Israelites returned because of this proclamation, carrying the offering taken in each region of Babylon where the captives lived.[4] For these returning Israelites, the book of Chronicles would give them the information they needed for rebuilding the temple.

Ezra 1:5–11: The returning Israelites came back with purpose and with materials for rebuilding the temple. King Cyrus returned the things Nebuchadnezzar had taken from the temple under the supervision of his treasurer, who gave them to Sheshbazzar, the prince of Judah (vv. 5–8). The items totaled 5,400 and are listed in verses 9–10. Sheshbazzar took responsibility for returning them all to Jerusalem (v. 11), where they would be used by Zerubbabel in rebuilding the temple. Some scholars suggest that Sheshbazzar and Zerubbabel were the same person because both were listed as having laid the foundation of the temple (Ezra 3 and 5).

Ezra 2: Chapter 2 records that Zerubbabel led the group of exiles back to Judah.

Closing

Genesis 12:1–3 states that God will bless those who bless His people. Possibly this was why King Cyrus was willing to return the articles stolen from the temple—to bless God's people. We too must continue to bless Israel. How do we do that today? In Romans 15:25–27, Paul stated, "If the Gentiles have shared in

---

[4] Warren W. Wiersbe, *The Bible Exposition Commentary: Joshua–Esther* (Colorado Springs: David C. Cook, 2003), 604.

their spiritual benefits, then they are obligated to minister to Jews (the Israelites) in material needs" (v. 27). How do we bless them? By giving to meet their material needs without any thought of return benefit for ourselves.

The Daily Word

Nothing is impossible for God. While the Israelites were captive in Babylon, the Lord put it on the heart of Cyrus, the pagan king of Persia, to issue a proclamation for God's people to return to Jerusalem and rebuild the house of the Lord. The Lord's promise given to Abraham continued to be fulfilled.

No matter what your situation looks like, remember God is a promise keeper. Even in hopeless situations, God remains faithful. He used the power of a pagan leader to allow the Israelites to return to their homeland, fulfilling His promises. God can use anyone because He is an all-knowing, all-powerful, omnipresent God. If He says it in His Word, He will do it. Today if you feel like giving up, *hold on to hope*. Hold fast to the hope found in Christ. Ask the Lord to help you during this time of need. Do not grow anxious or weary; rather rest in God's promises. The Lord will not let you down.

The Lord put it into the mind of King Cyrus to issue a proclamation throughout his entire kingdom and to put it in writing. . . . "Whoever is among His people, may his God be with him, and may he go to Jerusalem in Judah and build the house of the Lord, the God of Israel, the God who is in Jerusalem."
—Ezra 1:1–3

Further Scripture: Genesis 12:2; Deuteronomy 7:9; Hebrews 10:23

Questions

1. Read Ezra 1:4. What does this instruction remind you of (Exodus 3:21–22)?
2. King Cyrus proclaimed that God has appointed him to build a house for God in Jerusalem. Why do you think God is appointing a foreigner to oversee rebuilding His house?
3. Who arose to go and rebuild the house of the Lord? What was given to them to take with them (Ezra 1:6–11)?
4. What happened to those who could not prove their family lineage (Ezra 2:59, 62)? What did they have to wait for?
5. What did some of the heads of families offer (Ezra 2:68–69; 2 Corinthians 9:7)?
6. What did the Holy Spirit highlight to you in Ezra 1—2 through the reading or the teaching?

Lesson 121: Ezra 3—5

Promise Keeper: Rebuilding the Temple

Teaching Notes

Intro

The Israelites had been in captivity for 70 years but had now been released to return to their homeland. From 1 Chronicles and 2 Chronicles, they learned how the Israelites came to be in captivity and what they had to do to get back to the Lord. King Cyrus had released the Israelites (from Persia, formerly Babylon) and given them permission to rebuild their city Jerusalem and their temple.

Teaching

Ezra 3:1: Ezra didn't talk about their journey, but just announced that in the seventh month the people gathered in Jerusalem. Alexander Maclaren commented, "It is a strange narrative of a journey, which omits the journey altogether . . . and notes but its beginning and its end. Are these not the main points in every life, its direction and its attainment?"[1] Genesis 12:4–5 gave a similar description of Abram's journey. That's the beauty of faith . . . we have to depend on God as we make the journey.

Ezra 3:2–3: Ezra listed the names of the men who began to build the altar of God. Jeshua and Zerubbabel were the spiritual and civil leaders of this group of Israelites. They offered burnt offerings to God every morning and evening even though they feared the surrounding people. They worshipped and celebrated the Festival of Booths as if the temple had been completed.[2] They chose to live as though the temple were completed because it would take a while to rebuild it. An assembly like this had not taken place for 70 years (the period of captivity). They built this altar on the foundation that had remained while they were away. Again, this echoed Abram's actions in Genesis 12:7 when he built an altar to the Lord as soon as he arrived in Canaan. In Matthew 6:33, we're told to seek God first and then all things will be provided. So, when we come into a new

---

[1] Alexander Maclaren, *Expositions of Holy Scripture* (Grand Rapids: Baker, 1974), 1:77.

[2] John MacArthur, *The MacArthur Bible Commentary* (Nashville: Thomas Nelson, 2005), 524.

job, new marriage, have kids, or whatever the circumstance is, we don't have to be concerned about the things we need. We only need to be concerned about seeking the Lord. For the Israelites, the altar fanned the flames of their faith so they could do what they needed to do.

Note that even though they feared the people, this fear did not prevent them from setting up the altar and worshipping God. Who were the surrounding people the Israelites feared? According to MacArthur, these were the settlers brought in by the Assyrians and Babylonians when the Israelites were deported. When the Israelites returned, the settlers saw them as a threat.[3]

Ezra 3:4–6: The Israelites celebrated the Festival of Booths based on what the Law required as described in Numbers 29. They were celebrating and seeking the Lord even though the temple had not yet been rebuilt.

Ezra 3:7–13: In these verses, the Israelites laid the foundation of the temple. They paid the stonecutters and artists. They brought cedar wood from Lebanon as authorized by King Cyrus. Isaiah 60:10–14 said that foreigners would build their walls and kings would serve them and that the glory of Lebanon— its pine, fir, and cypress—would come to Israel to beautify God's dwelling place.

In the second month of the second year, they began to build. They appointed the Levites to supervise the work (v. 8). According to Wiersbe, this meant they spent seven months gathering the materials and preparing to build.[4] In Psalm 11:3, David wondered what the righteous could do when the foundations were destroyed. Here, Jeshua and Zerubbabel led Israel to rebuild on the foundations (vv. 9–10). Remember even though this book is named for Ezra, Ezra was not yet in Jerusalem. This building effort was led by Jeshua and Zerubbabel, and this temple was known as Zerubbabel's temple.

Some of the people thought Zerubbabel was the coming king. In Haggai 2:23, the Lord said He would take Zerubbabel and make him like His signet ring. Zechariah 4:6–10 described Zerubbabel in similar language, which also led some of the people to believe he was the coming king. The prophets had told Israel to get excited when they saw Zerubbabel rebuilding the temple. But Zerubbabel wasn't the coming king—he pointed to the king.

When the builders laid the foundation of the temple, the priests and Levites took their positions to praise the Lord. As David had instructed (v. 10), they sang and praised God because His faithful love endures forever (v. 11).

---

[3] MacArthur, 524.

[4] Warren W. Wiersbe, *The Wiersbe Bible Commentary: Old Testament* (Colorado Springs: David C. Cook, 2007), 737.

Psalm 136:1 reminds us that God is good and that His love is eternal. Practically speaking, you could just be coming out of bondage, captivity, a hard situation, an illness, or financial challenge. No matter what you have done or faced, God is truly a *Promise Keeper*. In Genesis 12, God chose the Israelites. Now He says He hasn't forgotten them or forsaken them—they are still His chosen people. This is our phrase for Ezra—God is the *Promise Keeper*. And after 70 years of captivity, the Israelites are reestablishing themselves by seeking the Lord.

How did rebuilding the temple point to the Messiah? Second Corinthians 1:20 says, "For every one of God's promises is "Yes" in Him." God's promises are ultimately fulfilled in Christ. This was a foreshadowing of Christ, the ultimate *Promise Keeper*. God didn't forget about His chosen people as the Israelites came out of captivity, and even in a fallen world, He hasn't forgotten about you and me. God keeps His promises as we continually seek the Lord.

Many of the older priests, the Levites, and family leaders, who had seen the first temple, wept loudly (v. 12). This implies that they were saddened when they did not see the same splendor of Solomon's temple in the new one (1 Kings 5—7). As MacArthur said, this temple was smaller and less beautiful without the riches of David's and Solomon's days and the Ark of the Covenant was also gone. An altar was not the same as the Ark. An altar was where they made offerings, but the Ark was where the presence of the Lord dwelled. The older men were weeping because the Shekinah glory of the Lord was not there.[5] At the same time, the younger ones shouted with joy because they were excited to be walking into something new. Psalm 126:1–6 was written as a song celebrating Zion's restoration.

Closing

We have to fan the flames of faith and seek unity when we see God doing something good. We should never despise small beginnings because God is keeping His promise through His children.

In Ezra 4, the Samaritans opposed the rebuilding of the temple and King Artaxerxes stopped the building. But in Ezra 5, Zechariah and Haggai delivered their messages from the king, and the temple building was resumed. When God is doing something new, opposition will come from without and from within.

---

[5] MacArthur, 524.

The Daily Word

After seventy years of captivity, the people returned to Jerusalem to rebuild the Temple. When the new foundation was completed, the people praised the Lord with shouts of joy and thanksgiving: "For He is good; His faithful love to Israel endures forever." However, while some praised the Lord, the older men who remembered the past foundation wept loudly as they recalled and grieved what Israel had done, what God had to do, and all that had been lost.

God restores all things in your life when you come to Him. He laid the foundation of the earth, and as you follow Him, He is your foundation and solid rock. There may be seasons when you must rebuild your foundation. You may be coming out of bondage or leaving a season of bitterness, a season of hopelessness, or even a season of discipline. As you rebuild your foundation in the Lord, you will praise Him as you find joy for new beginnings and what lies ahead; but you may also grieve what happened in the past. Continue to recall His promises of yes and amen. *He is good and His faithful love endures forever.* The Lord is mighty to save, gives strength to the weak, and fights your every battle. When the world seems like slippery sand, may Christ alone be your firm foundation. In Him, you will not be shaken.

They sang with praise and thanksgiving to the Lord: "For He is good; His faithful love to Israel endures forever." Then all the people gave a great shout of praise to the Lord because the foundation of the Lord's house had been laid. But many of the older priests, Levites, and family leaders, who had seen the first temple, wept loudly when they saw the foundation of this house, but many others shouted joyfully. —Ezra 3:11–12

Further Scripture: Psalm 62:6; Matthew 16:18; 2 Corinthians 1:20

Questions

1. Why were the people fearful of the local residents as they rebuilt the altar? Despite their fearfulness, they kept building. How does this encourage you to keep obeying the Lord and to be a consistent witness for Christ?

2. What were three things the people did in unity (Ezra 3:1, 9, 11)? What was their main goal to accomplish together? Are we seeing unity in the church today (Philippians 2:2)? Why or why not?

3. Do you agree with the statement, "The greater the opportunity, the greater the opposition" (1 Corinthians 16:9)? How do you see that playing out in chapter four? How are we to respond when we know the Lord has called us to something (Philippians 1:6)?

4. What were a few schemes the enemy tried to use to halt the rebuilding of the temple in chapter four? How did the Israelites respond to each one?

5. How did the people first respond, in chapter five, when they were asked who gave them permission to rebuild the temple? Do you claim allegiance to Jesus when opposition comes? Why is it more difficult at certain times than others (John 18:25)?

6. What did the Holy Spirit highlight to you in Ezra 3—5 through the reading or the teaching?

Lesson 122: Ezra 6—8

Promise Keeper: Ezra Returns to Jerusalem

Teaching Notes

Intro

In the book of Joshua, the Israelites moved into the Promised Land. During the period of the judges, the Israelites didn't listen to anyone until God brought in someone to save them, then they did the same things all over again. The story of Ruth was a highlight moment during that time. Then in 1 Samuel and 2 Samuel, we saw the anointing of Saul and David. In 1 and 2 Kings, Solomon built and instituted temple worship, but because of sin the kingdoms were divided into Israel and Judah. Then 1 and 2 Chronicles repeated the history of the kings. Now we're studying Ezra, which could be part of 1 and 2 Chronicles since Ezra wrote all of them. After years of exile and captivity, Israel is going back to the Promised Land. They travelled 900-plus miles from Persia back to Jerusalem.

When the Israelites returned to the land, they began to rebuild the temple, but opposition stopped their work. So, they asked King Darius to look for confirmation that King Cyrus had sent them to rebuild the house of God.

Teaching

Ezra 6:1–10: King Cyrus' decree to rebuild the temple in Jerusalem and to return the gold and silver articles to God's house was found. King Darius then ordered Tattenai, the governor of the region, to let the Israelites rebuild the house of God on its original site (vv. 6–7). Darius further ordered the cost of the temple to be paid from the royal revenues and that all supplies be given to the priests in Jerusalem as they were requested (vv. 8–10). God used a nameless person to find a scroll in an obscure place so His plan could continue. The Israelites rebuilt the temple on the same site on Mt. Moriah where Abraham was prepared to sacrifice Isaac. This same land was the site of the threshing floor that David purchased from Oman. This was the same location where Solomon constructed the first temple. And because of a scroll found in a fortress, the Israelites got to walk out God's promise that says, "Yes, I'm with my people. I will have this temple rebuilt."

Ezra 6:16: The Israelites, the priests, the Levites, and the people celebrated the dedication of this house of God with joy. All of this happened because King Darius humbled himself as described in Proverb 21:1, allowing God to channel the heart of a king to do as He wanted. God is the *Promise Keeper*.

Ezra 7:8: Although the temple had been rebuilt, it was not as great and grandiose as the temple Solomon had built. In this chapter, Ezra led a group of exiles into Jerusalem. Now Ezra actually entered the picture. He took a different route from the one that the first group of exiles had taken.

Ezra 8:1–14: Ezra listed the names of the family leaders who returned with him from Babylon to Jerusalem. Ezra listed eighteen men who led about 1,500 others along with women and children. This group was not as large as the group that had returned 80 years earlier with Zerubbabel and Jeshua. Ezra listed the heads of each family (Zechariah in verse 3, Eliehoenai in verse 4, Shecaniah in verse 5, etc.), a list that was also included in Ezra 2. The family members in this list were tied to those men listed in Ezra 2.

Ezra 8:15–20: Ezra gathered all these descendants to camp for three days at the river that flowed to Ahava. Among those gathered there, Ezra found no Levites. Ezra, using this time to prepare them to cross the river and return to Jerusalem, asked Iddo, chief of the Nethinim, who were descendants of the Gideonites and served as temple servants, to send people to help.[1] Iddo then sent 38 Levites and 220 Nethinim to lead the Israelites returning with Ezra. Why was it so important for the returning Israelites to have Levites? The Levites were appointed by God to offer sacrifices for the people and to care for the temple. These men were gathered before they left for Jerusalem. This is a key part of leadership. Ezra was confident that he had heard from the Lord, so he trusted others to do the work. He didn't follow them or micromanage them but trusted God that they would find the Levites and the Nethinim to do the work.

Ezra 8:21–23: Additionally, Ezra proclaimed a fast by the Ahava River so the Israelites could humble themselves before God, asking Him for a safe journey for them and their possessions. MacArthur said they would soon begin a long journey along a road frequented by thieves.[2] Ezra did this because he didn't want to ask King Darius for protection because the Israelites had told Darius that God would protect them. In Nehemiah 2:7–8, Nehemiah asked King Artaxerxes for letters to the governors along the Euphrates to grant his group

---

[1] John MacArthur, *The MacArthur Bible Commentary* (Nashville: Thomas Nelson, 2005), 529.

[2] MacArthur, 529.

safe passage on their journey to Jerusalem and to Asaph for timber to rebuild the gates, city wall, and houses. Ezra didn't get protection from the infantry and cavalry, but Nehemiah asked for it. At times, as believers, we need to ask for help. In Acts 23, Paul was glad that Roman soldiers guarded him in his journey from Jerusalem to Caesarea. You are not weak when you request protection on your journey. Ezra and the Israelites fasted (this meant no food) and asked God, and He answered them.

Ezra 8:24–30: Ezra selected twelve of the priests along with Sherebiah, Hashabiah, and ten of their brothers to carry their possessions back to Jerusalem. Ezra was radically trusting God to protect them and their valuable possessions on this journey. They had a large amount of money, but they received ultimate protection from Yahweh because He keeps His promises. God heard their request and He answered them.

Ezra 8:31–36: They set out for Jerusalem on the twelfth day of the first month. God strengthened them and protected them along the way. They rested in Jerusalem for three days after their arrival, and then, on the fourth day, they delivered everything to Meremoth the priest. All the items they had brought with them were accounted for. Then they offered burnt offerings to God. They also delivered the king's edicts to the governors in the region so the governors would support the Israelites and the house of God.

Closing

In Ezra 6—8, the money was delivered to the temple, the people were starting to worship the Lord, and tomorrow, we'll close out the Book of Ezra and see how God keeps His promises.

The Daily Word

About eighty years after Zerubbabel and Jeshua led a group of exiled Israelites back to Jerusalem, Ezra returned with a different Israelite group. Before their return journey, Ezra proclaimed a fast for all to humble themselves before the Lord, asking for a safe journey for the travelers and their possessions. This group traveled without a protective infantry or cavalry, seeking the powerful hand of the Lord for protection. Along the journey, the Lord strengthened them and protected them from potential enemies and any ambush. The Lord answered their prayers for the return journey to Jerusalem!

The Lord is enough for the journey He is leading you on. Whether you are returning to Him, following Him in a new calling, or pressing on in perseverance, do not fear and do not tremble. Lay your worries and your concerns at His feet. Consider fasting. Trust that the Lord will protect you and strengthen you. The Lord will cause your enemies to fall by your side. Press on, seek the Lord, and walk in humility as you go along your journey! He is with you and for you. He is your light and salvation. Rest in His faithful promises today. The Lord sees you and is with you!

We set out from the Ahava River on the twelfth day of the first month to go to Jerusalem. We were strengthened by our God, and He protected us from the power of the enemy and from ambush along the way. So we arrived at Jerusalem and rested there for three days. —Ezra 8:31–32

Further Scripture: Psalm 27:1–3; 2 Thessalonians 3:3; 2 Timothy 4:18

Questions

1. Was the temple built during King Darius' reign the same size and magnificence as the temple built by King Solomon (1 Kings 6:2–3)?

2. Why do you think there was a significant difference in the number of animals sacrificed at the dedication of this temple compared to the temple built by Solomon (1 Kings 8:63)?

3. In Ezra 6:18, to which book of Moses were they referring?

4. Ezra 7:6, 10 describe Ezra as a skilled scribe in the Law of Moses and stated God's hand was upon him. If we prepare our hearts to seek and obey the Lord the way Ezra did, would it be noticeable to others?

5. Could the tax-exempt law for the church today have come from Ezra 7:24?

6. What did the Holy Spirit highlight to you in Ezra 6—8 through the reading or the teaching?

Lesson 123: Ezra 9—10

Promise Keeper: Confession and Repentance

Teaching Notes

Intro

Our phrase for the book of Ezra is *Promise Keeper* because God promised the Israelites that they would be able to return to their homeland after 70 years of captivity, and in this book, we see that God kept that promise. Second Corinthians 1:20 emphasizes that God not only keeps His promises, but that His promises are kept in Christ. Today, we'll look at Ezra 9 and 10 as we wrap up this book.

Teaching

Ezra 9:1–3: The leaders reported to Ezra that the people of Israel, including the priests and the Levites, had intermarried with the women from the surrounding lands "so that the holy seed has become mixed with the surrounding peoples" (v. 2). In Joshua 3:10, the Israelites were told that God would dispossess all their enemies who lived in the Promised Land. Yet when the Israelites returned to Jerusalem, Ezra learned that the Israelites were now marrying their enemies. When Ezra heard this, he was devastated.

Ezra 9:4–15: While others gathered around him, Ezra sat in devastation until it was time for the evening offering (v. 4). Then he fell on his knees before God and cried out to God (vv. 5–15). How quickly the Israelites went from hallelujah and revival to the need for a time of serious repentance.

Ezra 10:1: Warren Wiersbe stresses the importance of never underestimating the power of the prayers of one person.[1] James 5:16–18 points out the urgent prayers of a righteous person can have a powerful effect. The power of prayer is attractive, because it points people to the Lord. Here we see that Ezra prayed and confessed the sins of his people as they gathered around him and wept

---

[1] Warren W. Wiersbe, *The Wiersbe Bible Commentary: Old Testament* (Colorado Springs: David C. Cook, 2007), 748.

bitterly with him. Ezra's actions portrayed a broken and contrite spirit, such as David described in Psalm 51:17. So when we come to the Lord in prayer, we cannot come with a spirit of pride and arrogance. We have to come with a humble and broken spirit. Ezra came to the table with lamenting and mourning. Wiersbe points to James 4:9–10, which describe an important aspect of Ezra's prayer.[2] Our laughter has to change to mourning and our joy to sorrow, when we humble ourselves before God so that He will exalt us. This is the process of a man of God who understands the condition and plight of his country and turns to the Lord. This is a picture of a move of God through a man of God, drawing people to God. The Israelites surrounded Ezra because of his prayers and the conviction of their sins. As another example, Genesis 39:9 describes Joseph's response to Potiphar's wife when she attempted to seduce him. Joseph recognized that any sin would be a sin against God. In Psalm 51:4, David acknowledged his sin was against God and God alone. In 2 Corinthians 7:9–10, Paul emphasized that grieving over sin leads to repentance, and repentance leads to salvation. Conviction should produce repentance, and repentance should produce change.

Ezra 10:2–4: Shecaniah took ownership and stepped up to confess to Ezra that the people had been unfaithful to God by marrying foreign women but also maintained that there was still hope for Israel. The people would make a covenant to take action—they would send away their foreign wives and children. The Israelites' repentance led to action. Shecaniah voiced the commitment of the Israelites to this action, but stated that they needed Ezra to get up and lead the charge (v. 4).

Ezra 10:5–6: Ezra led the priests, Levites, and people of Israel in taking an oath to send away their foreign wives and children. Ezra instructed them to do what they had said they would do, then spent the night fasting and mourning over Israel's unfaithfulness.

Ezra 10:7–8: They issued a proclamation calling all exiles to report to Jerusalem, further stating that anyone who failed to appear would forfeit their possessions and be excluded from Israel. As these things took place, Ezra continued praying and fasting. Wiersbe describes a method that produces change.[3] First, you have a humble praying leader. Second, you have a willing people. Then, you have a faithful committee—the group that executes a plan of action. Why was this so

---

[2] Wiersbe, 749.

[3] Wiersbe, 749.

important for Israel? Because God had set them apart as His special people and they needed to be in line with the Law.

Ezra 10:9–44: The men of Judah and Benjamin gathered in Jerusalem. On the twentieth day of the ninth month, Ezra stood before them and urged them to confess their unfaithfulness to God and then separate themselves from their foreign wives. The people agreed to do what Ezra said. But due to the sheer number of people who had to repent and the drenching rains, they asked to be allowed to return home and report to the leaders in their towns. The Israelites did what was proposed (v. 16). The leaders began their investigation on the first day of the tenth month and finished three months later. Wiersbe and MacArthur calculated that over a hundred people were found to be offenders, which included priests, Levites, singers, gatekeepers, and others.[4] These men agreed to send their wives away.

These were the people who were supposed to be leading others in worshipping the Lord. From this we can conclude that there is no sin that can be hidden from the Lord. Genesis 3:7–8 explained that Adam and Eve tried to cover up their sin and hide from God. In Psalm 32:3–4, David said that when he kept silent about his sins of adultery and murder, his bones became brittle from his groaning. He knew God's hand was heavy on him so his strength drained away. When we try to hide our sin from God, it becomes a heavy burden that weighs down on us. Ultimately, God designed us to gain freedom from this burden by confessing our sins to God so He can take away our guilt (Ps 32:5–7). Did you see the switch? David went from hiding his sins to seeking God as his hiding place.

We cannot hide our sin from God. In 1 Samuel 16:7, God emphasized that He sees the heart. He always knows what is in your heart and what you're trying to hide. Psalm 69:5 says our guilty acts are not hidden from God. Numbers 32:23 says we can be sure that our sins will catch up to us. In Luke 12:1–2, Jesus warned His disciples to be on guard against the yeast of the Pharisees by saying, "There is nothing covered that won't be uncovered, nothing hidden that won't be made known." Romans talks about God judging the secrets of the heart. First Corinthians talks about how God brings things to the light. Proverbs 28:13 describes everything Ezra was trying to accomplish in this book. When there is sin in the camp, "The one who conceals his sins will not prosper, but whoever confesses and renounces them will find mercy" (Proverbs 28:13). Ezra and the Israelites needed mercy. Second Chronicles 7:14 describes what happened here.

---

[4] Wiersbe, 749. John MacArthur, *The MacArthur Bible Commentary* (Nashville: Thomas Nelson, 2005), 532.

They humbled themselves and cried out to God, and He heard their prayers and healed their land.

Closing

First John 1:9 gives an awesome picture of how God keeps His promises through the Messiah, who is His Son, Jesus Christ. Ezra called for a time of confession and repentance. The same applies to us. When we come before the Lord in Christ and acknowledge our sins, then He is faithful to forgive us and cleanse us.

The Daily Word

Ezra became aware of sin in Jerusalem: the people of Israel, the priests, the Levites, even the leaders and officials, had intermarried and been unfaithful to the Lord. Ezra was devastated over Israel's sinful ways. In response, he prayed, confessed, and wept in humility before the Lord. As the people witnessed Ezra's brokenness, they joined him in confession and repentance. They brought their brokenness and hidden sins before the Lord. The Lord used Ezra to lead the people forward with a plan to change their lifestyles, and they received God's grace and strength.

The Lord promises healing when you come before Him in humility and brokenness. If you are hiding a sin, most likely you feel the weight of your disobedience. It sits on your shoulders or forms a pit in your stomach. No sin is hidden from the Lord. Go ahead and let go of it. Tell the Lord everything in humility and brokenness. *Then take action and turn away from your old ways.* God promises that when you release your sin to Him, you will find mercy and forgiveness. The Lord removes your guilt, your shame, and your sin as far as the east is from the west. He wants you to walk in freedom. He loves you. Just come before Him today.

While Ezra prayed and confessed, weeping and falling facedown before the house of God, an extremely large assembly of Israelite men, women, and children gathered around him. The people also wept bitterly. Then Shecaniah son of Jehiel, an Elamite, responded to Ezra: "We have been unfaithful to our God by marrying foreign women from the surrounding peoples, but there is still hope for Israel in spite of this. . . . Get up, for this matter is your responsibility, and we support you. Be strong and take action!"
—Ezra 10:1–2, 4

Further Scripture: Psalm 32:3–5; Proverbs 28:13; 1 John 1:9

Questions

1. Why didn't Ezra seem to be aware of the Israelites' intermarriage practices (Ezra 9:3)?

2. How can we, as Christians, effectively express our disapproval of the sin that goes on in the land as Ezra did?

3. Has there ever been a time in any generation that you believe God has not been faithful to leave a remnant? If so, when and why do you believe this way?

4. How did Ezra's lament spark confession and revival among the Israelites?

5. How was 2 Chronicles 7:14 played out in Ezra 10?

6. What did the Holy Spirit highlight to you in Ezra 9—10 through the reading or the teaching?

Lesson 124: Nehemiah 1—2

Builder: God Will Grant Us Success

Teaching Notes

Intro

Our word for the Book of Nehemiah is *Builder*. In my seminary courses, Dr. Howard Hendricks shared that the book of Nehemiah is a picture of how true spiritual leadership can function as the people returned to rebuild the temple and the city. The name Nehemiah means "Jehovah comforts" and appears nowhere else in the Bible outside of the book itself. Jewish tradition accepts Ezra the prophet as the book's author as well as the author of the book of Ezra. Possibly, the books of Ezra and Nehemiah were written as one book and were divided later with Nehemiah entitled 2 Ezra.[1]

God used both the Persians and the Babylonians to bring His judgment of 70 years in exile upon the Israelites for their unfaithfulness to His covenant (Jeremiah 25:11)[2]:

- 722 BC—The Assyrians deported the people of the ten tribes of Israel (the northern kingdom) and spread them throughout the known world (2 Kings 17).
- 605–586 BC—The Babylonians destroyed Jerusalem and deported all but the very poor of the remaining tribes (2 Kings 25).

During these 70 years in captivity, world leadership had changed, and the Babylonian empire had fallen to the Persians. In Ezra, King Cyrus of Persia allowed the first group to return to Jerusalem to rebuild the temple (Ezra 1:1–2). In Nehemiah, more exiles returned to rebuild the city wall around Jerusalem.

Nehemiah served as cupbearer to King Artaxerxes. Zerubbabel and Jeshua were part of the first wave of returning exiles (Ezra 1—6) and led the work to rebuild the temple in Jerusalem with a second wave of exiles (Ezra 7—11). Ezra

---

[1] John MacArthur, *The MacArthur Bible Commentary* (Nashville: Thomas Nelson, 2005), 518, 533.

[2] MacArthur, 533.

returned with the second wave. The Book of Nehemiah records the third wave of returning exiles to rebuild the city wall of Jerusalem. MacArthur states that in the Book of Nehemiah, "Careful attention to the reading of God's Word in order to perform His will is a constant theme."[3] How did they know exactly what to do when rebuilding the city wall of Jerusalem? They consulted the Word of God. Another constant theme in the book is the obedience of Nehemiah in completing the work as well as facing opposition while being obedient.[4] It's amazing that it only took 52 days to complete the rebuilding. The hand of God is constantly on this whole book. The timeline of the book is[5]:

- 445 BC (Nehemiah 1—12)—Covers only one year and tells of Nehemiah's first term as governor (serving from 445–433 BC).
- 425 BC (Nehemiah 13)—After 20 years that were not covered, chapter 13 gives the ending of Nehemiah's story and his second term as governor from 425 or 424 BC to probably 410 BC.

In Nehemiah 1, while in the city of Susa, Nehemiah encountered some men who had come from Judah, and he asked about the remnant that was left behind in Jerusalem. He found out the city walls had been destroyed and the remnant was no longer safe. Nehemiah wept over the conditions and turned to the Lord in prayer and fasting. Nehemiah knew something had to change and asked God for His help. When was the last time you wept and mourned over your city and your country? Nehemiah 1:5–11 shows Nehemiah's heart for his people, his city, and his country.

Teaching

Nehemiah 2:1–10: During the spring of 445 BC, Nehemiah, as the king's cup-bearer, served King Artaxerxes wine, and the king noticed Nehemiah was sad and asked him why (vv. 1–2). Nehemiah explained he was mourning over the ruin of his city where his ancestors were buried (v. 3). When the king asked what Nehemiah wanted to do, Nehemiah prayed and then requested that he be allowed to return to Judah to rebuild the city in honor of his ancestors (vv. 4–5). The king asked how long Nehemiah would be gone and Nehemiah gave him a specific time (v. 6). Queen Esther was the wife of King Xerxes and stepmother to King Artaxerxes, and she possibly influenced her stepson to allow the exiles to begin to return to Israel.[6] Nehemiah also asked the king to give him letters to

---

[3] MacArthur, 534.

[4] MacArthur, 535.

[5] MacArthur, 535–36.

[6] MacArthur, 538.

the governors of the regions he would travel through, to grant him safe passage (v. 7). Then Nehemiah asked for a letter for the keeper of the king's forest so he could get timber for the rebuilding. Nehemiah was asking the king for support for the rebuilding project, and the king granted everything Nehemiah asked for. Nehemiah gave God the credit for the king's support (v. 8). At Nehemiah's request, the king sent soldiers with him, providing Nehemiah safe passage to Jerusalem (v. 9). When Nehemiah arrived in Jerusalem, Sanballat the Horonite and Tobiah the Ammonite heard of Nehemiah's presence and were "greatly displeased" (v. 10). The opposition to Nehemiah's work came immediately.

Nehemiah 2:11–20: Nehemiah waited three days before taking a few men and surveying the walls of the city at night (vv. 11–15). He took time to assess his community before he let anyone in Jerusalem know why he was there (v. 16). When he completed his assessment, Nehemiah explained the situation to the people in Jerusalem and challenged them to help him rebuild the city wall (v. 17). He shared with them how God's hand brought him to them. The people accepted his challenge and were encouraged (v. 18). Those in opposition of the work began to mock the people of Jerusalem and suggested they were in rebellion against the king (v. 19). Nehemiah replied that the Lord would be the One who would give them success because they were His servants (v. 20).

Closing

As a cupbearer, Nehemiah was only a servant of the king, but he had access to the king. We all have a role to play, regardless of how we function in society. We all have access to God through prayer and fasting, and through His strength, we too can be successful in whatever role He has given us.

How will you respond to opposition? The answer for each of us who feel called to rebuild our city is found in Nehemiah 2:20: "The God of heaven is the One who will grant us success. We, His servants, will start building."

The Daily Word

Nehemiah wept and grieved over the destruction of Jerusalem. The walls were broken down and the gates burned. After Nehemiah spent time mourning, fasting, and praying before the God of heaven, the Lord led him before the king. The king asked Nehemiah: "What is your request?" First Nehemiah prayed. And although Nehemiah was fearful, he boldly requested to be sent to Judah to rebuild the city. Something that seemed impossible happened, as it pleased the king to send his cupbearer, Nehemiah, to go to Jerusalem!

Do you weep for the state of your nation? Or maybe destruction has hit closer to home, and you grieve for your marriage or the relationships in your family. As you grieve, seek the Lord and follow Nehemiah's example. He was only a cupbearer in a seemingly unpowerful position, and he was fearful. Nevertheless, he humbled himself, prayed, and sought the Lord. The Lord made the impossible, possible. As you seek the Lord regarding the destruction around you, *expect Him to show up with an answer*. He promises to hear your prayers. And then, as He opens up the doors, press on in confident obedience. The Lord will strengthen you.

When I heard these words, I sat down and wept. I mourned for a number of days, fasting and praying before the God of heaven. —Nehemiah 1:4

Further Scripture: Psalm 5:3; Nehemiah 2:8b; 1 John 5:14

Questions

1. Can you think of any other people in the Bible who sought after the Lord through prayer and fasting (Matthew 4:2; Luke 2:36–37; Acts 13:1–3)?

2. Was God faithful to answer their prayers? Has there ever been a time in your life when you sought the Lord in this way, and if so, what was the result?

3. In Nehemiah 1:8–9, Nehemiah reminded God of what He said to Moses. How often do you pray God's promises? Do you think God has to answer these prayers?

4. What was Nehemiah's position, and do you think this had any significance on the decision that the king made regarding Nehemiah's request?

5. What was the result of Nehemiah's prayer? Do you think God went above and beyond Nehemiah's expectations?

6. How did God use Nehemiah to answer his own prayer (Nehemiah 2:6)? Has God ever used you in an unexpected way to be the answer to your own prayer?

7. What did the Holy Spirit highlight to you in Nehemiah 1—2 through the reading or the teaching?

Lesson 125: Nehemiah 3—4

Builder: Be Serious! Be Alert!

Teaching Notes

Intro

Our phrase for Nehemiah is *Builder*. Nehemiah was obedient to God and cared about the conditions of his city, Jerusalem, and the people who lived there. He received permission to go to Judah and lead the work there to repair the city wall. Nehemiah 2:20 sums up what we've seen so far in chapters 1 and 2: "The God of heaven is the One who will grant us success. We, His servants, will start building." After assessing the damage, Nehemiah led the people to begin the work on the wall (chapter 3). They began the work with the gates: the Sheep's Gate (vv. 1–2), the Fish Gate (vv. 3–5), the Old City Gate (vv. 6–12), the Valley Gate (v. 13), the Dung Gate (v. 14), the Fountain Gate (v. 15), the Water Gate (vv. 26–27), the Horse Gate (v. 28), the East Gate (vv. 29–30), the Inspection Gate or Miphkad Gate (v. 31), and back to the Sheep Gate (v. 32).

Teaching

Nehemiah 4:1–6: Walking out God's calling draws opposition (Hebrews 11:36). Sanballat became "furious" when he found out the work on the wall was taking place, and he mocked and ridiculed the Jews in front of his colleagues and the powerful men in Samaria. Sanballat called the Jews "pathetic," made fun of their religious traditions, and questioned their ability to bring back to life the burned stones of the wall (vv. 1–2). Then Tobiah the Ammonite joined in with mocking the Jews efforts, saying any wall they built would not be strong enough to even hold the weight of a fox (v. 3). In response, Nehemiah prayed and asked God to turn all their threats back on them (vv. 4–5). The people continued to work on the wall despite the opposition they faced (v. 6).

Nehemiah 4:7–14: The threats and mocking of the enemies continued through the first seven chapters of Nehemiah. Sanballat and Tobiah brought others who were angry with the work on the walls—the Arabs, the Ammonites, and the Ashdodites (v. 7). They plotted together how they might overthrow Jerusalem

(v. 8). In response, Nehemiah led the people in prayer and then stationed guards around the clock (v. 9). There was so much rubble and trash to clear away before the wall could be rebuilt that laborers were already frustrated and tired from their work (v. 10). The combined enemies tried to intimidate the Jews, telling them they would never know what had happened until they had already been defeated (v. 11). The Jews felt they were being attacked from all sides (v. 12). So Nehemiah sorted the people by family groups in those areas of the wall that were most vulnerable and armed them with swords, spears, and bows (v. 13). Then he challenged the people to not be afraid of their enemies because the Jews had the support of "the great and awe-inspiring Lord." They were to fight for their countrymen, their families, and their homes (v. 14).

Nehemiah 4:15–23: Their enemies found out the Jews created a work schedule in which half the men worked, and the other half stood guard with spears, shields, bows, and armor (v. 16). The laborers carried their loads of supplies with one hand while holding a weapon in the other while the builders each worked with their swords strapped at the waist (vv. 17–18). Nehemiah kept a trumpeter with him at all times since the work was so spread out. The trumpet sound would draw the workers to rally together to fight their enemies with God (vv. 19–20). The work continued from daybreak until dark, and all the workers stayed inside Jerusalem at night to be part of the city's protection (vv. 21–22). Nehemiah and his workers never took off their clothes to rest but carried their weapons, even while washing (v. 23).

Closing

The people of Jerusalem faced significant opposition while they worked on the wall. They faced opposition by threat of death, by fear, by ridicule, and by intimidation. They survived it through prayer and persistence—by serving as watchmen. Dave Butts outlined the work of the watchman:

1. Watchmen stand their posts with "an intensity that must be shared . . . day and night . . . never silent . . . give yourself no rest" (Isaiah 62:6–7).
2. Watchmen must stand their posts with their eyes open. That includes open spiritual eyes as well, which is done through prayer and being watchful to discern what God is doing (Matthew 26:40–41).
3. Watchmen must be aware of the actions of the enemy (2 Corinthians 2:11).
4. Watchmen must work to discern the needs of God's people.[1]

---

[1] Dave Butts, "The Task of a Watchman," Harvest Prayer Ministries, https://www.harvestprayer.com/resources/personal-2/task-of-watchman/.

Be on guard for yourselves and for your teaching (Acts 20:28; 1 Timothy 4:16). "Be serious! Be alert! Your adversary the Devil is prowling around like a roaring lion, looking for anyone he can devour" (1 Peter 5:8).

The Daily Word

Nehemiah and all the people followed the Lord and worked together to rebuild the city's wall. But then *opposition from the enemy came.* Enemies plotted together to fight against Jerusalem and brought confusion and discouragement to the people. At this point, Nehemiah led the people in prayer to God. They were not afraid of the enemy. They remembered God called them to rebuild the wall, and Nehemiah encouraged them: "Do not be afraid!" The Lord gave them wisdom for a plan to stay on guard day and night, and they trusted He would fight for them.

As you walk obediently with Jesus, the enemy will come your way, devising plans to discourage and confuse you. You may think: *This is too hard—am I really following the Lord?* Be firm in your calling. Remember when the Lord confirmed the work of your hands. Stand strong in Him and remain alert. The Lord will fight for you and will give you wisdom. The Lord will protect you in battle when you feel surrounded by enemies. The Lord promises He is greater in you, than the one who is in the world. You can do this! You will not be destroyed.

After I made an inspection, I stood up and said to the nobles, the officials, and the rest of the people, "Don't be afraid of them. Remember the great and awe-inspiring Lord, and fight for your countrymen, your sons and daughters, your wives and homes." —Nehemiah 4:14

Further Scripture: Acts 20:28; 2 Corinthians 2:11; 1 Peter 5:8–9

Questions

1. In Nehemiah 3, do you think it was by accident that specific people built each section of the wall, or do you think there was a purpose behind it?

2. In chapter 4, what did Nehemiah do when he heard that Sanballat and Tobiah had conspired to fight against Jerusalem? What did Nehemiah and the workers do in response?

3. What part did Nehemiah play in building the wall (Nehemiah 4:4–5, 16–23)?

4. What did the Holy Spirit highlight to you in Nehemiah 3—4 through the reading or the teaching?

Lesson 126: Nehemiah 5—6

Builder: Experiencing Opposition

Teaching Notes

Intro

As you are doing what God has called you to do, you will experience opposition. Jesus said if we follow Him, we will experience persecution. Jesus said as we follow Him, people will say false things about us. Warren Wiersbe observed, "Under Nehemiah's gifted leadership, the people completed the rebuilding of the walls. Now all that remained to do was the restoration of the gates and the strengthening of the community within the walls."[1]

Harry Truman famously said, "If you can't stand the heat, get out of the kitchen." The enemy will always send opposition against leaders. In this chapter, opposition came as the work was almost done.

Teaching

Nehemiah 6:1–4: Since the doors were not yet in the gates, there was still a small gap in the wall. But the enemies did not know that. They only knew that the wall was nearly finished, so they tried to oppose Nehemiah one more time. As you are almost done with the task the Lord has given you, the enemy will try to get you to do a few things. First, the enemy will try to get you to compromise.[2]

Nehemiah's enemies repeatedly sent him a message to try to lure him into the Ono Valley to harm him. But each of the four times they sent their request to Nehemiah, Nehemiah replied that he would not come because he was doing a great work. Their request was persistent because they wanted Nehemiah to compromise. It's almost as though they said, "You're almost done. What harm will it do to come?" The enemy wants us to compromise just a little to begin to pull us off of the work the Lord has called us to do. Before long, a little compromise leads to drifting, and soon we find ourselves a long way off from where God wants us to be.

---

[1] Warren W. Wiersbe, *Be Determined: Standing in the Face of Opposition* (Colorado Springs: David C. Cook, 1992), 83.

[2] Wiersbe, 84.

Nehemiah 6:5–7: Wiersbe states that if we resist compromising, the enemy will slander us.[3] Nehemiah's enemies created a gossip mill to try to intimidate him. John MacArthur noted, "Official letters were typically rolled up and sealed with an official signet by the letter's sender or one of his assisting officials."[4] The fact that this letter was "open" was a sign of disrespect and open criticism. It was also a sign that its contents were public knowledge.

What was in the letter became gossip that spread quickly. The letter's charge was that Nehemiah had betrayed the trust of the king of Persia. When Nehemiah was granted permission to return to Jerusalem, he gave the king a definite time-frame for the work to be completed before his return to Persia. If the king were to hear the charges in the letter, he would feel Nehemiah had betrayed him in order to set himself up as king. The king would most likely send troops to take care of the problem . . . if the accusations were true, that is.

Nehemiah 6:8–9: When slander happens, don't get distracted. Every time compromises and slander were thrown at Nehemiah, he leaned on his relationship with the Lord. Nehemiah constantly talked to the Lord. The Psalmist wrote, "I have heard the gossip of many; terror is on every side. When they conspired against me, they plotted to take my life. But I trust in You, Lord; I say, 'You are my God'" (Psalm 31:13–14). Proverbs 4:27 encourages us, "Don't turn to the right or the left; keep your feet away from evil." Don't let the comments of gossipers get to you. Stay the course in your work.

Nehemiah 6:10–14: Wiersbe states that when distractions and slander fail, the enemy will make threats against us.[5] Nehemiah went to visit Shemaiah who advised him to hide in the temple because his enemies were coming to kill him. Nehemiah realized Shemaiah was working for Tobiah and Sanballat to again try to distract him from his work on the city walls. Since they could not draw Nehemiah out from the city, they attempted to make him retreat into the temple. But Nehemiah was not a priest. He knew he could not go into the temple like that. Israelites could seek refuge at the altar outside the temple, but they could not go into the temple (Exodus 21:13–14). This was a temptation to distract and discredit Nehemiah. No one would think to look for him there because they all knew he wasn't supposed to be there.

If Nehemiah were to hide in the temple, it would also discredit the boldness with which he had acted in the eyes of the people. Nehemiah would be like every

---

[3] Wiersbe, 86.

[4] John MacArthur, *The MacArthur Bible Commentary* (Nashville: Thomas Nelson, 2005), 542–43.

[5] Wiersbe, 88.

other disloyal Jew. He would have sinned, and his leadership would have been undermined in the eyes of the people.

Nehemiah 6:15–19: Wiersbe notes the enemy will not give up.[6] It only took fifty-two days for Nehemiah and the people to rebuild the walls, but Nehemiah's enemies challenged him throughout every single one of those days. Wiersbe observed, "Many a careless Christian has won the war, but afterwards lost the victory."[7] The enemy knew the task was done, but they still persisted in opposing the work. Even after the work on the wall was done, some of the Jews began gravitating to Tobiah, Nehemiah's enemy. Through letters to the nobles of the Jews, Tobiah still tried to intimidate Nehemiah. The people lost their focus on their task and to the one whom they were committed.

Closing

When the work was done, the people's allegiance shifted from Nehemiah to the enemies who had opposed them. Your ultimate loyalty in the work that God has called you to is to Christ. Other things, even good things like family, can be a distraction from the task that you have been called to by God. When we experience victory, it is important for us to not settle and get comfortable because God may want to press on and do even more. Don't win the war and neglect God's victory.

The Daily Word

Nehemiah and the builders pressed on in their calling to rebuild the wall. The fifth attempt to harm and discourage Nehemiah came when rumors were spread. The enemy continued to intimidate and dispirit the builders, so the work on the wall would not be finished. Nehemiah remained strong in the Lord. He stayed focused on the task, and the Lord granted him wisdom and discernment not to give in to the enemy's threats. After fifty-two days, the Israelites completed the wall. This intimidated their enemies, who lost confidence. In the end, the Israelites' enemies recognized it was the Lord God who built the wall.

Where is the enemy attempting to discourage you as you do what the Lord has called? Pursuing a unified marriage? Giving generously from your finances? Discipling a new believer? As you walk with the Lord, in His power, *the enemy will come after you.* Stay focused. Don't turn to the left or the right. Don't look back. Don't compromise. Seek the Lord for discernment of good and evil. If you feel like you can't bear up under the pressure, remember that your strength comes

---

[6] Wiersbe, 89.

[7] Wiersbe, 89.

from the Lord God Almighty. *He will fight for you.* You will complete all the Lord has called you to, and others will see it was the Lord's doing, not your own. To Him be the glory forever and ever. Amen!

Then I replied to him, "There is nothing to these rumors you are spreading; you are inventing them in your own mind." For they were all trying to intimidate us, saying, "They will become discouraged in the work, and it will never be finished." But now, my God, strengthen me. —Nehemiah 6:8–9

Further Scripture: Nehemiah 6:15–16; Psalm 31:13–15; Proverbs 4:26–27

Questions

1. When you read Nehemiah 5:1–5, do you notice many differences in our time period compared to Nehemiah's? Do you think these passages could be for today also? Why or why not?

2. In Nehemiah 6:10–13, a prophet gave Nehemiah a word, but Nehemiah realized it was false. What does the Bible say about false prophets (Deuteronomy 18:20; Matthew 7:15; 2 Peter 2:1)?

3. Nehemiah finished the wall in 52 days. The Israelites enemies were frightened and humiliated. Why? With God the Israelites were able to finish the wall in record time.

4. What did the Holy Spirit highlight to you in Nehemiah 5—6 through the reading or the teaching?

Lesson 127: Nehemiah 7—8

Builder: Public Reading of the Law, Festival of Booths Observed

Teaching Notes

Intro

Nehemiah 7 contains the list of the exiled men. In verse 1, the wall had been rebuilt, the doors installed, and the gatekeepers, singers, and Levites were appointed to their duties. The work was done, and everybody was in place. Beginning in verse 7, the Israelite exiles were listed. Beginning in verse 39, the priests were included. Beginning in verse 43, the Levites were included. Beginning in verse 44, the singers were included then in verse 45, the gatekeepers were included. In verse 46, the temple servants were listed. In verse 57, even the descendants of Solomon's servants were listed. Basically, God revealed that He never forgets the faithful, and here the faithful who came back from exile were listed along with the roles they played. With everything in place, it was time to hold a Bible conference. Warren Wiersbe stated that Israel was a "people of the Book" who needed to learn to delight in the Word of God.[1] Nehemiah wanted the exiles to focus on the Lord now that they were free. Psalm 1:2–3 emphasizes this point. With this purpose in mind, Nehemiah called for Ezra, who was the best teacher in the land.

Teaching

Nehemiah 8:1: The people gathered in the square in front of the Water Gate. They asked Ezra to bring out the Book of the Law of Moses, which Ezra had returned to Israel thirteen years before. Now they were shifting from Ezra's private study of the law to public study. Wiersbe said this chapter describes three responses to the Word of God, with verses 1–8 emphasizing that we must understand the word of God.[2]

---

[1] Warren W. Wiersbe, *The Wiersbe Bible Commentary: Old Testament* (Colorado Springs: David C. Cook, 2007), 775.

[2] Wiersbe, 775.

In John 15:3, Jesus told the disciples they were clean because of the word He spoke to them. Ezra was reading the Word of God to the people as they stood by the Water Gate. Hearing the Word of God has a cleansing and refreshing effect on people. This event in Nehemiah is a foreshadowing of the cleansing that happens when we talk to Jesus. Ephesians 5:26 says Jesus made the church holy by cleansing her with the washing of water by the Word. When the Word of God was reinstated back in Ezra and Nehemiah's time, the Israelites were being washed by the Word of God. When we dig into the Word of God, we experience a cleansing. When the Word is released, it is powerful and cleansing. It is refreshing when we understand it. In John 7:37, Jesus cried out, "If anyone is thirsty, he should come to Me and drink!" Jesus is the Word (John 1:1–4, 14). Jesus promised, "The one who believes in Me . . . will have streams of living water flow from deep within Him" (John 7:38). When we come to Jesus, we can be refreshed in the Spirit of God.

Nehemiah 8:2–8: Ezra brought out the Book of the Law and read from it from daybreak until noon while the people listened attentively. As *Nelson's Commentary* states, that's six hours.[3] Ezra stood on a high wooden platform and opened the book in full view of the people. The people stood up and lifted their hands before bowing down and worshipping the Lord. They truly respected the Word of God. First Timothy 4:13 tells us to give attention to the public reading, exhortation, and teaching of God's Word until Jesus comes back. When we give respect to God's Word, our understanding will grow. As the Word was read, the Levites explained the law to the people (v. 7) so the people could understand it (v. 8).

Nehemiah 8:9–12: In addition to understanding the Word, Wiersbe said we must rejoice in it.[4] Why would Nehemiah and Ezra have to tell the people not to weep? They were weeping because they realized they had not been worshipping the Lord or keeping the standards He asked them to keep. But Nehemiah urged the people to celebrate instead of grieving. They should rejoice because their strength would come from the Lord. They were experiencing a move of God, and Nehemiah wanted them to rejoice in it. Because the people understood the Word of God, they had a great celebration. Jeremiah said God's words brought joy and delight to him (Jeremiah 15:16). God's Word has the power to help us fight depression and loneliness. Psalm 19:8 says the Word of the Lord

---

[3] Earl D. Radmacher, Ronald B. Allen, and H. Wayne House, eds., *Nelson's New Illustrated Bible Commentary* (Nashville: Thomas Nelson, 1999), 594.

[4] Wiersbe, 775.

makes the heart glad and the eyes light up. When we're in the Word, our hearts are glad. Psalm 119:162 encourages us to rejoice over God's promises.

Nehemiah 8:13–18: In addition to understanding and rejoicing in the Word, Wiersbe said we also need to obey it.[5] The next day, the people continued to gather to study the Word of the law. When they discovered that the Lord had commanded Moses that Israel should dwell in booths during the festival (Leviticus 23), they went into the hill country to gather branches from leafy trees to make booths. They realized they had to be doers of the Word, so they went out, gathered branches, and built booths for themselves. Israel had not celebrated like this since the days of Joshua. With great joy, they celebrated the festival for seven days, with Ezra reading the book of the law every day. True revival involves digging into the Word of God, which impacts our emotions, leading to action. In Matthew 28:18–20, Jesus instructed His followers, "Go, therefore, and make disciples of all nations, baptizing them in the name of the Father and of the Son and of the Holy Spirit, teaching them to observe everything I have commanded you." We won't see a true revival until we do the Great Commission, until we actually act upon the Word of God. Maybe we don't need seminary or school, we just need to understand the Word of God and rejoice in what He's doing so that we can actually obey it. James 1:22 tells us to be doers of the Word and not hearers only.

Closing

If we want to see a true move of God, we must be doers of the Word. While that can include many things, it must include Matthew 28. We actually could see a revival if we acted out what we understood.

The Daily Word

After Nehemiah rebuilt the wall, he gathered the people together and opened the Book of the Law of Moses the Lord gave Israel. The people stood and listened to the reading of the Word. Certain Levites translated and explained the Word, so the people could understand it. Nehemiah encouraged the people to celebrate all they learned from God's Word. Indeed, the joy of the Lord was their strength! This joy motivated the people to not merely listen to the Word of the Lord but to obey it as well.

Why is it so hard to open the Word of God and actually read it? You walk by it, you see it sitting on the bookshelf, you carry it in your backpack or purse all day long. You even have it on your phone . . . but you get distracted. You neglect

---

[5] Wiersbe, 775.

to open it and actually read it. Today, open the Word of God and read a verse or two. The Israelites were strengthened with joy by reading the Word, and it motivated them to action. If you are feeling down, lonely, nervous, unmotivated, or in need of guidance, *open the Word of God*. Allow God's truth to settle in your heart. The joy of the Lord will be your strength!

Ezra opened the book in full view of all the people, since he was elevated above everyone. As he opened it, all the people stood up. Ezra praised the Lord, the great God, and with their hands uplifted all the people said, "Amen, Amen!" Then they bowed down and worshiped the Lord with their faces to the ground. —Nehemiah 8:5–6

Further Scripture: Nehemiah 8:10; Psalm 19:8; Jeremiah 15:16

Questions

1. What is the definition of a watchman? Why did Nehemiah assign watchmen to the gate? Where else were watchmen used (Jeremiah 6:17)?

2. How did they decide if a certain people group were families of priests (Nehemiah 7:64–65)? Where else was this used (Exodus 28:30; Numbers 27:21)?

3. Why did the people celebrate the Festival of Booths (or Tabernacles) (Nehemiah 8:14)? How did they prepare for the festival? What did they do during the festival?

4. What did the Holy Spirit highlight to you in Nehemiah 7—8 through the reading or the teaching?

Lesson 128: Nehemiah 9

Builder: The Grace of God

Teaching Notes

Intro

Why do we spend so much time in the Old Testament and studying the historical books? George Santayana said, "Those who do not remember the past are condemned to relive it."[1] So if we don't learn from the folks in our past, how can we ever grow? Do you remember the old church cliché; history = His story? During this time, Zerubbabel and Jeshua led the people in rebuilding the temple while Ezra and Nehemiah led the people in rebuilding the walls and the city. With everything in place, Ezra began reading the Word of God to the people. They were going over His story. In the books of Ezra, Nehemiah, and Daniel, there are three major prayers considered to be national prayers of Israel. We read Ezra's prayer for the nation in Ezra 9, and today, we'll read Nehemiah's prayer for the nation in Nehemiah 9. We'll read Daniel's national prayer in Daniel 9. It's important to understand each of these prayers is based on 2 Chronicles 7:14.[2]

Teaching

Nehemiah 9:1–6: Warren Wiersbe referred to these verses as "the greatness of God."[3] As the Israelites assembled, they were fasting, wearing sackcloth, and had put dust on their heads (v. 1). According to John MacArthur, they were cultivating a demonstration for their sin because they truly mourned for where they were.[4] Those who were the descendants of Jacob (Israel) separated themselves from the foreigners (v. 2). It had been thirteen years since Ezra first read the Word of God to them, and now these men under Nehemiah called on those who had married foreigners to recognize their sin and separate

---

[1] Warren W. Wiersbe, *The Wiersbe Bible Commentary: Old Testament* (Colorado Springs: David C. Cook, 2007), 778.

[2] Wiersbe, 778.

[3] Wiersbe, 778.

[4] John MacArthur, *The MacArthur Bible Commentary* (Nashville: Thomas Nelson, 2005), 547.

themselves from their foreign wives.[5] In the presence of the greatness of God, they confessed their sins. For one-fourth of the day—that's three hours—they read the Word of God, and then for another three hours, they confessed their sins and worshipped God (v. 3). In 1 Timothy 4:13, Paul told believers to focus on public reading. The Levites stood on a raised platform and encouraged Israel to stand up and praise God (vv. 4–5). In their prayer, they focused on God as the creator (v. 6). They recognized that God was incomparable and the One who truly created all things.

Nehemiah 9:7–12: As Wiersbe suggests, these verses shift from the greatness of God to the goodness of God.[6] In His goodness, God chose Abram (v. 7) and gave him the land of the Canaanites (v. 8). Sixteen times in this chapter, we see the word "give" because of God's goodness. The covenant with Abraham was based on God's faithfulness. God promised this land to Abraham and his descendants (Genesis 15:18; Exodus 3:8; 33:2). In Nehemiah 9, the people honored what God had done for them. They remembered what God had done for their ancestors when He brought them out of Egypt (vv. 9–12). Through all of these layers—the creation, the covenant, the exodus, the Red Sea—they kept building until they got to the point where their city had been rebuilt. These events revealed God's goodness to them. The people coming back into Jerusalem where the temple had been rebuilt needed to know God's story in all of this.

Nehemiah 9:13–21: These verses described the events that occurred at Mt. Sinai. God gave them good commands (v. 13), the Sabbath (v. 14), and spoke to them through Moses. He gave them bread and water and then told them to go in and possess the land He had given them (v. 15). But their ancestors were stiff-necked and refused to listen to God's commands or remember His wonders (vv. 16–17). Instead, they appointed a leader to take them back to Egypt and to bondage (v. 17). Nehemiah knew the people of his day faced the danger of repeating the mistakes of their ancestors. But Nehemiah recalled God's goodness in forgiving them because He didn't abandon them in the wilderness even when they made an idol and worshipped the golden calf (vv. 18–19). Instead, God sent His Spirit to instruct them and did not withhold manna or water (v. 20). God provided for them in the wilderness for 40 years (v. 21). Nehemiah reiterated what Moses had written in Deuteronomy 8:4 when he recalled that "their clothes did not wear out and their feet did not swell."

---

[5] MacArthur, 547.

[6] Wiersbe, 778.

Nehemiah 9:22–25: These verses recounted Israel's entrance into the promised land under Joshua, the son of Nun. God gave them the land (v. 22) and multiplied their descendants (v. 23). God subdued their enemies (v. 24). The word "subdued" brings to mind the truth in Exodus 15:3, "The Lord is a warrior; Yahweh is His name" (NLT).

Nehemiah 9:26–30: These verses describe the days from the judges to the time of the Babylonian captivity. They were disobedient and rebelled against God; they killed His prophets (v. 26). God then handed them over to their enemies until they cried out to Him (v. 27). This became their pattern of behavior (v. 28).

Nehemiah 9:31–38: After considering the greatness of God and the goodness of God, Nehemiah called them to experience the grace of God.[7] He reminded them that because God is gracious and compassionate, He did not destroy or abandon Israel (v. 31). In verse 32, the phrase "so now" implies that great revival took place as Ezra read the Word of God. Nehemiah emphasized that as they experienced revival, they should remember the great, mighty, and awe-inspiring God who keeps His gracious covenant. They couldn't take what happened to them and their ancestors lightly. As MacArthur pointed out, Nehemiah's prayer turned to a present confessing of unfaithfulness.[8] By going through the history of everything that the Israelites had experienced, they realized they were no better than their ancestors (vv. 35–36). They realized that they had gotten to this point because of their unfaithfulness. In verse 38, they made a renewed commitment to the Mosaic covenant. In view of all of this, Israel was all in. They realized what God had done to get them to that point, they confessed the sin in their lives, and they made a binding agreement to God. As MacArthur said, they made a pledge and a promise to obey God and repented of the sins of their fathers because they didn't want to go back. They wanted to see change.[9]

Closing

The Word of God will do the same thing for you if you allow it to be part of your life. God is looking for a little remnant who realizes how big God is, how great He is, how good He is, and that the grace of God is still in our lives so we can now walk out our ministry.

---

[7] Wiersbe, 778.

[8] MacArthur, 548.

[9] MacArthur, 548–49.

The Daily Word

The Israelites assembled, fasted, wore sackcloth, and put dust on their heads as a sign of mourning for their sins and spiritual condition. Then they prayed and praised the Lord. They spent time remembering God's faithfulness to the covenant He made with Abraham. They confessed their disobedience and recognized the Lord's compassion. He rescued and delivered them. He never abandoned them because He kept His gracious covenant. As a remnant, they made a binding agreement to follow the Lord.

The Lord will never abandon you. He will never leave you. God is your deliverer and your rescuer. He is a compassionate God. The Lord hears you when you cry out in distress. Maybe you feel abandoned by someone—a parent, sibling, or friend. Maybe even by God. However, unlike the others, *the truth is God will never abandon you.* He promises He will be with you always; nothing will ever separate you from His great love. Nothing. God's love is a free gift you receive by saying, "Yes, Lord, I receive Your grace." No binding agreement necessary. Today, accept His free gift; believe His promises.

You warned them to turn back to Your law, but they acted arrogantly and would not obey Your commands. They sinned against Your ordinances, which a person will live by if he does them. They stubbornly resisted, stiffened their necks, and would not obey. You were patient with them for many years, and Your Spirit warned them through Your prophets, but they would not listen. Therefore, You handed them over to the surrounding peoples. However, in Your abundant compassion, You did not destroy them or abandon them, for You are a gracious and compassionate God. —Nehemiah 9:29–31

Further Scripture: Deuteronomy 31:8; Romans 8:38–39; Ephesians 2:8–9

Questions

1. The Israelites had just finished the Feast of Tabernacles where they were filled with great joy. Why, in verse 1, were the people fasting and dressed in burlap?

2. How had the Israelites, according to the prayer, responded to God's great kindness, great mercy, and great goodness (Nehemiah 9:18, 26)? What did their rebellion lead too (Nehemiah 9:37)?

3. Why was it important for the Israelites to confess not only their sins but also the sins of their fathers/ancestors? When was the last time you examined yourself and confessed the sins the Lord revealed to you (2 Corinthians 13:5)?

4. In what four ways was God's greatness described in verse 6?

5. How is verse 33 a great model for confession? How does this verse also affirm the righteousness of God? How are believers to confess today (James 5:16; 1 John 1:9)?

6. What did the Holy Spirit highlight to you in Nehemiah 9 through the reading or the teaching?

Lesson 129: Nehemiah 10

Builder: Continuing the House of the Lord

Teaching Notes

Intro

It feels like we have flown through Nehemiah! The topic or theme for this whole book is *Builder*. This is a very practical book. Nehemiah was rebuilding the city of Jerusalem. At the end of Nehemiah 9, there was a group of people who had studied through the history of Israel. In chapter 10, this group decided they wanted a document that showed they wanted to follow God. This document was signed and sealed.

Teaching

Nehemiah 10:1–27: These verses list all the people who were committing and submitting to the Word of God. They were all in!

Nehemiah 10:28–30: You begin to see the separation of the Israelites as the people of God. This includes everyone who was obeying the law of God by literally separating themselves from worldly things and people. There were two major areas of separation. The first separation was marriage. There tended to be this theme of the Israelites being super tempted by the women of the enemy or foreign peoples. The problem was that as the Israelites came into foreign lands and married foreign women, they became worldly and disobeyed the Word of God.

So the Israelites would not let their daughters marry those outside the faith. The application for us here is that we must make ourselves different. When you start aligning yourself in relationships or marriages that are not equally yoked, the relationships don't work (Exodus 34:10–17). I think foreign marriages had been the downfall of Israel since the beginning. It's never worked! Marriage is very important! We are to be separate and distinct as followers of the Lord.

Nehemiah 10:31: The second area of separation is through the Sabbath. God wanted and still wants His people to rest. The Sabbath should not be a day of misery but a day of rest. I think we need to ask ourselves, "Can I depend upon the Lord to fully rest for an entire day?" What led the Israelites into Babylon was not resting on the seventh year—not taking a Sabbath. This would have been a huge statement for Nehemiah and the others to say, "Yes, we will adhere to the Sabbath."

Nehemiah 10:32–39: In the Israelites process of submission and separation, we see their support for the house of God. They came up with self-imposed commands to give to the house of the Lord. They did this in order to keep the people focused. It was written, "We will not neglect the house of our God" (v. 39). I feel like this chapter is a summary of God's desire for His people. God longs for His people to submit to the Word of God, to separate themselves from worldly things, and to continue to support the house of the Lord.

I want to look at the different offerings mentioned in these verses. Warren Wiersbe broke up these offerings in the following way:[1]

The temple tax (vv. 32–33).

- In the Book of Exodus, these taxes were used to make silver sockets and other things for the temple.
- In the New Testament and present day, giving would go to pay salaries (Luke 10:7); share with the needy (1 Corinthians 16:1–3); and show the practice of good stewardship (2 Corinthians 8:9).

The wood offering (v. 34).

- The fire on the brazen altar was to be kept burning (Leviticus 6:12–13).
- The Israelites cast lots to see who would give this offering.
- There was a lot of wood needed!

The firstfruits (vv. 35–37a).

- The firstfruits are giving to God the first and the best.
- These offerings were redeemed by sacrifices of the ground (Exodus 23:16), the trees (Leviticus 19:23–25), and sons (Numbers 18:15).
- All these things are about contributing to the house of the Lord (Jeremiah 2:3)!

---

[1] Warren W. Wiersbe, *The Wiersbe Bible Commentary: Old Testament* (Colorado Springs: David C. Cook, 2007), 686–87.

- God's firstfruits are the Israelites. They are to be giving of themselves. Later in 1 Corinthians 15:23, we see Christ is the ultimate firstfruits who sacrificed His life for ours.

What does this mean for us today? These are the ways you can help support the temple and the house of God[2:]

- God expects each one of us to give from our firstfruits.
- If you have a business think, "What can I give first?"
- Giving should be joyful (2 Corinthians 9:7).
- We should give as we have been given (Matthew 6:2–4; 1 Corinthians 16:1–2).
- What I love about the principle of firstfruits giving is that you are giving what you have!

The tithes (vv. 37b–39).

- The Jews tithed to the temple (Numbers 18:23–32; Deuteronomy 26:11).

Closing

If the Israelites were going to move forward with the work given to them, they needed to submit to God's Word, separate themselves, and support the house of the Lord. All of these things pointed and still point to God's presence. Just because a physical building stops growing, the house of the Lord does not stop growing.

The Daily Word

The Israelites submitted to Yahweh and made the decision to walk in His ways. They committed to separate themselves from others in the area because they were children of God, followers of Yahweh. It's one thing to say, "We love the Lord and read His Word," but they needed to *live their lives differently from those who did not follow God.* The Israelites vowed to obey and follow God's Word through marriage, honoring the Sabbath, and supporting the house of the Lord with their firstfruits.

---

[2] Steve Diggs, "Three Key Principles of Godly, Biblical Giving," Crosswalk, September 25, 2006, https://www.crosswalk.com/family/finances/three-key-principles-of-godly-giving-1426486.html.

If you truly love the Lord your God with all your heart, soul, and mind, then your behavior, your actions, and the way you spend your time, resources, and talents will be transformed. As a New Testament Christian, your faith is not about a list of laws and rules. Rather, it's a matter of daily yielding your heart to the Lord and receiving His grace and power that transforms you into His image. *Does your life resemble Christ or the world?* If you remain in the world, then you will resemble the world. But as you remain in Christ and walk in the Spirit, you will bear much fruit: love, joy peace, patience, kindness, goodness, faithfulness, gentleness, and self-control. As the world sees the fruit of the Spirit displayed in your life, they will know something is different about you. That difference is Jesus empowering you!

The rest of the people—the priests, Levites, gatekeepers, singers, and temple servants, along with their wives, sons, and daughters, everyone who is able to understand and who has separated themselves from the surrounding peoples to obey the law of God—join with their noble brothers and commit themselves with a sworn oath to follow the law of God given through God's servant Moses and to carefully obey all the commands, ordinances, and statutes of Yahweh our Lord. —Nehemiah 10:28–29

Further Scripture: John 15:4; 2 Corinthians 3:18; Philippians 1:27

Questions

1. The governor, leaders, priests, and Levites signed and put their seal on a document, making an agreement in writing. Who was this agreement made to? What were the things they committed to? What things have you committed yourself to in service to God?

2. What does it mean in Nehemiah 10:29 when it says, "They took on themselves a curse and an oath to walk in God's law" (NASB)?

3. According to Nehemiah 10:30, is it wrong to marry people of other ethnicities (2 Corinthians 6:14: Colossians 3:11)?

4. The people pledged to give a third of a shekel yearly for the service of the house of God. Find the value of a third of a shekel. What was this money specifically used for?

5. This chapter talks about the firstfruits, which are to be brought into the house of the Lord. What do the firstfruits foreshadow? Support your answer with several Bible references.

6. What did the Holy Spirit highlight to you in Nehemiah 10 through the reading or the teaching?

Lesson 130: Nehemiah 11

Builder: Nehemiah's Leadership

Teaching Notes

Intro

In Nehemiah, new life was coming because people were ready and watching. In chapter 11 we see that as Jerusalem grew, people were moving out to the "suburbs," to towns just outside the city. It was necessary for some of the Israelites to make a sacrifice and live in the city. To decide who would live in Jerusalem, the people drew lots. This is what we are going to see in Nehemiah 11. The beautiful part is that Nehemiah was so organized and structured, he was able accomplish all these things.

Teaching

Nehemiah 11:1: The leaders of Israel stayed in the center of Jerusalem. One out of ten people agreed to live in the city as well. Commentator Warren Wiersbe wrote, "[Nehemiah] knew that the nation of Israel could never be strong as long as Jerusalem was weak. But Jerusalem could not be strong unless the people were willing to sacrifice."[1] After the city was built Nehemiah knew his work was still not done. He recognized what it meant to govern over this area. Nehemiah called upon the people to live in Jerusalem.

Nehemiah 11:2: The people praised those who volunteered to move to Jerusalem. All the tribes came back together to build up the city wall, but then went back home. It's interesting that it seemed like the people did not want to live in Jerusalem, the city they just built! Why do you think that is? Nehemiah needed people to be a part of the change in Jerusalem.

Nehemiah 11:3–36: These verses are the start of a list of all the people who were going to live in Jerusalem. These were the people who were going to help be a part of change in the city. There are two tribes back in Jerusalem—Judah

---

[1] Warren W. Wiersbe, *Be Determined: Standing Firm in the Face of Opposition* (Colorado Springs: David C. Cook, 1992), 143.

and Benjamin. The rest of the ten tribes were scattered elsewhere. As you read through this passage you see the numbers of people living in Jerusalem. These men and women had a unique role in preserving the city of Jerusalem. These people are why you and I can go into Israel today. What an awesome picture!

Nehemiah 11 is all about sustainability in the community. The people trusted Nehemiah as their leader. They saw how God was moving in his life and trusted Him. In Lovett H. Weems Jr.'s article, "Ten Leadership Lessons from Nehemiah,"[2] he provides ten things we can learn from Nehemiah:

1. God's leader responds to a call.
    - Nehemiah knew his calling to rebuild the city wall came from God (Nehemiah 2:12b).
    - Nehemiah obeyed the call and came to survey the needs for rebuilding (Nehemiah 2:11–16).
    - A leader will always respond to a call!
2. God's leader cares for the people and their situation.
    - Once Nehemiah responded to the call, God's heart could be seen behind it.
    - Nehemiah saw himself as a part of the situation, using terms like "we" and "us" (Nehemiah 2:17, 20).
    - Nehemiah identified that he and the people of Israel were one when he said, "We are in trouble."
    - As a true leader, Nehemiah understood the issues and chose to go through the trouble instead of shying away from it.
3. God's leader helps define the reality of the situation.
    - As God's leader, Nehemiah recognized issues, but not in a prideful or arrogant way.
    - Nehemiah evaluated the situation the people of Israel were facing (Nehemiah 2:17).
    - Nehemiah led the people to discuss all that needed to be done and the reality of the challenges they faced.
4. God's direction and vision are sought by the leader and people.
    - Nehemiah depended upon the direction and vision for the work to be done to come from the Lord. We too have to seek His will for direction.
    - Nehemiah was constantly praying.
5. Prayer is essential to know God's will.

---

[2] Lovett H. Weems Jr., "Ten Leadership Lessons from Nehemiah," Church Leadership, April 17, 2019, www.churchleadership.com/leading-ideas/ten-leadership-lessons-from-nehemiah/.

6. God's vision is simple.
   - God's vision to Nehemiah was really simple—rebuild the wall.
   - A vision needs to be as simple as it can be.
   - Nehemiah stayed the course of God's vision.
   - A vision or direction might look differently from what you thought, but the vision is still the same.
7. God's leader builds a team.
   - Because Nehemiah had the trust of the people, he was able to create a team to lead the work.
   - The only way the Israelites could complete God's vision was that the people committed to use the talents God gave them to do the work (Nehemiah 2:18b).
   - We too have been gifted different talents from God to help complete His work.
8. God's leader keeps the real purpose before the people.
   - Nehemiah helped the people to realize that what they were doing was not just rebuilding a wall but reestablishing their position in Israel as God's people.
   - Nehemiah never kept anything from the people of Israel.
9. God's leader is not discouraged by adversity.
   - As the Israelites worked, they were made fun of and threatened by their enemies.
   - Nehemiah was personally threatened.
   - However, Nehemiah understood that what he was doing for God was important (Nehemiah 6:3).
10. God always has another vision.
   - The original vision was to rebuild the wall, but once it was completed, it was time to seek God's vision for the next steps.
   - God always has another vision that builds on top of what He has already established.

Closing

Be the change. The remnant of the Israelites moving to Jerusalem were able to be a part of the change. I encourage you today, please don't stop praying for the peace of Jerusalem. God still has big plans for this city!

The Daily Word

The Israelites returned to Jerusalem, the Holy City. They rebuilt the wall and the city itself. Again they worshipped Yahweh and submitted to His ways. They even sacrificed their land and firstfruits to Him. Now it was time to embrace where the Lord brought them by getting settled and structured in order to bring about sustainability as a nation. Nehemiah remained a strong leader the people followed to walk out God's plan and purpose for the nation of Israel.

There's a time for everything. Settling means commitment, which can be hard. Have you fully embraced the season you are in? In order for a house to feel more like *your home, you must settle in*. Unpack boxes. Paint the walls. Hang up pictures. Host a party for friends. Are you attending a new church? Maybe it's time to introduce yourself to the pastor, go to the membership class, offer to help in the nursery, or serve as a parking attendant. When you settle in somewhere, sustainability will likely occur. And that's a good thing! It means you have committed to the change. Change is not something to fear if you know it's from the Lord. Embrace the season the Lord has you in, and as you do, His peace will sustain you.

Now the leaders of the people stayed in Jerusalem, and the rest of the people cast lots for one out of ten to come and live in Jerusalem, the holy city, while the other nine-tenths remained in their towns. —Nehemiah 11:1

Further Scripture: Proverbs 16:3; Jeremiah 17:7; Luke 9:62

Questions

1. Why did the Jews cast lots to bring one out of ten people to live in Jerusalem?
2. In Nehemiah 11:1, Jerusalem was referred to as the holy city. The reference "holy city" can also be found in Revelation 21:2, and refers to what?
3. The king (Artaxerxes) had issued a command that the singers be given a daily portion. Why do you think he specified this particular group to make sure they had daily provision?
4. How do you see Nehemiah's actions, in the book of Nehemiah, reflect Christ?
5. What did the Holy Spirit highlight to you in Nehemiah 11 through the reading or the teaching?

Lesson 131: Nehemiah 12

Builder: The Joy of Jerusalem

Teaching Notes

Intro

This week, we'll finish the last two chapters of Nehemiah and the entire book of Esther. That means we will be finishing our study of the historical books. The one word for the book of Nehemiah is *Builder*. Nehemiah was called to rebuild the city walls in Jerusalem, which foreshadows Jesus the Messiah rebuilding the church. Just as God used Nehemiah to build the walls, He wants to use believers to build His church (Matthew 16:18). Wiersbe notes, "God uses many people with different gifts and skills to get His work done in this world . . . [so] we give our bodies to the Lord so that He can use us as His tools to accomplish His work."[1] The first 26 verses of chapter 12 list all the people who came back with Zerubbabel to work on rebuilding the temple and the wall. All of these people gave themselves to God, and it was important to Nehemiah that their names be recorded. Wiersbe divides this chapter into two sections: giving ourselves to God and giving our praise to God.[2]

Teaching

Nehemiah 12:1–25 Giving ourselves to God: Zerubbabel and Jeshua led those who went back to rebuild Solomon's temple after it had been destroyed. With them came 22 leaders (vv. 1–7) and eight Levites (vv. 8–9). The Levites stood opposite each other leading praise songs. In verses 10–11, the descendants of Jeshua were named. Beginning in verse 12, the priests were named (vv. 12–21). The high priests were named in verse 22, and Nehemiah even mentioned the reign of King Darius of Persia, possibly because the king helped pay the temple expenses. Nehemiah explained that the sons of Levi had been recorded in the Book of Chronicles (v. 23). In verse 24, the chiefs of the Levites are listed, with

---

[1] Warren W. Wiersbe, *Be Determined: Standing Firm in the Face of Opposition* (Colorado Springs: David C. Cook, 1992), 146.

[2] Wiersbe, 143–46.

the gatekeepers listed in verse 25. These were in the days of Joiakim and the days of Nehemiah and Ezra (v. 26).

Nehemiah 12:27–47 Giving our praise to God: As they prepared to dedicate the completed wall around Jerusalem, the Levites were called from all over Israel to Jerusalem to lead the dedication with gladness, thanksgivings, and singing (v. 27). Also, the sons of the singers gathered (vv. 28–29). Tom Constable explains, "Nehemiah enlisted Levites from all over Judah to guarantee that the dedication service would be properly grand."[3] Then the priests and Levites purified themselves, the people, the gates, and the wall (v. 30). Wiersbe describes this as the movement of those who worked on and watched over the wall, now becoming the worshippers at the wall.[4]

In Nehemiah 6, the work on the wall was completed, and revival broke out in chapters 8–10. In Nehemiah 7:4–5, Nehemiah documented that Jerusalem had few people living in it. In chapter 11:1–2, the people cast lots to determine who would move to Jerusalem to repopulate the city. These are the reasons why the dedication of the wall was delayed. Once everything was in place, the dedication took place. The word "dedication" in Hebrew means "Hanukkah," which comes from the process of dedicating the temple after its desecration by the Syrians.[5] In this dedication, singing praise songs was mentioned eight times, giving thanks six times, rejoicing seven times, and the use of instruments three times. The celebration was huge! The act of thanksgiving "means 'public acknowledgement,' 'to declare aloud, in public, to another.'"[6]

After purification, Nehemiah brought the princes of Judah up onto the wall and appointed two great companies to give thanks going in opposite directions on the wall (v. 31). Nehemiah called up additional people to join the first company, some with the musical instruments of David who were led by Ezra (vv. 31–36). Then the second company, including the choir, went behind Nehemiah on the other side of the wall (vv. 37–39). The two companies gave thanks as they moved along the wall (vv. 40–42). Both groups came together at the temple where they offered sacrifices and rejoiced (v. 43). Wiersbe states, "The people were bearing witness to the watching world that God had done the work, and

---

[3] Thomas L. Constable, *Expository Notes of Dr. Thomas Constable: Nehemiah*, 58, https://planobiblechapel.org/tcon/notes/pdf/nehemiah.pdf.

[4] Warren W. Wiersbe, *The Bible Exposition Commentary: Joshua–Esther* (Colorado Springs: David C. Cook, 2003), 690.

[5] Earl D. Radmacher, Ronald B. Allen, and H. Wayne House, eds., *Nelson's New Illustrated Bible Commentary* (Nashville: Thomas Nelson, 1999), 599.

[6] Radmacher et al., 599.

He alone should be glorified."[7] They rejoiced so greatly it "was heard far away" (v. 43b). Charles Fensham describes the importance of the day in this way: "The dedication of the newly built wall of Jerusalem is a climax to the books of Ezra and Nehemiah."[8] In verses 44–47, the people took steps to provide for the priests, Levites, singers, and gatekeepers after the dedication.

Closing

The Jews recognized they had gone through a lot, and they didn't want to go through it all again. Constable emphasizes the importance of this event: "This was the greatest day in the history of the restoration community. Israel was now back in the land more securely and more faithful to God than it had been since the first exiles had returned. Nehemiah had succeeded in rebuilding the walls of Jerusalem, reestablishing the Mosaic Law as Israel's authority, and reorganizing the temple ministry in harmony with God's will."[9]

Here's a question for us to consider: If God has radically changed our lives, how can we remotely stay quiet? This picture of the dedication is a picture of how God wants us to worship Him.

The Daily Word

Nehemiah led the people in a joy-filled dedication of the wall around Jerusalem. They had come out of exile, worked together, and rebuilt the wall of Jerusalem. It was time to celebrate! They gathered together as purified people and gave thanks with singing and the sound of trumpets.

Every day, you wake up to a new day and the opportunity to dedicate your life to the Lord as a living sacrifice. So praise the Lord! The Lord gives you life! The Lord gives you hope! The Lord gives you great joy and strength! The Lord offers the free gift of salvation and eternal life to all who believe in Him by faith! Perhaps you have a new baby, a new home, a new job, or a new work project. Dedicate your new season to the Lord. Sing a new song to Him. Blow a trumpet or pick up a guitar, and make a joyful noise to the Lord. And if others hear you as you dedicate your life to the Lord . . . so what? Let them hear and wonder, *What is that joyful noise of praise?*

---

[7] Wiersbe, *Bible Exposition Commentary*, 691.

[8] F. Charles Fensham, *The Books of Ezra and Nehemiah*, New International Commentary on the Old Testament (Grand Rapids: Eerdmans, 1983), 257–58.

[9] Constable, 60.

On that day they offered great sacrifices and rejoiced because God had given them great joy. The women and children also celebrated, and Jerusalem's rejoicing was heard far away. —Nehemiah 12:43

Further Scripture: 2 Samuel 7:29; Psalm 98:4–6; Romans 12:1–2

Questions

1. Why were the Levites throughout the land asked to come to Jerusalem?
2. Which part of the procession did Ezra lead? Which way did they go and what gates did they pass before proceeding to the temple (Nehemiah 12:31–37)?
3. What do you think was the most important thing about the dedication service (Psalm 68:32–35; Hebrews 13:15)?
4. Who was the one most responsible for this dedication service even taking place?
5. What should the joy of the Lord lead us to do (Nehemiah 12:44–47)? Do you see this kind of joy for the Lord in your own congregation? Why or why not?
6. What did the Holy Spirit highlight to you in Nehemiah 12 through the reading or the teaching?

Lesson 132: Nehemiah 13

Builder: The Surprise Ending of Nehemiah

Teaching Notes

Intro

This is our last lesson in Nehemiah. We have just studied how God moved through the people to rebuild the wall of Jerusalem and how the people rejoiced and praised God when the work was completed (Nehemiah 12). Between chapter 12 and chapter 13, Nehemiah served as governor of Judah for 12 years (Nehemiah 5:14). Nehemiah then returned to Persia as he had promised King Artaxerxes, probably for about a year. *Nelson's Commentary* explains, "On the day after [Nehemiah's] return, he discovered what became the surprise ending of his book; namely, that those devoted and dedicated people had tripped over temptation, fallen into sin, and lain down in disobedience."[1] In chapter 12, the people celebrated what God had done in their lives and worshipped in praise and thanksgiving. In the absence of Nehemiah for one year, the people had completely lost their way. General William Booth of the Salvation Army said, "I want you young men to bear in mind that it is the nature of a fire to go out; you must keep it stirred and fed and the ashes removed."[2]

Teaching

Nehemiah 13:1–3: In the first two verses, the assembled priests read from the Book of Moses before the people. They discovered that Ammonites and Moabites (the people descended from Lot) should never be allowed to be part of the congregation of God because they had not welcomed the children of Israel, shared food with them, but instead hired Balaam to curse the Israelites (Numbers 22:1–24:25). When the Jews heard the law, they separated out all foreigners from their midst (v. 3). They were returning to what was instructed in the Pentateuch (Deuteronomy 23:3–4).

---

[1] Earl D. Radmacher, Ronald B. Allen, and H. Wayne House, eds., *Nelson's New Illustrated Bible Commentary* (Nashville: Thomas Nelson, 1999), 599.

[2] William Booth; quoted in Warren W. Wiersbe, *The Bible Exposition Commentary: Joshua–Esther* (Colorado Springs: David C. Cook, 2003), 693.

According to the Abrahamic Covenant God made with Abraham, God would bless those who blessed the Israelites and curse those who cursed the Israelites (Genesis 12:3). The Ammonites and the Moabites had cursed the Israelites. This act is a foreshadowing of Jesus' teaching on the sheep and the goats (Matthew 25:31–46). I believe there will be a judgment on the nations that do not support Israel. We must seek nations that will support Israel.

Nehemiah 13:4–9: Eliashib the priest was related to Tobiah, who with Sanballat, had opposed the work on Jerusalem's wall (Nehemiah 2:19, 4:3, 6:10–14, 13:4). Eliashib had prepared a large space for Tobiah (the enemy) to stay within the temple (v. 5). While Nehemiah was away from Jerusalem, Eliashib, the high priest, allowed the enemy to dwell in several rooms in God's temple. Nehemiah did not find out about Eliashib's actions until he received leave from Artaxerxes to return to Jerusalem (vv. 6–7). Nehemiah threw all of Tobiah's possessions out of the temple and ordered the rooms to be purified and the things of God's house to be restored back to those rooms (vv. 8–9). *Nelson's Commentary* explains the purification would have included "washing, scouring, and sprinkling with blood."[3]

Nehemiah 13:10–14: Nehemiah also discovered the Levites and singers had not been given their portions to live on, so they had returned to their own fields (v. 10). Nehemiah rebuked the temple officials for not taking care of the temple servants, gathered the servants together, and put them back to work (v. 11). This was obviously a spiritual issue. Today, the church needs to be rebuked for withholding from God what belongs to Him! Nehemiah called for the people to bring their tithes, which had not been brought to the temple earlier. He appointed trusted men who would accept and then distribute those tithes to the temple servants (vv. 12–13). Nehemiah prayed to God and asked that his actions be remembered (v. 14).

Nehemiah 13:15–22: Then Nehemiah saw the disobedience of the people—working in the vineyard, transporting stores of grain to sell, and purchasing fish and merchandise from the Tyrians—all on the Sabbath (vv. 15–16). This becomes a theme in Nehemiah. In order to bring about reformation, a season of rebuke was necessary.

Nehemiah rebuked the nobles of Jerusalem who had allowed this and profaned the Lord's day (vv. 17–18). Nehemiah ordered that the gates of the city be closed just before the Sabbath began and not reopened until after the Sabbath ended. He also posted guards at all the gates so that no goods could enter the

---

[3] Radmacher et al., 600.

city (v. 19). Some merchants tried to camp outside the wall, but when Nehemiah threated them with force, they did not return on the Sabbath (vv. 20–21). Nehemiah instructed the Levites and the guards to be purified in order to keep the Sabbath holy. Nehemiah again ended his actions with a prayer that God would remember his work (v. 22).

Nehemiah 13:23–31—The next issue Nehemiah encountered was intermarriages with pagans. Half the children born as a result of the marriages could not speak Hebrew, which meant they could not read Scripture and did not know the Lord (vv. 23–24). Nehemiah rebuked and cursed them, beat some of the men and pulled out their hair, forcing them to take an oath that they would not allow their sons and daughters to marry foreigners (vv. 25–27). Even one of the grandsons of Eliashib the high priest had become son-in-law to Sanballat, another one of Judah's enemies (v. 28). Nehemiah prayed God would remember those who had defiled the priesthood and God's covenant (v. 29). Nehemiah then purified everything and assigned specific duties to each priest and Levite (v. 30). Nehemiah led the people in a time of giving the firstfruits—the best of the best—back to God (v. 31).

Closing

God used Nehemiah, and Nehemiah was completely obedient to God in the process. God wants to use each of us as well. When we begin to function as the builders of the church of the Lord, not even the forces of Satan will be able to overpower it (Matthew 16:18b).

The Daily Word

After the dedication of the wall, Nehemiah went back to assist King Artaxerxes in Babylon, later returning to the Israelites. When Nehemiah left for Babylon, the people were praising the Lord and devoted to His ways. However, during Nehemiah's absence, the people gave in to temptation, turned away from the ways of the Lord, and walked in disobedience to their God. Once again, Nehemiah brought hope. He sought the Lord and prayed without ceasing on behalf of the people. *The Lord used Nehemiah to rekindle the flame for the Lord inside the people, and they turned their hearts back to Him.*

Just like a blazing fire will go out if left unattended, believers, if left alone, will most likely lose their passion and purity for the Lord. As you follow Christ, you are to remain diligent, be fervent in spirit, and serve the Lord. Just as iron sharpens iron, people sharpen each other. Continue to abide in the Lord and in His Word. Spend time with other believers. Stretch your faith. *What do you need to do today to stoke your fire for the Lord?* God longs for you to keep the fire inside you ablaze so that the world will know of His great love.

While all this was happening, I was not in Jerusalem, because I had returned to King Artaxerxes of Babylon in the thirty-second year of his reign. It was only later that I asked the king for a leave of absence so I could return to Jerusalem. Then I discovered the evil that Eliashib had done on behalf of Tobiah by providing him a room in the courts of God's house. I was greatly displeased and threw all of Tobiah's household possessions out of the room.
—Nehemiah 13:6–8

Further Scripture: Proverbs 27:17; Romans 12:11; 2 Timothy 1:6

Questions

1. Why were the Ammonites and the Moabites not permitted to enter the Assembly of God (Deuteronomy 23:3–4)?

2. What were some promises the Israelites made to the Lord that they failed to keep (Nehemiah 10:28–31, 39; 13:1–11, 15–27)?

3. A man named Tobiah is mentioned in verses 4–5. Who was Tobiah, and why was Nehemiah upset that he was given access to several rooms in the temple (Nehemiah 2:10, 19; 4:3; 6:10–12, 17, 19)?

4. What was the problem with the children of the interracial marriages not knowing how to speak Hebrew? Is there a difference between how a believer and a nonbeliever speaks? What are some examples (1 John 4:5–6)?

5. What did the Holy Spirit highlight to you in Nehemiah 13 through the reading or the teaching?

Lesson 133: Esther 1—2

The Despised One: Finding the King's Favor

Teaching Notes

Intro

This is the beginning lesson on the final historical book. This is our 332nd lesson this year. Esther is an exciting book. The one word for the book of Esther is *The Despised One*. Mordecai was a Jew and was the despised one. Ultimately, that will bring a picture of the Messiah who became *The Despised One*.

Only the books of Esther and Ruth in the Old Testament were named after women. There are no quotes from Esther in the New Testament. This is also true with Song of Songs, Obadiah, and Nahum. Esther's name in Hebrew was Hadassah (Esther 2:7) which means "myrtle" or "myrtle tree" and possibly came from a Persian word for "star" or a Babylonian love goddess called Ishtar.[1]

Scholars do not know who authored the book of Esther, although Mordecai, Ezra, and Nehemiah are all possibilities. MacArthur notes, "Whoever penned Esther possessed a detailed knowledge of Persian customs, etiquette, and history, plus particular familiarity with the palace of Shushan."[2] Further, the author understood the Hebrew calendar, Hebrew customs, and Jewish nationalism, and so was possibly a Persian Jew who later returned to Israel. The book closes out the historical books, and only Ezra 7—10 and the books of Nehemiah and Malachi are placed later historically. The book of Esther ends around 473 BC during the Persian period of history from 539 BC to 331 BC and before King Ahasuerus was assassinated. Ahasuerus ruled from 486–465 BC. The book of Esther covers the years 483–473 BC. It's important to note that Ahasuerus also went by his Greek name, Xerxes, and was the father of Artaxerxes who allowed Nehemiah to return to Jerusalem. The events documented in Esther took place after the first group of Jews, led by Zerubbabel, returned to Jerusalem following 70 years in Babylonian captivity, and before the second group of Jews led by Ezra returned.[3] Zerubbabel led the Jews to rebuild the temple, then the events of Esther took place. The

---

[1] John MacArthur, *The MacArthur Bible Commentary* (Nashville: Thomas Nelson, 2005), 553.

[2] MacArthur, 553.

[3] MacArthur, 553.

second group of Jews returned to rebuild the city, and then the third group under Nehemiah returned to rebuild the city wall.

Some consider Esther to be a controversial book. Within the book of Esther, the name of God is never mentioned. However, Esther is included in the Megillah, along with Song of Songs, Ruth, Ecclesiastes, and Lamentations. These five books are the Megillah, and they are read in the synagogue during five special celebrations. Esther is read during the celebration of Purim.[4]

Esther's uncle Mordecai was from the tribe of Benjamin, and Haman, the man who became his enemy, was an Agagite (3:1). One thousand years before these two met, the Israelites had left Egypt (1445 BC) only to be attacked by the Amalekites (Exodus 17:8–16). Although King Saul was told to kill all the Amalekites, he allowed King Agag to live. The prophet Samuel later killed Agag with the sword (1 Samuel 15:32–33). Because he was a descendant of Agag, Haman hated the Jews. In Esther, Mordecai and Haman continued to live out the battle of Exodus 17. MacArthur describes the book of Esther as a chess match between God and Satan, using Mordecai, Esther, and Haman as the chess pieces.[5] When we talk about the despised one in the book of Esther, we're talking about Mordecai, who was the foreshadow of the coming Messiah (Psalm 121:4).

In Esther 1:1–12, Queen Vashti refused to appear before the king. The king was furious and consulted with his wise men to decide what to do. They counseled him to remove Vashti from the king's presence and that her crown be given to another (vv. 13–22). Chapter 2 presents the king's plan to find another queen.

Teaching

Esther 2:1–4: After the king had cooled down from his anger and embarrassment of Vashti denying his request, the king's assistant suggested they make a nationwide search for beautiful young women for the harem at Susa. While in the harem, the young women received beauty treatments in preparation for meeting the king, and the king would choose the woman who pleased him (vv. 1–4). This was no beauty pageant, because the women did not come as volunteers and they had no choice about their futures. The women who were not chose to be queen would have spent the rest of their lives in the harem. They existed in the harem only "to bring pleasure to the king."[6]

Esther 2:5–11: Mordecai was a descendant of Shimei, possibly the man who yelled curses at David and those who accompanied him (2 Samuel 16:5–13), and Kish may refer to Saul's father (1 Samuel 9:1). Mordecai had been taken into

---

[4] MacArthur, 554.

[5] MacArthur, 554.

[6] Earl D. Radmacher, Ronald B. Allen, and H. Wayne House, eds., *Nelson's New Illustrated Bible Commentary* (Nashville: Thomas Nelson, 1999), 605.

captivity in Jerusalem and then taken to Babylon (vv. 5–7) and he was the legal guardian of his orphaned cousin Hadassah (or Esther) whom he had adopted as his daughter (v. 7). *Nelson's Commentary* explains that those in captivity or just dwelling in foreign lands usually had two names, their Hebrew name, which was considered sacred, and their secular name, which reflected their adopted culture.[7] Esther and other young women were taken to the harem and placed under the supervision of Hegai (v. 8). Esther impressed Hegai and gained his extreme favor. Hegai sped up the beautification process for Esther, chose seven female servants to serve her, and gave her and her servants the best quarters in the harem (v. 9). Esther did not tell anyone that she was Jewish at Mordecai's request (v. 10). Meanwhile, Mordecai walked by the harem's courtyard daily to check on her (v. 11).

Esther 2:12–20: The women went through an entire year of beauty treatments before each one went before the king (v. 12). Each woman was given whatever she wanted to take with her to see the king (v. 13). The woman went to the king in the evening to have sexual relations, and in the morning, she was taken to a second harem under the king's eunuch, Shaashgaz. The woman never again saw the king unless he requested her by name (v. 14). *Nelson's Commentary* explains that these women were "destined to live as though they were widows for the remainder of their years."[8] When Esther's turn came, she brought with her only what Hegai suggested. She won approval in the sight of everyone who saw her, including the king who loved her more than any of the other young women (vv. 15–16). The king crowned Esther queen and held a great banquet for her, inviting his officials and staff (v. 18). No one knew Esther's background (vv. 19–20). "Both Josephus and the Jewish Rabbis exaggerated the beauty of Esther and elaborated on her virtues and piety. The Rabbis held that Esther was one of the four most beautiful women in history along with Sarah, Rahab, and Abigail. Josephus maintained that Esther 'surpassed all women in beauty' in the entire habitable world."[9]

Esther 2:21–23: Mordecai was given the responsibility of sitting at the King's Gate. There he heard two of the king's eunuchs plotting to kill the king (v. 21). Mordecai told Queen Esther, and she told the king on Mordecai's behalf (v. 22). The eunuchs were found guilty and hanged (v. 23). These three verses set the stage for all that follows in this book.

---

[7] Radmacher et al., 606.

[8] Radmacher et al., 607.

[9] Edwin M. Yamuchi, "The Archaeological Background of Esther," *Bibliotheca Sacra* 137:546 (April–June 1980): 99–106.

Closing

God used a queen to put her cousin in a place of authority, allowing him to hear about a potential assassination, which would then radically change the direction of the people of Israel. God continually put people in place, for His time and for His purpose, which was to save His people.

The Daily Word

Queen Vashti refused to do as King Ahasuerus ordered. Consequently, she was removed as the queen. The search for a new queen began. After several months of beauty treatments, the king loved the unlikely candidate, Esther, an orphan given the Hebrew name Hadassah at birth. Her uncle, Mordecai, adopted her and watched over her, even from the palace gate. Esther won more favor and approval from the king than any other young woman. She had the king's attention and respect. So, when Mordecai overheard two men plotting to assassinate the king, he told Esther to tell the king, thus saving the king's life.

The Lord uses the most unlikely people, at the most unlikely times, to do His will. You may wonder why you are in the season you are in. You may feel as though you are not adequate for a job or position. You may question the timing. But take a deep breath. Receive this season as a gift with a purpose from the Lord. God has a reason, and if you are willing to yield to Him and His plans, He will use you for great purposes in His time. Don't question, try to figure out, or manipulate the situation. Simply trust the Lord, walk in integrity, and do the next right thing. God puts people in place for a specific time and purpose. Just take one step at a time, and do not worry. *Walk it out.*

When Mordecai learned of the plot, he reported it to Queen Esther, and she told the king on Mordecai's behalf. When the report was investigated and verified, both men were hanged on the gallows. This event was recorded in the Historical Record in the king's presence. —Esther 2:22–23

Further Scripture: Ecclesiastes 3:1; Lamentations 3:25–26; Habakkuk 2:3

Questions

1. Why do you think Queen Vashti denied the king's request to come before the court in Esther 1:12? What was her punishment?
2. Why do you think Esther told no one of her background? Ultimately, did this work in her favor?

3. How did Mordecai save the king's life (Esther 2:19–23)? What happened to the men who plotted against the king?
4. What did the Holy Spirit highlight to you in Esther 1—2 through the reading or the teaching?

Lesson 134: Esther 3—4

The Despised One: Called for Such a Time as This

Teaching Notes

Intro

Today we continue the study of Esther. In chapters 1—2, we read about Queen Vashti who humiliated her husband King Ahasuerus (also known as King Xerxes), and he took away her crown. The most beautiful young women in Persia were selected to spend one year in the harem in preparation for going to the king as he looked for someone to replace Vashti. Esther, a young Jewish woman, was one of those chosen to go before the king, and she was chosen to be the next queen. Esther's uncle and adoptive father was given a place of authority at the King's Gate. While there, he heard of a plot to assassinate the king. He passed on the information to Esther who then told the king, and the plotters were found guilty and hanged. Our phrase for Esther is *The Despised One,* and it begins to come into play in chapters 3—4.

In chapter 3, King Ahasuerus honored Haman, an Agagite and Amalekite, who was an enemy of the Jews. Haman was promoted over all the other officials (v. 1). The king ordered his entire staff to bow and pay homage to Haman, but Mordecai refused to do so (v. 2). Other staff members asked Mordecai why he refused, and after several days, they reported his refusal to Haman to see if Mordecai's actions would be tolerated. Mordecai refused to bow because he was a Jew (vv. 3–4). When Haman found out, he was enraged, and because Mordecai was a Jew, he planned to destroy all the Jews in the kingdom (vv. 5–6). Because Mordecai refused to bow down, Haman deceived the king and asked him to proclaim a decree that the "disobedient ethnic group" be annihilated, and in return, Haman promised the king that he would pay 375 tons of silver into the royal treasury (vv. 8–9). The king agreed and gave his signet ring to Haman, and the decree was written and sealed exactly as Haman dictated (vv. 10–12). The letters were sent to each province that they were to "destroy, kill, and annihilate all the Jewish people . . . and plunder their possessions on a single day" (v. 13). The potential numbers of Jews that were being targeted throughout the Persian Empire could have been as many as 15 million.[1]

Teaching

Esther 4:1–4: When Mordecai heard about the decree, he put on sackcloth and ashes and went into the city mourning and crying loudly and bitterly (v. 1). He could go no further than the King's Gate because he was wearing sackcloth (v. 2), and the Jewish people mourned and fasted through the entire kingdom (v. 3). Edmund Burke says, "All that is necessary for the triumph of evil is that good men do nothing."[2] Mordecai began to do something immediately instead of letting evil prevail (Proverb 24:11–12). As believers, we cannot be neutral!

The fasting in verse 3 was a corporate fast. The Hebrew root for fast means "to abstain from food" and "at times from drinking, bathing, anointing with oil, or sexual intercourse. In essence, fasting acknowledges human frailty before God and appeals to his mercy."[3] *Nelson's Commentary* explains fasting was commonly done in the ancient world and used in "mourning for the dead, intercessory prayer, repentance and contrition for sin, and times of distress."[4] Examples of fasting in the Old Testament include: the Day of Atonement (Leviticus 16:31), and the commemoration of the destruction of Jerusalem (Zechariah 8:19). Fasting can last for one day (1 Samuel 7:6), seven days (1 Samuel 31:13), or 40 days (Exodus 34:28).

Esther 4:5–12: Esther heard what Mordecai was doing and sent him clothes to replace the sackcloth (v. 4). When Mordecai refused the clothes, Esther sent one of the king's eunuchs, Hathach, to find out what was going on (v. 5). Mordecai told Hathach everything about the decree and Haman's gift of money in return for the annihilation of the Jews (vv. 6–7). Mordecai even gave Hathach a copy of the decree to give to Esther and asked her to plead with the king to save their people (vv. 8–9). However, Esther sent Hathach back to Mordecai to remind him that if she went before the king without his summons, she could be killed and in fact the king had not summoned her for 30 days (vv. 10–12).

Esther 4:13–17: Mordecai sent another response to Esther, asking if she really thought she would be safe since she lived in the palace. He asked her to consider

---

[1] Warren W. Wiersbe, *The Bible Exposition Commentary: Joshua–Esther* (Colorado Springs: David C. Cook, 2003), 722.

[2] Wiersbe, 723.

[3] Earl D. Radmacher, Ronald B. Allen, and H. Wayne House, eds., *Nelson's New Illustrated Bible Commentary* (Nashville: Thomas Nelson, 1999), 608.

[4] Radmacher et al., 608.

if God had put her in the role of the queen to be able to intervene in this time (vv. 13–14). Mordecai pointed out three facts: (1) Being a palace resident was no guarantee she would be delivered from death; (2) her silence wouldn't prevent deliverance from coming from some other source; and (3) her being in the palace was not an accident and that she was there "for such a time as this" (v. 14) (Genesis 50:20). Most scholars believe that God is in this book, even if His name is not mentioned. Huey suggests, "The book implies that even when God's people are far from him and disobedient, they are still the object of his concern and love, and that he is working out his purposes through them."[5] Now Mordecai had Esther's support, and she asked him to assemble all the Jews in Susa to fast for three days. Esther and her female servants also fasted, and after the fast Esther would go before the king, even at the cost of her life (v. 16). Mordecai did everything as Esther requested (v. 17). Wiersbe points out that this was a matter of life and death for Esther because everything was already against her—the law of the Persians, the governmental decree, and her gender because of the king's attitude toward women.[6]

Closing

Esther was not the only one in the Bible who was willing to do God's will no matter the cost. Paul wrote that his life didn't matter as long as he continued to testify to what the Lord had done in his life (Acts 20:24). Esther was willing to let go of everything—her crown, her kingdom, even her life to do God's will (Luke 14:33). Jesus also told His disciples that they needed to deny themselves in order to follow Him (Matthew 16:24).

Remember that all this started because Mordecai refused to bow down to Haman. How do you get to the point that you're willing to do whatever it takes, regardless of the consequences? Romans 8:31 answers this question: "If God is for us, who is against us?"

The Daily Word

King Ahasuerus promoted Haman the Agagite in rank and even gave him the king's signet ring, enabling Haman to enforce decisions. Esther's uncle, Mordecai, refused to bow down to Haman as ordered, which enraged Haman. Therefore, Haman ordered all Jewish people to be destroyed. Mordecai heard this decree and brought it to Esther's attention. Mordecai encouraged Esther to go before the king and personally plead with him to save her people. Even though this action would put her own life at risk, Esther recognized her strategic position as queen

---

[5] F. B. Huey Jr., "Esther," in *The Expositor's Bible Commentary: 1 Kings–Job*, ed. Frank E. Gaebelein and Richard D. Polcyn (Grand Rapids: Zondervan, 1998).

[6] Wiersbe, 725.

was *for such a time as this*. She courageously agreed to go before the king in an effort to save her people, saying, "If I perish, I perish."

You may have an opportunity to stand up for the Gospel, risking your reputation, financial or promotion opportunities, friendships, or perhaps even your life. You can choose to be quiet or take a bold, courageous stance for Jesus, with an Esther mindset saying, "If I perish, I perish." As a believer, you are called to deny yourself, pick up your cross, and follow Jesus. *Sometimes that means doing the difficult thing.* Regardless of the cost, *trust God.* Live in such a way you are willing to let go of your life for God. *For such a time as this*, the Lord has placed you where you are today. Remember, God is with you. God is for you. He is worthy of it all.

"If you keep silent at this time, liberation and deliverance will come to the Jewish people from another place, but you and your father's house will be destroyed. Who knows, perhaps you have come to your royal position for such a time as this." Esther sent this reply to Mordecai: "Go and assemble all the Jews who can be found in Susa and fast for me. Don't eat or drink for three days, day or night. I and my female servants will also fast in the same way. After that, I will go to the king even if it is against the law. If I perish, I perish." —Esther 4:14–16

Further Scripture: Matthew 16:24; Acts 20:24; Romans 8:31

Questions

1. Why didn't Mordecai bow down before Haman? What was Haman's response to this?

2. How does Haman's edict of destroying the Jewish nation compare to Genesis 49:10? What does this promise tell us?

3. Why do you think the city of Shushan/Susa was confused? By sitting down to drink, were the king and Haman proud of themselves? Why or why not?

4. What did the Holy Spirit highlight to you in Esther 3—4 through the reading or the teaching?

Lesson 135: Esther 5—6

The Despised One: Pride Before the Fall

Teaching Notes

Intro

There is a great old movie that covers chapters 5—6, which could give a visual look into these chapters. There is also Laura's Daily Word devotional that can lead you to look at the daily passages with a different focus. There are multiple ways God leads us to connect to these passages. We saw yesterday that letters had been sent to all the provinces with the king's decree that all the Jews throughout the kingdom would be annihilated and their possessions plundered on one day. Mordecai found out and let Esther know what was going on. At the end of chapter 4, in verse14, Mordecai says to Esther that who knew but that God had brought her to the palace for such a time as this. Esther told him to assemble all the Jews in Susa to fast for her before she went before the king.

Teaching

Esther 5:1–8: On the third day of fasting and praying, Esther donned her royal clothing and stood in the courtyard where the king could see her (v. 1). The king saw her, motioned her into his presence with his scepter, and asked her what she wanted (vv. 2–3). The king said he would give her anything up to one half of his kingdom (Mark 6:22–23). Why did Esther not immediately tell the king about what Haman was doing? Wiersbe suggests: (1) it wasn't the right time to inform the king because he was unprepared to hear it; (2) it wasn't the right place to expose Haman's actions in the king's throne room; (3) Esther wanted only Haman to be present with her and the king when she told the king what Haman had done; and (4) the king had yet to find out that he had never rewarded Mordecai for exposing the plot to assassinate the king five years earlier and finding that out would prepare the king to receive Esther's news.[1] This can be seen as a picture of King Jesus waiting for us to prepare and to come into His presence.

---

[1] Warren W. Wiersbe, *Be Committed: Doing God's Will Whatever the Cost* (Colorado Springs: David C. Cook, 1993), 135–36.

Queen Esther was ready to give up everything to enter into the king's presence. She risked everything.

Esther asked only that the king and Haman would come to a banquet she had prepared for them (v. 4). Esther was radically prepared for the king and Haman to come to her banquet. The king and Haman hurried to attend (v. 5). Once again, the king asked Esther what she wanted and, once again, offered up to half his kingdom (v. 6). Esther asked only that the king and Haman return the next day for another banquet (vv. 7–8). Wiersbe states Esther's actions gave evidence of God's sovereignty: (1) God prevented Esther from immediately telling the king about Haman's deceit; (2) God directed the king's responses to Esther by leading him to accept her invitation to the second banquet; and (3) God prevented any of the people who knew that Esther was a Jew to share that information with Haman.[2]

Esther 5:9–14: Haman left the first banquet, full of joy and in good spirits over being honored by Queen Esther but came across Mordecai at the King's Gate who still refused to rise before him. Haman's good spirits turned to rage and anger toward Mordecai (v. 9). Remember the hatred between Haman and Mordecai had its roots in the actions of the Amalekites against the Israelites on their exit from Egypt. Haman was a descendant of King Agag, an Amalekite, and Mordecai was a descendant of the tribe of Benjamin (Exodus 17:8–16).

Haman controlled his anger until he got home, and then he sent for his friends and family to come hear him talk about how wealthy he was, how he had been promoted over all other royal staff and officials, and how Queen Esther had invited only him to a banquet with herself and the king (vv. 11–12). Yet, despite all the good things that had happened to him, Haman was obsessed with the fact that Mordecai had not shown him the respect he deserved (v. 13). Actor John Barrymore said, "One of my chief regrets during my years in the theater is that I couldn't sit in the audience and watch me."[3] Doesn't that sound like Haman who was on a complete ego trip about how much power and authority he had been given, and was unwilling to accept anything less than honor from the people below him (Genesis 3:4–5; Proverbs 6:16–19; 16:18; 29:23)?

Haman's wife and friends told him to build a 75-foot-tall gallows and then the next morning, ask the king to hang Mordecai on it. They encouraged Haman to go and enjoy the banquet the next day. Since Haman liked the advice, he went ahead on that same day and had the gallows built, confident he could get the king to do as he wanted (v. 14). Note that the flesh always is impatient to push through its own agenda, but if something is of the Lord, there is no reason to

---

[2] Wiersbe, 137.

[3] Quoted in Wiersbe, 138.

rush or to try to force. Haman pushed everything forward so he could be rid of Mordecai sooner.

Closing

Wiersbe points out that Haman was controlled by his false confidence, pride, and malice.[4] William Barclay wrote that "pride is the ground in which all the other sins grow and is the parent from which all the other sins come."[5] Malice turns into revenge, and that truly grieves the Holy Spirit (Ephesians 4:30–32; Colossians 3:8). In Esther 6, Haman is humiliated by the king honoring Mordecai.

The Daily Word

Mordecai saved King Ahasuerus' life after overhearing an assassination plot at the King's Gate. And yet Mordecai neither sought nor received recognition for his life-saving actions. Mordecai chose to walk in humility and integrity. Haman, on the other hand, always looked out for his own interest. When the king asked Haman how to honor someone, Haman assumed it was himself the king wished to honor and replied with an extensive plan. Haman walked in pride with the expectation of reward for himself. Haman's plan for honor backfired as the king at last honored Mordecai with honor and dignity throughout the city square.

As a follower of Christ, you are not to look out for your own interest or think of yourself more highly than others. Keep in mind, *the Lord despises the proud but gives grace to the humble.* If you know you have done something worthy of recognition, it is best not to "toot your own horn." God sees you. He knows every move you make. You will receive honor from Him. As you walk in humility, He will exalt you. Today, make the choice to walk poor in spirit and see the Lord move in your life!

Haman entered, and the king asked him, "What should be done for the man the king wants to honor?" Haman thought to himself, "Who is it the king would want to honor more than me?" —Esther 6:6

Further Scripture: Proverbs 27:2; Philippians 2:3; James 4:6

---

[4] Wiersbe, 138–39.

[5] Quoted in Wiersbe, 139.

Questions

1. When Esther was preparing to risk going before the king, what did she put on (Esther 5:1)? How are we, as believers, to clothe ourselves because we are in the King's presence (Romans 13:14; Galatians 3:27; Colossians 3:12–14; 1 Peter 5:5; Revelation 19:8)?

2. As Haman recounted his riches and all the ways he had been exalted by the king, what kept him from enjoying this favor (Esther 5:11–13)? What keeps you from being satisfied with what you have been blessed with?

3. Why did Haman plot Mordecai's death? According to Psalm 37:12–13, how did the Lord respond to this behavior, and why?

4. In Esther 6:2–3, the king discovered how Mordecai had saved his life and that he had not been thanked or honored for his actions. How does this point to Christ?

5. The king wanted to exalt Mordecai, so Haman was forced to honor him publicly (Esther 6:10–11). How do we see this foreshadow Christ in Philippians 2:9–11?

6. What did the Holy Spirit highlight to you in Esther 5—6 through the reading or the teaching?

Lesson 136: Esther 7—8

The Despised One: Hasten with the Message

Teaching Notes

Intro

For the book of Esther, our phrase is *The Despised One*. Although the book bears the name of Esther who saved the lives of all the Jews in Persia, her uncle Mordecai was also an important part of the story. And Mordecai was the despised one. Mordecai was the one who found out about the decree that would annihilate all the Jews. Mordecai was the one who sat outside the King's Gate in ashes and sackcloth while mourning, and he was the one who convinced Esther to do whatever she could to protect the Jewish people in Persia. The crisis the Jews were facing was the result of Haman, a royal official and a descendant of King Agag and the Amalekites, who became angry when Mordecai refused to bow before him in respect. Enraged, Haman didn't just want to destroy Mordecai but to annihilate the entire Jewish population living in Persia.

In chapter 6, the king passes the night before Queen Esther's second banquet for him and Haman by reading the book of daily events. There the king found the report that Mordecai had prevented the assassination attempt on his life (vv. 1–2). When the king asked what honor had been given to Mordecai, he was told nothing had been done (v. 3). Haman arrived at court ready to ask the king to have Mordecai hung on the gallows (vv. 4–5). Instead, the king asked Haman what he should do to honor someone. Since Haman thought the honor would be his, he told the king to give the man a royal garment and a horse that the king had ridden, clothe the horse, and then parade the man through the city, proclaiming he was being honored by the king (vv. 6–9). The king accepted Haman's plan but told Haman to give that honor to Mordecai (v. 10). Haman did so. After being honored, Mordecai returned to his place at the King's Gate (vv. 11–12). Haman, however, returned home and told his wife and friends what had happened (vv. 12–13a). They told Haman that his own downfall was certain (v. 13b). Even as they talked, the king's eunuch arrived to take Haman to Queen Esther's banquet.

Teaching

Esther 7:1–6: When the king and Haman arrived at Queen Esther's banquet, the king told Esther again that he would give her anything she wanted, even up to half his kingdom (vv. 1–2). The queen responded that if she had the king's approval, she wanted only that her life and the lives of her people to be spared (v. 3). Esther was sensitive to understand when the right time was to release her word to the king. Esther explained that her people had been "sold out to destruction, death, and extermination." She went on to tell the king that if her people were only going to be sold into slavery, she would not have even bothered him (v. 4). The king had no idea who or what she was talking about (v. 5). Esther pointed out that evil Haman was the one guilty of planning the destruction of her people. Haman stood terrified before the king and the queen (v. 6)

Esther 7:7–10: The king was so angered by what he had heard that he left the banquet and went into the garden. However, Haman remained with Esther because he realized the king was planning something terrible for him (v. 7). As the king returned, he saw Haman falling on the couch where Esther was reclining and wondered if Haman would actually violate the queen while the king was still in the palace. After the king finished speaking, Haman's face was covered (v. 8). One of the eunuchs told the king that Haman had already built a gallows at his house for the execution of Mordecai. The king commanded that the gallows be used for Haman instead (v. 9). Haman was hung on the gallows and the king's anger subsided (v. 10).

Although Haman was dead, the king's decree was still in effect. All of the provinces had already received a copy of the decree stating that they could kill the Jews on a specific day. God's hand was on His chosen people, even as it appeared that Satan was trying to wipe out the Abrahamic Covenant found in Genesis 12:1–3. This was one of the times that anti-Semitism tried to wipe out a huge population of the Jews. Although we don't often take biblical history and bring it forward to modern times, it's almost impossible not to read the story of Esther and Mordecai and not think about the Holocaust (the mass slaughter of the Jews by Hitler during World War II). During the Holocaust, six million Jews were murdered. Why would one man like Hitler want to annihilate the Jews? Why did Haman want to annihilate the Jews? At Auschwitz, one of the largest of the concentration camps, approximately one million Jews were put to death. In Treblinka, approximately 925,000 Jews were killed. At Belzec, more than 434,000 were killed. At Sobibor, around 167,000 were exterminated, in Poland, more than two million were killed, and, in the Soviet Union, another two million were killed.[1] The list could go on and on, and these were people killed in many of

---

[1] United States Holocaust Memorial Museum, https://encyclopedia.ushmm.org/content/en/article/documenting-numbers-of-victims-of-the-holocaust-and-nazi-persecution.

our lifetimes. Altogether, over six million Jews were killed during the Holocaust, and I believe Satan tried to use Hitler to wipe the Jews off the earth. Even today, Satan is still trying to find another Haman, another antichrist spirit, to annihilate God's chosen people. The former Iranian dictator Ahmadinejad said, "There's no doubt that the new wave [of attacks] in Palestine will wipe off this stigma [Israel] from the face of the Islamic world." How would it feel to be the country of Israel, knowing every day that Iran wants to wipe your entire nation off the map? This evil spirit is still here today and it's because of the despised ones. There's an anti-Semitic language out there that refuses to acknowledge Israel even exists. That's why Mordecai paints a true picture of the coming Messiah. Mordecai was the one who wouldn't bow down and instead refused to give in to the enemy. That's exactly what Christ does, even as *The Despised One* (Mark 12:10; John 1:11; 1 Peter 2:4). Mordecai pointed to Christ (1 Corinthians 1:28–31).

Esther 8:1–8: The same day that Haman was hanged, the king gave Queen Esther Haman's estate (v. 1). The king then took the signet ring from Haman and gave it to Mordecai, appointing Mordecai to a high state in the royal house (v. 2). Esther fell at the king's feet and begged him to revoke the evil decree from Haman (v. 3). The king held out his scepter to Esther, so she stood before him and begged the king to send out a royal edict to revoke the documents Haman had sent out (vv. 4–6). Since it was impossible to revoke the first degree, the king told her that she could write whatever she wanted in the king's name and seal it with his signet ring and it too could not be revoked (vv. 7–8). Esther was in agreement and did whatever she could to save her people (Isaiah 62:2–6). Esther was not afraid to ask (James 4:2)! That's what I would want for all of you, for me, for all of us here—don't be afraid. Be bold enough to ask!

Esther 8:9–17: Mordecai summoned the royal scribes and sent out a new edict to each province, written to each ethnic group in their own language (v. 9). The edicts were sealed with the royal signet ring (v. 10). The edict gave all the Jews in the kingdom permission to defend themselves, to kill, and even annihilate anyone hostile to them on the day the first royal decree said they
were to die (vv. 11–12). Couriers rode horses throughout the kingdom with haste, delivering copies of the new edict which made the first decree worthless (vv. 13–14). Mordecai went out from the king's presence in a royal robe of purple and white and with a gold crown, and the city of Susa rejoiced. The Jews celebrated and rejoiced in every province and city (vv. 15–17). They were pre-celebrating because they already knew they had won. This is the only time you will see other ethnic groups professing to be Jews.

Closing

Whitcomb wrote,

> It has often been observed that this [fourteenth verse] provides a remarkably cogent illustration of missionary work today. God's death sentence hangs over a sinful humanity, but He has also commanded us to hasten the message of salvation to every land. Only by a knowledge of, and response to, the second decree of saving grace through the Lord Jesus Christ can the terrible effects of the first decree of universal condemnation for sin be averted.[2]

The first decree for each of us is that we are destined for sin and death. But the second decree cried out the good news that Christ came to earth and died on the Cross for our salvation. We should be the couriers (Luke 2:20)! Jesus told the church to go (Matthew 28:19–20).

The Daily Word

Queen Esther sat down at the feast with the king and Haman. For the third time, the king said to the queen, "Whatever you ask will be given to you. Whatever you seek, even to half the kingdom will be done for you." This time, Queen Esther spoke directly to the point and asked for two things—for her life to be spared and for her people to be spared. The Lord moved the king to grant Esther all she requested and even more. The Jewish people were saved. Esther was saved. And Esther's uncle, Mordecai, even received a place of honor in the palace. The time was right, and Esther received the answer for which she had prayed and fasted.

God can still do the impossible today. The Lord moves as the "Esthers" of this generation rise up in boldness, courage, and dependence on God alone. Esther didn't depend on her good looks. She didn't depend on her position. She fasted and prayed and then asked an entire people group to join her, all while depending on a faithful God. God does the impossible when you have faith, even faith as small as a mustard seed. Pray precise and direct prayers, fast, seek the Lord, and wait for His timing. You may not know how big God can move until you take a leap of faith. Take courage and don't be afraid. *Go ahead and take that step of faith that makes you say, "But what if . . . ?"* Have faith because the Lord is with you!

---

[2] John C. Whitcomb, "Esther," in *The Wycliffe Bible Commentary*, ed. Charles F. Pfeiffer and Everett F. Harrison (Chicago: Moody, 1962), 107.

> **Queen Esther answered, "If I have obtained your approval, my king, and if the king is pleased, spare my life—this is my request; and spare my people—this is my desire." —Esther 7:3**
>
> Further Scripture: Matthew 14:27–29; Matthew 17:20; John 14:14

Questions

1. After reading Esther chapter 7, read Proverb 26:24–27. How do these verses in Proverbs describe Haman?

2. The decree was carried urgently per the king's command to spread the good news throughout the empire. How should we be carrying the good news to those who are perishing?

3. The one who was despised in the book of Esther ended up exalted. How was he a type of Christ (Isaiah 53:3; John 15:24–25; Acts 2:36; 5:30; Philippians 2:8–9)?

4. It was the law of the Medes and Persians that a decree written in the name of the king and sealed with the king's signet ring could not be revoked. How did King Ahasuerus and Mordecai render the edict to annihilate the Jews powerless (Esther 8:8–12)? How does this compare to the sentence of death mankind was under due to sin, and how it was rendered powerless?

5. Read Psalm 37:10–11 and describe how you see this proven out in Esther chapter 8.

6. What did the Holy Spirit highlight to you in Esther 7—8 through the reading or the teaching?

Lesson 137: Esther 9—10

The Despised One: The Deliverance of the Jews

Teaching Notes

Intro

This is the last lesson in Esther, and the last lesson in the twelve historical books: Joshua—*Commander*, Judges—*Judge*, Ruth—*Kinsman Redeemer*, 1 Samuel—*Anointed One*, 2 Samuel—*Eternal Throne*, 1 Kings—*Something Greater*, 2 Kings—*Surviving Seed*, 1 Chronicles—*Son of David*, 2 Chronicles—*Royal Throne*, Ezra—*Promise Keeper*, Nehemiah—*Builder*, and Esther—*The Despised One*. All of these phrases point to the coming Messiah (Matthew 5:17). In Esther, God used Mordecai, the despised one, and his cousin, Esther, to save the Jews from annihilation in Persia (1 Corinthians 1:28–31). The first edict to kill the Jews could not be rescinded, but the second decree changed the Jews' situation. Constable explains, "The king gave the Jews permission to defend themselves by killing their enemies. Evidently this meant that they not only met attack with resistance, but in some cases, they initiated attack against those who they knew would destroy them."[1]

Teaching

Esther 9:1–4: Both edicts went into effect on the same day, but the Jews' enemies were not able to overpower the Jews and instead were overpowered by the Jews (vv. 1–2). The Jewish people clearly had a better weapon—the people were afraid of the Jews (Esther 8:17; Jeremiah 30:16). Other examples of this in the Bible include:

1. Jacob on the road from Shechem to Bethel, when all the people in the cities that were around them were terrified of the Lord and left them alone (Genesis 35:5).
2. When Israel entered the Promised Land, the nations in the land already feared them (Deuteronomy 2:25; Joshua 2:8–11; 5:1; 9:24).

---

[1] Thomas L. Constable, *Expository Notes of Dr. Thomas Constable: Esther*, 63, https://planobiblechapel.org/tcon/notes/pdf/esther.pdf.

Sadly, that same fear does not exist in most people today. Romans 3:18 says, "There is no fear of God before their eyes." As Pharaoh asked, "Who is Yahweh that I should obey Him by letting Israel go? I do not know anything about Yahweh, and besides, I will not let Israel go" (Exodus 5:2).

Verses 3–4 state that all the officials in Persia's provinces helped the Jews because they were afraid of Mordecai, who had great power in the palace and was becoming more powerful throughout Persia. Mordecai, the despised one, had become powerful. This is the picture of Christ, *The Despised One*, dying on the cross and then being raised from the dead in glory and power (1 Corinthians 15:54–57).

Esther 9:5–10: The Jews destroyed their enemies with the sword. They killed 500 men in the citadel of Susa, including the ten sons of Haman (vv. 5–10). However, the Jews took no plunder in their victory. Remember when God told Saul to strike down all of the Amalekites, including the animals, but Saul disobeyed and allowed King Agag and the best animals to survive (1 Samuel 15:17–23)? The Jews in Persia also faced the Amalekites, and they destroyed their enemies, but they refused to keep any of the animals or the things that had belonged to them. The Jews had learned something in their time in Persia. Commentator Baldwin explains, "The deliberate decision not to enrich themselves at the expense of their enemies would not go unnoticed in a culture where victors were expected to take the spoil. The very novelty of such self-denial would be remarked upon and remembered and taken as proof of the upright motives of the Jewish communities."[2]

Esther 9:11–32: The king was told how many were killed, and he asked Esther what else she wanted (vv. 11–12). She asked that the Jews in Susa be given one more day to complete the decree against their enemies and that the bodies of Haman's sons be hung on the gallows (v. 13). The king granted her requests (v. 14). The Jews assembled the next day and killed 300 more men but still took no plunder (v. 15). The Jews throughout the provinces killed 75,000 of their enemies but took no plunder as well (v. 16). The Jews in the provinces fought on the thirteenth day of the month of Adar and rested on the fourteenth day. The Jews in the city of Susa fought on the thirteenth and fourteenth days and then rested on the fifteenth (vv. 17–18). Each group celebrated the victory on the day they rested. Therefore, Mordecai sent letters to all the Jews throughout the province and ordered the celebration on the fourteenth and fifteenth days of the month of Adar each year, as the days that "their sorrow was turned into rejoicing and their

---

[2] Joyce G. Baldwin, *Esther*, Tyndale Old Testament Commentary (Downer's Grove, IL: InterVarsity, 1984), 105.

mourning into a holiday" (vv. 20–22a). The celebration included fasting, giving of gifts, and rejoicing (v. 22b).

This was the creation of the Festival of Purim (v. 23). Evil Haman had selected the date for the annihilation of the Jews by casting lots (or "Pur"), so the festival was named after that (v. 24; Proverb 16:33). Verse 25 begins the summary of the book of Esther—what Haman plotted for the Jews happened to him and his sons instead. The feast of Purim commemorates all these things for the Jews of Persia and for all Jews to come (vv. 26–32). The Feast of Purim is still celebrated today.

Closing

The despised one brought about deliverance for the people of God. Mordecai, a humble man, was lifted up in rank to be second only to King Ahasuerus, and he continued to speak for his people and seek their welfare (Esther 10:3). What a perfect picture of Jesus, *The Despised One*, who brings deliverance to the people of God today and intercedes for us!

The Daily Word

Once again Esther went before the king asking for favor. She asked that the Jewish people be given one more day to kill their enemies and hang Haman's sons. The king gave orders for this to be done. Mordecai recorded these events and ordered the people near and far to celebrate the fourteenth and fifteenth days of the month Adar every year because, "During those days the Jews got rid of their enemies." That month, sorrow turned into rejoicing and mourning turned into a holiday. It was to be two days of feasting, rejoicing, and of sending gifts to one another and to the poor.

How great it is to celebrate! You celebrate the birth of Christ at Christmas and His death and resurrection at Easter. *But what if you celebrated a special day in your relationship with Jesus?* The day you said *yes* to Jesus and went from death to life? Perhaps the day you broke free from the bondage of unforgiveness, pain, or bitterness? As a follower of Christ, you can celebrate these moments in your spiritual journey just as much as a birthday or anniversary. The Lord promises to turn your mourning to dancing and ashes to beauty. Celebrating provides a time to look back and remember how the Lord has moved in your life. Today, think of a day to celebrate in your own walk with the Lord, and then throw a party, spend time in worship and praise to the Lord, or give a gift to someone who needs to know Jesus loves them!

He ordered them to celebrate the fourteenth and fifteenth days of the month Adar every year because during those days the Jews got rid of their enemies.

That was the month when their sorrow was turned into rejoicing and their mourning into a holiday. They were to be days of feasting, rejoicing, and of sending gifts to one another and the poor. —Esther 9:21–22

Further Scripture: Psalm 30:11–12; Isaiah 61:3; Luke 15:22–24

Questions

1. In Esther 9:1, what edict or order was given by the king (Esther 8:11–12)? Why did the king make this edict?

2. Who was Mordecai a descendant of and how was he related to Esther (Esther 2:5–7)? What position did Mordecai hold?

3. What was Queen Esther's request of the king in chapter 9? Did the king grant Esther's request? Why do you think he did this?

4. What feast was established to celebrate the Jews getting relief from their enemies? How did they celebrate this? Do the Jews still celebrate this today? How does this celebration reflect our own liberation from the enemy?

5. What did the Holy Spirit highlight to you in Esther 9—10 through the reading or the teaching?

Contributing Authors

Dr. Kyle Lance Martin
Kyle Lance Martin is the founder of Time to Revive, a ministry based in Dallas, Texas, whose mission is to equip the saints for the return of Christ. His heart's desire, aside from loving his wife and four kids, is to engage people with the Word of God directly in their own environment. Kyle believes when people turn to the Messiah in humility and have a willingness to walk in the Holy Spirit, they can know and experience the calling of being a disciple of Jesus Christ. Kyle received his master of biblical studies from Dallas Theological Seminary and his doctor of ministry in outreach and discipleship from Gordon-Conwell Theological Seminary.

Pastor Gordon Henke
Gordon Henke is a pastor from northern Indiana, serving the church for 25 years. His passion is the studying of the Word. With confidence in the truth of the Word, he passionately helps people boldly share their faith.

Pastor Tom Schiefer
Tom Schiefer is the senior pastor of Nappanee First Brethren Church in Nappanee, Indiana. Prior to accepting a call to pastoral ministry, he was a band and choir director in Ohio. In the context of these two careers, he loves to orchestrate the Word of God, and the message it contains, into harmony with people's lives.

Pastor Fred Stayton
Fred Stayton is the lead pastor of Sonrise Church in Fort Wayne, Indiana, and has a passion for turning the hearts of fathers back to their children. Fred and his wife, Cheryl, have six children and one grandchild.

Ryan Schrag
Ryan Schrag is the national director for Time to Revive and has a heart to "equip the saints for the return of Christ" in the United States. Prior to joining full-time ministry, he was formerly the owner/operator of a lawn care business.

Wesley Morris
Wesley Morris is the Georgia state chairman for Time to Revive. A former construction worker turned pastor, he now trains and equips people to encounter Jesus and boldly share their faith.

Josh Edwards

Josh Edwards is the Minnesota state chairman for Time to Revive and leads worship both nationally and internationally. For the past 20 years he has been leading worship and speaking to the body of Christ about his heart's desire to see the church united, revived, and equipped to do the work of the ministry.

Shawn Carlson

Shawn Carlson is the executive director for Time to Revive. He has a strong desire to see people grow closer to Jesus through the study of God's Word and the carrying out of His mission.

Matt Reynolds

Matt Reynolds is the president of Spirit & Truth, a ministry aimed at equipping believers and churches to be more empowered by the Spirit, rooted in the truth, and mobilized for the mission. After serving as a local pastor for 13 years, Matt responded to a missionary calling to pursue Spirit-filled renewal in the church.

Larry Hopkins

Larry Hopkins is a businessman and entrepreneur in Dallas, Texas, who loves studying and discussing God's Word. He has a heart for revival, which stems from his love and desire for the Bible.

Pastor Kyle Felke

Kyle Felke is a former pastor in northern Indiana. He grew up in a home where both parents were teachers, which instilled in him a passion for teaching. This, combined with a love for Jesus, led him to pursue a biblical education and pastor a church in northern Indiana.

Contributing Authors

The Pentateuch
Kyle Lance Martin

The Gospels
Kyle Lance Martin
Josh Edwards
Ryan Schrag
Matt Reynolds

The Historical Books
Kyle Lance Martin
Wesley Morris
Josh Edwards
Pastor Gordon Henke
Pastor Tom Schiefer
Pastor Kyle Felke
Larry Hopkins

Acts
Kyle Lance Martin
Pastor Gordon Henke
Pastor Tom Schiefer
Wesley Morris
Shawn Carlson

The Wisdom Books
Kyle Lance Martin
Pastor Gordon Henke
Pastor Tom Schiefer
Wesley Morris
Ryan Schrag
Pastor Fred Stayton
Shawn Carlson
Josh Edwards

Paul's Letters
Kyle Lance Martin
Pastor Gordon Henke
Pastor Tom Schiefer

Wesley Morris
Shawn Carlson
Josh Edwards
Ryan Schrag

The Major Prophets
Kyle Lance Martin
Pastor Gordon Henke
Pastor Tom Schiefer
Pastor Fred Stayton
Ryan Schrag
Josh Edwards

General Letters
Kyle Lance Martin
Pastor Fred Stayton
Shawn Carlson

The Minor Prophets
Kyle Lance Martin
Josh Edwards

Revelation
Kyle Lance Martin
Pastor Gordon Henke
Pastor Tom Schiefer

Printed in the USA
CPSIA information can be obtained
at www.ICGtesting.com
LVHW021743171223
766680LV00006B/135